Praise for *Known and Unknown* by D

"The first political memoir of the Information Age."

—Gordon Cr

"Readers might be appreciative to find themselves in possession of a serious memoir, more in keeping with the older Washington tradition of Dean Acheson or Henry Kissinger." —Kimberley Strassel, *The Wall Street Journal*

"Don Rumsfeld creates an entertaining masterpiece. . . . In short, this work cannot be recommended too highly. It is a unique portrait of a half-century of American government from the inside out." —Stephen Laib, *The Intellectual Conservative*

"An insider's view." —Walter Pincus, *The Washington Post*

"I'm rereading portions of *Known and Unknown*. I've read it through the first time, and now I'm using it like a reference book for history." —Greta van Susteren

"Those who believe in what I would call the accepted Iraq narrative . . . will either have to produce commensurate written texts that substantiate these assertions or prove that Rumsfeld's ample paper trail and meticulous documentation are at odds with his performance as secretary." —Victor Davis Hanson, *City Journal*

"I would heartily recommend it. I don't think anybody could go buy a book written by anybody who has been more intimately involved, closer to power, for as many years, has been through as much, has known all of the power players as you have. It is amazing."

—Rush Limbaugh

"[Rumsfeld] describes the highs and lows of a long and dramatic career and discloses some behind the scenes details that may shock you." —Sean Hannity

" 'Dismissive' is a word often used to describe Rumsfeld, but 'dismissive' perfectly describes his critics, who are unwilling or unable to re-examine their own assumptions in the light of new or overlooked information and fresh perspective provided by Rumsfeld, in his exceedingly well-documented work. With its hundreds of annotations and supplementary documents, *Known and Unknown* is a significant contribution to the historical record. It is, as Rumsfeld once noted about similar memoirs, 'only from one perspective,' but it's a unique and valuable perspective, a serious work that deserves consideration by any serious student of recent history." —Jamie McIntyre, former CNN Pentagon correspondent

"It is a terrific book. . . . Let me tell you something, it is absolutely fascinating. He's very blunt in talking about people and issues and so forth, you'll really enjoy it, in my humble opinion."

—Mark Levin

ABOUT THE AUTHOR

Donald Rumsfeld was the thirteenth and twenty-first U.S. secretary of defense. He currently chairs the Rumsfeld Foundation, which supports leadership and public service at home and the growth of free political and free economic systems abroad. The Rumsfeld Foundation funds microfinance development projects, fellowships for graduate students interested in public service, linkages between young leaders from Central Asia and the United States, and charitable causes that benefit the men and women of the U.S. armed forces and their families.

Married in 1954, he and his wife Joyce have three children and seven grandchildren. They currently reside in New Mexico.

Donald Rumsfeld

Known and Unknown

A MEMOIR

SENTINEL

SENTINEL
Published by the Penguin Group
Penguin Group (USA) Inc., 375 Hudson Street,
New York, New York 10014, U.S.A.
Penguin Group (Canada), 90 Eglinton Avenue East, Suite 700,
Toronto, Ontario, Canada M4P 2Y3
(a division of Pearson Penguin Canada Inc.)
Penguin Books Ltd, 80 Strand, London WC2R 0RL, England
Penguin Ireland, 25 St. Stephen's Green, Dublin 2, Ireland
(a division of Penguin Books Ltd)
Penguin Books Australia Ltd, 250 Camberwell Road, Camberwell,
Victoria 3124, Australia
(a division of Pearson Australia Group Pty Ltd)
Penguin Books India Pvt Ltd, 11 Community Centre, Panchsheel Park,
New Delhi—110 017, India
Penguin Group (NZ), 67 Apollo Drive, Rosedale, Auckland 0632,
New Zealand (a division of Pearson New Zealand Ltd)
Penguin Books (South Africa) (Pty) Ltd, 24 Sturdee Avenue,
Rosebank, Johannesburg 2196, South Africa

Penguin Books Ltd, Registered Offices:
80 Strand, London WC2R 0RL, England

First published in the United States of America by Sentinel, a member of Penguin Group (USA) Inc. 2011
This paperback edition with a new preface published 2012

10 9 8 7 6 5 4 3 2 1

Credits for photographs in the inserts appear on pages 733–37.

Map illustrations by Jeffrey L. Ward

THE LIBRARY OF CONGRESS HAS CATALOGED THE HARDCOVER EDITION AS FOLLOWS:

Rumsfeld, Donald, 1932-
Known and unknown : a memoir / Donald Rumsfeld.
p. cm.
Includes bibliographical references and index.
ISBN 978-1-59523-067-6 (hc.)
ISBN 978-1-59523-084-3 (pbk.)
1. Rumsfeld, Donald, 1932- 2. Cabinet officers—United States—Biography. 3. United States. Dept. of Defense—Official and employees—Biography. 4. United States—Politics and government—1945–1989. 5. United States—Politics and government—1989- 6. War on Terrorism, 2001-2009. 7. Iraq War, 2003- I. Title.
E840.8.R84A3 2011
352.293092—dc22
[B]
2010042050
Printed in the United States of America

Set in Minion Pro
Designed by Amy Hill

To Joyce

"What one needs in life are
the pessimism of intelligence
and the optimism of will."

*—former Belgian ambassador to NATO and
dean of the North Atlantic Council, André de Staercke,
as quoted in Rumsfeld's Rules**

* I first gathered the sayings and thoughts that collectively would become known as "Rumsfeld's Rules" while I served in the U.S. Congress in the 1960s. I continue to accumulate them to this day. Some rules are original. Many are quotes or variations of ideas from others. If known, the original source is credited. Readers will find examples of the rules scattered through this book.

Contents

Preface to the Paperback Edition

In the early morning hours of May 2, 2011, shots rang out inside a walled compound on the outskirts of Abbottabad, Pakistan. At the end of the decidedly one-sided firefight, three terrorists were dead. Among them was the al-Qaida leader who had become the face of terrorism in the twenty-first century, Osama bin Laden. With well-placed bullets from the team of Navy SEALs, the decade-long manhunt for the world's most wanted terrorist came to a close.

When the news broke, it was gratifying to learn that the man we had tracked in the months and years after the 9/11 attacks had finally met his end. Years earlier it had become something of a routine that when I awoke for my day at the Department of Defense my wife Joyce would ask, "Don, where's Osama?" "We're working on it, now go back to sleep," was invariably my reply. Joyce's almost daily needling was a sure way to bring a smile to my face at 4:30 a.m., but it was also a reminder that many millions of Americans were demanding the answer to the exact same question.

Bin Laden's death was met with jubilation across the United States. In lower Manhattan and in front of the White House, thousands gathered in spontaneous celebration. They waved flags. They held candles. They sang "God Bless America." This country hadn't seen such an outburst of patriotism since the days immediately after the attacks that Bin Laden had himself initiated. Here, it seemed, was the perfect bookend, an echo of the bipartisan unity America saw from the steps of the U.S. Capitol building to university campus vigils nearly a decade earlier. Understandably, many wondered if the welcome news meant our country had at long last reached the end of the conflict that had begun on 9/11.

The hardcover edition of my memoir was published eleven weeks before Osama bin Laden's demise. From his possible presence at Tora Bora in December 2001 to a later occasion when we were convinced that the tall man in flowing white robes we were watching on a video feed from an overhead Unmanned Aerial Vehicle (UAV) was undoubtedly the man we were after, *Known and Unknown* chronicles the efforts of those in the U.S. intelligence community and in the Defense Department to find and capture or kill the target known in military shorthand as "UBL." The man and his terrorist organization that cast a pall over the first decade of the twenty-first century also played an outsized role in the latter chapters of this book. To support my book, I had over 4,200 declassified documents released, many dozens of which refer to Bin Laden and al-Qaida. (The Web site www.rumsfeld.com has received over 39 million hits as of this writing.)

Though much difficult work remains to be done, particularly in combating the radical Islamist ideology championed by al-Qaida and in curbing the regime support for terror from Iran to Syria, Bin Laden's death was a singular accomplishment in the struggle against radical Islamism.

This was made possible in large measure by President George W. Bush and an administration that undertook the political risk to put in place the policies necessary to go on the offensive against Islamist terrorism. President Barack Obama and his administration also deserve the credit for having the courage to authorize the raid and, more important, the wisdom to leave in place the vital tools they inherited and that made Osama bin Laden's death possible.

But more than any president and any administration, it is the men and women of the U.S. military and the intelligence community who merit our nation's appreciation. Bin Laden's death was made possible by their tireless efforts spanning a ten-year period. It was made possible by those who served in Afghanistan where they sent Bin Laden and al-Qaida into retreat and toppled its state sponsor and host, the Taliban government. It was made possible by those who served in Iraq where American persistence and grit defeated al-Qaida in Anbar province in 2006 and helped the Iraqi people form the democratic government they proudly elected under a constitution they had drafted. It was made possible by those who served at detention centers in Guantánamo Bay and elsewhere where key pieces of information were collected that allowed the United States to dismantle much of al-Qaida and capture or kill a large fraction of its senior leaders, including Osama bin Laden.

It is to honor those individuals who have served and sacrificed in the wars that followed the attacks on September 11, 2001, that I am donating all of the proceeds that I receive from the sale of my memoir, *Known and Unknown*, to nonprofit organizations that support our troops and their families. A complete list of the military charities we are proud to be able to support can be found at www.rumsfeldfoundation.org.

Writing this book provided me an opportunity to travel to more than seventy-five events over the last year, many of which were held on U.S. military bases from California to Florida to Japan and South Korea. It has been a welcome opportunity to meet literally thousands of men and women who served our nation in the days after 9/11 and their families and to shake their hands, and sign photos taken of us years earlier in Afghanistan, Iraq, and elsewhere around the globe. Most of all, it has been an opportunity to look each of them in the eye and thank them for all they have done to protect our nation. I will be forever grateful for having had the privilege of serving alongside such inspirational and talented men and women.

History assures us that young men and women will continue to be called on to defend our nation and our way of life in the decades ahead. The death of Bin Laden was an important moment in our history, to be sure, but the struggle against Islamist extremism is far from over. Much less is it won. Our country's military engagements in Afghanistan and Iraq are drawing to a close, but, let there be no doubt, America will be challenged elsewhere. From Iranian nuclear weapons to China's increasingly aggressive military stance to cyberattacks to an Islamist resurgence in the wake of the so-called Arab Spring, there are looming dangers. And those are just a few of the "known unknowns." And for every possible threat we can identify, there are others that are not and will not be anticipated or predicted—the even more challenging "unknown unknowns."

At some point in the not so distant future, America will be surprised to learn that those who wish us and our way of life harm have not surrendered. When that day comes, I have no doubt but that the dedicated men and women who volunteer to serve in our military, in our intelligence services, and in positions of responsibility for our nation's security will once again step forward courageously. May we all continue to be grateful for their service.

—Donald Rumsfeld,
December 2011

Author's Note

An internet search of "known unknown" in the autumn of 2010 resulted in more than three hundred thousand entries, a quarter million of which were linked to my name. There is an entry on Wikipedia. The reference has been turned into "poetry." That poetry has been set to music. And that was just on the first page of the search results.

Yet for a phrase seemingly so well known, there is some irony in the fact that its origins and meaning remain largely unknown.

The phrase first became publicly linked to me in early 2002. Toward the end of one of my Pentagon press briefings, a journalist told me that "reports" were suggesting the absence of a link between Saddam Hussein's regime and terrorists seeking weapons of mass destruction. These unidentified reports, the questioner suggested, were evidence of a lack of a "direct link."

Putting aside the substance of the reporter's question—at least for the moment—I raised a larger point about the limits of human knowledge. I responded:

> Reports that say something hasn't happened are always interesting to me because as we know, there are known knowns: there are things we know we know. We also know there are known unknowns: that is to say we know there are some things [we know] we do not know. But there are also unknown unknowns—the ones we don't know we don't know. And if one looks throughout the history of our country and other free countries, it is the latter category that tends to be the difficult one.

At first glance, the logic may seem obscure. But behind the enigmatic language is a simple truth about knowledge: There are many things of which we are completely unaware—in fact, there are things of which we are so unaware, we don't even know we are unaware of them.

Known knowns are facts, rules, and laws that we know with certainty. We know, for example, that gravity is what makes an object fall to the ground.

Known unknowns are gaps in our knowledge, but they are gaps that we know exist. We know, for example, that we don't know the exact extent of Iran's nuclear weapons program. If we ask the right questions we can potentially fill this gap in our knowledge, eventually making it a known known.

The category of unknown unknowns is the most difficult to grasp. They are gaps in our knowledge, but gaps that we don't know exist. Genuine surprises tend to arise out of this category. Nineteen hijackers using commercial airliners as guided missiles to incinerate three thousand men, women, and children was perhaps the most horrific single unknown unknown America has experienced.

I first heard a variant of the phrase "known unknowns" in a discussion with former NASA administrator William R. Graham, when we served together on the Ballistic Missile Threat Commission in the late 1990s. Members of our bipartisan commission were concerned that some briefers from the U.S. intelligence community treated the fact that they lacked information about a possible activity to infer that the activity had not happened and would not. In other words, if something could not be proven to be true, then it could be assumed not to be true. This led to misjudgments about the ballistic missile capabilities of other nations, which in some cases proved to be more advanced than previously thought.

The idea of known and unknown unknowns recognizes that the information those in positions of responsibility in government, as well as in other human endeavors, have at their disposal is almost always incomplete. It emphasizes the importance of intellectual humility, a valuable attribute in decision making and in formulating strategy. It is difficult to accept—to know—that there may be important unknowns. The best strategists try to imagine and consider the possible, even if it seems unlikely. They are then more likely to be prepared and agile enough to adjust course if and when new and surprising information requires it—when things that were previously unknown become known.

I also encountered this concept in Thomas Schelling's foreword to

Roberta Wohlstetter's book *Pearl Harbor: Warning and Decision,* in which Schelling identified a "poverty of expectations" as the primary explanation for America's inability to anticipate and thwart the Japanese attack on Hawaii.[1] Schelling's message was as clear as it was prescient: We needed to prepare for the likelihood that we would be attacked by an unanticipated foe in ways that we may not imagine. Going back in history, the influential nineteenth-century German military theorist Carl von Clausewitz emphasized the challenges of dealing with incomplete or faulty intelligence and the inevitability of surprise.[2] Some with an interest in philosophy have made note of a line attributed to Socrates: "I neither know nor think that I know."[3] This has been interpreted to mean that the beginning of wisdom is the realization of how little one truly knows.

One known unknown for me was how to write a book. I had never tried to do so before. I didn't know whether or how to incorporate the hundreds of thousands of pages of primary source documents in my personal archive. I still have my parents' almost daily letters to each other during World War II, hundreds of notes on the reasons I cast my votes while serving in the Congress during the 1960s, and my detailed memos of my meetings with President Ford as White House chief of staff to ensure that his requests and directions were executed. I also have some twenty thousand memos humorously characterized as "snowflakes" from my tenure as secretary of defense in the George W. Bush administration, some recording momentous decisions, others simply scheduling a time for a haircut. Thousands more documents reside in classified archives at the Library of Congress, the State Department, and the Department of Defense.

Despite its challenging volume, I decided my archive could augment my personal recollections. On the one hand, the documents would add detail and context to my memories, and on the other, they would cause me to more rigorously challenge what I remembered. A portion of my archive will be available in digital form on my web site, **www.rumsfeld.com**, which accompanies and supports this memoir. I have also released and will continue to release additional documents not directly cited in this book but of historical interest nonetheless.

My life has spanned more than one third of the history of the United States. As I thought more about this memoir and a title, the idea of the known and the unknown seemed to fit. Not only are there things in this book people believe they know about my life, but there are also things that may surprise and differ from what many may have read or heard or assumed. The same holds true about many of the events I observed—from my years in Congress during the civil rights struggle and the Vietnam War era, through the Cold War and my service as secretary of defense during the age of terrorism. The known and the unknown are what I have attempted to present in this memoir—that slice of our amazing country's history of which I have been privileged to be a part.

—Donald Rumsfeld,
December 2010

PART I

Lessons in Terror

"The wind in the tower presages the coming of the storm."

—*Chinese proverb, as quoted in Rumsfeld's Rules*

Baghdad

DECEMBER 20, 1983

"Ambassador Rumsfeld, may I present to you his Excellency, Saddam Hussein, the President of Iraq."

As his aide announced him, the infamous Iraqi leader approached me confidently. Like other strongmen who pose as popular revolutionaries, Saddam wore military fatigues with a pistol on his hip. Saddam's "revolution," of course, was in reality a coup in which he arrested or murdered his political opponents.

He was above average height and build, and his hair and mustache were so black that I wondered whether he dyed his hair. It was December 20, 1983, the only time I met the man who would become known as the "Butcher of Baghdad."

Saddam stopped a few feet in front of me and smiled. I extended my hand, which he clasped. The cameras rolled.

© GETTY IMAGES (NEWS)

In later years, this inelegant video still became one of the most widely viewed political images on the internet.[1]

My trip to Baghdad that winter as President Reagan's envoy—my official title was Personal Representative of the President of the United States in the Middle East—was the highest-level contact by any U.S. official with Iraq's leadership in twenty-five years. None of us in the Reagan administration harbored illusions about Saddam. Like most despots, his career was forged in conflict and hardened by bloodshed. He had used chemical toxins in the war he initiated with Iran three years earlier. But given the reality of the Middle East, then as now, America often had to deal with rulers who were deemed "less bad" than the others. The sands constantly shifted during evaluations of our country's potential friends and possible foes. And in 1983, at least, some leaders in the region seemed even less appetizing to deal with than Saddam Hussein.

Iraq's Baathist regime was at the time the bitter adversary of two nations that threatened the interests of the United States—Syria and Iran. Syria, under President Hafez al-Assad, was a leading supporter of international terrorism and occupied portions of Lebanon, a country that when left to its own devices favored the West. Iran had been a close friend of the United States until the 1979 coup by militant Islamists led by a radical cleric, Ayatollah Khomeini. The subsequent abduction of sixty-six Americans at the U.S. embassy in Tehran by pro-Khomeini revolutionaries poisoned U.S.-Iranian relations and further damaged the troubled presidency of Jimmy Carter, whose response appeared hapless.*

Iraq sat between these two menaces—Syria and Iran. It must have taken a good deal of effort, or more likely some mistakes, for America to be on the bad side of all three countries. By 1983, there was a clear logic in trying to cultivate warmer relations with Saddam Hussein's Iraq. The tide of the Iran-Iraq war had turned against Iraq. Iran was launching human mass wave attacks—children as young as twelve were sent marching toward Iraqi lines, clearing a way through minefields with their bodies. Whatever misgivings we had about reaching out to Saddam Hussein, the alternative of Iranian hegemony in the Middle East was decidedly worse. The Reagan administration had recognized this reality and had begun to make lower-level diplomatic contacts with the Iraqis some months earlier.

My unusual visit had begun a day earlier, under equally unusual circumstances. In the late evening of December 19, 1983, I traveled to the Iraqi Foreign Ministry building in Baghdad with a small staff for a preliminary

* Most of the hostages were held until January 20, 1981, the day Reagan was inaugurated president.

meeting with Saddam's deputy prime minister, Tariq Aziz. Our group—which included Bill Eagleton, the experienced chief of the United States Interests Section in Baghdad, and Robert Pelletreau, a senior State Department official—had helped to prepare me for the visit.

But as we exited an elevator and started down a hall on an upper floor of the Foreign Ministry headquarters, two armed, unsmiling Iraqi guards broke me off from the group. While my startled staff was led straight down the hall, I was turned down a dark corridor to the right. I couldn't help but wonder for the briefest of moments how many Iraqi citizens had been taken alone down dark hallways by men with guns, wondering what might be next.

I was led into a bright but windowless room. The walls were padded in what looked to be white leather. Standing alone was a medium-sized, gray-haired man in thick horn-rimmed glasses, wearing military fatigues and a pistol on his hip.

"Welcome, Ambassador Rumsfeld," he said in flawless English. "I am Tariq Aziz." He motioned for the guards to leave us and we stood across from each other.

Tariq Aziz later became a familiar figure in Saddam's regime, the man who often appeared on television to defend his government. But Aziz was certainly not the typical Middle Eastern official. His manner was erudite and polished. He had been educated at Baghdad University's College of the Fine Arts and seemed to live quite comfortably as an Assyrian Christian in a Muslim country. He was one of Saddam's most trusted senior officials—which, considering Saddam's rampant paranoia, was no small achievement—and one of the few to survive long in his orbit. As a sign of his stature, he was serving in the dual roles of deputy prime minister and foreign minister.

It was never explained to me why the Iraqis decided to part with the arrangements we had agreed on and pull me away from my staff. My sense was that Aziz thought we could be more direct without others present. That indeed turned out to be the case.

For the next two-plus hours we had an intense, candid, rapid-fire discussion about my mission to Baghdad and the relationship between our two countries. Aziz seemed well versed on the Reagan administration and my role as the President's envoy. I found myself favorably impressed by his knowledge and interest in the world beyond Iraq.

Our long conversation covered a host of issues. Most important was our mutual interest in keeping both Syria and Iran contained. Iran was of particular interest to Aziz, for understandable reasons: He had survived an assassination attempt a few years earlier that had been attributed to Iranian agents, an attack that Saddam used as one of the pretexts for launching the Iran-Iraq war. Aziz asked for our help in dissuading America's friends and allies from supplying arms to Iran. I told him, as Reagan administration officials had previously, that any efforts to assist Iraq were hampered by the regime's use of chemical weapons and human rights abuses.[2] I had questions as to exactly how Iraq might be helpful to us. Nonetheless, it was still clear that Iran's leadership, due to their bitter hostility toward the United States and their history of holding Americans hostage, remained unapproachable.

I made the point that the United States and Iraq had some shared interests. "It seems unnatural," I said, "to have a whole generation of Iraqis growing up knowing little about America and a whole generation of Americans growing up knowing little about Iraq." Aziz nodded in agreement.

My meeting with Saddam, which took place the next morning, has been the subject of gossip, rumors, and crackpot conspiracy theories for more than a quarter of a century, particularly after I was involved in the administration that removed him from power in 2003. Supposedly I had been sent to see Saddam by President Reagan either to negotiate a secret oil deal, to help arm Iraq, or to make Iraq an American client state. The truth is that our encounter was more straightforward and less dramatic.

As I met with the Iraqi leader, we sat at opposite ends of a gold and burgundy-upholstered couch amid plush surroundings. The large room had intricately carved wooden doors and walls inlaid with marble. In a country where the people didn't receive reliable electricity or water, it was discordantly ostentatious.

Our meeting was considerably more formal than my long session with Aziz. This time I wasn't pulled off alone. Two members of our mission were included—Bill Eagleton and Robert Pelletreau—along with Aziz and an Iraqi interpreter.

The war with Iran was naturally uppermost in Saddam's mind. Iraq's capital, Baghdad, was a mere one hundred miles from the Iranian border and suffering frequent shelling and rocket attacks. Even the presidential complex where we were meeting was protected by sandbags and barriers. Though Saddam was in a difficult situation, he made no direct request for American military assistance. Like Aziz, Saddam said he was concerned about other nations providing military and financial assistance to Iran and clearly hoped that the United States might have some influence with them.[3] In addition, at the State Department's request, I discussed a proposal to funnel Iraqi oil through a pipeline that ended in Aqaba, Jordan.[4] Saddam said he would consider the idea but indicated it would require American assurance that Israel would not attack it.[5] Though officially most Arab nations didn't even acknowledge Israel as a nation, they tended to view its formidable military with respect.

Saddam indicated a surprising amount of openness to cooperation with the West. "France in particular," he said, "understood the Iraqi view."[6] Over the years that followed, that particular remark came to my mind on more than one occasion, and I never had cause to doubt it.

At one point, Saddam motioned me over to a window and pointed toward a tall building on the city's skyline.

"See that building?" he asked, as we looked out at Baghdad's sprawling vista. I nodded.

"When an elevator in that building breaks, where do we look to have it repaired?" he asked. I waited for his conclusion.

"I look for help in the West," he continued. His point was clear: Iraq needed the West to make his country part of the modern world. Looking back, I wonder how much of our recent history would have changed if his perspective at the time had outweighed his other goals and appetites.

As Saddam and I began to discuss the prospects for U.S.-Iraqi relations, he said something quite interesting.

"It seems unnatural," he said, "to have a whole generation of Iraqis growing up knowing little about America and a whole generation of Americans growing up knowing little about Iraq."

I concealed a smile. Those, of course, were my exact words late the night before. Certainly Saddam's repeating them was no coincidence. I didn't know how Saddam had heard my statement—if Aziz had told him personally or if, as was not at all unlikely, the room Aziz and I met in was bugged. In any event, I was pleased and encouraged that he repeated it so pointedly. I began to think that through increased contacts we might be able to persuade the Iraqis to lean toward the United States and eventually modify their behavior.

After Saddam repeated my words back to me, I nodded. "I agree completely," I replied, as if it were the first time I had heard those thoughts.

Over my decades of public service I received a number of unusual gifts from foreign leaders and heads of state, but none was stranger than the one Saddam presented to me. It was a videotape that may well have been put together specifically for my visit, though the production values weren't going to win it any Oscars. The tape contained two to three minutes of amateurish footage of Syria's dictator, Hafez al-Assad, reviewing Syrian troops and applauding. Then it showed people purported to be Syrians strangling puppies. This was followed by a line of young women biting the heads off of snakes. The video appeared edited in a way that indicated Assad was present and applauding these gruesome acts. I suspect Saddam wanted me to see the Syrians, and Assad in particular, as savages. Considering the Assad regime's history, that wasn't a difficult sell.

After about ninety minutes, Saddam thanked me for coming, and I expressed my appreciation. As odd as it might sound, he came across as rather reasonable. For his part, Saddam seemed gratified to have had a visit by a senior American official representing President Reagan. He knew it would increase his stature both at home and in the region.

I did not expect that Saddam's regime would play such a prominent role in our country's future—and in my life—in the years ahead. After a hiatus of seventeen years, U.S.-Iraq diplomatic relations were reestablished in 1984 shortly after my meeting. We had convergent interests: America could assist Iraq by discouraging other countries from selling arms to Iran, and Iraq could assist America by holding the line against an ascendant radical Islamist and terrorist-supporting regime in Iran. Ultimately, of course, the United States was unable to reorient our relations with Iraq, and my visit to Baghdad was something of a side event. America's primary concern in the region at the time was not Iraq but the small, troubled nation of Lebanon, which was being ripped apart by terrorism and civil war. No experience better prepared me for the challenges I would face many years later, as secretary of defense in the George W. Bush administration, than the crisis in Lebanon. Many times, in fact, I looked back on the hopes and disappointments of that period, the consequences of which still reverberate.

CHAPTER 1

Smiling Death

On October 23, 1983, as dawn broke in the Middle East, a water delivery truck was headed for an American military facility at Beirut International Airport. The truck had been hijacked and loaded with explosives, the equivalent of some twelve thousand pounds of TNT.[1] An eyewitness who caught a glimpse of the driver characterized him as "smiling death" for his chillingly cheerful expression as the truck headed toward his target—a four-story building that housed sixteen hundred men and women in uniform and flew the flag of the United States of America.[2] After the truck barreled through the building's entrance, it ignited an explosion so massive that it briefly lifted the entire structure into the air, until it collapsed upon itself. A second bomb, targeting French military personnel, had gone off almost simultaneously, killing fifty-eight.

By the time the rubble settled, 241 Americans were dead.* They had been part of a Marine contingent and multinational force deployed to Lebanon to serve as a check on the warring factions of that country. The Beirut airport bombing was the largest loss of Marines in a single incident since the Battle of Iwo Jima in World War II. And until September 11, 2001, it was the worst terrorist attack ever committed against American citizens.

* The casualties included 220 Marines, 18 Navy corpsmen, and 3 Army soldiers.

At the time of the Beirut attack I was home in Chicago and serving as chief executive officer of G. D. Searle & Co., a pharmaceutical company. As I watched the pictures of the huge plume of smoke over the bomb site on television, I was stunned by the scale of the attack. So was President Reagan, who appeared grief-stricken as one after another flag-draped coffin containing murdered Americans returned home. The Marine barracks bombing, Reagan later said, was the saddest day of his presidency and maybe the saddest day of his life.[3]

Many groups immediately claimed credit for it, but eventually the attack was linked to a fledgling terrorist group backed by Iran and Syria. The group called itself Hezbollah, Arabic for "Party of God," even as they committed this brazen act of mass murder. The bombing clearly had been intended to spark an American withdrawal from Lebanon so that Syria, Hezbollah's sponsor, which already occupied a third of the country, could gain even more influence.*

In an effort to show America's resolve, Vice President George H. W. Bush was dispatched to Beirut. "We're not going to let a bunch of insidious terrorists, cowards, shape the foreign policy of the United States," Bush vowed.[4] As I watched the scene, I was uncomfortable with his word choice. I have never thought people willing to drive a truck bomb into a building and kill themselves were "cowards." Rather, I saw them as dangerous fanatics willing to do anything for their cause. I did agree with him that we should not let terrorists shape the foreign policy of the United States.

As America continued to bring the dead home, there was a profound sense that the country should respond forcefully to the atrocity. In the aftermath of the attack, the most powerful nation in the world did not.†

With no substantive military response in the offing, the only other way the United States could react to the terrorist challenge was through aggressive diplomacy. The President decided that a fresh set of eyes might be useful in the Middle East, and that it would at least demonstrate his and our country's concern.

Shortly after the Beirut bombing, I received a phone call from Secretary

* The alleged mastermind of the attacks—Imad Mughniyeh—was indicted in absentia by a U.S. grand jury. Immediately after the Beirut bombing he took flight and could not be found. Mughniyeh became one of the world's most wanted terrorists. Over the decades he was linked to a number of other high-profile attacks until he was killed, ironically, by a car bomb in Syria in 2008.

† Eventually, the Pentagon settled on an air strike against the Sheik Abdullah barracks in Baalbek, Lebanon, on December 4, 1983. The result was that the Syrians sustained little damage and the United States looked ineffective.[5]

of State George Shultz, who I first had met in 1969 when we served in the Nixon administration, and who had been a friend ever since. Shultz was President Reagan's second secretary of state, replacing Alexander Haig, another colleague of ours from the Nixon years. A former Marine with a low-key demeanor, Shultz spoke plainly. He said the President needed to appoint a new special envoy to the Middle East to work on the Lebanon crisis and help with the American response to the terrorist attacks. Shultz said they wanted someone who had standing outside of the government. "I'd like you to do it," he said.

If I agreed, the task would be to support the Lebanese government, to work with our allies on encouraging the Syrians to ratchet down their aggressive behavior, and to signal America's commitment to the region.

I knew the history of presidential envoys to the Middle East was not a happy one. I had observed the challenges of America's diplomacy in the region over my years in Congress and my service in the Nixon and Ford administrations, during which a number of experienced foreign policy officials worked in the region with hopes of breakthroughs, generally to return disappointed. I requested and received a leave of absence as CEO of Searle. Then I prepared to go to Washington to meet with President Reagan as he coped with the biggest national security crisis his administration had yet encountered.

Ronald Reagan had been in office for more than two years when he faced the Lebanon crisis. I had come to know him when he was governor of California and I was serving in the Nixon and Ford administrations. I was used to seeing him on television or being with him at more formal events when he had the aura of a movie star. Instead, as I entered the Oval Office on November 3, 1983, he looked quite different. The President welcomed me into the room with horn-rimmed granny glasses perched on his nose and a stack of papers in his hand, which he referenced occasionally while talking.

The caricature often used by Reagan's critics was that he was good-hearted but not particularly bright—an "amiable dunce," one said. I had heard the same charge of low candle power made against nearly every Republican president in my adult lifetime, usually by those on the other side who couldn't imagine how anyone intelligent could possibly disagree with them. In Reagan's case, as in others, the caricature simply wasn't true. The President was not a detail-oriented manager, to be sure. He enjoyed telling a humorous anecdote, even during the most serious of meetings. He lacked the hard-charging style so often common among Washington politicians, and his approach took some getting used to. But as I came to know Reagan over the years, it was clear that he had the strong, long-range strategic sense so essential to successful leadership. Now that Reagan's letters and other writings have been published, it is instructive to see his insightful mind at work.

Some presidents allow themselves to get lost in minutiae. Reagan's predecessor, Jimmy Carter, was a famous micromanager. Ronald Reagan didn't have that problem. He knew where he wanted to lead America, and set the course for his administration around large principles. He left it to others to sort out the details while standing ready to provide course corrections and calibration as necessary. While that didn't always serve his best interests, for the most part it worked exceedingly well.

"My idea of American policy . . . is simple," he told aides when asked his view on the Soviet Union. "We win and they lose." Critics scoffed at that statement as simplistic bravado, but in truth it was a big idea, bold and transformative. For a number of years before Reagan took office, the architecture of the federal government and the foreign policy establishment had been built around the notion of peaceful coexistence, or "détente," as it was called, with the Soviets. It was not fashionable to look at the Cold War as a win-lose proposition. The Soviet Union was considered more an unfortunate fact of life. But Reagan knew that major strategic changes in U.S. policy could be made by a president who had thought the subject through, was determined to redirect policy, and had an effective team of senior officials ready to implement his vision. The ultimate confirmation of his wisdom toward the Soviets, of course, is that President Reagan accomplished what he set out to do.

With regard to the crisis in Lebanon, Reagan's words were similarly straightforward, even if things ended up turning out quite different than he'd initially hoped. On the Middle East, Reagan's instincts were consistent with his policy against the Soviets: to use American strength to protect and encourage the aspirations of free people and to deter those who would break the peace. The President said we could not allow terrorists to drive us from Lebanon. At the same time, he was aware that when it came to the maneuverings of the Middle East, the United States was holding a difficult hand that would require substantial time and patience to play successfully. Those two commodities were in short supply. Reagan's major national security focus was the Soviet Union, as it should have been at the height of the Cold War. For the time being at least, his goal in the Middle East was to try to bring about some modest degree of stability.

I told Reagan I would do my best to represent our country's interests in the region. He thanked me for agreeing to come onboard at a difficult time for the country and pledged his support for the mission. Yet it was apparent that the "mission" wasn't all that clear.

Throughout the Lebanon crisis, Reagan got the rhetoric right—he declared that America would not cower in the face of terror or abandon our friends in the region—but I could tell from our first meeting that formulating a consistent policy was going to be more difficult. It was hard to plant a standard toward a goal when there was little or no solid ground in which to set it.

After our discussion in the Oval Office, President Reagan and I walked to the White House press briefing room, where he introduced me as his special envoy to the Middle East.[6] The press began with typical Washington-style queries. They noted that I was Reagan's third Middle East envoy in three years, the latest diplomat being sent out to undertake the Sisyphean task of rolling a boulder up a never-ending hill. Why, some wondered, would I take such a "no-win job"? I responded that I simply wanted to be helpful, despite the difficulty of the challenge. But what I didn't say was that I also had to try to manage expectations. As I told George Shultz, "I promise you will never hear out of my mouth the phrase 'The U.S. seeks a just and lasting peace in the Middle East.' There is little that is just, and the only things I've seen that are lasting are conflict, blackmail and killing—not peace."[7] I thought the best I could hope for was to make some modest progress. Under the circumstances I knew that even keeping things from getting worse in the Middle East could be valuable.[8]

Because I wasn't on the federal payroll, I had hoped that would free me from some of the burdens of the federal bureaucracy. That was wishful thinking. A Department of State functionary decided I had to be classified technically as an "unpaid government employee." As such, a legal title was needed for me so that they could determine which classification applied. Was I a State Department expert or a consultant, or did I fall into some other category? It was finally concluded that I was to be considered an expert. I was uncomfortable with that classification. Anyone who claims to be an expert on the Middle East is starting off on the wrong foot.

I did know Lebanon's plight was agonizing, and that it had worsened since civil war broke out there in 1975. I had been serving as secretary of defense in the Ford administration when the Department of Defense (DoD) assisted in the evacuation of American citizens from the country. The Lebanese civil war ultimately claimed 150,000 lives, and by 1983, the loss of life was already monumental—"comparable to the United States losing ten million of its citizens," Reagan declared that December.[9] Hundreds of thousands of the most successful and educated Lebanese fled the country. The countryside outside Beirut came under the control of Lebanese militias that had little or no allegiance to the central government.

Complicating matters further, by the time of the 1983 Beirut bombing a large fraction of the country was occupied by Lebanon's neighboring and rival foreign powers, Syria and Israel. The Syrians had a proprietary attitude toward Lebanon, which they considered part of greater Syria. Israel had invaded in June 1982 to protect its territory from the Palestinian terrorist camps that were operating inside Lebanon. The Syrians resented the Israeli occupation, the Israelis resented the Syrian occupation, and the Lebanese resented being occupied by anyone. In the middle of all this hostility was a small contingent of American military personnel as part of a multinational peacekeeping force.

From a safe distance in Washington, it was easy for American leaders to say that we'd never let terrorists defeat us in Lebanon or push us to withdraw. But it became apparent that fulfilling that pledge would have required far more than Americans were prepared to muster. There was little appetite anywhere—in the administration, in Congress, or among the American people—to increase our military commitment to Lebanon, especially after the outrage over the Beirut bombing dissipated.

Lebanon, I soon learned, was also the subject of intense debate even within the administration. Many in the Pentagon, including Secretary of Defense Caspar Weinberger, favored an early and complete withdrawal from the country. The American troops still on the ground were in largely indefensible positions and were being targeted by the Syrian-backed extremists. Because of the dangers they faced, the troops' movements were severely restricted. They were using, as Weinberger later put it, "fruitless tactics in pursuit of unreachable goals."* During his trip to Beirut after the bombings, even Vice President Bush, who publicly expressed support for our presence, privately

*I had known Weinberger from our time in the Nixon administration. He had served as director of the Office of Management and Budget (OMB), where he was known as "Cap the Knife" for his cost-cutting efforts, and later as secretary of the Department of Health, Education, and Welfare (HEW). When he became Secretary of Defense, he had a different task. The Carter administration had systematically reversed the DoD budget increases James Schlesinger and I had initiated under President Ford, and when Reagan came in, the DoD budget needed to be increased. Cap and I were friends, and when he died in 2006, Colin Powell, who had been one of his senior military assistants, and I delivered eulogies.[10]

characterized the pleas of Lebanon's president for American support unpersuasive.[11]

On the other side of the issue was Secretary of State Shultz, who favored maintaining an American military presence to help stabilize the Lebanese government. The unpleasant alternative to that, Shultz pointed out, was to have the country become a client state of Syria or an ungoverned haven for terrorists and extremists. Shultz's position was bolstered by a number of our strongest allies in the region. King Hussein of Jordan, for example, made it clear that if the United States were to leave Lebanon, we would essentially be out of the Middle East dynamic. Of greater concern, the King felt that without an American counterweight in Lebanon, Syria would likely turn its attention toward Jordan, and then to Saudi Arabia. Saddam Hussein told me during our meeting in Baghdad that he believed the United States had been indifferent to Syria's initial invasion of Lebanon and had "let this group of lunatics bash each other."[12] It was an experience to be on the receiving end of a lecture from Saddam Hussein, especially when he might have been right.

I gravitated toward Shultz's view. I believed that since we were there, we should keep some forces on the ground, and do so without specifying a time limit. And we needed to encourage our coalition partners—the British, French, and Italians—to stay for a period as well. It was in all of our interests to try to help the Lebanese build some internal unity and develop the capability to better defend themselves. If the Syrians saw that we would not be run out of Beirut, they might be more amenable to negotiations with the Lebanese government. Importantly, this was where President Reagan had come down as well.

Unfortunately, the administration's strategy faced another major impediment, namely the United States Congress. During the late phase of the Vietnam War, Congress had passed the War Powers Resolution, which required a withdrawal of American military forces deployed to another country within sixty to ninety days absent the explicit authorization of Congress.* The resolution, despite its questionable and still untested constitutionality, undercut the President's ability to convince troublemakers of America's staying power. It was clear to anyone with a newspaper that Congress wanted out.

So with the Reagan administration internally split over the policy, with Syria poised to exploit Lebanon's chaos, with American deaths from the attack on the Marine barracks still being mourned, and with a ticking

* Every presidential administration since Richard Nixon's has held that the War Powers Resolution is unconstitutional.

clock in the form of Congress ever present in our minds, I was sent to Lebanon to try to work out the problem. It brought to mind an observation former Israeli Prime Minister Shimon Peres once made to me: "If a problem has no solution, it is not a problem to be solved but a fact to be coped with over time."

CHAPTER 2

Into the Swamp

"WELCOME TO LEBANON, MR. RUMSFELD." © 1983 GEORGE DANBY

For years, Beirut had been known as the "Paris of the Middle East"—a favored destination of Western and Arab tourists. Its high-rise hotels along the Corniche and its magnificent port made it a symbol of a modern Middle East. That, of course, was before their civil war began in 1975. I thought I had been prepared for what I would see on my arrival in Beirut eight years later, but the physical devastation was much worse than I had expected. By the time of my visit in late 1983, large sections of downtown and portions of the port had been reduced to rubble. Once elegant hotels were pockmarked from rockets and bullets. Even the presidential palace was scarred by rocket attacks. That was where I first

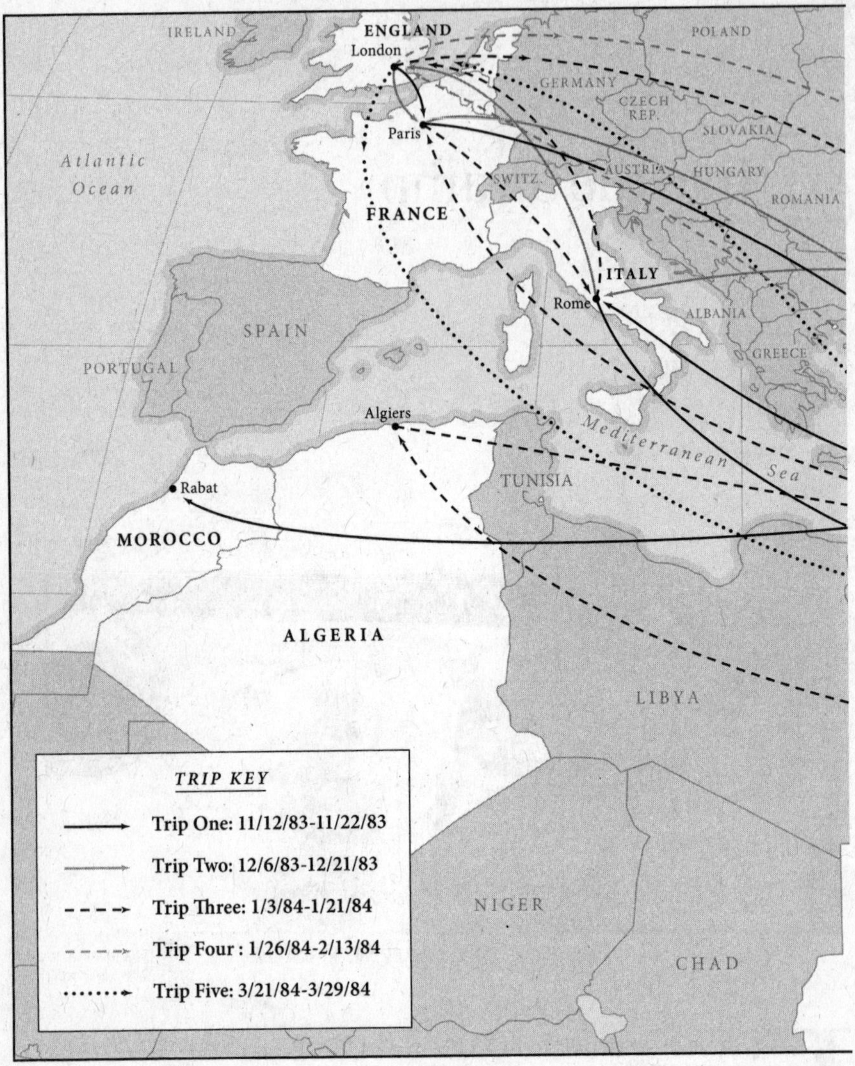

I traveled throughout the region five times during my brief tenure as President Reagan's Middle East envoy.

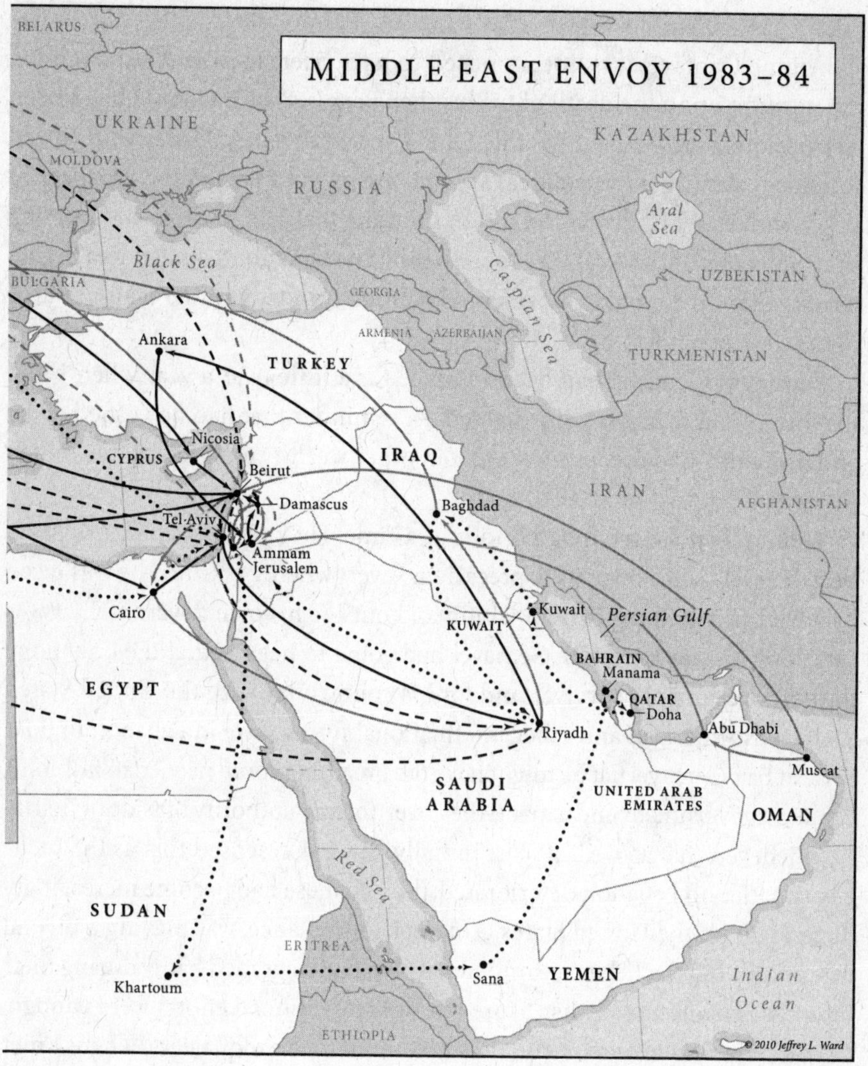
MIDDLE EAST ENVOY 1983–84
BELARUS
UKRAINE
MOLDOVA
RUSSIA
KAZAKHSTAN
Aral Sea
Black Sea
BULGARIA
GEORGIA
Caspian Sea
UZBEKISTAN
ARMENIA
AZERBAIJAN
TURKMENISTAN
Ankara
TURKEY
Nicosia
CYPRUS
IRAQ
Beirut
Damascus
Baghdad
IRAN
AFGHANISTAN
Tel Aviv
Ammam
Jerusalem
Cairo
Kuwait
KUWAIT
Persian Gulf
BAHRAIN
Manama
QATAR
Doha
EGYPT
Riyadh
Abu Dhabi
Muscat
SAUDI ARABIA
UNITED ARAB EMIRATES
OMAN
Red Sea
SUDAN
ERITREA
Khartoum
Sana
YEMEN
Indian Ocean
ETHIOPIA
© 2010 Jeffrey L. Ward

met Lebanon's beleaguered leader, who was struggling to hold his shattered country together.

Amine Gemayel was not supposed to have been president but assumed the position upon the death of his brother, Bashir. Bashir Gemayel had been a radical politician for the Middle East: a young dynamic leader who vowed to reform the Lebanese political system and even broached the prospect of peace with Israel. That was the sort of thinking that didn't win friends among the potentates of the Arab League. Bashir's assassination—linked to a Syrian terror group—resulted in his reserved, serious-minded brother taking charge of the shaken nation.

President Gemayel had been in office for a little over a year when I first met him. He was impeccably dressed—a reminder that had he wished to, he and his family had the resources to join other wealthy émigrés on the French Riviera.

Gemayel spoke for long periods at a time. He knew his country's prospects, as well as his own, were precarious. Everywhere he turned he was faced by adversaries and rivals, both within and outside his own government. I was struck by his raw emotion. Gemayel had come to believe that the only hope for his government's survival, and for his country, lay with the United States. As long as American and other multinational forces were in Lebanon to hold Syria at bay, Gemayel felt he might have the breathing room needed to fashion a coalition government and expand the government's authority outside of Beirut.

I believed that as well, at least initially. But I also sensed that as the security situation in Lebanon deteriorated, the Lebanese had become increasingly dependent on the United States. America, for instance, was playing a pivotal role in training the Lebanese military, which had degraded badly during their internal struggles. Yet I wasn't sure our well-intentioned efforts were enough. On one trip I went to visit the Lebanese military headquarters, where I met with their leadership and our American trainers. Our people seemed to be training the Lebanese for conventional actions against professional combat units rather than for engagements with militias and small terrorist cells. As I wrote Secretary Shultz, I wondered if we were preparing the Lebanese military to fight the right battles.[1]

I also wondered whether the United States was playing too prominent a role in Lebanese politics. By the time I arrived on the scene, there seemed to be an expectation that we would help select the Lebanese cabinet, notwithstanding our country's limited familiarity with the intricacies of Lebanese politics. To me, this was the diplomatic equivalent of amateur brain surgery.

The likely result would be having a government seen as a puppet of the United States. As their dependence was increasing, a growing number of Americans back home weren't sure how much they were willing to put on the line for that small country so far away.

Lebanon's President sensed this. Although the Reagan administration spoke of its commitment to his country, Gemayel was unconvinced—and understandably so. He could not be certain that the United States would fulfill its promise to protect the Lebanese. As a result, Gemayel feared he could be forced to choose between making an arrangement with either Israel or Syria to try to keep his government intact. Neither of those choices was acceptable to large factions of the Lebanese people. An arrangement with Israel would damage Lebanon's relations with its neighboring Arab nations. Gemayel, like most of his countrymen, also was wary of the Israelis and their intentions, and expressed the fear that Israel could devour his country "like a mouthful of bread." Being at Syria's mercy was an even worse alternative; mercy was not a defining characteristic of the Syrian regime. I noted that if Israel could eat Lebanon like a mouthful of bread, the Syrians could gobble up Lebanon like a potato chip.[2]

During my first twelve days in my new post, I held twenty-six official meetings in nine countries, traveling over twenty-five thousand miles, to develop a better understanding of America's options for our involvement in Lebanon. On the twelfth evening, weary and not feeling particularly enlightened, I put down some initial thoughts on the situation in a cable to Secretary Shultz I titled "The Swamp."[3] It was not a cheerful title; but it conveyed my sense of the region as a dangerous, shifting place inhospitable to American interests. My initial assessment was that we needed to lighten our hand somewhat in the Middle East, but to proceed carefully so as not to further upset the situation. Specifically, I wrote Shultz that we should:

- close the gap between inflated perceptions of our abilities and reality;
- never use U.S. troops as a "peacekeeping force," we were too big a target; and
- keep reminding ourselves that it is easier to get into something than it is to get out of it.

Contrary to what I expected when I first departed for Beirut, and despite my sympathy for the Lebanese people, I was left with the sense that there was little upside to our engagement. "My nose tells me that the odds are strongly stacked against us," I advised Shultz. "I wish we hadn't gone in. We need to be looking for a reasonably graceful way to get out."[4]

The ensuing months saw more violence in Lebanon, as extremists linked to Syria and Iran hoped to accelerate a U.S. withdrawal. In early 1984, terrorists murdered one of the most prominent Americans in Lebanon—Dr. Malcolm Kerr, president of the American University of Beirut. Since we also had to be near the top of the terrorists' wish list in the region, those charged with providing security for our team were particularly attentive.* Being assigned to stand inches away from high value American targets in the region was not exactly a formula for a long life.

I normally would have worked from the U.S. embassy in Beirut. But it had been closed after a bombing several months earlier that had killed sixty-three people. So instead my staff and I worked out of the American ambassador's residence some distance from the capital. Unfortunately, the ambassador's residence was hardly more secure than the embassy had been. It was shelled periodically, but there was no basement or shelter. As a result, during some of the attacks we spent time working under a staircase, which provided the best available cover.

One evening I left the ambassador's residence to go to a small shack in the complex that contained the communications equipment needed to contact Washington, D.C. Our mission's indispensable chief of staff, Tom Miller, and Ambassador Reg Bartholomew were with me. The shack contained two small rooms, a phone, and several radios. There was a small window with an air-conditioning unit in it. Just outside the shack, a SUV was parked near a tree.

When I made contact with the Secretary of State, he told me that he just had spoken with my wife, Joyce, who had been seeing reports on Chicago television and in the newspapers about the bombing and rocket attacks in Beirut, some of them in the areas where I was located.

"I talked with Joyce and reassured her," Shultz said confidently. "I told her you had the best security possible and you were safe."

At almost that exact moment, there was a loud explosion. A 122 millimeter Soviet-made Grad rocket hit the car just outside the shack. The impact

* The military adviser in Lebanon was Brigadier General Carl Stiner, a pivotal figure in the development of U.S. special operations forces.[5]

of the explosion blew the air conditioner out of the window and across Tom Miller's shoulder. A typewriter flew between Bartholomew's and my heads, and I was thrown to the floor. As I scrambled back to continue the call with Shultz, I realized the phone line was dead. We, fortunately, were not.

In late December 1983, Secretary of Defense Weinberger received crucial support for a prompt and complete withdrawal of U.S. forces from Lebanon in a study commissioned by the Pentagon. It placed responsibility on the military commanders on the ground for failing to have adequate security safeguards and noted that the Marine force "was not trained, organized, staffed, or supported to deal effectively with the terrorist threat in Lebanon."[6] The report recommended that the Marines in Lebanon be withdrawn.

After the report was published, President Reagan acknowledged that the Marines' mission in Lebanon was difficult. "We recognized the fact at the beginning," Reagan said, "and we're painfully mindful of it today. But the point is that our forces have already contributed to achievements that lay the foundation for a future peace, the restoration of a central government, and the establishment of an effective national Lebanese Army."[7] Asked if the United States planned to stay in Lebanon to see this work through, the President responded, "[W]hile there's hope for peace we have to remain."[8]

My own doubts about our ability to remain were growing. As I often do when dealing with a seemingly intractable problem, I developed an options paper. In the case of Lebanon, the exercise helped me think through whether we should persevere or, conversely, recognize that the potential for a positive outcome was limited and look for the best way to reduce American forces with as little damage to Lebanon and to our friends in the region as possible. In tough national security decisions, I've often found that there are seldom good options—only the least bad. This was the case in Lebanon. I estimated that we had a roughly 60 percent chance of accomplishing our goals in some form. These were not great odds, but I felt they were better than the alternative of a hasty withdrawal that would leave Lebanon to the control of the Syrians and further damage the reputation of our country. This was, after all, not quite a decade after our hasty withdrawal from Saigon at the end of the Vietnam War.

At the same time, a vigorous public debate was going on in Congress about whether to extend the mandate for U.S. troops in Lebanon—and if so, for how long. The Middle Eastern parties with whom we were negotiating learned all the details about the congressional debate by reading our newspapers. The Syrians were in effect being alerted that they probably had a winning hand.

Republican Senator Barry Goldwater was never one who had to be coaxed to offer his opinion. "We're not helping one bit," he said bluntly, "risking the lives of American Marines serving over there, trying to keep peace, when they've got a bunch of jackasses who want to kill each other. I'd get out of there and let them shoot."[9]

Also troubling was the position of Illinois Senator Charles Percy, the chairman of the Senate Foreign Relations Committee. He was from the opposite end of the Republican spectrum from Goldwater and had previously been inclined to stick it out in Lebanon. But Percy was now saying withdrawal from Lebanon should take place "as soon as possible."[10] Indeed, there was a growing impression that a withdrawal might be ordered at any moment.

The way Syria operated during the Lebanon crisis provided an interesting insight into how smaller nations can manipulate a superpower. It also was a cautionary lesson for me in the future about how to deal with totalitarian regimes opposed to America's national security interests.

The Syrian dictatorship possessed in the extreme two qualities particularly dangerous in a military adversary—ruthlessness and patience. Like all dictatorships, the regime had the advantage of not needing to cater to its domestic opinion. It could do whatever it deemed expedient to achieve its goals. The Syrians had been playing a diplomatic game with us for decades: doing just enough to look accommodating or coming up just shy of being too provocative. They played the international media like skilled poker players—offering public words of support for peace efforts so as to be seen as not unreasonable. The Syrians would float friendly diplomatic overtures to give the regime deniability when negotiations went off-track, as they had intended all along. This left them free to pursue their hostile interests behind the scenes: destabilizing the Lebanese government and supporting armed militias and terrorist groups. At other points, the Syrians dropped any pretense of cooperation and became immovable. Even during negotiations, Syrians and their then allies, the Druze, directed relentless artillery and rocket fire on the civilian population of Beirut.

The Syrians were savvy about the U.S. government. A Jordanian official told me the Syrians had analyzed America's War Powers Resolution carefully. They knew that congressional support for our involvement in Beirut was fragile and vulnerable to the slightest shift of activity in the region.[11] The Syrians believed correctly that they had the ability to force such a shift at their pleasure.

The obvious mixed signals the Syrians were receiving from Washington undoubtedly heightened that belief. Secretary Shultz and I observed that the Syrians were the most reasonable whenever the United States flew reconnaissance missions over their territories. They seemed sensitive to the proximity of American military power. When our flights were suspended, the Syrians became more intransigent. In mid-December 1983, the Department of Defense halted the reconnaissance flights without informing the State Department or our mission. It was done just at the moment we were trying to achieve concessions from the Syrian government. Even worse for American credibility, after assuring President Gemayel that the United States was going to continue to exert pressure on the Syrians, we heard through the grapevine that someone in the Department of State had tried to set up a separate, secret channel to make conciliatory overtures toward the Syrians. Here I was telling the Syrians there could be consequences for their actions while someone back in Washington was telling them just the opposite. Our delegation was blindsided.

None of these activities put me in a strong position when I arrived in Damascus on January 12, 1984, for my first meeting with one of the chief puppet masters behind the chaos in Lebanon, Syrian President Hafez al-Assad. In the best of worlds, Assad would be amenable to easing Syria's interference in Lebanon's political system and ending their support for terrorist groups. Neither prospect was likely, especially when America's negotiating position was weak. The best we could hope for was to have Assad believe he might pay a price if he went too far against American interests.

Known as the Sphinx of Damascus, Assad was a man of studied discipline and ruthless calculation. He once ordered the leveling of the entire Syrian town of Hama, murdering an estimated ten thousand to forty thousand of his own people in the process.

Assad received me in his villa south of Damascus, where he had been recovering from a heart ailment. In our three-and-a-half-hour meeting (not long by Assad standards), he plied me with a steady stream of coffee. I tried to point out the strength of America's position. I presented Assad with an overhead satellite photo of his capital city, including his presidential palace. In 1984, satellite photography was not as well known or accessible as it is today, with anyone able to use Google Earth. Back then overhead imagery was the exclusive purview of only a few technologically advanced governments, particularly ours. I gave Assad the photograph less to acknowledge his hospitality than to remind him that we were watching from above.

When our discussion turned to the business at hand, Assad was intractable. He was critical of our policy in Lebanon and in the Middle East generally. Assad expressed little sympathy for our concerns about terrorism in the region. He recited the trope that "one man's terrorist was another man's revolutionary." The American revolutionaries I had grown up admiring hadn't made a practice of killing civilians or paying suicide bombers.

In the case of Lebanon, the supposedly indecipherable Sphinx of Damascus was anything but. Time was on his side, and he knew it. What's more, he knew we knew it. My meeting with Assad underscored the folly of democratic countries trying to face off with a dictator unless that country is resolved and unified, with the firm purpose to see the mission through to the end.

When I later met with our coalition partners to report on our efforts, none suggested that they had that kind of staying power. Only France, which had a longstanding relationship with Lebanon, had an interest in continuing to try to stabilize the country.

When I met with British Prime Minister Margaret Thatcher, she made it clear as only she could that when it came to U.S. policy on Lebanon, she was at best a reluctant team player. I had long been a fan of "the Iron Lady," as the Soviets called her. I found that her stern reputation masked a dispassionate realism—which was certainly visible in her approach to the Middle East. In our meeting, she bore to the heart of the issue with crisp, unforgiving precision. She was skeptical of Lebanese President Gemayel's ability to expand his coalition and, in a break from the American position, equally skeptical of Israel's role in the standoff. She believed that our coalition lacked a clear mandate. She did not favor taking a tough stance with Syria because she believed that we needed them for a successful Middle East peace effort.[12] She noted that even when the United States challenged Syria, some American officials behaved in a way that signaled to the Syrians that we lacked the will or cohesion to actually follow through. A mixed message was the worst kind to send to an authoritarian regime, she noted. In that, as in many things, she was absolutely correct. If anyone left our meeting with an impression other than that the Prime Minister would be happy to be done with the whole business at the soonest possible opportunity, they hadn't been listening. In her public statements Thatcher was more diplomatic, offering words of solidarity with her political soul mate, President Reagan. But she also indicated what I knew well: Our time was running out.[13]

By the end of January 1984, as our Congress and most of our allies were ready to pull out, all hell was breaking loose in Lebanon. Emboldened by

America's mixed signals, the Syrians and the Druze stepped up their shelling of Beirut, causing increased civilian casualties. At the airport, our Marines were hunkered down behind new defensive barriers, under such restrictive rules of engagement that they were free to do little other than defend themselves. But rather than stiffening American resolve, the attacks seemed to be accelerating interest in withdrawal, at least among members of our government.

I got a taste of the mood in Congress when I went up to Capitol Hill to brief members. The Speaker of the House, the formidable Democrat Tip O'Neill, with whom I had served in Congress years before, had arranged for me to meet with the freshmen Democratic members. O'Neill understood how complex and challenging the situation was. His newly elected members were of a different sort. As I was going in to meet with this group, Tip pulled me aside. "Don't look for much help from me on this, Don," he warned. "I'm working with some crazies here." By now America's Lebanon policy had become simply a matter of arranging the details of an inevitable departure from the country.[14]

Retreat did not come easily for Ronald Reagan. "[T]he situation in Lebanon is difficult, frustrating, and dangerous," Reagan said in a radio address to the nation in early February 1984. "But that is no reason to turn our backs on friends and to cut and run. If we do, we'll be sending one signal to terrorists everywhere: They can gain by waging war against innocent people."[15]

As the President was making his strong public statements, members of his national security team were working to move the United States in a sharply different direction. An internal National Security Council (NSC) review of the Lebanon policy called for the prompt withdrawal of most American peacekeepers. But in a show of support for Lebanon, it also called for increasing American military training and support to the Lebanese Armed Forces, which would leave about five hundred military personnel on the ground.[16] Considering the alternatives, that sounded better than outright withdrawal. I believed that at least a residual presence could be helpful in sending a message that we were not going to simply depart hastily in defeat. I saw the situation in terms of flying a damaged plane: We could either crash land with a precipitous withdrawal or gradually reduce our presence in a controlled landing. I hoped that by the latter, we could salvage something, however modest, from our effort.

A couple of days after the issue appeared settled, George Shultz departed for meetings in South America and the President went to California. Meanwhile, fighting escalated in Lebanon, particularly around Beirut. On February 7, Reagan's national security officials convened an emergency meeting to discuss the Lebanon situation anew. With Reagan away, the meeting was chaired by Vice President Bush who, as I was told, with the support of Secretary of Defense Weinberger and White House Chief of Staff Jim Baker, pressed for the immediate withdrawal of all of our forces, including the trainers and advisers just agreed to, from Lebanon.[17] When informed of the recommendation, the President apparently acquiesced.

I was traveling in the region when Robert (Bud) McFarlane, Reagan's new national security adviser and a former Middle East envoy, delivered the news. "[T]he situation on the Hill is becoming explosive," he told me, in what might have been the understatement of the year. He insisted that the Congress would not agree to a residual presence of any U.S. forces at the Beirut airport, and that the administration needed "to act before the Congress confronts us with a very restrictive resolution or other problems."[18]

I understood the dynamics in Washington pretty well, but I was disheartened that the American effort was ending so precipitously. It was similar to watching the American withdrawal from Saigon at the end of the Vietnam War, one of the low moments for America in recent history. At the time, I suspected that if Reagan and Shultz had been present at that NSC meeting, the decision might have come out differently.

Now it fell to me to deliver the disappointing news to President Gemayel. It was among the saddest tasks I have had to perform. After talking with McFarlane, I traveled to the presidential palace in Beirut. The palace had taken four direct hits that morning. Windows were broken and the long white drapes were blowing out in the wind. As I walked to the President's office, I stepped around a pool of blood from a palace guard who had been hit in the shelling. I was reminded again of the personal courage Gemayel displayed by remaining in Beirut.

The Lebanese leader was amazed to learn that America had arrived at this decision. Though I knew he had cause to doubt the depth of the American commitment to his country, he appeared to have not imagined that we would desert him altogether. Being involved in diplomacy on behalf of the United States, I came to appreciate the perspectives many other countries have toward us. It sometimes seems to me we are looking at each other from opposite ends of a telescope. Smaller nations seem to look at us from the small end, through which we look enormous, even omnipotent. Americans have a tendency to look at other countries from the other end, and so their concerns seem smaller to us. This has colored the impression of our country in the Middle East, and indeed in the rest of the world: The view seems to be that if the United States can put a man on the moon we ought to be able to do almost anything if we really want to. Many believe that if we don't achieve a goal they want, it is because we aren't trying hard enough. That seemed to be Gemayel's view.

Even though he was clearly down, the Lebanese leader was not ready to give up. He said he would remain in Beirut and do his best to try to pull together a workable coalition government. He explained his predicament and the serious problems he faced: trying to keep the ethnically and religiously diverse Lebanese army together; maneuvering to keep the Syrians off his back; and trying to persuade the Lebanese people to come together to save their country.

Trying to maintain his dignity, he urged that I ask President Reagan to reconsider his decision to withdraw.[19] "I want to be very frank," he said. "I am not trying to run away from my responsibility. . . . Now it is a matter of saving my country."

I could provide Gemayel with no reassurance. I knew the decision would not be reconsidered. The United States had been one of Lebanon's close allies. As I left him to his fate, I felt what he felt: America had not lived up to its promises.

To my surprise, the statement from the White House announcing the American withdrawal was couched in buoyant optimism. "[A]fter consultation with our MNF [multinational force] partners and President Gemayel, and at his request, we are prepared to do the following," the statement began. It outlined a series of steps the administration was taking to further help the Lebanese. "We will stand firm to deter those who seek to influence Lebanon's future by intimidation," the statement added, pledging support for the Gemayel government. The steps, the statement said, "will strengthen our ability to do the job we set out to do and to sustain our efforts over the long term."[20] From the language, one could have been forgiven for thinking the new decision being announced was a victory for the Lebanese government. The reality was Gemayel would now be alone facing Syria and the centrifugal forces pulling apart his country.

The day after the White House statement, the Syrians and their allies stepped up their artillery and rocket attacks against the presidential palace, the American ambassador's residence, and other targets in the hills overlooking Beirut. On February 8, more rounds of artillery landed near the ambassador's residence. The United States did not mount any military response to these attempts to kill or injure our ambassador and his staff. I asked Washington about the new and tougher rules of engagement that had been approved by the President in the event American personnel continued to come under attack in Lebanon. I argued for a military response of some kind. The battleship USS *New Jersey* eventually began a shore bombardment using its sixteen-inch guns. But the retaliatory strike came late and was well off target. The shelling's only effect was to signal American ineffectiveness, quite the opposite of what the President intended.*

At the end of March 1984, I stopped in Beirut for a final meeting in Lebanon with President Gemayel. Our encounter took place at midnight and lasted an hour and a half. Knowing now that the administration would not reconsider its decision to withdraw, Gemayel felt defeated. There was an air of despondency in his voice, followed by moments of resignation. After the dozens of hours we had spent together in the heat of battle, when our hopes had been higher, it was a sad parting. With the Syrians gaining an upper hand in his country, I thought it might be the last time I would see the courageous but disheartened Lebanese President.†

Despite Shultz's and my hopes for an orderly evacuation, the departure of American forces from Lebanon ended up appearing frantic. Our withdrawal was met with despair by the Lebanese people and with ridicule from the French.[21] The Italians left as soon as we did, and even the French, despite their disparagement of the American pullout, followed shortly thereafter. Lebanon and Israel never forged a satisfactory arrangement. Syria would remain in Lebanon for the next two decades, just as Hafez al-Assad had intended.

I returned to Washington on March 29, 1984, having worked hard on the complex and intractable issues in the region but disappointed in the outcome. While some would point a finger at Lebanon's failings, it is also true that the withdrawal of American troops, our inability to match actions with our pub-

* The shelling from the *New Jersey* kicked up dust but did no damage whatsoever. As I learned from my former senior military assistant, Vice Admiral Staser Holcomb, then serving as commander of U.S. naval forces in Europe, the President's orders to respond to the shelling had come down the military chain of command "through multiple sets of clenched teeth." In other words, no one had been insubordinate, but the reluctance at each level had the effect of substantially modifying the response Reagan intended.

† The dangers confronting the Gemayel family did not end with the murder of Bashir, and they did not disappear after the United States withdrew from Lebanon. Amine's son, Pierre, was openly critical of Syria's influence in his country. Twice elected to the country's parliament, Pierre was serving as Lebanon's industry minister when he was assassinated on November 21, 2006.

lic statements and our hopes, and a lack of firmness by the administration in the face of congressional pressure had contributed to the outcome.

There were many decisions and judgments that had led our country to this point. For one, the administration may not have fully appreciated the staying power and determination of a regime like Syria's. We approached a dictatorial regime from a position of weakness. Ruthless actors do not follow our modes of behavior. For example, one assumption in our negotiations with Syria was that their forces would withdraw from Lebanon if America could get Israeli forces to do so. That proved to be incorrect.

We experienced the risks of allowing our friends to become dependent on the United States. The Lebanese military could not fill the vacuum after America withdrew, at least in part because they had not been trained for the type of fighting they'd face. The other problem was the difficulty of having a national military force in a country with strong ethnic divisions. The government of Lebanon wasn't able to achieve the cohesion necessary to provide effective leadership and, as it turned out, rested too much of its hopes on a continued American presence.

The experience with Lebanon confirmed my impressions of the Middle East as a tangle of hidden agendas, longstanding animosities, and differing perceptions operating above and beneath the surface. The hope that moderate Arab states, such as Saudi Arabia, Egypt, Jordan, and others, might play a constructive role in the crisis also proved to be misplaced.

I was troubled by the unrealistic expectations some in the region had of the United States, of the ways and how rapidly we could assist them if their neighbors took aggressive actions. In my travels, I was often warned by Gulf leaders about the looming dangers posed by Iran and Syria, and, potentially, by Iraq. I explained the need for our friends to undertake planning to deter aggression. I urged them to be prepared beforehand—and not found wanting after a new crisis arose. While I found the Saudis and Bahrainis somewhat receptive, the Kuwaitis, for one, were less so. Many leaders seemed to believe that American forces would be able to appear magically from over the horizon and deliver them from Iran's or Iraq's clutches; these beliefs encouraged them to do relatively little about their own defenses.

The difficulty in coordinating the military and political elements of the U.S. government and the Congress also became apparent during the Lebanon crisis. It pointed out just how important it is for there to be a tight linkage between our country's diplomatic and military capabilities if America is to successfully meet its national security objectives.

While some believed that a decade after Vietnam, America had finally shed the baggage of our involvement in Southeast Asia, it seemed the American body politic was still a prisoner of the Vietnam experience. The country was able to deal with short operations such as the evacuation of American citizens from Grenada, which had occurred almost simultaneously with the Marine barracks bombing. But it was not well prepared to address the more complex challenge we faced in Lebanon. Our government—the Department of Defense as well as the Congress—and the media were still focused on yesterday's war, reacting to the Vietnam experience but not confronting the growing problem of international terrorism.

Perhaps the most important lesson was that our government had not yet developed a full appreciation of the devastating effectiveness of terrorism as an instrument of policy against us and, indeed, against any free nation. We were on defense when we needed to be on offense. After the Marine barracks truck bombing, the immediate reaction was to do everything possible to defend against a similar attack. Cement barriers were put on the grounds around buildings, so that trucks with explosives couldn't easily run into our buildings as they had before. The terrorists started using rocket-propelled grenades (RPGs), lobbing them over the cement barricades. So to defend against RPG attacks, embassy buildings along the Corniche in Beirut were next draped with a metal mesh to keep them from hitting the building. Because the mesh worked reasonably well, it wasn't long before terrorists began hitting the soft targets, namely Americans and other Westerners going to and from their work.

It should have been clear: The way to successfully deal with terrorists is not only to try to defend against them, but also to take the battle to them; to go after them where they live, where they plan, where they hide; to go after their finances and their networks; and even to go after nations that harbor and assist them. The best defense would be a good offense.

Beirut demonstrated to me the profound truth that weakness is provocative. Our withdrawal from Lebanon contributed again to an impression among our friends and enemies of a vulnerable and irresolute America. This, of course, was President Reagan's concern all along.

One observer of our pullout from Lebanon was a young Saudi. The American response to the Beirut terrorist attack, Osama bin Laden observed, demonstrated "the decline of American power and the weakness of the American soldier, who is ready to wage cold wars but unprepared to fight long wars. This was proven in Beirut in 1983, when the Marines fled."[22] Osama bin Laden said he first conceived his attack on the World Trade Center during that period.

Referring to the destruction of the Marine barracks and the bombing of the U.S. embassy in Beirut, Bin Laden later noted, "When I saw those destroyed towers in Lebanon, it sparked in my mind that the oppressors should be punished in the same way and that we should destroy towers in America—so they can taste what we tasted and so they stop killing our women and children."[23]

We were already entering a new age of terrorism, although many didn't fully appreciate it. In September 1984, after U.S. forces had withdrawn from Lebanon, the U.S. embassy annex was nearly destroyed by a bomb, the third major attack on Americans in Lebanon in three years.

A month later, Prime Minister Thatcher barely escaped assassination by the Irish Republican Army. She was in her hotel room when a bomb exploded, destroying the bathroom she had been in only moments earlier. Her would-be assassins left Mrs. Thatcher a chilling note that I've reflected on many times since. "We have only to be lucky once," they wrote to her. "You will have to be lucky always."

Within weeks of Thatcher's hairbreadth escape, George Shultz and I each delivered speeches on our recent experiences in the Middle East and the rising danger posed by terrorists. On October 17, 1984, I was awarded the George Catlett Marshall Medal presented by the Association of the U.S. Army. In my acceptance remarks, I summarized my conviction that the United States and free people everywhere needed to come to grips with terrorism as a preeminent threat of the future:

> Increasingly, terrorism is not random nor the work of isolated madmen. Rather, it is state-sponsored, by nations using it as a central element of their foreign policy. . . . A single attack by a small weak nation, by influencing public opinion and morale, can alter the behavior of great nations or force tribute from wealthy nations. Unchecked, state-sponsored terrorism is adversely changing the balance of power in our world.[24]

Just a week after I gave my speech, George Shultz sounded a similar note of caution. He warned against America acting as a global Hamlet while terrorism was on the rise. "The magnitude of the threat posed by terrorism is so great that we cannot afford to confront it with halfhearted and poorly organized measures," Shultz warned.[25]

In a preview of what President George W. Bush would call for less than two decades later, Shultz urged that America pursue a policy goal of preempting terrorist atrocities. He recommended strengthening U.S. intelligence capabilities, demonstrating a willingness to use force when and where needed to confront terrorism, and deploying the full range of measures available to our country.

"We will need the flexibility to respond to terrorist attacks in a variety of ways," Shultz advised, using words that mirrored ones a future president would use, "at times and places of our own choosing."

The Beirut bombing and its aftermath remain seared in my mind as the beginning of the modern war waged by Islamist radicals against the United States of America. It was one of those rare moments when our country was awakened, however briefly, to the dangers foreign elements could pose to our interests. Another of those moments would occur on a bright September morning in 2001. But the first, for me, took place much earlier—on a December afternoon when I was just a boy.

PART II

An American, Chicago Born

"I am an American, Chicago born . . .
and go at things as I have taught myself. . . ."

—*Saul Bellow,* The Adventures of Augie March[1]

Cook County, Illinois

DECEMBER 7, 1941

In the carefree days of the early 1940s, when I was not yet ten years old, my life centered on school, chores, and, for entertainment, the family radio. Sometimes I'd tune in to *Captain Midnight,* which was about a U.S. Army pilot and his dangerous adventures. But it was another program that fully captured my imagination. Countless times I hurried into the living room so I wouldn't miss its famous opening to the sounds of the "William Tell Overture":

> A fiery horse with the speed of light, a cloud of dust, and a hearty "Hi-yo, Silver!" The Lone Ranger! With his faithful Indian companion, Tonto, the daring and resourceful masked rider of the plains led the fight for law and order in the early West. Return with us now to those thrilling days of yesteryear. The Lone Ranger rides again.

For many young boys in the quiet villages on the outskirts of Chicago, where the biggest neighborhood news usually was the search for a missing dog, the American West offered mystery and excitement. My friends and I sent in for the Lone Ranger's six-shooter ring and deputy badge. And we learned the Lone Ranger credo: "I believe that to have a friend, a man must be one. That all men are created equal and that everyone has within himself the power to make this a better world. That God put the firewood there, but that every man must gather and light it himself." Seven decades later, it is still not a bad philosophy.

The radio also was our portal into the world of professional sports. In the fall, that meant football. My father and I cheered on our favorite team, the Chicago Bears. The Bears were fighting it out one Sunday at Comiskey Park when the announcer on Chicago's WENR radio station interrupted the action with a bulletin. "Flash: Airplanes from the empire of Japan have launched a surprise attack on the territories of Hawaii." A U.S. military base called Pearl Harbor was in flames.

NBC Radio broke from its regular programming to air a live report from Honolulu: "We have witnessed this morning . . . the severe bombing of Pearl Harbor by enemy planes, undoubtedly Japanese. The city of Honolulu has also been attacked and considerable damage done. This battle has been going on for nearly three hours. . . . It is no joke. It is a real war."[2] Hawaii was not yet an American state, but I had a vague idea of where it was. I didn't know anything about Pearl Harbor or what it meant to the United States Navy. But I could feel that something terrible had happened. I saw it in my parents' faces and heard it in the tense voices reporting the news of the attack. From that moment on, much of what was on the radio, in the newspapers, in talk on the streets, and in school centered on the attack.

For two years, Americans had followed the conflicts raging in Europe and Asia, but from the comfortable distance provided by two vast oceans. Many remembered the heavy American losses in World War I a little more than two decades earlier and wanted no part in another territorial dispute far away. That sentiment was especially strong in Chicago. The city was the national headquarters of the antiwar America First Committee. With more than eight hundred thousand members, it was one of the largest antiwar organizations in American history. The America Firsters appealed to many young Americans, including some whose paths I would cross in later life—a student at Yale Law School named Gerald Ford as well as a young John F. Kennedy, who sent the committee a check.* The America First Committee was one of the early casualties of the Pearl Harbor attack. Its membership dwindled almost overnight. And many of its supporters—Ford and Kennedy among them—soon went off to war.

Throughout the rest of that Sunday, our family huddled around the radio, listening to the latest news. New reports were coming in every hour:

> President Roosevelt's announcement of Japanese air attacks on United States Pacific bases staggered London, according to a dispatch just received, and London now awaits Prime Minister Churchill's promise to declare war on Japan within the hour. . . . Political lines have been almost

*The Kennedy who most aided the cause of the America Firsters was Joseph P. Kennedy, John's father and a former U.S. ambassador to Great Britain. Returning to the United States in 1940, he announced that the British would have to seek an accord with Nazi Germany. "Democracy is finished in England," he was quoted in a notorious front-page article. "It may be here."[3]

> wiped out. Senator Wheeler of Montana, a leading isolationist says, "We must do the best we can to lick Japan." . . . And the *Chicago Tribune*, one of the leading isolationist papers prints this headline for tomorrow morning: "OUR COUNTRY: RIGHT OR WRONG."[4]

The next day, the American people heard from the President. Having first been elected four months after I was born, Franklin Delano Roosevelt was the only president I had known. There was something about Roosevelt's voice that added to his authority. He had a formal, almost aristocratic tone. He certainly did not sound like any of our friends in the Midwest. Throughout the Great Depression, he had been a voice of reassurance, including to my parents. Outlining the indictment against the Japanese empire, he spoke slowly and deliberately. Every syllable was carefully enunciated, as if the words themselves were missiles of outrage and anger. That gave him a singular quality as America heard for the first time the words that have now become so familiar to history: "Yesterday, December 7, 1941—a date which will live in infamy . . ."[5]

The President asked Congress for a declaration of war. The fate of democracy now hung on America's success. A war that millions at home had wanted to avoid was going to be fought, and many Americans would die in the cause. The conflict would change the lives of Americans across the country, including a boy in Illinois who wondered if we'd be able to return to the carefree world of *The Lone Ranger* again.

CHAPTER 3

The Last of Spring

Don Rumsfeld
January 11, 1946

My Autobiography - Page 1.

My name is Donald Henry Rumsfeld. I was born in St. Luke's Hospital in Chicago, Illinois, on the ninth of July in the year 1932.

In the desperate, hardscrabble years of the Great Depression, 1932 was, as the historian William Manchester described it, "the cruelest year" of them all.[1]

Even resilient, industrial Chicago had not been spared the Depression's ravages. On the edge of the Loop, the city's downtown business district, thousands of those left unemployed and homeless constructed a Hooverville of scrap metal shanties and cardboard tents, named as such to disparage the president who was blamed for the economic woes. Alleys and streets were given new names like Prosperity Road and Hard Times Avenue.[2]

On July 9, 1932, the *Chicago Tribune* noted grimly that the Dow Jones Industrial Average had closed the day before at 41.22—the lowest point recorded during the Great Depression. This was the day I was born—on what may well have been the bleakest day of the cruelest year of the worst economic catastrophe in American history. Born in St. Luke's Hospital in downtown Chicago, I was the second child of George and Jeannette Rumsfeld. As I later recorded in my first and only other attempt at an autobiography (at age thirteen) I came home from the hospital to find I had a two-year-old sister, Joan.[3] Since my family moved a great deal during our early years, Joan tended to be a frequent playmate and one of my closest friends.

Our mother, Jeannette, was a small woman, but her stature belied a feisty intensity. A teacher by training, she was a stickler for proper grammar. While she was kindhearted, she was also a formidable taskmaster. One vivid memory of my mother occurred when we lived briefly in North Carolina. In the South teachers taught by rote, as opposed to the progressive education I was used to in Illinois, in which students were encouraged to learn at their own pace. As a result I was far behind my Southern classmates. When told that I was in danger of being held back a grade, Mom bridled. She told my teacher that I would attend summer school and that she would tutor me personally to get me up to speed. Every day, Mom and I went through drills to make sure I learned my division tables. It wasn't my favorite summer, but I learned enough to make it to the next grade.

My father, George Rumsfeld, was the kind of man any young boy would look to as a role model. I certainly did. He was the most honest and ethical person I knew, and I often sought his advice. One of the reasons he might have worked so hard to be a good father is that he knew what it was like not to have one. John von Johann Heinrich Rumsfeld left the family and divorced my father's mother soon after his birth. From an early age, it was up to my father and his older brother, Henry, to help support the family. Dad started as an office boy at the age of twelve and worked hard for most of his life, always with an upbeat manner, often whistling, and without complaint. He seemed to have a sense of urgency about things and was never one to waste time. Sometimes he'd take me to the public golf course near twilight for his version of speed golf—playing nine holes in what I remember to be less than forty-five minutes, never stopping to take a practice swing.

My earliest years were spent in the city of Chicago, which by then had become known as a settling place for large numbers of European immigrants, industrious frontiersmen seeking a second chance at fortune, and for sizable numbers of African Americans, who emigrated from the South. Yet amid the city's diversity, Chicagoans shared a common trait: a decidedly unfriendly attitude to the pretensions of aristocratic Europe. Many in Chicago were Irish at the time, and local politicians gloried in mocking the English, and the British seemed to reciprocate. "Having seen it," the British writer Rudyard Kipling sniffed after visiting Chicago, "I urgently desire never to see it again. It is inhabited by savages."[4]

There was some truth to the notion that the city was not for those with delicate sensibilities. The city gave America Al Capone, the St. Valentine's Day Massacre, the Black Sox Scandal of 1919, and its legendary machine politics—denizens of its cemeteries were known for voting early and often. Chicago's residents took a certain pride in their rough-and-tumble ways. It was a city where one's value was measured not so much by pedigree but by sweat. "Chicago," American writer Lincoln Steffens once wrote, quite correctly, "will give you a chance."[5]

My father had spent most of his youth and first years of marriage in modest apartments in the city and was eager to move his family to a house in the suburbs. When I was six, we moved to nearby Evanston, home of Northwestern University, and then finally to a house in Winnetka, a small suburb to the north. These moves were not idle decisions but ones that my father, quite typically, had carefully thought through. Dad believed that the areas where the schools were considered the best tended to be areas where property values would increase. Winnetka, in the New Trier High School district, was such a place. We shared our house with Dad's mother, Lizette, and her mother, Elizabeth. The older women, who had raised Dad, often spoke to each other in German.*

These days Winnetka is a well-to-do bedroom suburb of Chicago, but in the 1930s the town was economically diverse. Our neighborhood was a mix of businessmen with families and immigrant and working-class families: construction workers, a train conductor, an electrical power line worker, a gardener, and a cleaner among them.

I guess because my parents were energetic people, I must have inherited that characteristic at an early age. In addition to my studies, I played third base on Conney's Cubs, our village hardball team, which was sponsored by the local pharmacy. I joined the Cub Scouts when I was seven, and enjoyed excursions to hike, fish, and canoe. As far back as I can remember I had odd jobs. I was not yet ten when I determined that I would earn enough money for my first Schwinn bicycle. I delivered newspapers, mowed lawns, and sold magazine subscriptions, including the Norman Rockwell–covered *Saturday Evening Post*. On Saturdays I earned a hefty twenty cents for delivering a neighbor's homemade sandwiches to the employees at the Winnetka Trust & Savings Bank. When I finally earned enough money for my red Schwinn, it seemed the most perfect thing in the world. For kids in our neighborhood, our bikes were freedom. We could go anywhere we wanted. At least until it was time to come home.

* The Rumsfelds trace their roots to a small farm on the outskirts of Sudweyhe in Lower Saxony. Members of our family can still be found there. In the late nineteenth century, my great-grandfather Johann Hermann Rumsfeld, a merchant seaman, immigrated to America. After settling initially on the East Coast, his son John von Johann Heinrich eventually made his way westward to Chicago.

All in all, mine was a fairly typical childhood in a small Midwestern town in the 1930s. Before Pearl Harbor.

Shortly after the Japanese attack, my father volunteered to join the Navy. Dad was not an ideal recruit. He was thirty-eight years old, well past the age draft boards were seeking. He had a slight frame that made him appear frailer than he was. The Navy recruiting office turned him away.

Instead of giving up, Dad embarked on an effort to gain weight. He ate banana splits, milk shakes, and anything else that would pack on pounds. After undertaking this regimen, Dad went back to the recruiting office and tried again.

It may have helped him that the war was not going well. The recruiting office finally said yes and told the determined man with the German name to prepare to deploy for officer training. His decision meant a big change in our lives.

After his ninety-day training assignment in Quonset Point, Rhode Island, Dad was commissioned, and our family moved to a blimp base near Elizabeth City, North Carolina. Navy blimps were used to spot German U-boats stalking Allied merchant ships in the Atlantic. My father didn't want to spend the war in North Carolina though, and quickly requested a transfer to sea duty. Eventually his request was granted, and he was assigned to the USS *Bismarck Sea* (CVE-95), a baby flattop, or escort carrier, in the final phases of completion at a shipyard near Bremerton, Washington. Originally, my parents decided that the family would return to Illinois. But Mom didn't want to be that far away from Dad, and at the last minute she decided we would travel with him until he went out to sea. So we moved next to East Port Orchard, Washington, then briefly to Seaside, Oregon, while the ship was being completed.

In 1944, after the *Bismarck Sea*'s shakedown cruise, the Navy transferred my father to the USS *Hollandia* (CVE-97), which was also preparing to deploy to the Pacific theater. The reassignment turned out to be fortuitous. After Dad went off to sea with the *Hollandia*, the *Bismarck Sea* was sunk by a kamikaze attack. More than three hundred people onboard were killed.

With our father at sea, my mother, like so many wives whose husbands were off at war, had to manage the family by herself. She learned to drive for the first time after Pearl Harbor, and wasn't particularly comfortable with it. Heading south from Oregon, we drove through San Francisco. Mom was so nervous about driving up and down that city's famous hills in our green 1937 Oldsmobile that she made Joan and me get out of the car and walk in case she lost control of the vehicle trying to work the clutch and floor stick shift.

Without having a chance to consult Dad, she bought a tiny house on C Avenue in Coronado, California, not too far from the naval air station. It was a big decision for her to make, with little money and less experience in such matters. Throughout the war, she was careful with purchases. Mom once wrote to my father that out of the $190 she had for the month, the family's expenses totaled $186.37.*

We were fortunate to be in Coronado with so many other military families in roughly the same circumstances. Mom became good friends with the wives of others in the crew of the *Hollandia*. They shared their worries and their news with one another. Many of the kids I went to school with had fathers or older brothers deployed, so we shared a special bond.

We followed the news of the war by poring over maps in newspapers, listening to radio reports, and watching the short newsreels that played in movie theaters before the feature presentations. Everyone I knew in Coronado supported the war effort with a sense of common purpose. We planted Victory Gardens, where we grew our own vegetables. With earnings from odd jobs, I bought coupons or stamps for war bonds. I collected paper, rubber, and metal hangers to be recycled into war materials. My mother saved frying oil to be used for munitions. No one could buy new car tires, because rubber was being used for military vehicles, so old tires were retreaded. The government rationed such staples as gasoline, sugar, butter, and nylon. There were few complaints—there was a sense we were all in it together.

As the war went on, we would spot small flags in people's windows with a star that signified someone in that house was in military service. When a serviceman was killed, those flags would be replaced with ones that had gold stars.

My parents were not accustomed to being apart, and it wore on both of them. Mom wrote letters almost every day. Dad would respond on the thin, onion-skin paper known as V-mail, the "V" standing for victory. Sometimes letters would fall apart as they came out of the envelope, because parts had been cut out by the censors aboard the ship to avoid giving the enemy intelligence if the mail was intercepted. As a result, we never knew where Dad was or what he was doing, but we were happy to receive his letters because that way we knew he was safe.

* She itemized her expenses for Dad, including $70.00 for the house payment, $6.52 for gas and electricity, $2.60 for water; $8.37 for milk; $47.00 for six months' taxes, and $7.00 for my new pair of shoes. Mom supplemented our income by working as a substitute schoolteacher. The tight finances were yet another challenge that she—like so many other military wives—was facing on her own.[6]

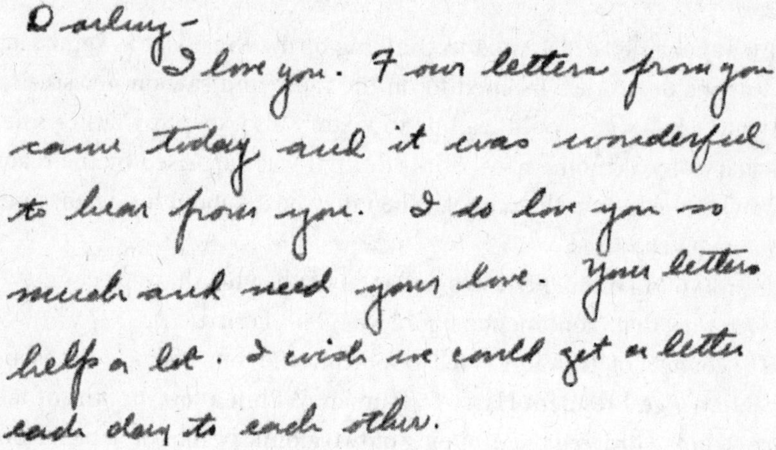

Darling—

I love you. Four letters from you came today and it was wonderful to hear from you. I do love you so much and need your love. Your letters help a lot. I wish we could get a letter each day to each other.

Letter from Jeannette Rumsfeld to George Rumsfeld, November 14, 1944.

"Well Darling, so long for now," Dad wrote to my mother in August of 1944. "I love you and don't think I'll ever want to leave you or the kids again when this war business is over."[7]

Around my father's birthday, Mom wrote, "We didn't have cake on your birthday—I didn't want it without you. We just thought of you all day and talked about you and thought you many birthday wishes. . . . I want more time with you—all I can have—and as soon as possible."[8]

Mom updated Dad on Joan and me. "[Don] is the type of person who needs to keep busy and he does keep busy," she wrote in one letter. "Don said this evening at dinner that he has three ambitions. He would like to become a 'band leader' like Harry James [at the time I played the cornet in the junior high school band]—an 'architect' and a 'flying Naval Officer.'"[9] As it turned out, I would only fulfill one out of three.

In one of my letters to Dad, I updated him on what I was sure he needed to know. Softball was in season and I was going out for right or center field. Even though Dad was at sea in the Pacific Ocean, I did have my priorities. "Would you please try to get me a . . . fielder's mitt if you can?" I asked. "I miss you a lot," I added. "Take good care of yourself."[10] I couldn't wait for him to come home.

A dramatic moment for me came quite unexpectedly when I was working on a school play in the courtyard of Coronado Junior High School. An urgent announcement came over the loudspeaker: President Franklin Roosevelt had died.

I had become accustomed to thinking of the President as indomitable. He was the person we listened to on the radio and saw on newsreels, the one who I believed would lead us to victory and keep my father safe. As shocked as I was by the news of his death, I was surprised by the reaction of a few of the kids in the school. When they heard about his death, some of them seemed cheered.

In my young mind, FDR was tied to my father, his ship, our country, and the war. Now that monumental figure was gone. I cried.

The conduct of the war now fell to someone the country knew almost nothing about, Vice President Harry S. Truman. Within a few months of taking office, Truman ordered the dropping of two atomic bombs on Japan. None of us knew what an atomic bomb was other than that it was a powerful explosive, and there was something called fallout from the massive detonation. For many Americans, including our family, the bombings meant that the long bloody war, a war that had cost sixty million lives, might soon be near its end.

After the second bomb was dropped on the Japanese city of Nagasaki, Dad wrote my mother a letter. "There is much conversation among the crew about the possibility of a Jap surrender, based on nothing concrete of course, as we have no information other than that from the radio," Dad told her. "All of us think, however, that there is a good likelihood of it happening not far in the future. It is wonderful to contemplate."[11]

His hope was fulfilled a few days later. On August 15, 1945, newspapers carried variations on the headline: "JAPAN SURRENDERS, END OF WAR!" I was selling the San Diego newspaper at the Coronado ferry dock with that message emblazoned on the front page. I sold out every copy of the paper that day, though in retrospect I wish I'd kept one. V-J Day meant my father would be coming home.

At first the USS *Hollandia* was scheduled to go to Japan as part of the occupation force. But the ship was assigned instead to bring back to the United States the survivors of the USS *Indianapolis,* which had been sunk in the Pacific by a Japanese submarine. It was a terrible disaster. Approximately three hundred U.S. naval personnel went down with the ship. Of the nine hundred or so men who had made it into the water, only about three hundred were rescued after nearly five days with no food or water, facing exposure and shark attacks. So the USS *Hollandia* returned to the United States on September 26, 1945—stopping first to drop off the wounded survivors of the

Indianapolis, then coming into port the following day to disembark the *Hollandia*'s crew.

When we received word that the ship was coming in, my mother drove us up to meet Dad. Mom, Joan, and I watched the ship disembark the passengers and crew. Finally, my father came off the ship. For this thirteen-year-old boy, all was suddenly right with the world.

After my father died in 1974, I found a wrinkled letter among his papers that seemed to sum up as eloquently as anyone could what his service and the service of so many others had meant to the country. The letter was signed by Secretary of the Navy James Forrestal, who later became our country's first secretary of defense. I assume it was sent to wartime personnel when they left the Navy for civilian life. Forrestal wrote that he had timed the letter to arrive after Dad was formally discharged from service "because, without formality but as clearly as I know how to say it, I want the Navy's pride in you, which it is my privilege to express, to reach into your civil life and remain with you always."[12] Decades later, when I served as one of Forrestal's successors as secretary of defense, I framed that letter, hung it in my office, and thought of it often when other young men and women were sent off to war in distant lands.

With my father officially discharged, we drove back to Illinois. Dad went right back to work at the same real estate firm he had started with at age twelve. He spent his days as a residential real estate salesman and then made extra money by buying houses in areas with good school districts, fixing them up, and then selling them for a profit. As a result, we lived in six or seven different houses over the next few years, including three houses on the same street in Winnetka. Because we were constantly refurbishing our homes, many nights when I came home from school I would help steam, soak, and scrape off the old wallpaper and put up new wallpaper in its place. After our work was done, Dad would put the house on the market to sell it, and he'd start over again in a new place.

I liked high school and studied hard. I played as many sports as I could. In my freshman year I entered the intramural wrestling tournament, and made it to the finals. By my senior year, I was co-captain of the varsity wrestling team with my friend Lenny Vyskocil, and our team won the Illinois state title for the first time in our school's history.

Over the years people have asked me about my many years as a wrestler, and even tried to make it a metaphor for my approach to life. The fact is that wrestling happened to be a sport I was suited for. As with most activities,

I found that the harder I worked at wrestling, the better I got, and I began to understand the direct link between effort and results.

In high school, I met Marion Joyce Pierson. Our friendship developed in a larger group of our friends, who would gather at the local diner. Hamburgers, fries, milk shakes, and the jukebox seemed a way of life on Friday and Saturday nights. Joyce and I were both elected class officers in our junior year. Through that year, I became increasingly aware of her spirited but unassuming style. Her eyes had a certain twinkle, as if they were concealing a wise insight or a humorous thought. We started dating when we were seniors, and it was an on-again, off-again relationship for most of the year.

As I considered college, I received proposals for wrestling scholarships from a number of the Big Ten universities, which I weighed carefully. But the dean at my high school, Fred Kahler, suggested that I go to Princeton. He had gone there, and Princeton, in his mind as a proud alumnus, was the best place for me. Until that moment, I had thought of the Ivy League as a place for the wealthy or connected, and I didn't know which of those categories I fit into less.

When I learned that Princeton did not give athletic scholarships, I told the Dean I couldn't afford to go there. Undeterred, he told me to fill out the application forms and take whatever tests were needed, and he promised to speak to the scholarship committee to get me aid based on need. I almost certainly would not have attended Princeton without his dogged encouragement.

The class of 1954 was not only all male, but all white. Well over half of our classmates in college had gone to prep school and had already taken a number of the required first-year courses. Those of us who came from public schools had a tougher road. Nearly every day I would go from classes straight to the library, then to football or wrestling practice, and then back to the library to study late into the evening.

My Princeton scholarship covered tuition and fees but not books, or the cost of the dorm, food, or transportation. I soon learned about a naval ROTC program that paid for almost all expenses and also provided fifty dollars a month in spending money. Along with it came a commitment to serve a minimum of three years upon being commissioned an ensign in the regular Navy at graduation.

As part of that NROTC program, I spent six weeks every summer on training duty. In 1952, after completing my Navy training aboard the USS *Wisconsin*, my roommate, Sid Wentz, and I caught a space available on a free military flight to Frankfurt, Germany, and traveled around Europe for two weeks. These were countries I had read about as a youngster during the war. Seven years after World War II had ended, I was struck by its lingering impact. Some bombed areas hadn't been repaired. Even the stalwart British were still contending with rationing.

Meanwhile, the world had entered a new war—the Cold War. It featured clashes between surrogates and espionage rather than outright military confrontation between the two superpowers. Then war broke out on the Korean peninsula. In 1953, when I was again on a summer Navy training cruise, I received a letter from my folks telling me that my close friend and wrestling teammate from high school, Dick O'Keefe, had been killed in the conflict. Even more painful was the knowledge that Dick died when the war was all but over. Over seventeen thousand UN casualties, mostly American, occurred during the final weeks of the conflict, as each side made every effort to advance their positions while a cease-fire was being negotiated.

One of the major fears during the Cold War's early days was that Communists would infiltrate Western governments. Indeed, one of the reasons the Truman administration stepped up to assist Western Europe economically through the Marshall Plan was out of concern that desperate countries might be ripe for a communist takeover. There were reports of Communists in high-ranking posts in the U.S. government. By far the most engrossing, even transformative, episode during this period involved an admitted former Communist named Whittaker Chambers. Chambers had decided to defect to the American side and was cooperating with our government. It must not have been an easy choice for him, because he still believed that the Soviets would ultimately prevail in the Cold War.

As part of Chambers' effort to supply information to the United States government, he volunteered the information that Alger Hiss, a high-ranking State Department official, was a Communist spy. Hiss angrily denied the charges, and nearly everyone in the correct circles supported him. Polished, well dressed, and articulate, Hiss had clerked for Supreme Court Justice Oliver Wendell Holmes and attended the Yalta Conference with President Roosevelt as part of the State Department delegation. Chambers did not compare well to Alger Hiss in newspaper photographs or newsreels: He was an overweight, unkempt figure with bad teeth who admitted to having aided the Soviet cause. Far fewer people seemed to believe him than Hiss.

In congressional hearings, Hiss contended he had never known Chambers. He was convincing. It seemed that if Chambers turned out to be telling the truth, Hiss would have to be the best liar in the world. Apparently he was. The connection between them seemed to be confirmed when Chambers testified in a secret session that Hiss had once mentioned to him about seeing a rare bird called a prothonotary warbler, which Hiss later independently acknowledged, completely unaware of the implication of his admission. To the surprise—and continued disbelief—of some, Hiss was eventually convicted of perjury.

I was fascinated by the case for many reasons, and its lessons stuck with me. When Hiss was convicted, I saw how completely wrong the conventional wisdom—as well as first impressions—could be. I also observed how determined many people, some thought to be the wisest among us, were to discount all evidence of Hiss' guilt, even after he was shown to be deceptive. I also learned the name of a Californian serving on the congressional subcommittee who supported Chambers' cause, and who helped break the case. He was a tenacious young member of Congress named Richard Nixon.

The Hiss case gave a new level of legitimacy to the concerns about Soviet espionage expressed by many conservatives. That cause was taken up by Senator Joseph McCarthy, a Republican from Wisconsin. The tension between McCarthy's aggressive tactics and others in the government came to a head during the famous Army-McCarthy hearings, as a Senate committee looked at potential Communist infiltration into the armed forces. Once again I was riveted.

A lawyer for the Army named Joseph Welch called McCarthy to account after the Senator verbally attacked one of Welch's young associates during a hearing. Welch then famously asked, "Have you no sense of decency, sir?" It was a good question—or, more accurately, a statement of fact. For the first time I observed the ugly sight of members of Congress unfairly browbeating a witness to advance their political interests.

The events had particular interest for me, because I was studying politics and government. In hindsight, I wish I had majored in history. A few members of the faculty in the political science department were far to the left. I was struck by the way one professor in particular seemed to disdain the private sector as rife with corruption and unethical behavior. The business world was an abstraction to him. He seemed to have little concept of what hardworking, ethical people like my father did every day.

Students at Princeton were required to write a senior thesis for graduation. I chose as my subject President Truman's seizure of the steel industry two years earlier, during the Korean War. In *Youngstown Sheet & Tube Co. v. Sawyer*, Sawyer being Truman's secretary of commerce, the Supreme Court ruled that Truman's wartime seizure of the industry had been unconstitutional. I argued in my thesis that the Court's decision was "timely and reassuring."[13] It hadn't provoked much discussion outside legal circles at the time, but the 1952 case would become an important decision about the limits of executive power in wartime.

As we prepared for our graduation in March 1954, I attended our senior class banquet. The speaker was a Princeton alumnus and the former governor of Illinois, Adlai Stevenson. He was best known for being the unfortunate Democrat to run for the presidency against the popular Republican, Dwight D. Eisenhower, two years earlier. Stevenson was frequently considered an aloof intellectual—an "egghead" in the parlance of the 1950s. "Eggheads of the world, unite," Stevenson once replied in a play on Karl Marx's famous quote, "You have nothing to lose but your yolks!" I couldn't help but admire his good humor and perspective.

Stevenson's speech that evening had more influence on me than any I had heard before. I knew I would next be serving in the Navy, but I was not certain whether I would stay in it and if not, what I wanted to do with the rest of my life. It might seem strange considering my later career that the one who so strongly sparked the idea of public service for me was a liberal Democrat and self-proclaimed egghead. But his comments came to me at a formative time in my life and a turning point for the country. With an armistice reached in Korea in 1953, America had just ended its involvement in a second war in a decade. Mounting concerns about communism, nuclear exchanges, and the possibility of more armed conflict were intensified by the first test of the hydrogen bomb, a weapon one thousand times more powerful than the atomic bombs of World War II.

Stevenson put the future into an important and new context for me. He talked about the responsibility of citizenship in whatever path we might choose, and the stark consequences awaiting us all if we failed in our responsibilities. "If those young Americans who have the advantage of education, perspective, and self-discipline do not participate to the fullest extent of their ability," he warned, "America will stumble, and if America stumbles the world falls."[14]

He reflected on the weighty responsibility of the American people in our democracy to be involved in helping to guide and direct their government. He said, "For the power, for good or evil, of this American political organization is virtually beyond measurement. The decisions which it makes, the uses to which it devotes its immense resources, the leadership which it provides on moral as well as material questions, all appear likely to determine the fate of the modern world.

"Your days are short here," he added in closing, "this is the last of your springs. And now in the serenity and quiet of this lovely place, touch the depths of truth, feel the hem. You will go away with old, good friends. Don't forget when you leave why you came." Stevenson's eloquent and inspiring words opened my mind to the need to look squarely and thoughtfully at each new experience, and to know I'd have to answer to myself at each leave-taking.

CHAPTER 4

The Longest of Long Shots

I tended at a still young age to be deliberative when it came to important decisions. I was one who tried to weigh the pros and cons, to look at things from different points of view, and then to make a careful choice. A woman can have a wonderful way of changing all that.

Upon graduating from college, I was ready for the Navy. Having been entranced with the idea of flying at an early age, I requested and was assigned to the naval flight school in Pensacola, Florida. Since there were no female students at Princeton in those days, and I studied or worked most of the time, and with little money, I had had practically no dates. So I thought it would be a fine thing to go off to the Navy unattached. But then there was Joyce.

We had kept in touch since high school, and I had seen her briefly on holidays when we both happened to be home. She was attending the University of Colorado and had an active social life there, with many friends and suitors. And my idea of going off to the Navy and hoping Joyce might wait around ran straight up against the news that she was having romances out West. So I invited her to come out to Princeton during her spring vacation and then again for my graduation.

The morning after I arrived back home in Illinois from graduation, while having breakfast with my parents, I thought about my immediate future. On the one hand was the prospect of being a happy bachelor in the Navy, young and unattached. But then a moment of total clarity presented itself. Without discussing it with anyone, I rose from the table. "I'll be back in a bit," I told my parents.

I went to find Joyce and asked her to marry me. There was little buildup, little suspense, and at ten o'clock in the morning, it wasn't very romantic. But it felt right. I didn't know who was more surprised when I proposed—Joyce, me, or her parents. When she told her folks the news, Joyce's dad summed up the prevailing mood. "I'll be damned," he said, shaking his head.

Getting engaged the day after you got home from college may seem almost quaint now. Even in the 1950s things were starting to change. *I Love Lucy* hovered at the top of the Nielsen ratings for its six seasons, starting in 1951, but tensions burbled under the surface of Lucy and Ricky's happy home life. Back then, their interracial relationship was unusual, as was Lucille Ball's performing while pregnant. The word "pregnant" was not considered appropriate for use on television. The stars themselves divorced when the show ended. Rock and roll was viewed with suspicion by the establishment—Elvis Presley was threatened with arrest for obscenity by the San Diego police if he moved his body during his performances. Marilyn Monroe emerged as a new, modern movie star whose sex appeal and real-life dramas threatened to overshadow her acting. But it would take some years before these changes were brought home to Joyce and me. Our experiences were far removed from the glitter and glamour of popular music and films.

I did have one brush with the spotlight, however. While I waited for my flight-training class to begin in Pensacola, I was assigned to the Naval Air Station in Atlantic City, New Jersey—now as a newly engaged twenty-one-year-old. Soon after I arrived, Atlantic City was hosting the 1954 Miss America Pageant. These lovely young contestants were in need of escorts to the pageant ball. The pageant's sponsors looked to the men of the United States Navy for help. When a call went out for forty-eight young officers to serve as escorts for the Miss America contestants, I felt it was my patriotic duty to volunteer. I was assigned to that year's Miss Indiana.

As it happened, 1954 was the first year that they televised the Miss America Pageant, so it received a good deal of publicity across the country. The big news was that the actress Grace Kelly would appear. Joyce's friends were among the viewers that night. Watching their television sets, more than one of them was heard to inquire, "Isn't that Don Rumsfeld dancing with that beauty contestant?" As one might imagine, it was not long before that news made its way to Joyce. Thankfully she took it all in stride—as she has been able to take a great many things in stride over the many decades that followed.

Marion Joyce Pierson and I were married on December 27, 1954. As of this writing, I have spent more than 80 percent of my life with the pretty girl with twinkling eyes I first met at the age of fourteen. Newly married, Joyce and I would tackle Navy life together. Our first of many houses was a standard-issue cinder-block box at the end of the runway at NAS Whiting Field—a tiny place with a kitchen and bathroom on one side of a small sitting area and a bedroom on the other.

During flight training, I flew SNJs, the kind of single engine propeller aircraft now found only in air museums. My father was concerned about my flying, having seen a number of aircraft crash during the war. He had a point. Sadly, we lost several friends over those years. Still, I loved everything about flying—the freedom, the speed, the excitement. "More than anything else the sensation [of flying]," Wilbur Wright reportedly said, "is one of perfect peace mingled with an excitement that strains every nerve to the utmost, if you can conceive of such a combination." I knew what he meant. I felt like I could have continued on as a naval aviator for the rest of my life.

My strong hope had been that I would be assigned to single-engine aircraft, preferably as part of an aircraft carrier–based fighter squadron. But the month I completed my carrier qualification and was headed to advanced training, the Navy had not met its quota of multiengine seaplane pilots, so that is where I was slotted. It was the bad luck of the draw. I tried to get my assignment changed, but the Navy needed multiengine patrol-plane pilots, and that was that. It was an early lesson in the reality of dealing with a large bureaucracy.

I then asked to be transferred back to Pensacola to serve as a flight instructor, since that was the only way I could get back into single-engine aircraft, even if it was the training command. My request was granted, but just as Joyce and I were preparing to leave, my orders were changed. I was sent to Norfolk, Virginia, where one of my assignments was to train for the 1956 Olympics in wrestling. After winning the All-Navy Wrestling title and qualifying for the final Olympic tryouts, however, my shoulder separated while wrestling at the Naval Academy. My Olympics hopes, such as they were, were over.

My disappointment was overtaken by a much more important event. On March 3, 1956, at Portsmouth Naval Hospital, our first child, Valerie Jeanne, was born, and our small family soon moved to Florida, where I began my assignment as a naval flight instructor. Later I was selected to be an instructor of flight instructors. At the age of twenty-four I was the youngest in the group and the most junior in rank. It was an excellent assignment and an honor, but it wasn't the carrier duty I wanted.

Toward the end of my three-and-a-half-year commitment, I requested a transfer from the regular Navy to the Naval Reserve, where I would be able to keep flying as a "weekend warrior" but would also be able to pursue a career in the private sector. I loved flying, so much so that I probably would have been happy if I could have found a civilian job as a crop duster or a bush pilot in Alaska. But I also had responsibilities, and they were brought home to me almost immediately when Joyce came down with hepatitis from a flu shot with a dirty metal needle before the days of disposables. It took the better part of a year for her to get well. With a very sick wife, no job, no health insurance, and an infant child, we went back to Chicago and moved in with Joyce's parents, and later with my parents, while I looked for work.

With the help of the Princeton alumni job placement office, I started interviewing. I was offered several starting jobs with corporations in Chicago. Then I heard that a first-term U.S. congressman from northeastern Ohio, David Dennison, was looking for an administrative assistant.

My earlier impression of Washington, D.C., had not been a good one. After my college graduation, Joyce and I had traveled there to attend a wedding. While there we went to a session of the U.S. Senate. Both of us, with our interest in politics and government, were expecting to witness great matters of state being debated. As it turned out, there was almost no one in the U.S. Senate chamber. The aged Senator Carl Hayden—who had been the last territorial sheriff of Arizona before it became a state—was presiding, and from time to time was dozing off. Only one other senator was on the floor: Wayne Morse of Oregon, who was talking about music. Henry Clay and Daniel Webster they were not that day.

I had never met a congressman before I met Dave Dennison, and he was exactly what I'd hoped a congressman would be. He was a thoroughly decent human being—honorable, intelligent, sincere, and hardworking. Though I had no legislative experience, I think he identified with me. We had both been wrestlers, and his brother also had served as an instructor of naval flight instructors. After my interview, I excitedly told Joyce, "I would pay to be able to work for this man."

From the start, Dennison and I had a good working relationship. I was called on to organize and follow up on meetings with constituents, write legislative briefs, newsletters, press releases, and scripts for his radio program. Though he seemed content with my performance, I found the job difficult. I had not written anything since college, except for an occasional letter home.

I had spent the previous three-and-a-half years flying airplanes and had literally never worked in an office in my life. The closest I had come was when I mopped the floors of a dress shop every week to make money while I was in high school. During those first challenging months I felt like I was scrambling every day. Almost every night I would go home with my stomach in knots.

In 1958, Dennison was up for his first reelection. He asked me to move my family to Ohio to help. It was a tough year for Republicans. A nasty recession was underway, and with President Eisenhower in the White House, Republicans were getting most of the blame. On top of that, Dennison's opponent accused him of unethical practices. He criticized the Congressman for having had his wife temporarily on his congressional payroll (for a brief period, performing responsibilities for which she was fully qualified) and for leasing a portion of his law office as his congressional district office. Each was legal, but Dennison's opponent made it sound like corruption. He fought against the allegations, but in a bad year those charges tipped the scale. All through election night we agonized, watching the down-to-the-wire contest. In the end, the congressman lost the election by 967 votes, about one switch vote per precinct. Seeing an able, honorable congressman lose his seat by such a narrow margin for what was unfair criticism was crushing.

After Dennison lost, I went to work for Congressman Robert Griffin, a Republican from Michigan. I also enrolled in Georgetown Law School. But Dave Dennison called me back to Ohio to help him try to win back his congressional seat. Joyce was pregnant again at the time, but she was also a tough battler for causes and people she believed in. When I asked her about going back to Ohio and getting involved in another tough political race, she quickly replied, "Let's do it." She gave birth to our second daughter, Marcy, while we were on the campaign trail in Warren, Ohio, in March 1960.

Once again, Dennison's dedication wasn't enough to turn the tide, and he lost by a narrow margin, while Massachusetts senator John F. Kennedy edged out Richard Nixon in the race for president. I was now 0 for 2 in political campaigns. I felt like I'd had enough of politics for the time being, so we returned home to Illinois, ready to start doing something else, or so I thought.

I had been settled at the Chicago-based investment banking house A. G. Becker for about a year when a rare opportunity presented itself. In late 1961, the incumbent Republican congresswoman in our district, Marguerite Stitt Church, announced that she was not going to seek reelection. Her husband, Ralph, was first elected to Congress in 1934, when I was two years old, and when he died in 1950, his wife was elected to the seat and held it subsequently.

Since the seat was open for the first time in almost three decades, it was seen as an opportunity for both parties that was not likely to be open again for the foreseeable future. The Republican candidate had an advantage because the district, while fairly diverse, had been Republican for a long time. Twelve or thirteen candidates announced they would run for the GOP nomination. Among them were several prominent local figures, each with a decent chance of winning.

I had toyed with the idea of running for Congress now and again. One of the people who encouraged the idea was New Jersey Congressman Peter Frelinghuysen, who represented the Princeton area. When I worked on Capitol Hill, he asked me to lunch. While we were talking, he asked when I was going back home. He did not think I should spend my career as a congressional staffer, but instead suggested that I might return to Washington one day as an elected official. It seemed unusual that a senior member of Congress would take such an active interest in a young staffer's career. His suggestion stuck in my head.

If I wanted to run in my home district, this might be the only chance I'd have in several decades. I was twenty-nine years old. I had never held elected office. I had been away from my home district for ten years, since 1950, when I left for college. I did not seem to have anything that could even remotely be considered a political base.

My parents thought the idea of running for Congress was almost unbelievable. Having lived most of his life in Chicago, Dad had the impression that politicians were crooks. My mother didn't see how someone my age could possibly succeed Mrs. Church, who was forty years older. I was the longest of long shots. The savvy political reporter for the *Chicago Sun-Times* predicted I would run seventh out of seven.

I did have a few things going for me, however, the most important of which was our many friends from school in the area. The campaign team we put together was like a reunion. But it was not, to be sure, in any sense a finely honed operation. In our initial meeting around a table in our kitchen, we had a long discussion about strategy and position papers. Then, just as the meeting broke up, someone asked, almost as an afterthought, "Won't we be needing some money?" Laughing at how inexperienced we were, we each put in fifty dollars and managed to scrape together the formidable sum of four hundred dollars.

Ned Jannotta, a friend from New Trier High School and Princeton, became the campaign manager. He had also been away for many years in college, the

Navy, and business school and was not even registered to vote. Brad Glass, another friend from high school and college, became our campaign treasurer. As a former All-American tackle on Princeton's football team and a national intercollegiate heavyweight wrestling champion, he could be persuasive.

Another friend from high school, Hall "Cap" Adams, agreed to handle our advertising. He had printed up pocket-sized campaign cards designed for me to hand out to voters. I thought carefully about what my positions should be and managed to condense what I believed at age twenty-nine and what I believe today into twenty-three words onto the card. The policy portion read: "firm foreign policy, strong defense and a freer trade policy, effective civil rights measures, reduction of the debt, incentives for increasing economic growth."

My parents, despite initial skepticism, quickly became enthusiastic supporters. Dad let us use a vacant house he was in the process of fixing up as our temporary campaign headquarters. My mother even spoke on my behalf. "I have heard many comments about your performance on behalf of your wayward son. I'm sure it was not a pleasant task, but the victory was well worth

the many hours you spent working toward it. I am delighted with your stamina," I wrote my mother after she gave a talk supporting me at the Women's Republican Club of New Trier Township.[1]

Joyce and our friends went to work on making the candidate more presentable. For one thing, it was clear early on that I wasn't a very good public speaker. Ned Jannotta and Joyce arranged to use an empty hall one evening so I could practice and they could critique me. I went up on the stage and gave my stump speech to the almost empty hall, over and over, while they would yell, "Stand up straight!" and "Get your hands out of your pockets!" and "Quit popping the microphone!" until I started doing a bit better. I found public speaking was like anything else: Unless you have some remarkable natural talent—which I didn't—when you're starting out, you don't do it very well. But if you work on it and work on it, you can get better. I used to say it is like training an ape. If you do it right you get a banana and if you do it poorly you don't. And pretty soon you start doing it right.

I had to deal with the impression that at twenty-nine I simply was too young to be a congressman. It was a particular problem since the incumbent, Mrs. Church, was so much older. So I traveled around the district as often as possible with Joyce so voters would see that I was married. As it happened, the election two years earlier of the young President Kennedy proved helpful to me. Kennedy had successfully overcome questions about his age and inexperience. The youthful image he and his family projected proved to be a winning asset.

To get my name out, Jannotta and I decided to meet with prominent local leaders and ask for their public endorsements. The idea was that their endorsement would create a ripple effect, so their friends and colleagues would learn they had endorsed me, which might encourage them at least to hear me out as well. We decided to think big and looked for one of the most prominent business leaders in the district. Donold Lourie, the chief executive officer of Quaker Oats, became an early target. My mother again was helpful; she had known Lourie's mother years before. Another stroke of luck was that Lourie had been an All-American football star at Princeton. The meeting was of pivotal importance to my campaign, and I was going to use every possible advantage I could. So I gathered together my friends Ned Jannotta, Brad Glass, and Jim Otis—all of whom had been on Princeton's varsity football team—and brought them with me.

Lourie was delighted to meet his fellow Princeton football alums—maybe too delighted. All he wanted to talk about was Princeton football. But I did manage to pry in a request for his help. Lourie graciously said he would give it some thought. I figured I had little to lose by indicating my sense of urgency. "Let me explain our situation," I said. "The primary election is the second Tuesday in April. I need your support now, so I can use your support to get others to step up."

I told him I wanted to publish his name in a local newspaper advertisement with the names of some other prominent citizens who were endorsing me. Then I said that when people asked him why he was for Rumsfeld, he had to be ready to make my case. It was a lot for me to ask a major businessman who had met me only a half hour earlier, but we needed his help and we needed it then, not later.

As I continued to press—maybe press my luck—Lourie again said he would get back to me. Not long after, he contacted us and said he'd sign on. It was, as expected, a major boost—one of the area's most prominent citizens had put his backing behind a young unknown who was not the favored candidate of the Republican organizations in the district. It caused others to wonder why, and take a look. Soon community leaders in the district indicated they were backing me. Among them was Dan Searle, the CEO of the pharmaceutical company G. D. Searle & Co. He came on as our finance chairman and helped open the door to contributors and community leaders. Chuck Percy, the head of Bell + Howell, came onboard and led me to Arthur Nielsen, Jr., who signed on as chairman of the Rumsfeld for Congress Committee. By the election in early April, we had recruited some fifteen hundred volunteers and mounted a grassroots effort with everything from "Rumsfeld for Congress" earrings to cartops and bumper stickers to help to get the word out.

In those days newspaper endorsements were important. The biggest paper in the district, the *Chicago Tribune*, already had a candidate. They had endorsed the front-runner in the GOP primary, a prominent state legislator named Marion Burks. But the *Tribune*'s major rival, the *Chicago Sun-Times*, had not endorsed anyone yet. We knew that the *Sun-Times* was not likely to back the same candidate as the *Tribune*, so I took a gamble that I might be able to persuade that paper to throw its support behind me.

The paper was owned by the legendary Chicagoan Marshall Field. As it happened, the father of a close friend of Joyce's and mine from high school, Carolyn Anderson, had a business connection to Field, and he arranged for me to meet him. Field made himself available for about three minutes. He was on his way out of town but said he would ask the editors of both of his papers, the *Sun-Times* and the *Daily News*, to meet with me, and then it was up to me to persuade them to support me. The editor of the *Sun-Times* was a well-known, crusty, old-time journalist named Milburn "Pete" Akers. He agreed to see me that morning and at least give me a hearing.

I found my way to Akers' office and faced a large, somewhat disheveled man sitting behind a desk piled with papers. Akers started peppering me with questions right away: Who was I? What had I done? Who had I met in the congressional district? What places had I visited? Who was supporting me? Why was I running? And so on. It was all done in a courteous but penetrating way. I answered the questions as best I could. But I had never done anything like this before and was somewhat dazed by the encounter. I left our meeting without any idea what Akers might decide.

In fact, he got on the phone the moment I left and started checking out my answers. Not surprisingly, Akers wanted to talk to his numerous contacts to see what they thought of me. The political editor of the *Sun-Times*, who had predicted I would run seventh in a field of seven in the GOP primary, had to change his prediction when a month later, to his certain amazement, his paper, thanks to Akers, endorsed me for Congress. And the battle was on between Chicago's two morning papers—the *Sun-Times* and the *Tribune*.

From there on out, whenever my name was mentioned in the *Sun-Times'* editorials, it said that I was thirty years old, which was not yet the case.[2]

"Mr. Akers, I'm grateful for the mention," I told him on the phone, "but there's a problem. You keep writing that I'm thirty, but I'm only twenty-nine."

"I know that," Akers replied, matter-of-factly. "But you will be. And thirty sounds better."

After the *Sun-Times* endorsement, a number of the original candidates in the Republican primary dropped out. By late March it came down to a four-man race between the two who were by then the front-runners with strong newspaper support—Burks and me—and two other candidates. Burks was the favored candidate, having garnered the endorsement of a number of the big Republican Party township organizations. He used what he saw as his strengths in the race against what he saw as my weaknesses, homing in particularly on the charge that I wasn't a hard-right conservative. In one of his campaign ads he repeatedly labeled himself as a conservative and noted that he was "the only candidate qualified by experience, maturity, and political philosophy to represent the citizens of the 13th Congressional District."[3] Burks, however, also had to deal with unproven allegations involving financial management issues at an insurance company that he had chaired.

By the day of the primary election it was looking like I might actually win. We were mobilizing an army of volunteers, finally raising some campaign funds, and had important endorsements.* It was a surprising showing for a group of young people who started the campaign in a kitchen scraping together four hundred dollars. Because I'd managed two losing campaigns for Dave Dennison, failing by the thinnest of margins, however, we weren't going to take anything for granted until all the votes came in. I won with 67 percent of the vote on April 10, 1962. "RECENT POLITICAL UNKNOWN IN SWEEPING WIN," reported the *Chicago Daily News*.[4] Joyce and I were still amazed at the thought that we had actually won. We knew we had little time for celebrating as we quickly turned our attention to the November general election.

Since the district was Republican leaning, I felt we had a good chance. Our campaign team was energized and enthusiastic, and I could feel traction as we went into the fall. But then historic events intruded. In late October, Adlai Stevenson, by then America's ambassador to the United Nations, gave a dramatic presentation to the UN Security Council. Complete with fresh aerial photographs to prove the Kennedy administration's case, he asserted that the Soviet Union had been secretly planning to install nuclear weapons on the island of Cuba, ninety miles from the United States. For many days, as American forces imposed a blockade against the Soviet ships en route to Cuba, the world stood closer to the brink of nuclear confrontation than at any time yet in the Cold War. Politics didn't matter anymore. Americans stopped thinking about an election that was but a few weeks away and focused on the Cuban missile crisis.

When the confrontation ended and the Soviet ships turned around, President Kennedy received a sizable boost in popularity. I thought it might propel Democrats to victory in races around the country, even where they weren't favored to win. I was also running against a man with a good name for a Democrat in 1962: John A. Kennedy. He was not related to the President, though it probably didn't bother him all that much if some voters thought otherwise.

In the final days of my 1962 general election campaign I had no sense of what would happen. We kept working and worrying. On election night, when I prepared for a close vote, I was stunned again. We had won by a sizable margin. I was thirty years old and headed to the United States Congress. It was

* Our entire primary campaign cost a whopping twelve thousand dollars. It was at the time the most money that had been spent in that district on a congressional race.

quite a night for our entire family. But most of all I remember the expression of amazement on the faces of my parents. Something had happened in the life of their son and in their lives that was beyond anything they had imagined.

I had been a newly elected member of the Republican freshman class for about fifteen minutes before I was asked to make waves. Shortly after my victory, Congressman Bob Griffin telephoned. I assumed my old boss was calling me to offer his congratulations. Instead, he told me he was in the early stages of an effort to unseat the third-highest-ranking Republican in the House, Charles Hoeven of Iowa, as the chairman of the Republican conference. Griffin had put together a small group that thought the party needed fresh blood and new ideas if they were to stake a claim on becoming the majority party sometime in the future. Of course, as a member of the leadership, Hoeven had strong backing for reelection. But Griffin and his team had a candidate they thought might be able to beat Hoeven. Their candidate was his colleague and friend from Michigan, Gerald R. Ford.

I had met Ford briefly while I was working as a staff member in Griffin's office and had a positive impression of him. But as one might expect, opposing the entrenched party leadership was not something a newly elected, unknown freshman—not yet even sworn in—clamored to do. To make things even dicier, Griffin acknowledged that Ford hadn't yet agreed to run. He was waiting to determine how much backing he could expect. My assignment, if I chose to accept it, would be to round up support from as many newly elected members for a man who wasn't even sure he would make the race.

This was unusual business for someone who hadn't yet set foot in his new office. But Griffin argued that the mission was worth the risk. The thought of having Republican leaders who seemed to accept, or at least not be uncomfortable with, a state of permanent minority status was discouraging. Republicans had made a lackluster showing in the 1962 midterm elections when historically the out-of-power party should have made reasonable gains. I knew from my experiences working for two Republican congressmen how frustrating it was to be in the minority, and particularly to feel that your leadership wasn't mustering the energy and determination to fight back.

So I told Griffin I was onboard and went to work urging other incoming Republican members to support Gerald Ford for conference chairman. With the showing of support we assembled, Ford decided to run for the post, which he eventually won by a vote of 86–78.

As expected, our renegade effort left a lasting impression on the other members of the Republican leadership.

"I was picked as the lamb for the slaughter," Congressman Hoeven said after his loss to Ford. "This should serve as notice to [other party leaders] that something is brewing."[5] As it turned out, Hoeven's warning proved prophetic.

PART III

The U.S. Congress: From Camelot to Quagmire

"[W]e stand today on the edge of a New Frontier—the frontier of the 1960s—a frontier of unknown opportunities and perils—a frontier of unfulfilled hopes and threats."

—John F. Kennedy, 1960 acceptance speech

The White House

FEBRUARY 25, 1966

For nearly ninety minutes, the President of the United States fired a barrage of confident-sounding words at us. He was up and down from his chair like an oversized yo-yo that had been wound too tight.

"Now I don't want to hear any of y'all leave here and say you haven't been briefed!" he insisted in his booming Southern drawl.[1]

The briefing Lyndon Baines Johnson was providing to members of Congress that frigid February morning was a last-minute affair. My office had received an invitation to the White House late the previous afternoon. It was on a Friday, a day when there were no votes scheduled in the House of Representatives, which meant that many members of Congress would be out of town. Yet because of the profound importance of the subject—the war underway in the country LBJ called "Veet-NAMM"—I was one of more than one hundred members of Congress who braved the snowy Washington roads to hear what the President had to say.

We were gathered in the East Room ostensibly to receive an update from Vice President Hubert Humphrey on his recent trip to Southeast Asia. But from the start this seemed more like a political presentation. The Vice President was a warm, lively person, filled with optimism, and his remarks held true to his character. Yet despite Humphrey's enthusiasm, the presentation was thin on new information and heavy on upbeat platitudes. "We no longer need to be afraid to speak of victory," Humphrey told us at one point, as LBJ looked on approvingly. "The tide has turned."[2] Anyone following the media knew that casualties in Vietnam were mounting, which did not seem to mesh with the administration's assertions of impending victory. In fact, the war would go on for nine more years.

In addition to the Vice President, Johnson had his senior national security officials in attendance at the morning session, including the courtly southerner Secretary of State Dean Rusk, the cerebral Secretary of Defense Robert McNamara, Ambassador Averell Harriman, and Deputy CIA Director

Richard Helms. This was a command performance. And there was no doubt in anyone's mind as to who the commander was.[3]

Though LBJ was supposed to turn the briefing over to the Vice President, he never relinquished control. Humphrey spoke with almost continuous interruptions from the President. Throughout the meeting, Johnson gave the impression of a man sitting on the lid of a volcano that kept erupting. Overall, it did not seem like a presentation from a confident administration.

With only a small number of U.S. military advisers on the ground, the Vietnam War had not been an issue in my first campaign for Congress in 1962. After Johnson became president and the American war effort expanded, I was willing to support a more robust military campaign in Vietnam, as were many others in Congress. But it was becoming difficult to support the administration, since their policy was increasingly unclear. The President seemed to vacillate between the left flank of his party, which wanted concessions to the enemy—some were even beginning to talk of withdrawal—and those on the right who supported a more decisive military effort. LBJ would give a speech about negotiating and working things out with the North Vietnamese. Then the next month he'd give another speech asserting that the road to peace was not the road of concession or retreat and criticizing those who disagreed as "nervous Nellies." The military would announce a bombing pause that could last for weeks. Then bombing suddenly would commence with ferocity. Even at this meeting, President Johnson's team again was offering up the word "victory" without providing their definition of the term.

Though the meeting was supposed to be a frank exchange between the executive and legislative branches, during the first half of the question-and-answer session I watched White House aides walk through the attendees, seeming to place questions with friendly members of Congress. I was thirty-three years old, in my second term in Congress, and far from an expert. But I had a question in my mind and decided to ask it. I began by mentioning some of the earlier questions raised by other members that I felt had not received adequate answers. I noted Congressman John Young of Texas had asked, "Why, in view of all of the power, the airplanes, the bombing, the manpower, the billions of dollars, have not the Viet Cong quit?" Humphrey's response had been that the Viet Cong still believed we might pull out. I then pointed out that Secretary of State Rusk had said much the same: The Viet Cong still thought they would win and America would fold up in defeat as the French had in Vietnam twelve years earlier.

"So my question is: Why are the Viet Cong not convinced of our national will?" I asked. "In what ways have we failed to convince them of this determination, and what is being done, or can be done, to convince them?"[4]

Since he was supposed to be leading the briefing, I addressed my question to Vice President Humphrey. But before he could answer, LBJ popped up from his chair and jabbed his big index finger toward me.

"I'll tell ya what'll convince 'em!" he almost shouted. "More of the same like we've given 'em!"[5]

"Like the bombing pause?" I asked skeptically.

"For the past thirty days, we've stepped up bombing!" Johnson raged. "The Reds have seen twenty thousand casualties!"

LBJ knew all the details of the bombings then underway. The press was reporting that he was personally selecting targets from the West Wing of the White House, and that assessment seemed correct. I assume the idea was to demonstrate the close involvement of the commander in chief in the war, but for me it was an enduring lesson about the perils of trying to micromanage a war from thousands of miles away. Long before this briefing, I noticed that LBJ tried to preempt any second-guessing of his Vietnam strategy by quoting then Speaker of the House Sam Rayburn's comment during World War II. "If General Marshall doesn't know more than I do in this area," Rayburn supposedly said, "then we've been wasting a whale of a lot of money at West Point all these years." In other words, Johnson was suggesting that the military knew best and others ought not to question the military brass. I understood that I knew far less about what was going on in the war than the President and his advisers, but I didn't think he had answered my question, so I followed up.

"Well, Mr. President, if we have been doing this since the conclusion of the pause," I continued, "is there any hint or indication that we are, in fact, being successful in convincing them? Is the message getting through?"

LBJ looked at me for a moment in silence. "No," he eventually conceded, "there isn't."

The President became more subdued—his moods could change rapidly—and his deep-pocketed eyes turned somber.

"Look, no man wants to end this war as badly as I do," he said. His softer tone might have garnered some sympathy. That was, until he quickly added, "I've got a lot riding on it."

Those words summarized the last hour of the briefing, which consisted of an elaborate and rambling effort to cast blame for the unhappy situation wherever President Johnson could. First, it was Congress' fault. He referred more than once to the Gulf of Tonkin Resolution, which had passed the House of Representatives in August 1964 by a vote of 416–0.[6] Johnson clung to that vote like a life preserver. He carried a dog-eared copy of the resolution in his pocket, which he pulled out to recite some of its lines. He particularly liked to emphasize one phrase in the resolution: "approves and supports."

"That's two words," he said, "and they are both there."

Of course, it wasn't that simple. When I voted for the Gulf of Tonkin Resolution, I did have some concerns about its language—I worried it might be interpreted too broadly by LBJ—and in hindsight I should have considered the words more carefully.[7] But even then I had not anticipated it would be interpreted as a blanket justification for anything the President chose to do. LBJ clearly believed many of the people who voted for the Gulf of Tonkin Resolution now wanted to bail out on him, and he would have none of it. He seemed to be trying to convince the Democrats that they would be alright in the upcoming elections if they stuck with him. And he threatened Republicans who publicly opposed his policies that he would "land on them with both feet."[8]

But according to LBJ, it wasn't just Congress that deserved blame for the situation in Vietnam. Johnson sought to tie the conflict to his predecessor, President Kennedy, who sent military advisers into Vietnam in the early 1960s, and to the Kennedy cabinet that Johnson had inherited. He pointedly noted that Secretaries Rusk and McNamara were both Kennedy appointees. I wondered if they felt ill at ease as the President spoke. LBJ then invoked former President Eisenhower, saying that "Ike" had supported his actions in Vietnam. Johnson even referenced consulting about the war with the Pope. I was half convinced he would have placed some of the blame on his wife, Lady Bird, if he could have thought of a way to do so. I watched in amazement—even embarrassment—as LBJ went on with his "woe is me" harangue.

As I listened to him personalize the growing criticism of the war, I thought to myself that Vietnam wasn't LBJ's personal problem. It was our country's. A Johnsonian phrase, "a stuck pig squeals," came to mind.

Looking back on that encounter from different circumstances, I was probably too harsh in my assessment of LBJ. During the Cold War—only a few years after the Soviets tried to place nuclear missiles in Cuba—the Communists were testing American resolve on several continents. It was hard, if not impossible, to ignore the challenge the Communists were posing in Southeast Asia. But it was a tall order to explain that to the American people, and to try to convince them that it was worth fighting a long, costly war in a small country so many thousands of miles away.

In any event, the President did not make it easy to be sympathetic to him.

Indeed, that memorable meeting in February 1966 marked in my mind the beginning of a downward path for Lyndon B. Johnson and his administration. It was certainly a moment of clarity for me in terms of how I saw Vietnam. The war in Southeast Asia would slowly poison the remainder of the 1960s, a decade that had started out with such promise.

CHAPTER 5

"Here, Sir, the People Govern"

—Alexander Hamilton

After I had begun serving in the U.S. House of Representatives, I was sent a doctoral dissertation about the Congress. The thesis was that the representatives elected to Congress tended to reflect the kind of people who lived in their districts. At the time my district had the highest level of education and the highest annual earned income in the United States. From that one might have inferred that it said something about me to have been elected by such a bright, affluent population in one of the largest districts in the country. But, in fact, the dissertation asserted that I was the one who broke the rule. The paper said something to the effect of "Rumsfeld is distinguished principally by his total lack of social, financial, and political standing in the community."

As I read the passage one night, I nudged Joyce, who was asleep.

"Listen to this," I said, and I read her the critical lines.

"Go to sleep, Don," Joyce responded. "It's tough to argue with."

Though the 1960s are commonly remembered for drug use, permissiveness, and the hippie counterculture—"if you can remember anything about the sixties," one wag joked, "you weren't really there"—that was not how the decade started. It was a time of energy and opportunity, with a dynamic leader who seemed to offer both in generous supply. Although I was a Republican, it was hard not to be caught up in the excitement and glamour that John F. Kennedy brought to the country. The young, seemingly vital president—he was elected at forty-three—implored Americans to "get this country moving again." And America responded.

The astronaut John Glenn circled the Earth. The Freedom Riders began their daring bus rides in the South. Judy Garland embarked on her legendary comeback tour at Carnegie Hall. The satirical novel *Catch-22* was published. American women were gaining their voice, leading to the rise of the feminist movement. There was a sense that with this young, exciting president to lead them, Americans could go anywhere.

I was ready to serve in Washington, D.C. Early on I took a tour of the Capitol building—that exquisite monument to America's heritage; I walked along the rich marble floors and gazed up into the splendid dome of the rotunda and studied the large statues, two from each state in the Union. I felt fortunate every day to be a member of Congress. At the age of thirty, it was quite a privilege to be the human link between half a million people and their federal government.

I found the 434 members I served with interesting as individuals. I soon came to believe that by knowing them, I was learning about our country. They varied in energy, integrity, and intelligence. But the important thing was that they did represent the people of their congressional districts, and each one was there for that reason. Some clung to the vestiges of an earlier era. There were still spittoons on the floor of the House chamber for those who chewed tobacco, and every member was issued one. There was a strong deference to seniority and paying one's dues. Indeed, the attitude of many of the old bulls of Capitol Hill was that newly elected members should quietly stay in their place until we'd been around for a while—like a decade or two.* I gravitated toward a different group.

Because I had decided to help Gerald Ford defeat one of the old bulls in a leadership contest, I had earned the enmity of another member of the leadership, the second-ranking Republican in the House, Congressman Les Arends. Arends was one of the oldest of the old bulls, having been in Congress since 1935. Making matters worse, Arends was also the chairman of the Illinois GOP delegation. Among other privileges, he played the deciding role in all committee assignments for members from our state. I had been hoping for a spot on the Foreign Affairs, Armed Services, Appropriations, or Ways and Means committees. But helping Don Rumsfeld, a member of the

* There were some memorable characters. I was once on the House floor reading a bill that we were about to vote on later that day. Congressman John Byrnes of Wisconsin, well known as a serious legislator, came up to me. "Don't start reading that stuff, Don," he said jokingly, "or you'll never make it around here."

GOP rebellion that threatened him, was at the bottom of Arends' agenda. He adopted the philosophy of "don't get mad, get even."

Instead, I was assigned to what was considered one of the less important committees—the House Committee on Science and Astronautics, also known as the Space Committee. I was disappointed with the assignment but never had any regrets about supporting Ford for the leadership. Because the space race was heating up between the United States and the Soviet Union, the committee turned out to be more interesting than I had expected.

In 1957, the Soviets had launched *Sputnik*, the first satellite to orbit the earth, and the American people were surprised to find our country having to catch up to the Russians in an area where we had presumed superiority. President Kennedy had proposed a sharp increase in America's investment in our space program. He put forward an ambitious proposal—to have the United States "commit itself to achieving the goal, before this decade is out, of landing a man on the moon and returning him safely to the earth."[1] The audacious promise captured the country's imagination. In a can-do era, Americans felt, why shouldn't we be able to go to the moon?

As a member of the subcommittee on manned space flight, I spent time with the men selected to accomplish President Kennedy's bold pledge, including Neil Armstrong, years before he became the first person to take "one giant leap for mankind." I admired their professionalism and their courage.

I understood the appeal of having an American walk on the lunar surface. I also knew that the administration was attempting to blunt criticism from its left that space would become the next frontier in the Cold War by making a point of emphasizing NASA's peaceful, civilian missions.[2] But I looked at the idea of a lunar landing somewhat differently. Was that, I wondered, the best use of finite resources? The Soviets were not worried about demonstrating peaceful intentions. Indeed, they announced that they had no interest in putting a man on the moon and concentrated on less dramatic but more practical efforts, such as manned orbital missions and satellite technology. By making the possible military use of space a lower priority, I was concerned America might allow the Soviets to gain superior capabilities in reconnaissance, intelligence, and communications, and in the process also develop the ability to destroy or neutralize other nations' capabilities.

Another person shared that concern. Dr. Wernher von Braun was one of the brilliant scientific minds on our side. Two decades before I met him, he was Germany's leading rocket engineer. Hitler rallied his forces after their defeat at Stalingrad with the help of von Braun's V-2 rocket, called Hitler's "wonder weapon," that claimed thousands of lives. Thankfully, von Braun's achievement came too late to turn things around. After the war, while other German scientists defected to or were captured by the Soviet Union, von Braun arranged the surrender of hundreds of his top German scientists to our American troops. This action, too, stirred anger. "He behaved like a traitor," said one critic. "He smashed up half of London and other cities and he went crawling off to America with Germany's secrets and became a hero."[3]

Von Braun went to work for the U.S. Army, becoming in 1960 the first director of the Marshall Space Flight Center in Huntsville, Alabama, where I visited as a member of the Space Committee. It was ironic that only twenty years earlier Germany and the United States had been locked in a terrible world war and now von Braun and his team were working with America to master space.* The charismatic and confident von Braun shared our conviction that the Soviets posed a threat to the world, and he committed himself to assisting our space program. Through his work, the United States developed the Saturn V rocket—"the most powerful machine ever made by man," it was called—which propelled our astronauts into outer space.[4]

I never strayed far from the principles I had written on my first campaign card in 1962. I resisted expansions of the federal government and was supportive of tax relief. I didn't believe that either party had a monopoly on wisdom—or on any particular issue—and I still don't. For example, I supported the establishment of the Peace Corps as well as some environmental protection legislation. I also expressed reservations about the House Un-American Activities Committee's use of subpoena power.

I found myself becoming friends with individuals with other points of view, such as John Dingell, a Democrat from Michigan, and the political activist Al Lowenstein, whom I had first gotten to know on Capitol Hill in the late 1950s. Lowenstein knew everyone in the liberal pantheon from Eleanor Roosevelt to Norman Thomas to Bobby Kennedy. He was an early critic of America's involvement in Vietnam, took part in protest marches, and led civil rights activities with

* Around the same time I found myself in similar circumstances regarding Japan. My father had volunteered to serve in the Navy in World War II and was assigned to the Pacific theater against the Japanese, then our bitter enemies. Less than two decades later Japan had embraced democracy and a Western economic system. I began involving myself in issues related to Japan, and began a long relationship with the people of that country. I helped establish the U.S.-Japan Parliamentary Exchange Program during the 1960s, which was designed to develop closer ties between legislators, businessmen, journalists, and scholars from both countries. I stayed engaged with Japan over the decades, serving on President Reagan's Commission on the Conduct of United States/Japan Relations from 1983 to 1984 and as a member of the board of trustees of the Japan Center for International Exchange from 1990 to 2001.

a passion. But unlike some on the far left, Al was a fierce anticommunist who steered away from those radical groups that were aligned with Soviet ideology.

We were an odd pairing—me with my crew cut and conservative suit and tie and Lowenstein with rumpled hair and untucked shirttails—but we forged a friendship. I found him humorous, passionate, and interesting. We got together when we were both in Washington, which was not often, since Al was constantly traveling all over the globe. He had a habit of sending us postcards in his almost unreadable scrawl. And just before our third child, Nick, was born in 1967, Al was with us at home timing Joyce's contractions.

During his first uphill battle for a seat in Congress, against the Democratic establishment's preferred candidate, he sent me a letter joking about the repercussions if he won. "I intend to join you if not on the Space Committee, then wherever else they put people who defeat Manhattan congressmen in primaries," he wrote.

"Best of luck," I replied. "If you want me to come in and campaign against you, I will be happy to."[5] In return for a contribution he had made to my first congressional primary, I sent him a fifty-dollar contribution—for the Democratic primary only.[6] I had no doubt he would be a lively addition to Congress if he won a seat, which he finally did in 1968.

Shortly thereafter, and to my regret, our relationship soured. In 1970, Lowenstein ran for reelection against a tough Republican opponent. His campaign wanted to use our friendship to demonstrate that he was not as radical as his opponent suggested.[7] Among other things, he was accused unfairly of being involved in the Black Panthers and of echoing the line of the enemy in Vietnam.

Wanting to help my friend, I gave an interview in which I made the point both that I wasn't endorsing Lowenstein but that some of the characterizations being pinned on him were not consistent with my knowledge of him. "I don't subscribe to the theory that an individual who raises questions about national issues, including war, is undermining support for the men in uniform who are executing that policy," I told a reporter.[8] "I have never known him to advocate working outside the system and I certainly have never heard him advocate the use of violence."

If I had still been a member of Congress, that would have been one thing. But by then I was a senior aide in the Nixon administration and was referenced as such by the *Long Island Press*. The interview caused much more of a flap than I had anticipated. Al's GOP opponent was furious and contacted the White House, demanding that I issue a retraction.

I was busy, so I asked my assistant, Dick Cheney, to handle the issue.

Cheney was focused more on the need to elect Republicans to Congress than on my friendship with Al, and he drafted a strong statement of support for his opponent, who was then able to make it look as if Lowenstein had distorted his relationship with me for political gain.

I'd like to think that if I'd dealt with the matter personally I might have found a way to meet the needs of both friendship and politics. I've always regretted how the situation ended up. Al wound up losing the campaign. He was understandably unhappy with me, and it hurt our friendship. I learned that the political world sometimes made things difficult for friends.

Of all the presidents I've observed close up, John F. Kennedy was probably the most charismatic. He radiated warmth and good humor, and his televised press conferences usually offered glimpses of both qualities. The first time I had a conversation with him was at a House of Representatives' annual party in 1963.The privilege of escorting the President around and introducing him fell to Congressman Albert Thomas, a Democrat from Texas and a friend of Vice President Lyndon Johnson. A thirty-year veteran on Capitol Hill, Thomas was first elected just after I was born.

"Mr. President, this is the best young Republican that we have had around here in years," Thomas said, introducing me to President Kennedy. "He's not very good at paddleball, but he's a great guy."

Lean and smartly attired, President Kennedy reached out to shake my hand. "It's nice to meet you, Congressman," he said, with his distinctive Boston accent. "What district are you from?"

"The Thirteenth District of Illinois," I replied, "north of Chicago."

"That's Mrs. Church's old district, isn't it?"

"It is, Mr. President," I replied.

"They sure did beat me in that district," he said, smiling.

We chatted for a bit, and then he moved on. I was not surprised that Kennedy, with his acute political instincts, knew my district off the top of his head.

Joyce and I received our first invitation to the White House during the Kennedy administration. Joyce found me at one point and said she had had an interesting conversation with the nicest man. She knew he looked familiar, but she couldn't quite place him. She pointed to him across the room. It turned out to be Dean Rusk, the Secretary of State. We were not accustomed to meeting such people socially.

Later that evening I saw President Kennedy standing in the hall, close to the elevator that went up to his private quarters. He looked different from the athletic, handsome man I had met some months before. His face was a bit puffy. I would read later that it may have been caused by the medication he took for his back pain. Though he was the same engaging president, he seemed tired. I never spoke with him again.

Sometime after that visit to the White House, I was back home meeting with a group of Chicago-area businessmen. Even though Kennedy, unlike many of the Democrats who succeeded him, recognized the relationship between tax relief and economic growth, he was met with wariness by the business community.* Though Kennedy's victory over Richard Nixon three years earlier had been narrow, I felt he was going to be tougher to beat as an incumbent. He was already putting his political organization in place, which apparently was what had taken him to Dallas, Texas, that November morning.

As I was speaking to the Chicago group, a waiter came into the room, walked up to my host, and whispered into his ear. The host looked at me. I could tell something was wrong.

"Excuse me, Congressman," he said, a look of disbelief crossing his face. "President Kennedy has just been shot." Our meeting promptly ended, as we sought out more information about what had happened.

At first, word was that Kennedy had been taken to Parkland Memorial Hospital, where he was receiving blood transfusions in a frantic effort to save his life. Reports also surfaced that Texas Governor John Connally was wounded, which was true, and that LBJ was shot, which turned out to be false. Finally, word reached newscasters that a Catholic priest was delivering last rites to the President. At 2:38 p.m. Eastern Time, CBS newsman Walter Cronkite, in one of the iconic moments of that day, pulled off his horn-rimmed glasses as he announced, with a catch in his voice, the news of Kennedy's death.

We like to believe our institutions can survive great trials, but in the hours after a cataclysmic event like the assassination of a president, it was difficult to shake doubt. The fact that our young president—just forty-six years old—was suddenly gone left Americans feeling that time had stopped. Shops and banks closed. Trading on the stock market was halted. People were crying openly on the streets. Schools were let out with children walking out of their classrooms weeping. Special memorial services were planned for churches and synagogues across the country.

*There was a story circulating at that time about a meeting the President had with a group of industrialists. After issuing an optimistic prognosis for the country, Kennedy said, "If I were not President, I would be buying stock right now." "Sir, if you were not President," a man at the end of the table retorted, "I would be buying stock too."

In sorrow, anger, and confusion, citizens started blaming right-wing hate groups, segregationists, and the South for the murder, even though the assassin proved to be an avowed leftist. I watched with grief as the scenes from the assassination played over and over on the television screen: the President slumping forward in the open-top car, clutching his neck; Mrs. Kennedy, in a pink dress, inexplicably climbing onto the back of the moving limousine, only to have the Secret Service jump onto the car and prod her back into the seat; Lyndon Johnson sworn in aboard Air Force One, with a shocked Mrs. Kennedy and my friend, Congressman Thomas, behind him. One scene after another took place as if in slow motion, as Americans came to terms with the reality that this had happened.

Along with other members of Congress, I attended the memorial service for the late President in the Capitol Rotunda on Sunday, November 24. That afternoon in the standing group of members of the House, Senate, cabinet, Supreme Court, and diplomatic corps, I watched as people walked by the President's casket to pay their respects. There was a solemnity to the moment, a peaceful quiet.

I was standing toward the back of the group when I heard static coming from a radio being held by a Capitol policeman.

I eased over to him and asked, "What's happening?"

"Oswald's been shot," he whispered. A Dallas nightclub owner, Jack Ruby, had gunned down Kennedy's alleged assassin, twenty-four-year-old Lee Harvey Oswald, in an underground parking area as Oswald was being moved from his holding cell to another facility. The shooting took place on live television before millions of viewers, another shock for a country already on edge.

Kennedy's death soon gave way to the birth of the Kennedy legend, more powerful and more lasting than his presidency. It started with a deeply moving memorial service, modeled after Abraham Lincoln's. So well crafted, it was almost like watching a movie, except, of course, that it was painfully real. It all added to a sense that something magical—Camelot—had been lost.

For all John Kennedy's personal charm, however, little had been accomplished in his all too short presidency. On the foreign policy front, the administration's record was thin. There were the talks with Soviet leader Nikita Khrushchev in Vienna, where Khrushchev came away with the impression that Kennedy was young and inexperienced. There was the failed Bay of Pigs invasion of Cuba that added to the impression of American weakness. Then followed the construction of the Berlin Wall and the Cuban Missile Crisis, both of which seemed to have been at least in part a result of an emboldened Khrushchev deciding to test America's new young leader.

On the domestic side, few legislative initiatives linger on in history. Kennedy wasn't in office long enough to build a substantive legacy, and he had been hampered by the powerful Southern, pro-segregation oligarchs who dominated congressional Democrats.

The nation felt a profound sense of loss. For some Americans, the sense of shock and grief we all shared turned to disillusionment and anger. Indeed, what I remember of the decade of the sixties—riots, demonstrations, marches, and angry protests—seemed to have its start in Dallas, Texas, on November 22, 1963. The hopes and the growing sense of grievance among millions of Americans who believed they had been cheated fell onto the shoulders of a man who seemed, in style and temperament, to be John F. Kennedy's near polar opposite.

During my first year in the House of Representatives, I was among a group of congressmen invited by then Vice President Johnson to his home in the Spring Valley area of the District of Columbia. While his wife, Lady Bird, was the picture of graciousness and dignity, LBJ assumed his hosting duties like he did most things—with intense, backslapping, slightly over-the-top behavior.

During our visit he corralled us up for a personal tour. As he led us through his house, pointing out this memento and that, a special moment was reserved for what seemed to be his favorite room: the master bathroom. It was admittedly an impressive sight—in fact, I'd never seen a bathroom quite like it. As I recall, there were a number of contraptions built around the toilet—a mirror and lights attached to arms that pulled out, along with a magazine rack and at least one telephone. Johnson showed a Texas-sized pride in his trappings—modesty tended to elude him. He clearly relished impressing visitors with his bathroom's operational capabilities. He also liked keeping people off balance, and suddenly being shepherded into the Vice President's bathroom command center certainly had that effect.

To join the Kennedy ticket—a marriage of political convenience—Lyndon Johnson had left his post as the powerful Senate Majority Leader, which had made him arguably the most influential man in Washington, and became vice president, where he was not only virtually powerless, but visibly so. Johnson never seemed to fit in with the Kennedy team, and the differences in style were sometimes striking. He was a bit like a loud, slightly out-of-tune banjo being plucked in Harvard Yard. His relationships with members of the Kennedy administration, particularly Bobby Kennedy, were prickly. A proud man like Johnson must not have liked the feeling that he needed the members of the Kennedy team.

Despite his occasional coarseness, LBJ had a gift for smooth talk when it suited him. It was part of the patented Johnson treatment—his good cop–bad cop routine—in which he sometimes played both roles simultaneously. I suppose this may have been what had made him such a formidable leader of the Senate, which he managed with a mix of patronage, forcefulness, and a generous helping of guile.* When his almost shameless flattery failed him, Johnson deployed a strong arm. He was a large man, in both size and personality, and was not shy about touching people. I'd see him physically grab the arms of members of Congress he was trying to persuade. He'd wrap his massive hands around people's shoulders and lean into them until about all they could see was his oversized earlobe next to their faces.

Because LBJ had been such an effective Senate leader, I fully expected him to be a successful president. I hoped he would be. The country was in a difficult, dangerous place and needed him to succeed. Lady Bird later reflected that she believed her husband might have been better served if he had replaced the Kennedy team with a team of his own.[9] But for the most part, LBJ probably would have been better off if he had never taken the vice presidency. He might have become known as the most effective Senate leader in history. However, his congressional experience did help him realize what had to have been his most important accomplishment as president—one that many Americans thought was all but impossible. And it was by far the most important vote I cast in the United States Congress.

The issue of civil rights was not a priority for constituents in my congressional district, which had a modest minority population. But it was a priority for me. When my father was in the war and stationed briefly in North Carolina, segregation and racial tensions were facts of life, a situation vastly different from the suburbs of Chicago. In rural North Carolina, as a boy, I once watched from the other side of a fence while black and white students from different schools confronted one another by waving the sharp edges of broken glass bottles. An even worse situation broke out after some black citizens attempted to enter the segregated white movie theater. It was sad to see the

* For a rich lesson in Texas politics and U.S. history, it is worth listening to the historian Michael Beschloss's compilation of LBJ's secretly recorded tapes in *Taking Charge: The Johnson White House Tapes, 1963–1964* and *Reaching for Glory: Lyndon Johnson's Secret White House Tapes, 1964–1965.*

hostility. When I worked for Congressman David Dennison of Ohio in the late 1950s, I learned more about civil rights issues. Dennison had been a supporter of the 1957 Civil Rights Act proposed by the Eisenhower administration, an admirable effort that unfortunately became much reduced in scope because of the opposition of Southern Democrats in the Senate.

Back in early 1962, I had included my support for "effective civil rights measures" in my original campaign platform because I wanted the voters to know that the issue was important to me, even if it weren't yet a major issue for them. But in the coming months and years, as protests and demonstrations increased, civil rights became an issue all across the country, except not in the way I had hoped. As a result of the violence seen on television, many in the country and some in my district began to equate civil rights with civil unrest.

Since my father was a local real estate agent, I came to know a number of area realtors. If they had a position on civil rights at all, it tended to be for the status quo. Their clients were often concerned that property values would go down if minorities moved into their neighborhoods. Some of my supporters preferred I stay away from the issue.

At the height of efforts to pass civil right legislation, I was invited to be part of a meeting with a group of black leaders to hear their thoughts. The meeting was arranged by Clarence Mitchell of the NAACP, a civil rights pioneer who did a great deal to advance the cause of black Americans. He was on Capitol Hill so often that he was dubbed the 101st senator. Mitchell brought with him a number of African American leaders, including Jim Farmer from the Congress of Racial Equality, the Reverend Ralph Abernathy of the Southern Christian Leadership Conference, and the Reverend Martin Luther King, Jr.

The group was realistic about the challenges they faced but determined to achieve change. They wanted more pressure placed on the Johnson administration. Though President Kennedy had publicly supported civil rights, they noted, he had not been willing to tackle the Southern Democrats in Congress. In fact, Kennedy's hesitancy about the issue had inspired Dr. King to take his cause to the streets of Washington for his stirring "I have a dream" speech in August 1963. With other members of Congress, I went to a balcony in the Capitol to listen to King's speech over the radio while we looked out over the sea of humanity on the Mall. The peaceful crowd stretched out from the Lincoln Memorial, where King was speaking.

As protests increased, the issue of the civil rights legislation became even more controversial. The *Chicago Tribune* editorialized against passage.[10] The paper even put the term "civil rights" in scare quotes, as if there were something suspicious about the phrase. The editorial page labeled a number of the black leaders working to pass the legislation "racial agitators" and cautioned Americans about the bill's potentially adverse consequences. The bill being considered by Congress, one *Chicago Tribune* editorial claimed, was "a license for virtually unlimited civil disorder" and would turn "communities over to street mobs" while making black Americans "a privileged class."[11] It was scary stuff for many nervous white suburbanites who had few interactions with black Americans.

I thought I could make a case to my constituents that civil rights legislation was a means to better the lives of all Americans rather than a ticket to anarchy. I promised I would weigh any legislation with an eye to our Constitution. I also let them know that I was well aware that no piece of legislation, no matter how well meaning, could end bigotry, racism, or other human weaknesses. "These problems—human by definition—must and can only be solved finally by human beings—not governments or laws, but in the churches, clubs, schools, businesses, and homes," I wrote.[12]

When civil rights legislation came before the House, a long, heated debate ensued. My records show a total of 111 amendments were brought forward—some designed to strengthen the legislation, others to gut it, and still others designed to make it more moderate so it could garner enough votes to pass.[13] The 1964 Civil Rights Act ultimately was approved by the House on February 10, 1964, by a vote of 290–130. Ninety-six Democrats and thirty-four Republicans opposed the bill. I was a proud member of the majority.

After the bill passed the House, Democrats staged a filibuster in the Senate. Though a majority of senators tended to support civil rights legislation, they had failed over the years to obtain the two-thirds supermajority needed to cut off a filibuster. In 1964, Johnson was ready to try again.*

Over those tense, dramatic days, Senate Republicans and moderate Democrats together worked to garner the votes needed to end the filibuster. Senator Everett Dirksen of Illinois, the Republican leader, skillfully led the effort in support of the legislation. The situation seemed to change by the hour as senators worked to pry loose that elusive sixty-seventh vote. Many prominent senators joined the bill's opposition, including Tennessee's Al Gore, Sr., and Robert C. Byrd of West Virginia, who filibustered against the legislation for fourteen hours and thirteen minutes.

Typically, President Johnson was in the thick of things. He used all of the

* The supermajority needed to stop a filibuster was changed from 67 votes to 60 votes in 1973.

skills he had honed as Senate majority leader to help ensure the bill's passage, first making sure that it got to the floor and later arm twisting to get every possible vote. As the historic debate unfolded, some of us from the House went over to the Senate to watch. When the Senate roll call reached the necessary sixty-seventh vote, cheers broke out in the Senate chamber. After years of frustration, this historic legislation had passed the United States Congress. Dirksen summed up the battle by paraphrasing Victor Hugo. "Stronger than all the armies," he said, "is an idea whose time has come."

I was grateful and proud that the Republican Party had proved indispensable in passing the civil rights legislation. Indeed, one of the generally overlooked facts in the history of the civil rights movement was that in the 1960s a higher percentage of Republicans in both the House and the Senate supported the legislation than did the Democrats, and that without the leadership of Senator Dirksen, it would likely not have passed.* I had hoped that the robust and critical level of support by the GOP for civil rights would lead to a revival of the party's historically close relationship with minority voters. For many decades after the Civil War, black voters had voted with the party of Lincoln, but that changed during the New Deal days of the Franklin Roosevelt administration.

A few years later, when I was still in the House, I urged civil rights activist James Farmer to seek a seat in Congress as a Republican. If he had been elected in his heavily Democratic Brooklyn district—admittedly a long shot—he would have been the first black Republican in the House of Representatives since the 1930s. Farmer was a masterful orator and a charismatic presence—one of the heroes of the movement, who organized the Freedom Rides that led to the desegregation of busing. Farmer had been linked to a socialist group in his youth. Some of my Republican friends took issue with my support for Farmer's candidacy—some unfairly calling him "a renowned black militant."[14] Farmer had pledged to vote for the GOP leadership and was the only hope we'd ever have of picking up that seat in New York City, so I didn't see what the fuss was about. I worked successfully to persuade Gerald Ford and New York City Mayor John Lindsay to support him.[15] My concern about civil rights issues no doubt led to my developing a reputation with some in the media as a "liberal-leaning" Republican.[16] This was considered by the press to be a compliment.

Though I admired President Johnson's important role in the civil rights

*In the House 80 percent of Republicans voted in favor, compared to 61 percent of Democrats. In the Senate, the numbers were similar—82 percent of Republicans in favor versus 69 percent of Democrats.

battle, that was about as far as I went in supporting his legislative programs. A self-described Roosevelt New Dealer, he wanted the initials "LBJ" to be remembered as fondly as FDR's in the history books, and promptly proposed a host of big government programs under the rubrics of the War on Poverty and the Great Society. I thought most of his initiatives, which promised more power for bureaucrats in Washington, were not well considered. But Republicans did not have large enough numbers in Congress to slow even marginally the rush of Great Society legislation.

Moving into the presidential election less than a year after John Kennedy's assassination, LBJ was on a quest for his own validation, an electoral triumph that he hoped would shatter all records. The year 1964 was my first reelection campaign and the first presidential campaign I was involved in as an elected official. As it turned out, I had a front-row ticket to a Titanic-sized defeat.

The Democrats knew it would be hard for a still-grieving country to turn its back on the man who had been John F. Kennedy's handpicked vice president, and they made the most of their advantage. At the 1964 Democratic National Convention, the slogan emblazoned across the stage wasn't exactly subtle. Playing off of a line in Kennedy's well-known inaugural address—"Let us begin"—the Johnson convention theme was: "Let us continue." LBJ's acceptance speech referenced his predecessor six times. Notably the word that would be his eventual undoing—"Vietnam"—did not merit a single mention, despite the 23,300 American troops there on the ground.

If it seemed like voting against LBJ would be a vote against John F. Kennedy, Johnson apparently was fine with that. The Republicans, in effect, were battling two presidents at once: one martyred and one sitting. That meant the GOP needed to run a pitch-perfect campaign. What we got was quite the opposite.

The Republicans did not have many outstanding widely known contenders in 1964. The man who once had seemed likely to be the front-runner, Richard Nixon, had suffered an embarrassing defeat in his race for governor of California two years earlier. By all accounts, including his own, he was through with politics. After losing his bruising gubernatorial bid, Nixon bitterly told the assembled press corps, "You won't have Nixon to kick around anymore."[17] He seemed to reiterate the sentiment in the congratulatory note he sent to me (and, I assume, to other victorious Republican candidates) that year. "As I leave the political arena," Nixon wrote, "I am greatly heartened by the fact that you will be in there fighting for our cause."[18]

Nelson Rockefeller, the governor of New York, was making his second run for the presidency but was considered too liberal to win the nomination. Governor Bill Scranton of Pennsylvania, a former member of Congress and a fine public servant, started too late to make a viable run. That left Senator Barry M. Goldwater, who locked up the delegates needed to win the nomination after a long, well-organized effort.

I didn't know Barry Goldwater at the time, though I had been uncomfortable with his opposition to the 1964 civil rights legislation. Goldwater believed that moral issues were not the business of the legislative branch. I saw his point but thought that if we sat back and waited for good intentions to kick in on civil rights, we might be waiting a long time. I generally agreed with him, however, on economic issues and on national security. I had no doubt in my mind that his administration would have been considerably better for our country than a rerun of President Johnson's.

Goldwater had a reputation for being outspoken, which I found refreshing in a politician. But in Goldwater's case, it occasionally meant trouble for him. He would make comments like, "Sometimes I think this country would be better off if we could just saw off the Eastern Seaboard and let it float out to sea."[19] His humorous line played well in the west and with conservative audiences but wasn't helpful for a man who needed to win over some Easterners to get elected.

For his running mate, the Arizonan picked one of my colleagues in Congress, Representative William Miller of New York. Miller was a good man, diligent and serious. But that's not why he was chosen. Goldwater selected Miller, he blurted out one day, because "he drives Lyndon Johnson nuts."[20] It was a less than presidential rationale for selecting a vice presidential nominee.

The Johnson campaign's strategy soon became clear—to exploit Goldwater's outspokenness and try to depict him as a dangerous crackpot who would take America into a nuclear war. Subtlety was not a Johnson strong suit. The infamous "Daisy" ad on television that the Johnson campaign aired—showing a little girl counting daisy petals as a nuclear bomb, presumably launched by Goldwater, went off behind her—was undoubtedly the most cynical campaign ad ever aired by an incumbent president. It also was among the most effective. Though it was only shown as a paid ad once, the controversy it stirred up ensured that it was aired over and over again by news organizations and became etched in voters' minds. The Johnson campaign didn't stop there. They ran ads showing someone tearing up a Social Security card, implying Barry Goldwater intended to abolish Social Security. Capitalizing on his vote against civil rights, they also prepared a commercial showing a Ku Klux Klansman saying, "I like Barry Goldwater. He needs our help." Even the media started to criticize the Johnson campaign's vicious tone.[21]

Goldwater didn't help himself. After being characterized as a right-wing extremist for months, he decided to challenge the premise of the criticism. At the Republican National Convention in San Francisco, I watched Goldwater deliver his now well-known acceptance speech, in which he declared that "extremism in the defense of liberty is no vice. . . . Moderation in the pursuit of justice is no virtue."[22] Goldwater, true to form, stubbornly refused to distance himself from those remarks—which his opponents suggested were an admission of his extremism—while the Johnson team reveled in their good fortune.

Though LBJ had not mentioned the words "Vietnam" or "communism" once in his convention address, Goldwater went after both in his usual frank manner. "Make no bones of this," he warned his audience. "Don't try to sweep this under the rug. We are at war in Vietnam." He accused LBJ of failing to define a strategy for victory in the conflict.[23] And he cautioned the country about the expansive aims of the Soviets. The substance of his remarks was lost in the furor over the charge against him of extremism.

It soon began to look like Goldwater might lose so badly that many otherwise safe Republican House and Senate seats were in jeopardy. At that moment, in fact, I was being attacked by my Democratic opponent, who was trying to paint me as even more right-wing than Goldwater.* To avoid giving my opponent any ammunition, a supporter suggested I come up with some plausible excuse to stay clear of appearing with Goldwater. But Goldwater was our party's nominee, and though I didn't see eye to eye with him on civil rights, I certainly intended to vote for him. I thought it would be disrespectful and misleading not to show up when he came to my district to give a speech in Evanston, Illinois.

When I arrived at the meeting, it was clear that the Goldwater supporters were pleased that their local congressman was showing his support. After experiencing months of criticism of their presidential candidate, including from many Republicans, someone, at least, was on their side. When Goldwater arrived I greeted him warmly, knowing the photo of our appearance

* My Democratic opponent was a businessman, lawyer, and former vice president of the University of Chicago. He called me "more negative than Goldwater" and concluded that the "Goldwater-Rumsfeld attitudes and voting records are negative, irrelevant, and unsuited to our times. They seem to me doctrinaire and extreme."[24]

together would likely appear in my opponent's next brochure. I made sure to smile.

As the Senator began speaking, he turned to introduce the state and local officials gathered on the platform. Then he turned toward me. Goldwater glanced at his notes and said, "And I'd like to thank your fine congressman, Don Rums-*field*." No doubt some people on Goldwater's staff winced at the mispronunciation. Not I. Goldwater had just proved to the press that he really didn't know me very well.

With nothing seeming to go right for the Goldwater campaign—he was down by double digits in nearly every national opinion poll—I still held on to the slender hope that we might win a few more seats in the House and Senate for voters who wanted a check on the excesses of the Johnson administration. Instead, the Republicans ended the election in considerably worse shape. Thirty-six Republicans in the House were defeated, and our minority hit a low of 140 seats out of 435. We were outnumbered by the Democrats by more than two to one. I was one of the fortunate ones able to hang on, winning by what must have looked like a comparably comfortable margin of 57 to 43 percent. That turned out to be the closest of my four elections to Congress.

My fellow Republicans and I were a dwindling, lonely group in the House of Representatives. Though Democrats long had outnumbered Republicans in Congress, after the 1964 election there were so many Democrats in the majority that when all the members were in attendance, the Democrat side spilled over across the aisle into the Republican side of the chamber. The press suggested the Republican Party was on a course toward permanent minority status. The entrenched GOP leadership appeared to regard this state of affairs as a fact to be accepted rather than a problem to be solved. I saw the situation differently.

CHAPTER 6

Young Turks

After the Goldwater defeat, a small group of like-minded Republicans in Congress began considering what to do next. Some thought we needed a fresh approach in the House Republican leadership. We had made a start with the election of Congressman Gerald Ford as the Republican conference's chairman in 1963. Now we could either accept the status quo or keep working for change.

The first call I placed the day after the elections was to a veteran in our party, Congressman Tom Curtis of Missouri. Curtis had been a mentor of sorts to me since I first came to the House. He was a sober, scholarly type who would become interested in an important issue, consult the leading national experts on the subject, develop a conviction, and then pursue his position aggressively. I liked that approach. He had a tenacity that sometimes grated on opponents, but he also had in abundance the best qualities of a legislator—he was principled, studious, honest, and courageous. Just elected to his eighth term, Congressman Curtis shared my concerns about our party's situation. We agreed to meet in Washington with a few other members to talk about what might be done next.[1]

The legend surrounding those days—among those who followed it—was that those of us who met in the aftermath of the 1964 elections had mutiny on our minds from the beginning. But my recollection is that no one at our early meetings was talking about trying to oust the House Republican leadership.

After talking with a few congressmen, including Bob Griffin, Charles Goodell, and Bob Ellsworth, we decided to encourage adoption of a reform agenda that would pose a more aggressive challenge to the Democratic majority and provide Republicans with a sharper contrast in the next congressional elections.

The Republican leader, Charlie Halleck, and his number two, Minority Whip Arends, both resisted the idea. Halleck was a decent man, a staunch conservative, and a supporter of civil rights. But he had been elected to Congress in 1934 and was a symbol of a different era. Arends continued to resent my defiance of his authority as the chairman of the Illinois delegation. Both remembered that Griffin, Goodell, and I had been involved in the earlier effort to unseat another member of the leadership in favor of Gerald R. Ford.

As chairman of the Republican conference, Ford was wary of opposing his fellow members of the leadership. But when evidence of substantial support of the reform agenda emerged among rank-and-file Republicans, Ford signed on. The groundswell of GOP enthusiasm for a new, invigorated agenda didn't seem to move Halleck. He didn't take the substance of our proposals seriously. Rather than participating in the reform effort, he spent his time trying to ensure he had enough votes to keep his job.[2] Appearing with Ford at a press briefing, one reporter noted that Halleck "seemed nervous and apprehensive, constantly deferred to Ford, and literally kept looking over his shoulder."[3]

Halleck's actions won him few if any fans among the reform minded. If Halleck had enthusiastically embraced our idea and worked to incorporate the concerns of the "Young Turks," perhaps his fate would have been different. He acted like the entrenched, inflexible member of the old guard—exactly what we did not need.

"Halleck has played his cards wrong," reported the columnists Bob Novak and Rowland Evans.[4] Indeed, I didn't see how he could have played them any worse. Ironically, Halleck's paranoia about a leadership challenge led him to act in ways that made a challenge all but inevitable. Along with several other members of the House, I concluded that it was time for Halleck to go. Once again the Young Turks turned to the man we thought had the best hope of beating Charlie Halleck in a leadership contest. And once again our candidate was reluctant to seek the post.

Gerald Ford, by his own admission, was not a bomb thrower, nor was he anyone's image of a political revolutionary. We had to work hard to convince him that running for the post of Republican leader was in the party's best interests. Due to Ford's pronounced reluctance, not everyone in our group was enthusiastic about the idea of a Ford candidacy. Tom Curtis, for one, thought he was not resolute enough. But despite the qualms expressed by some in our group, it finally came down to one hard fact. Ford was the only one who had a reasonable chance of defeating Halleck. So several of us pressed Ford hard to run, until he finally agreed.

At a press conference announcing his candidacy, Ford made it clear that the upcoming battle was not personal. "It is a question of having new, dynamic, bold, innovating leadership," he explained. "It is a question of using all the talent that we have available among Republicans in the House."[5] I had strong reason to agree with Ford's remarks—I had helped to draft them.

I had not worked closely with Ford during my first term in Congress, but intense political contests have a way of forging friendships. Throughout the Ford-Halleck contest, I came to appreciate Ford's strengths that were sometimes overlooked. Once he made up his mind to run, Ford proved to be a smart and tenacious campaigner. He was also unfailingly likable, even by his opponents. That meant that when members looked for someone to blame for the GOP revolt, they turned not to the genial Ford but to those of us considered to be running things behind the scenes. I quickly received attention as one of the primary agitators. One Democratic congressman put it somewhat facetiously, "Rumsfeld held the dagger that Ford plunged into Halleck's back."[6]

For the next month the Ford and Halleck forces battled. Halleck was saying we needed to stay the course, he had the experience to help us win a majority, the Goldwater disaster was a fluke, and other comments he felt might appeal to specific members of the Republican conference. The Ford message, by contrast, was as effective as it was simple: It was time for a change.

I kept our group's daily tabulation of where we believed each of the 140 Republicans stood on the Ford-Halleck race. Every morning we made assignments for our "whips" to talk to the members, to try to find out what they seemed to be thinking at the moment, where they stood, where they thought others stood, and to revise and adjust our latest head count. At the end of each day I would log in their reports as "for Ford," "leaning Ford," "undecided," "unknown," "leaning Halleck," or "for Halleck." The race was so close, and so many members were noncommittal, that we could never be certain of the exact count. It seemed that it could come down to a vote or two.[7]

Though we were a reform-minded group, the Ford campaign team was not above playing old-school politics. This was the United States Congress, after all. We crafted a strategy for the vote-rich Ohio delegation that would have made Charlie Halleck proud. Among the Buckeye State's GOP delegation were a number of old-timers who initially favored Halleck. But we had an advantage Halleck didn't. Gerald Ford was the ranking minority member on the House Appropriations Committee, which had significant power over determining how and where tax dollars were spent. We pointed out to the large Ohio delegation that if Ford became the Republican leader, by tradition he would step off of the committees on which he served. Once he vacated his senior position on the appropriations committee, the next in line for that powerful position was Representative Frank Bow, from the great state of . . . Ohio. It was a strong incentive for the Ohio members to vote for Ford.

With the January conference approaching, we thought we might still be behind by a few votes. At that point, one bloc of uncommitted votes was in the Kansas delegation. And it just so happened that my next door neighbor in the Cannon House Office Building was a friend of mine from Kansas named Robert Dole. A World War II veteran who lost the use of his right arm in combat, Dole was a hardworking legislator and a wonderfully witty man. He and I would often walk together from our offices over to the House floor when a vote was called. We both often worked on Saturdays if we were not back in our congressional districts, and sometimes brought our children to the office with us. Dole and I were fiscal conservatives concerned about waste in the federal government and occasionally worked together to highlight the spending excesses of Congress. After I turned to Dole for his help in the leadership race, he invited Ford to speak to the Kansas delegation to help swing a few precious votes our way.

Gerald Ford was on the verge of an upset, but we couldn't celebrate just yet. As the vote approached, I became concerned that some members—in an abundance of caution—might be leading both sides to believe they would be with them. So on the day of the balloting, I made a point of sitting right next to a key congressman from Ohio to try to make sure we kept his delegation in our camp.

With Halleck and Ford both present, the vote was taken. We each wrote our choice on a ballot and turned it in. When the ballots were counted, we noticed something unusual about the tally. While there were only 140 Republican members, there had been 141 votes cast. For a moment, it seemed we were back in Chicago. It was clear that a second vote was needed. This time each of the members would be observed carefully as they brought their ballots up to the box. When the final results came in—with everyone voting just once this time—the outcome was what we had hoped. Ford had won, by a vote of 73–67. We were elated. Ford was pleased as well, but, as was his way, also modest. He immediately reached out to Halleck and his supporters.[8]

From the time he first came to Washington, Ford's goal had been to become Speaker of the House of Representatives.[9] History, of course, had other plans for him. If Ford had not made that run against Halleck, he would not have become the House Republican leader, nor would he later have been selected by President Nixon as vice president when Spiro Agnew had to resign. Indeed, it can probably be said that the man who was never elected president by the American people became president of the United States by the narrow margin he received to become House minority leader on January 4, 1965.*

Our informal group that had helped elect Ford to the leadership continued to press for many of the reforms we had been urging. We were hopelessly outnumbered by Democrats in the Congress who liked things the way they were and by some Republicans who didn't want to make waves. At one point we stood in front of the Capitol with a large banner showing the last time the rules were changed in the House—1909. We called these "horse-and-buggy rules." Over time our group was dubbed Rumsfeld's Raiders. Our tactic was to make parliamentary moves at opportune moments during legislative debates to try to enact some of our reform planks. Our proposals included the establishment of a House ethics committee, the opening of more congressional hearings to the public, and the recording of yea or nay votes on spending bills rather than the more typical unrecorded, anonymous voice votes.†

By 1966, Republican fortunes were on the rise, thanks in part to a reinvigorated GOP as well as the drooping popularity of LBJ as the public focused more on Vietnam. In the midterm elections that November a string of Republicans were elected across the country—notably Governors George Romney of Michigan and Ronald Reagan of California. Republicans gained forty-seven seats in the House, which brought to Congress a number of bright freshmen members: William Steiger of Wisconsin and Edward "Pete" Biester of Pennsylvania particularly stood out. Both were fine examples of legislators willing to dig down on issues and consider legislation on its merits. They thought as I did about the Congress—rather than serving as a stepping-stone to the Senate or the White House, there was important work to do where we were.‡

* The following Christmas, Ford graciously gave me a copy of his book about Lee Harvey Oswald, *Portrait of the Assassin* (Ford had served on the Warren Commission that had investigated the Kennedy assassination). Ford inscribed it: "To Don Rumsfeld in appreciation of your fine friendship and wonderful loyalty and to express my deep gratitude for your assistance, cooperation and leadership in the rugged days of 1965."

† These efforts eventually took shape in the Legislative Reorganization Act of 1970.

‡ We were friends outside work as well. Bill Steiger, Pete Biester, and their wives became close friends of Joyce's and mine. The Biesters lived a few blocks from us, and our children went to the same

Another new member who supported some of our reform efforts was George Herbert Walker Bush, the son of Senator Prescott Bush of Greenwich, Connecticut. Bush attracted notice by managing to secure a coveted seat on the Ways and Means Committee as a first-term congressman. Bush and I would find each other in the same circles many times in the years that followed.

Our group's renegade activities also caught the attention of a young Republican who was looking for a job on Capitol Hill. In 1968, Dick Cheney had won an American Political Science Association Congressional Fellowship and applied to be an intern in my congressional office. To this day Dick contends he flunked our first interview—and has gotten a good deal of mileage over the years in telling his amusing but completely inaccurate version of our first meeting, calling it the worst interview of his life. The fact is that I didn't take him as an intern at the time because my office needed a lawyer, not a budding academic. I thought he seemed like a fine person, bright and talented. But I confess that as he left my office that day, I had no expectation that I'd be working so closely with him over so many decades.

Not long after Gerald Ford won the top Republican leadership post in the House in 1965, he received a phone call from President Johnson. LBJ wasted no time in applying the Johnson treatment to prod the new GOP leader to support his policies on the war in Vietnam. After bellowing, "Congratulations!" Johnson expressed annoyance that Ford had stated, accurately, that Republicans were not getting much in the way of actual information from the White House about the situation in Vietnam.

"There's not anything that we know that we don't want you to know," LBJ assured him. The President then tried to persuade Ford that the key to increasing the number of Republicans in Congress was to go along with the administration on the war. "I think it will get you more Republican seats than anything else, if you show that you are not picayunish and not fighting," he advised.[10]

He was a "Ford man," the President said, but of course he couldn't say so publicly.[11]

No matter how heartfelt Johnson's remarks might have been, I found it hard to believe that bolstering the ranks of his Republican opposition in the Congress was part of LBJ's agenda.

---

schools. Steiger had had solid experience in the Wisconsin state legislature as well as excellent political instincts. It was a real loss when he died shortly after his fortieth birthday in 1978, from complications of Type 1 diabetes.

When it came to the Vietnam War, the Republican Party was in something of a quandary—and Johnson knew it. Republicans in Congress were likely to be the last ones to counsel retreat in the face of Communist aggression. I too was sympathetic to the Kennedy and Johnson administrations' expressed aims in Vietnam—to check Communist expansion—as were most Americans in the early years of the war.

But I started to have concerns in May 1965, when a Vietnam War appropriation bill came before the House, and President Johnson urgently requested an additional $700 million for the Department of Defense. The vote turned into a proxy fight between supporters and opponents of the war. I could see no reason for Johnson to try to ram through an appropriations bill so quickly. It seemed to me it was another maneuver designed to show the American people that Congress supported the war. But in the end, I voted for the appropriations, basing my decision, as I wrote at the time, "on the more fundamental fact that we cannot know what is in the mind of the President and certainly we cannot function if we operate on the assumption that his motives are bad." I concluded, "Frankly, I do not have the vaguest idea whether I voted properly or improperly."[12]

Shortly after our memorable White House briefing in February 1966, it was clear that the war in Vietnam had become the single most important issue facing the country.[13] Many members of Congress were questioning Johnson's credibility, including his use of the Gulf of Tonkin Resolution to justify any action he took.[14] While LBJ and others in the administration would offer comforting words like "the tide is turning" and that there is "light at the end of the tunnel," for the first time in history the world was watching a war on television and was beginning to sense that the words did not match what they were seeing. The administration's rhetoric gradually evolved into clichés associated with what was beginning to feel like a failing effort.

As I had seen firsthand, President Johnson avoided difficult questions about the conduct of the war from members of Congress and the press. He believed that media reporting was providing aid and comfort to the enemy and said as much. I concluded that if I wanted to better understand what was going on in Vietnam, I should go there myself.[15]

In May 1966, our House Subcommittee on Foreign Operations and Government Information traveled to Vietnam to look into charges of waste and mismanagement of taxpayer dollars by the Agency for International Development (AID). I saw this trip also as an opportunity to talk to the troops without a filter and to hear from the military and diplomatic leadership in Vietnam firsthand.

Almost immediately I observed one telling sign about our difficulties in Vietnam. When we arrived at the AID office in Saigon, the television set wasn't working. The picture was on but there was no sound. The AID employees tried to fix the set, but couldn't. Then someone tried to ask the Vietnamese personnel on duty there for assistance. But none of the Americans around were able to communicate with the Vietnamese to tell them what was needed. If the folks on the ground at AID were not able to communicate well enough with the Vietnamese they worked with to fix a television set, I wondered how they could work together to win a war.

The language barrier extended well beyond the AID office. We were told that of 260,000 U.S. personnel then stationed in Vietnam, roughly 1,500 could speak some Vietnamese.[16] While language differences could be manageable in a conventional war, they posed particular difficulties in a conflict where U.S. forces needed to appeal to local populations for support.

There were other revelations ahead. When our delegation traveled to the port of Cam Ranh Bay, we noticed a mammoth construction project underway. I asked an engineer how many U.S. troops the new port facilities would be capable of supporting. The answer was, up to a half million. Since there currently were fewer than three hundred thousand troops in Vietnam, this suggested that the administration might be preparing for a sizable increase in the U.S. military presence in the period ahead. This would have been stunning news to the American people. During the presidential campaign in 1964, in fact, Johnson had suggested that Goldwater, not he, would expand the war if he was elected president.

In South Vietnam the briefings we received from military leaders, including General William Westmoreland, were discouraging. We received little information on efforts to build up the military, political, and economic capabilities of the South Vietnamese. I thought it was easy for the administration to order the American military, largely made up of draftees, to Vietnam, but it was a vastly more difficult task to marshal diplomatic or economic experts who could help the Vietnamese develop the capabilities they needed to be able to sustain themselves.

It was clear that the Vietnam War was an unconventional conflict that the American military and other elements of our government were not well enough organized, trained, equipped, funded, or staffed to manage. The enemy America was fighting didn't have to win a single direct engagement with our military to survive, and they never did. Indeed, it was in their interests not to fight our kind of battle at all. They would ambush American troops on Monday and go back to harvesting rice on Tuesday. They would selectively engage our forces when it suited them, but generally avoid direct confrontation, because they knew they would lose. Their strategy was simply to hold on and make the war costly enough so that the Americans and our allies would eventually call it quits.

Further, there seemed to be little success in engaging in the ideological component of the conflict. The Viet Cong were fighting for something. Ho Chi Minh promised his followers economic progress, while the United States had been portrayed as promising only more bombs and bloodshed. Unquestionably, the people of Vietnam would have been vastly better off free of a repressive Communist regime and with freer political and economic systems. But neither we nor the Vietnamese we were supporting had developed an ability to communicate that truth persuasively. We were fighting dedicated ideological revolutionaries who would not surrender their Marxist ideology or bargain away at the negotiating table their hope for a united, single Vietnam under Ho Chi Minh.

By increasing American troop levels still further in the country, we were increasing the number of targets, which would lead to more casualties and further undermine support for the war at home. The U.S. approach seemed to be playing into the hands of the enemy—with more military bombardments and more American troops and without successfully enabling our South Vietnamese allies to take on more of the burdens of the fighting. In a report to my constituents I noted that it was unlikely that the United States "could 'win' this type of insurgency war for the South Vietnamese."[17]

Despite our country's good intentions, I was concerned that we were creating a dependency on the part of the South Vietnamese.[18] During one of my stops in the country I visited a training facility where American flight instructors were teaching Vietnamese pilots how to fly. It seemed to me that it would have made more sense to teach the Vietnamese pilots how to be flight instructors, so they could train other Vietnamese pilots. As long as Americans were the ones training the Vietnamese, they would remain dependent on us to keep turning pilots out.

There was growing sentiment in Congress, particularly among Democrats, that the best way to express their objection to the conduct of the war was to deny it funding. That wasn't how I saw it. My view was that even if one disagreed with the way the policy was being implemented, as I and others increasingly did, the best way to respond was to recommend corrections at the policy level.[19] I wished Congress could be more involved, on a substantive level, rather than simply yanking the purse strings shut when displeased.*

In September 1967, I cosponsored a resolution to bring the conduct of the war to the House floor for debate and discussion. Resolution 508 proposed to determine if "further congressional action is desirable in respect to policies in Southeast Asia."[21] I didn't think anyone knew with certainty what the balance should be between the branches on these matters. I was not proposing specific reforms; rather, I was suggesting that Congress undertake a study of the topic.† Unfortunately, at the request of the administration, a majority of Democrats blocked Resolution 508 from consideration.

On a number of occasions I joined other members of Congress in expressing concern about what appeared to be the White House's attempts to manage the news on the war. This was an understandable inclination on the administration's part, since no doubt they felt the media coverage of the war was unfair. But the administration made matters worse with their seeming reluctance to provide much, if any, documentation that would have given members of Congress a better sense of what was taking place.[23]

By this time, I had become a cosponsor and advocate for the Freedom of Information Act (FOIA), authored by Congressman John Moss, a Democrat from California. The legislation, which passed unanimously in 1966, was crafted in reaction to the Johnson administration's behavior. As a Democrat, Moss was in the awkward position of promoting a bill that went against the express wishes of the President, so I helped him develop the legislation and move it through the House. For me, support of the bill came down to one long-held belief: Good judgments require accurate information.[24]

I'm still a supporter of FOIA. But once I joined the executive branch of government in 1969, I began to understand the costs our well-intentioned law imposed. Under FOIA, for example, it often proved difficult to differentiate between the many legitimate requests for information and frivolous fishing expeditions by those who want to bury government in paperwork or those with an ax to grind. Federal officials spend many hours and considerable

*In his August 21, 1858 debate with Stephen A. Douglas, Abraham Lincoln pointed out, "And so I think my friend, the Judge, is equally at fault when he charges me at the time when I was in Congress of having opposed our soldiers who were fighting in the Mexican War. . . . You remember I was an old Whig, and whenever the Democratic party tried to get me to vote that the war had been righteously begun by the President, I would not do it. But whenever they asked for any money, or land warrants, or anything to pay the soldiers there, during all that time, I gave the same votes that Judge Douglas did."[20]

†On June 2, 1965, I testified before the Joint Committee on the Organization of the Congress and raised a series of questions about the balance in responsibility between the executive and legislative branches of government.[22]

expense trying to decide what information is and is not releasable under FOIA. We wanted to pass a law to solve an immediate problem. In retrospect, I wish we had been able to better understand the long-term ramifications of the legislation we were championing.

The situation in Vietnam, and the demonstrations against the war and the draft, strengthened greatly my support for a transition to an all-volunteer military. The draft had been in place since World War II. By the mid-1960s, many young Americans were asking why they were being forced to fight in a war they did not understand and that they did not see as critical to our country's security. Since the various draft exemptions—being a college student, a teacher, married, or a conscientious objector—seemed to favor the more affluent, the draft also exacerbated racial and social tensions in the country. In October 1967, one of the largest antiwar demonstrations in the Washington area was held on the steps of the Pentagon, with many protesting that conscription was unwarranted, discriminatory, and unfair. I agreed with them.

In our free system of government, I believed, conscription was appropriate only when there was a demonstrated need.[25] A volunteer system offered many advantages. First and foremost, it would preserve the freedom of individuals to make their own decisions about how they wished to live their lives. Volunteers who chose to enter the military would be more likely to make it a career, instead of serving for a short period. It also would avoid the implicit discrimination and the inherent inequities caused by the various deferments and exemptions in the draft system.

Because of my interest in a volunteer military, I was invited to be part of a conference at the University of Chicago convened to discuss the topic. There I met one of the most passionate proponents of the all-volunteer system, the economist Dr. Milton Friedman, who I would turn to many times over the years for advice and guidance. Friedman's belief in the power of freedom was inspiring, and he felt the same way about giving people the choice to serve in the U.S. military as he did about giving them a choice about their education. Other participants on the panel included Senator Edward Kennedy and the anthropologist Margaret Mead, both of whom favored continuing the draft.

Many arguments were offered to bolster both sides of the issue. Some contended that without the draft we would not be able to recruit enough troops. My view was that in every other activity in our society, in both the public and the private sectors, we were able to attract and retain the personnel needed without resorting to compulsion. It was done simply by paying them a competitive market wage. The critics also contended that it would be too expensive to pay the men and women in the U.S. armed forces what would be paid in the private sector. My response was why should government pay those serving in our military less than a competitive wage, namely, what the market says they are worth? Specifically, why should government draft only some and then say, in addition, we will pay you only 50 percent or 60 percent of your worth? No one ever had a good answer to those questions.[26]

As members of the Joint Economic Committee, Tom Curtis and I proposed and held a hearing on whether or not the military draft was still necessary and whether a volunteer military was or was not economically feasible. One Pentagon official testified that the Department of Defense had as its objective "to obtain as many or all of its personnel through voluntary means."[27] But that wasn't what was happening in practice, and they knew it. I tried to test the willingness of members of Congress to study the feasibility of ending the draft by offering a nonbinding resolution. The resolution stated simply that it was "the sense of Congress" that the draft should be enforced "only when necessary to insure the security of this Nation."[28] With bipartisan opposition, I was not able to get it considered—it later fell to the Nixon administration to pursue the issue.

I came to believe it was only a matter of time before the federal government and the country would have to take the idea of an all-volunteer military seriously. I was convinced then, and remain convinced now, that if the country had had a volunteer system in place during the Vietnam War, the level of violence and protest across the country would have been considerably less.

The conventional wisdom is that because of the opposition to the Vietnam War, Lyndon Johnson's political fate was sealed by early 1968. In fact, at first things were looking pretty good for President Johnson. Though later changing his mind, one of LBJ's chief rivals for the Democratic nomination, Robert F. Kennedy, had announced he would not challenge Johnson in the Democratic primaries. The nature of some of the more radical antiwar demonstrations seemed to have increased sympathy for Johnson across Middle America, and he was holding steady in the polls. Like many, I was amazed to see pictures of American celebrities, such as Jane Fonda, expressing solidarity with the North Vietnamese. It is one thing to oppose a war policy. It is quite another to support the enemy. Indeed, even though I thought President Johnson brought some of his problems on himself, I didn't like to see any president so hounded, and I certainly did not like to see our troops besmirched.

Then, in January 1968, North Vietnamese and Viet Cong forces broke a truce during their country's Tet holiday. Their surprise offensive consisted of assaults on more than a hundred cities across South Vietnam. In military terms, the Tet Offensive was not a victory for the Viet Cong and the North Vietnamese. But military victory was not the enemy's intent. Their effort was targeted at war-weary Americans watching the bloodshed on their TV screens. And the message was unmistakable. The enemy was telling the American people, "We will never give up." Toward the end of the Johnson administration, I had mistakenly accepted as credible the certainty in the media that the 1968 Tet Offensive had been a defeat for America and the South Vietnamese. But, in fact, after the initial surprise, our forces had pushed back effectively. The fury of the Tet Offensive, coupled with the fact that the mighty U.S. military was taken by surprise, made a powerful impression. At home, Americans were ill prepared for the shocking images from the attacks and the increasing impression that the United States might actually lose the war.

A few weeks later, *CBS Evening News* anchor Walter Cronkite traveled to Vietnam. Returning to the United States, he aired a special commentary on February 27 that may have been the single most devastating moment for the Johnson administration in the long years of the Vietnam War. Cronkite soberly concluded that we were "mired in stalemate" and needed to negotiate with the Viet Cong. After the broadcast aired, the President was reported to have said, "If I've lost Cronkite, I've lost middle America." It was undoubtedly true.

On March 31, the President appeared before television cameras for an address from the Oval Office. He talked about making 1968 "the year of decision in South Vietnam—the year that brings, if not final victory or defeat, at least a turning point in the struggle." By then there had been so many turning points, so many decisive moments, so many tides turned that it seemed to ring hollow. LBJ then uttered words that deliberately had not been included in his teleprompter text, surprising everyone but those closest to him. "With America's sons in the fields far away, with America's future under challenge right here at home, with our hopes and the world's hopes for peace in the balance every day," he said, "I do not believe that I should devote an hour or a day of my time to any personal partisan causes or to any duties other than the awesome duties of this office—the presidency of your country. Accordingly, I shall not seek, and I will not accept, the nomination of my party for another term as your president."[29]

The war in Vietnam had been a test of political wills. But it was not our enemy's will that had been broken. The turmoil of the year had left the Johnson administration in ruin and American policy on the war uncertain. It also abetted a most unlikely political comeback.

PART IV

In Nixon's Arena

Provence, France

AUGUST 8, 1974

The French seaport of Saint-Tropez was the landing site for Operation Dragoon during World War II, where the Allies began their drive to liberate southern France from Nazi control. A decade later the town again achieved notoriety as the setting for a film that launched the career of actress Brigitte Bardot. With its pristine beaches and skies as clear and blue as the nearby Mediterranean, it soon became a haven for European glitterati.

If there was anything the Rumsfelds were not, it was part of the glitterati. We passed through the town's narrow, winding roads in an aging but resilient maroon Volvo.[1] Our three young children were squeezed together in the backseat, and our trunk was stuffed with bags and suitcases. Our destination was Grimaud, a small, sleepy village where Ambassador André de Staercke, the distinguished dean of the North Atlantic Council, had a vacation home.

While most Americans were transfixed by the Watergate scandal we were thousands of miles away from those epic events. As the U.S. ambassador to the North Atlantic Treaty Organization, I had to fly back to Washington for meetings periodically. But for the most part Joyce and I were removed from the day-to-day Watergate developments that spring and summer. We were living in Belgium, where the news on TV was in either French or Flemish, and I didn't speak either language. Two of our children were in neighborhood Belgian schools, and I couldn't even read their report cards. We received English newspapers, of course—the *International Herald Tribune* and some British papers—but we weren't able to keep up to speed with events in Washington as one would expect today with the internet and cable TV.

Instead, during that period I had been deeply involved in helping alleviate a dispute teetering on the verge of war between two of our NATO allies, Turkey and Greece, over the island of Cyprus. Every once in a while I would turn on the local television and see pictures of President Nixon and sometimes hear an announcer say recognizable names like "Hahl-dah-mann" and

"Err-leek-mann" in a thick accent. I didn't need to speak Flemish to know that what they were describing wasn't good.

But that was half a world away. And when tensions lessened over Cyprus, I welcomed the chance for some time away from official business with my family. En route to Grimaud, Joyce purchased a copy of the *International Herald Tribune.* She was so absorbed in it that I noticed she wasn't paying the slightest attention to the picturesque countryside along the French coast.

"Don," she finally said, with a tone of unusual insistence, "I think you should stop and read this."

I knew that what had caught Joyce's attention had to be something to do with Watergate, but we didn't talk about those problems in the car, because mentions of the scandal seemed to bother our seven-year-old son, Nick, who had met Nixon several times. I had taken Nick with me on my last visit with the President in the Oval Office before leaving for NATO headquarters in Belgium. Having the undivided attention of our nation's commander in chief—who allowed Nick to sit in his chair—had left a strong impression on him. So Joyce and I avoided discussing accusations against the President when Nick was within earshot.

I was not all that eager to learn the bad news, either, so I kept driving until we reached a beach where our kids could go swimming. I took Nick's hand and walked with him across the white sand. As our son saw for the first time what passed for typical swim attire for women on a Mediterranean beach, his expression was one of amazed innocence. He had not seen anything like that along the shores of Lake Michigan. It was another reminder that the Rumsfelds were a long way from home.

Eventually, I sat down on the sand and turned my attention to the newspaper. President Nixon, the reports said, might be close to resigning. Despite his deteriorating political and legal situation, I never thought he'd actually have to surrender the office. I thought at worst he might be forced to accept a reduced presidency with less influence. Knowing the tenacious Richard Nixon, I found it hard to envision him giving up. If the news stories were accurate, however, it seemed that my friend from my days in the Congress, Vice President Gerald R. Ford, could become president of the United States.

Early that evening we arrived at Ambassador de Staercke's house. De Staercke had assembled an eclectic group for dinner, including the Belgian ambassador to the United Kingdom, Baron Robert Rothschild, and Brigitte Bardot's business manager. While the gravity of the situation in Washington, D.C., had become clearer to Joyce and me, the European dinner guests were surprised by the *Herald Tribune's* assessment that the situation might be coming to a head. To the Europeans, Watergate seemed a relatively minor problem. Even Nixon's secret tapings in the White House were shrugged off as not particularly unusual.

My secretary at NATO headquarters in Brussels, Leona Goodell, telephoned de Staercke's house to tell me that an aide from Vice President Ford's office was trying to reach me, and shortly thereafter his call came through. The Grimaud telephone switchboard was not used to receiving calls from the White House, and our dinner companions began to appreciate the seriousness of the matter. The Vice President's aide made it clear that Ford wanted me to fly back to Washington at once. We all stayed up and listened to President Nixon's dramatic remarks to the nation. "I have never been a quitter," the President said solemnly. Then Richard Nixon did exactly that, announcing that he would resign his office at noon the very next day. The man who had spent much of his adult life in pursuit of the White House was suddenly, and quite unexpectedly, returning to his home in San Clemente, California.

CHAPTER 7

1968: Year of Turmoil

The familiar portrait of Richard Milhous Nixon is of a bitter, haunted figure who became the first American president to resign. I worked for a notably different Richard Nixon, conferring with him dozens of times as a member of his cabinet and periodically in smaller meetings. Nixon had serious failings, which became all too evident when his secret tapes were revealed. But I knew him to be a thoughtful, brilliant man—certainly one of the brightest presidents I observed. He was indeed a paradox who managed to reach the apex of power and then came crashing down, which I suppose is why decades later so many Americans still find him fascinating.

By 1968, during my third term in Congress, Richard Nixon was on the road to an improbable political comeback. His second presidential bid took place during one of the more tumultuous years in modern American history—a year punctuated by the escalating debate over Vietnam. The Tet Offensive, which had sealed the fate of President Johnson, accelerated the nearly continuous protests outside the gates of the White House. Marchers were routinely chanting things like "Hey! Hey! LBJ! How many kids did you kill today?!" There were so many protests, in fact, that the President had difficulty leaving the White House. That year saw 16,592 Americans killed in the war—the highest number of any year of that conflict.

Our country was rocked by violence and heartbreak. On April 4, 1968,

Martin Luther King, Jr., the man in whom so many Americans had placed their hopes, was assassinated in Memphis, Tennessee. Joyce and I were in Florida with our family when we heard the news and flew back to Washington immediately. His death sparked an ugly backlash. Things were so tense that we had to show identification to National Guardsmen before they would let us cross the bridge from National Airport in Virginia into Washington, D.C. As we drove into the nation's capital, we saw rioting in the streets, with buildings and cars set on fire. The next school day the city decided to keep the public schools open, leaving us with the indelible image of our twelve-year-old daughter, Valerie, serving as a school safety monitor on one corner of the street while National Guardsmen with guns at the ready stood watch on the others.

That June, Senator Robert F. Kennedy was assassinated in Los Angeles, just after winning the California Democratic presidential primary. His death, along with King's, stirred up the still vivid memories of his brother's assassination. The succession of murders, combined with a war with mounting casualties and the frequent and often violent demonstrations in Washington and around the nation, gave many of us a palpable sense that the country could be spiraling out of control.

Amid anger and protest, Nixon offered himself as a source of reassurance and stability. For voters it was a welcome change from the anguished presidency of Lyndon Johnson. But because he had been defeated in two high-profile elections during the past decade, he had to battle the impression that he was a loser.

When Nixon's law partner and close associate, John Mitchell, asked me to head up the Nixon campaign in Illinois I declined, telling him I wanted to watch the race for a bit. It seemed to me that Nixon had spent much of his adult life getting ready to do something but not actually doing much besides running for the next office and serving in the standby role as vice president for eight years. As the campaign developed I was increasingly impressed by his steadiness and focus. Eventually, I agreed to be an assistant floor leader for Nixon at the 1968 Republican convention in Miami, and then as a surrogate speaker for him in the presidential election.

On the third day of the convention Mitchell, by then Nixon's campaign manager, sent me a note asking that I attend a meeting in Nixon's suite at the Hilton Plaza Hotel to discuss his vice presidential selection. The private gathering, with most of the leading figures of the Republican Party, would start immediately after the balloting for president was concluded. It was an unexpected invitation for a thirty-six-year-old congressman who did not know the candidate well, and in fact had been slow to support him, but I accepted with interest.[1]

After Nixon's nomination, which ran late into the evening, I drove to the Hilton and made my way to his suite. Twenty-one people were gathered there, including such Republican luminaries as former Governor Thomas Dewey of New York, the 1944 and 1948 Republican presidential candidate; Senator Strom Thurmond of South Carolina, the Dixiecrat's presidential candidate in 1948; and Senator Barry Goldwater of Arizona, seemingly well recovered from his 1964 defeat. I was the youngest and without question the least experienced person in the room.

Nixon soon arrived and shook hands with everyone. Never one for small talk, his greetings went rather quickly. Nixon seemed quite energetic despite the late hour. He sat in a swivel chair toward one end of the room. The rest of us were seated in an oblong circle.[2] Nixon leaned back in his chair and extended his feet onto the edge of a coffee table.

I was impressed with how he handled himself as he held forth—he was businesslike and authoritative. He started off by giving his vision of the coming campaign, which he expected to be another close one. In considering possible vice presidential candidates, Nixon pointedly said he would not do what John F. Kennedy did in 1960 by picking Lyndon Johnson. I took that to mean he didn't want a running mate who was a regional candidate chosen to help the ticket carry a particular state. Instead, Nixon said he wanted someone with broader appeal. I assumed he wanted to set aside individuals with close ties to the party's left or right wings.

"I don't want to select someone who will have the effect of dividing this party," Nixon said in his baritone voice.[3] From time to time he fiddled with his watchband as he spoke. He asked us to indicate who we believed would run best in our part of the country.[4] "Now let's go around the room," he said. He first looked to Congressman Sam Devine of Ohio, sitting to my immediate left. "Sam, start it off," Nixon said.

I figured Devine would talk for a while to give me a chance to collect my thoughts. No such luck. Sam said he had responded to a written request from Nixon with his choice of a running mate—and that he had nothing further to add. Then Nixon and the room full of Republican luminaries turned to the next person in line. "Don, what do you think?" Nixon asked. I barely knew most of the Republican bigwigs in the room, including Nixon, but now it was my turn.

I had something of a problem, as Nixon seemed to have just ruled out some of the people I thought would run best in my area in Illinois, most of whom were identified as being toward the left of the party: Charles Percy, Nelson Rockefeller, and John Lindsay. I had opposed Rockefeller as a presidential candidate that year, but as a vice presidential candidate I thought he might bring some strength to the ticket in places like Cook County. The Republican Party was still recovering from 1964, and I felt our local candidates would have a better chance to win in 1968 if we broadened the GOP base. I also thought it would be useful to have a vice presidential candidate who could help the party make inroads in the northern, industrial, urban, and particularly the suburban areas. A candidate who would demonstrate an interest in the problems that were of concern to people in America's cities—education, crime, drugs, and the enduring racial divisions—might attract more independent-leaning voters. I said that Senator Charles Percy in particular would be helpful in my home state, which promised to be a bellwether. I then went on to say that I thought it would be a mistake to pick a candidate from below the Mason-Dixon Line. The South was still polarized, and I thought that it might send an unfortunate message that Republicans were not supportive of civil rights. I said this knowing that one of the most prominent Southerners in the party, Strom Thurmond, was sitting only a few feet away.*

On several occasions during the discussion, Nixon would ask, "What about Volpe?" or "What about Agnew?" John Volpe was the governor of Massachusetts. Spiro T. Agnew was the recently elected governor of Maryland. Nobody seemed to know much about either of them. But as the discussion went on, it occurred to me that Nixon very likely had all but made up his mind to select either Volpe or Agnew before any of us had arrived.[5]

It was nearly five o'clock in the morning when the meeting finally ended. As I headed out, I passed Nixon, who was standing alone. He shook my hand. Then he said something I wasn't expecting.

"You've got an easy district," he observed. "I'd like to have you come with me [on the campaign trail], and I want to talk to you about it." I told Nixon I was willing to do what I could to help. I also pressed the case against picking a Southern candidate for vice president.

Nixon thought for a moment. "Don, I'm afraid we're all going to have to give a little on this one," he said.[6]

*Thurmond made a strong pitch for his favorite candidate, a rising star in the conservative wing of the party: California Governor Ronald Reagan. Since Reagan, like Nixon, hailed from California, the ticket would lack geographic balance. Congressman John Rhodes of Arizona also threw out a name no one else had mentioned: Congressman Gerald Ford. But Ford, like Reagan, had few backers among GOP elders.

When I got back to my hotel room near dawn, Joyce, typically, got right to the point. "Well, who is it?" she asked.

"You won't believe it," I replied. I told her it looked to me that it would be Volpe or Agnew with an outside possibility of Senator Mark Hatfield of Oregon. Hatfield was a friend, and of the three the one I would have preferred. He had been suggested by the Reverend Billy Graham. Joyce thought for a moment and then, with a puzzled look, asked the question that the entire world would soon echo: "Agnew?"

When Nixon announced Governor Agnew's selection the following day, he said he had based his decision on three criteria. First, Nixon claimed, Agnew was qualified to become president. Second, he said Agnew would be a good campaigner; and third, if they got elected Agnew would be able to manage domestic policy.[7] To my knowledge, Agnew was not particularly noted for those qualities. More than anything Nixon seemed pleased that he had selected someone so unexpected, catching everyone off guard. And indeed the choice of Agnew was so startling that it stunned even Agnew.[8]

Though I remained impressed with Nixon, I found his selection process disappointing. The weakness of his vice presidential choice eventually caused great problems for him down the road. Nixon's real criterion did not seem to be competence or experience but rather finding someone who did not elicit opposition from any quarter. His intent may have been to preempt criticism, but if so, it was shortsighted. That no one spoke against Agnew was not an indicator that he had no flaws, but rather that no one yet knew of his shortcomings.

In late August, the Democrats held their nominating convention in Chicago. The Nixon team asked me, as the only local Republican congressman representing part of Chicago, to join what they called the "Republican listening post." The plan was to be ready to exploit in the media whatever openings the Democrats might offer.* We were located at the Chicago Conrad Hilton Hotel. Our group consisted of a young Nixon speechwriter and future Pulitzer Prize–winning columnist, Bill Safire, another top speechwriter and talented rising star named Pat Buchanan, Republican Governor John Love of Colorado, and me.

*I was later named cochairman of the Republican truth squad, along with Senate Minority Leader Hugh Scott. Our small team of senators, governors, and congressmen followed Vice President Hubert Humphrey around the country and held press conferences after his appearances to get Nixon's positions into local media at the same time Humphrey was getting coverage. True to form, the genial Humphrey would occasionally stop by to see us and say hello, even as we were preparing to counter his presentation.

As it turned out, we didn't have to do much, if any, truth squadding. The Democrats suffered through one of the worst conventions in modern history. Inside the convention hall there were heated debates over the Vietnam War and attempts to cut off the microphones of some of the speakers. Outside, thousands of demonstrators gathered in protest marches—including a large crowd in Grant Park across the street from our hotel. From our windows we could see demonstrators holding candles or carrying signs protesting President Johnson and the Vietnam War. Joyce came into the city to join us, and we watched from our hotel room. After a while we decided to go down and see what was happening up close. Joyce and I talked a reluctant Governor Love, a dignified man from an earlier generation, into going into Grant Park with us.

The majority of protesters were not anarchists, revolutionaries, or violent. Most were young, not much older than our eldest daughter. I understood their point of view, since I had my own concerns about the conduct of the war. But there were troublemakers sprinkled among the groups that were looking to incite a showdown with the police.

Later that night, when we were back in the hotel, Joyce and I looked out of the windows again. The demonstration began to take a less peaceful turn. Some in the crowd started to attack the police, hoping to provoke a violent confrontation that would garner press attention. The vastly outnumbered Chicago police tried to keep the crowd under control. Finally, the police deployed tear gas. The gas filled the lobby of the Hilton and eventually made its way through some lower floors. As the situation grew more tense, some officers took tougher actions. Police in robin egg blue helmets charged into the demonstrators, wielding night sticks and dragging some of the troublemakers to police vans. Other officers pinned people against the wall of the Conrad Hilton and, in the process of subduing them, some hotel windows were broken.[9] The agitators in the crowd responded with more violence.

As the rioting continued, members of our listening post checked in with Richard Nixon and reported on what was happening. The unfolding disaster in Chicago understandably captured his attention. He asked a number of questions and expressed dismay at the level of violence. Like many politicians, Nixon was interested in gathering information about his political opponents—a few years later, of course, the country would find out just how interested.

The harmful aftereffects of the chaos in Chicago lingered for months. It cast an unwelcome shadow on the Democratic convention and on Hubert Humphrey's presidential campaign. What the country saw on television was ugly, and the political fallout was substantial. What I witnessed left a painful memory and a lingering sense of sorrow about what had happened in Chicago, one of America's great cities and my hometown.

I was struck by the fact that Nixon was running against a Democratic opponent who in many ways was his opposite. Aptly labeled "the happy warrior," Humphrey was upbeat and engaging. He was also tough. Reciting the litany of previous incarnations of a new Nixon persona in 1952, 1956, 1960, and 1962, Humphrey noted, "Now, I read about the new Nixon of 1968. Ladies and gentlemen. Anyone who's had his political face lifted so many times can't be very new."[10] I had a feeling a Humphrey-Nixon debate would not help our side.

The Nixon campaign agreed—the candidate had not forgotten his difficulties debating John F. Kennedy in 1960. That September, Bryce Harlow, a friend and well-known Washington figure, came to my congressional office. Harlow was working hard on the Nixon campaign. He told me that Nixon did not want to give Humphrey the chance to debate and to untether himself from the unpopular Johnson. Furthermore, Democrats in Congress, at Humphrey's and LBJ's urging, were proposing to suspend the equal time provisions so that Governor George Wallace would be able to participate without any other third-party candidates. Wallace, a segregationist candidate from Alabama, was running for president as an independent. His candidacy promised to siphon support from Nixon in the south, and like Humphrey he was quick and entertaining in a debate format. Harlow told me Nixon was disinclined to give Wallace any airtime and that he considered it unfair for just one third-party candidate to be included.

Harlow asked me to help stop the suspension of the equal-time provisions that would have allowed for the three-way debate. I thought we had substantial common interests on the issue: I agreed with Harlow's political assessment that a three-way debate was the worst scenario for Nixon, and I disapproved of the Democrats' last-minute attempt to jury-rig the rules. I also thought this might be an opportunity for my group in Congress to get some attention for the issues we wanted to advance. "Rumsfeld's Raiders" were pushing a reform package that included measures popular with the public, such as campaign finance reform and a ban on the use of political contributions for personal enrichment.

As Harlow set himself up in Ford's minority leader office, just off the House chamber, we crafted a campaign of legislative maneuvers to stall the suspension of equal-time provisions. Any member could stop business in the House of Representatives by requiring the clerk to call the roll in order to have a majority of members (a quorum) present. So before the debate legislation came up for a vote, one of us would ask for a quorum call and the rest of us would work to ensure that there were never enough members present on the House floor for debate or votes to continue. From noon on October 8 until well into the next day our group arranged for thirty-three consecutive intentionally unsuccessful quorum calls.

This was not well received by the Democratic Speaker of the House, John McCormack. He threatened to send out the Capitol police force to physically round up members and lock them in the chamber. At one point, Congressman John Anderson of Illinois was barred from leaving the House floor—leading to a bizarre scene in which a member of Congress was pounding on the doors of the House chamber, shouting that he was being held hostage by the Speaker.

In addition to the repeated calls for a quorum, we also managed to arrange votes on a series of amendments to the legislation that dragged things out even further. LBJ must not have been pleased. We were outmaneuvering the legislative master himself.

Before we were done, we kept the House in session all night in what became the longest continuous session of the U.S. House of Representatives since the battle over the Missouri Compromise of 1820. Some of the tradition-conscious Republican leadership considered our efforts unseemly, but Minority Leader Gerald Ford stood apart and cheered us on. Our effort was dubbed "The Longest Night."

Our goal was to delay the bill because we knew we did not have the votes to defeat it. We were trying to hold out for two days so Senate Republicans could make a similar effort and prevent the bill from being voted on before Congress was set to adjourn on October twelfth. It worked. The bill was shelved indefinitely. Humphrey and Nixon never debated, nor did Governor George Wallace. Our efforts caught Nixon's attention, and the candidate let it be known that he was grateful for our assistance.

A week later, Nixon invited me to accompany him on a campaign swing through the South and Midwest, where I got to know him a bit better.[11] Despite his somber, pensive, and businesslike demeanor, Nixon showed himself to be an engaging stump speaker. He worked at it, meticulously preparing his notes beforehand. At one point he became so involved in his speech that he nearly fell off the crate he was standing on.

Toward the end of one flight, Nixon called me into his private compartment. Then fifty-five, his hair, touched with gray, was receding. He got right down to the business of the campaign and asked me where I was scheduled to speak over the closing weeks. I told him I was going to New York, New Jersey, and Pennsylvania.

"That's good," he said, putting on his master political strategist hat. "Stay out of Illinois." Though he might have been elected president in 1960 if Illinois had tilted to him over Kennedy, Nixon seemed to think he would win the state this time.

On the next leg of our trip we had a longer conversation.[12] Nixon was relaxed as we spoke. He seemed to want to know more about me—he asked me if I smoked, and I told him I did smoke a pipe. He expressed irritation at the campaign and what he considered to be Humphrey's attempts to characterize him as a racist. "If I did that to Humphrey I'd never hear the end of it in the press," Nixon mused. "Do you think I should debate him?"

"No, I don't," I replied.

He told me his advisers were telling him to hit Humphrey harder in his speeches. I told him I thought he was doing fine. Humphrey was a likable character, and I didn't think that being harsh to him would be a good strategy. Later Nixon received kudos in the press for appearing on the popular entertainment show *Laugh-In*—something of a precursor to *Saturday Night Live*—and saying the show's catch phrase, "Sock it to me!" The fact that Nixon was willing to appear on the show demonstrated to many of his critics that he was able to take himself less seriously and have a little fun.

As Nixon had predicted, the election was close—his victory margin was less than 1 percentage point, making the 1968 presidential election one of the tightest in American history. Richard Nixon had risen from the political grave.

CHAPTER 8

The Job That Couldn't Be Done

"For the past five years we have been deluged by government programs for the unemployed, programs for the cities, programs for the poor," Nixon observed in his convention speech in Miami. "And we have reaped from these programs an ugly harvest of frustration, violence, and failure across the land." To cheers, Nixon said it was time "to quit pouring billions of dollars into programs that have failed in the United States."[1]

One of the chief targets of the Nixon speech was the Office of Economic Opportunity (OEO), which had started under John F. Kennedy as a small set of experimental programs run out of the Executive Office of the President. The agency had been lassoed by his successor, LBJ, as part of what he grandly called his War on Poverty.

Under Johnson, who thought on a mammoth scale, OEO ballooned. At one point it administered Community Action Programs, Head Start, the Job Corps, Legal Services, and the Volunteers in Service to America, or VISTA (a domestic Peace Corps) as well as programs to help senior citizens, Native Americans, migrants, neighborhood health centers, and drug treatment centers, plus others, a number of which evolved into their own independent activities over time.

As a member of Congress I voted against the 1964 legislation that established the Office of Economic Opportunity.[2] I was uncomfortable with OEO programs being run out of the Executive Office of the President rather than being housed in the relevant cabinet departments and agencies. It seemed like another layer of bureaucracy on top of the existing department bureaucracies.

As OEO grew during the Johnson administration, so did its opposition. When Nixon took office, it was clear that Johnson's lofty goal of eradicating poverty was failing. Hundreds of millions of dollars were being spent, and it proved difficult to identify and track progress. There was also an air of radicalism in some of the OEO programs. When I first walked through the OEO offices I saw posters of the Marxist Che Guevara proudly displayed on the walls. In some parts of the country taxpayer dollars were going to radical and violent "Black Power" groups. An additional controversy was that OEO provided funds to community groups, intentionally bypassing the locally elected governors and mayors. This led to resentment of OEO by state and local officials of both political parties.

Though Nixon ran on a platform hostile to the OEO, he decided after his election he would not abolish it outright, but instead would try to reform it. Racial tensions were high, and many groups had their hopes set on the success of OEO's mission. Nixon thought OEO might somehow be redirected into more realistic and effective activities. When he was searching for someone to run the agency, now the scourge of most conservatives in his base of support, Nixon turned to his top domestic policy aide, Daniel Patrick Moynihan, for suggestions.

Pat Moynihan was creative, entertaining, and one of the smartest individuals I had ever met. As the saying went, Moynihan wrote more books than most people had read. He had applied his considerable intellect to the Department of Labor during the Kennedy administration, and later had written on Lyndon Johnson's vision of the Great Society. A Democrat with an independent streak, he was now working for Kennedy's old rival, Richard Nixon, as an expert on urban and minority affairs.* I thought it said something laudatory of Nixon that he saw the merit of bringing Moynihan into his confidence.

Moynihan had keen political instincts. Who better, he proposed, to run an agency disliked by Republicans in Congress than . . . a conservative Republican from Congress? Pat knew I had voted against OEO but that I had supported civil rights legislation and had shown an interest in tackling reform. He strongly recommended that Nixon appoint me. It was an unorthodox choice.

* Moynihan later served as ambassador to India and to the United Nations before being elected to the United States Senate from New York, holding the seat until 2000, when he retired.

My reply to the request from the new president was also unorthodox: "No." I was not thinking about leaving Congress at the time, though I was still tangling with the old guard. In early 1969, for example, I had run for chairman of the House Republican Policy Committee. I thought I had support all lined up when, at the last minute, my longtime nemesis Minority Whip Les Arends persuaded Bob Taft of Ohio to run against me. Taft won by one vote, but I still enjoyed my work and wasn't much interested in joining the Nixon administration in an assignment that seemed almost destined to fail.

Nixon's aides continued to press me as they put together their new administration. I continued to resist. Finally, I wrote a straightforward, detailed memo to the Nixon team outlining why I was not the right choice to run OEO:

> 1) The probable reaction to the appointment of a white, Ivy League, suburban, Republican Congressman from the wealthiest Congressional District in the Nation, with little visable [sic] management experience and little public identification with poverty problems, and who voted against the poverty program when it was first proposed would be harmful for the Nixon Administration. . . .*
> 2) The job that the Administration wishes to have done on OEO, as I understand it, is the liquidation of the Johnson poverty approach. The development of the Nixon approach to these problems would essentially be the responsibility not of OEO but of [other] Departments. . . .
> 3) In a political situation, which this is, it would seem that the best approach would be to use a person identified as a liberal when one wishes to retrench and reorganize.[3]

I figured I would not hear about Nixon's proposal again. Then one Sunday that spring, as Joyce and I were having dinner with our kids, the telephone rang. Before long I was talking to President Nixon. It was the first time a president of the United States had called my home.

"Don," Nixon said, "I want to invite you and your wife down to Key Biscayne to talk." I told the President I would be willing to meet with him in Florida, where Nixon occasionally vacationed. When we got off the phone I told Joyce about the conversation.

"Well, it's settled," she said simply. She liked the OEO idea even less than I did, since it meant leaving Congress to run an agency I was ambivalent

* The census had determined that my congressional district's residents, while not the wealthiest in the country, did have the highest annual earned incomes.

about at best. But she concluded immediately that I was unlikely to leave a meeting with the President of the United States without committing to accept the job.

The reserved Nixon spent his decades in politics having to push himself to be in the public eye. Even while supposedly relaxing in sunny Florida, he was formal and businesslike. As I noticed in our earlier meetings, he could be less than easy in his personal interactions. When Nixon met Joyce, for example, he acknowledged her with a smile. "Don," he said, "I'm glad to see you brought your daughter." Nixon would repeat that quip on more than one occasion.

If not warm and easy in personal relationships, on a professional level President Nixon proved persuasive. As we met in Florida in April 1969, Nixon told me he needed me to take the OEO job. "The agency needs to be run right," he said. "And you'll have my full support." As I made my case for not taking the post, Nixon kept telling me he did not agree and that I was the right man for the job. He left the impression that he had a personal interest in my future. And when the President told me he needed my help, I found it hard to keep up the fight. Nixon persuaded me to take on an assignment I didn't want, at an agency I had voted against, with a mission that Nixon didn't like, for a purpose that was still unclear.

As our discussion on OEO was ending, I told the President that I'd recently returned from a second trip to Southeast Asia. Referencing Johnson's credibility problems on the war, I suggested that Nixon examine carefully the American military's bombing of the Viet Cong and North Vietnamese targets in neighboring Laos. The Johnson administration's silence on the issue left the American people unaware of the bombing campaign. Our friends in the region—the governments of Laos and Cambodia—insisted that American officials not reveal that they had given approval to bomb in their countries. Had it become public, Laos and Cambodia would have had to protest the very activity they had approved. The problem, as I told Nixon, was that while our friends were cooperating they were protecting themselves. By continuing a secret bombing campaign, Nixon would not be protecting himself.

"President Johnson got into trouble for not telling the truth," I noted. "Your administration does not want to fall into the same pattern."

Nixon listened intently and nodded. I hoped the message got through.

Having agreed to the President's request, we encountered an unanticipated problem that put my nomination in question. The Constitution prohibits individuals from receiving a government salary outside Congress if the salary for that position was increased during their time in Congress. While I had been serving, Congress had raised salaries for federal posts, including the director of OEO, which made me ineligible to receive the new salary for that position. Nixon's legal staff discovered the issue and asked the Justice Department to look into the matter. A young assistant attorney general arrived at my house on a Sunday afternoon to discuss a possible solution. The suggestion was that I not receive a salary as director of the OEO and instead be paid as an assistant to the president in the White House. At the President's suggestion, I was also to be made a member of the President's cabinet. I can still picture that lanky lawyer sitting at our small dining table, discussing the issue. As it turned out, I owed the start of my service in the executive branch of the federal government to the fine legal mind of William Rehnquist, a future chief justice of the United States.[4]

During my early months at the Office of Economic Opportunity, I had my first protracted encounter with the national media, and the episode left an indelible impression on me. On September 22, 1969, I opened the *Washington Post* to a column by Jack Anderson. Anderson was a syndicated columnist, appearing in nearly one thousand papers across the country. His pieces sought to offer a glimpse of Washington to average Americans, and he especially enjoyed targeting politicians and government officials. That morning I was in his crosshairs.

The column's title caused a sensation: "ANTI-POVERTY CZAR EMBELLISHES OFFICE."[5] "Anti-poverty czar Donald Rumsfeld has wielded an economy ax on programs for the poor," Anderson wrote. "He has used some of the savings to give his own executive suite a more luxurious look, thus reducing the poverty in his immediate surroundings."

Anderson's column, which reached as many as forty million readers, could not have come at a worse time. I was trying to forge relations with the agency's employees, many of whom were skeptical or downright hostile to Republicans. I also wanted to try to give the OEO some credibility among its critics as being well run, to try to earn support in Congress.

Anderson's column damaged those efforts badly, painting a portrait of me as a stereotypical fat-cat Republican, in stark contrast to my predecessor in the job, President Kennedy's wealthy brother-in-law Sargent Shriver, who was portrayed as being sensitive to the mission of OEO. "Under Sargent Shriver, the anti-poverty director's office was unique in government," Anderson noted. "There were no carpets, and the furnishings were prim." Anderson's claims included the following:

> To be prepared should his budget-cutting efforts prove tiresome, he had added a bedroom to his executive suite. Expensive lamps now give a soft, restful glow to the walls that were once lit by fluorescent tubes. . . . And as evidence of his new Cabinet rank, Rumsfeld has added the ultimate in executive status symbols: a private bathroom.[6]

One could see why the piece was irresistible to critics. It was undoubtedly given to Anderson by an insider who didn't like the reforms I was implementing to make OEO more efficient and leaner. There was only one problem: Anderson's story was not true. In fact, as far as I could tell, not a word of that column was accurate, with the exception of the correct spelling of my name. Anderson had not bothered to make a simple phone call to confirm his facts or even to ask for a comment.

I had learned in managing Congressman Dave Dennison's 1958 campaign how even the appearance of wrongdoing could be terribly damaging. A newspaper article, no matter how false, can stick to a public figure for decades. The old axiom about the press is that a politician should never engage in battle with an opponent that buys ink by the barrel. But I had to do something. So I dictated a four-page response that addressed the Anderson column point by point, including:

> QUOTE: "Anti-poverty czar Donald Rumsfeld has wielded an economy ax on programs for the poor . . ."
>
> COMMENT: 1969 FY expenditures were $1.7 [billion]. The Nixon Administration request for $2.8 billion . . . is still pending before Congress. That is not an "economy ax."
>
> QUOTE: "Expensive lamps now give a soft, restful glow to the walls that were once lit by fluorescent tubes."
>
> COMMENT: The fluorescent tubes are still there. Three lamps, GSA issue, are not in Rumsfeld's office, but in the reception area on the 8th floor. There is not a lamp in Rumsfeld's office, either expensive or cheap, restful or not restful.
>
> QUOTE: "And as evidence of his new Cabinet rank, Rumsfeld has added the ultimate in executive status symbols: a private bathroom."
>
> COMMENT: . . . There is no private bathroom. There are two bathrooms on the 8th floor where Rumsfeld's office is located—one for ladies and one for men. Rumsfeld uses the latter.[7]

After my secretary typed up my response, I invited Anderson to read it and to take a tour of my office. After he saw with his own eyes that his entire piece was false, I was under the naïve impression that he would correct his column with the same fanfare that his original column received. But, quite the contrary, he informed me that while he regretted the error, he had recently inherited his column from longtime columnist Drew Pearson. Anderson said he feared that if he admitted he had run a totally false column, some of the newspapers in the syndicate for his column might drop it.* Obviously, he was more concerned about his paycheck than the damage the article did to me or the truth.

The episode was like a body blow and left me with a deep caution of the press. Years later, when I left government and moved back to Chicago in 1977, the Anderson story would still haunt me. Joyce and I would run into people who, while generally friendly and complimentary, wondered why I had built that fancy bedroom and private bathroom at the expense of the poor.

Our plan was to have OEO serve as a laboratory for experimental programs, not as an entity that managed large operations in perpetuity. For example, OEO had tried a number of innovative approaches to education. Under my predecessors, to their credit, OEO had launched an experiment providing school vouchers for parents. The plan had the support of my friend Milton Friedman.[9] Friedman and I believed that school vouchers could lead to an improvement in public education by giving parents choices rather than forcing them to send their children to a particular school.[10] OEO also had supported an experiment in performance contracting for teachers, an idea that was bitterly opposed by the politically active teachers' unions.

I also served on a committee President Nixon established to encourage and guide school desegregation policies as required by the Supreme Court's landmark 1954 decision *Brown vs. Board of Education of Topeka*. The committee was originally chaired by Vice President Agnew, which offered an early glimpse for me of Agnew in a substantive setting. I did not come away impressed. He soon lost interest in the issue, did not seem particularly knowledgeable on the substance, and rarely came to the meetings. The chairmanship was assumed by another member of the committee, the Secretary of Labor and a rising figure in the Nixon administration, George Shultz. Shultz

* It was cold comfort some years later when Jack Anderson finally confessed that his column on me was among his biggest mistakes.[8]

quickly became a friend. Also a Princeton graduate, and a former Marine, he was not flamboyant—though rumor has it that he has a tattoo of a Princeton tiger on his backside.

The President thought well of Shultz. Nixon had a collection of favorites who would go up and down in his level of interest, depending on his priorities at the time. Early on, at least, Shultz was one of them. "Keep your eye on Shultz," Nixon told me at our meeting in Key Biscayne. "He's going to be a star."

Shultz skillfully moved the heated debates about school desegregation away from emotionally charged, confrontational discussions toward more practical approaches. Our effort to peacefully desegregate schools in the South, supported by the President, deserves to rank high in the Nixon administration's domestic record.

In addition to dealing with policy matters at the Office of Economic Opportunity, we often had to face the raw public emotion provoked by the thorny social issues of the time. A day at OEO without a protest, a demonstration, or a bomb threat was a good day. There were times when my courageous secretary, Brenda Williams, would have to move her desk in front of the door to prevent protesters from breaking into our office on M Street.

On one occasion in November 1969, some fifty people barged into a conference room during a staff meeting, protesting the hiring policies of the Legal Services program. Terry Lenzner, the program director, escorted the group to a room on another floor so our meeting could continue. A pugnacious young Democrat, Lenzner had captained the Harvard football team some years before. He was not one to back down from trouble. When Lenzner tried to leave the group, the protesters blocked the door, effectively holding him captive.

I was notified of the problem and went down to the room. Wedging myself in past those blocking the doors, I took Lenzner's arm and told him we were leaving.[11] I then told the protesters they had the right to express their views, but we were not going to conduct the government's business under threats or intimidation, and that if they didn't leave the building, they would be arrested. That, of course, was exactly what some of them wanted. I obliged them and called in the local police. I was later told that I had caused the arrest of a major fraction of the graduating class of Howard Law School. As it turned out, among them was a young law student by the name of Jerry Rivers, later better known as Geraldo Rivera. It was but one example of the hostility and divisions that some of the OEO programs had caused in the country.

Considering the many issues in the agency's purview, I had to delegate enormous amounts of responsibility to keep OEO operating. As a congressman, I had not had a large staff. But at OEO I understood well the importance of having talented assistance. Among others, the group I recruited and worked with included Christie Todd Whitman, a future governor of New Jersey and later administrator of the Environmental Protection Agency (EPA); Bill Bradley, then the talented New York Knicks basketball star and a future U.S. senator; Ron James, who later became a senior official in the Department of the Army; and Max Friedersdorf, an outstanding director of congressional relations in the Nixon, Ford, and Reagan administrations.

Two others stand out. Frank Carlucci, for one, was an enormously capable man I lured from a promising career in the Foreign Service. I first knew Carlucci when we were on the varsity wrestling team at Princeton during the early 1950s. Frank went from there to the U.S. Navy and then the State Department, where he led an initiative that reduced the number of personnel at the U.S. mission in Brazil by a large fraction. His ability to move into an entrenched operation and reorganize it caught my attention.

Another excellent decision was hiring a serious young man from Wyoming. After interviewing with me six months earlier, Dick Cheney had gone to work for my good friend Congressman Bill Steiger of Wisconsin. I knew Steiger was impressed with his work. When I was nominated as the director of OEO, Steiger suggested that Cheney write a strategy memo to assist me in my confirmation hearings. It focused on what I sensed and heard was needed for a successful OEO: better accountability. Once I was confirmed by the Senate, I asked Carlucci to call Cheney and bring him aboard as my special assistant. Cheney had been thinking of returning to the University of Wisconsin to complete his doctorate in political science, but he took the job. Together, Carlucci, Cheney, and I—three future Republican secretaries of defense—labored to fix a cornerstone of Johnson's Great Society.

The well-worn recent media caricature of Dick Cheney as a rigid ideologue is unfamiliar to those of us who know him well. I've known him from his start in the federal government. At first Cheney was one of the many bright young staffers around the OEO office, but in short order he proved indispensable. The words "steady" and "unflappable" were frequently applied to him—and with good reason. Dick was an enormous help as we wrestled with the many heated controversies in which OEO had become embroiled over its short life. In fact, the more difficult the situation, the more Dick seemed to like it.*

Because of OEO's mission and its position as the centerpiece of the Johnson antipoverty legacy, many prominent people were interested in its activities and agreed to serve on its advisory board. One of them was Sammy Davis, Jr., often introduced as "the world's greatest entertainer." Sammy and I became friends. One memorable night the entertainer came to visit us at our small row house in Washington. It was only twenty-eight feet across; the second floor had two small bedrooms. We took the door off the upstairs closet so we could fit in a small crib when our son, Nick, was born.

"This is a nice place," Sammy said, when he entered our front room. "Let's see it."

"You just did," Joyce replied with a smile.†

Some months later, Joyce and I were in Nevada, where I was giving a speech. It happened that my trip coincided with Sammy's hundredth performance at the Sands Hotel & Casino. After his spectacular show, Sammy told Joyce and me he would not be performing the next night and wanted us to go to dinner with him. He said he would arrange for us to see the best entertainer in Las Vegas which, considering Sammy's fame, was quite a compliment. So that evening we went to the International Hotel and were seated at a front row table—Sammy, his lovely wife Altovise, Joyce, and me.

Before long, the entertainer whom Sammy had extolled came onstage. Wearing a sequined jumpsuit and alternating between the ridiculous and the sublime, he promptly took command of the large audience. He sang songs of every genre, and that evening I became an Elvis Presley fan.

I could see that Elvis was a masterful showman. The audience was enthralled. Periodically he would take a silk scarf, wipe his brow, and toss it to the screaming crowd. At one point he threw a long, scarlet scarf in our direction. Sammy's wife caught it and handed it to Joyce.

* I asked Cheney to work on a dispute involving a community action program in eastern Kentucky. He found himself smack in the middle of an old-fashioned Southern political blood feud between an influential Democrat, Treva Howell, and Republican governor Louie Nunn. Both were leveling serious allegations of wrongdoing at each other. The charges were so serious that I told key Nixon aide John Ehrlichman that the FBI needed to become involved. Ehrlichman said he intended to send what he called his "own people from the White House" to investigate. I told him that getting the White House involved in investigations of that type was one of the dumbest proposals I could imagine and that I would ask the FBI to look into it myself, which I proceeded to do. FBI Director J. Edgar Hoover found that neither Howell nor Nunn had broken the law. Ehrlichman's team of investigators gained greater fame—or infamy—in subsequent years as "the White House plumbers."[12]

† When our family of two adults, three children, a dog, and a cat moved out a few years later, we were amused but not surprised to find that our house was advertised for sale as "suitable for a bachelor."

After the show, Sammy took us backstage to Elvis' dressing room. The room was filled with all sorts of people—fans, friends, members of his entourage, and showgirls. Eventually Joyce and I became separated in the crowd. After a while, she spotted me in what had to have been an unexpected place—standing in a corner of the room talking intently with the king of rock and roll.

After Sammy introduced us, Elvis pulled me aside. He wanted to discuss what I thought was an unlikely subject—the United States Army. Some years earlier he had served with the Third Armored Division in Germany for seventeen months. He wanted to share his thoughts about the armed forces and the pride he had in his service. Something of an admirer of Nixon, he was also interested in discussing the administration. Around that time, Presley had sent a letter to Nixon asking to help with the illegal narcotics trade. This led to the famous meeting between Elvis and the President in the Oval Office of the White House.

I imagine there weren't a lot of people in Elvis' normal circle with whom he could have a serious conversation about the military. I was impressed that years after his service he still cared so much about the Army. It certainly wasn't the sort of conversation I expected to have when I walked into his dressing room, but it was a welcome reminder that patriots can be found everywhere.*

During my tenure as director of OEO, we were successful in saving and strengthening some worthwhile programs by reallocating funds to them from less successful projects. We spun off functioning programs to other federal departments. We didn't perform miracles there, though I believe we did some good for the poor and for the country.

Even though many well-intentioned people at the agency worked hard to find solutions to the problems of poverty, easy answers were in short supply. During those tough times I could always count on Joyce to provide some good-humored perspective. She knew how often I would come home feeling disappointed that a program had not worked out better.

One night when I came home late, I went to the refrigerator and found a note taped to the door. Joyce had written, I am sure with a smile: "He tackled the job that couldn't be done; with a smile he went right to it. He tackled the job that couldn't be done—and couldn't do it."

* Even today, particularly on Sundays when we do not get to church, Joyce and I listen to a recording of Elvis singing gospel songs. He remains one of our favorite singers.

CHAPTER 9

Counsellor

After I left the Office of Economic Opportunity, Nixon appointed me Counsellor to the President, a general advisory position in the White House. I continued as a member of the cabinet, and I moved full time into an office in the West Wing. I began to see the President and his top aides far more regularly than I had while at OEO.

I soon noticed that Nixon liked to ruminate away from the Oval Office. He often took refuge in a separate private office in the Old Executive Office Building, the massive nineteenth-century building adjacent to the White House. There he would meet with small groups of aides to talk about whatever might be on his mind. I would find him there dressed in a suit and tie, his feet up on a stool, the ever-present yellow pad in his lap, thinking his way through a problem.

In 1970, the country remained in turmoil. Tension over Vietnam remained high, and the situation flared in the spring after the so-called incursion into Cambodia—a phrase that seemed to conjure up a sightseeing visit more than the armed invasion it was. On May 4, students at Kent State University shut down the campus with a massive demonstration protesting the administration's action in Cambodia, which students feared would widen and extend the war. In an attempt to control the chaos, Ohio National Guardsmen opened fire, killing four people and wounding others. The incident precipitated a nationwide student strike at more than four hundred colleges and universities—involving as many as four million students.[1] Nixon, troubled by the mass demonstration, appeared at the Lincoln Memorial at an early-morning student protest and talked to a group of them who had made camp there. His visit was dismissed by a growing and vocal legion of critics, but I thought it demonstrated an interesting aspect of the President's character that he was willing to put himself in the middle of such a scene.

On May 15, protests at the historically black Jackson State University in Mississippi turned violent, and two more students were killed. Shortly after these shootings, Cheney (who continued to work as my assistant after I left OEO) and I traveled to Mississippi to get a sense of what might happen and to reach out to the families.[2] We found a fluid, unstable situation—everyone was holding his breath waiting to see what might happen next. It was a tense moment, as the country watched Americans—young students and equally young National Guardsmen—turn on one another. The disorder continued across the country for many months, until campuses finally reopened that fall.

Members of Nixon's cabinet had their own personal experiences with young people expressing opposition to the war and wanting to be part of the so-called youth movement, which was characterized by wearing long hair, beads, and tie-dyed shirts. This provided a challenge for some parents in the cabinet, since most Sundays Nixon invited our families to the White House for a church service, and parents had to work overtime to make sure their children looked presentable enough to read scripture or shake hands with the President. Our own children were friends with some of the antiwar demonstrators, and it was not exactly easy for them to reveal that their dad worked for Richard Nixon in the White House. Valerie once told me that she was thinking of joining one of the demonstrations. "Okay, do it," I said bluntly, "if you believe in what you are saying." But I told her I didn't want her to join a protest simply because she wanted to be part of her crowd. She decided not to go.

Now that I was at the White House full-time, there was speculation in the press and elsewhere that I had moved into President Nixon's inner circle. That was an outsider's perspective. Inside the White House the situation was more complex. Nixon had more than one so-called inner circle—and he would swing back and forth among them, depending on his interests and moods. He also used the various circles for quite different purposes.

There was, of course, the well-publicized duo in the Nixon White House, consisting of Bob Haldeman and John Ehrlichman. They appealed to Nixon's political bent, his toughness, and his long-held resentment of those he called the Washington elites. Haldeman and Ehrlichman's German surnames led the press to dub them the Berlin Wall for their reputation as a united front protecting the President and, it was implied, keeping others out. My experience was that Haldeman and Ehrlichman had quite different personalities and working methods.

As chief of staff, Haldeman was the aide closest to the President. He was a trim man with a crew cut, brisk and methodical, but rarely unpleasant. I liked his meetings, because they tended to be substantive and efficient. I also had a reasonable certainty when I dealt with him that he was providing an accurate version of President Nixon's wishes and views, which made me comfortable with the guidance he offered. Because of his closeness to Nixon, Haldeman might have been the one person who could have stepped in and stopped Nixon's decisions regarding the management of the Watergate scandal. Nixon sometimes said things he hadn't thought through. What he needed was someone to talk him out of those thoughts. I suspect Haldeman's fault might have been in not insisting to his boss that he was wrong.

Ehrlichman was less pleasant to deal with. He seemed to have a high degree of certainty about his views that bordered on arrogance, a trait that did him no favors as he gathered more influence in the White House. Certainty without power can be interesting, and even amusing. Certainty with power can be dangerous. It was never clear to me whether Ehrlichman was basing his guidance to others on the President's views or his own. I did not follow his guidance without checking his suggestions out with others, and then only if I agreed with them.

One person who made his way through the Berlin Wall was Chuck Colson. He served as Nixon's special counsel and seemed to become increasingly close to him as the 1972 election approached. A former Marine, a troubleshooter, and a self-described hatchet man, Colson was bright and tough. The President boasted that Colson would do anything for him, including walk "right through doors."[3] Nixon no doubt valued Colson's loyalty, but in my experience unquestioning obedience rarely serves a president well.

There was another group—another so-called inner circle—in the White House that included former California lieutenant governor Bob Finch, Pat Moynihan, George Shultz, and me. We were what Bill Safire once described as "youngish intellectual types" who appealed to Nixon's inner policy wonk. Unlike members of the Haldeman group, each of us had backgrounds in elected office, government, or academia that predated the Nixon administration. We all respected the President, but none of us awoke every morning planning to bash through closed doors for Nixon's political purposes.

During his early years as president, Nixon tried to merge these two groups into meetings Haldeman called FRESH, constituting Finch, Rumsfeld, Ehrlichman, Shultz, and Harlow.[4] We were an informal sounding board for Nixon on policy and political issues. It was an interesting opportunity to watch Nixon's mind at work. He was a strategic thinker, often looking two or three steps ahead of a given decision and always musing about and considering a full range of options.

There were, of course, times that Nixon would rant about something that had angered him. He'd go on about members of the press or certain administration figures who weren't carrying the ball well enough. I wasn't surprised to learn that sometimes I was the subject of these harangues. Contrary to the impression from the secret Nixon tapes—and the occasional deleted expletives—I did not find the President anywhere near as profane as some portray him. As historian Stephen Ambrose noted, most of those expletives were milder words, like "crap" and "hell" and "damn."[5]

One of the things I took occasion to discuss with the President was the administration's outreach to minorities—a perennial problem for Republicans and something government needed to be attentive to if it hoped to be truly representative. Some people blamed the widening gap between minorities and the GOP on Nixon's Southern strategy, a political effort that sought to win the votes of Southern Democrats, many of whom tended to be unsympathetic to civil rights legislation. Whether the strategy was a good idea or not, the fact is that the Democratic Party had successfully engaged in exactly that sort of maneuvering for decades—these voters were called "Southern Democrats" for a reason.

While I did not favor racial quotas, I believed it was important for the administration to make a serious effort at diversity. In the Nixon administration there were too few individuals from minority groups involved in policy-making positions at a time when issues with significant racial ramifications—school desegregation, riots, inner-city school problems, and drugs—were front and center. I suggested that the White House form a group to monitor minority hiring, marshal aid to black colleges, and focus on other efforts in support of minorities—including speaking to minority organizations.

In making my case to the President, I cast it in political terms that I thought might appeal to him. Strained relations between the Nixon administration and minorities, I noted, were eroding support for his priorities, such as the economy and ending the war in Vietnam. "A critical factor in altering the present perception of the Administration is hiring," I suggested in one memo. "Minority groups will be far more likely to see the administration in a favorable light if they are in fact a part of it."[6]

As the tapes have revealed, Nixon occasionally made offensive remarks about minorities. I didn't know exactly how he felt, however, since my experience was that his comments seemed in part generational, and I found his actions regarding minorities were not consistent with his sometimes inappropriate words. Nixon generally seemed to agree with my arguments about minority outreach, and his administration made serious efforts in that regard, including the major effort on school desegregation and the successful work by Bob Brown, Nixon's White House lead on minority affairs.

President Nixon occasionally gave me assignments that involved foreign policy, which he knew was among my interests. He also thought my having that exposure could be helpful if I sought a seat in the United States Senate—which was a frequent suggestion of his. He thought many Republicans in the Senate were weak-willed and poor advocates for his policies. He wanted people he considered his protégés to get to the Senate and "toughen them up." I tended to put off his suggestions that I run for a Senate seat in Illinois. But Nixon did persuade George H. W. Bush to run for a seat in Texas, a campaign Bush lost.

In September 1970, the President asked me to be a member of the U.S. delegation to the funeral of Egyptian President Gamal Abdel Nasser. Nasser, a close Soviet ally, was the beneficiary of millions of dollars in Soviet arms. As a result of our country's strained relations, no senior American foreign policy official was assigned to the delegation.

The large population of Cairo had at least doubled for the funeral of their leader. Many delegations from around the globe gathered in a huge tent to await the official events. For hours, passages from the Koran were broadcast over loudspeakers. Egyptian women on the mobbed streets wailed in a ritual chant. I left to see what was going on in the streets and ended up with the crushing mob of mourners following Nasser's body across the Nile.

While in Cairo our group met with the then Vice President and acting President, Anwar Sadat. We were advised in our Department of State and intelligence briefings that Sadat was unremarkable and not likely to successfully succeed Nasser as president. As it turned out, he proved to be a bold, courageous leader who successfully mended Egyptian relations with the West and moved the Soviet troops out of Egypt in short order.

In the spring of 1971, the President proposed that Bob Finch and I go to Europe and North Africa to discuss the growing illegal drug problem. As we prepared to leave, Nixon made an unexpected request. Stressing the need for the utmost secrecy, the President asked us to pass a message to a Romanian official that Nixon wanted to establish a channel of communications with the leadership of the People's Republic of China. We were to ask that Chinese leaders make contact with Nixon through Major General Vernon Walters, then the U.S. defense attaché in Paris. It was an unusual request to make—and I didn't know if Secretary of State William Rogers was privy to it. But Nixon sometimes had people doing things in secret. As it happened, the Romanian official in question was traveling and we were not able to pass along the message. But Nixon had given us an early indication that he had decided to make a direct and bold overture to China.

It was during this period that I first worked with National Security Adviser Henry Kissinger. I was impressed with Kissinger's uncommon ability to arrange matters as he wanted them. Kissinger was not in anyone's circle within the White House and over time became a force unto himself. The conventional wisdom about the Nixon-Kissinger relationship was that they worked as equals, or even that Kissinger was the teacher and Nixon the student. Though Kissinger is now properly recognized as a critical figure in modern American foreign policy, he did not enter the Nixon administration with that same stature. Kissinger had come from an academic world of theoretical rather than practical experience. By contrast, Nixon had real-world experience and had been actively engaged with foreign leaders in scores of countries for decades. If anything, at the outset, Nixon was the professor and Kissinger the student, though an unquestionably brilliant one at that.

A problem that came up time and again was something I would become familiar with over the ensuing decades: the complicated relationships between the National Security Council, the State Department, and the Defense Department. Once at a cabinet meeting a discussion arose as to how State, Defense, and the NSC were working together. Kissinger, then serving as the National Security Adviser, scribbled a note and handed it to me with a smile. It said, "As a team of barracudas."[7]

Tensions appeared to come to a head in one meeting, when Kissinger expressed his concern that the State Department was doing things without coordinating them with the National Security Council, meaning him. Specifically, he believed that Secretary of State Rogers had communicated with the Soviet leadership without his knowledge. Haldeman, who was not intimidated by anyone, even the formidable Kissinger, responded that Kissinger had done the exact same thing when he met with Soviet ambassador Anatoly Dobrynin without informing Rogers. Kissinger bristled at Haldeman's suggestion. He rumbled that he had only spoken to foreign officials outside of regular channels when the President directed him not to inform the State Department. He was, of course, ignoring the possibility that Rogers had also acted at Nixon's direction. In any event, Kissinger then stormed out of the room.[8]

Fifteen minutes later, Kissinger returned. He informed the group that Haldeman's comment was "inadmissible." Cryptically, he added that he was now reconsidering "the other matter" he had discussed with Haldeman. I later learned that the other matter Kissinger referred to was choosing between resigning from the faculty of Harvard to stay on in the Nixon administration—and losing tenure—or returning to academia. Kissinger, who at times used the threat of resigning as a bargaining chip, was suggesting that he might change his mind and return to Harvard unless Secretary Rogers stopped dealing with foreign governments without his knowledge.

Ultimately, Kissinger would replace William Rogers as secretary of state while retaining his position at the NSC. During the period when Henry wore both hats, all he had to do was talk to himself to ensure good communications between State and the NSC. But a president benefits from a range of viewpoints. I thought Kissinger was most effective, and President Nixon and the country better served, when he was filling a single post.

I preferred having more substantive responsibilities to functioning as a general adviser and troubleshooter in the White House. The President and I had several conversations during this period in which we discussed possible future assignments for me, such as U.S. special trade representative, deputy secretary of state, and U.S. ambassador to NATO.[9] He seemed to enjoy these discussions, which were an opportunity for him to be actively involved in mentoring younger members of his administration.

In fact, the President frequently considered staff shake-ups, possibly to make sure he always had fresh eyes looking at important issues—and also, I suspect, to keep people on their toes. It was something of a hobby for him—like a general war gaming moves on a map.

To this end, shortly after the 1970 midterm elections, the President called a small group to Key Biscayne for a day-long meeting.[10] He was now looking ahead to his 1972 reelection campaign and told us he wanted to make some personnel changes in the administration. He mused aloud about all sorts of possibilities. As the meeting went on, I stepped out to the men's room. When I returned, the President looked at me.

"Don, we're going to make Rogers Morton Secretary of the Interior and make you Secretary of Housing and Urban Development," Nixon said matter-of-factly. He was going to fire the current secretary of HUD, former Michigan governor George Romney. Another former governor in his cabinet, Walter Hickel, Secretary of the Interior, was going to be fired as well.

I looked around the room. The idea of my going to HUD apparently was fine by everyone else. I wondered what had happened in my absence to lead to this strange idea. I said I'd have to think about it, knowing that as a congressman I had voted against making Housing and Urban Development a cabinet-level post.[11]

A day or so later, I talked to Attorney General John Mitchell and told him my views. I said I thought it was unwise for the President to replace two former governors in his cabinet at the same time. I pointed out that Romney, for one, came from the key state of Michigan. As it turned out, Nixon had a bumpy time in the press when he announced his planned dismissal of Hickel at Interior. Fortunately, knowing he would get still more flak if he fired Romney, the Hickel bumps reinforced my arguments and ended the President's idea of my going to HUD.

With the 1972 presidential campaign in mind, Nixon soon had another thought for me. He suggested that I become chairman of the Committee to Reelect the President, which had the unfortunate acronym of CREEP. Running Nixon's reelection campaign might have seemed like a prestigious assignment at the time, but I had no desire to be a full-time political operative.

I tried to turn the President down in a lighthearted way. "Mr. President," I said with a laugh, "I'm pretty sure you're going to run your campaign, and to the extent you don't have the time, John Mitchell will run it, and to the extent he doesn't, Bob Haldeman will. So you certainly don't need me at that post. The organ-grinders will all be in the White House." I didn't have any desire to be the trained monkey.

Nixon smiled. "Well, let's think about it some more," he said. For whatever reason, that idea too was dropped.

Later the President raised the idea of my becoming chair of the Republican National Committee. I felt once again that it would be Nixon, Mitchell, and Haldeman who would be calling the shots, and that whoever was at the RNC would be little more than an adornment. It was not the job for me.

I was well aware that repeatedly saying no to a president posed risks, risks that increased each time I did it. My pattern of turning down job offers did not seem to please Haldeman or Ehrlichman. I'm sure they began to think that I wasn't a team player. And I suspected that Nixon probably was beginning to feel the same way.

As the 1972 election drew closer and politics took over, the group in the White House that Joyce and I were close to, the academics and policy-oriented people like Shultz and Moynihan, became less involved than they had been at the beginning of Nixon's term. The other circle—Haldeman, Ehrlichman, and later, Colson—were the ones who seemed to have his ear and confidence.

In one sense, this was a natural development. The Haldeman group was attuned to Nixon's increased focus on his reelection. We were not. But the theory put forward by some, that this group unduly influenced the President by appealing to his resentments is inconsistent with my experience. Maybe it's because I was younger and he was the president of the United States, but I seldom observed Nixon being unduly influenced by anyone. He may have had his enablers, but Nixon seemed to me to be the one in the lead.

As the campaign proceeded, I did sense a change in mood at the White House, and not for the better. At the end of one meeting I watched the President walk off with Haldeman and Colson. There was nothing particularly unusual about that, since they were frequently together. But for some reason I was increasingly uncomfortable with what was going on at the White House. Something didn't feel right.

By the early 1970s the rate of inflation, though not high by historical standards, was a growing political issue. As was typical in Washington, there was pressure on politicians to do something, if for no other reason than to demonstrate the government's concern about a problem. The Democratic majority in Congress came up with a solution that seemed politically attractive but was unwise: They passed legislation giving the president the power to impose wage and price controls on the country.

My suspicion was that Congress passed the legislation never imagining that President Nixon would actually use the power, but rather to put him on the spot politically, and to demonstrate that the Congress was doing something about inflation. The Democrats hadn't counted on John Connally, the charismatic former governor of Texas. Connally was well-known for having been hit by one of the bullets fired at President Kennedy by Lee Harvey Oswald. A Democrat who switched to the Republican Party in 1973, he was a prominent, if not dominant, figure in the Nixon cabinet. Nobody seemed to have the effect on Nixon that Connally did. Indeed, the President appeared to hang on his every word.

Connally, a protégé of LBJ's, liked big, bold action. When wage and price control legislation first came up, Connally's staff at Treasury drafted a memo urging the President to veto it on philosophical grounds. "Why are we doing this?" Connally demanded, when he saw their memo. "If a legislature wants to give you a new power—you take it. Put it in the corner, like an old shotgun. You never know when you might need it."[12]

Six months later, to almost everyone's amazement—and certainly to mine—Connally had successfully persuaded Nixon to grab that old shotgun and pull the trigger. The dollar was weak, inflation seemed to be getting worse, and Connally recommended presidential action.

In August 1971, the President held a confidential meeting with his economic team at Camp David. Nixon had long blamed an economic downturn for his narrow loss to Kennedy in 1960. Now that he was president, he was determined to not have the economy ruin his chances for reelection. At the meeting, the President agreed to the approach recommended by Connally.

Nixon demanded absolute secrecy about his decision until he was ready to unveil it. In the first phase of the program, Nixon planned to announce a ninety-day freeze on wages and prices in the United States. He also would sign an executive order to create an economic stabilization program, a pay board, a price commission, a health advisory board, a rent-control board, and various other new government entities.[13] All of them would be overseen by the Cost of Living Council, to be chaired by Secretary of the Treasury Connally, which would include most of the non–national security members of the President's cabinet.[14]

In my view, imposing wage and price controls may have been politically expedient, but it was probably the worst policy decision the administration made. I thought the proposal would subvert the free market's ability to allow consumers and producers across the United States to determine prices based on the laws of supply and demand. This couldn't be done by any centralized planning or planner, no matter how brilliant.[15]

The President needed a director for the Cost of Living Council (CLC) to administer what was called "Phase Two" of the program. Nixon, with the advice of Shultz, decided I was the man for the job. I'd told him I wanted to be involved in policy, and this was clearly a policy position. It just happened to be one I did not agree with. George Shultz, who had moved from being Secretary of Labor to director of the Office of Management and Budget, informed me of the President's decision. He urged me to accept the post.

"I don't believe in wage and price controls," I told him.

"I know," he said. "That's why you need to do the job."

Shultz told me he wanted a director of the program who would work to make sure the new controls were temporary and did as little damage as possible.[16] So for the second time in the Nixon administration, I agreed to take on a presidential assignment that seemed like a no-win position, and which ran counter to my beliefs.*

If the goal was to end wage and price controls as soon as possible, I saw a first step in that direction: the need to ensure that we did not hire a permanent staff that would want to perpetuate itself. Instead, I borrowed individuals from other departments and agencies—called detailees—particularly individuals who understood the dangers of wage-price controls, and who could be sent back to their home departments with the stroke of my pen.

Second, I emphasized from the outset that Congress passed the Economic Stabilization Act for the sole purpose of dealing with inflation. Not only did I believe that such an intrusion by the federal government would undermine the free market system, I feared that it presented government officials with the almost irresistible temptation to use that power for political ends.[17] Some wanted the controls to be used to break labor unions. Others wanted them to be used to strengthen unions. I ruled out all of those ideas immediately. Furthermore, I insisted that we would not use these new statutory powers to favor or punish any given constituency for political gain.

We established a tiered system based on the size of the companies to be regulated. We freed smaller companies from the controls, placed only modest reporting requirements on medium-sized companies, and focused on the larger companies that could better handle the burdens. They had the resources of large law, accounting, and lobbying firms to effectively deal with the federal government.

Our nonpolitical, nonpartisan approach to the work of the cost of living program did not sit well with everyone. The different interpretations of how the powers of the CLC should be used led to some difficult encounters. Joyce could often tell who was on the other end of the phone based on

* The Cost of Living Council (CLC) did have one attraction: It was an education. It brought together the administration's finest economic experts—including Shultz, Arthur Burns, Herb Stein, Paul McCracken, Ezra Solomon, and Marina Whitman. Larry Silberman, then the Undersecretary of the Department of Labor, and James Lynn, the Undersecretary at Commerce, worked closely with me as well to help figure out what we could do to implement the President's directives without damaging the economy. Dick Cheney, who had asked for his own area of responsibility, came on board as director of operations.

how much colorful language I used. When Ehrlichman called, he would rail against the decisions of various entities that made up the Economic Stabilization Program. I had to explain repeatedly that once the President gave them the powers to make decisions, we had little choice but to live with them.[18]

From the outset, I was deeply concerned that the CLC would be tarnished with allegations of political favoritism and corruption. As a result, we spent a great deal of effort trying to make sure that that did not happen. During the time that I was director of the Cost of Living Council, to my knowledge there was only one accusation that a staff member might have a conflict of interest. When I heard about it, I sent it straight to the Justice Department, where it was promptly found to be groundless. In a presidential election year—especially in the Nixon administration that particular election year—I considered it an amazing, indeed an almost unbelievable, accomplishment that there was not one instance of wrongdoing. Public officials generally don't get credit or awards for avoiding potholes, but our group at CLC deserved an award for the many bad things that did not happen on our watch.

A consequence of my service as director of the CLC was that it put still further distance between Nixon's closest political aides and me. Not being deeply involved in the 1972 campaign, however, turned out to be a considerably bigger blessing than I could possibly have imagined.

As the election year heated up, Nixon was heading toward what some political experts said would be a close reelection fight. During much of the prior year, Nixon's job approval rating had hovered at just under 50 percent in the Gallup polls. While I personally liked the eventual Democratic nominee, South Dakota Senator George McGovern, I did not believe he would be a strong candidate for president. I came to know him while I was serving in Congress. He was to the left of the country, and his platform seemed weak. But McGovern did have an advantage, the same advantage Kennedy and Humphrey had had in Nixon's previous contests: He projected warmth.

I wrote a memo for the President, noting that McGovern's "warmth, concern, [and] decency are appealing." I suggested that the administration seek opportunities to highlight Nixon's interest in the problems of ordinary Americans. I believed Nixon did care about improving people's quality of life but that he just preferred to view and discuss things in theoretical, rather than personal, terms. That didn't always come across positively in that new media age. "A danger for our Administration is in its competence we seem harsh, in our strength we seem tough, in our pragmatism we seem goalless and idealless." Finally, I offered a warning, perhaps reflecting concerns I was starting to have about operations at the White House. "The campaign," I wrote, "must scrupulously avoid going 'over the line.'"[19]

Even if anyone had listened to that advice, it came a bit late. On June 19, 1972, three days after I sent that memo to the President, the *Washington Post* published a front-page news story with a headline: "GOP SECURITY AIDE AMONG FIVE ARRESTED IN BUGGING AFFAIR."[20] The story linked an attempt to place listening devices at the Democratic National Committee headquarters in the Watergate Hotel to an aide at the Committee to Reelect the President.[21]

I attended the regular White House senior staff meeting in the Roosevelt Room that morning.* Several expressed curiosity about the piece in the *Post*. There were differing ideas as to how to deal with the article. Some wanted to confront it as a news story that needed to be managed—in other words, as a public relations problem. My instinct was to get to the root of what had happened and get the situation resolved. Years later, Chuck Colson recalled my comment in the meeting: "If any jackass across the street [at campaign headquarters] or here [in the White House] had anything to do with this, he should be hung up by his thumbs today. We'd better not have anything to do with this. It will kill us."[22] I don't remember if that was precisely what I said, but if anything that was an understated version of my thinking.

Despite the drumbeat of news stories that began to appear in the *Post* on that subject, the Watergate break-in was not uppermost in voters' minds during the 1972 presidential campaign. However, I did notice troubling signs when the Watergate matter came up in conversations. Joyce and I attended a meeting in the fifth-floor auditorium of the Old Executive Office Building for those Nixon had selected to serve as surrogate speakers for his campaign, including many from his cabinet and key members of Congress, such as Goldwater, as well as Joyce and some other cabinet wives. Ehrlichman offered the group what seemed to me to be tortured responses to some of the questions being raised in the newspapers about Watergate and the campaign. After the meeting I advised Joyce never to repeat Ehrlichman's recommended talking points, because I felt they did not have the ring of truth. Joyce had had the same reaction.[23]

*Most of the regular attendees were at the senior staff meeting on June 19, 1972: Shultz, Moynihan, Harlow, Haldeman, Colson, Ehrlichman, and press secretary Ron Ziegler.

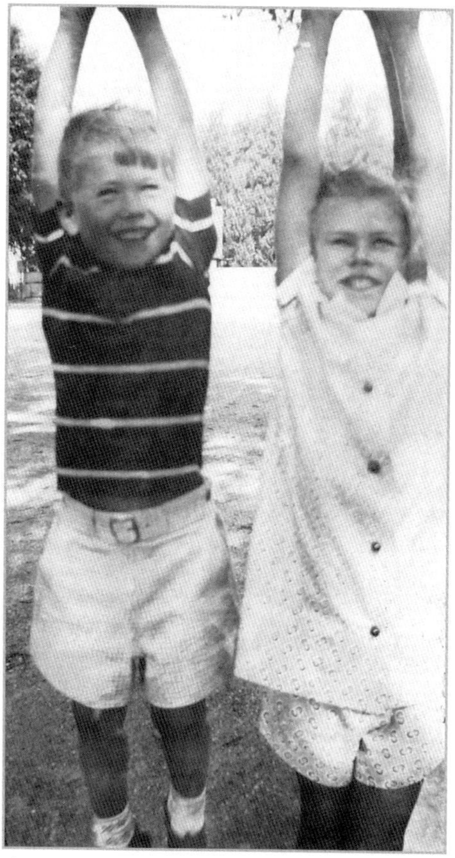

1

With my sister Joan, c. 1938.

2

Lt. George Rumsfeld and Jeannette Rumsfeld, Coronado, California, c. 1944. Like so many others, our lives were changed by Pearl Harbor and World War II. We were not surprised by Dad's decision to volunteer for the U.S. Navy. He lived by the simple rule, "Do the right thing."

3

Becoming an Eagle Scout was an important activity for me as a young man (top center). As a guide at the Philmont Scout Ranch, I came to know New Mexico.

4

The Princeton University Varsity wrestling team in 1953 (fourth from left). Wrestling brought home to me the relationship between effort and results.

5

With Joyce, June 1954. Quite a month! I graduated from Princeton, was commissioned an ensign in the U.S. Navy, and asked Joyce to marry me. She said yes.

6

The airplanes I flew when serving in the Navy are now all in museums (author upper right).

In my first campaign for Congress, Joyce and our two daughters, Marcy and Valerie, frequently hit the trail with me in an effort to make me seem more established than my twenty-nine years suggested.

PUBLICAN
FOR CONGRES
JAMES

8

With campaign manager Ned Jannotta after winning the 1962 Illinois 13th District primary election. When the results came in at our headquarters, the volunteers and I were amazed.

9

During the 1962 general election campaign for Congress, former President Dwight Eisenhower visited Illinois. I attended a lunch in his honor. During coffee whoever was sitting next to him got up so I could have a picture with Ike, who graciously put me at ease. It was the first time I had met a president.

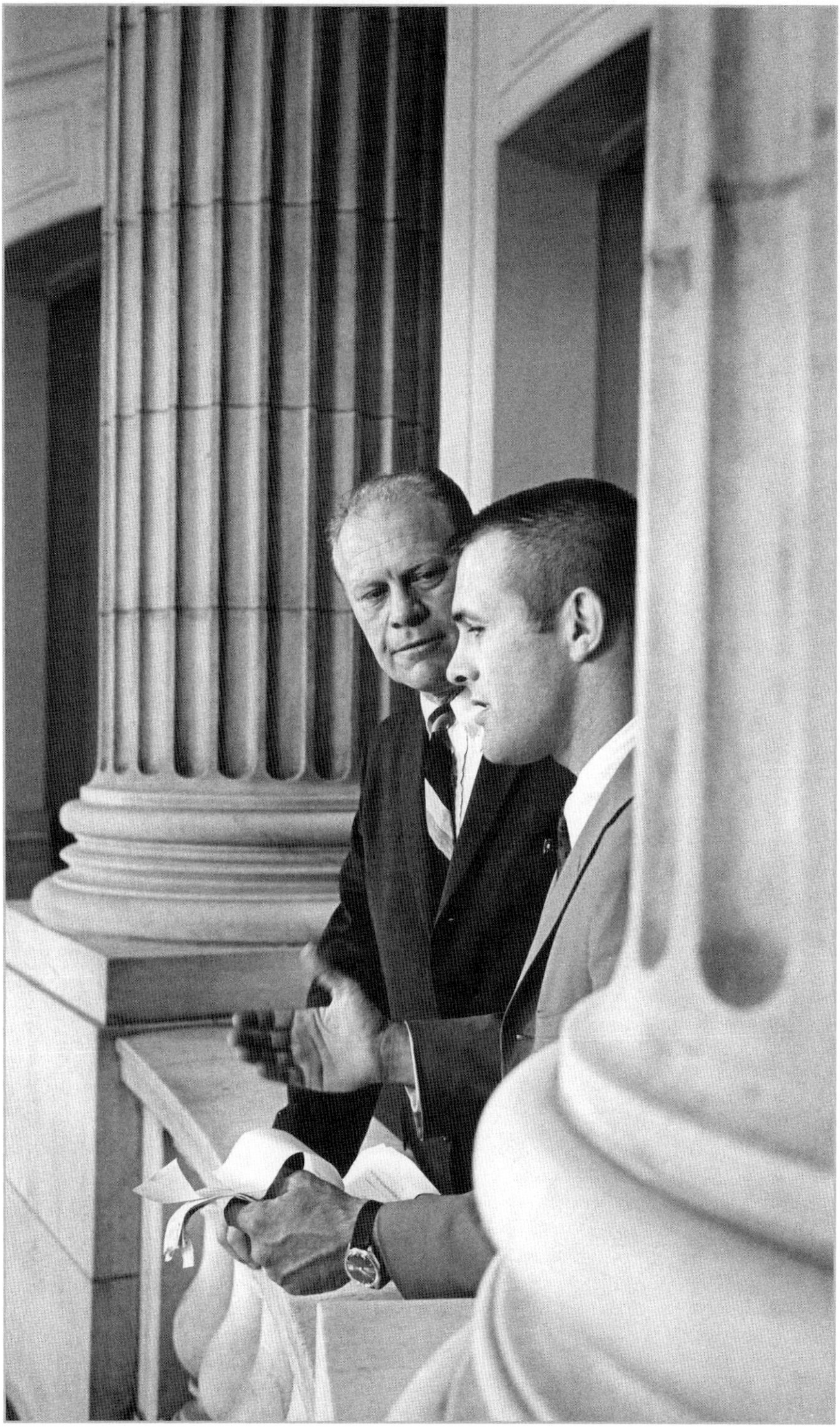

NORMAN MATHENY/1964/*THE CHRISTIAN SCIENCE MONITOR* (WWW.CSMONITOR.COM)

With House Minority Leader Gerald Ford outside the Speaker's Lobby of the United States House of Representatives. If our paths hadn't crossed in the years we served in Congress, both of our lives would have turned out quite differently.

11

As a member of the Manned Space Flight Subcommittee in the U.S. House of Representatives in the 1960s, I met with many of our country's pioneers in space. I introduced Marcy to Gus Grissom (right), the first man to fly twice beyond inner space. We were joined by the irrepressible Vice President Hubert Humphrey (center). Grissom died some months later in a test of Apollo I.

12

Just days after Martin Luther King, Jr., was assassinated in Memphis, Tennessee, Congress passed a bill to strengthen the 1964 Civil Rights Act. I was honored to receive one of the pens President Johnson used to sign the bill.

© BETTMANN/CORBIS

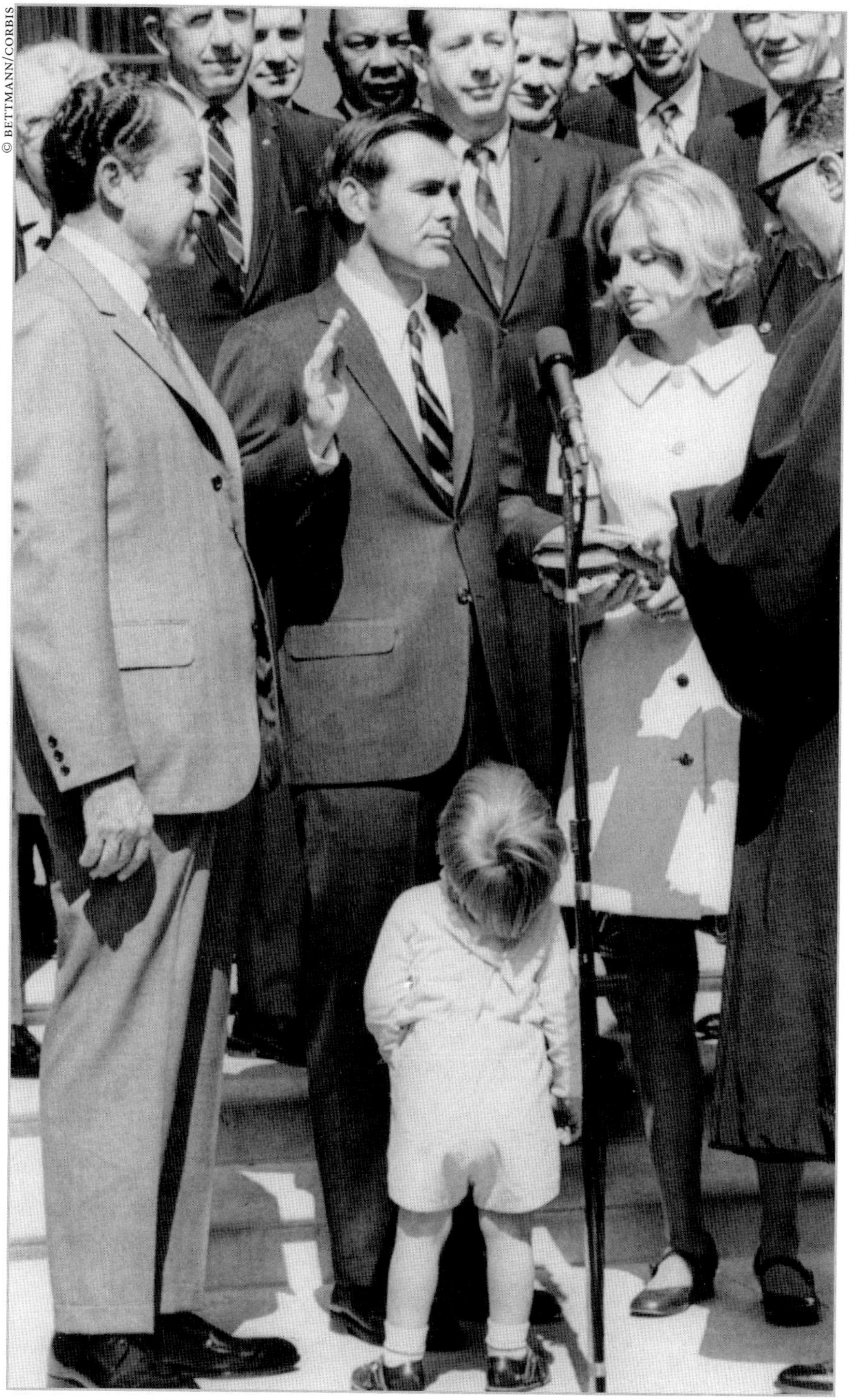

13

An official White House swearing-in for a member of the president's cabinet is generally a formal occasion. Our three-year-old son, Nick, had other ideas. Joyce held the Bible but kept her eyes on him, wondering what he might do next as President Nixon tried not to laugh.

14

Director of the Office of Economic Opportunity, c. 1969. Finding myself at the helm of an organization whose founding I had opposed was a challenge. But I believed that properly managed and with more modest goals, OEO could be an effective experimental laboratory for innovative anti-poverty programs.

15

At a farewell dinner for Bryce Harlow (left) and Daniel Patrick Moynihan (center). Harlow and Moynihan were examples of the varied and outstanding talent President Nixon attracted to his administration. Moynihan stood out as an intellectual giant whose good humor and enthusiasm for life was infectious. Harlow was unquestionably the administration's most seasoned expert on the presidency and the workings of the federal government.

In the Nixon and Ford administrations, Kissinger seemed ever-present.

17

(Above): During a spring 1972 trip with Bob Finch, we managed a side visit to the legendary El Cordobés. He had come from a poor orphanage outside Córdoba to become the world's greatest matador. We went to his ranch in the countryside, where he invited me into the ring for the testing of the bulls. One newspaper inaccurately characterized my bull as "a small bewildered cow." El Cordobés howled with laughter when I tried to explain my technique—while wearing with good humor the Nixon tie clasp I had given him.

18

19 

The Taos Indians had been working for years to reclaim the sacred Blue Lake in a forty-eight-thousand acre tract of land in the Sangre di Cristo Mountains near Taos, New Mexico. I was privileged to be present at the ceremony when President Nixon signed the legislation to return it to them.

(With left to right) President Nixon, John Mitchell, John Erlichman, Charles Colson, Bryce Harlow, Bob Haldeman, and Bob Finch at Nixon's Key Biscayne home. The President was constantly adjusting the members of his administration to assure he was getting a stream of fresh ideas.

20

In Cairo for President Nasser's 1972 funeral with (left to right) John McCloy, who had served as the High Commissioner of Germany after World War II; Robert Murphy, the renowned "diplomat among warriors"; and Elliot Richardson. Then-acting President Anwar Sadat impressed us as thoughtful, serious, and ready to open avenues of communication with the West.

21

President Nixon could be both considerate and generous with his time. When I was preparing to leave for Brussels as the new U.S. ambassador to NATO, he asked me to stop by the Oval Office on my last day in Washington and to bring our son, Nick, with me. It was a glimpse of Nixon most people did not see.

With President Nixon and Henry Kissinger when Nixon attended his last NATO meeting in Brussels, just weeks before his resignation.

22

23

24

We had scheduled a family vacation for the beginning of August 1974. Joyce was determined to have some time together. We learned of President Nixon's imminent resignation from the *International Herald Tribune*.

25

When I returned to Washington to serve as chief of staff in 1974, President Ford was determined to keep the White House involved in big issues. The warm and brilliant Dr. Herman Kahn moved seamlessly from discussing economics to nuclear strategy to future trends. Ford's engagement in the discussion might have surprised his critics.

26

With Vice President Nelson Rockefeller, March 1975. The feeling was mutual.

The Watergate issue proved little more than a nuisance in 1972. Concerns about a close election were misplaced. Nixon won in a landslide, losing only Massachusetts and the District of Columbia. His stunning 23 point margin—60.7 percent to 37.5 percent—was one of the most decisive presidential victories in U.S. history. The President's reaction to his overwhelming victory was not what most people might have expected. It certainly wasn't what I expected.

The morning after his reelection, Nixon held a cabinet meeting. I assumed the purpose would be to thank everyone for their help in the campaign, and to talk a bit about his goals for his second term.[24]

The meeting started off well. Nixon walked into the White House cabinet room to an enthusiastic standing ovation. The President beamed and urged us to take our seats. But the applause continued. For a moment, as he soaked in our congratulations, Nixon paused and gripped the back of his chair in the middle of the large oval table.

Whatever celebratory emotions he may have felt at that moment quickly dissipated. He spoke with his usual precision. He did thank us all for our work, but then quickly moved on to abstract policy discussions. Referring to the most prominent campaign issue, the ongoing conflict in Vietnam, the President said that he had complete confidence that his administration would bring peace. "Richard Nixon doesn't shoot blanks," he said.[25]

He remarked at length on what he said was his favorite period of history, which oddly enough was the British parliamentary debates of the 1850s. He mentioned Winston Churchill's father. "He was a brilliant man," Nixon said, "whose career was ruined by syphilis."

He talked about the rival British prime ministers William Gladstone and Benjamin Disraeli. Gladstone was in office longer, Nixon observed, but Disraeli had a more brilliant record. The President informed us that Disraeli once described Gladstone's government as "an exhausted volcano." This was a roundabout way for Nixon to make what I took as his central point; namely, that some from his first-term administration were tired. This was a special problem, Nixon added, because second presidential terms usually did not measure up to first terms.[26]

Then, to his by now somewhat subdued audience, the President announced he was going to spend the next few weeks on what I knew was his favorite pastime—thinking about the role each of us would play, if any, in his second term. He said he did not want to be merciless, but that "the government needs an enema." The President then nodded to his chief of staff. "Bob will take over now," he said, looking at Haldeman.[27] Nixon left the room to another, considerably more muted, round of applause.

After the President left, Haldeman rather abruptly announced that Nixon wanted everyone's resignation by the end of the week. He said this was customary in a second term, and that Nixon would be making decisions to accept or reject the resignations in the days ahead. He handed each of us an unsigned memo with the subject heading "Post-Election Activities." It was all very businesslike, as was Haldeman's way.

"While it is recognized that this period will necessarily be a time of some uncertainty," the memo stated, "this will be dispelled as quickly as possible." That was not a particularly comforting thought. Nor was what followed. "Between now and December 15, please plan on remaining on the job, finishing first-term work, collecting and depositing Presidential plans, and making plans for next term. This is not a vacation period."

We were asked to put together a book describing our current assignments, and I sensed that we might well be writing job descriptions for the people replacing us. "This should be as comprehensive as possible," the memo instructed.[28]

All in all the meeting deflated the cabinet's enthusiasm for Nixon's impressive victory. Many of them had worked hard to support the President, and most had served as surrogate speakers. His behavior let down some and angered others. Most everything about it—the judgment it revealed, the timing, the tone—was insensitive and unwise.

Immediately after the meeting I told Haldeman he might want to be careful about asking for resignations from anyone at the Cost of Living Council, because almost none of us had wanted to be there in the first place. If we did submit our resignations, we would mean it, and the President would be faced with the problem of trying to manage the economic stabilization programs with a whole new team—if he could find people willing to do it. I added that he should also be aware that there may be situations like that elsewhere in the administration, where his broad, sweeping request for resignations could boomerang badly. Haldeman came back to me a few hours later, undoubtedly after talking to the President, and said he understood and retracted his earlier request, saying I should not ask for the resignations of those at the CLC.

President Nixon soon departed for Camp David to ponder the upcoming staff shake-ups that had been so indelicately telegraphed.* He had his key

* By the time he was done, Nixon had accepted fifty-seven resignations and made thirty new appointments.[29]

people with him—Haldeman and Ehrlichman, along with George Shultz—a reassuring sign that Nixon still held Shultz in high esteem. Regrettably, if the President had listened to Shultz more often, and more closely, his second term might have been quite different.

I was ready to leave the administration and had been thinking of going to the private sector. I started consulting with friends back in Chicago about what I might do, and I told Shultz my intentions. As I was deliberating, the President asked me to come to Camp David to meet with him before I made any firm decisions. So in late November 1972, I went up by helicopter, flying north along the Potomac River to the Catoctin Mountain of Maryland, with no idea of what might result from my visit. I met first alone with Shultz and Ehrlichman to give them my thoughts. Then we joined the President in his office for about an hour.

Nixon quickly went to business. He again urged me to run for the U.S. Senate seat from Illinois. He told me he would endorse me for the GOP nomination in 1974, even in a crowded primary. Running for the Senate still didn't feel right to me. I had come to understand that I would prefer an executive position more than a legislative role, having by then served in both.

On several occasions, President Nixon and I had talked about the possibility of a foreign policy post. At this meeting, Nixon told me he was going to appoint Elliot Richardson as Secretary of Defense, and that Pete Peterson, the Secretary of Commerce, would probably go to NATO as the U.S. ambassador. As a result, I assumed that the NATO position, which Nixon had discussed with me previously, was out. That had all but decided it for me, since I knew I did not want to remain in the White House.

The President understood that I was starting to move on to other plans. "Don, we will find the right spot," Nixon assured me as the meeting drew to a close. "To use the chess analogy, I want you to know that you are not a pawn."[30]

A few days later, the Peterson nomination was scratched, and the President informed me he wanted to nominate me to serve as U.S. ambassador to NATO after all. While I knew he had reservations about the way the NATO alliance was functioning, and that Europe hadn't exactly been at the epicenter of his foreign policy in his first term, the President spoke positively of NATO as a good place for me. In one conversation he said that NATO was more interesting and substantive than other ambassadorial posts because it dealt with many countries rather than just one.[31]

Because of NATO's collective security approach—an attack on one member nation was to be considered an attack against all—the alliance had served as an effective deterrent against the Soviet Union. As such, the NATO headquarters in Brussels tended to be a prestigious destination for Europe's most seasoned diplomats. I told the President I would be pleased to be nominated for the post.

The assignment had two important attractions: First it was an opportunity to serve in a new field, and to learn, which I had always enjoyed. Second, I would be out of the White House. My preference to be out of Washington seemed counterintuitive to some. After the public announcement on December 2, 1972, *Washington Post* reporter David Broder wrote: "Much of official Washington was surprised" by my selection.[32] It was true enough that a former congressman from the Midwest who had primarily worked on domestic and economic policy issues might not have been the obvious choice for NATO ambassador.

Others in town, who measured people's power solely in terms of their proximity to the Oval Office, thought I had ruined my career by leaving for Europe right after President Nixon's landslide reelection victory. They could not see why anyone would voluntarily leave the cabinet and the White House—the seat of world power—to move so far from what they believed to be the center of the universe. But I had worked in two administration posts for close to four years. I had served in the White House and the cabinet, and I was uncomfortable with the thought of staying. I knew the White House was no longer the place for me.

CHAPTER 10

NATO and Nixon's Fall

REPRINTED WITH PERMISSION OF *THE DALLAS MORNING NEWS*

As much as he appreciated the symbolic importance of NATO, Nixon found the alliance frustrating. It operated by consensus—requiring unanimity in any major decision—and Nixon didn't have a great deal of patience for policy making by committee. Unanimity is hard to achieve in any organization, and it was not easy with a group of the most respected diplomats from fourteen other nations operating on instructions from their capitals, each with different country histories, needs, cultures, and languages, not to mention lingering animosities toward one another after two world wars.

The move to Brussels, Belgium, where NATO is headquartered, turned out to be a treasured experience for our family. But first we had to overcome some initial qualms. Our oldest child, Valerie, was sixteen and had been looking forward to learning how to drive. In Belgium, driver's licenses weren't available until the age of eighteen. So before we left, a friend volunteered to teach her the basics. In our old car with the knob on the floor stick shift missing, Richard B. Cheney kindly and skillfully moonlighted as Valerie's driving instructor in parallel parking.

The neighborhood schools in Belgium taught in French and Flemish. None of them would pass a building code anywhere in the United States. Sharp hooks protruded from walls, the rooms were in disrepair, students were crammed in. Their school, École Hamaïde, where Marcy and Nick went, emphasized the idea that education was a serious business. Every morning the headmistress, dressed in black and wearing a stern look on her face, would formally shake every child's hand as they entered the building—sending the message that it was time to get to work. But at the end of the day, she would bid each of them farewell with a smile and a hug, signaling it was time to have fun again. The school taught responsibility. The students performed the cleaning tasks, not a team of janitors. Joyce and I often have reflected that in that old building our children received what was very likely the best education any of them ever had.

Not all of the aspects of my new post were unqualified advantages. For a time, Joyce and I didn't have a car in Brussels while our car was being shipped over from Washington. As ambassador I had the services of a car and a driver for official business.

I discovered later that someone at the Department of State had sent an agent from the inspector general's office to quiz the embassy drivers about our use of the government car for personal errands. Some at the State Department apparently did not like a political appointee in a post that they felt should be held by a career Foreign Service officer, and they thought that anything they could find that might pose an embarrassment was to their advantage.[1]

There had been a pattern of such traps being set for political appointees by some members of the permanent bureaucracies. I first saw this at OEO with the false leak to the press about my alleged office "redecoration." In Brussels, I also learned later that someone in the Department of State had authorized the building of a swimming pool and a tennis court at the NATO ambassador's residence where we were living. Envisioning a headline about Rumsfeld's efforts to turn the ambassador's residence into a posh resort, I canceled their plans as soon as I learned about them.

My predecessor as ambassador, David Kennedy, had served at NATO less than a year, and the post had been vacant for over eight months prior to his arrival. I would be Nixon's third ambassador to NATO. This alone suggested to the alliance that the administration's interest in it was at best modest. In advancing our country's priorities, I knew I was going to need all the help I could get. And I found guidance from what some might consider an unlikely source: the French. In my experience, France's perplexing, and sometimes irritating, public opposition to American policy initiatives seemed more often to be nationalist public relations for the French domestic audience than expressions of real policy differences. Charles de Gaulle, for example, had withdrawn France from NATO's military command structure in 1966 and forced it to take its headquarters—along with the American and allied forces stationed there—out of France. The act was more a political ploy than a real demonstration of French independence from NATO. The move infuriated then President Johnson. Johnson instructed Secretary of State Dean Rusk to ask President De Gaulle if his actions toward the forces also meant that we would have to take home all of the American servicemen buried in cemeteries across France who had fought and died for that country's liberation from the Nazis. This was President Lyndon Baines Johnson at his best.

When I arrived at NATO, however, it was clear that the French saw the alliance's value, and wanted a somewhat greater voice in its activities, while still staying apart from the military command structure. I was most fortunate to benefit from the counsel and friendship of the distinguished and seasoned French ambassador to NATO, François de Rose.

The aristocratic François was a delightful blend of intellect, integrity, and good humor. He spoke several languages fluently, including English, which he spoke better than I did. He and his beautiful, vivacious wife, Yvonne, were a generation older and had a vastly more sophisticated lifestyle than the Rumsfelds. Yet we connected and became lifelong family friends. When tensions would flare between the strong-willed Kissinger and the mercurial French Foreign Minister, Michel Jobert, it would fall to de Rose and me to see that their differences did not disrupt our work. In a time-honored diplomatic tradition, François and I frequently resorted to calculated ambiguities that allowed both Washington and Paris to interpret NATO communiqués and declarations as they saw fit.

The situation back in Washington was taking on a more ominous tone. On April 30, 1973, the so-called Berlin Wall collapsed at the White House as fallout from the unfolding Watergate scandal: The President had requested the resignations of Bob Haldeman and John Ehrlichman. The *Washington Post* called the resignations "dramatic" and "devastating," and they certainly came as a shock to me. I knew how central each had been to Nixon personally. Their departures, along with looming criminal charges against both men, foretold what lay ahead. Democrats were now beginning to use the word "impeachment" publicly.[2]

That summer I was amazed to read that President Nixon had secretly taped his conversations in the White House and the Executive Office Building. Nixon apparently believed that recording his every word was a good idea, that it would secure his place in history. It certainly did that—but not in the way he intended. I found the secret taping deceitful. All of us offered him candid advice totally unaware that we were being taped, while he, of course, could calculate his remarks.*

On my periodic trips to Washington on NATO business, I didn't spend much time with the President. By then he was devoting more and more of his hours to his role as the defendant in an impeachment investigation. But I came away with a strong impression that the White House was under siege.

As the scandal grew, our allies began to raise questions about America's increasingly weakened president. Compounding the problem was the fact that the political situations in many NATO countries were also unstable. Some NATO members had government coalitions holding power by two- or three-vote margins in their parliaments. Italy, for example, had already changed governments some thirty-plus times in the twenty-nine years since the end of the World War II. The Netherlands at one point was unable to form a government for many months. With so much political instability in Europe, many there counted on America to be a rock of confidence and reassurance. Now that image was slipping.

Even the status of the U.S. military in Europe was coming into doubt. In 1973, Democratic Senator Mike Mansfield renewed his effort to remove important portions of our forces from Europe by passing a legislative amendment, which the Nixon administration vigorously opposed. The NATO nations were unlikely to fill any vacuum that would be left by an American withdrawal. Our allies even then were still recovering—psychologically, economically, and politically—from World War II.†

As a believer in the principle that weakness is provocative, I worried about the signal that a partial withdrawal of American troops from Western Europe would send. It might be seen by the Europeans as the first step in a full withdrawal and, even more worrisome, it could provoke the Soviet Union into taking an even more aggressive posture on the continent. In July 1973, it looked like the legislation might pass, so at the request of the administration I hurriedly flew to Washington to testify against the amendment in Congress.[3] Mansfield's effort was defeated, if narrowly. Though the Senate debate made the Europeans

* At the time I was unaware that Henry Kissinger was also taping his phone conversations with others. Presidents Kennedy and Johnson had also done so.

† We were often reminded that most of the representatives at NATO had experienced the war firsthand. Joyce experienced this when she paid a social call on the wife of Marcel Fischbach, Luxembourg's ambassador to NATO. To make conversation, Joyce asked Madame Fischbach how she had met her husband. Mrs. Fischbach replied matter-of-factly that when Luxembourg was occupied by Germany, the Nazis would round up young unmarried girls and send them to the Nazi officers' clubs for entertainment. Since at that time they were leaving married women alone, her parents had taken the precaution of arranging for her to marry a man she barely knew—Marcel Fischbach.

nervous, it might also have had the positive benefit of reminding them that they needed to step up and be more willing to invest in their own defense. Unfortunately, that was a message that many Western Europeans resisted.

On October 10, 1973, in a surprise announcement, Spiro T. Agnew resigned as vice president after he was charged with bribery. I had never had a particularly high opinion of Agnew's performance, but even I was startled by the allegations of graft.

Soon thereafter, names began to come up as possibilities to replace Agnew. On Friday, October 12, I was in the ambassador's residence in Belgium when I received a call from a reporter from NBC in Washington. He said he had information that I was going to be named vice president. I thought it was laughable. Then a college classmate of mine, Marty Hoffmann, who was serving as general counsel of the Department of Defense, called and told me the same rumor. After that, we received a dozen or so calls in rapid succession. The BBC said they had it on highly reliable authority that Rumsfeld was to be the nominee. A man from Senator Charles Percy's staff then called and said my name was "all over the Senate."[4]

A media frenzy was now underway, with wild rumors flying around every name suggested by almost anyone. Around 1:00 a.m. in Belgium, Armed Forces Radio reported that another widely mentioned candidate, Gerald R. Ford, was now out of the running. Then CBS, covering multiple bets, reported that the vice presidential nominee would be former Secretary of State Bill Rogers, former Secretary of Defense Mel Laird, or me. I suspected that my name was being thrown into the mix intentionally by Nixon or his staff to either heighten my visibility as a possible Senate candidate some day or, more likely, as a diversion—to make his announcement of someone else an even bigger surprise. Convinced it would not happen, I went to bed. Shortly thereafter, two or three cars with press people and cameras arrived and camped out in front of our house. This got Joyce's attention. She nudged me. "Are you sure it's not you?" she asked.

At 2:00 a.m. Brussels time, the cars outside our house started to disperse. In the East Room of the White House, after enjoying the guessing game that had surrounded his choice, President Nixon announced that he intended to nominate House Minority Leader Gerald R. Ford to be vice president. I hoped Ford's honesty and forthrightness would help to shake off the ugly mood from Agnew's resignation and the Watergate mess, and reestablish the reputation of the administration.

The vice presidential speculation now over, my attention was on other things. In early October 1973, the Yom Kippur War had broken out. The war began when a coalition of Arab nations—led by Egypt—launched a surprise attack on Israel. As tensions rose, I received a phone call from NATO Secretary General Joseph Luns. The tall and imposing Dutchman was an adept manager of the range of personalities and priorities represented by the fifteen permanent representatives to NATO.

Luns told me he had received a call from the Italian ambassador to NATO, who had received a call from a foreign ministry official in Rome, who had received a call from an Italian senator, who had been called by an alarmed woman in his constituency. The woman had been awakened suddenly by lights and loud vehicle movements at a military facility near her home where American forces were stationed.[5] They all wanted to know what was happening. Like them, I had no idea.

I phoned Washington and learned that our forces at the military facility in Italy were being mobilized by the President to assist with supplies for the Israelis. Though Italy, of course, was a NATO ally, Italy's ambassador to NATO didn't know a thing about it, nor did anyone else at NATO, including, quite obviously, Secretary General Luns and me. Ever since I had arrived in Brussels, I had stressed the importance of trust and consultation within the alliance, but here we had not lived up to our promise. It was an awkward episode.* But more than that, I saw it as a sign that the strain of Watergate was affecting the White House. I doubted the administration would have made such a misstep if we had been in top form.

Predictably, the Soviet Union sought to capitalize on the difficulties of its principal adversary. Under the leadership of General Secretary Leonid Brezhnev, the Soviets were playing a double game across the globe. They pursued a sizable military buildup at home and engaged in aggressive activities in Africa, Latin America, the Middle East, and Asia, all the while proclaiming their desire for peace and détente. Many in the West, and many NATO members, accepted the Soviet's rhetoric at face value. Some in Western populations seemed willing to blame their own governments, and particularly the United States, as the real source of the tension and instability in the world. With Soviet encouragement, millions around the world marched in protests—they marched not against Soviet aggression but against the United States and other NATO nations.

* As the Watergate problems grew, and as the Yom Kippur crisis escalated, top aides like Secretary of State Henry Kissinger, Secretary of Defense Jim Schlesinger, and Al Haig (who had replaced Haldeman as White House chief of staff) exchanged diplomatic notes under Nixon's signature. At one point, senior officials decided to raise the Defense Condition level—a decision made at the height of the crisis when an embattled President Nixon was reported to be asleep.

Yet even in Western Europe, for all the complaining about America among the elites, the United States still held a special meaning. One Belgian friend told me privately that when his daughters were pregnant, the best thing he could do for them was to arrange for them to be in the United States around their delivery times so his grandchildren would at least have the option of being American citizens. Notably, but unnoted, was the fact that nobody was clamoring to get visas to give birth in the Soviet empire.

At the end of 1973, Joyce and I decided it would be a good idea for our children to get a glimpse of the kind of oppressive societies that NATO was defending America against. So, over the New Year holiday, we took a train with our children and our friends, John and Carolyn Twiname and their children, behind the Iron Curtain to Soviet-controlled Czechoslovakia. As the American ambassador to NATO, I was not unfamiliar to the Soviets. In some communiqués they referred to me colorfully as "Nixon's running dog." To avoid diplomatic awkwardness, I traveled to Czechoslovakia as a private citizen.

We could all feel the change of mood as we crossed the border from a free and prosperous West Germany into Czechoslovakia. Outside the windows we saw massive steel barriers placed to deter Western tanks. Communist officials came onto the train, unapologetically went through passengers' bags, tossed aside the contents, and left us to repack our luggage.

After arriving at the train station in the town of Pilsen, we went to the hotel we had been assigned to by the Communist authorities. We were followed as we walked around the city, which was gray and grim. Store windows revealed sparse stocks—a shoe store with only a handful of pairs of shoes in the window. Religion being disfavored in the Communist bloc, a church we visited was nearly empty, save for a few elderly women in babushkas, praying in silence.

For our New Year's Eve dinner we went to a neighborhood restaurant. We were having a good time, and as the evening progressed many of the patrons began singing and dancing. People came over and danced with our son and daughters. I sang what I remembered of a Czech folk song I had learned from the co-captain of our high school wrestling team, Lenny Vyskocil, whose relatives had come to America from Czechoslovakia.

At one point the bartender pointed to a man he said wanted to meet me. Trying to avoid the attention of the authorities who were observing us, the man led me toward the men's room. I took my son, Nick, with me, thinking that he might provide some cover. For all I knew the man might be going to tell me he wanted to defect.

When I found him in the bathroom, I couldn't understand a word he was saying. He became animated and started taking off his shirt.

"What in the world is going on?" I wondered.

Once he was bare from the waist up, he turned to show me his back. There was a tattoo of what looked like a Pacific island with a palm tree and an American flag on it.

I left the room unclear about his message. The bartender told me that the man had wanted to see me because as a boy he had been befriended by an American soldier during World War II. The American had been killed later in the war, and the Czech, valuing his friendship with that soldier, had the tattoo put on his back in honor of his lost friend. And he wanted at least one American to know how he felt about our country.

I returned to our festive table, where everyone was continuing to have a good time with the Czech patrons. A bit later, the room grew quiet. The music stopped. People moved away from us. Apparently a Czech or Soviet security official who had not been pleased with the festivities had signaled that the evening was over.

Joyce tugged on me. "We should go," she said.

It was a sad farewell to a wonderful New Year's Eve, with friendly people repressed by their puppet government and their Soviet overlords.

The following June, President Nixon came to Brussels for a major NATO summit with the other fourteen heads of state. This turned out to be his last trip abroad as president. As he came down from Air Force One, I greeted the President and his delegation at the foot of the stairs. It had been some time since I had seen Nixon. He appeared to be in a pleasant mood, and I wondered if he was simply grateful to be out of Washington and away from the Watergate problems for a while. The foreign arena was a break for him, and it was the forum in which he was usually at his best.

I escorted him and Secretary of State Kissinger to an airport reception hall, where I had assembled the senior American officials and staff from the U.S. NATO mission. I thought it might boost Nixon's morale to meet some friendly Americans and, at the same time, give our hardworking staff a rare opportunity to shake hands with the President.

Roughly three quarters of the NATO staff assembled were American military officers or senior enlisted personnel. The rest were some of the Defense and State Departments' finest civilian officials. Nixon went down the line and graciously shook hands and exchanged brief pleasantries with each of them.

After his greetings to them, I left with Nixon and Kissinger and climbed in the President's limousine. We rode in the backseat and headed to the American ambassador to Belgium's residence, where Nixon would be staying while in Brussels.

Once in the car, away from the press and cameras, Nixon's face fell. His mood changed.

Referring to the NATO staff members he had just met, Nixon snapped, "They're a bunch of fairies." The President apparently had assumed that the NATO staff was composed of State Department people. His White House prized "machismo and toughness"—as Chuck Colson once described it—and Nixon tended to view people in the State Department as lacking grit.[6]

I was taken aback by Nixon's mood and derogatory comment. Only a moment before he had seemed friendly to the staff I had worked so hard to recruit from both State and Defense. They were fine public servants, and I felt protective of them. So I spoke up and told the President that he was mistaken.

"Those folks are mostly military," I said. "They just didn't have their uniforms on." They were exactly the kind of hardworking people Nixon tended to appreciate.

Of the small numbers who were from the Department of State, I noted, "They're fine folks. I handpicked everyone, and they are doing an excellent job for the country." Nixon looked out of the window, his face sullen. Perhaps in private, with people he knew, he allowed the strain of the events in Washington to show. When we arrived at the ambassador's residence, the President got out of the right side of the car. Back in public, he was smiling and cordial again. I moved to get out from the opposite side. As I exited, Kissinger followed behind me. He grabbed my arm, gently tugging me to the left side of the car. When he was sure the President was out of earshot, Kissinger said to me quietly, "Rummy, we don't argue with him anymore."

A few weeks later, Nixon's second chief of staff, Al Haig, called me from the White House.[7] During the last months of Watergate, he, as much as anyone, held the administration together. The phone reception was weak, and I heard a clicking noise throughout the conversation. Maybe it was just a sign of the times, but I had the impression that someone might be listening in.[8] Haig asked if I might consider returning to the White House to serve again as a counsellor to the President, to help out. It was becoming an all-hands-on-deck moment. I knew, however, that returning to Washington was the last thing I wanted to do. I had been at NATO for fourteen months at that point. I valued my relationships with my NATO counterparts and felt I was contributing something useful for our country and the alliance. I told Haig it wouldn't make sense for me to come back so soon.

Belgium undoubtedly seemed a world away to those in Washington mired in Watergate, but NATO was also embroiled in a serious crisis. Two of our NATO allies, Greece and Turkey, had a long history of differences over Cyprus, an island inhabited by both Greeks and Turks. Their disagreements had come to a boiling point during the summer of 1974, when Turkey invaded Cyprus. The dispute posed a difficult dilemma for the alliance.* NATO was established as a military alliance to deter and defend its member states against external threats—not conflicts between its members. Because Washington was consumed with Watergate, I received little or no guidance during much of the crisis.

I was being urged by Secretary General Luns to assert the weight and influence of the United States to help resolve the issue; he may have assumed that I had the authority to do that, and also undoubtedly hoped that the United States had the capability to step in and calm those ancient and intractable differences.[9] That was not the only reason I declined to return to Washington when Haig called. It wasn't at all clear what I could conceivably do. At the end of our phone call, Haig told me he understood my reasons for not returning to Washington, and as far as he was concerned the matter was settled.†

As a result, I was not present at the White House less than three weeks later, on August 8, 1974, when President Nixon announced his resignation. Nor was I present to see that now famous wave Nixon gave as he prepared to board Marine One—smiling, with his arms raised in an awkward swoop, and his fingers curiously signaling "V" for victory.

I had, however, seen a similar wave by Nixon some years earlier when he gave a speech in San Jose, California. It was an episode that had stuck in my mind. Outside the large hall there was a sizable gathering of angry anti-Vietnam war protesters held back by a fence. As Nixon came out to get in his car in the motorcade, they shouted at him and waved hostile signs.

Instead of getting into his car, Nixon climbed atop something so he could be better seen by the mob. Then he had made the same gesture that he made

* As a consequence of this serious dispute, Greece withdrew its forces from NATO's military command structure. They were readmitted in 1980.

† Nixon noted in his memoir that "Don Rumsfeld called from Brussels, offering to resign as Ambassador to NATO and return to help work against the impeachment among his former colleagues in Congress." My guess is that Haig may have told Nixon this to try to lift his spirits.[10]

as he left the White House—the same forced grin, the same swoop of the arms, the same "V" for victory.

The message was clear, both times: Richard Milhous Nixon was determined not to let his opponents get the best of him.

In the years immediately after Nixon's resignation, there was a sense among a number of us that we had emerged from a shared disaster. When Bill Safire sent me the book he wrote about his days in the Nixon administration, *Before the Fall*, he inscribed it: "To Don Rumsfeld—fellow survivor."

Another survivor of Watergate, in a way, was Richard Nixon himself. Anyone who saw and felt the physical impact on Nixon of Watergate and the long impeachment process, capped by his resignation, exile, and subsequent serious illness, had to be surprised by his truly amazing comeback. But he was a most unusual human being. He seemed unable to accept defeat. Instead, he went to work using his impressive strength and fine mind to contribute to the national and international dialogue on important public issues.

I don't know to this day how to reconcile the man I knew with the tragedies that he inflicted on himself and the nation. Like the man, the Nixon era defied easy definition. His administration provided vital support for a range of initiatives that variously won support and opposition from both sides of the aisle—welfare reform, block grants to states, the all-volunteer military, the Environmental Protection Agency, and the Equal Employment Opportunity Commission, to name a few. The man loathed by the left and elites nominated the Supreme Court justice who authored the majority opinion in *Roe v. Wade*. The Republican leader targeted with loud and sometimes violent demonstrations by thousands of young Americans pressed successfully to give eighteen-year-olds the right to vote. The cold warrior who came to prominence as a fierce anticommunist and a scourge of Soviet spy Alger Hiss made a historic overture to Communist China and pursued détente with the Soviet Union. The public figure who would suffer the ultimate political disgrace also won one of the greatest electoral triumphs in American history less than two years before. The man who so often seemed introverted and lonely, and served by a small cadre of strongmen, also brought into his orbit a truly impressive and diverse array of talent who would affect the course of America for many decades thereafter.

On a personal level, the Nixon presidency changed the course of my life. Nixon offered me my first opportunities to lead large government enterprises in both the domestic and economic areas, and eventually to participate in our nation's foreign and national security policy by representing our country overseas. Moving out of the legislative branch of our federal government to serve in the executive offered a new and completely different view of government, one that informed my public service in the decades that followed.

In the years after his humiliating resignation, I talked to Nixon occasionally. In 1982, he invited me to a dinner at his home in Saddle River, New Jersey, where he was hosting his longtime friend King Hassan II of Morocco. It had been nearly a decade since I had last seen Nixon. He looked and acted the same—still quite formal and still deeply interested and engaged in public issues. Nixon prided himself on those dinners. He described various courses as they came along, and told the gathering about the White House events at which some of the dishes previously had been served. He gave a formal toast, much as he would have had he still been president. After presenting a typically thoughtful, well-informed assessment of the world, he asked the King to give a thumbnail sketch of the then current leaders in the Middle East, which Hassan proceeded to do with fascinating insight and candor.

A year later, in August 1983, the former President phoned me at my office in Illinois. It was quite early, about 7:30 a.m. Nixon was already hard at work on a book he was writing and wanted to talk about the Defense Department and the national security issues he was writing about. He called DoD a "hydra-headed monster" and a "three-ring circus" and wanted to know what could be done to improve its performance.[11] He was still offering me advice, and apparently still guiding others on their career paths. He advised me, interestingly enough, to become secretary of state one day and not to return to the Department of Defense after my time there in the Ford administration. Nothing seemed too small to pique his interest. In one conversation he had decided that I should stop wearing glasses and use contact lenses instead.

In 1994, two decades after relinquishing the presidency, Richard Nixon suffered a stroke. Once he was hospitalized, his condition appeared to improve. Then quite suddenly it worsened, and after eighty-one proud, defiant years, he slipped into unconsciousness, and finally into death.[12]

News of the former President's passing struck a somewhat unexpected chord with millions, including with me. Nixon had been a pivotal political figure for more than a generation. His funeral was a major event. A national day of mourning was declared by President Clinton, as tributes to Nixon poured in from across the country and the world, even from some who had been his bitter enemies.

On April 27, 1994, Joyce and I flew to California to attend the memorial service at Nixon's presidential library in Yorba Linda. So many from his administration had gathered there that it was like turning a page to the past. The Reverend Billy Graham, with whom I had sat in Nixon's hotel suite all those many years ago as Nixon quizzed the attendees for advice about a running mate, officiated at the service. He hailed Nixon as "one of the greatest men of the century." Spiro Agnew, the man Nixon chose as his running mate in 1968, made a rare public appearance, looking solemn and sad. Haldeman had died a year earlier, but Ehrlichman and Colson were there, aging, and somber. Like Nixon, Colson had spent his later years working to achieve peace and reconciliation in his life. After his release from prison, to his great credit, Colson embarked on a prison ministry program that won acclaim and admiration. Any differences with them seemed so long ago.

Henry Kissinger, who became a national figure during the Nixon presidency, and who stood by Nixon in the final days of Watergate, delivered a touching eulogy. "He achieved greatly and he suffered deeply," Kissinger pointed out, "but he never gave up." And, in the front row, were all the living presidents. Each of them—Ford, Carter, Reagan, Bush, and Clinton—had been affected by the Nixon presidency in one way or another. A few, including the sitting president, Bill Clinton, had started their careers in fierce opposition to him. Yet as Clinton saluted his once disgraced predecessor as a "statesman" who sought peace, all was forgiven and forgotten, at least for that day.[13]

After the service, I greeted Nixon's daughter Julie Nixon Eisenhower. She loved her dad, and all who knew Nixon could see that she and her sister, Tricia, were the lights of his life. It was a difficult day for Julie. As she gave me a hug, she whispered sweetly, "I think he would have liked it."

Her comment struck me, since during the service I had turned to Joyce and quietly said pretty much the same thing. "I can almost see President Nixon smiling," I whispered.[14]

The man from Whittier, California, who seemed to have struggled so mightily in a search for acceptance, had finally achieved it.

Time and perspective had softened most everyone's view of the Nixon era. But his resignation had left the nation reeling. And as so many mourners praised so much of his legacy and focused largely on his achievements, I took a moment to notice someone else at the gathering. As usual, Jerry Ford sat quietly, humbly, avoiding attention or accolades. Yet he was the man who had to pick up the shattered shards of the Nixon administration and pull a bitterly divided country together. And I had been summoned back to the White House all those years ago to help him.

PART V

Javelin Catcher: Inside the Ford White House

"The role of White House Chief of Staff is that of a javelin catcher."

—Jack Watson, White House Chief of Staff to President Jimmy Carter, as quoted in Rumsfeld's Rules

The Philippine Sea, West Pacific Ocean

DECEMBER 18, 1944

In his early thirties, Lieutenant Gerald Rudolph Ford had sandy blond hair and the build of the lineman he had been on the University of Michigan football team.* Like thousands of Americans, Ford had volunteered for the United States Navy shortly after Pearl Harbor. By the spring of 1943 he was aboard an aircraft carrier, the USS *Monterey,* as it steamed toward the Pacific theater and war.

As part of the U.S. Pacific fleet, Ford's ship helped secure Makin Island in the Gilberts, participated in strikes in the Battle of the Philippine Sea, and launched air strikes against Japanese-occupied Wake Island. In various battles the ship survived, but it was a force of nature, not of man, that almost sent the carrier—and Gerald Ford—to the bottom of the sea.

On the outskirts of the Philippine islands on December 18, 1944, a typhoon tore at the *Monterey*. As Ford raced to his battle station on the bridge in the early morning hours, the storm forced the ship into a dramatic roll, pitching Ford toward the edge of the deck. To keep from being thrown overboard to certain death, the athletic Ford managed to slow his descent and twist onto a catwalk belowdecks.[1]

The violent storm caused a series of fires that threatened to engulf the ship. Amid the chaos of flame, winds, and seas, the fleet's admiral, William Halsey, advised the *Monterey*'s captain to abandon ship. But the crew instead embarked on a desperate effort to save their carrier. For seven punishing hours, working on a bucking ship in 100-knot winds, Lieutenant Ford led a fire brigade to fight the blazes. When the typhoon finally passed, the Third Fleet had lost 3 destroyers, 150 aircraft, and almost 800 men. But the USS *Monterey* and all but one of its crew survived.[2] In the years that followed many people would underestimate the genial, even-keeled Jerry Ford, but those on the *Monterey* that day would not be counted among them.

* Ford turned down contract offers to play professional football for the Detroit Lions and the Green Bay Packers to attend Yale Law School.

The surviving but battered *Monterey* became the aircraft carrier on which Navy pilots in training at Pensacola, Florida, made their first carrier landings. Hundreds of naval aviators landed on that ship over the years, and on June 5, 1955, I was one of them. It means something to me that the aircraft carrier I first landed on as a fledgling naval aviator was the same ship whose history was intertwined with a man I came to admire and respect.

My connection to Ford began with one aircraft carrier and ended five decades later with another. In 2006, when I was serving as secretary of defense, the Navy decided to name its newest aircraft carrier the USS *Gerald R. Ford*. The great ship was the first in a class of America's largest and most capable carriers, a fitting tribute to a fine officer who had given so much of his life to the service of his country. In late November that year, Joyce and I decided to fly to Rancho Mirage, California, to see President Ford. By then, almost immobile, he wasn't able to get up to greet us—but when he heard my voice at the door he called out, "Rummy!" with much of the enthusiasm and strength he'd always had. I had brought along USS *Gerald R. Ford* baseball caps and an artist's rendition of the new carrier. His response was typical—humble and proud.

I reflect with great pleasure on our decades-long voyage from the USS *Monterey* to the USS *Gerald R. Ford*. In the interim President Ford and I would serve together on another type of vessel—the ship of state—in the wake of a quite different kind of storm.

CHAPTER 11

Restoring Trust

"Trust leaves on horseback but returns on foot."

—As quoted in Rumsfeld's Rules

Roughly two hours after President Nixon made his emotional departure from the White House on August 9, 1974, I touched down at Dulles International Airport just outside of Washington, D.C., having flown from Europe in haste at then Vice President Ford's behest.

I was met at the gate by Dick Cheney, whom I had asked to be available to give me a hand and bring me up-to-date. Also present was an assistant from Ford's vice presidential office. He carried a sealed envelope from Bill Scranton and Tom Whitehead, informing me that Ford had appointed me chairman of his transition. The letter suggested that I come at once to the presidential transition office in the Old Executive Office Building.[1]

It seemed natural that as a longtime member of the Congress, Ford would first turn to friends and associates from the House to help him as he proceeded to put things in order. Still, I had no idea what my role would be as Ford's transition chairman. There was no precedent for what Ford was facing: taking over a corroded presidency in the middle of a term, after having never been elected either president or vice president. I likened his situation to stepping into the cockpit to pilot a large, damaged aircraft at thirty thousand feet and being expected to take it to its destination and land it safely.

Ford's circumstance would inevitably have posed unique burdens. But that was the least of his problems. With all that the country had gone through over the prior decade—bitterness and division caused by Vietnam and Watergate, the resignations of Vice President Agnew and then President Nixon, political assassinations, bombings, student protests, sit-ins, the rise of the drug counterculture, the youth revolt, militant organizations, anarchists—it was not certain that the country would hold together. There was an ugliness in the air, a cynicism, that was worse than any I'd experienced before in my life. And the challenges of leading the nation had fallen to a man who never desired the job, had no mandate from the voters, and was burdened by the suspicion that came with being Richard Nixon's handpicked successor.

Less than two hours earlier, as my plane was making its initial descent to Washington, Ford had taken the oath of office and famously assured the country that its "long national nightmare" was over. But in fact it was not over, least of all for him. From Gerald Ford's first day as president to his last, the shadow of Richard Nixon clung stubbornly to the White House. The Watergate investigation continued. An unprecedented criminal trial of the former president—a "trial of the century"—loomed. Every statement that came out of the White House was scrutinized, questioned, and doubted. That the country managed to become steady amid all this is a lasting tribute to Gerald Ford as a leader and as a human being.

When I arrived at the White House that afternoon, I barely had time to exchange greetings with the other members of the transition team before we were called to the Cabinet Room to meet with the new President. The contrast between Ford and his predecessor was notable. Ford was open, down-to-earth, and comfortable with himself, joking with his staff that the Marine Corps band didn't have to play "Hail to the Chief" when he entered the room. The rousing University of Michigan fight song would suffice.[2] If the new President came across as something of a Boy Scout, he did so honestly. Indeed, he was the first and only Eagle Scout to serve as president of the United States.

Even as he found the responsibilities of global leadership dropped unexpectedly into his lap, Ford looked untroubled and upbeat. "Good to see you, Rummy!" he greeted me.[3]

"Hello, Mr. President," I responded. It was the first time I'd addressed a friend by that title.

Though it was a relief to see Ford seemingly so comfortable with his new responsibilities, tensions promptly became apparent. Ford found himself between two distinct factions in the White House: his own small vice presidential staff, most of whom were counseling him to make a clean break from the previous administration, and the large Nixon staff still in the White House, few of whom were urging Ford to make major changes. Ford faced a choice between reassuring the country and the world that there would be continuity and the markedly different choice of moving sharply from the discredited Nixon administration to a fresh and new Ford administration untainted by the Watergate scandal. Ford leaned heavily toward the continuity camp. In fact, the President advised us in his first meeting with our transition team that he already had made several decisions in that regard, some of which to me seemed not to have been fully thought through.

The night before he took office, for instance, he went out on the front lawn of his home in Alexandria, Virginia, to announce that Henry Kissinger would remain in his dual roles as secretary of state and national security adviser.[4] Though I am sure Ford believed the announcement would be reassuring to the world—and I have no doubt that it was—the timing left an impression that the soon-to-be President felt he needed Kissinger so urgently that he couldn't wait until he was sworn in to make the announcement. It made the President seem dependent on his prominent secretary of state.

The next day, at the President's first meeting with our transition team, he told us that he would not be asking for the resignations of anyone in the Nixon cabinet or White House staff. He was concerned that anyone he asked to leave might be thought to have some link to the Watergate scandal. Kindness was a defining trait of Ford's life. He didn't want to put the stigma of Watergate on anyone unfairly. He had also decided that he would keep Al Haig on as White House chief of staff. So within hours of becoming president, Ford indicated that he planned to keep the Nixon administration intact—Nixon's cabinet and those of his advisers not facing criminal charges.

As Ford filled us in on his decisions, he told us that he expected his friends "to give me hell" when we disagreed with him.[5] I was deeply concerned about the approach he had just announced, and I found an early opportunity to tell him so. "Mr. President, you can't argue with your position that if someone in the cabinet is doing a good job they shouldn't be removed," I said to him. "But let me argue it anyway."

I told him it was tough to govern in the best of times and this was the worst of times. If he maintained what was seen as a discredited administration, the impression would be that it was business as usual in Washington, D.C. He needed to make enough changes fast so that all of those who stayed on would be seen as having been selected by him. All of those who left would be seen as leaving not because of any Watergate taint but simply because a new president wanted to bring in his own team.

"That's interesting, Don," Ford replied. He said he did want his own people, but he didn't want to get rid of anyone currently at the White House except for reasons of performance.

I countered that I believed that in this unusual situation that was exactly the wrong approach. I urged him instead to sit people down and say that his decision to make a change was not a question of their performance, but that he needed his own personnel. Ford said he'd consider the idea but wasn't about to make any changes soon.[6]

As for Al Haig, I thought both the President and Al would have been better served had Ford promptly announced that Haig would stay on for a brief transition period and then return to the military. The decision to keep Haig as chief of staff complicated both Haig's and the transition team's work. How could our group reach a decision that ran counter to the chief of staff's? The situation also was a difficult one for Haig, since some of those who had worked for Ford on his vice presidential staff viewed Haig and his associates as "Nixon people" who might be making decisions not necessarily in the new President's best interest. Some on Nixon's staff, in turn, saw the Ford team as amateurs and, as such, time-consuming distractions. But Ford did not relent on this matter, either. I was quickly beginning to appreciate a quality of President Ford's that I had not fully understood when we were in Congress. Once he made up his mind, he could be stubborn. This left our transition team little to do except work on administrative and lower-tier personnel issues.

One early and highly visible indication of Ford's presidential decision making would be his nomination for vice president, the country's third in two years. The nominee would have to be confirmed by both houses of a Democratic-controlled Congress. Ford consulted with people from both parties and I recommended that the selection be a figure well known to the public, to avoid any more unsettling surprises.[7] Among the more serious contenders were George Herbert Walker Bush of Texas, then serving as the chairman of the Republican National Committee, and Nelson Rockefeller, the former governor of New York. Rockefeller was being strongly recommended by two of Ford's most influential advisers, Mel Laird and Bryce Harlow. At

Ford's request, I was the third person asked to fill out the extensive paperwork required to be considered for his vice presidential nomination.

Bush had been appointed by President Nixon to serve as party chairman, which was his position at the height of the Watergate scandal. That had to have been one of the toughest jobs in Washington at the time, and I recalled that Nixon had once talked to me about the post. Now I was grateful I wasn't there. Bush offered an image of an energetic and athletic fifty-year-old with a pedigree. But his association with Nixon and the Watergate scandal, coupled with the fact that he was an untested national candidate, were drawbacks. Bush left no doubt that he wanted the vice presidency, however, and, unlike the other possible candidates, he set up a high-powered "war room" in a nearby hotel to promote his candidacy.[8]

Rockefeller had broader name recognition as a two-time presidential contender and a scion of one of the most prominent and wealthiest families in America. His celebrity offered a sizable advantage, but he had his problems as well. There would be an exhaustive examination of his personal finances were he to be nominated for the vice presidency, and no one was quite sure what members of Congress might find.[9] Rockefeller also had to deal with a news story claiming he had an illegal slush fund for dirty tricks against the Democrats.[10] Far more problematic for Rockefeller was the strongly negative feelings he engendered among conservatives in the Republican Party who viewed him with suspicion and dislike.

It was an honor to be considered, but I did not take the suggestion that I was a vice presidential contender all that seriously. Given that Ford was from Michigan and I was from neighboring Illinois, selecting me didn't make much sense politically, and I was less well-known than Bush or Rockefeller. I had already informed Ford that I was eager to return to Brussels.

The President told me that he was determined to announce the selection in his own way.[11] He felt rather embarrassed about the way the Nixon team had handled his nomination, with a big production in the East Room and widespread speculation about who might emerge from behind the curtain with Nixon—speculation that the Nixon staff seemed to encourage. Ford did not indulge in such high drama.

Eleven days after taking office, President Ford announced his selection of Rockefeller at a small gathering in the Oval Office.[12] He had gone with a well-known figure, again seeking to offer reassurance to the American people. Rockefeller "showed his usual self-assurance," as one reporter put it, and his remarks suggested that he expected to undertake more duties than other vice presidents had in the past.[13]

That same morning Ford explained his selection of Rockefeller to me.[14] At the time I thought Rockefeller was probably a reasonable choice. I expected Rocky to be an energetic and helpful addition to the administration. "[T]here was general agreement," one newspaper noted, "that the conservative new President from the Middle West had broadened his base of support and increased his chances for being elected in his own right in 1976, if he runs, by choosing a moderate Easterner with considerable influence and resources."[15] The nomination of Rockefeller, another paper remarked, made for a ticket "that only an economic disaster can defeat in 1976."[16]

Just before announcing his selection, Ford placed a call to San Clemente, California. He wanted to give Nixon the courtesy of hearing the news first.[17] Reaching out to the former President was a typically gracious thing for Ford to do. But if I had known Ford was planning to call Nixon, for whom Ford repeatedly expressed sympathy and admiration, I would have advised against it.[18] I didn't think it was in Ford's interest to put himself in the position of seeming to need Nixon's blessing on his choice. Though Ford's overture to Nixon did not get much attention, in retrospect it might have served as an early sign of the difficulties Ford was about to create in regard to his fallen predecessor.

As I prepared to return to my NATO post in Brussels, I was worried about the new administration. I was so concerned that I hand carried a memo the transition team prepared on the topic of personnel to the President. We urged Ford to build visibly what would be seen as his own team. Noting that the failure to do so was the very mistake that Lady Bird Johnson believed LBJ made after succeeding John F. Kennedy, we warned, "Without full attention by you to personnel matters, there will not be a true Ford presidency."[19] My worry was that Ford's presidency would be seen not as his, but as a Nixon-Ford presidency.

Ford did want to distance himself from what was seen as the imperial presidency of Richard Nixon, but instead of changing personnel, he attempted to change the White House's management structure. Ford attributed the misjudgments in Watergate to having everything filtered to the President through his chief of staff, Bob Haldeman. My view was different. I believed the problems that plagued Nixon's administration were not caused by how decisions were made but by the decisions themselves. The chief of staff system was reasonably efficient and had been developed in the Eisenhower administration, which did not come to the same unfortunate end as Nixon's. To change the perception of an insular White House and a rigid "Berlin Wall," Ford settled on what he called the "spokes-of-the-wheel" approach. To this day, I shudder at the phrase. The idea was that a large number of his staff and cabinet—the spokes—would report directly to him—the hub—instead of having a chief of staff coordinate the process.

However laudable the intent, the spokes-of-the-wheel approach was an unworkable way of managing the modern White House. Ford enjoyed interaction and give-and-take with a wide and varied group of people, and that was helpful, but this organization approach essentially allowed any senior staff or cabinet official to walk into the Oval Office at any time to discuss any subject. Many would end up leaving such a meeting with what they sincerely believed to be presidential authorization but without the necessary coordination with other White House staff or cabinet members who had responsibilities in the matters discussed with the President. An open door policy could work for a member of Congress, or even for a vice president whose staff is small, but a president has too many demands on his time to listen to every staff member's suggestions, wade through every disagreement, and then ensure that the relevant personnel are involved, or at least informed.

With Ford having done little to settle the differences that were already growing between the Ford and Nixon camps in the White House, I expected the difficulties to be plentiful. I knew that a dysfunctional White House such as the one that was evolving would be a dangerous place.

But this advice, like a number of the recommendations of our transition team, was too late. And at least for a while it seemed that there was no need for the President to do anything different from what he was doing. He was liked by the press, by members of Congress, and by the public. A headline in *Newsweek* magazine summed up the prevailing conventional wisdom with the words: "THE SUN IS SHINING AGAIN."[20] Ford became president on August 9, and his honeymoon reached its apex on September 1, 1974, when a Gallup poll gave him an approval rating of more than 70 percent. It was as if the country had taken a look at the honest, open Ford and breathed a sigh of relief. No more distrust, no more suspicions. That proved short-lived.

On September 8, 1974, one month after he took office, with no advance notice to the country, Ford made a decision that left nearly everyone who heard it stunned. Those of us who knew Ford well—and who had heard his periodic expressions of sympathy for Nixon—probably should have at least suspected that he might consider the possibility of a pardon. Nonetheless, it had never occurred to me. In fact, at Ford's first cabinet meeting a few weeks earlier, he seemed to rule out the idea and said the subject should not even be discussed.[21]

As he announced the pardon, totally out of the blue on a Sunday morning, Ford referred to Nixon and his loyal family, saying, "Theirs is an American tragedy in which we all have played a part."[22] The President spoke about Nixon's plight with obvious sincerity and sympathy—the charges against him being a "sword" over his head. But it was a sympathy that the public did not share at that moment. For myself, I still felt respect for Nixon and for the many accomplishments of his administration, but I also felt disappointment over how his presidency had ended. He had not been truthful with the nation, which had caused grave harm to our country.

The stunning news shook Ford's inner circle. The press secretary he had just recruited and announced, Jerry terHorst, resigned in protest. Among the general public, the pardon provoked a vicious reaction. Many Americans at the time believed that Nixon had been involved in the cover-up and was getting away with it. Ford's own motives came under scrutiny, with the suggestion that the pardon might be the result of a secret deal. Al Haig's continuing presence as White House chief of staff seemed to give credence to the allegation, since Haig had been involved in persuading Nixon to step down. Suddenly a suspicious figure, Ford plummeted precipitously in the opinion polls.

Knowing Ford as well as I did, I was convinced he would not have been part of a deal with Nixon.[23] Instead, I thought this had been a decision that Ford had made without consulting very many others and without carefully considering how and when it might best be done and what the impact might be on him personally. Accepting that the pardon was the right thing to do—and by now even many of Ford's harshest critics have since conceded that it was—there is little question but that it could have been handled in a better manner.* For one, Ford might have surfaced the notion with key leaders in the House and Senate, to keep them from being stunned. He might have talked it over with a trusted group of aides to ensure his announcement and

* Senator Edward Kennedy was one of the harshest critics of the pardon, skirting close to accusing Ford of complicity in Watergate: "Do we operate under a system of equal justice where there is one system for the average citizen and another for the high and mighty? It is the wrong time and the wrong place and the wrong person to receive a pre-indictment pardon. And it has led many Americans to believe that it was a culmination of the Watergate coverup." It was not the first or only time Kennedy was wrong. In 2001, Ford received the Profile in Courage award from the John F. Kennedy Library, and Senator Kennedy praised him in quite different terms.[24]

tone were properly calibrated and supported by his staff. But he appeared to have done none of those things.

Nixon did little to help. His six-paragraph statement accepting the pardon stopped short of admitting any guilt in the Watergate matter. "No words can describe the depths of my regret and pain at the anguish my mistakes over Watergate have caused the nation," he said. He might have tried harder to find some.

As those decisions were made, my focus was elsewhere. I had already returned to Brussels on August 22, 1974—the day after the transition team submitted our report and the day before our daughter Valerie departed for her first year of college. While I followed what was happening in Washington, D.C., I also had my hands full at NATO with the ongoing Cyprus crisis.

Then, on September 16, 1974, my father died at the age of sixty-nine. He was not only my father, but also a close friend. I sometimes called him George, as you would a pal. When I married Joyce, he was my immediate choice as my best man.[25]

His death was a blow, even though it was not altogether unexpected. Alzheimer's had started to set in when he was in his early sixties. The disease can be toughest on the spouse, and it was certainly hard for my mother. They had had a lifetime love affair. When Dad's condition deteriorated, my sister, Joan, and I encouraged Mom to make the difficult decision to move Dad to a nearby nursing home, for his safety. For the last year of his life, Mom spent most of every day there with him, even though he no longer recognized her.

When I traveled to the States from Belgium, I would stop in Washington to handle my NATO business and at the end of the day fly to Chicago to see my parents. My father's brain was working in ways that made him agitated. But sometimes while I was with him there would seem to be a small spark of recognition. He would smile and I would think, or at least hope, he might have had a moment of clarity and happiness as he recognized me or my mother. But just as quickly as that moment came, it was gone. When I left him I would wonder to myself if what I had taken to be recognition had been there at all.

I was at my parents' home outside Chicago preparing for my father's funeral service when I received a call from the White House operator, who then brought President Ford on the line. His voice was full of warmth and concern. The President said he wanted to express Betty's and his sympathies to me and to my family.

Then he went on to say, "I know this is not an ideal time," but if I was up to it he had some rather urgent business that required my attention. He said that he had decided he needed to replace Al Haig as chief of staff after all. He made it clear that he wanted me to take the post. Ford said he was having problems managing some of the staff, including his longtime aide Bob Hartmann.[26] He was a seasoned newspaper man who had worked closely with Ford since 1968 and had become Ford's chief of staff when Ford became vice president. Hartmann's role had now changed drastically, and the President said Bob was having difficulty adjusting to it. I sensed that Ford was working hard to spare Hartmann's feelings.

Ford knew that I had a strong desire and intention to stay at NATO and, equally, to not work again in the White House, having been there for four years previously. But the President asked me to come to the White House to talk with him about it before I returned to Brussels.

On September 22, 1974, I found myself back in the Oval Office. President Ford said again how sorry he was about my father. He knew I had always looked up to him as a man of integrity, much as Ford had to the man who raised him. Ford's biological father had left his mother when he was a baby; his stepfather, Gerald Rudolph Ford, Sr., raised the boy as his own, even giving his stepson his name. For a moment it didn't matter that I was talking to the President of the United States in the Oval Office. We were two friends talking fondly about the men who shaped us.

Eventually he turned to the business at hand. Things had not been going well for the President, and he knew it. It was not only the negative reaction to the pardon, although the immediate damage from that decision was difficult to overestimate. The economy was worsening. Relations with Congress had soured. The Rockefeller nomination as vice president was not well received by a large number of conservatives and was being delayed in the congressional confirmation process by an exhaustive investigation into his personal finances. On top of all that, the Republican Party's prospects in the upcoming 1974 midterm elections were at best gloomy, which did not bode well for Ford's agenda.

The President now conceded that his spokes-of-the-wheel approach was not working and would not work. The Hartmann faction was unfriendly with the Haig faction, and others in the White House seemed caught in between. Only a few weeks after informing the country that Nixon's White House chief of staff, Al Haig, would stay on indefinitely, Ford would have to do something he never liked to do—change his mind.

The President said that while he could not be seen as abandoning outright his very public decision to reject the Nixon-Haldeman staffing system in favor of his spokes-of-the-wheel approach, he agreed that he would move toward a proper staff system gradually. His solution was, at the outset, to call whoever replaced Haig the "chief coordinator." I was not impressed with that idea, because it would signal to others in the White House that the new chief of staff was not actually in charge of the staff. But I understood Ford's reasoning.

The President went on to say that if I took the post, it would be only temporary, perhaps six months or so. He added that if a cabinet position became open that I found interesting, that would be an option. After an hour and a half of going through the pros and cons, it was time to make a decision. In the end Ford made it an issue of patriotism. He was the President of the United States, and he insisted he needed me to do the job.[27]

Finally, as I continued to express reluctance, Ford smiled. "Come on, Rummy," he prodded. "Say yes. I have a golf game."

I smiled back at him. "Okay," I said, "I'll do it."[28]

Joyce, as usual, took the news in stride, though she was sad to leave her friends in Belgium. "This time," she jokingly said, "I'm not going to try to save the world." She was hoping to just get through the next few months, so I could help the President get settled in, and then we might go home to Illinois.*

* I was pleased to learn that I would be succeeded at NATO by the distinguished diplomat David K. E. Bruce. Bruce had been the head of the Office of Strategic Services (OSS) in Britain during World War II and had had the unique distinction of having served as ambassador to Germany, France, and the United Kingdom. Bruce's appointment signaled Ford's serious commitment to the alliance.

CHAPTER 12

A Rocky Start

On my first day back in the White House, I moved into the chief of staff's West Wing office, where Haldeman had presided during the height of the Nixon years and where Haig later, with Henry Kissinger, worked near miracles to hold the United States government together.

Many in the White House remained spooked by Watergate and its ghosts. In the months since Nixon's departure, listening devices were still being found in the Oval Office and elsewhere in the White House complex. As I started to get settled in my new office, my secretary opened a desk drawer and found a tape with a note attached, designating it as "Presidential Tape—March 8, 1971." I immediately delivered the tape to Phil Buchen, the new White House counsel, and even insisted that he sign a receipt as evidence that we had turned the tape over as soon as it had been discovered.[1] Only the day before that, a safe had been discovered in the cupboard next to the fireplace in my new office.[2] An uninventoried safe in Haldeman's office could have had anything in it—papers relating to Watergate, more Nixon tapes, possibly evidence that could lead to new indictments. The mystery of the Haldeman safe was heightened when we discovered that no one knew how to open it. Wanting to make sure the safe was transferred from my office and properly handled, I asked my stalwart assistant, Dick Cheney, to accompany the safe and ensure that everything went by the book.

After all the drama, Cheney reported back that under the supervision of Secret Service agents, the safe had been blown open with explosives and was found to be empty. Still, the time and energy we wasted in taking the necessary precautions on this and many other matters were but an example of the ongoing costs of Watergate. It also helped me begin to realize that Ford's pardon of Nixon, irrespective of the unfortunate way it was handled, might have been the right decision. The President never would have been able to move his own agenda forward as long as Nixon's prosecution was in the offing.

In those early months, former President Nixon's difficult adjustment to his San Clemente exile came up on my radar screen repeatedly. After he left the presidency, Nixon was extremely ill and hospitalized on a number of occasions with near fatal blood clots. Frank Gannon, who was helping Nixon with his memoirs, confided in me his hope that Nixon would live long enough to bring the book to completion.[3] One of Nixon's aides during the transition, his former press secretary, Ron Ziegler, called me several times to discuss Nixon's predicament. During one call he told me that children on the beach were throwing "dog dirt," to put it nicely, at Nixon's home.[4]

One problem we encountered with regard to Nixon involved the growing number of people on the federal government payroll who had found their way to San Clemente. No one knew how to handle arrangements for a resigned president, but we had agreed in consultation with the Congress to allot the former president a small staff to ease his transition. We thought the number of staff hovered around twenty, but like all things involving the government, the numbers kept getting bigger. I learned during my first week on the job that Nixon's staff had ballooned to more than sixty, meaning that the number our staff had been giving the press was wildly inaccurate. If that became public, I feared it would look like Nixon was establishing a mini-presidential operation. As I discussed the matter with Ford, who was as amazed as I was to hear of it, he said that we had to help Nixon figure out a different arrangement.[5] I knew the "we" meant me. I had several difficult conversations with Ziegler, and we were able to persuade Nixon's senior staff to reduce the size of their payroll.[6]

As I settled into my office, I returned to my usual routine. Most of the day I worked at a stand-up desk. I found it an easier way to keep focused over my twelve- to fifteen-hour days. I had a Dictaphone at the ready, into which I would dictate memos that my staff transcribed and sent out. In the Nixon administration, these memos were typed on yellow paper—giving rise to their nickname: yellow perils. At the Ford White House my memos became known as snowflakes, presumably because they were now printed on white paper and fell on the staff like a blizzard. The memos were my way of reaching out to those in the organization, to keep work moving along, and to communicate the President's instructions. Oral comments can be forgotten or pushed down the priority list. With written memos I could assign a task, keep a copy, and track the progress.

I also followed the advice I had given President Ford earlier, when he assumed the presidency, by promptly bringing in some new faces to work with the talent that was already there. One of them, of course, was not all that new to me. By this time, Cheney and I had worked together in three different assignments—the Office of Economic Opportunity, the Cost of Living Council, and the Nixon White House. But our time in the Ford White House would prove to be our most challenging yet.

Echoing my practice with Cheney, I encouraged every senior staff member to find a deputy they could trust, who could help take some of the load off them, and, if possible, over time become interchangeable with them. This made some uncomfortable. Many in senior roles prefer to guard their access to the president and are reluctant to give authority to a deputy. I thought we all needed to remind ourselves that none of us were indispensable.

When I asked Dick to serve as my top assistant (he would later become deputy chief of staff), he reminded me about a couple of arrests he had had for drinking and driving after he got out of college and was working on power lines in Wyoming. The arrests had come up in his FBI background check when he came to work for me in the Nixon administration in 1969, and after discussing them with him, I had hired him anyway. Dick pointed out that serving as my assistant in the Ford White House would be a far more visible position. He did not want the President or me to be surprised when the clearance process turned up his arrests again, and said he'd understand if either Ford or I thought it might prove an impediment to his being hired. Shortly thereafter I briefed the President on the issue.

"Do you think this is the guy you need for the job?" Ford asked.

"I do," I replied.

"Then bring him aboard," Ford said. That settled that.

Throughout the hectic months that followed, Dick helped to make a nearly impossible job often enjoyable. Our back-and-forth banter was our way of getting through the difficult and hectic times. No assignment was too small if it eased the burden on the President. We weren't always saving the world.

Indeed, one early problem that Dick and I were involved with was trying to find a way to keep the sun off Ford's neck when he was working in the Oval Office. It took days for the proper curtain to be found.[7]

On the first occasion that I scheduled Cheney to substitute for me on a trip with the President, I dictated a note to Cheney joking, "I perjured myself and told [the President] that Cheney was a tremendously able guy in whom I had complete confidence."[8] Ford and Cheney had different personalities, and at first I was not sure how they would gel. The President was a gregarious sort who liked to smoke a pipe and tell stories. Cheney was cerebral; on trips he was perfectly happy reading a book or, more likely, a series of work-related memos. When the two of them returned I asked the President how the trip had gone. "Dick is great!" Ford replied. He admired Cheney's businesslike manner. "He comes in, he's got ten items to cover, he covers them and he leaves."[9] I was pleased that the two seemed to get on so well, because I was hoping Cheney not only would be able to take more of the burden off of me, but also might eventually replace me.

Cheney and I agreed that we needed to tighten the ship for the administration to be successful. We couldn't afford a sluggish bureaucracy or a string of independent operators. Naturally our approach tended to make the sluggish bureaucrats and independent operators less than pleased.

We decided to trim the size of the White House staff. By the time Nixon left, it had more than doubled, from about 220 people to 510, not counting the additional hundreds of so-called detailees who were theoretically on loan to the White House from the departments and agencies, most of them from the Department of Defense. Lyndon Johnson had also made extensive use of the practice. Whenever I visited the West Wing during Nixon's second term, while I was serving at NATO, I would see people in the hallways and meetings and wonder who they were—and what in the world they were supposed to be doing.

Always wary of comparisons to Nixon's imperial presidency, Ford endorsed my proposed belt tightening—at least, most of the time. It was a quite different story when I briefed him on my plans for a similar reduction of the First Lady's staff in the East Wing. He seemed fine with it—that is, until I suggested that he broach the subject with Betty that evening.

"Oh no, Don," Ford said with a chuckle. "This is your plan. You go up and settle it with her."[10]

I then suggested to Cheney that he might be the best one to raise the subject with the First Lady, but he knew exactly what I was up to. Despite our reputations as taskmasters, neither Cheney nor I had the persuasiveness to successfully turn the indomitable Betty Ford. "Predictably," President Ford later noted, "the size of the East Wing staff hardly changed at all."[11]

Other challenges were more nettlesome than staff size. One involved Henry Kissinger. As I feared from the day Ford announced Kissinger would stay on in both of his posts, Ford's approach to Kissinger was at times deferential. Kissinger often arrived late for Oval Office meetings with the President, sometimes by as much as twenty or thirty minutes. Perhaps tardiness had not been an issue in the waning days of the Nixon presidency, but things had to be different now.

After Kissinger failed to arrive at the scheduled time three days in a row, I raised the matter with Ford, who had also taken notice. The President suggested we change the meeting time to accommodate Kissinger. That was the wrong approach. Ford's tolerance of repeated late arrivals by his cabinet or staff sent a bad signal.[12] I told Kissinger and his staff that things had to change, which they did, at least with respect to the President's schedule.

Going back to my time in the Nixon administration, I had noticed that the National Security Council was not well connected to the cabinet and the rest of the White House staff. But foreign policy decisions had consequences outside the State Department and NSC bureaucracies. They often involved Congress, the press, complicated legal issues, as well as other departments and agencies. Ford's economic advisers needed to have an opportunity to weigh in on international economic issues. Ford's press secretary needed to be able to communicate to the public the administration's foreign policy actions and decisions. Perhaps because foreign policy had become largely his sole domain during the tumultuous years of Watergate, Kissinger was not accustomed to coordinating with others. Further, with Kissinger holding two of the three national security posts, Defense Secretary James Schlesinger was marginalized. This problem was exacerbated by the fact that Ford and Schlesinger did not work well together. On any number of occasions I made an effort to see that Schlesinger was included in major decisions, urging Ford to see him. I was only partially successful.*

The one-sided national security process led to at least one major embarrassment for the Ford administration. In 1975, the prominent Soviet dissident Aleksandr Solzhenitsyn came to Washington to attend a banquet put on by

*Three weeks after I became chief of staff, I told the President he needed to meet alone with Schlesinger to get his "unvarnished" views on arms control negotiations with the Soviets before he issued guidance to Kissinger, who would be conducting the talks. I discovered a week later that Ford had decided to just call his secretary of defense and inform him of the guidance that he had given to Kissinger, who by then had already departed for Moscow.[13]

the labor federation, the AFL-CIO, in his honor. Solzhenitsyn was one of the most powerful voices of opposition in the Soviet Union. Because he told the truth about the Marxist system—his book *The Gulag Archipelago* denounced the evils of totalitarianism in the sharpest terms—he was a constant irritant to the Soviet leaders. Key conservative senator Jesse Helms tried to arrange a meeting between Solzhenitsyn and President Ford as a sign of America's support for the dissident's efforts.[14]

Kissinger vehemently opposed the meeting. He felt the symbolism of the President meeting with Solzhenitsyn could set back U.S.-Soviet relations, which he was trying to bolster in the lead-up to a meeting in Helsinki scheduled for the following month. Kissinger was even reported to have characterized Solzhenitsyn as a "threat to world peace."[15]

Cheney and I urged Ford to meet with the Soviet dissident.[16] Cheney put together a memo stating the reasons. "[T]he decision not to see Solzhenitsyn is totally out of character for the President," Cheney pointed out. "More than any President in recent memory, he's the man who's willing to see anyone, talk to anyone and listen to anyone's views, no matter how much they may differ from his own." I was impressed with the memo. Up to that point Cheney had dealt mainly with domestic issues, but now he was engaged with foreign policy as well.

At first Ford sided with his secretary of state, as was his tendency on foreign policy matters. Kissinger, of course, was not trying to hurt Ford. He was providing his advice as a secretary of state. He wasn't a politician. Nor was he as tough on the Soviets as some others in the administration. And because Ford only rarely consulted with the obvious counterpoint to Kissinger—Secretary of Defense Schlesinger—the President often heard only one set of views.

Ford's refusal to meet the most famous dissident in the world led to an outcry that extended well beyond the conservative movement. Realizing his mistake, Ford belatedly agreed to the meeting. But Solzhenitsyn at that point declined the invitation, embarrassing the White House even further. Political columnists Rowland Evans and Bob Novak chronicled the damage in a column in the *Washington Post* titled, "Snubbing Solzhenitsyn." They blamed the public relations debacle on a "lack of informed political consultation, gross insensitivity, equivocal explanations, [and] just plain bad manners."[17] It was hard to disagree with that assessment.

Another ongoing challenge to the proper functioning of the White House was Ford's chief speechwriter and former chief of staff, Bob Hartmann.

The President knew Hartmann had not adjusted well to his new role—or, more important, to Ford's.[18] As one of the few wholly Ford people on the White House staff, Hartmann had been a loyal friend to the President for a number of years. Ford didn't want to upset him. That gave Hartmann, still serving as Ford's chief speechwriter and political adviser, the space to continue to operate pretty much how he wanted, leading to frustrations among the others on the staff. Hartmann, who had seen his influence diminished in nearly every other area, guarded most speeches as matters that were between only the President and him, even though they required meticulous coordination and review by relevant senior administration officials.

Working with Hartmann, the President embarked on a program called Whip Inflation Now or WIN. Inflation hovered at above 10 percent. The price of gas had jumped sharply, from thirty-nine cents a gallon in 1973 to fifty-three cents in 1974. The Dow Jones Industrial Average had lost a third of its value. The American people clearly wanted something to be done about the economy, and Ford decided to take action. The idea behind WIN was to treat the nation's economic woes like an enemy and to spark a public campaign to help defeat it, with bumper stickers and lapel pins.

The President decided to introduce his new economic proposal to the public in a televised address to Congress in early October 1974. The final draft of the speech arrived in my office four hours before the President was to deliver it. As I skimmed the text, I found it unimpressive.[19] The speech urged Americans to make up "a list of ten ways to fight inflation and save energy." Hartmann wanted the President to wear a big red WIN button during the speech. I agreed with Ford's determination to do something about the economy, and to try to engage the public. But to deliver a speech that sought to address a severe economic downturn with gimmicky catchphrases and buttons was not, in my view, presidential.

Knowing how the speech shop operated, I suspected that the draft of the speech sent so late to my office might not have been vetted properly by the President's economic advisers or experts in the Treasury Department.[20] I called Alan Greenspan, chairman of the President's Council of Economic Advisers, to check if he had seen it. Greenspan said he had received a copy of the speech only a few hours earlier. He and his staff had worked hard to try to improve it in the brief time they had, but the speech still contained errors and misstatements. He could only vouch for the accuracy of about four fifths of it. Even with his last-minute edits, Greenspan felt the speech was high risk.

I went in to see Ford and urged him to cancel the speech. Because the networks had cleared airtime for the President, I suggested that he instead give a five-minute address discussing the economic problems facing the country, and then say he was not yet satisfied with the economic programs presented to him but was committed to finding the best possible policy. I reiterated my concerns about Hartmann's speechwriting operation.

Ford heard me out, but since he had already authorized Hartmann to go forward with the idea, he was reluctant to back down. "Don," he finally said, "I think it is a good program."

"Okay," I replied. "I wouldn't have felt right if I didn't at least give you this thought."[21]

The response to the speech was not what Ford had hoped. Wearing a pin to defeat inflation became a national punch line. Ford was disappointed by the negative reaction to his speech both in Congress and in the country. I felt sorry for him, but it was a self-inflicted wound and still another sign that the spokes-of-the-wheel approach the President had selected at the outset was not working.

As chief of staff I tried to keep my personal views on the substance of policy issues out of my advice to the President unless asked. I wanted to serve as an honest broker. But since my days in Congress, I had views on the economy and the limited role government should play. During my time in the Ford administration I came to know a young economist at the Department of Treasury named Arthur Laffer, who further focused my views. At one dinner I had with him and Dick Cheney, Laffer outlined his view that higher tax rates did not necessarily translate into higher tax revenues. On a cocktail napkin he sketched out what later became famously known as the Laffer Curve to illustrate his point.* Put simply, the theory that the higher the tax rate the greater the revenues to the government is disproved by the fact that if the tax rate were at the highest rate—100 percent of earnings—government revenues would drop precipitously. If everything one earned was to be confiscated by the government, people would have little if any incentive to work.

Laffer advised what seemed counterintuitive to many then (and even today) that the administration might need to *reduce* tax rates to achieve higher revenues, since that would leave more money in the hands of those who create the jobs and therefore expand the economy. That night gave quantitative

*There are conflicting reports on exactly when this event took place—Jude Wanniski states that it was in December 1974 and that Dick Cheney and I were both there. In 2004, Wanniski gave a different account on an internet blog. Memory can be a tricky thing. As it happens, my calendar indicates the dinner was on September 16, 1975, and I have a personal note about Art sketching the curve that night on a napkin.[22]

context and rationale for my inclination toward lower taxes coupled with fiscal responsibility. Laffer's approach would also appeal to one of the Republicans soon to be running for president—Ronald Reagan.

When Ford offered Rockefeller the vice presidency in August, he had indicated—or at least he had left Rockefeller with the impression—that Rockefeller would have broad responsibilities for domestic policy. I was concerned by any vagueness in such matters and convinced that the President needed to provide clarity, and fast. "It seems silly now," I conceded to Ford, "but mark my words, it will be a monstrous problem, and you will spend all your time trying to unsort it unless you address it now."[23] If Vice President Rockefeller was in charge of domestic policy and Secretary of State Kissinger was in charge of national security policy, I thought, what exactly was President Ford's area of responsibility? I suggested that Ford even consider giving Rockefeller a cabinet department to run as part of his duties, so he would have a clear area of management responsibility.[24] The President considered the idea but decided against it.

Ford was eager for Rockefeller to feel accepted in the White House as he, on occasion, had not in the Nixon administration. "I want us to embrace him, make him feel at home," he said.[25]

After Rockefeller was confirmed in December, the new Vice President met with Ford in the Oval Office. With his shock of gray hair and distinctive dark-framed glasses, Rockefeller was an energetic and powerful presence. The President said he wanted the two of them to work closely together. "Do you have anything else to add, Don?" he asked me.

"I do, Mr. President," I said. "I think it would be very bad if anyone had the understanding that I was acting as the doorkeeper between you and the Vice President." I suggested that the two of them agree that Rockefeller should have walk-in privileges with Ford, without including me in the meetings. They both agreed to this, although Rockefeller did say he wanted to stay in close touch with me.[26] Additionally, I expressed the hope that Rockefeller and his staff, if they saw a problem, would act promptly to address it before another news cycle passed. "I think we all ought to agree that we'll pick up the phone and get any problem that seems to be building sorted out immediately," I said.[27] Shortly thereafter, I showed Rockefeller and his two sons around the White House, which was then decorated for the Christmas season. Reflecting on the early interactions between Ford and Rockefeller, I told Cheney cheerfully, "They are off to a good start." Rockefeller, I added, "is such an enthusiastic and decent person."[28]

It was not long, however, before my relationship with the Vice President went south, somewhere below Chile, as a matter of fact. Ours turned out to be the most difficult personal relationship I experienced in all of my years in the executive branch of the federal government.

It didn't help our relationship that Rockefeller and I understood our respective roles quite differently. I saw my job as helping to make sure that the President received a full range of advice on policy questions, even when the advice contradicted the views and initiatives of others, including those of the Vice President. Rockefeller, by contrast, seemed convinced he was an autonomous factor, alongside the President, who had been delegated domestic responsibilities by Ford and, therefore, whose activities and advice should not be challenged by anyone.*

Looking back at how I had suggested Rockefeller as a possible vice presidential nominee to Richard Nixon in 1968, I realized how mistaken I had been. Though I have had to deal with many strong-willed people in government and managed to get along with them, Rockefeller was quite different. His chief of staff, Ann Whitman, once said that the Vice President "acted as if he were President. He'd come back from a meeting announcing that he was going to run the White House."[29] More than one observer thought Rockefeller still had his mind set on the office he by then had sought three times. Bill Moyers, a onetime aide to Lyndon Johnson, memorably quipped, "I believe Rocky when he says he's lost his ambition. I also believe he remembers where he put it."[30] A man of vast inherited wealth who was accustomed to getting his way, he would badger and pester subordinates until they said what he wanted to hear.

The situation worsened considerably when the Vice President came forward with his own energy proposal. It bore Rockefeller's unmistakable imprint: It was big, ambitious, complex, and as the Vice President modestly contended, billed to resolve America's energy woes for the foreseeable future. It did have some attractive aspects, such as an emphasis on conservation. But, after studying it, I was concerned that this kind of giant, amorphous proposal could become a "Christmas tree" in Congress—an opportunity for members to tack on amendments funding their pet projects.[31] Rockefeller proposed a $100 billion "quasi-public corporation" called the Energy Independence Authority that would finance energy projects—the idea being that

* Rockefeller considered himself the head of the Domestic Council, which Nixon had created in 1970. Theoretically, the Domestic Council would do for domestic policy what the National Security Council did for the President's national security policy.

funds from the government would incentivize innovation in the private sector. With no guidelines, some of those loans could potentially go to people who were friends of people in the White House, and likely friends of Rockefeller's. In short, this looked to be a political, financial, legislative, and ethical time bomb.

I suggested to the President that he ask the relevant experts in his administration to review and comment on Rockefeller's proposal, such as the Office of Management and Budget, the Department of the Treasury, and others. When Rockefeller learned I had made the suggestion and was circulating his proposal in the White House staffing system, he became furious, convinced I was trying to scuttle his plan and sabotage him.

As it turned out, many in the administration had concerns about the proposal. Several people on the staff urged me to persuade the President not to introduce it.[32] Alan Greenspan came out vocally against the plan, warning that it "creates a large potential for real or perceived corrupt practices. . . . There are realistically no limits to the types of projects it can assist, and virtually no limits as to the kind and amount of assistance it can offer."[33] Rockefeller resorted to his usual responses when questioned by anyone: strong-arm tactics, bullying, and anger at any who disagreed.

Around the same time, Rockefeller's personal poll numbers were dropping, which he found inexplicable.[34] Ford was differing with him on emergency funding to bail out New York City, then in a financial crisis caused by local mismanagement. This led to an unfortunate headline: "FORD TO CITY: DROP DEAD."[35] Ford decided he did not want to oppose Rockefeller on the energy plan at the same time as he was opposing him on the New York City financial bailout.* Rockefeller led Ford to believe he had support for his energy proposal within the administration, which was hardly the case, although he may well have believed it, since few in the administration were willing to incur his wrath by disagreeing with him.

The plan's arrival on Capitol Hill was at first heralded in the press as a triumph for the powerful Vice President against his imagined White House adversaries, a perspective undoubtedly promoted by Rockefeller.[37] But support for his mammoth energy bill cooled once people read it. Not surprisingly, criticism of Ford, rather than Rockefeller, began appearing in the press, for his endorsement of what was characterized as a "horrendous mistake" and a "stunningly bad idea."[38] Congressional support evaporated steadily,

* The President was absolutely correct on this issue. At one meeting, Ford asked if anyone was in favor of giving New York City a bailout before it defaulted. I replied not just no—but hell no.[36]

until eventually a vote was held on a much-reduced version. Even that was resoundingly defeated in the House of Representatives.[39]

Gerald Ford, who allowed the avoidable political embarrassment to happen, wound up taking the political blame for Rockefeller's unwillingness to work with others in the administration. Time and again over those months I would consult with Cheney about how we could deal with Rockefeller. It is amusing now to consider those who thirty years later would call Dick Cheney an "imperial vice president."[40] Back in the Ford years, Cheney and I had to deal every day with the real thing.

Not having expected to become president, Gerald Ford had to grapple repeatedly with tough questions without the tested support system most new presidents have already established over the course of their campaigns. Ford didn't have a tested policy team or a national platform. On the other hand, Ford was also unusually free of the constraints of special interest groups and political supporters who generally help a candidate get elected, and as a result have had a hand in shaping his policies.

I thought we might have something of an opportunity if we invited America's most innovative thinkers to meet with Ford to discuss major issues that were sometimes lost in the day-to-day details of being president. Dr. Robert Goldwin, a former dean of St. John's College in Annapolis, Maryland, who had served with me when I was at NATO, agreed to come back to the White House to serve as a special consultant to the President. Dubbed the administration's intellectual in residence, Goldwin arranged meetings for Ford with leaders from academia on topics ranging from welfare, unemployment, and crime to global hunger.*

The President engaged in the discussions Goldwin arranged with enthusiasm and insight. Ford's open and friendly manner, combined with the fact that he did not have a conniving bone in his body, caused him to suffer unfairly from suggestions that he was dumb. Or, as Lyndon Johnson once put it, "That's what happens when you play football too long without a helmet."[41] But that most certainly was not the case. Ford was a graduate of the University of Michigan and Yale Law School. He had served on the House Appropriations Committee for twenty-three years and had an encyclopedic knowledge of the federal budget.

In light of the caricatures of Ford that were gaining traction in the press, I thought Ford needed to give the American people a sense of the direction he

* For example, one luncheon included Gertrude Himmelfarb, Edward Banfield, Herbert Storing, and Thomas Sowell.

wanted to take the country.[42] What did he want his presidency to be about? What were his policies and priorities? If Ford didn't seize the initiative to define his presidency, I feared that others were going to define it for him.

Cornelius Crane Chase was the son of a Manhattan book editor and a concert pianist. When he was a youngster he was expelled from two private schools, and he worked odd jobs, such as cab driver, motorcycle messenger, busboy, and produce manager. But it was as a television performer that Cornelius Chase, better known by his nickname Chevy, found his calling. Chase became a nationwide celebrity for his humorous caricature of President Ford as a well-meaning but clumsy oaf who couldn't seem to get anything right. Chase's popular parody on *Saturday Night Live* did damage to the President's image throughout his presidency. Even though Ford and others on the staff tried to laugh it off, the attacks hurt politically.

The episode that cemented that aspect of the President's image occurred when we were on a trip to Salzburg, Austria, in June 1975 to meet with Egyptian President Anwar Sadat. As Air Force One arrived at the airport, it was raining. The mobile steps that had been wheeled up to aircraft's door had not been fitted with nonskid safety strips. As the President and Mrs. Ford exited the plane, a crew member handed the President an umbrella. Ford took the umbrella with one hand and thoughtfully took Betty's arm with his other. This, of course, meant Ford did not have a hand on a railing.

Joyce and I were exiting the same stairs behind them when I saw the President slip and fall down the last few steps. Ford bounced up quickly, but that hardly mattered. I knew the widely televised stumble was going to be a disaster. The picture of Ford's fall appeared on page one of what seemed like every newspaper in the world and was replayed on television over and over again. In the face of this embarrassment, Ford could have blamed any number of people. But Ford, true to form, wasn't mad at anyone but himself. The Salzburg stumble was, of course, a gift to Chevy Chase. "He [Ford] had never been elected . . . so I never felt that he deserved to be there to begin with," Chase later said. "That was just the way I felt then as a young man and as a writer and a liberal."[43]

The truth was that Ford was very likely the best athlete to serve in the modern presidency. As president, he swam regularly, played golf, and was an accomplished skier and an aggressive tennis player. He had a bad knee from his football days, and like all of us, he stumbled from time to time. Unfortunately when he stumbled, it was for all the world to see.

The President had real strengths and one of Ford's most important assets was the First Lady. Betty Ford was a gracious, lively, and entertaining woman whom the President clearly adored. She helped set the standard for modern first ladies by talking openly about controversial public issues, a role that traditionally was not considered the province of a president's wife. Mrs. Ford expressed her support for the Equal Rights Amendment, for example, and for legalized abortion. She talked openly about her battle against breast cancer, as she did in later years about her struggle with alcoholism.[44] All of this was unorthodox stuff for the mid-1970s. Not everyone who supported President Ford welcomed Betty's outspoken views. Some even thought it made the President look weak, because he couldn't seem to "control his wife," as was said back in those days. A few urged me to ask Ford to encourage Betty to withhold some of her opinions.

I had a different perspective as a husband of an independent woman and a father of two independent-minded daughters. It seemed to me you'd be yelling into the wind to suggest that somebody like Betty Ford ought not say what she believed. From a political standpoint, Mrs. Ford's remarks probably even helped the President. The First Lady's frankness about her personal struggles no doubt encouraged many Americans to seek treatment for similar problems and made them feel less alone. Years later, the treatment center for addiction that bears her name has been a lifeline to thousands and a living testament to her courage and candor. Further, her husband's obvious comfort with Betty's directness highlighted the Fords' respectful as well as devoted relationship. Mrs. Ford, in fact, proved so popular that Republicans printed up campaign buttons that read "Betty's Husband for President!" Still, Ford's presidency would continue to be buffeted by Chevy Chase's parodies or some other extraneous factor. We were losing ground. Time was short, and Ford needed to make the presidency his own.

When Ford became Nixon's vice president, he had all but ruled out a run for the presidency.[45] But by the spring of 1975, he had changed his mind.* Ford was growing more confident in the office. He was becoming a more skillful executive every day.

Several months later, I was with Ford in California when his presidency almost came to an abrupt end. On September 5, 1975, we were heading for a meeting with California's governor at the state capitol in Sacramento. As we were walking, a woman aimed a gun only a few feet from the President.[46] A Secret

* Ford once explained to me the reasons for his initial reluctance. When Nixon asked Ford to become vice president, Nixon told Ford that he wanted his favorite cabinet member, John Connally, to be the Republican standard-bearer in 1976, presumably after Nixon's full eight years in office.

Service agent spotted her, wrestled the gun from her hand, and forced her to the ground. "It didn't go off," she kept saying, as police swarmed in to arrest her. "It didn't go off. Can you believe it?"[47] The would-be assassin was Lynette "Squeaky" Fromme, a follower of the notorious mass murderer Charles Manson.

A few weeks later, on September 22, 1975, we were in San Francisco for a full day of events. After a speech at the AFL-CIO, we left the building by a freight elevator, which had doors that opened from the top and bottom. When we stepped out, the top door malfunctioned and came down hard. Ford, the tallest person among us, was struck on the head. He went down in a crouch, briefly stunned, then stood back up. He seemed fine, although the blow had left a cut on the bald spot above his forehead. It looked like a red neon sign. I suspected we had just made Chevy Chase's night.

We resigned ourselves to another round of jokes and made our way toward the lobby when I suggested the President walk fast and not shake hands. Ford agreed and walked briskly toward the back door of his limousine. We proceeded to the St. Francis Hotel, where his doctor treated the wound with cold packs. Before long, it was time to head to the airport. The mark on his head was less noticeable at this point, but I still wasn't taking any chances. Again, I recommended he head straight to the car, which he did. This time, as we came out of the building, we heard the crack of a gunshot. The President ducked.[48] Standing just behind him, I ducked as well. A Secret Service agent pushed Ford into the backseat of his limousine. I followed the agent, and we landed on top of the President, on the floor of the car, as it sped off.

As our motorcade continued to speed to the airport, I heard Ford's muffled voice from below. "C'mon, Rummy, you guys get off," he urged. "You're heavy!"

It was the second assassination attempt in less than a month. This time the would-be assassin was Sara Jane Moore. A Marxist radical, she had been picked up by the local police a day earlier on an illegal handgun charge but had been released.[49]

Moore was standing across the street, about forty feet from the President, when she fired. An alert bystander, Oliver Sipple, saw the revolver and reached out to deflect her aim.[50] The bullet came within inches of the President's head—and my own—striking the wall of the hotel behind us. "I do regret I didn't succeed, and allow the winds of change to start," Moore said immediately after the shooting. "I wish I had killed him. I did it to create chaos."*

* Moore later said she was blinded by radical political views. Her concession would have been small consolation had she killed the President. She was released from prison in 2009.[51]

When we arrived on Air Force One, we could not take off immediately because we had to wait for the First Lady, who had been on a separate schedule. No one had told her what had happened, so when Betty came onboard, she asked the President innocently, "How did they treat you?"[52]

After the events of the day were described, she was as calm as her husband. In fact, they handled the situation so well that we were even able to take a moment to lighten the mood somewhat. As the Fords laughed, I chimed in that I thought I deserved a good deal of credit for handling the event so skillfully that "not one single person noticed that the President had bumped his head again."

As much as we wanted to make light of the situation, however, we knew it was deadly serious. The President's natural response was to be brave and defiant in the face of would-be assassins.[53] But it never left my mind that twice in a matter of weeks, two deranged individuals got close enough to President Ford to kill him.[54]

In October 1975, I was with the President in Connecticut when yet another incident occurred. As the presidential motorcade moved through Hartford en route to the airport, the local police department failed to block one of the intersections at the base of a hill. When the President's car was crossing that intersection, a car with four teenagers rammed into the side of the presidential limousine. Those of us seated in the backseat—the President, our host, and me—were thrown to the floor.

Taking no chances, the Secret Service followed their normal procedure and had the motorcade start up fast to get the President out of possible further danger. As we sped away, the lead car in the motorcade had to stop suddenly to avoid a pedestrian. Our limousine slammed into the rear of the lead car, again jostling us around in the backseat. Then, as we stopped suddenly, the Secret Service car behind us, which had been racing to keep up, slammed into the back of our car. We were thrown around in the backseat for the third time.

While no one was seriously injured, the near comic chain reaction seemed to be a metaphor for an administration whose troubles were piling up. Coming off the midterm elections, which were bad for Republicans, we had every reason to believe that 1976 was going to be another tough election year. There were even some suggestions in the press that the GOP was an endangered species on a trajectory of perpetual decline.[55] The administration was not performing up to its potential. I felt an urgent need to get it on a better track.

CHAPTER 13

An Agonizing Reappraisal

On October 22, 1975, Dick Cheney and I met with the President in his study, just outside the Oval Office. We discussed some possible scenarios for the 1976 campaign if, as expected, Governor Ronald Reagan were to challenge Ford in the Republican primaries. There was also discussion of the unpleasant possibility that Ford might lose the nomination, which gave him another chance to decide if a nasty primary contest was really something he was up for.

"Look, I'm running," Ford said with a strength and decisiveness that pleased me. "It will be a tough race, but I'm not going to pull a Johnson [and bow out]. It will be bloody right down to the last gong if Reagan runs."[1]

I had raised the troublesome issues I saw with him many times: a poorly coordinated speech shop; an unmanageable vice president; a marginalized secretary of defense leading to an unbalanced NSC; press leaks; and the like. He knew that I thought his White House needed significant changes if he were to have a successful presidency, fend off the Reagan challenge, and win in the general election.

Apparently change was on the President's mind as well—but instead of the administrative fixes I had been proposing for months, he was thinking of personnel changes.

"You know, there are funny things you think of just before you go to sleep," he said. He told us he had gotten so angry at Secretary of Defense Jim Schlesinger over a recent dustup Schlesinger had had with a senior Democratic congressman who was a close friend of Ford's that he told Cheney and me that he was considering replacing Schlesinger with Rockefeller and naming George H. W. Bush as his vice president. I had listened to President Nixon muse on various occasions about possible cabinet shake-ups during his administration. These generally proved to be simply ideas tossed out to see how others would react. And indeed, as Ford talked, he sounded like he was thinking more about after the election, if he won his own term.[2] What Ford did not know at the time was that I was planning one last-ditch effort to convey my sense of urgency to him.

In Ford administration lore, the events that soon followed became known as the Halloween massacre. According to some press accounts, I played a driving role, arranging for the President to dispatch all of my enemies in one swoop so that I could be vice president. The massacre mythology, in fact, became one of the building blocks of my image in some quarters as a master behind-the-scenes operator. The facts of those next few days tell a far different and less tidy human story.

Since the day I arrived as chief of staff, I had been planning to leave the White House by 1975. The President and I had originally discussed my staying for six months. It had now been a year. After almost two decades in government service, I was ready to leave and find a way to pay for college tuitions for our children. I began to talk to a few close friends back home in Chicago about what I might do in the private sector when I left the administration. At the same time, I cared about President Ford and wanted him to succeed.

Over the course of several weeks, I prepared a memorandum for the President that became a lengthy and somewhat repetitious collection of the same advice and recommendations I had been making since the day he took office. I took Cheney into my confidence and asked him to look at it. He not only agreed with the sentiments, but added his own touches, and said he would like to sign on to it as well. The memo grew to be almost thirty pages long, and I thought hard about whether and when to give it to the President. One of the rules I developed as a chief of staff was, "Don't accept the post or stay unless you have an understanding with the President that you are free to tell him what you think 'with the bark off' and you have the relationship and the courage to do it." I ultimately decided that I owed it to Gerald Ford to follow my own rule.

I tried to prepare Ford for what was coming. On the evening of Thursday, October 23, when Cheney and I met with him, the President had a cold and seemed discouraged. I gave him a draft of our memo to review, so he could prepare to discuss it, since it was long. Because of the sensitive nature of the document, I asked him to read it and give it back to me personally the next morning, so there wouldn't be a copy in the White House staffing system.

As Ford thumbed through it, I explained to him that the concerns expressed in the memo were not just Cheney's and mine—many on the White House staff had problems with the way the system was working. On the one hand, we all thought highly of President Ford personally. We believed it was important for the country that he win the election. However, we were worried that the administration was not working as it should be, and that that might make his reelection impossible.

Parts of the administration were moving in different directions and at different speeds. The White House gears were grinding against each other, causing unnecessary friction in interpersonal relationships. This was not the fault of the individuals involved. I told Ford squarely that I believed it was the result of the way he had organized the White House.[3]

"This is not very encouraging," Ford said.

"Well, hell, it's not," I replied. "But it's solvable."

With that, Dick and I took our departure.[4]

The President gave the draft memo back to me the next morning, a Friday. He told me he wanted to see Cheney and me Saturday morning, and then Kissinger and me later the same afternoon. He added that what he had in mind for that meeting would require that I get along very well with Kissinger.[5]

Later that evening, I told Ford that after our morning meeting he might not want to go ahead with whatever he was planning, since I was considering leaving the administration. Ford didn't yet know that Cheney and I had decided we would attach letters of resignation to the finished memo.[6] We wanted the President to know that we couldn't serve him properly under the current circumstances.

Saturday, October 25, was a beautiful Indian summer day. Cheney and I went into the Oval Office shortly after eleven to review our completed memo with the President. We had pulled together a list of eight major issues we believed put Ford's administration and reelection in jeopardy, including the President's reputation as a nice person but an ineffective chief executive, administrative disorder in the White House, and a lack of clear priorities.

I set out specific suggestions to improve the running of staff meetings, the calendar, and scheduling—all issues that had caused the President headaches for the past year but which he had been reluctant to allow me to fix. Among other things, our memo outlined: possible scenarios for the upcoming presidential primary campaign and fundamental problems in the administration; problems with the workings of the National Security Council; and the need for better coordination with the speech shop and with the Vice President.

Because we wanted to underscore the seriousness of the memorandum and its recommendations, we included the following:

> With that background, and because of our deep sense of these problems, the only way to conclusively make the case and demonstrate the importance we attach to the kinds of changes recommended, is to assure that there will be absolutely no question in your mind that anything said below would affect us in any way or be to our advantage. . . .
>
> Therefore, our resignations are attached.

There was nothing in the memo I had not said to the President a number of times before—and of course, he had seen an earlier draft on Thursday evening. But the weight of all of it together in a single memo, along with our resignations, got his attention. Ford did break into a broad smile as he read the P.S. I had attached at the end: "If you can take this load and still smile, you are indeed a President."[7]

Ford handed the memo back to me and told us that he had to think about it. He went on to discuss normal administrative issues, as if this was any other morning meeting.[8] Cheney and I left the Oval Office not knowing what would happen next.

A few hours later I went back in to meet with the President and Kissinger, as scheduled. Ford seemed relaxed and confident. We sat on the couches, he in his chair in front of the fireplace. After a few pleasantries, the President calmly announced he had decided to make some major personnel changes. He informed us he had decided to replace Bill Colby as CIA director with George H. W. Bush, whom he would bring back from China, where he was serving as the U.S. emissary. He planned to nominate Elliot Richardson to be secretary of commerce, to replace the ailing Rogers Morton. Then he told Kissinger that he would be surrendering his role as national security adviser but remain secretary of state. The President added that he would be asking Dick Cheney to be the new White House chief of staff. Then he looked at me. "Don," he said, "I want you to replace Jim Schlesinger as secretary of defense."

After reciting this list of major moves, Ford stopped and looked at us to gauge our reactions. There was a long pause. I don't recall that Henry or I had a word to say, which was something of a first for both of us. "In truth," Kissinger later wrote, "there was not much to say, since the President did not invite any discussion."* But within a few minutes, Kissinger found his voice. He expressed his concern that removing him as national security adviser could diminish his authority in international relations. He thought he would no longer be seen as a White House insider close to the President, and that it could look like he was being demoted. He made an impassioned plea that his deputy, Brent Scowcroft, be the one to replace him on the NSC to avoid that appearance.

The President looked at me. "What's your reaction?" he asked.

I was taken aback. The memo I had given him earlier contained numerous examples of how he might improve things in the White House for the better. However, while I had argued for fashioning a Ford team early in his presidency, such a dramatic shuffling of his cabinet this late was not among my recent suggestions. Still, I did not doubt that the memo Cheney and I had presented to him may have played a role in getting Ford to move—albeit in the President's own direction. "That's a pretty big load," I said. "I want to think about it."

After talking it over with Joyce, I went to the President the following day and told him I did not think I should go to the Defense Department. I said the time to have made major changes in his cabinet had been soon after he had taken office. Now he was within a year of the upcoming 1976 presidential election, and a Democratic-controlled Senate would need to confirm his nominees. The dramatic changes could smack of desperation. I also cautioned against removing Schlesinger. I told the President I thought that Schlesinger was a darn good secretary of defense and that I didn't know of a national security issue about which I disagreed with him. Were I at the Defense Department, I told him, I would likely be advocating policies similar to those Schlesinger had been pressing.

Ford pointed out that Schlesinger and Kissinger did not get along, and he believed that Kissinger and I would have a more collegial relationship.† I said

* Ford describes the scene in a similar fashion in his autobiography: "Kissinger and Rumsfeld were stunned by the sweeping nature of these changes. Both expressed doubts."[9]

† President Ford had another reason for wanting me to take the post. He wrote: "Defense, I told Rumsfeld, was the place he ought to go. With his experience and ability, he could convince Congress to appropriate necessary funds for the military."[10]

that if I were in the Pentagon, I would have no problem agreeing or disagreeing with Kissinger and having the President resolve any differences.

I reminded Ford that he and Kissinger had not sufficiently included Schlesinger in the interagency process. I told him that whoever might go to Defense would need to have an opportunity to give the President the Defense Department's views and recommendations. I was also concerned that Brent Scowcroft might not be an independent national security adviser because he had worked so closely with Henry. But Kissinger was suggesting he might resign if Scowcroft did not replace him in that role.[11]

Ford's assurances did not convince me I should accept the nomination. If I decided to stay in government, I was ready to have a substantive, policy-oriented position, as opposed to a staff post in the White House. On the other hand, I knew the decision to replace Schlesinger would likely be portrayed in the press as a palace coup and that could be damaging to both the President and me. But Ford was not taking no for an answer. He clearly intended to take charge of his administration.

Before deciding, I spoke to Kissinger and expressed concern that if I went to the Department of Defense, it might prove difficult for him. Kissinger had made a habit of reflexively blaming the Pentagon for leaks adverse to him and the State Department. I told him that I probably couldn't control leaks any better than Schlesinger, and that I was concerned he would go haywire on every leak he saw in the press. "You see a couple of those and you will flip out and the President will be misserved," I said. "It strikes me that the only person you could have over there would be a perfectly submissive person. . . . I have never learned to kiss fannies very well, and I don't intend to start now." Kissinger assured me that that would not be the case, and that he thought we could work together well.[12]

I asked Ford's permission to discuss the issue with Cold War strategist Paul Nitze. When I was ambassador to NATO, Nitze had come to Brussels periodically to brief the North Atlantic Council on the strategic arms negotiations with the Soviet Union and would stay at our guest house. I came to think of him as a man of many dimensions, immense talent, and long experience.* There were few who understood the Cold War and the dangers posed by the Soviet Union better. Coincidentally, as I later learned, Nitze had been the one

*In 1963, I had spoken out against President Kennedy's appointment of Paul Nitze to be secretary of the Navy when I was in Congress. I had read of some of the recommendations of a panel he had chaired, which I considered too conciliatory toward the Soviets. After I learned that he had been asked to chair the committee specifically to try to improve the recommendations, I apologized to him. We became warm friends.[13]

person who James Forrestal, the first secretary of defense, consulted before agreeing to leave Franklin Roosevelt's White House to serve as secretary of the Navy (a post Nitze would later fill).

When I told him about Ford's proposal, Nitze, a friend of Schlesinger's, told me I had no choice but to accept. In his view, it was not a difficult question. The President had to have a secretary of defense who could do the job. Second, that person had to be confirmable by the U.S. Senate, and third, it had to be someone with whom the President could work with comfortably. Nitze told me I had to accept, since I was the only one who met those three key criteria.

On November 2, a Sunday, President Ford left for Florida for meetings with President Anwar Sadat of Egypt. At my request, Cheney went with him. Someone had leaked the story of Kissinger losing his NSC hat, and we were told it would be published the following Monday in *Newsweek*.[14] Ford was concerned he would lose control of the announcements, and his decisions would come out piecemeal instead of as an overall plan. Aboard Air Force One, Ford asked Cheney to find a way to get me to agree to take the job at Defense. Cheney said he would try.

That Sunday afternoon I took our son, Nick, to the Washington Redskins' football game. It was a chance to be with him and to be away from the phone.

After the game, Nick and I went out to our car, and I found that I had lost my keys. A couple was pulling out of the parking lot, and I asked them if they could give us a ride into Washington. I could see the woman whisper a muffled no to her husband, but he asked where we were going. I told him we were heading up to Pennsylvania Avenue. He said that was the way they were going, and we could get in.

As we approached the White House, he asked where we wanted to be dropped off. I said, "Pull in here," and he realized he had just pulled up to the White House West Wing entrance. The couple had no idea who I was or that I worked for the President.

I asked them if they had ever been inside the White House. When they said no, I asked if they would like to come in. The guard waved us through, and the man parked out front. I took them into the West Wing and gave them a tour of the Oval Office, the Cabinet Room, the Roosevelt Room, and my office, thanked them for the ride, and escorted them out. As they left, I wondered what sort of conversation they had on the way home. I can almost hear the husband saying to his wife, "And you wanted to say no!"

I was told that Cheney was trying to get in touch with me on the phone. He told me Ford needed my answer before the *Newsweek* story appeared the next morning. Realizing that my limited time was over, I remembered Nitze's admonition and finally agreed to take the job.

Before he left for Florida, the President had met with CIA director Colby and Schlesinger about their leaving the administration. I imagined neither meeting was enjoyable for any of them, but I was impressed with the forthright, take-charge Gerald Ford I was now witnessing. He met with them himself, rather than asking someone else to do it. I found that classy.

The circumstances surrounding George H. W. Bush's nomination to be director of the CIA is a particularly stubborn chapter of the myth that I had stage-managed Ford's staff reorganization. Typical of this "Rumsfeld takes out Bush" storyline was the view expressed in a sympathetic biography of Bush, *George Bush: The Life of a Lone Star Yankee:* "Rumsfeld, who took over as secretary of defense in the administration's cabinet shake-up that fall, had a motive for shunting Bush off to the CIA. . . . Rumsfeld took a backseat to no one . . . and steered his organizational system to 'diminish the influence of all potential rivals at the White House.'" The Bush biography cited a memo I wrote to the President in 1975 that "lauded" Bush's qualifications for the job at CIA. From this memo the author argued that "Rumsfeld was more than a contributor to the Bush transfer. He was a promoter."*

At the President's request, I provided him with a memo listing strengths and weaknesses of twenty-three potential CIA candidates, one of whom was Bush. At the end of this long list, the memo included the senior staff's rankings of the candidates listed. Rather than promoting Bush, I put him "below the line."[16] That meant that I recognized his qualifications for the job but that he was not on my personal short list of top recommendations to the President.

I understood why Bush might be a reasonable candidate for the position. He had served in Congress and had good relationships in both parties. It made sense to put a former legislator in the post, since it looked like the principal responsibility for the new CIA director during that period would be to deal less with intelligence matters and more with the Congress during difficult ongoing investigations. The investigations centered on covert programs authorized by several of Ford's predecessors as president that had been leaked and that had appeared in the press under a series of sensational headlines.

* Bush obscured the situation somewhat in his own book by putting the allegation in the words of an unnamed "former House colleague," who told him, "'I think you ought to know what people up here are saying about your going to the CIA. . . . They feel you've been had, George. Rumsfeld set you up and you were a damned fool to say yes.'" By repeating the myth instead of setting the record straight, Bush in effect endorsed it.[15]

One article described a program authorized by President Johnson to investigate ties between antiwar groups and foreign supporters, which continued during the Nixon administration. The CIA had monitored some ten thousand American citizens, a newspaper claimed. The reports also focused on a 1973 CIA review that documented the Agency's covert operations stretching back a quarter century. The list included alleged assassination plots against foreign leaders authorized during the Kennedy and Johnson administrations. The explosive document tracing these activities was quickly given the title the "Family Jewels."[17] I was amazed by the allegations and shared President Ford's desire to have a CIA director in place who had some credibility with Congress.

Bush was eager to return to a high-profile post in the United States.[18] His wife, Barbara, later noted that Bush was "thrilled" when he was asked to take the job at CIA.[19] My distinct impression was that he not only was greatly pleased, but also that he had actively sought the assignment.

The Bush nomination engendered a controversy when Democrats in the Senate insisted that he agree not to be a vice presidential candidate in 1976 before they would consider his nomination. The senators argued that the CIA had been politicized, its credibility damaged, and Bush was a former Republican National Committee chairman with obvious political ambitions.

When I heard about the demand, I told President Ford that I thought he and Bush should not agree to the Senate's request. I said any president ought to be able to select anyone he wants for vice president, including Bush. Ironically, Ford told me that it was Bush who insisted that he agree to the senators' condition, because he was afraid he could not be confirmed otherwise and he badly wanted to be CIA director.* In his autobiography, Ford recalled that what actually took place was not what Bush later contended. "[E]ven though Congress held all the cards, I was tempted to fight," President Ford later wrote. "But Bush himself urged me to accept the Democrats' demand."[21]

It has always amazed me that Bush's version of what took place has consistently been contrary to the facts, even when the actual version of what took place had been attested to in writing by Gerald Ford, not only in his book but also in our later personal correspondence. After the failure of President Bush's nomination of John Tower to be secretary of defense in 1989, my name was circulated in the press as a possibility for the post.[22] The pushback from the Bush White House was fast and strong—with my imagined role in sending

* Bush contended that it was President Ford's decision to exclude him from consideration for vice president. Bush is quoted as saying, "I told Ford I'm not going to do that, but if you want me in this job enough you will make the caveat."[20]

Bush to the CIA cited as the reason. I thought it highly unlikely that I would be asked to serve in his administration. Nonetheless, I was getting tired of reading the falsehoods surrounding the matter, and I wanted to set the record straight. So that spring I wrote to President Ford asking how he remembered the episode.[23] Ford responded: "It was my sole decision to send George Bush to the CIA. George wanted to come back from China and Bill Colby wanted to leave the CIA because of the Church and Pike [Intelligence] Committee hearings. . . . It was George Bush's decision to agree not to accept any Vice Presidential nomination. I, reluctantly, agreed with his decision."[24]

Another Halloween massacre myth has gained currency over the years: that I engineered the effective firing of Vice President Nelson Rockefeller, presumably to clear the way for me to be the vice presidential nominee.[25] After I differed with him on policy matters, Rockefeller began making a series of accusations against me. This continued, and indeed escalated, even after the Ford administration ended, when he continued to engage in ridiculous charges.*

I suppose it is always easier on one's ego to say you were tripped rather than that you fell. But the reasons for President Ford's decision to remove the Vice President from the ticket were obvious: He was increasingly unpopular across the country. Ford found "ominous" a poll showing that 25 percent of Republicans would not vote for Ford if Nelson Rockefeller were his running mate.[27] The reality was that Rockefeller might not have been able to win the vice presidential nomination at the 1976 Republican convention even if Ford were to have recommended him. And if Ford did try, it might have led to an ugly, divisive fight that could have caused him to lose the presidential nomination to Governor Ronald Reagan.

On October 28, 1975, President Ford told Cheney and me that he had met with Rockefeller and "suggested" that Rockefeller announce that he would not be a candidate for vice president. This was news to me. Of course, when the President of the United States makes such a suggestion, it isn't a suggestion at all. Ford said Rockefeller responded positively and offered to do anything the President wanted. The President took Rocky up on his offer to help by asking Rockefeller to serve in a second term as secretary of the treasury or

* In a 1977 interview Rockefeller said, "The third thing that I have no proof of but I have no way of explaining the event that ensued except by surmising what I will say to you and that is that Rumsfeld had something on the President that he could use and that the President for whatever reason did not want to come out. And therefore it was virtually if not in actual fact a blackmail situation."[26]

secretary of state if Kissinger left. But having just said he'd do whatever Ford asked of him, Rockefeller said no.

A few weeks later, his rejection festering, Rockefeller began to lash out wildly. At a meeting with Republican Party officials, where he was supposed to help motivate the senior party leaders, he instead berated them, holding them responsible for his removal from the Ford ticket. "You got me out, you sons of bitches," he raged. "Now get off your ass."[28] His was a rather unorthodox motivational technique.

I was not surprised when I, too, became the target of Rockefeller's anger and disappointment. By this point, Rockefeller increasingly seemed to be troubled and embittered by his frustrated ambitions.

Although I saw Ford's cabinet moves as a sign of his growing confidence, and welcomed his decisiveness, ultimately it may have put him in a weaker position than if he had waited until after the 1976 election. Many conservatives were delighted with the removal of Rockefeller from the ticket but saw the firing of Schlesinger as a victory for Kissinger, who they distrusted for his approach toward the Soviet Union. Earlier in 1975, Ford had led Ronald Reagan in a primary contest by more than twenty points among Republicans, but by the close of that year, Reagan had inched ahead.

Announcing his candidacy for the Republican nomination, Reagan made no mention of President Ford. But when he said it was time for "progress instead of stagnation; the truth instead of promises; hope and faith instead of defeatism and despair," it was clear enough to whom he was referring.

More than a year earlier, Gerald Ford had taken office with the daunting task of steadying the nation and righting its course. With his integrity and warm, open manner, he had helped to dispel the demons of Vietnam and Watergate. But at the same time, a few of his key early decisions had imperiled his chances of reelection. They had led to what was being characterized as the Nixon-Ford administration by his opponents. And in selecting Rockefeller, he seemed not in tune with his party. Now President Ford faced a new challenge that was almost as daunting as those weeks after Nixon's resignation: a fight for his political survival.

This, however, was not to be my fight. I was leaving the White House to face my own new set of challenges: helping to steer America through a simmering Cold War and to begin to recover our nation's standing after the humiliating withdrawal from Vietnam.

PART VI

Fighting the Cold War

"History teaches that weakness is provocative. Time and again weakness has invited adventures which strength might well have deterred."

—*Rumsfeld's Rules*

Washington, D.C.

MARCH 4, 2009

As I prepared to write this memoir, it occurred to me that it would be helpful to invite some of my former colleagues to talk about our experiences together. I thought it would help jog my memory and ensure that I took into account the perspectives of others. Unfortunately, the list of those from my earliest decades in government who were still alive was dwindling. One absence was most notable of all.

Gerald R. Ford died just after Christmas in 2006, his beloved Betty at his side. I was honored to be among those he had asked to deliver a eulogy.[1] Notably, so was the man who defeated Ford in his 1976 quest for election in his own right, Jimmy Carter. With time and perspective, many of Ford's onetime adversaries embraced him with appreciation and affection. Though I could no longer talk with President Ford about our experiences together, there were others from that era who I thought could help shed some light on those years, including someone with whom I differed markedly from time to time.

In the early months of 2009, with our days of active government service ended, Henry Kissinger came to visit. Henry was eighty-five and I was seventy-six. We had been friends for well over thirty years.

As we talked about my work on this book, Kissinger, an accomplished historian and author, went out of his way to be helpful. He provided some transcripts of telephone conversations we had had. And perhaps sensing my reluctance to dwell on our long-ago disagreements, he urged me to write the book as I remembered our relationship back then. "Tell it like it happened, Don," he prodded. "Don't gloss things over. I didn't," he added, with emphasis.

At various points over the years Kissinger had referred to me as a skillful, even ruthless, bureaucratic infighter. When the Nixon tapes became public, he was quoted making other tough, colorful comments in the heat of the moment. Kissinger called me when some tapes were to be released and apologized for some of the things he had said. I told him not to worry. I added that, at the time, I occasionally felt the same way about him. I said it with a smile, but it also happened to be true.

Time and distance can change and mature one's perspectives. Several years after the Ford administration ended, Joyce and I ran into Kissinger again at a reception. Joyce laughed when she saw him. She remembered when he liked to flash the peace sign to suggest, tongue in cheek, that she was a bleeding heart liberal on the Vietnam War. "Henry, I can't believe it," she said, as she hugged him affectionately, "I'm actually glad to see you!"

After Kissinger completed his memoir of the Ford administration in 1999, he sent me a copy of his book. The inscription was a perfect summation of our relationship: "To Don Rumsfeld, an occasional adversary and a permanent friend."

When I returned to government service in 2001, I invited Henry to join the Defense Policy Board. He was routinely involved in advising me on national security issues. I also arranged for him to be able to meet regularly and privately with President Bush.

But Kissinger and I had never worked as closely together as we did in the final year of President Ford's administration as the secretaries of state and defense. Though our perspectives varied, sometimes sharply, together we helped the President manage a Cold War, hold a resolute stance against Communist aggression, and work to rebuild America's defenses and standing after our country's withdrawal from Vietnam.

CHAPTER 14

Unfinished Business

I was still serving as White House chief of staff on April 29, 1975, when America's long and vexing involvement in Vietnam came to a close. A few weeks earlier President Ford had implored the Democratic-controlled Congress to authorize aid to our ally, the beleaguered South Vietnamese. He and Kissinger hoped the funds could bolster the South enough so it could arrange some sort of a truce with the North Vietnamese. But the U.S. Congress had had enough of Vietnam.

When Ford heard that Congress had rejected his request, he was furious. "Those bastards," he snapped.[1] An evacuation of all of our forces was now inevitable.

Vietnam was the first war in our history that the American people were able to watch unfold on television. That fact made a big difference. As such, we were all witnesses to the heartbreaking scene of U.S. forces executing a humiliating exit while our Vietnamese allies of more than a decade of war faced an uncertain future at the hands of the triumphant Viet Cong and North Vietnamese.

Throughout that long, sad day, I was with President Ford at the White House as he monitored the withdrawal. The American ambassador to Vietnam, Graham Martin, updated us on the number of Americans still waiting to evacuate, as well as the number of Vietnamese clamoring to leave. The second number kept growing.

Many of the Vietnamese who had worked with our forces were

understandably desperate to flee from the advancing Northern forces, making use of rafts, small boats, whatever they could find to escape. When our Marines temporarily opened the gates to the embassy in Saigon, thousands of local citizens tried to force their way in, only to be physically pushed back. Martin and his team understandably found it difficult to turn our Vietnamese allies away.[2] As Martin's wife departed by helicopter, she reportedly abandoned her suitcase so that space could be made for one more South Vietnamese woman to squeeze onboard.

Eventually it was decided that only American citizens could be airlifted in the short time remaining. The indelible image from that day is the heartbreaking photograph of desperate Vietnamese at a building across from the American embassy, trying to crowd aboard a helicopter departing from its roof. Those who had helped America during the war knew what was coming for them. It was an ignominious retreat for the world's leading superpower.

David Kennerly, the White House photographer who had earned a Pulitzer Prize for his Vietnam War photography and understood the power of images as well as anyone, put it succinctly to those of us gathered in the Oval Office with the President that day. "The good news is the war is over," he said. "The bad news is we lost."[3]

Secretary of State Kissinger believed that Ambassador Martin would be the last American to leave the country.[4] After word was received that Martin had been airlifted out of the South Vietnamese capital, Kissinger announced to reporters, "Our ambassador has left, and the evacuation can be said to be completed."[5] As it turned out, that wasn't quite true.

After hearing Kissinger's statement, Secretary of Defense Schlesinger advised us of the problem. The contingent of U.S. Marines assigned to prevent the panicking Vietnamese from flooding our embassy was still on the ground. Somehow there had been a misunderstanding. Kissinger and Schlesinger each considered the other's department responsible for the miscommunication. The President felt Schlesinger bore responsibility and said he was "damn mad" about it.[6] The last thing Ford needed was another public disagreement between his two top national security cabinet officials.

I discussed the issue in the Oval Office with Ford, Kissinger, and Ron Nessen, the White House press secretary. A few in the room felt we should not issue a correction because the Marines were expected to be airlifted out soon, at which point Kissinger's statement would be accurate. I disagreed. What if the Marines were overrun and unable to get out? In any event, what we had told the American people simply was not true. That mattered.

"This war has been marked by so many lies and evasions," I said, "that it is not right to have the war end with one last lie."[7]

The President agreed. He sent Nessen down to the press room to issue a statement saying that the evacuation had not been completed after all.

Kissinger was not pleased about the correction and again vented his anger at Schlesinger. He wanted the Defense Department to be blamed publicly for the miscommunication.* So the war in Vietnam ended in much the way it had been carried out—with recriminations and regret.

Since my years in Congress, I had had concerns about our country's involvement in Vietnam—to the point that both President Nixon and Kissinger viewed me as something of a dove on the subject. I hoped they would find a way to bring the war to an orderly close. It seemed to me that we had lost opportunities to actually win the war. During the Nixon administration, I supported the President's and Defense Secretary Mel Laird's policy of Vietnamization, which put the emphasis on enabling the Vietnamese to take charge of their own affairs. Even in the final days of the war, there was at least a possibility that we might have been able to salvage something worthwhile from the effort had Congress approved the resources to support the South Vietnamese government—and particularly to fund its army—for a longer period.[9] But Congress was not ready to go against the strong antiwar sentiment in the country.

With the war's unfortunate end, a great many in our military and among the American people swore they would never again get involved in the tough, bloody business of counterinsurgency. Many wanted to turn inward, ignoring conflicts waged by the Soviet Union and its proxies. Instead of bringing us peace, I feared the chaotic conclusion of Vietnam could result in an even more deadly escalation of the broader Cold War struggle. The withdrawal from Vietnam became a symbol of American weakness—a weakness our adversaries would highlight for years—and an invitation to further aggression.

Even after the pullout from Vietnam, President Ford pleaded with Congress to at least provide military aid to the anticommunists in the region so they could defend themselves. Those pleas, too, were rebuffed. As such, the victory of the Viet Cong was accompanied by the rise of Communist forces in neighboring Laos and Cambodia. Khmer Rouge guerrillas captured the Cambodian capital of Phnom Penh and swiftly murdered the members of

* By the next day Kissinger had cooled down. After a meeting with the President, he said, "Don, I want you to know that I believe you handled the matter last night just right. . . . We would have ended up in a pissing match within the government, and we don't need that." He concluded saying, "I owed you that and wanted you to know it." Kissinger could be a fierce bureaucratic battler, but he also was a man of integrity who would admit when he had erred.[8]

the prior Lon Nol government and their families. As many as two million people were massacred in Cambodia's now infamous "killing fields," with the carnage often attributed to America's abandonment of the region.

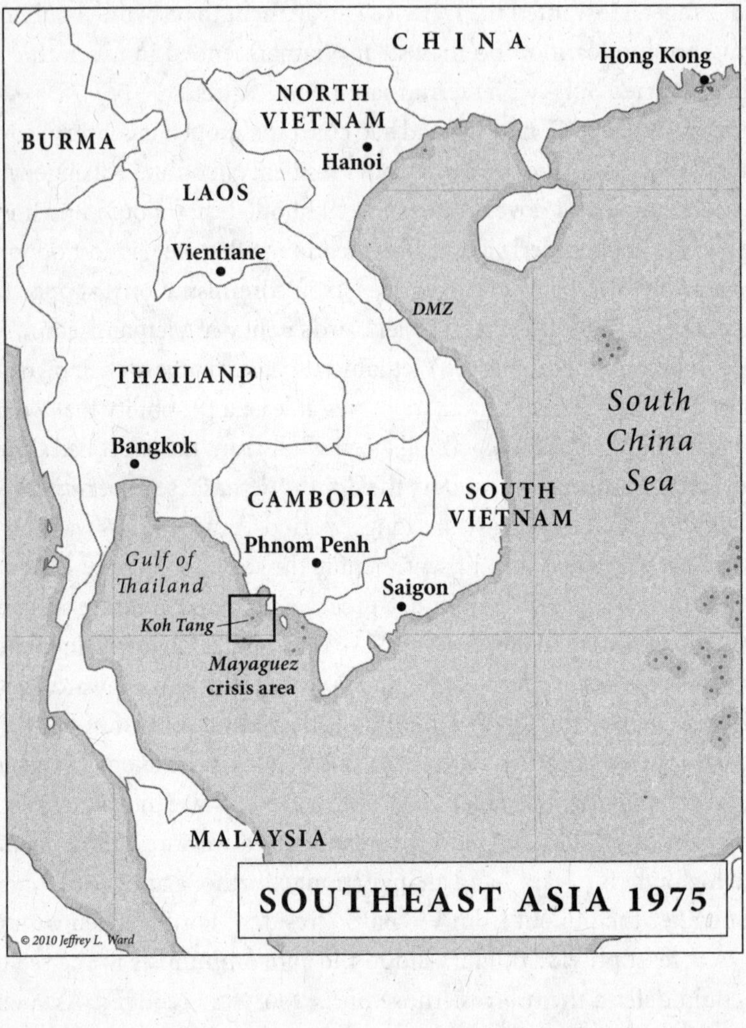

Yet only days after the final U.S. helicopter departed Saigon, America was on the verge of being drawn into another conflict in Southeast Asia. On May 12, 1975, at around 7:15 a.m., those of us at the White House received alarming news: Khmer Rouge gunboats had seized an American merchant vessel, the SS *Mayaguez*, in the Gulf of Thailand, which had more than three dozen crew members onboard.

Ford quickly convened an NSC meeting and asked me to attend. With Kissinger and Schlesinger present, Vice President Nelson Rockefeller argued for an immediate, robust military response. I thought that was premature, since we were still trying to locate the captured ship. Kissinger favored "tough talk" and a demand to free the ship.

My first concern was typical of a chief of staff; I thought it preferable to quickly develop a clear range of options for the President. I recommended acknowledging the incident but saying as little as possible so as to preserve those options until he had decided on a course.

The President decided to go with Henry's approach.[10] Ford publicly declared the capture of the *Mayaguez* an act of piracy. Absent the immediate release of the crew members and the vessel, the President warned, "the most serious consequences" would follow.[11] There was speculation that some, if not all, of the hostages had been taken to the nearby island of Koh Tang, so the President ordered a military blockade around it. Three Cambodian gunboats that chose to defy the blockade were sunk.

As the crisis continued, Ford asked my views on his options. In a meeting on May 14, I presented the President with a memorandum outlining what I saw as the possible courses of action.[12]

We understood that American forces would need to take the island where we believed the Khmer Rouge held the hostages, but I suggested that we plan to get all American troops out within forty-eight hours to avoid drifting into a longer term presence there. Vice President Rockefeller suggested that B-52s bomb targets on the mainland. I suggested we not use the massive, four-engine bombers, since they were associated with damage inflicted across Vietnam and had caused negative reactions in the region and in America. I thought a better approach would be to see if we could use Navy aircraft from the USS *Coral Sea,* which was headed toward the area. Carrier-based aircraft could strike with precision and reduce the potential of civilian casualties.[13]

"The longer the delay," I cautioned, "the weaker the U.S. looks, the greater the danger to the lives of the people, and the greater the likelihood that the critics will get into the act."

That afternoon the President gave the order for a three-prong attack: a Marine helicopter assault on Koh Tang Island; strikes on the mainland by attack aircraft from the USS *Coral Sea;* and a naval interdiction operation to try to recapture the *Mayaguez.*[14] U.S. Marines stormed the beach on Koh Tang and encountered withering fire from entrenched Khmer Rouge positions.

An hour or two into the operation, we received word from Schlesinger that the destroyer USS *Wilson* near Koh Tang had been approached by a Thai fishing boat. The boat held men waving their clothing, in lieu of white flags. It was the crew of the *Mayaguez.* The Khmer Rouge, undoubtedly fearing more reprisals, had released all of the crew.

While the crew was being rescued and the *Mayaguez* recovered, the Marines were engaging the enemy on Koh Tang. By the end of the mission, eighteen U.S. Marines had been killed. The names of the American military who died are etched into the Vietnam War Memorial in Washington, D.C. The official total of American dead in the entire Vietnam conflict stands at 58,261.

President Ford's actions over the *Mayaguez* were the first steps toward rebuilding American credibility.[15] When I became his secretary of defense months later, I remembered the *Mayaguez* crisis and its lessons. To our enemies, post-Vietnam America looked like a weakened nation, which encouraged them to act in provocative ways.

CHAPTER 15

Turning On the Lights

As I prepared to meet with the members of the Senate Armed Services Committee who would vote on my confirmation as secretary of defense, I telephoned Senator Barry Goldwater for advice. In the years since his unsuccessful bid for the presidency in 1964 and our awkward encounter in my congressional district, I'd come to know and respect him. He had become a senior statesman in the Senate and was one of the congressional leaders who, in the final days of Watergate, helped Nixon face the reality that he would have to resign.

I asked Goldwater how he thought my nomination was being received. "Don, it's going to be fine," Goldwater replied. "I have been talking to some of the senators."

"Do you foresee any problems?" I asked.

"There are a few who have questions," he conceded. Some, for example, were worried that as the youngest secretary of defense in history, I wouldn't be tough enough to hold my own against Kissinger.[1]

"Well, what are you saying to persuade those folks?" I asked him.

"Don, I'm telling them the truth," Goldwater responded, his voice a soft growl. "I'm telling them that you're going to be the best damn secretary of defense they've ever seen, and that if you aren't, I'll kick your ass up between your shoulder blades."

On Wednesday, November 12, 1975, I entered room 1114 of the Dirksen

Senate Office Building, which was named for my old Illinois colleague in the Congress, to testify at my confirmation hearing to become the nation's thirteenth secretary of defense.* The hearing was dominated by the urgent national security issue of the day: the Cold War. Millions of Americans have since come of age without knowing the fear of a nuclear exchange between two superpowers. But as I went through the confirmation process, the Soviet Union posed what was widely considered, as President Kennedy had put it, a "clear and present danger."

In anticipation of a possible nuclear attack, a number of American homes were built with bunkers in which families could seek refuge from nuclear fallout. Children practiced survival drills in schools in the event of a nuclear strike. The U.S. Capitol building had so-called safe areas stored with supplies of food in the event of an attack. Many public officials believed, as I did, that the Soviet Union's ambitions were aggressive, its agents were global, and its supporters were on the offensive.

While America had been preoccupied in Southeast Asia, the Soviets had broadened their empire-building efforts to nearly every continent of the world. The Soviets still held a firm grip on the occupied nations behind the Iron Curtain. They were funneling arms to nations and to anti-democratic revolutionary groups in the Middle East, Latin America, Africa, and Asia.

Around the time of my confirmation, the African nation of Angola took center stage. Supported by money and weapons from the Soviet Union and thousands of Cuban troops, Marxists threatened to seize control of the country. In late November 1975, President Ford and Secretary Kissinger made a strong public push for official support of pro-Western forces in Angola. Congress responded by doing exactly the opposite. They passed an amendment effectively prohibiting the United States from providing assistance to Angola.[2] Ford was outraged.†

Without American assistance to fend off the Marxist rebels, Angola became a Communist dictatorship. More worrisome, the Soviet Union came

* As was tradition for nominees, I was introduced to the Senate Armed Services Committee by the two senators from my home state: Senator Charles Percy, a Republican from my old congressional district, and Senator Adlai Stevenson III, a Democrat. I had known Senator Percy for many years, and Senator Stevenson was the son of the man who had so sparked my interest in public service some two decades before.

† Ford was so angry that he uncharacteristically started questioning the personal fortitude of members of Congress. I cautioned Ford against that kind of rhetoric. I told him that was the kind of thing LBJ would say. "There is something about that chair," I said, pointing to the one behind his desk, "that makes presidents begin to act and talk in a way to make them seem tough." I urged Ford instead to approach his critics like Eisenhower did—in sorrow rather than in anger, and to rise above them rather than to sink to their level.[3]

away believing it had a free hand on the continent of Africa, and possibly elsewhere. Nations friendly to America began to wonder, as the South Vietnamese and their neighbors had, whether American assurances of aid and security were reliable. Indeed, within the next few years, South Vietnam, Cambodia, Laos, Nicaragua, Grenada, Ethiopia, and Afghanistan would come under Communist domination. "The general crisis of capitalism is continuing to deepen," Soviet leader Leonid Brezhnev proclaimed in 1976.[4]

A period of heightened concern over espionage preoccupied our allies in Europe. Intelligence officials saw Soviet influence behind desertions in the Dutch army. There were concerns about reports that Soviet sleeper cells in Western Europe were waiting to be activated by Communist powers in the Warsaw Pact.[5] "There is afoot an enterprise of demoralization of armies on a French and European level," the French Secretary of State for Defense warned.[6]

Soviet leaders were speaking soothingly, if deceptively, of their hope for reconciling with the West. Brezhnev, for example, had declared in the 1960s, "The Soviet Union is ready to develop Soviet-American relations in the interests of our peoples, in the interests of strengthening peace."[7] Important segments of the American public—including some in Congress, academics, and opinion leaders—believed him. Sympathy for the Soviets was a longstanding sentiment among the American elite.*

In the quest for a warmer relationship with the Soviets, a new word entered the popular lexicon: détente, a French word for relaxation or thaw. Though the word became identified with President Nixon and Henry Kissinger, the policy had been introduced earlier, during the mid-1960s, when the Johnson administration sought to reduce tensions with the Soviet Union as America escalated the conflict in Vietnam. Nixon decided it was worth exploring whether détente with the Soviets was a realistic policy. This led to a series of summit meetings and treaty signings. They were public relations coups for both sides, but the photo ops rarely, if ever, resulted in improved Soviet behavior.

Though President Ford was considerably more savvy about the Soviets

* Around the time I was born, a *New York Times* reporter, Walter Duranty, won a Pulitzer Prize for his coverage of the Stalin era. Some of his articles were headlined: "INDUSTRIAL SUCCESS EMBOLDENS SOVIET IN NEW WORLD POLICY," "RED ARMY IS HELD NO MENACE TO PEACE," and "STALINISM SOLVING MINORITIES PROBLEM." Duranty's reports from Moscow denied allegations that Stalin's regime had starved its citizens—"There is no famine or actual starvation, nor is there likely to be"—and offered uncritical reporting on Stalin's show trials of political dissidents ("You can't make an omelette without breaking eggs"). Though much of the reporting proved to be false—and precisely in line with what Stalin wanted the world to believe—Duranty's Pulitzer has never been revoked.[8]

than he was given credit for, he leaned toward continuing the Nixon strategy Kissinger advocated. Schlesinger, by contrast, was less enthusiastic. Like Schlesinger, I was not necessarily opposed to high-level meetings between Soviet and American leaders. However, I was concerned that projecting a relaxation of tensions between the United States and the Soviet Union could leave the wrong impression with the American people and our allies. It might feed the perception that we could minimize the Soviet Union's global ambitions, which in turn could lead the American people and the Congress to believe that the defense budget could be reduced—even while we knew that the Soviets were increasing theirs.

My confirmation hearing quickly became an airing of differences over détente within the Ford administration, the Congress, and the country. A number of conservative senators wanted to have me on record opposing Kissinger's policy. Others hoped that I'd signal a greater affinity than Schlesinger had for the Kissinger view. I told the members of the committee that I believed détente had become a code word for both the proponents and opponents of the policy.[9] The Soviets weren't incapable of reason, but we needed to understand that they looked at the world differently than Americans did. Because they were accountable to no one, the Soviet leaders had no obligation to tell the truth to their citizens, to us, or to the world. It seemed dangerous to me to try to predict their actions or their strategy based on thinking it would be a mirror image of how we in our free system might act if we were in their circumstances. By the end of the hearing, most senators were left with the accurate impression that my views were not dissimilar from Schlesinger's.

Only two senators voted against my confirmation—Jesse Helms, a conservative Republican from North Carolina, and Richard Stone, a Democrat of Florida.* I entered the Department of Defense in 1975 with the feeling that I had good support in the Congress. The department would need that support badly, because, in the aftermath of America's withdrawal from Saigon, the morale of our military was at a low point.

Though no doubt a large portion of the country remained proud of our military in the aftermath of Vietnam, some of the loudest voices equated members of our armed forces with mass murderers and war criminals. In ways that would have been unheard of during World War II and that would not be countenanced today, some Americans hurled obscenities or spit at

* Helms later said he voted against my confirmation to register his protest against President Ford for firing Schlesinger instead of Kissinger.

men and women in uniform. Even with America's withdrawal from Vietnam, protests and marches continued against the military.

At the forefront of some of the demonstrations were two Catholic priests, the Berrigan brothers.[10] In the 1960s they had picketed the homes of Secretary of Defense Robert McNamara and Secretary of State Dean Rusk. They led efforts to chain themselves to the doors of the Pentagon and to throw blood at the entrance.[11]

In 1976, Philip Berrigan brought a group of protesters to our house near the Washington-Maryland border. For days they demonstrated around the clock on the sidewalk, shouting, "Murderer!" We worried about our younger children, Marcy and Nick, going to and from the house through the aggressive demonstrators. At one point, Joyce opened our windows and played Beethoven's "Ode to Joy" at the highest volume to keep up her spirits and to try to drown out the protesters' chants. When they started digging a grave in our front yard, Joyce called the police. Three were arrested for destroying private property.[12]

At the trial, Joyce's only support in the courtroom was our eldest daughter, Valerie, who was home from Connecticut College.* Valerie was conflicted in a way I expect was typical of many young people at the time. She had been part of a student group at college that had invited Daniel Berrigan, Philip's brother, to speak about the war (although it had not been her choice to invite him). To her surprise, she had found his remarks not unreasonable. But though she walked across the courtroom and shook hands with Daniel at his brother's hearing, Valerie believed the protestors' destruction of our property had crossed a line well beyond lawful dissent. A public official ought not to have to serve as a doormat for every malcontent with a gripe against the government. Thanks to Joyce, the protesters were convicted.

In the grim atmosphere of the post-Vietnam period, the Cold War, and the relentless demonstrations, I tried to lift the spirits of the twenty-three thousand military and civilian personnel who worked in the Pentagon. I made an early effort to take in the daunting physical terrain of the building by walking through it. I found the experience depressing. To save energy, many of the sockets in the long hallways lacked bulbs. Much of the seventeen miles

*I called lawyers at the Pentagon and at the Department of Justice to ask for assistance. Contending that the demonstrators were protesting at a private residence, not on government property and that they had a permit to do so, both sets of lawyers unhelpfully said it was not a matter for the U.S. government—even though the only reason the protesters were at our house was because of my position as secretary of defense.

of dark corridors had bare walls, making the atmosphere dreary at best.[13] Though they had every reason to be proud of its history and their service, there was little to inspire the men and women of the department into feeling that they were working in a great and historic institution.

I decided to turn on the lights—literally, with new bulbs and bright hallways. I asked that paintings depicting scenes of U.S. military history be dusted off, brought up from basement storage rooms, and hung on the mostly naked walls. We dedicated corridors to commemorate historic moments, missions, and people. My former NATO colleague, Secretary General Joseph Luns, traveled from Belgium to participate in the official opening of a new corridor honoring the NATO alliance.

In an attempt to demystify the Department of Defense, I had the Pentagon opened up for public tours, much like the White House and Capitol building. The tours allowed people from across the world to get a sense of what was taking place there and what the men and women of the armed forces had achieved.

Unfortunately, as I assumed my duties, I did not enjoy the support of outgoing Secretary Schlesinger who, understandably, was hurt by his removal. Our relationship previously had been friendly.* But the inaccurate rumors that I had been involved in masterminding his firing were gathering steam and no doubt contributed to our uneasy relationship.

I also found myself in an uncomfortable relationship with the number two at the department, Deputy Secretary Bill Clements, who had hoped to be appointed secretary of defense himself. Clements had on occasion bypassed Schlesinger in his dealings with the White House and the State Department, even boasting to reporters that he had greater influence at the White House on defense policy than his boss.[14]

Heading into a presidential campaign, I could not make significant personnel changes—particularly with someone as politically well connected as Clements.† Fortunately, the Pentagon at the time had statutory positions for two deputy secretaries, and the second slot was vacant. I recommended former congressman and NATO ambassador Bob Ellsworth to fill it. His principal responsibility would be to deal with DoD's share of issues that resulted from the ongoing congressional investigations of the intelligence community.

* In fact, when I was still serving as ambassador to NATO, Schlesinger had asked me if I would be willing to be considered for the post of secretary of the Navy, which I had declined, not wanting to leave NATO then.

† Clements' wife was the Republican National Committeewoman from Texas.

While some Americans questioned everything the military did, there was another segment of the country that was inclined to do the opposite. There was a tendency to be so proud of the men and women in uniform that we thought of military leaders as infallible. Having served for close to twenty years in the regular Navy and the reserve, I had a healthy respect for the military and an appreciation for military advice.* But as secretary of defense my role was different. "The U.S. Secretary of Defense is not a super General or Admiral," I wrote in Rumsfeld's Rules. "His task is to exercise leadership and civilian control over the Department for the Commander-in-Chief and the country."

Control wasn't what a lot of people had in mind, however. I quickly faced what successive secretaries of defense have faced: a powerful set of forces known as the iron triangle—a network of entrenched relationships among the military and civilian bureaucracies in the Defense Department, the Congress, and the defense industry. With more or less permanent positions, those in the iron triangle knew that the secretary of defense and the department's political appointees of either party were temporary. They could delay and simply wait out policies they did not favor. One responsibility in serving as head of the Defense Department is to look as far down the road as possible, point the department in the direction it needs to go, and then, to the extent possible, build momentum that will be hard to reverse.

Among the most important issues that faced us at the Pentagon in the mid-1970s was the selection of a new main battle tank for the Army. At the time, the expectation was that the new tank would be used to defend against a Soviet invasion of Western Europe. As ambassador to NATO, I had worked to achieve a higher level of standardization of military equipment among our NATO allies as a way to save taxpayer dollars and improve logistical efficiencies. NATO standardization also helped to offset the Soviets' advantage of a free hand to standardize weapons systems among the Warsaw Pact countries. Early in my tour at the Pentagon, I issued a memorandum to the department that set forth the importance I placed in standardization, and that I expected planners working on the new main battle tank to follow that lead.[15]

The Pentagon, however, was going in a different direction. Late in the afternoon of July 20, 1976, Deputy Secretary Clements and Secretary of the Army

* When I became secretary of defense I was a captain in the Navy reserve. Since I concluded I would not be able to activate myself in the event the President called up the reserves, I transferred from the active reserve to the standby reserve.

Martin Hoffmann asked to see me, along with a number of other senior officials. They were in sharp disagreement over competing tank proposals from Chrysler and General Motors.

The Army leadership strongly recommended the General Motors tank design, which had a standard diesel engine and a 105 millimeter howitzer cannon, the weapon size the Army had used for years. The Army had no doubts its position would prevail. Its leaders seemed to assume my role in the decision would be to approve their recommendation. In fact, they were so certain of their position that they had already sent out a press release to members on the relevant congressional committees announcing that General Motors had won the contract. It was a classic example of the iron triangle in action.

However, Deputy Secretary Clements and Undersecretary of Defense for Research and Engineering Dr. Malcolm Currie had come to a different conclusion. They favored Chrysler's design: It could be filled with a larger, 120 millimeter cannon and it had, for the first time, a turbine engine instead of a diesel. They pointed out that our major NATO allies—including the British, French, and West Germans—had tanks with 120 millimeter cannons. They also argued that the turbine engine would be more agile and efficient than the diesel.

I listened to both sides in the assembled group in complete amazement. This was the biggest weapons decision for the Army in years. Yet they had arrived in my office with conflicting positions without giving me any advance warning or briefing to allow me the time to make an informed decision. Further, both sides insisted that I decide that complicated issue, which would have such long-term consequences for our country's fighting force, then and there. I was notably unhappy about being put in that impossible position. After listening to their arguments, I told them I was going to delay a decision for a period of weeks until I could make an informed judgment. I needed more than fifteen minutes to decide the fate of a major weapons system that would serve the country for many decades.

Army officials were stunned at my reaction. "This can't be delayed," they argued. "The press releases announcing the decision are already out. Everyone's going to be furious. Capitol Hill will explode." Of course, I knew they were right. Angry contractors would take their grievances to Congress and the press. Members of Congress on both sides of the issue would be outraged.

I replied: "I'd rather deal with an explosion on Capitol Hill and in the press than with the problems our country will have if we make the wrong decision." I told the Army to pull back its premature press releases. I added that I would release a statement of my own announcing that the decision would be delayed.*

Soon, various reports appeared in the press that civilians in the Office of the Secretary of Defense had defied the advice of the United States Army. That had the benefit of being true, except that it wasn't nameless "civilians," it was one civilian in particular.[16] This led to a ferocious pushback from elements in the Army, active and retired, as well as in the Congress and the media.[17]

As I studied the issues in the days ahead, I concluded that Clements and Currie had been right in opposing the Army's recommendation. Although some were still steaming, Hoffmann and some of his senior Army tank officials began to pull together to help move my decision forward. Not surprisingly, some on Capitol Hill were less than persuaded. A number of congressional districts and states stood to benefit from one or the other tank, and their representatives in Congress aggressively argued their positions. Threats of issuing congressional subpoenas for testimony were tossed around.[18] Accepting all the pyrotechnics, I tried to make sure the goal remained clear: to get the tank that would best serve our armed forces and our country well into the next century.

The XM-1 tank contract taught me that overruling a recommendation by the military services would almost certainly lead to upheaval and come at the cost of additional scar tissue. It also proved the rule that "if you do something, someone won't like it." But the decision to delay was the right one.

The contract with Chrysler was announced on November 12, 1976, fourteen weeks after that meeting in my office. The episode over the XM-1 tank, now known as the M-1 Abrams tank, was an important lesson in reexamining fundamental assumptions on which we based our decisions. Over time, the turbine engine proved to be successful. And the additional benefit of NATO standardization on the 120 millimeter cannon served to strengthen our collective security and to reduce costs. Some fifteen years later, the main battle tank I had authorized in 1976 was used in battle for the first time—except not in Western Europe as had been contemplated, but in Kuwait and Iraq during the 1991 Gulf War. The tank performed brilliantly.

* William "Gus" Pagonis, then a major in the Army office of legislative affairs, was given the unpleasant assignment of going up to Capitol Hill that night to retrieve what turned out to be the Army's incorrect press release. Pagonis went on to be a three-star general who served years later during the Gulf War and saw firsthand the M-1 tanks in action.

CHAPTER 16

Hold the SALT: Tension over Détente

By 1976, the national security team that President Ford had inherited and then reassembled proved to be a capable group. It included several figures who would leave their imprint on American foreign and defense policies for decades: Secretary of State Kissinger, National Security Adviser Brent Scowcroft, CIA Director George H. W. Bush, and White House Chief of Staff Dick Cheney.

While Kissinger emerged from the Ford cabinet shake-up unenthusiastic about losing his second hat as national security adviser, he characteristically found humor in his situation. While briefing congressional Republican leaders on foreign aid around that time, he joked, "I've been so busy figuring out what jobs I have left that I haven't had time to study this."[1] In truth, President Ford's surprise moves flummoxed the wily Kissinger—a man not easily flummoxed. So entrenched was his well-deserved reputation as a master strategist who could predict the actions of leaders like moves on a chessboard, that some people even assumed he had to be the one behind the Halloween massacre, to eliminate me as an obstacle in the White House.[2] Surely, some reporters contended, Ford's moves had to have been part of some grand Kissinger plan. And if it was not Kissinger's plan, then it must have been Rumsfeld's. Once again, the conspiracy theorists prevailed in the press, and the conventional wisdom didn't give Ford the credit he deserved.

Privately, Kissinger thought it was "scary" to, as he put it, "monkey around with the whole NSC machinery when things are going reasonably well."[3] Kissinger, who had worked for Vice President Rockefeller and knew him to be his unfailingly strong ally in the Ford White House, at first believed Rockefeller's assertions that I was behind his removal from the NSC post.

"The guy that cut me up inside this building isn't going to cut me up any less in Defense," Kissinger told Treasury Secretary Bill Simon immediately after the shake-up.[4] If in fact Kissinger was angry, it did not last. Indeed, one of Ford's stated reasons for moving me to the Department of Defense was that Kissinger and I were able to work together.

My relationship with Kissinger changed when I moved to the Pentagon. As secretary of defense, I was now a statutory member of the NSC. Since the days he had elbowed out Bill Rogers as secretary of state in the Nixon administration, Kissinger had become accustomed to making national security decisions with the President pretty much alone. As Kissinger knew well, my relationship with Ford went back to our days in Congress. I also wasn't hesitant to express my views. Perhaps because Kissinger wasn't either, the presumption, particularly in the press, was that we would be in constant conflict.

Though differences did exist, they were not many and they were on substance. One point of tension was unavoidable. Kissinger and I led institutions that were different in mission and makeup: One focused on sustained diplomatic engagement; the other focused on preparing for, deterring, and, when necessary, engaging in military conflict. Given the different perspectives, I thought it particularly important that Kissinger and I base our dealings on a common understanding of the facts and an open flow of information. This led to an early test of our relationship. As a former ambassador and State Department official, I knew that the distribution of sensitive cables sent to Washington from overseas posts would often be narrowly restricted by the Department of State, despite the fact that some needed to be read by a wider group of senior national security officials. I asked my staff to prepare a chart that tracked the flow of the restricted-distribution cables from the State Department to the Pentagon.[5] The tracking chart made clear that the sensitive cable traffic to DoD had decreased precipitously.

With the chart in hand, I met with Kissinger and not too subtly suggested that he open the flow of information to the Pentagon. He knew well that information was power. Kissinger seemed, or more likely acted, surprised by the statistics and vowed to improve the situation. Still, there never was the free exchange of information that I sought. It was a sign that even our good personal relationship had its limits.

I knew I had to do all I could to persuade Congress and the public that the United States had to bolster its military capabilities if we were to deter the Soviets in the years ahead. We needed to ensure peace not only by being strong, but by being perceived as strong by those who would do harm to our country and our allies. I was all for fiscal responsibility, but in this case I was certain that an increase in the U.S. defense budget had to be the administration's highest priority. This effort was controversial in some circles—even within the White House and Pentagon.[6] As I campaigned to increase defense investment, there was a consensus within the Democratic-controlled Congress that the proposed defense budget would be cut by $5 billion to $6 billion, or about 5 or 6 percent.[7]

During my first weeks at the Pentagon, I met with Andy Marshall, the Defense Department's Director of Net Assessment, the Pentagon's internal think tank, which examined the relative strengths of the United States and the Soviet Union.* Marshall demonstrated that the Soviet Union had been gaining ground relative to the United States. America had been slipping toward a position of rough equivalence. The projections of future trend lines did not bode well for the United States.

I compiled the data into a booklet called *Defense Perspectives* that provided an easy to understand set of statistics, charts, and graphs—numbers of personnel, tanks, helicopters, submarines, ships, and the like. The data told an important story: While the United States and the USSR were still roughly equivalent in their respective capabilities, the trend lines were clearly adverse to America, and if our respective levels of investment were to continue, we would drop below the band of rough equivalence.[9]

In addition to the *Defense Perspectives* booklet, I organized briefings, which I led along with John Hughes, a respected, long-serving intelligence officer at the Defense Intelligence Agency. Hughes had briefed President

* Marshall's assessment pointed out areas where the United States retained advantages over the Soviet Union: for example, in the quality of its missiles and in the potential for significant improvements in missile capability. The Soviets, however, were poised to move ahead in the areas of air defenses and civil defense preparedness. They had constructed elaborate underground systems beneath large housing projects, where a significant fraction of their urban industrial population could find shelter in the event of a nuclear conflict. Even if large numbers of their citizens were killed in a nuclear conflict, the Soviets were making the investments necessary to survive as a country. Communist leaders did not reach the top posts in the Soviet Union by worrying about the lives of a few hundred thousand of their people.[8]

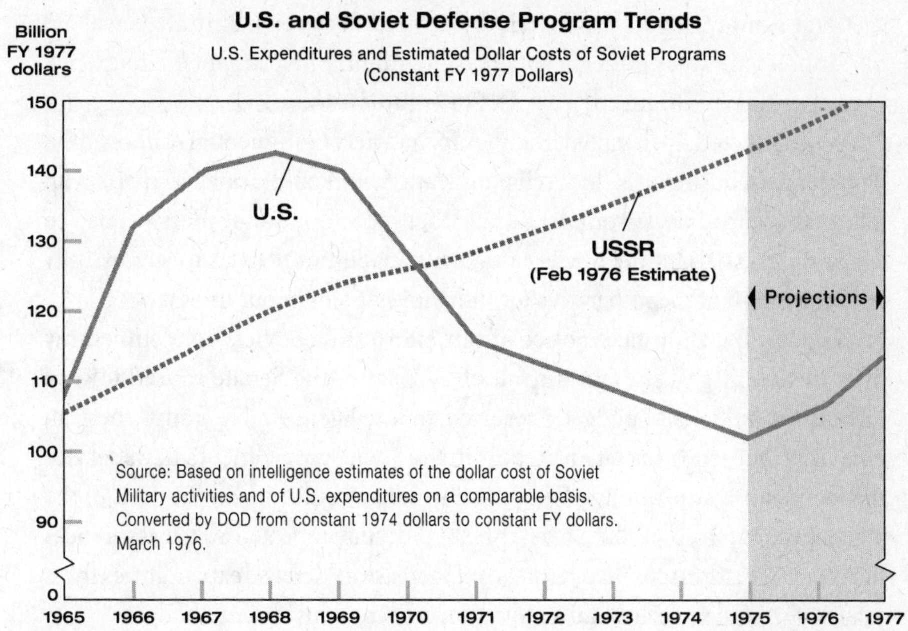

Kennedy and his national security team during the Cuban Missile Crisis.* He prepared classified overhead photography from U.S. satellites and other sources that showed in vivid, powerful pictures the Soviet military buildup. The Hughes presentations—at varying degrees of classification, depending on the audience—gave an impressive visual texture to the data we had assembled.[10]

Beginning in early 1976, I began to host early evening briefings for small groups of senators and congressmen in the Roosevelt Room of the White House, directly across from the Oval Office. We called them "smokers" back in those days, since many of us still smoked cigars or pipes. Our invitations to the White House for a private, classified briefing were well received. Attendance was excellent. President Ford and other senior national security officials would drop by, giving the briefings added weight and a sense of unanimity within the administration.[11]

* The Hughes briefing on Cuba, on February 6, 1963, had been carried on national television. Hughes' use of aerial photographs taken from U-2 spy planes was considered revolutionary at the time. By the time Hughes was working with me, the technology had developed to the point that we had satellite images as well. With new high-resolution cameras, we had to be cautious. They made an overwhelming case, but making them public would have revealed sensitive information about our surveillance capabilities to the Soviets.

After one of the briefings, Congressman Les Aspin of Wisconsin, a Democrat and senior member of the House Armed Services Committee, walked out impressed. An opponent of increasing military investment, he muttered, "I can see I'll have to invent a new set of arguments."[12]

We conducted unclassified briefings for a variety of influential Americans—labor leaders, business leaders, religious leaders, and public policy experts with national security backgrounds. I knew that more opinion leaders needed to know the facts about the Soviets' military capabilities if I was to successfully convince them of the imperative for more investment in our military.*

Moscow began to take notice of our efforts. The Soviets condemned my briefings as "disgraceful." In the fall of 1976, after the Senate moved toward increasing the defense budget, I received an intelligence cable from American officials in Moscow that cited a report in the Soviet government's news service that condemned me "for justifying the US military build-up on the basis of the 'hackneyed myth about the 'Soviet threat' . . . despite repeated Soviet assurances that the USSR threatens no one, does not increase its defense expenditures from year to year and seeks instead a reduction of all nations' defense budgets."[13]

The record is now clear that the Soviets lied about their defense budget. The Soviet government was attempting to achieve strategic military superiority over the United States at the expense of the nonmilitary sectors of its economy. The Soviets were successful in this approach for a period of time, but they now were rattled by having their buildup revealed to the world. The Soviets' strong and disingenuous reaction was powerful evidence to me that we were on the right track.

I could feel we were gaining traction. The Ford administration proposed an increase in the defense budget for fiscal year 1977, and Congress appeared to be moving in our direction. While the increase was modest, it was a marked change from the earlier series of decreases, and it was the first increase in real terms in the U.S. defense budget in almost a decade.[14] It was a reassuring achievement, especially for an administration that was under fire from all sides in an election year, and with the Congress controlled by the opposition party. The powerful facts we had marshaled and presented proved to be persuasive. Had President Ford been reelected, I have no doubt that our defense buildup would have continued. As it happened, however, after four

*I also had the briefing presented to our NATO allies. At my request, the NATO Secretary General appointed a Danish intelligence officer to develop a NATO-classified version of my briefing and then take it to all of the NATO capitals. My goal was to encourage our allies to increase their own defense budgets, which were declining. Our success in getting the Europeans to increase their defense expenditures was modest, but we did slow their decreases.

years of the Carter administration's inattention, it was left to Ronald Reagan to increase defense investments appreciably.

My situation as a new secretary at the Department of Defense was made more complicated because of the approaching presidential primary and general election campaign. I felt that a secretary of defense should not involve himself in domestic politics. That was easier said than done in a gripping and contentious primary challenge that hinged on national security issues.

Ronald Reagan declared his candidacy against the President two days after I was confirmed. Having become acquainted with California Governor Reagan when I was director of the Office of Economic Opportunity, I knew his campaign was not to be dismissed lightly. He was an effective executive, had an impressive talent for communication, an able staff led by Ed Meese and Judge Bill Clark, and was developing a growing list of influential supporters around the country.

At first, Reagan avoided direct attacks on Ford, focusing instead on the administration's policies and, more specifically, on Henry Kissinger.[15] Reagan took direct aim at the administration's foreign policy by forcefully redefining "détente" as an American concession to, and accommodation of, the expansionist Soviet Union. As Reagan mounted his offensive, the term "détente" was becoming poisonous. To conservative critics the term encapsulated American fecklessness and a sense that America was a declining power in the world.

Well into the primary campaign, the President stubbornly kept using the term even when he knew it was hurting him politically. Ford eventually realized that his spirited defense of détente was not worth the damage it was causing his election chances. "[L]et me say very specifically that we are going to forget the use of the word détente," he said. "The word is inconsequential. What happens in the negotiations between the United States and the Soviet Union, what happens in the negotiations between the People's Republic of China and the United States—those are the things that are of consequence."[16]

The primary election season did not start out well for Governor Reagan. Written off by the Eastern establishment and short on funds, Reagan lost most of the early primaries. The Californian seemed to be headed for his last stand in the March 1976 North Carolina primary. Reagan seized on what initially had seemed a relatively obscure issue: the negotiations to turn over the Panama Canal to the Panamanian government. Reagan said, "[W]e bought it, we paid for it, it's ours, and . . . we are going to keep it!"[17] The line drew loud applause, perhaps because it represented a reassertion of American will that many felt had gone missing since the fall of Saigon. The North Carolina results—Reagan beat the sitting president of his own party by six points—startled the political pundits and the Ford campaign team. And it soon put me in an awkward position.

Building on his success, the California governor fashioned yet another issue that resonated with many Americans who felt the United States was slipping into a position of weakness. In the face of the Soviet threat, Reagan said, "The evidence mounts that we are Number Two in a world where it's dangerous, if not fatal, to be second best."[18] What Reagan could not have known was that he had zeroed in on the issue at the center of an ongoing internal debate Kissinger and I had been having in front of Ford.

Six days after Reagan's victory in North Carolina, I met with the President and Kissinger in the Oval Office to discuss this very issue. Kissinger disagreed with any public admission of the unpleasant facts I was marshaling; namely, that after nearly three decades in the Cold War, the U.S. military capability trend lines relative to the capabilities of the Soviet Union were adverse to us, and the Soviets' overall capability was now roughly equivalent to ours. Absent a clear and sustained shift in our defense investment, the trend lines, favorable to the Soviets, would put them in a position of superiority in the years ahead.

"The impression that we are slipping is creating a bad impression around the world," Kissinger avowed. I also wondered at the time if he took Reagan's criticism personally, since he had presided over most national security issues for the past seven years.[19]

"But it's true," I rebutted.

"Then we have to define our goals," Henry said. "It is inevitable that our margin since '60 has slipped. Are we trying to maintain the same margin as we had in 1960 or to maintain adequate forces?"

"We have been slipping since the '60s from superiority to equivalence," I countered. "And if we don't stop, we'll be behind."

I believed Reagan's incendiary claim that America was the "number two" power was not yet technically correct, but it was clear to me that absent increases in our overall defense investment, his assertion would eventually become true.

Kissinger's immediate goals and mine were in conflict here. Kissinger wanted the perception of American superiority to aid his negotiating positions and to reassure our allies, and for the strong diplomatic position it would provide as he worked on arms agreements with the Soviets. In contrast,

I needed us to acknowledge the truth of the U.S. decline in our relative capability so that the American people and Congress would support the increases in defense investments necessary to reverse the adverse trends.

President Ford listened intently to our back-and-forth discussion. This was the type of spirited, open exchange that was healthy and needed, and which had been missing on foreign and defense policies in the past.

"I don't think [I] should say we are slipping," Ford finally decided. "I can say we need to redouble our efforts. I don't want to say we are getting behind. I'll say we have a challenge, we have rough equivalence and we've got to keep up." The President also decided to criticize the Democratic Congress for its reductions in defense spending.

"I think the posture to take is that Reagan doesn't know what he's talking about and he's irresponsible," Kissinger advised.[20]

Even though Kissinger was bothered by the California governor's unrelenting attacks, I thought Reagan was making a critically important point. The only thing irresponsible would be to dismiss it.

Kissinger and I also found ourselves in different corners on his negotiations with the Soviets over a second Strategic Arms Limitation Treaty (SALT II).* The debates over the arms-control agreement sometimes made me feel, as I later described it, "like the skunk at the garden party."[21] Ford hoped to sign a second treaty before the end of his term and, I suspected, before the presidential election in November.

I was concerned that the Soviet Union had not proven to be true to its word in previous negotiations. The Soviets were not forthcoming about the level of their defense expenditures. They also appeared to have been violating at least the spirit of the first SALT by concealing missile silos and other military infrastructure. All of this was to say nothing of their aggressive activities on several continents that threatened international peace and security and seemed designed to undermine American interests.

I was certainly comfortable delaying a new treaty if a satisfactory resolution to my concerns could not be reached. This of course had the effect of making me the administration's hawk, and positioning me as out of step with Kissinger and his allies, Rockefeller and Scowcroft. My reluctance to sign on

* The first SALT, signed in 1972, included a ban on antiballistic missile systems that could bring down an enemy's nuclear ballistic missiles after they were launched. To begin development of a missile defense system, President George W. Bush and I led the effort to repeal the Anti-Ballistic Missile Treaty in 2001.

to Kissinger's positions in obtaining an agreement without the Department of Defense's support proved frustrating for him. Kissinger was used to the Pentagon's opposition to his proposals, but they had not been much of a problem for him in the past given the tepid relationship between Ford and Schlesinger. He was unhappy that I was putting doubts into the President's mind, and he accused me of using delaying tactics to scuttle his negotiations with the Soviets. "Rumsfeld was skillful at deflecting every controversial issue into some bureaucratic bog or other," Kissinger noted later, giving more weight to what he considered my bureaucratic skills than the substantive merit of my arguments.[22] He thought that was a criticism of me. I felt it was a compliment when it came to the risk of an arms control agreement that, in my view, was not in our country's best interest.

The discussions within the administration over SALT were even more difficult for me in light of my relationship with Rockefeller. At one meeting in mid-February 1976, we listened to a long presentation by Kissinger on the status of the SALT negotiations, which Rockefeller responded to by banging the table in approval.

When I laid out the Department of Defense's position, Rockefeller kept interrupting me. He had a well-developed practice of trying to throw people off with bullying tactics. Now that he was a lame-duck vice president, he was even more caustic. A couple of times, as I was speaking, he snapped, "Don, what's your point?"

Exasperated, I finally said, "Mr. Vice President, I've been listening for one hour and fifteen minutes, and I am proceeding in my own way to lay out my points." And I continued to do so. Rockefeller's behavior laid bare the tensions over the hoped-for deal with the Soviets favored by the liberal wing of the party, for which Rockefeller was the poster boy.

A key, if controversial, issue in the debates over SALT was the fate of America's cruise missiles.* Cruise missiles varied in ranges, could be armed with nuclear or conventional warheads, and could be launched from land, sea, or air. Their unusual flexibility made them particularly attractive as a weapons system. It also made them a serious complicating factor in negotiations to limit the size of our nuclear arsenal.

* Cruise missiles did not have a natural constituency even in the U.S. military, which made them susceptible to being bargained away in arms negotiations. One reason for this was that no one military service clearly benefited from expenditures for them, and the funds for them would have to come from one of the service's budgets. As a result, no military service was ready to argue for the program at the expense of their other budget priorities. That left me as one of the few advocates for cruise missiles at the time within the Pentagon.

America had a measurable lead in cruise missile technology. The Soviets would have to expend large amounts of their resources to keep up with us, so the Soviets wanted us to promise to curtail our cruise missile development in a SALT II treaty. An agreement could have been achieved if Ford had been willing to acquiesce to these demands. Kissinger and Rockefeller, and others eager to sign a treaty with the Soviets, were ready to agree to that. I was uncomfortable agreeing to limit an advantage, the exact nature of which, at that time, we could not predict.[23]

In one meeting Kissinger tried to blame the Joint Chiefs for intransigence on the cruise missile issue. They were not the impediment, I told him—I was.[24] I urged the President to delay any treaty that required restricting our cruise missile technologies as part of the deal. The Defense Department needed more time to assess the merits of the treaty's specific provisions before agreeing to them.

That Kissinger and I had differing views on the arms treaty with the Soviets posed a problem for Ford. The President needed support from the conservative wing of his party and a few hawks in the Democratic Party, like Senator Henry "Scoop" Jackson of Washington state, to get a treaty ratified in the Senate. If the Joint Chiefs testified against the treaty or the Secretary of Defense resigned because he could not support it, its prospects for ratification would be dim.

Ford made clear to me that he was unhappy with our position in the Defense Department. Undeterred, Ford approached the Soviets with a proposal to continue negotiations while pushing the final status of cruise missiles for a separate discussion at a later date. Brezhnev rejected Ford's suggestion outright, calling it a "step backward." The Soviet leader wrote in March 1976 that "someone is deliberately trying to put roadblocks on the way to reaching an agreement."[25] I had little doubt who the Soviet leader meant by "someone." The U.S.-initiated talks collapsed.

American public opinion leaned heavily in favor of arms reductions. Those who didn't support agreements with the Soviets tended to be characterized in the press as advocates of confrontation with the Communist empire. Paradoxically, I thought Soviet aggression and confrontation could become more likely if we passed a SALT II treaty that conceded too much. The Soviets might be emboldened by our weakness.

In 1979, two years after he had left office, Gerald Ford came to visit me in Chicago. I drove to the airport to pick him up. He was bringing Joyce and me one of the golden retriever puppies from his dog, Misty. He also had just completed his memoir, *A Time to Heal.* Sitting in the backseat of the car on the way to my house, Ford handed me an autographed copy of his book.

Placing his other hand on my arm, he said gently, "Don, you are not going to like everything in this."

I asked why.

"Because I placed responsibility for our failure to get a SALT agreement on you and Brezhnev," he replied.

I smiled. "Well, Mr. President," I said, "I can live with that."

CHAPTER 17

The 1976 Defeat

The year 1976 saw not only the two hundredth anniversary of the Declaration of Independence but also a surprisingly close presidential election. The attraction of a virtually unknown candidate for the Democratic nomination for president, Jimmy Carter, resonated with many voters in a way that it might not have in any other year. His simple promise, "I'll never lie to you," appealed to a country still furious over Watergate and Vietnam.

Gerald Ford, despite being burdened by the characterization of his tenure as the Nixon-Ford presidency, had become a solid, decisive executive. He was no longer the surprised occupant of a shattered, discredited presidency that he had to rebuild. Now it was his office, and he wanted to keep it.

Reagan's run for the Republican nomination continued to gain traction. He was winning a number of states and putting Ford on the defensive. At one point, the President's close advisers considered the possibility that President Ford might lose the Michigan primary. It was never discussed publicly, of course, but if Ford were rejected by Republican voters in his home state, the embarrassment could leave the President little choice but to consider dropping out of the race. Fortunately Ford won the Michigan primary convincingly.

Ford and Reagan then engaged in a series of primary duels, each in search of the magic number of delegates needed to clinch the nomination. By the time of the Republican National Convention in Kansas City, where one of the two would be nominated, it looked like Ford would win, and the process of selecting a replacement for Rockefeller began.*

For the third time in three years, I found myself being discussed for the vice presidential nomination. Ford again asked me to fill out the extensive paperwork, including the dozens of pages of disclosure forms required for background and financial checks. I knew well that I made no more sense as a running mate for Ford than I had the last time he'd considered me.

Some weeks before the Republican convention, my mother sent me a newspaper article that indicated that the medical therapy of choice for tonsillitis in the 1930s was radiation treatment, which could lead to cancerous thyroid tumors. She told me that I had been radiated for tonsillitis when I was a child. After I read the article, I showed it to the White House doctor, who examined me and said he saw no problem. Several weeks later, as I was shaving, I noticed a bulge in my throat. Knowing that it could be a malignant tumor, I decided to schedule surgery before the Republican National Convention was to begin on August 16, 1976, further eliminating me from serious vice presidential contention.

I was at Bethesda Naval Hospital recovering from the surgery when Dick Cheney called me from Air Force One. He and the President were on their way to the Kansas City convention. Because of the operation, I wasn't able to talk yet, so Joyce took the call. Dick asked how I was doing, and then passed along a message from the President.

"Tell Don that we're going to win the nomination and keep him in his job," Cheney said. It was a graceful way to tell Joyce and me what I already believed. I was not going to be Ford's vice presidential choice. His selection turned out to be a friend from my days in Congress, Bob Dole of Kansas.

At the convention, President Ford defeated Governor Reagan on the first ballot by 117 votes. A narrow victory for a sitting president, but it was preferable to the alternative.

With the economy in recession, the pardon of Nixon still a sore point, and a long, heated primary campaign just over, Ford started the fall campaign behind the Democratic candidate, Georgia's governor, Jimmy Carter, by thirty points in the polls. This was just two years after many of the most prominent political reporters and experts in Washington had

* As he had in August 1974, President Ford asked me and many others for a list of people to consider for vice president. I suggested George Shultz, Mel Laird, John Connally, Howard Baker, Bill Brock, Jim Buckley, George H. W. Bush, and Bill Scranton.[1]

proclaimed the then likely Ford-Rockefeller ticket as virtually unbeatable.[2] But Ford wasn't giving up. With the assistance of Cheney, a Texas politico named Jim Baker, and the excellent campaign team they put together, Ford battled his way back into contention.

On September 23, 1976, in Philadelphia, Ford and Carter met for their first presidential campaign debate. Most voters thought Ford won that encounter. He seemed knowledgeable and likable, while Carter appeared vague on the issues.[3]

It was on foreign policy that the second debate, and perhaps the election, turned. During the encounter, reporter Max Frankel began to ask Ford a question, "Mr. President, I'd like to explore a little more deeply our relationship with the Russians. . . . We've virtually signed, in Helsinki, an agreement that the Russians have dominance in Eastern Europe . . ."

"There is no Soviet domination of Eastern Europe and there never will be under a Ford administration," the President declared.

Frankel was visibly startled. "I'm sorry, could I just follow—did I understand you to say, sir, that the Russians are not using Eastern Europe as their own sphere of influence in occupying most of the countries there and making sure with their troops that it's a Communist zone?"

Ford would not back down. "I don't believe, Mr. Frankel, that the Yugoslavians consider themselves dominated by the Soviet Union," he said. "I don't believe that the Romanians consider themselves dominated by the Soviet Union. I don't believe that the Poles consider themselves dominated by the Soviet Union."[4]

I understood what Ford was thinking. Every year during the Cold War, members of Congress would commemorate Captive Nations Week. This was an opportunity to express America's solidarity with those who lived in nations trapped behind the Iron Curtain. Ford, along with other congressmen representing districts with large numbers of Eastern European immigrants and their families, would recognize Captive Nations Week by describing the nations in the Eastern Bloc as being captive to the Soviet Union, and by adding that we refused to concede that those nations would be permanently subjugated. "Permanently" was the operative word Ford had left out in his response to Frankel in the debate. Without the context of Captive Nation's Week, it came across as if the President was naïve about foreign policy, and that he did not know or would not admit that the Soviet Union was subjugating the Eastern Europeans, of which he was of course well aware.

I immediately knew it was a disaster. I called Cheney and urged him to get the President to correct himself fast. Apparently Cheney and Scowcroft had already tried repeatedly but failed. The next day, Ford agreed to issue a clarification, but the damage had been done.

Two weeks later a Pentagon public relations fiasco brought the Department of Defense to the center stage of the campaign, if only briefly. I had formed a close working relationship with the chairman of the Joint Chiefs, General George Scratchley Brown, who had a distinguished military career.* But unlike many military officers who reach high posts in the Pentagon, Brown had little patience with bureaucratic procedures and little political polish. He tended to say what he thought, including things that, on reflection, might have been better left unsaid.

In April 1976, Brown had what he assumed was a private conversation with a cartoonist. He mused that the Shah of Iran, a U.S. partner, had an insatiable appetite for weapons because he had "visions of the Persian Empire." He said that the military capabilities of Great Britain were "pathetic," with nothing more than "generals and admirals and bands." Brown gave a few other choice opinions, including some offensive comments about U.S. support for Israel. Many months later, a few weeks before the presidential election, his remarks made their way to the press. I winced when I read them.[5]

Jimmy Carter demanded that Brown be reprimanded. Ford called me and said we needed to decide quickly on whether to keep Brown or fire him, making it clear he leaned to the latter.[6]

"Let me try to handle it," I said. "Give me one more news cycle, and I will see if I can put this behind us." I called in Brown and told him that the President and I both believed the things he said had been inappropriate, but that Ford had given me a brief opportunity to see if I could help the situation.

I proposed that we go down to the Pentagon press room and give a brief statement, making clear that we understood the comments were regrettable. Brown agreed and we headed to the lion's den.

I told the Pentagon press corps that General Brown's comments were inappropriate, and that "the absence of a reprimand should not be taken as an endorsement of obviously inelegant phraseology."[7]

Brown stepped forward after a reporter asked, "Is there any suspicion at

* His most notable combat experience occurred during World War II when, in August 1943, as part of the 93rd Bombardment Group, Brown took part in a famous bombing raid against the Ploesti oil refineries in Romania, which were providing oil to Nazi Germany. Eleven planes in his bombardment group, including the lead plane, were shot down during that dangerous mission. Brown was credited with helping to bring back the surviving aircraft safely.

all in your mind that there may be something political about the timing in all this? What do you think?" The reporter posed this question since Brown's comments had not appeared in the press until six months after he said them, right before the presidential election.

"I'm not in a position to judge," Brown replied. "I do think it's a little strange . . ." I had no idea what Brown was about to say next, but I had a sinking feeling it wouldn't do him any good. So I stepped up next to him, put my arm around him, and with a big smile I said, "He's not in a position to judge, he's exactly right, I agree with him completely."[8]

General Brown and the assembled reporters broke out in laughter. And with that, I ended our press conference, and the General and I made our escape. The story died, George Brown remained as chairman of the Joint Chiefs of Staff for the remainder of his full term, and a fine officer's career was not tarnished by an early dismissal or presidential reprimand.

On the night before the 1976 presidential election, Joyce and I attended a dinner at the home of the legendary publisher of the *Washington Post*, Kay Graham. Another guest at the dinner was the Democratic National Committee and Carter campaign chairman, Bob Strauss. As the evening drew to a close, the Strausses and the Rumsfelds were leaving the dinner at the same time.

"You know, Don," Bob said, "the only thing worse than losing tomorrow would be to have it go on one more day."

I knew what he meant. The election contest—from the beginning of the Reagan challenge to the general election fight against Carter—seemed to have gone on forever.

It was not until the early hours of the morning after the election that NBC finally declared Governor Jimmy Carter the winner. The closeness of the result—two percentage points in the popular vote—made Ford's loss even more painful. After campaigning tirelessly, the President's voice gave out on election night. As a result, Betty Ford had to read his telegram of congratulations to President-elect Carter, with the Ford family gathered around them.[9]

I felt terrible about the election loss—for a friend and a fine leader. I had no doubt that Ford would have proven to be a superb president in the next four years if he'd been elected. His margin of defeat was so narrow that almost anything might have changed the outcome. I couldn't help but wonder what might have been if he had made a fresh start when he first came in with visible high-level personnel changes that would have established a distinctive Ford presidency in the public's mind, or if Ford had selected someone other than Rockefeller as vice president, or if the Nixon pardon had been handled differently. Or what if he had achieved a politically expedient SALT agreement with the Soviets? Or if he had avoided the mistake about Soviet domination of Eastern Europe in the debate? But that was not how Gerald Ford thought. He looked forward, not back.

On November 5, 1976, three days after the election, Ford held a cabinet meeting. "I don't want any eulogies," he said. "We had a good team, and I was proud of you." Ford said we had an obligation to the American people to carry on the same efforts until his last day in office, on January 20, 1977. After about thirty minutes, the meeting ended with a round of warm applause.[10]

Gerald Ford could be proud of his tenure as president, brief though it was, for many reasons. He was an honest, open, hardworking statesman who had the qualities the nation desperately needed to exorcise the ghosts of Watergate and Vietnam. He was a steady commander in chief during the Cold War who pushed for greater defense investment. The presidency as an institution was in jeopardy after Nixon's resignation, and Ford had righted the foundering ship of state. Backlash over the Watergate scandal might have resulted in hasty, unwise restrictions on executive powers that could have had lasting adverse repercussions for our country, but President Ford prevented that from happening. He preserved the integrity of the office and handed it intact to his successor.

As saddened as I was over Ford's loss, I was more troubled by the man who would replace him. Jimmy Carter, a one-term governor from Georgia, would become president of the United States. On November 22, 1976, President-elect Carter asked to meet with me at Blair House, across Pennsylvania Avenue from the White House, to brief him and his national security team on defense matters.[11] Although I believed Carter was an intelligent man, and one who cared about the country, I worried that he seemed not well prepared for the presidency.

At our meeting, the Georgia governor was pleasant, and I saw a few flashes of his famous grin. He opened our meeting with a list of items he wanted to discuss, including the budget, decisions pending at the Defense Department, and an assessment of the military balance and trends.[12] Throughout the meeting Carter relied on notations on a piece of paper in front of him. There was little extemporaneous give-and-take.

At one point Carter asked a question about how he would know a ship was moved once he ordered it. It struck me as unusual in that this was a man who had graduated from the Naval Academy. I explained the process of issuing an order to the chairman of the Joint Chiefs who would then pass it down through the relevant commands and then down to captain of the ship. He asked again, "But how can you be sure it actually has moved?" I told him the first time it doesn't move, you fire those responsible. It was a strange exchange, suggesting a president focused more on details than strategy. It also seemed to signal someone with reservations about the military.

After the meeting, I told my staff that the President-elect was going into the toughest job in the world, and even though it might be tempting, I did not want them discussing anything about our meeting for a period of time. I thought Carter deserved a fair shot at success in his new responsibilities.

On December 10, 1976, I had a second meeting with the President-elect. He asked to come to the Pentagon to meet with the Joint Chiefs of Staff. He brought with him Senator Walter Mondale, the vice president–elect.

We provided Carter and his designated national security team with a top-secret briefing on Soviet capabilities. Our briefing had given many people, including a number of Democrats, considerable pause about the Soviet Union and its intentions. But if the briefing had a similar effect on Carter, he hid it well. After the session was over, the President-elect asked that I stay behind for a few minutes, along with Chairman Brown and the members of the Joint Chiefs.

When the room was cleared, Carter told us with a sense of excitement that he had received an "unprecedented" communication from the Soviets about their interest in an arms-control agreement. What led Carter to consider the contents unprecedented he did not say. Carter then informed us that he wanted negotiation rather than confrontation with the Soviet Union. The President-elect asked the members of the chiefs to give him a detailed appraisal of the flexibility he would have in negotiations with Brezhnev.[13] While I thought it appropriate that he was so straightforward with the chiefs about his intentions, focusing on how much the United States could concede to the Soviets struck me as worrisome, especially in light of the briefing he had just received.

My impression of Carter in action was of a new president determined to change much of what had been done in the Nixon and Ford years. It seemed his approach would be that faucets on were to be turned off, and vice versa. It was not an uncommon start to a new administration but it could be costly for the country if carried to an extreme. An example of this tendency was Carter's prompt canceling of the B-1 bomber program, the construction of which I authorized as one of my final acts as secretary of defense. This supersonic, swept-wing replacement for the aging, workhorse B-52 bomber carried a high price tag, but its flexibility and its capability to serve our country's needs for many decades convinced me it was a sound investment.*

Soon after Carter's inauguration, Joyce and I went with Dick and Lynne Cheney on a brief vacation on the island of Eleuthera in the Caribbean. After the hectic years following our meeting at Dulles airport in August 1974, we were starting to unwind. It was a pleasant transition for us all. We played tennis, boated, and spent time in the sun talking about life. Cheney grilled steaks and made chili.

After a long and tumultuous journey, we were out of government and unemployed. Our thoughts turned to the future. Though President Ford urged me to stay involved in politics, I was ready to move into the business world.[15] Dick was thinking about a number of possibilities, including elective office. The only thing I knew for sure was that Joyce and I were heading home to Illinois.

* Carter's successor, Ronald Reagan, wisely decided to reinstate the B-1, and it has remained a valuable weapon system for our country into the twenty-first century.[14]

PART VII

Back to Reality

"Washington, D.C. is sixty square miles surrounded by reality."

—As quoted in Rumsfeld's Rules

Riyadh, Saudi Arabia

NOVEMBER 18, 1983

Saudi Arabia's King Fahd was one of the forty-five sons of Ibn Saud, modern Saudi Arabia's founder. Fahd had ascended to the throne only a year earlier. One of the wealthiest men in the world, he received me amid plush furnishings, floors of marble, and walls etched in gold.

I had been the CEO of G. D. Searle & Co., a pharmaceutical company, for nearly five years when I took a leave of absence to serve as President Reagan's Middle East envoy. In that capacity I went on a mission to the Kingdom of Saudi Arabia, where I sought the ruling family's assistance on the crisis in Lebanon.

As we began our official talks, the Saudi king's servants brought tea out to us in the ornate formal throne room. I had quickly learned on my trips to the region that it was wise to ration my tea intake during these long meetings, and after a sip, I held my small cup aside.

After a few moments I looked up to find King Fahd staring at me with a puzzled look. He had noticed I wasn't drinking my tea, and like a good Middle Eastern host wanted to make sure it was to my liking. He thought I might want a sweetener.

"Canderel!" he called out, his arms thrust upward, accentuating his exuberance. My worlds collided.

Canderel was the European brand name for Equal, the tabletop sweetener produced by Searle that seemed like it had consumed much of the last five years of my life. Searle had waited for close to a decade for approval from the U.S. Food and Drug Administration to be able to market it. Now I was being offered it in a royal palace many thousands of miles from Searle headquarters in Skokie, Illinois.

Prince Saud, the young, Princeton-educated member of the royal family who was the new foreign minister, rose from his chair and walked over with a small dispenser of our company's new product.

I suspect King Fahd had no idea of my connection to the sweetener. But with a smile on his face, he said that his wife had him use it in his tea. The king, a large, joyful man, proclaimed proudly that he had slimmed down by several kilos as a result. His still sizable presence shook as he said it.

I don't recall what I said in response, but I certainly remember what I thought. I would have given anything for a video of the scene to use as a commercial. It would have been an award winner.

G.D. Searle was again becoming a healthy presence in the industry, thanks in part to the no-calorie sweetener in Equal and Canderel that over time became broadly known as NutraSweet. But it had only happened after a long period of legal uncertainty, as well as a revised business strategy. We restructured the company to position Searle back on an upward path. When I arrived there in the spring of 1977, the company's future was anything but bright.

CHAPTER 18

Searle's Sweet Success

G. D. Searle & Co. began in 1888, when a Civil War veteran and pharmacist, Gideon Daniel Searle, started a small company with a chemist in Chicago. Nine decades later, the business had become a global conglomerate. It had developed an impressive number of products: Dramamine, Metamucil, and Aldactone, as well as Enovid, the first mass-market oral contraceptive that would become known simply as the Pill. The company's rise into a major conglomerate had proved challenging. By 1977 the company had experienced weak earnings for eight straight quarters. Its stock price had fallen sharply, hitting a low of $10.75 per share, about half of its price a year earlier. Analysts wondered if its future was a long, downward slide. That concern had a way of getting shareholders' attention.[1]

So too did the choice of a new chief executive officer that year. Of all the people that the Searle board of directors could have selected to come in as the first non-family CEO, they chose a relatively young former public official with no background in the corporate world, let alone pharmaceuticals.

At the company's annual meeting where I was introduced to the shareholders as the future CEO, a middle-aged woman stood up.

"My name is Ethel Shapiro; I am a shareholder," she said. She noted that commentators were observing that little in my past experience made me a likely savior for the struggling pharmaceutical company.

"Mr. Rumsfeld," she asked bluntly, "why are you worth the $250,000 annual salary you will be receiving as CEO?" The amount was significant, to be sure. It was, in fact, four times what I had made as secretary of defense.

It was a fair question, and I suspected other shareholders might have been wondering the same thing.

"That sounds a lot like my mother," I replied, and many in the room laughed. As it happened, my mother was surprised by my decision to accept the Searle position. She believed I had established myself in government and wondered why I would want to get involved in an industry I knew little about and that had such obvious risks. She knew drug companies were often involved in complex and costly lawsuits. Searle, in fact, was at that moment undergoing a federal investigation into the accuracy of its research. Legal charges against the company had been filed and others were pending.

In answer to Mrs. Shapiro, I observed that I had not set my salary; the Searle board of directors had. I added that I was confident the board would have many opportunities to review my performance over time to determine whether I deserved that level of compensation. And I told her I would do my best to earn it.

It had not escaped my attention, or the Searle family's for that matter, that I had no relevant business or pharmaceutical industry experience. But I had been involved in managing large, complicated, international enterprises. Perhaps the deciding factor for the Searle family was my disinclination to shy away from making the tough choices that would be needed to get the enterprise on an upward path. The family knew me. Back in early 1962, not many people thought a twenty-nine-year-old with no experience in elective office could win a seat in Congress against a large field of more seasoned opponents. But Dan Searle did.

I, in turn, believed in Searle. Taking the reins of the pharmaceutical company was an opportunity to help develop products of value to people. My father, in particular, would have considered it honest and worthwhile work. There was some press speculation that I might be considering a run for the U.S. Senate from Illinois in 1980. To signal the seriousness of my commitment to the company, and to refute the speculation, I signed a five-year contract with Searle, even though the board of directors had not asked me to do so.

My time at Searle was a formative experience for me, unlike any challenge I'd ever faced before. It is in essence the story of a former government official unfamiliar with the daily workings of the business world finding his way. With the help of a superb team, I took the reins of a troubled company with great potential and developed a strategy to turn it around. We moved quickly to tighten budgets by reducing staff. We sold off entities not related to what we decided were our core businesses. We decentralized decision making and rigorously measured our progress against our goals.

Setting goals was the most important task we faced, because it forced us to decide what our priorities were. We also needed broad agreement on the priorities among the directors and senior managers so that everyone was pulling in the same direction. It was critically important to ensure that those goals and priorities were known throughout the organization.

When I arrived at Searle, one of the first things we did was to put together several task forces with a mix of employees, board members, and thoughtful people from outside the company to examine what I had decided were the key problem areas of the company's operations. They then offered specific recommendations. I knew Searle needed changes, but I didn't want change for change's sake. I needed to make sure the changes we were considering were the right ones. And I needed to make sure we could achieve broad support in the company to move forward with the changes.

After the review was complete, Searle's senior management and I agreed on our top priorities: focusing the company on its core businesses and laying the foundation for future growth. To achieve our goals, we decided we would trim excess layers of management and sell off subsidiaries that either were peripheral to Searle's mission or were unlikely to produce significant results. We resolved to work with the federal government to try to determine the fate of one especially promising product, aspartame. And we would invest significantly in research and development to ensure there would be more products in the pipeline in the years ahead.

Over my eight years at Searle, I became a believer in the rule that "What you measure improves." A corollary rule in the military is that "You get what you inspect, not what you expect." We needed to select the key metrics for each of the company's divisions that would be indicative of the company's long-term performance. While our goals included improving our earnings per share, leading to a higher stock price, the priorities we selected and measured had to be ones that would move us in the right direction. We decided to hold our own feet to the fire by publishing these metrics in our annual report so our shareholders could see our goals and how well we were doing in meeting them. Either our indicators were getting better or they weren't, and if they were, it would eventually be reflected in our company's overall value.

One of the single most important tasks of a senior executive is to recruit and rely on the right people. A rule I had observed was that "A's hire A's; B's hire C's." I've seen terrible organization charts that worked because of the people involved and impressive organization charts where the enterprise struggled because of the people involved. At Searle, I was looking for people who brought knowledge and expertise different from mine. I favored candidates with high energy and a sense of humor because I knew we'd be working long hours in a tough environment.

The senior management also needed to work well as a team. We could have the brightest, most capable people in the world, but if there was no commitment to the company's broader mission, their talents would not be enough. I learned that lesson as a midshipman on the USS *Wisconsin,* when the battleship ended up stuck on the New Jersey shore. A dozen tugboats tried to push the *Wisconsin* free. One tug would hit the ship, then another. It wasn't until all of the tugboats were organized in a coordinated effort that they put their bows against the hull of the battleship and pushed it free.*

At Searle, two people stand out as leaders of our team effort.† I invited John Robson to serve as Searle's chief operating officer. Robson had played a critical role in my congressional campaigns, was an accomplished lawyer, and also had public service experience as chairman of the Civil Aeronautics Board, among other appointments. He took the lead in legal and regulatory affairs and I trusted his judgment implicitly.

I also turned to Jim Denny, a man I'd known in college who was serving as the treasurer of Firestone Tire & Rubber Company. Denny's name appeared on a list of three candidates for the important position of Searle's chief financial officer from an executive search firm I had engaged. To my surprise—since I wasn't eager to hire an acquaintance—he turned out to be the unanimous choice for the job. Given my modest business background, I made sure Denny's office was close by. Not a day went by that I didn't step over to ask his

* Years later in a meeting with Chief of Naval Operations Admiral Elmo Zumwalt, I told him my story about the USS *Wisconsin.* "I was on that ship. I was the navigator," Zumwalt replied. Astonished, I asked him, "How the heck did you become an admiral with that foul-up in your record?" Zumwalt answered that he had warned against the mooring location but had been overruled by the Navy Department in Washington. I then asked if my account about the tugboats was what he remembered. "You are exactly right, but you left one part out: The tide came up." It was a lesson about the importance of teamwork, to be sure, but it is also best to have a little help from the Lord.

† Both Robson and Denny went on to have distinguished careers after Searle. John served as dean of the Emory Business School before going on to be deputy treasury secretary for the George H. W. Bush administration. Jim became chief financial officer for Sears, Roebuck & Co. and later chairman of Gilead Sciences. Their private investment activities, however, have been less exalted. The three of us banded together in the 1980s as TBM. Once when we were considering a project requiring legal disclosure, we were forced to disclose that TBM stood for "Three Blind Mice."

advice on business questions. Robson, Denny, and I were so engaged in what we were doing that we tended to overlook the traditional niceties of an executive suite. We were perhaps too informal for some directors who, as Denny later put it, "expected more than ham and Swiss on rye with cole slaw for their board meeting lunch."[2]

The board of directors, too, saw changes. A few of its members had joined when the company was still a family-oriented enterprise, rather than a global conglomerate. I worked to ease some members off the board, particularly those who were also in Searle's management, in favor of experienced outsiders who could bring the company a fresh and broader perspective.*

There is a danger that CEOs and senior executives can get too engaged in details, which can prevent them from having the necessary distance to see trends and the broader picture. When I was a flight instructor in the Navy I noticed novice pilots often took control of an airplane by grabbing hold of the stick too tightly and overcontrolling. As a result, the motion of the plane became jerky. It can be similar in any organization, whether in business or government. An executive who holds on to everything too tightly can lose sight of the larger issues. "Find ways to decentralize" is a guideline I included in Rumsfeld's Rules. "Move decision-making authority down and out. Encourage a more entrepreneurial approach." No one person can make all the necessary decisions in a large and complex enterprise. The best organizations have multiple leadership centers that are working in tandem toward the same goals.

Robson, Denny, and I encouraged the heads of Searle subsidiaries to tell us their priorities to increase their profits for the longer term. For example, we saw potential in one of Searle's units, then much less known than it is today.

Pearle Vision was first formed in 1961, when an optometrist named Stanley Pearle opened a store in Georgia that not only offered eye examinations but also could produce prescription lenses on-site and sold a wide selection of frames. The division's president, Don Phillips, embarked on a well-conceived plan that used the profits of existing Pearle Vision centers to build new centers and exponentially expand the franchise. The approach allowed us to increase the number of Pearle Vision centers from 240 in 1976 to more than

* Since Searle did business outside of the United States, especially in Europe, one of the people I turned to was a man whom I had always found a reservoir of good sense and unique perspectives, former ambassador to North Atlantic André de Staercke, the Belgian who had long served as the dean of the North Atlantic Council.

860 by 1981. We then franchised some of the centers to increase the incentives for store managers. Still later, we took a portion of Pearle Vision public while retaining a majority interest and management control. Our shareholders profited at each stage of the process.

To get clarity and insight into how things were really functioning at Searle I dug down into one division at a time. I had a habit of asking employees from senior managers to lab technicians direct questions, some of which may have seemed intrusive, but it was the best way I knew to gather the information I needed. On occasion, my approach made people uncomfortable, particularly if they didn't have ready answers. But more likely than not, they would have the answers the next time.

Like many companies in the mid-1970s, Searle had acquired numerous subsidiaries. Before I decided what to do with them I resolved to visit most of them personally. A number of the units were related only marginally to Searle's core businesses. One subsidiary's business was to produce and sell sperm from livestock. Its main source of revenue came from an aging bull named Astronaut. As fine a bull as he was, it was clear that this revenue stream was finite. Another was a centrifuge factory in France plagued by labor union activism. I had some inkling that the situation there was difficult when I was advised I should show up for my visit late at night, not during working hours. A visit by top management was not likely to be well received by the workers, I was told. Hostile labor conditions and weak earnings made the decision to divest an easy one.*

I decided to divest Searle of a number of its subsidiaries, even though I knew it would have the effect of temporarily reducing our revenues and earnings, since a number of these companies were profitable. Within a year I had directed the sale of twenty companies. One Rumsfeld Rule I developed is "Prune. Prune businesses, products, activities and people. Do it annually." Perhaps paradoxically, my intent was not to make Searle smaller through these divestments—I wanted to reinvigorate the company and invest in our core businesses to achieve growth.

To reduce costs and improve performance, we initiated a sizable reduction of Searle's corporate headquarters staff, which had the added benefit of decreasing the distance between the top of the organization and our customers.

*I cannot, however, claim to have sold the centrifuge company. Because of the power of the unions and French law, we weren't even able to give the company away. Our only solution was to pay the employees and the government so we would be permitted to transfer the business to the employees and be free of it.

In good times, the company was able to afford a growing corporate payroll, but times had changed. We needed to let some people go and move others from corporate headquarters to the divisions. Keeping in mind the memory of the way Bob Haldeman had summarily requested blanket resignations from Nixon's cabinet and subcabinet the day after his 1972 reelection, I wanted to treat our employees as fairly as possible.

It helped that the cost-cutting measures extended to all corners of the company, even to the executive offices. It was not a pleasant task for a new CEO to have to tell longtime members of the board of directors that it was necessary for them to leave the board, but the reality was that we needed new talent at the top if we were to succeed.

As the one making these decisions, I felt a responsibility to meet with as many of the people being let go as I could. I had already been out of a job several times in my life when I left the Navy and after several political campaigns, so I knew what it was like, particularly with a family to support. My words to them were what I felt would be helpful to me if I were in their shoes. I knew they would have to go home and explain their situations to their spouses, children, friends, and neighbors. I told them the truth—that the decision did not reflect on them. The reality was that the pharmaceutical industry and the company were both changing; U.S. companies, including Searle, needed to adjust to globalization. We were eventually able to provide many leaving Searle with outplacement assistance services to ease their transitions.

The rapid changes we were making at Searle caused heartburn for some, especially among our traditional investor base. I decided to freeze the company's stock dividend. This was not a uniformly well-received decision, particularly by shareholders who were accustomed to receiving dividend checks that increased over the years. The idea was to gradually move our shareholder base away from investors focused on dividends to investors more interested in the company's long-term growth.

I also decided to increase our investment in Searle's pharmaceutical research and development with the money we received from selling off some of our subsidiaries. One of my concerns was that the research and development division had too few promising new products in the pipeline. A number of the patents on existing products were expiring and would begin to face competition from generic drugs. I knew we needed to invest more if we were to be a successful research and development–based pharmaceutical company.

One of the more underappreciated aspects of the pharmaceutical industry is the time and investment put into research and development. Time and again the pharmaceutical industry has been singled out as a villain in corporate America and as the main culprit in escalating health-care costs. In fact, pharmaceutical and drug costs are less than 12 percent of the total of health-care costs.[3] I never cease to be amazed at people, particularly lifelong politicians of both political parties, most of whom have never created anything of value, savaging those who do. Successful pharmaceutical companies have to invest; that is to say they have to put at risk hundreds of millions of their investors' dollars in an effort to discover new therapies to save lives, extend lives, and improve the quality of lives, and, yes, also to try to make a fair return for their investors while doing so. More often than not, many years of trial and error result in dead ends. But with expensive facilities and talented researchers, breakthrough discoveries do occur. And even when efforts are unsuccessful, they learn what need not be tried again. Because of companies like Merck, Pfizer, Searle, Gilead Sciences, and others, millions of people in our country and across the globe are living longer, healthier lives.

During my third year at Searle, no doubt because of the cost-cutting measures I was implementing, I found myself included in a *Fortune* magazine cover story as one of the supposedly ten toughest CEOs in the country.[4] In some quarters it probably helps to be considered a tough boss. But I was uncomfortable with it.

I never thought that being tough was an appropriate or successful leadership approach, nor was it the way I managed. While I wanted everyone to feel the sense of urgency I felt, I found we achieved better performance when we treated everyone fairly and respectfully. Rather than being tough, my goal was to be effective, to achieve results, and to be willing to make difficult decisions even when there weren't obvious, attractive options. Searle was becoming a leaner and more focused operation, and we were increasingly able to leverage its strengths. If the message was coming across that the new CEO meant business, I had no problem with that. We had to drive forward and make the now slimmed-down company more profitable. There was one product in the pipeline that we knew could help significantly. The only impediment was the federal government, which was not a minor one.

One of the more unexpected things I discovered as CEO of a pharmaceutical company was that I had to think as much or more about the federal government than I did about our competition. I had known on an intellectual level that government was involved in the private sector in a great many ways, but it was only when I was actually in business that I felt the full impact. The government was a participant in practically everything we did—from the IRS to the Food and Drug Administration to the Department of Justice's antitrust division to the Federal Trade Commission to the Securities and Exchange Commission. We needed government clearance for almost all of our products. We also needed government approvals in each of dozens of other countries where Searle did business.

This was the case with the artificial sweetener Searle had discovered and had been developing for more than a decade. Aspartame was an example of the occasionally serendipitous results from research and development programs. In 1965, a Searle scientist was working on a treatment for ulcers involving amino acids. He happened to have some residual powder from two amino acids on his finger and accidentally discovered the sweet taste of the compound when he licked his finger to pick up a piece of paper.[5]

We knew that the products from aspartame could help the company, especially since there were questions being raised about the safety of the existing artificial sweeteners, notably saccharine. Searle had put aspartame through an extensive testing process, and the FDA had approved the product for commercial dry tabletop use in 1974. But a year and a half later, eighteen months before I joined Searle, the FDA took an almost unprecedented step when they issued a stay of their earlier approval of aspartame. The FDA had raised questions about Searle's overall research and development activities, which had complicated the situation considerably. There was press speculation that the Department of Justice might indict Searle over allegations that some of the company's research documentation might not have been in order.[6] Given the cloud cast over Searle, aspartame began to look much less promising than had been hoped.

I was learning a critical difference between the federal government and the private sector. People in the public sector tend to be praised and rewarded for their efforts or intentions, rather than judged by the results of their actions. What government does is assumed to be respectable and in the interests of the public. The FDA, for example, is criticized only if it errs and approves a drug that turns out not to be safe or effective—as it should be. But there is no criticism of the FDA if it delays the approval of drugs that are safe and could save or extend lives.

Unlike in government, good intentions are not what are rewarded in the business world—results are. What matters is outputs, not inputs—that is to say, in business millions of dollars in investment mean nothing unless there is a fair return. In government, progress is often judged by how much money is thrown at a problem. Federal education programs, for example, are more often measured by the size of the education budget, not by the results they are producing, such as the graduation rate. And regardless of its mistakes, the federal government does not go out of business. If businesses make mistakes, they suffer, lose money, managers are replaced, or the companies go into bankruptcy. So while the FDA could wait as long as it wished in delaying aspartame, Searle paid the price.

The FDA stay of approval gave competitors more time to research alternative products to aspartame. It allowed critics of the sweetener to engage in a public relations campaign, raising concerns in the minds of potential customers, investors, and employees. And, importantly, Searle's patent on aspartame continued to run, thereby shortening the number of years the shareholders would have the financial benefits of patent protection if and when the stay of approval was eventually lifted.

My view was that if Searle had been at fault over any of the research documentation issues that the government had raised, then we needed to figure out promptly what the problem was, fix it, and move on. The most harmful thing would be the continuing stalemate that was so costly to the company. Since there was a real possibility that the stay of approval on aspartame might never be lifted, we had to wean ourselves from the mindset that aspartame might be an answer to Searle's difficulties and focus on other solutions. The day-to-day management of the legal and regulatory issues surrounding aspartame was handled by John Robson.

After years of testing, the FDA's stay of approval for the dry use of aspartame was finally lifted on July 15, 1981. This was six years after the FDA stay of approval had been issued, which meant that Searle's investors had lost that many years of patent protection on what would become a major product.*

With FDA clearance, we moved ahead and invested in the necessary manufacturing facilities and plans to market aspartame under the trade name Equal. Equal became a national success in short order and then an international success under the trade name of Canderel. Millions of those light-blue packets found their way to supermarkets, homes, and restaurants. That

* Searle sought new legislation to help every company affected by an FDA stay of approval. In January 1983, Congress passed an amendment to the Orphan Drug Act that provided any product that had been approved, and was subject to a stay of that approval which was later lifted, an extension of their patent to compensate for the time lost during the period of the stay.

was only the start. There were even bigger things in store for aspartame and Searle, thanks to a company called PepsiCo.

In 1983, the FDA gave approval for wet use of aspartame, which meant it could now be used in liquids in addition to the dry use as a tabletop sweetener. As with Equal, Searle's creative marketing team decided to establish a brand name for its use in beverages. We called it NutraSweet and gave it a distinctive red-and-white swirl logo. It was one of the early examples of branding an *ingredient*, rather than a product, which thereby boosted the value of both.

The Coca-Cola Company had been among the first to use aspartame in its diet soda Tab. But the company did not use 100 percent aspartame, choosing instead to combine it with saccharin, which was less expensive and more readily available. As a result, we did not allow Coke to use our NutraSweet logo. But if Coke or Pepsi made the decision to go 100 percent NutraSweet in their diet colas, it could change the beverage industry—not to mention help Searle greatly.

As we negotiated with representatives of the soft-drink companies, CBS launched a new attack on aspartame. On the evening news, CBS anchor Dan Rather highlighted some discredited allegations for three nights running in January 1984. Searle had provided CBS and his producers with data and information about the safety of NutraSweet that they did not use. In a letter, Searle's general counsel blasted Rather for "patently absurd" reporting and "manipulative editing."[7] It may have been the first time Rather was caught up in such poorly researched journalism, but it would not be his last. Fortunately, the facts were on Searle's side. Aspartame had gone through one of the most extensive food additives tests in history to earn FDA approval.

Despite the CBS TV attacks, later in 1984 I was contacted by Don Kendall, the CEO of PepsiCo. Kendall confided that a small group at PepsiCo was involved in confidential discussions to abandon saccharin altogether and go with 100 percent aspartame in one of their diet drinks, enabling it to adopt the NutraSweet logo. This was a gamble for the company, since aspartame would increase Pepsi's costs and news reports like CBS's were not helpful in developing public confidence.

Nonetheless, Kendall was inclined to put 100 percent NutraSweet in every can and bottle of their biggest selling low-calorie drink, Diet Pepsi. He thought it would reinvigorate their brand and distinguish them from their competitors. He asked that Searle help share the cost and risks, agree to a reasonable price for aspartame, and provide a sufficient supply to Pepsi.

Knowing how important it was for one of the major cola companies to adopt the product, I agreed.[8]

Kendall was pleased. "Rumsfeld, you are a genius," he said, adding, "or at least I am going to make you look like one."[9]

With Kendall's decision on Diet Pepsi—and a substantial advertising campaign about the benefits of NutraSweet—aspartame became one of the most successful new products introduced in the United States during that period, with sales in excess of $700 million by 1985.

NutraSweet was sought out by people interested in managing their weight and maintaining healthier lifestyles. It is now in use in some five thousand products, reaching hundreds of millions of people in more than one hundred countries worldwide. I never forgot the many years and millions of dollars lost while waiting to get that stay of approval lifted by the government.

Over my first six years at Searle, the company's earnings per share, as well as its share price, had increased threefold. The overall picture had improved noticeably, but the core pharmaceutical business remained challenging. It did look like we would have some new products by the mid-1980s as a result of our increased investments in the late 1970s, but Searle was competing against larger companies worldwide that were able to outinvest us in research and development.[10] To better ensure a stream of new drugs in the decades ahead, the Searle family and the board of directors began to discuss the notion of a merger with another firm.

In the fall of 1985, we began talks with Monsanto, a company that had experience in research and development and was interested in moving into the pharmaceutical sector.[11] Though a merger seemed within reach, negotiations got bogged down in the hands of lawyers and investment bankers. I was concerned that over time the merger talks would get into the press. I decided to inform Monsanto that we would agree to the sale of Searle common stock, but only if Monsanto's investment bankers and lawyers could get an acceptable agreement signed and announced before the New York Stock Exchange opened the following morning. If not, the deal would be off. Sure enough, the deal was announced the next morning, shortly before the stock exchange opened.

I couldn't help but reflect on those early days at the company, by then more than eight years earlier, when many people—including my own mother—wondered if I had made the right decision to join it. But from the first day on the job I liked the idea of taking on a new challenge in an important industry.

Thanks to our restructuring plan and Searle's talented employees, we had achieved a solid comeback.

The stock price had increased from $12.50 when I took over to $65 per share, a compound annual return, excluding dividends, of 20 percent.* Searle's profits grew from $35 million in 1977 to $162 million in 1984.[12] I was pleased with the results and greatly valued my time with the company. But I was never completely out of politics and government. They had a way of drawing me back in, usually when I least expected it.

*During the same period, the Standard & Poor's 500 grew 12 percent.

CHAPTER 19

From Malaise to Morning in America

Since Joyce and I had left Washington in 1977, the national political scene had changed markedly. As President Carter's administration seemed to lurch from one crisis to another, his popularity cratered.

Since my meetings with Carter and his new team at the end of 1976, I had had two other noteworthy encounters with his administration. The first came in 1978, when Carter asked the CEOs of large Fortune 500 companies to support wage and price controls to deal with inflation, an effort akin to what President Nixon had attempted. Having been the director of Nixon's Cost of Living Council, I felt an obligation to share my experiences, even if the administration might not welcome them.[1] As diplomatically as I possibly could, I explained what I thought of Carter's plan, which was that it was unworkable and unwise. Carter ignored all warnings and went ahead with his "voluntary" wage price controls. Inflation soared anyway.

Then, in December 1979, not six months after Carter signed what he viewed as a landmark arms-control agreement, SALT II, with the Soviet Union's leader Leonid Brezhnev, Soviet tanks rolled into Afghanistan. The invasion stunned Carter, who seemed amazed that the country he saw as his partner in peace would be engaging in such warlike and expansionist behavior. Carter made an infamous and revealing statement that he had learned more about the Soviets in one week than he had during his entire administration.* I found

* Carter said, "My opinion of the Russians has changed most drastically in the last week [more] than even in the previous 2½ years before that."[2]

the idea that the President of the United States was surprised by the Soviet Union's capacity for mendacity and aggression embarrassing. The generally sympathetic *Time* magazine characterized Carter's comment as "strikingly naïve."[3]

After I had studied SALT II, I agreed to testify against it before the Senate Armed Services Committee. Given the Soviet Union's past behavior, it seemed to me dangerous to believe that the Soviets would not exploit the treaty in order to pursue their goal of military superiority.[4] Eager to ratify the treaty, Carter and his supporters in the Senate dismissed such sentiments, but only until the Soviet invasion of Afghanistan.

As the Afghanistan crisis threatened to unravel U.S.-Soviet relations, I was invited to attend a meeting at the White House with President Carter and Secretary of State Cyrus Vance. The gathering, on January 9, 1980, was billed as an insider discussion. When I arrived I found about forty people, including a range of current and former officials. The discussion was really more of a briefing.[5]

I was struck by the administration's tone. The Carter team had invested so much into believing that the Soviets were well-intentioned that they found it almost impossible to reverse course. They seemed proud that their subdued, diplomatic response to the Soviet invasion of Afghanistan had been, by their assessment, "measured" and "predictable," so as not to enflame the situation. But I saw little reason for them to be pleased. Telling the Soviets that, in effect, we would not respond to their provocations was tantamount to a green light for further aggression.

Those present from the administration seemed unclear about what they were going to do next. During his briefing, Secretary of State Cyrus Vance announced emphatically that it was U.S. policy to not sell weapons to the Soviet Union. I was astounded that the Secretary of State felt compelled to make that point.

As I expressed at the gathering, was anybody seriously suggesting or even contemplating selling arms to the Russians?[6]

When Carter spoke, his manner was grave. He suggested that the Soviet invasion was more serious than when the Soviets invaded Hungary in 1956 or Czechoslovakia in 1968. Someone even suggested reinstating the draft. Carter mentioned retaliatory options such as reducing the number of Soviet personnel allowed at their Washington embassy or restricting Soviet aircraft flights.

Though I was discouraged, I declined an opportunity to criticize the President before the television cameras that were outside the White House immediately after the meeting. With Soviet tanks rolling into Afghanistan, I felt it was not the time to highlight the Carter administration's mistakes.

Eventually, Carter ordered an embargo on grain shipments to Russia, which had the chief result of angering American farmers. The action also contradicted his previously stated position that "food should not be used as a weapon" in international disputes.[7] He also announced an American boycott of the 1980 Olympics in Moscow. Then, in an address to the nation outlining what apparently he thought to be his tough new policies, Carter offered this memorable line: "Fishing privileges for the Soviet Union in United States waters will be severely curtailed."[8] Winston Churchill he was not.

I believed that Carter should have increased the U.S. defense budget in response to the Soviet invasion of Afghanistan, set aside arms-control negotiations, worked with our NATO allies to encourage them to take an interest in problems outside the area covered by the NATO treaty, and provided assistance to Pakistan and other Afghan neighbors who could offer a hand to those Afghans resisting the Soviet forces. It also struck me that it might be helpful if Carter would stop making obviously inaccurate statements, such as that Soviet leader Brezhnev "shared our aspirations" when Brezhnev had demonstrated time and again that he did not.[9]

Proving again that weakness is provocative, on November 4, 1979, Islamist fundamentalists in Iran took sixty-six Americans hostage in the U.S. embassy in Tehran. Desert One, a U.S. attempt to rescue the hostages, ended with a tragic helicopter crash in the Iranian desert and the deaths of eight American servicemen. Between that failed mission and Carter's weak response to the Soviet invasion of Afghanistan, his decisions confirmed in the minds of many Americans that they had elected a president who lacked a sufficient understanding of the world we inhabited.

Ronald Reagan made his third run for the presidency in 1980. I readily agreed to serve as a member of his national security advisory committee during the campaign.[10] As one of the individuals Reagan was considering as his vice presidential running mate, I was asked to speak that summer at the Republican National Convention in Detroit. I pointed out the mistakes the administration was making, including canceling the B-1 bomber, as well as the importance of recognizing the Soviet military buildup and our need to match it. I said Carter was "sleepwalking during four years of America's decline."[11]

At the convention, I was assigned a handler from Reagan's campaign, whose assignment was to shadow me at all times so that Governor Reagan could reach me on the phone if he decided to select me.* But the vice presidential possibility getting the most talk at the convention was Gerald Ford. Ford had rebounded greatly in the public's esteem since his loss to Carter. Perhaps it was a case of buyer's remorse. Still, I thought having Ford as vice president was not a good idea for either Ford or Reagan. It suggested that Reagan needed someone to look over his shoulder. It also could have been awkward for Ford, having served as president, to be relegated to the number two spot. Some suggested that a Reagan-Ford ticket amounted to a sort of "co-presidency." It would be like putting four hands on the wheel of the ship of state, which was a sure prescription for confusion.

I received a phone call from Governor Reagan. "Don, I want to thank you for being willing to be considered," Reagan said, "but I've decided to go with George Bush."

"Thank goodness!" I said, to his surprise.

I had feared Reagan was going to say he'd picked Ford. As it happened, the Reagan-Ford talks had collapsed after the idea of a co-president began to surface on television.

I told Reagan I was pleased that he decided not to go with Ford.

"Oh no, Don," Reagan replied, "Jerry and I decided that together." It was typically generous of Ronald Reagan to put it that way.

No one was more skillful at surveying the damage of the Carter years—toppled allies, emboldened enemies, and a diminished America—than the Great Communicator. Reagan conjured up four years of gas lines and high unemployment following Carter's tax and spend economic policies. He declared that Iranian fundamentalists and Soviet aggressors had made advances as a result of American ineptitude. "Are you better off than you were four years ago?" Reagan asked the American people during the campaign. On election day, voters decided they were not, and put Ronald Reagan in the White House.

In the fall of 1982, as Searle was beginning to show a measure of success, I received a call from Ed Meese, who was counsellor to the president in the Reagan White House. The President and his new secretary of state, George Shultz, wanted me to serve as President Reagan's emissary on the Law of the Sea Treaty.

* Others mentioned were former treasury secretary Bill Simon, former New York Congressman Jack Kemp, and Reagan's close friend Senator Paul Laxalt of Nevada.[12]

The so-called United Nations Convention on the Law of the Sea was designed to codify navigation rights in international waters. But it had grown into something considerably more ambitious, with a provision that would put all natural resources found in the seabeds of international waters under the collective purview of the treaty's signers—a scheme that would result in substantial wealth being put into the hands of what was ominously called the International Seabed Authority.

Shortly after Reagan was inaugurated, he was invited to join a ceremonial treaty signing by some 160 nations in Jamaica. Reagan's first secretary of state, Al Haig, reportedly asked the President who he thought should represent the United States. To nearly everyone's surprise, Reagan announced he was not ready to agree to the treaty. Reagan believed rewards and investment incentives should go to those nations that had the specialized technology and capability to mine the ocean floor, not to the "Authority."*

Reagan's reversal of U.S. policy led to consternation at the Department of State, to which Reagan asked, "But isn't that what the election was about?" Once I heard that story I knew that we had a vastly different president in the White House.

I met with Reagan in the Oval Office to receive his guidance on my new assignment. The President was gracious and personable. He had instincts about what he wanted to accomplish but, not being an expert on the treaty, he did not get into the details.[14] Still, Reagan hit the important points he wanted me to convey to the leaders of the larger industrialized nations on my mission. It was the "experts," after all, who had put our country into this unfortunate position on the treaty in the first place. He wanted me to reset the American position and gain the support of key foreign leaders to join him in opposition to the seabed mining section of the treaty. All of the momentum, of course, was pushing those countries in exactly the opposite direction and toward the fanfare of the treaty-signing ceremony.

I made several trips to Europe and Asia to make Reagan's case. Two meetings particularly stood out as a study in contrasts. One was in Paris with France's socialist president, François Mitterrand. True to form, as I outlined President Reagan's objections to the treaty on free-market grounds, I could

* Dr. Robert Goldwin had written an article on the Law of the Sea in June 1981 that pointed out the potentially unfortunate consequences of the treaty. Goldwin wrote that John Locke did not define "common" resources as belonging to everyone; he defined them as belonging to no one, and that ownership derived from the labor expended to harvest the resources. Remove the reward for the labor and you remove the incentive to work. Goldwin's article so impressed me that I sent it to George Shultz, who had succeeded Haig as secretary of state.[13]

see Mitterrand growing increasingly enthusiastic about the aspects of the treaty we found most offensive.[15]

A few days later I met with Prime Minister Margaret Thatcher at 10 Downing Street in London. I explained my mission and Reagan's concerns. Quite briskly, Mrs. Thatcher bore right into the heart of the matter.

"Mr. Ambassador, if I understand correctly, what this Law of the Sea Treaty proposes is nothing less than the international nationalization of roughly two thirds of the Earth's surface," she began. "And you know how I feel about nationalization."

"I do indeed, Prime Minister," I responded. Mrs. Thatcher had made transferring nationalized businesses, from utilities to mining companies, back to the private sector a hallmark of her premiership.

She smiled. "Tell Ronnie I'm with him."[16]

Contrary to early expectations, Reagan ended up being quite successful in his efforts to defeat the seabed mining provisions in the Law of the Sea treaty. A number of the key countries I visited as his special envoy, including Germany, Japan, and the United Kingdom, did not sign. As of this writing, it still remains unsigned by the United States. The experience provided a useful lesson, as I indicated in Rumsfeld's Rules, that "in unanimity there may well be either cowardice or uncritical thinking."

In 1986, as Reagan neared the end of his second term, I started giving the possibility of running for president serious thought. I surveyed the field and felt that, based on my years of public service and my time in the private sector at a Fortune 500 company, I offered a breadth of experience that a number of the possible candidates lacked. I talked the idea over with Joyce and a few close friends—some of whom had been involved in my long-shot bid for Congress back in 1962—and decided to explore the possibility.

The logo for my brief presidential campaign was, appropriately, a dark horse.

I considered informing President Reagan personally about my decision, but I didn't want to put him in an awkward position, considering that his vice president, George H. W. Bush, was the leading candidate. Instead, I went to see one of Reagan's close friends and advisers, then Attorney General Ed Meese.

A respected figure among conservatives, Meese was a thoughtful man who always seemed to put loyalty to President Reagan ahead of his own ambitions. "Ed, I'm considering running for the nomination," I told him. "I thought I'd let you know."

Meese expressed his appreciation that I informed him personally. Although he said he was likely to stick with Bush, he welcomed me into the race. "It's important to have alternatives available in case something happens," he commented. I knew our conversation would find its way to President Reagan.

There was another person I wanted to speak to before I made any announcements. I flew out to meet with President Ford at his home in California. Despite Bush's considerable advantage as the sitting vice president, Ford felt the 1988 contest was open. Very kindly, he told me that he had been describing me to his friends as the "competent" choice.[17] But considering my time away from the public spotlight, Ford wondered how I could get from where I was to where I wanted to go.

Having participated in several presidential campaigns over the years, I was well aware that putting one together from scratch was a monumental undertaking, especially without being a front-runner and not currently in elective office or carrying a famous name. Bush had made light of the so-called vision thing, but I felt it was important for a candidate to be able to explain why he had decided to run for the country's highest office.

I believed my national security background qualified me to uphold the Reagan standard of "strong and decisive leadership" with respect to the Soviet Union and the other threats that were gathering around the globe.[18] I also wanted to focus on opportunities for all Americans, building on my experiences in Congress and the private sector.

My hope was to emerge at the top of the second tier of candidates, while the two front-runners, Bush and Bob Dole, faced off. It was a page from the playbook of my first congressional primary, when my plan had been to run ahead of the other second-tier candidates, and then try to persuade them to drop out and support me, leaving me in a one-on-one race with the front-runner. As in 1962, a great many things would have to fall my way for that plan to work. For one thing, the other second-tier candidates would have to falter. Second, I would have to raise sufficient funds to be able to hang on through Super Tuesday and beyond.

After having served by then as a member of Congress, an ambassador, White House chief of staff, secretary of defense, and a private sector chief executive officer, running for president was humbling. I remember going to speak to college Republicans at the University of Northern Iowa. The schedule my campaign group prepared said that three hundred students might attend. But almost no one showed up. The seats were empty, with the exception of the college Republican chapter president and a few of his friends. There, as at other events, my small staff may well have outnumbered interested voters.[19] I participated in all of the presidential candidate forums to try to boost my candidacy, but they received very little coverage, because Bush, wisely pursuing a front-runner's strategy, usually didn't attend.

It was hard to raise money with low name recognition, but of course it was hard to increase name identification without spending money. Ironically, the new public-financing laws enacted in the wake of Watergate, supposedly to keep money from distorting the political process, favored incumbents. It made fund-raising for lesser known candidates an even steeper uphill climb. I now was barred by law from contributing more than $50,000 to my own campaign if I wanted to receive federal matching funds, which I knew I would need. In Illinois, I needed to deposit $6,000 on a $600-a-month office. "Multiply that 1,000 times around the country," I said at the time, "and you see what candidates are experiencing."[20]

I soon became concerned about running a campaign deficit. I had read about Democratic Senator John Glenn's debt-ridden 1984 presidential campaign, and it raised concerns in my mind.[21] Knowing Glenn from his days as an astronaut, I called him and asked about his campaign experience. He told me he had given the maximum a candidate was legally able to contribute to his own campaign, so to pay off his debts he had to try to raise additional funds. But few new donors were reaching for their wallets to contribute to a campaign that had already ended in a loss, and many of those who had contributed to his campaign already had given the maximum the law allowed or they could afford. The result was that members of Glenn's campaign staff and a number of vendors were stiffed. It was a tough situation for an honorable man like Glenn, particularly since he had the financial capability to pay the debts personally. But many did not know the new campaign law prevented Glenn from doing so.[22]

If my campaign went on through the primary and we were not able to raise enough money, I knew I would be in the same position. As a conservative concerned about debt, the hypocrisy of running a campaign on a deficit was not appealing, particularly when I knew it would not be legal for me to personally pay it off. I concluded that I should not go forward, and announced my decision in April 1987, many months before the first primary vote was scheduled.

From the sidelines, I watched the campaign unfold. In the Iowa caucuses, Dole from neighboring Kansas won, but Pat Robertson was a surprising second. Bush ran third. Then came the New Hampshire primary, where Bush had his longstanding New England roots and connections, his family name, and the money that came easily to an incumbent vice president and front-runner, allowing him to flood the airwaves and pull out a win, in part by attacking Dole as a secret tax raiser. Dole's campaign began to falter.

At that point, I faced a decision. I could endorse no one, or I could endorse Bush, the likely winner, or I could endorse Bob Dole. I thought Dole would be a better president, so I endorsed him. So did Al Haig, another candidate who dropped out of the race about when I did. Bush went on to win the nomination and easily defeated his lackluster Democrat opponent, Massachusetts Governor Michael Dukakis.

For me, the bright spot in the new Bush administration was the secretary of defense. I had not spent much time with Dick Cheney since I left Washington in 1977. He had since been elected to Congress from Wyoming while I was working in Chicago. Contrary to what people might have expected, considering our relationship, I don't recall having any conversations with Cheney about the Defense Department during his four years in the Pentagon running it. He may have been sensitive to President George H. W. Bush's attitude toward me and kept his distance. In any event, Cheney and I were each busy with our respective careers, his in Washington, D.C., and mine in business ventures from New York to Silicon Valley.

CHAPTER 20

Our Rural Period, Interrupted

In 1988, fourteen years after my dad died, my mother, Jeannette, was in the passenger seat in a car accident. The doctors thought she would recover, but bedridden, her inactivity led to pneumonia. Mom died at the age of eighty-four. She was a wise, wonderful, supportive figure throughout my life. She had been healthy before the accident, and my sister Joan and I weren't ready to lose her. Still, I was grateful that each of our children had had an opportunity to know her well. At age fifty-six, both of my parents were now gone, which left me with a deep sense of loss.

In 1990, I became the chief executive officer of General Instrument Corporation (GI), a New York City–based supplier of electronics to the cable and satellite television industry. GI had been acquired in a leveraged buyout by Forstmann Little & Company. Ted Forstmann's unusual talent was in finding companies he believed could be significantly improved by bringing in new management. He raised money from investors, which he would then borrow against to get more funding, so he could purchase companies for what he believed was less than what they could be worth. Forstmann Little would eventually take the company public again at a higher value than its purchase price, pay the original investors and any loans, and use the profit to make still more acquisitions. GI was an interesting challenge, since I knew no more about electronics than I had about pharmaceuticals when I joined Searle. A scientist working for the company, Dr. Woo Paik, had developed a breakthrough technology: the world's first all-digital high-definition television. Once again Washington intruded. The Federal Communications Commission (FCC) effectively forced General Instrument and our partner, the Massachusetts Institute of Technology, to combine with Zenith, AT&T, Thomson, Philips, RCA, and NBC to form what was called the Grand Alliance for digital high-definition television. The theory was that we would collaborate on fashioning an American standard for HDTV and share in the royalties. Apart from the damage that decision by the FCC did to GI's leading position—since GI was the company that had developed all-digital HDTV—the government's unhelpful involvement also contributed to the delay of the technology's introduction in America for close to a decade.[1]

In 1992 William Jefferson Clinton defeated President George H. W. Bush when he sought reelection. Clinton, a young Democrat, was elected with less than half of the vote. An intelligent man with excellent political instincts, Clinton had a talent for locking you in his gaze and saying insightful things you were interested in hearing. He had a passion for domestic policy and could hold forth on the subtleties of single-payer health care without losing his audience. But Clinton had a manner somewhat different from presidents I had especially admired, such as Eisenhower, Ford, and Reagan. They were modest people who seemed almost surprised to be in the White House—in Ford's case, it was genuine surprise. By contrast, Clinton seemed to have been aiming for the presidency practically since childhood, and he appeared not at all surprised that he had attained it.

In his first four years in office, Clinton raised taxes on the American people after promising a tax cut—a reversal that had proven perilous for his predecessor. The Clinton team's military operation in Somalia ended in retreat and emboldened Islamist extremists. The administration responded indecisively to a series of terrorist attacks, including the first bombing of the World Trade Center in 1993. Having confronted the problem of terrorism as President Reagan's Middle East envoy, I couldn't help but think back to what had happened in Lebanon and how it had brought America's credibility into question.

Due to the policies of the Clinton administration—including a plan to have the federal government take over the American health care system—Republicans gained ground during the first years of his term. In 1994, the leadership of a then little known congressman from Georgia named Newt Gingrich brought the GOP control of the U.S. House of Representatives for the first time in decades. Gingrich combined the intellectual firepower of his academic background with a zeal for commonsense solutions. He could rattle off ideas like a machine gun.

The Republican wave continued through 1995. Bob Dole, then serving as the Senate minority leader, became the Republican presidential nominee. With Dole leading Clinton in early polls, a federal government shutdown was blamed on Republicans in Congress, damaging their image. The Clinton political machine launched tough attacks on Dole and the Democrats pulled ahead.

I watched the unfolding campaign from Chicago. I was sorry to see Dole struggling against the incumbent president. In the spring of 1996, Bob's wife, Elizabeth, called and asked me to come to Washington to help the campaign on policy issues. I agreed to do it on a part-time basis. I'd known Elizabeth since she had served in the Nixon administration. Strong and polished, she was an excellent partner for Bob.

Dole was struggling with the same problem that Gerald Ford had faced early on—he was a legislator by nature who had to make the transition to becoming a presidential candidate and an executive. There was so much to like and admire about Bob Dole the person, and certainly the legislator. But the traits that drew people to him and made him a lion in the Senate did not translate well to a candidate for president.

Having run for president three times, he was not always receptive to advice, especially from a campaign staff he hardly knew. On a flight aboard his campaign plane, Dole finally gave in to pleas from his aides to practice a speech with a teleprompter. So he proceeded to practice the speech by reading it—in silence. The staff stood there baffled while Dole practiced the speech in his head.

I spent my time on policy issues, working with longtime Minnesota congressman Vin Weber. Together we helped Dole craft a supply-side economic message by seeking input from some of the leading economic experts in the country, including Milton Friedman, publisher Steve Forbes, and Dr. John Taylor of Stanford University. The Dole proposal had as its centerpiece a 15 percent across-the-board tax cut for the American people. He argued that by letting people keep more of their own money, they could better stimulate the economy than the federal government could. Still, with the country seeming to be at peace and reasonably prosperous, Dole lagged behind Clinton.

In the late summer of 1996, languishing in the polls, Dole called me up one evening. He said he was going to announce me as the general chairman of his campaign. I laughed when I heard the idea, which seemed to have come out of nowhere. I reminded Dole that I had agreed to help out part-time on policy.

"Well, I've got to do it," Dole insisted. "I have to show we're doing something to shake up the campaign." Again I resisted, since I knew who was running the Dole campaign—the candidate and his large paid staff of professional managers. By the end of the conversation I thought I had made myself clear that I could not do it.

To my dismay, Dole went ahead the next day and announced that I was his chairman. I subsequently learned that Dole already had a campaign chairman—New Hampshire governor Steve Merrill—who apparently had not been informed of the change. Graciously, Merrill contacted me and said he was willing to assist the campaign in any way possible.

Within a month, Dole's supporters gathered in San Diego for a convention that they hoped would define his candidacy for the American people and dent Clinton's lead in the polls. In San Diego, I noticed that the relatively new twenty-four-hour television era had turned Washington politicians into celebrities. Republican delegates treated the most recognizable faces in the party as if they were movie stars. I also noticed another change from my days in Congress. As the size of congressional staffs had increased, so had their power. In the old days one dealt directly with a member of Congress on policy issues. By 1996, one often dealt with a member of the congressman's staff instead.[2]

The Dole campaign tried in vain to focus voters and the media on the character question the administration was battling. At one point, after citing a list of scandals and investigations against the administration, Dole blurted out, "Where is the outrage?" I understood his frustration. He felt the media was not holding the Clinton team to the same standard of behavior applied to other politicians.

The American people didn't share Dole's outrage, and President Clinton won reelection convincingly, though the final margin was closer than a number of the polls had suggested. Within weeks of Dole's defeat, there were rumors about the leading contenders for 2000. One name surfaced early—George W. Bush, the governor of Texas.[3]

After the campaign I went back to the business world, serving on various boards of directors. As the collapses of Enron and WorldCom demonstrated a few years later, one of the important roles of outside directors is to try to look around corners and identify any problems with a company's strategies or management. Because I held management to a high standard and asked a good many questions about operations, some CEOs considered me a difficult director. Others sometimes cheered me on. One CEO said to Joyce, "Don is a terrific director, but you sure as hell wouldn't want more than one of them on your board."

I became increasingly involved with a small start-up company in California named Gilead Sciences, Inc. Mike Riordan, a MD from Johns Hopkins University with an MBA from Harvard, started the company with a small venture capital investment. Eventually, Gilead produced one of the early AIDS treatment drugs. It later developed Viread (also called Tenofovir), the backbone of HIV treatment today, as well as Tamiflu, a flu drug. By March 1996, Gilead had moved from a market capitalization of zero to $1 billion, with $300 million in cash and several blockbuster drugs. Its stock was rising and the company was getting excellent reviews from security analysts.[4] This was a tribute to excellent science and, as always in the pharmaceutical business, a dose of good fortune. It was also a tribute to people willing to risk their careers on a small start-up company and the thousands of investors willing to risk their money on a long shot.

I liked the idea of working with a small group of bright, talented young people in Silicon Valley as they started the enterprise from scratch. Gilead had terrific potential and some brilliant minds, but so did other start-up biotech firms. I agreed to join the board early on, and eventually became the chairman. I helped recruit a superb group of top-flight people to the board to broaden its perspective and attract investment.

Our board brought broad experience to the talented young management team. These board members, with their relationships around the world, helped guide Gilead in its transition from start-up to a more mature player in a highly competitive industry.

I also made a pitch for Condoleezza Rice, who had served in the George H. W. Bush administration and was the provost of Stanford University, to join the board of directors.

"[W]e'd better get ourselves in the queue before she makes any public decisions about her future," I advised George Shultz.[5]

I pointed out that our company met in Foster City, California, a thirty-minute drive from Stanford. When I would see Rice at various events, I would jokingly pester her about joining Gilead's board. I sent her notes trying to make the case. "Condi," one began, "When are you going to call me up and say, 'Gee, Don, I would be delighted to join the Gilead Board. . . . Those are good folks, it is an interesting business, it is nearby, it only meets four times a year, so the answer is yes!'"[6]

Rice expressed interest but did not commit. She had decided to go on the boards of larger and considerably more prominent firms, such as Chevron. It was not long before she began advising George W. Bush, whose presidential prospects seemed bright.

In 1999, Bush asked to meet with me when I was serving as chairman of the Commission to Assess the Ballistic Missile Threat to the United States. The commission had been established by Congress to evaluate threats posed by ballistic missiles, particularly ones in the hands of rogue regimes. Bush was interested in the commission's work. He mentioned that Shultz had suggested that we meet.[7]

My earlier encounters with the younger George Bush in the 1970s and 1980s had been brief. Perhaps it is my midwestern roots, but I confess to a not very wise or useful bias about those who enjoy the inherited benefit of prominent names. Getting to know George W. Bush was a good lesson against letting personal stereotypes color your thinking about people. The Bush I met in his suite at the Capital Hilton in Washington had taken difficult steps to change his life, was serving as governor of Texas, and was working hard to be elected president of the United States.

I found him to be unlike the picture the press was drawing of him as uncurious and something of a slacker. He asked serious questions, was self-confident, and had a command of the important issues. Decidedly down-to-earth, with no inclination to formality, his demeanor was different from his father's somewhat patrician manner. Sometimes, as I'd learn over the years, George W. Bush would have his feet up on his desk and be chewing an unlit cigar. He pointed out that he'd grown up in Midland, Texas. He had a toughness, and he told me that he stood apart from "that Eastern establishment."[8] I left our 1999 meeting impressed.

After the disappointment of the Dole campaign, politics didn't tug on me as it once had, but national security issues did. I wasn't formally advising Bush, but at Rice's invitation I offered occasional thoughts.

Once, in a letter to Josh Bolten, who was then serving as the policy director for the Bush campaign, I offered some thoughts on national security. I warned against the idea of a "graduated response"—sending small numbers of troops and then escalating that number over time. "'Graduated response' didn't work in Vietnam for President Johnson," I observed. "If the U.S. is going to get into a fight, it is worth winning, and we should hit hard up front. Hoping for a measured, antiseptic war (immaculate coercion) to be successful," I cautioned, "is the hope only of the unschooled."[9]

I was slow to endorse anyone for the presidency in 2000. A complicating factor for me was that early on I had two friends in the race, Steve Forbes and Elizabeth Dole, so I preferred to stay out of the Republican primary battle.

There was, however, one presidential candidate running that year who I was quick to support: New Jersey senator Bill Bradley was waging an uphill campaign against Vice President Al Gore for the Democratic Party's presidential nomination. Having invited Bradley thirty years earlier to work with me at the Office of Economic Opportunity, my interest in his career had continued. When he announced his campaign against Gore, I sent him a contribution. I believed the thoughtful and honorable Bradley would make a considerably better president than Gore, whom I saw as lecturing and wooden. And so my first presidential campaign contribution in 2000 was to a Democrat, although I let Bradley know that I would not be with him in November.

Throughout the early part of the year I watched Bush with interest as he racked up primary victories, knocking out each of his rivals, including Senator John McCain of Arizona, a man with a hair-trigger temper and a propensity to fashion and shift his positions to appeal to the media. In May 2000, after the primaries were over, I joined a number of former national security officials at an event to endorse Bush. In attendance were Henry Kissinger and George Shultz, as well as Colin Powell and others. Together, we stood behind Governor Bush as he announced his plans for reducing the size of America's nuclear missile arsenal while deploying a missile defense system. The decisions about how to accomplish his objectives, Bush said, would fall to his secretary of defense.[10]

Unlike many presidential nominees, Bush selected an excellent running mate. He made a reasoned, sober choice of a well-known figure who might not offer him much near-term political advantage but who would be both a source of sound counsel and well prepared to assume the presidency if necessary. It was a surprise when Dick Cheney's name was announced—and in this case a pleasant surprise. Cheney was no longer my young assistant but the respected candidate who Joyce and I hoped would become the next vice president of the United States.

At Cheney's request, I traveled to Danville, Kentucky, in October 2000 to attend the debate between the contending vice presidential candidates, Cheney and Senator Joe Lieberman of Connecticut. It was an excellent debate between two fine, experienced, honorable, well-prepared public servants. I thought Dick got the better of it. His quiet competence was reassuring, and it was strengthened by his good humor, which most Americans had not seen.

In November, Joyce and I were invited to be with Dick and Lynne in Austin, Texas, for the election returns. By then I had lived through a good number of very close elections. The 1958 congressional campaign I managed was lost by an eyelash. In the 1960 presidential election, the balloting had seesawed all night between Richard Nixon and John F. Kennedy. Eight years later Nixon had barely defeated Hubert Humphrey, and in 1976 we didn't know if Ford had won or lost until the next morning. But the 2000 presidential election night lasted for more than a month, and it only lurched to a conclusion on December 12, 2000, when George W. Bush officially became the president-elect.

I certainly was supportive of the new President and Vice President, but at sixty-eight years old I thought at most I might help out on a part-time basis if asked, as I had with President Reagan. I was engaged with a variety of activities, including serving on the boards of the RAND Corporation and the National Park Foundation, as well as on several corporate boards. In December 2000 alone I attended six different board meetings in New York, Chicago, California, and Zurich, and was traveling periodically to Washington for government commission meetings. Joyce and I had agreed I would pare down some of my business activities over the next year and spend most of my time at our home in Taos, New Mexico, where our family tended to gather. "We are moving into our rural period," Joyce confidently announced to friends at our fiftieth high school reunion earlier in 2000.

As the Bush transition kicked into gear, I was still serving as chairman of the Commission to Assess United States National Security Space Management and Organization. We were examining how our patchwork of national security institutions dealt with issues in space—bringing me full circle to the issue I had first dealt with as a new member of Congress back in 1963, serving on the space committee.

I was at a meeting of the Space Commission in Washington in late December when Cheney called me. He told me he wanted to get together and that he preferred our meeting to be confidential; he would send a car and driver to bring me to the Madison Hotel downtown, where Cheney and the President-elect were meeting with people being considered for senior administration positions. I was taken into the hotel through the basement so that I would not encounter reporters or hotel staff.[11]

I assumed Cheney wanted my thoughts on candidates being considered for various national security positions. But as we started to talk, I realized

Dick was wondering if I would consider coming into the administration. He asked my views about two posts—CIA director and secretary of defense—saying the President-elect felt both were in need of attention, and that reforming them would be a priority for the administration. Cheney told me that Bush had not yet made decisions on who would lead either department. He had in mind several candidates for each post, and my name was on both lists.

After discussing the two departments, Cheney asked, "Don, if the situation is right and that's where the President-elect finally comes out, do you think you would be willing to take on a full-time assignment?"

That idea had not occurred to me before our conversation. I said I would have to think about it and talk to Joyce.

"Fair enough," Dick said. "Think about it, and if things develop, we'll want you to talk to the President-elect."

Later that evening, Cheney, trying to reach me, telephoned Joyce. She told Dick what she had told me: She would be up for whatever I might decide to do. When Cheney called me again, he said, "Don, I talked to the President-elect, and he'd like to meet with you down in Austin on Friday."

Cheney gave me a sense of how the administration was shaping up. It was already known that Colin Powell was going to be secretary of state. John Ashcroft was to be announced soon as attorney general. Condi Rice would be the national security adviser.

Apparently Bush was interested in my experience in government, my record in business, and my credentials with conservatives. But with the selection of Cheney as vice president and Paul O'Neill as treasury secretary, there was already talk of Bush relying on retreads from the Ford administration. I would be seen as yet one more.

Then, of course, there was the other matter. It was no secret to Governor Bush that his father's relationship with me lacked warmth.[12] Cheney said that at one point, when he was the head of Governor Bush's vice presidential search committee, my name had been raised as a potential running mate. But as Cheney put it, in his usual understated way, the Bush family "did not salute" the idea.

Still, Cheney was confident that President-elect Bush would make his own decisions about whether I was right for a position in his administration. "My preference is for you to go to DoD," Cheney said, adding, "You are Condi's and Colin's top choice for the job."

It was starting to look like Joyce's and my "rural period" might be postponed.

PART VIII

Leaning Forward

Austin, Texas

DECEMBER 22, 2000

The Bush-Cheney team was scrambling through its abbreviated transition period. When I was asked to meet with Bush on December 22, some of the people being considered for key positions were cycling through Austin.

The George W. Bush I encountered at the governor's mansion three days before Christmas was very much the man I had met previously: inquisitive, interested in national security issues, and comfortable with himself. A disciplined man who kept precisely to a fast-moving schedule, he was not much for small talk, which suited me fine.

I congratulated the President-elect on his victory, and he thanked me for my support during the campaign. "I know Dick told you I wanted to visit about a few things," Bush said. In particular, he was expecting to hear my thoughts on the Defense Department and the Central Intelligence Agency.

I was still surprised by Governor Bush's request to see me. He had to be aware that I did not have a close relationship with his father. I thought it spoke well of him that he was interested in meeting me himself to draw his own conclusions. Our meeting that December would be only the second substantive conversation we had ever had.

Bush first asked to hear my views about the Defense Department.[1] I ventured that the Department seemed to have drifted somewhat since the end of the Cold War. President Clinton had not seemed to have a comfortable relationship with the military, due in part to the accusation that he had evaded military service during the Vietnam War. Clinton's early foray into defense policy on the issue of gays in the military exacerbated the problem, with the Joint Chiefs of Staff, led by its then chairman General Colin Powell, taking the rare step of publicly exposing a disagreement with the President.[2] Once burned, Clinton seemed to have left the department largely to its own devices.[3]

That presidential remove, I suggested, had had consequences. It provided the senior officials in the Pentagon the latitude to operate relatively free of top-level strategic direction. Under those circumstances, moreover, various members of Congress were better able to promote their particular interests, sometimes at the expense of sound national policy. In the combatant commands, four-star admirals and generals had wielded considerable power, and for years had been called, I thought inappropriately, commanders in chief. To my thinking, the United States had only one commander in chief, and it was the elected president.[4]

"The task for the incoming secretary of defense will be to implement what you promised throughout the campaign," I said. "You will need to fulfill your pledge that 'help is on the way' for the United States military." If the President-elect hoped to achieve the goals for the Department of Defense that he had outlined over the course of his campaign, he would need a secretary of defense willing to adjust the arrangements that many in the Pentagon had grown comfortable with—that of a light-touch administration that sanctioned their activities from a respectful distance. The task for his new secretary would not be to simply tweak existing policies and practices at the margins.

Bush nodded in agreement. He had outlined ambitious plans for the United States military, emphasizing his view that it needed to accelerate its transformation toward agility, speed, deployability, precision, and lethality. Bush did not strike me as one who worried about ruffling feathers, but he had not served in Washington and had never had to tangle with a bureaucracy as entrenched and powerful as that of the Defense Department, the defense contractors, and congressional interests closely tied to the status quo. I cautioned that military officers as well as career civilian officials in Defense and throughout the executive branch would be wary of reforms that impinged on their acquired authority.

I highlighted an additional challenge to the President-elect. Many members of Congress wanted further cuts to the Defense Department budget. I was convinced the budget needed to be increased significantly to correct the shortfalls of the prior decade and to ensure a military force suitable for our nation's strategic requirements. America's armed forces had been reduced by more than half a million personnel. The defense budget had been cut by $50 billion in inflation-adjusted dollars from the time President Clinton took office in 1993. Yet while defense investment had been reduced sharply, as Bush had noted in his campaign, military deployments had tripled.

I raised other issues with him that I believed the department faced, including: the requirement to begin testing and deploying ballistic missile defenses; improvements to homeland security; a strengthened effort on information warfare; and the urgent need to improve our country's intelligence capabilities.[5] Some of these issues, particularly missile defense, had become polarized. I thought Governor Bush's record of reaching across the aisle to Democrats in the Texas state legislature boded well for garnering bipartisan support for national security programs.

In short, our conversation reflected my belief that the Department of Defense had some longstanding problems and that fixing them would unquestionably require breaking some crockery and bruising more than a few egos. I was direct about this with Bush. He was an experienced executive and politician and knew that what he had promised on the campaign trail with respect to defense policy was important and needed, but that it carried political risk—for the President and for his secretary of defense.

Bush considered those thoughts, and seemed to appreciate them. Unlike our previous meeting, he asked few questions. He appeared to be more interested in having me talk. He next asked my views on the CIA. Having previously served as secretary of defense, I assumed that if the President-elect was thinking about me for a position in his administration, it would most likely be at the CIA.

I thought Bush and the members of the National Security Council would need to exert a stronger hand in setting the intelligence community's priorities, to ensure they reflected the administration's policy objectives. How would the Agency, for example, balance its resources among collecting intelligence on rogue regimes pursuing weapons of mass destruction, analyzing trends in global warming, collecting energy price information, and considering the threats from AIDS or cyberwarfare? Would the CIA spend more or less resources hunting down war criminals in the Balkans or trying to track down terrorists? These were decisions on priorities that would need clear direction from the President and his senior advisers. My experience had led me to believe that direction had been lacking.

"Turbulence in the intelligence community has been a problem," I told him. There had been six CIA directors and seven directors of the Defense Intelligence Agency between 1987 and 2000. "If a corporation changed its management almost every other year," I said, "it would go broke—and it ought to." Bush laughed. I suggested that he nominate someone who could remain in the position long enough to make substantial progress.

Bush asked how I felt about taking a role in his administration. "I'm not eager to go back into government," I replied, "but I would consider it if you thought I could be helpful." However, I advised, there were a number of things he would need to be aware of before coming to a decision.

I cautioned him that after more than two decades in the private sector, running two Fortune 500 companies, serving on a number of boards of directors, and being involved in a number of nonprofit activities, my personal situation was complex and my business responsibilities were extensive. While not connected to major defense contractors, I did have ties to a number of companies, some of which did business, however loosely, with the federal government. Extracting myself from all of those relationships would be difficult—not to mention costly.

I also informed him that like many families across America, ours had not been immune to the problem of drug addiction. Two of our children, Marcy and Nick, had found themselves caught up in that personal torment, and the experience had been heartbreaking and difficult for Joyce and me. But by December 2000, Marcy and Nick were both in recovery. Marcy had been clean for more than a decade and was active in the community of recovering addicts. I wanted the President-elect to be aware of this, so I shared our family's experience with him, as I had with Cheney, who had known our children since they were little. Bush listened with understanding.*

"You might be better off considering candidates who had fewer complications in their lives," I suggested to him. Bush said he appreciated my position and asked me to forward to him or Cheney the names of people I thought might be appropriate for DoD or CIA. I promised to do so.

Before our meeting ended, I had one other thought I wanted to share. I had observed over the past few years that there were ways of behaving that could invite one's enemies to act aggressively, with unintended but dangerous consequences.[6] The American withdrawal under fire from Somalia in the early 1990s was an example. In like fashion, American leaders did not act forcefully in response to al-Qaida's fatal attack on the USS *Cole* in Yemen in 2000. The cumulative effect, I cautioned, suggested to our enemies that the United States was not willing to defend its interests. "Weakness is provocative," I said to the President-elect, who nodded in agreement. "But so is the perception of weakness," I added.

* Early in the administration, Bush came up to Joyce and asked, "What's your son addicted to?" It was a blunt question, to be sure—it was one of the first conversations Joyce had ever had with the President—but that was not unusual for George W. Bush. Perhaps reflecting on his own, well-known challenges with alcohol, he asked thoughtful questions and showed a comforting lack of any embarrassment over the issue. It quickly put Joyce at ease with the new President.

As I saw it, a decade of hesitation and half measures had undermined our national security. The incoming administration would need to give the country strategic direction and build up our defenses and intelligence capabilities. Anyone assuming those posts would need to have that in mind.

I wanted Bush to know that if he selected me I would not intend to simply preside over the department or agency. "Governor, if I were to serve in your administration I would be leaning forward," I said. "If you would be uncomfortable with that, then I would be the wrong man for the job."

CHAPTER 21

Here We Go Again

After my meeting with Bush, Joyce and I spent the Christmas holidays with our family at our home just north of Taos, New Mexico. Dick Cheney called me the afternoon of December 26 to talk about the names I had passed along for the CIA and the Pentagon. I had suggested that they consider Jim Woolsey, who had been Clinton's CIA director, and Bob Kerrey, the former Democratic senator from Nebraska for secretary of defense.[1] I liked the idea of someone who could give the administration bipartisan appeal. I also mentioned a CEO like General Electric's Jack Welch, who had been a successful manager and had a distance from politics. But I had another, more unorthodox notion that I wanted to suggest. "Dick, here's an interesting idea," I began. "What if—"

"Hold on, Don, I've got another call," Cheney interrupted. "Let me get back to you."

Ten minutes later Cheney rang me up again. "We don't need any more advice, Don," Cheney said. "That was the President-elect calling. He told me to tell you he wants you to be secretary of defense."[2]

"Actually before we were interrupted, I was going to suggest you as SecDef," I told Cheney.

It was an idea similar to one I had suggested to President Ford a quarter of a century before, that Nelson Rockefeller, in addition to being the vice president, might also have substantive responsibilities running a cabinet department. There was nothing in the Constitution that prevented such an arrangement. Cheney had run the Defense Department before. I felt that if anyone could handle both positions, it was Dick.

Cheney didn't sound surprised by the suggestion. "The President-elect had the same idea," he acknowledged. But Bush ultimately concluded that running a cabinet agency could conflict with bringing in Cheney as a key adviser on a wider range of policy matters and raised a question about having a sitting vice president regularly testify to Congress.

I told Dick I wanted to discuss Bush's offer with Joyce and think about it more before giving my answer. Later that day, I decided to accept the nomination. The young man who had joined me at the Office of Economic Opportunity as my special assistant back in 1969 would become one of the most influential vice presidents in American history. And to my amazement, I would go from having been the youngest secretary of defense in our country's history to the oldest.

When I left the Pentagon in 1977, the Carter administration reversed many of our decisions seemingly just because they were made by the prior administration. I was not going to do the same. I wanted to understand the rationale behind the Clinton administration's decisions before making changes.

Eleven days before the inauguration, I met with President Clinton's outgoing defense secretary, Bill Cohen. I had known him when he was a Republican senator from Maine and was eager to hear his thoughts. Measured and knowledgeable, he touched on more than fifty issues he expected I would have to deal with as his successor. A number of them proved prescient. He mentioned the threat posed by Iraq's attacks on U.S. and British aircraft in the northern and southern no-fly zones. Noting the recent terrorist bombing of the USS *Cole* in Yemen, he raised the dangers posed by al-Qaida and its leader, Osama bin Laden. He also suggested that it might make sense to appoint a combatant commander to be in charge of protecting the American homeland from attack.[3] Cohen's briefing was enormously helpful as I prepared to testify as a nominee for secretary of defense for the second time.

When I was nominated by President Ford in 1975, the major issue of the day had been détente with the Soviet Union. Now, with the Cold War behind us, there had been upbeat talk during the 1990s of a "peace dividend" that would allow the U.S. government to spend more on domestic programs by reducing investment in national security. Some analysts and scholars had argued that we were at the "end of history"—that the United States and its democratic principles were beyond ideological challenge in the world.[4]

If the world was moving steadily and irreversibly toward democracy and capitalism as some claimed, perhaps there was less need for a robust U.S. national security strategy. Focusing only on the short term and the immediate rather than taking time to consider longer-term potential challenges is an understandable temptation. There is often pressure for the seemingly urgent to crowd out the important. The post–Cold War holiday from strategic thought that characterized much of the prior decade turned out to be not a luxury but a dangerous misjudgment. Overconfidence had spawned complacency. U.S. intelligence capabilities had atrophied, and U.S. operations from Somalia to Haiti had communicated uncertain American resolve. The problems of Islamist extremism, the nuclear weapons programs of North Korea and Iran, the threats from ballistic missile programs, and the crumbling of the United Nations' containment measures for Iraq had been exacerbated.

I doubted we had reached a golden era when nations would pound their swords into plowshares. If there was anything new at the dawn of the twenty-first century, it was the status of the United States as the sole great power in the world, voluntarily shouldering enormous responsibilities for global humanitarian assistance, peace, and prosperity. Dean Rusk, the secretary of state during the Kennedy and Johnson administrations, once observed that "only one-third of the world is asleep at any given time and the other two-thirds is up to something."[5] Though to many our world seemed relatively peaceful, we needed to understand that the world of the twenty-first century, with weapons of unprecedented lethality and availability, is dangerous and untidy.[6]

Not surprisingly, many of the questions at my Senate confirmation hearing tended toward short-term political considerations rather than long-term strategic considerations. The most contentious issue was Bush's call to withdraw the United States from the Anti-Ballistic Missile Treaty. Among other provisions, the treaty, signed by the Americans and the Soviets during the Nixon era, barred even the testing of antimissile technologies, let alone any deployment. Bush wanted out of the treaty so we could proceed with the development of a missile defense program.

In 1983, I was present in the White House when President Reagan announced his ballistic missile defense initiative. Though critics on the left derided his plan as an attempt to achieve *Star Wars*–like armaments, Reagan was a strong proponent. Bush now hoped to carry Reagan's legacy forward by building on two decades of planning, research, and design, and get to the point of actually deploying an operational system.

With the Soviet empire gone, with the Russian government seeking improved relations with the West, and with a number of impressive technological advances, I was surprised to see what had changed in congressional discussions of the issue—practically nothing. Opponents of Bush's plan used arguments almost identical to those wielded against Reagan. Sometimes they were the same arguments from the same people.

Critics were still contending that a missile defense program was not technologically feasible. Increasingly, however, testing indicated that such a system could work. Of course the tests also included some failures. But as I learned from my time in the pharmaceutical business, the development of important products often requires years of trial and error, and a failure can be a valuable learning experience. A zero-failure mentality means no one will try anything, and nothing new will be developed.

Critics also contended the system would cost too much. I pointed out that the defense budget was less than 3 percent of our country's gross domestic product, and that missile defense was less than 3 percent of the defense budget. Was the prospect of protecting Los Angeles or Atlanta from a dictator with a rogue missile not worth that cost? It seemed that a number of the biggest spenders in Congress suddenly became penny-pinchers to block defense programs they opposed.

Some senators argued that missile defense would be destabilizing, and lead to a new arms race or alienate the Russians.[7] In answering their concerns on this score, I recalled lessons that had been reinforced when I chaired the Ballistic Missile Threat Commission. "The problem with ballistic missiles, with weapons of mass destruction . . . ," I suggested, "is they work without being fired."[8] To the extent that hostile regimes or terrorists could threaten

America, our interests, our friends, and our allies with ballistic missiles or chemical or biological weapons, they could alter our behavior and perhaps cause us to acquiesce to actions that we would otherwise resist. Further, our lack of a missile defense system encouraged enemies to invest in offensive missiles to which we remained vulnerable. With an increasing number of nations working to advance their ballistic missile technology, vulnerability was not a strategy I favored for America in the twenty-first century.

Those arguments made little headway with senators such as Carl Levin, then the ranking Democrat on the Senate Armed Services Committee. Over the years I would differ many times with Levin, who often wore his partisanship, like his half-glasses, right on the tip of his nose. Levin cloaked his passion with his studied prosecutorial demeanor but seemed curiously immune to reason on missile defense.

After forging no new ground on missile defense, the senators at the hearing turned to other matters. Senator Pat Roberts posed what I thought was the most interesting and important question at my confirmation hearing. "What's the one big thing that keeps you up at night?" the Kansan asked. There were a number of things I might have mentioned—North Korea, Iran, Iraq, nuclear proliferation, cyberwarfare, or terrorism. But if anything were to keep me up at night, I knew it was my concern about the quality of our intelligence. As I had said to Bush during our meeting in Austin, our country's most important national security challenge was "improving our intelligence capabilities so that we know more about what people think and how they behave and how their behavior can be altered."[9] We needed an ability to uncover what our enemies were thinking and what motivated them. I believed that with more knowledge of that sort we would be better able to alter an enemy's behavior before they launched an attack, rather than waiting and having to take action after an attack.[10]

The hearing ended on a pleasant note when my confirmation received the committee's unanimous support.* Among others, Senator Dick Durbin, a Democrat from my home state of Illinois, said positive words about my record in government and on the wrestling mat. I knew enough about Washington to suspect that, given the decisions ahead, such approbation was unlikely to last.

*There was one issue raised in early January 2001 when the *Chicago Tribune* ran a story about an exchange President Nixon and I had in the Oval Office. Nixon made some disparaging and offensive remarks about African Americans. The irony of the minor controversy was that in contrast to the *Chicago Tribune*'s vigorous opposition to civil rights legislation, as a congressman I had supported the bills throughout the 1960s.

Six days after the President was inaugurated, Joyce and our family were welcomed to the White House for my public swearing-in ceremony. I had been privately sworn in right after the inauguration parade so I could begin my duties at the Department of Defense immediately, but the public event was special for Joyce and me because of those who had gathered with our family. Judge Larry Silberman, a friend and colleague from the Nixon, Ford, and Reagan administrations, performed the ceremony. I was again in the Oval Office with Dick Cheney for the first time in twenty-four years.

"Don asked me to join him here in the White House staff, some thirty-two years ago, and [it] was a turning point for me, from the standpoint of my career," the new Vice President recalled.[11] "From that day on, he kept me busy enough so that I forgot about my graduate studies, gave up any idea of ever returning to academia, and set me on a path that I've never regretted."

Dick noted that we'd both gone on to hold jobs as White House chief of staff and secretary of defense. "Some regard him as the best secretary of defense we ever had," Cheney said. Then with a smile he added, "I would say he was one of the best."

To commemorate the moment, Vice President Cheney later sent me two pictures. One was of the two of us as young men when we worked together at the Office of Economic Opportunity in the Nixon administration. The second was a more recent picture of us from the swearing-in ceremony. At the bottom, Cheney had written, "To Don, here we go again."

CHAPTER 22

Dogs Don't Bark at Parked Cars

"If you are not being criticized,
you may not be doing much."
—*Rumsfeld's Rules*

My first day at the Pentagon included the ceremony that traditionally accompanies the arrival of a secretary of defense: a military parade and a nineteen-gun salute. It also included something I hadn't expected, a sign of the times. As I was getting settled in my office—the same one I'd occupied twenty-five years earlier—a young man walked in. "Mr. Secretary," he said authoritatively, "I'm here to give you your drug test."

He presented me with a plastic cup. As I went to the bathroom to follow through with the request, he added one more instruction. "Sir, please leave the door open." I laughed, but complied. As the young man departed, he said, "I can't wait to tell my girlfriend that I just did the drug test on a secretary of defense."

Back in 1975, one of my first acts in the Pentagon had been to turn the lights on—literally. I wanted to brighten up the halls with displays that conveyed the historical importance of the Department and the special privilege it was to be working in the Pentagon. In the quarter-century since I had departed, some had attached more to the meaning of privilege than I ever intended. Lunches for senior officials had become high-end affairs. The Pentagon even had a pastry chef, who displayed his colorful creations in glass cases in the hall just down from my office.

Another sign of how things had changed in the building were the Marine sentries posted at the door outside my office and the security detail that was assigned to follow me everywhere I went inside the Pentagon. These things made me uncomfortable. If the Pentagon was secure enough for the rest of the twenty-five thousand employees in the building to walk around without personal armed guards or sentries at their doors, I concluded it was secure enough for me. And if it wasn't secure enough, then we had even bigger problems than I thought.

Within days, I had removed as many of the vestiges of pageantry as I could with a few snowflakes. These short memos became my method of communicating directly with the individuals I worked with closely.[1] Some would say they developed into an unrelenting snowstorm. They were raw thoughts that I dictated into my still trusty Dictaphone. Some were trivial housekeeping, some were humorous, and, I admit, some missed the mark. Nonetheless, they reminded Department officials of what I believed needed to be done. I hoped they would encourage people to reach out to me in return. After I had sent a few snowflakes, the sentries at my door were soon gone. But I was never certain about the pastry chef.

Shortly after I arrived, I met with the Joint Chiefs of Staff to discuss my approach and what I hoped we could expect from each other. "I look forward to meeting with you frequently," I said. I added that I hoped our meetings would not simply be gripe sessions on anyone's part. It was often the case that military leaders got caught up in rivalries among the services. I wanted an open atmosphere in which we put the interests of the Department and the country first.

"I am not one to believe that everything that was done previously was wrong," I told the chiefs. "Indeed, I am assuming it is right." I had respect for them and their contributions, and I intended to build on the work they had done. "As I said in my confirmation hearing, there is a lot I don't know. I need to get briefed up, and I intend to do so."[2] I told the senior civilian appointees in the Department that they should seek out the chiefs' advice early and often and "find ways to ask them for their collective judgment."[3] Early on I established a new entity called the Senior Level Review Group (SLRG) that brought together the military chiefs and civilian leadership in the decision-making process.[4] We met regularly to discuss important policy issues facing the Department.

My first task was to consider candidates for the post of deputy secretary of defense. I knew the job could be more difficult with a second-in-command who was not on the same page. President Bush had requested through Cheney that I consider two candidates for deputy: Richard Armitage and Paul Wolfowitz. They were part of the group called "the Vulcans" that had advised Bush on defense policy issues during his campaign. I don't recall ever having met Armitage before, but from the start of our meeting he was brusque. It quickly became clear that since he wasn't going to be secretary of defense, as he had hoped, he preferred to be number two at the State Department, working alongside his friend, Colin Powell. I was happy to accommodate him.

Though the President was considering Wolfowitz for the ambassadorship to the United Nations, he seemed far more interested in serving as deputy secretary of defense. I knew Wolfowitz would be an unusual pick. He did not have the industry background or deep management experience traditional for successful deputy secretaries of defense.* I worried that a man with such an inquisitive, fine mind and strong policy interests might not take well to many of the crucial but often mundane managerial duties—making the hundreds of nonpolicy related decisions—that would come with the deputy post. Still I had had some success over the years in making unorthodox hiring choices. From my prior experiences with Wolfowitz, I knew that he would provide thoughtful insights. I expected to be able to take more time in the day-to-day management of the Department, though if we became engaged in a major conflict, that would have to change.

Wolfowitz was not confirmed by the Senate until March, two months after the presidential inauguration, a critical period in which we suffered from not having even a single Bush appointee confirmed and on the job with me in the Department.† The slow pace of Wolfowitz's confirmation turned out to be a model of swiftness compared to the other four dozen presidential appointees for the Pentagon. It took months and months—almost a full year—to have many of the President's nominees confirmed by the Senate. "The process is

* The traditional model of a secretary of defense and deputy secretary of defense was Mel Laird and his deputy, David Packard, who had cofounded Hewlett Packard and benefited from a long career in business.

† Secretary Cohen offered to be helpful in any way to smooth the transition, which I appreciated greatly. His deputy, Rudy deLeon, and a number of Cohen's senior staff graciously agreed to stay on during the many months it took to get President Bush's nominees selected, cleared, confirmed, and on the job.

outrageous," I lamented to the Joint Chiefs.[5] We suffered from the absences of secretaries of the Army, Navy, Air Force, the undersecretary of defense for policy, and the assistant and deputy assistant secretaries. These were people needed to carry out the work of the Department. The problem was not only the delay in the Senate. It also took months for the President's nominees to receive the security clearances they needed to undertake their work. The White House personnel office was painfully slow in vetting candidates. The cumulative effect was that on average we operated with 25.5 percent of the key senior civilian positions vacant over the entire six years of my tenure, causing serious harm to the Department's activities.*

Despite the dysfunctional clearance and confirmation process, I had to get going quickly on an assessment of the Department and, more broadly, America's circumstance in the world. I sought out someone whose advice I had valued during my first Pentagon tour: Andy Marshall was still working in the department, though his work was less in vogue during the prior Bush and Clinton administrations, in part because of his cautions on China and Russia. After a few weeks on the job, I asked him to join me for lunch—not privately in my office, but in the lunchroom where senior officials often grabbed a sandwich or a bowl of soup. In the status-conscious Pentagon, I wanted to send a message that I valued Marshall's thinking. Over lunch, Marshall warned that the Pentagon bureaucracy was as resistant to change as ever.

It was clear that there would be challenges, especially with some of the leaders in the Army. Some of its senior officers were aware that I had overruled the Army on the M-1 tank decision in the mid-1970s. Over time, the Army and other quarters of the Washington defense establishment had raised pointed concerns about what was characterized as *my* defense transformation agenda. Early on, a story line developed, possibly because of my work on the Space Commission and Ballistic Missile Threat Commission, that I entered the Pentagon with a pet theory about relying more on technology and less on traditional ground forces. This line became the framework for myriad news reports and books about various aspects of my tenure this time as secretary of defense. That myopic focus on technology as a way for some to try to describe my approach to the job was understandable. It was also, to paraphrase H. L. Mencken, simple, neat, and wrong.

In fact, the transformation agenda that I supposedly brought with me to the Pentagon in January 2001 was not of my making. In my first meeting with the chiefs, I made a point of asking for their thoughts on what they believed

* From the time we recommended someone for a position, it took the White House personnel shop seventy days on average to approve them, and then another fifty-two days for Senate confirmation.[6]

"transforming" could mean for the Department.[7] I had not written on the issue of defense transformation, nor did I consider myself in the circle of national security experts who had promoted the idea throughout the 1990s. I was, however, generally open to proposals for reforming and adjusting old institutions and making them more responsive to contemporary circumstances. This, after all, was what I had done during my earlier service in government, and in business.

The President had given me explicit guidance to make the Defense Department "lethal, light and mobile."[8] On the campaign trail, Bush had promised to direct his secretary of defense to begin "an immediate, comprehensive review of our military—the structure of its forces, the state of its strategy, the priorities of its procurement." He was reasonably specific about what he wanted the end result to be:

> Our forces in the next century must be agile, lethal, readily deployable, and require a minimum of logistical support. We must be able to project our power over long distances, in days or weeks rather than months. Our military must be able to identify targets by a variety of means—from a Marine patrol to a satellite. Then be able to destroy those targets almost instantly, with an array of weapons, from a submarine-launched cruise missile, to mobile long-range artillery. On land, our heavy forces must be lighter. Our light forces must be more lethal. All must be easier to deploy. And these forces must be organized in smaller, more agile formations, rather than cumbersome divisions.[9]

I knew that accomplishing even one of Bush's stated goals could preoccupy the Department and its leadership for years. Working toward all of them simultaneously in the Pentagon—an institution that moved with all the speed and dexterity of a half-million-ton oil tanker—would be formidable. People naturally prefer to cling to established ways of doing things. Change is hard. Large organizations especially favor practices they have already mastered, even if those practices, fashioned decades before, are outdated. But the problems we faced, by almost all accounts, were serious. There was an acquisition system with excessive costs and redundancies. Too little attention had been paid to military housing and other infrastructure, as declining defense budgets shifted priorities to preserving costly and, in some cases, out-of-date weapons programs. Yet the resistance to change remained. In my first months in office, more often

ILLUSTRATION BY TAYLOR JONES FOR *HOOVER DIGEST*

than not I heard from senior officials: "Don't change anything. Everything is fine."[10]

A searing reality was that there were people in the world who were working hard to think of novel ways to harm us. The key to transforming the Department, as I saw it, was through encouraging its civilian and military leaders to be more forward-looking, and to think freely, not conventionally. In my view, transformation hinged more on leadership and organization than it did on technology. Precision-guided weapons and microchips were important, but so was a culture that promoted human innovation and creativity. In the information age it was critical that we be able to transmit information rapidly to the people who needed it. More often than not what prevents that is not a computer or a piece of equipment, but outdated organization charts and layers of bureaucracy.

We couldn't afford to be constrained by the way the Department was organized, trained, and equipped today because our ever adapting adversaries were seeking to exploit our weaknesses tomorrow. I often noted that the United States then faced no peers with respect to conventional forces—armies, navies, and air forces—and, as a result, future threats would likely lie elsewhere. Even so, I accepted that we couldn't change overnight. I wanted to stress the gradual and continuing nature of the process. Transformation began before I arrived at the Pentagon, and I knew it would need to continue after I left. It was a continuum, not a discrete event.[11] "Transforming," as I saw it, was a better term than "transformation." The latter sounded as if an organization might go from being "untransformed" to "transformed" with a distinct end point, which was not the case.

I also understood that the President's objectives would face stiff resistance from the iron triangle of Congress, defense contractors, and the permanent DoD bureaucracy. What I had encountered in the 1970s was as strong as ever. As before, I anticipated resistance to any significant changes from some military officers—current as well as retired—who saw themselves as protectors of their service's traditions. Senior members of Congress would also fight changes for a variety of reasons: some to protect pork for their constituents; some to preserve the jurisdiction of their committees and subcommittees; some to lend a hand to friends within the Department; and some because they had honest disagreements with the President's agenda and about the best way forward.

A shift in Washington had taken place since I left the Pentagon in 1977. The relationship between the executive and legislative branches had evolved from proper congressional oversight to what was becoming legislative micromanagement. The Defense Department was receiving between four and eight hundred letters every month from members of Congress, in addition to countless phone calls. All of these inquiries initiated a flurry of bureaucratic activity to resolve them.

In a memo I drafted soon after my return to the Department, I wrote about the challenge posed by the increasingly intrusive role of the Congress. The Defense Department was "tangled in its anchor chain," I wrote. The memo continued:

> The maze of constraints on the Department forces it to operate in a manner that is so slow, so ponderous and so inefficient that whatever it ultimately does produce is late, wasteful of taxpayer dollars, and has the unintended result of leading to still more letters of complaint and calls of criticism from Congress, more critical hearings and more condemnation in GAO [General Accounting Office] reports, to be followed by a still greater number of amendments, restrictions and requirements to try to correct the seeming mismanagement. . . . Over time, the regula-

> tions and requirements that have been laid on are so onerous that . . . they are smothering incentive, innovation and risk taking.[12]

I was astonished, for example, to discover that the legislation authorizing the Department of Defense's budget had exploded from a bill totaling 16 pages in 1977 when I left the Pentagon to a whopping 534 pages in 2001.[13] I knew that Washington lobbyists had invested many years, sizable political contributions, and a great many golf games and private dinners to build intimate relationships with key members of the House and Senate, as well as with select DoD officials. "It is hard to imagine how a collection of such talented, intelligent, honorable, dedicated, patriotic people, who care about the security of the U.S. and the men and women of the armed forces, could have combined to produce such a mess," I dictated in a note to myself that May. "And yet, they conclude that nothing should be done to clean up the mess."[14] Well, I was going to at least give it a try.

As ambitious as the President's transformation agenda was, at its core was a humble recognition of the limits of our intelligence capabilities. I wanted everyone in the Department to be aware that, no matter how much information we collected and no matter how much we planned, surprise was inevitable. No large, complex plan ever gets executed as written. A belief that assumptions will play out as planned is a dangerous form of intellectual arrogance. It can lead to confusion and paralysis when those assumptions turn out to be wrong, as they often will. I believed the dangers that flow from error and surprise could be reduced if built into the plans was the expectation that not only will some anticipated problems be handled imperfectly, but that we will inevitably face problems that had not been anticipated. Indeed, I saw preparing for the inevitability of surprise as a key element in the development of defense strategy. We had to consider our vulnerabilities with imagination and ask ourselves the question Frederick the Great once posed to his generals: "What design would I be forming if I were the enemy?"[15]

A second critical task was to adapt operations as needed and shift resources quickly. That required us to have forces that were agile and could move rapidly. For these lighter forces to be as capable as more traditional heavy forces, far greater precision was required. And to take advantage of the improved precision of our weapons, our forces needed more accurate targeting intelligence.

We also had a responsibility to capitalize on advances in science and engineering. During many years of involvement with national security issues I had seen impressive technological breakthroughs used to vastly improve our military capabilities. When my father served in World War II, for example, it could take dozens of harrowing combat aircraft sorties to ensure that our forces could knock out a single military target. By 2001, however, technological advances had made it possible for a single aircraft to destroy multiple targets with precision on a single sortie.

Because new military systems would only be as good as the human beings who volunteered to operate them, we also needed to make better use of our most valuable asset: the men and women, military and civilian, who make up the Department. This led to one of my high-profile battles as secretary of defense.

For Defense Department civilian employees—some seven hundred thousand strong—the existing personnel system was a tangle of contradictory rules and regulations and, as a result, was counterproductive. The system did not move people into the positions for which they were best suited, nor did it reward good performance. As I knew well, the ability to hire and reward the most talented and move underperformers into other lines of work was essential to success in the private sector. Yet due to congressional restrictions and the influence of government labor unions, it was nearly impossible for senior DoD officials to recruit, promote, transfer, or replace civilian workers efficiently. As a result, instead of trying to fire underperforming workers and hiring new ones, managers were turning to uniformed military personnel and outside contractors, because they could be brought in rapidly to do a job and then be moved out when the job was done. Billions of tax dollars were supporting antiquated personnel systems that were undermining the important work of the Department of Defense.

We made it a high priority early on to address this by proposing a modern personnel system befitting one of the largest, most technologically advanced workforces in the world. I worked with a team at the Pentagon, led by a tenacious undersecretary for personnel and readiness in Dr. David Chu, and a determined secretary of the Navy in Gordon England, to develop and launch the National Security Personnel System. The new system permitted considerably more mobility among the Pentagon civilian workforce and instituted pay for performance. Bush offered his full support for the plan, yet it barely survived several union-led attempts to roll it back.* The Department and many of its civilian employees benefited from the changes Chu and England proposed, but it was met with vigorous opposition, especially from the employees' unions.

Those within the Department who felt the new system would not work in their favor tried to stir up fear and uncertainty among the workforce. Nobody likes to have their job performance reviewed or questioned—indeed, the Pentagon had become arranged in such a way that an effective review system was all but impossible. My determination to untangle the system and make it easier for supervisors to oversee their employees left me vulnerable to the charge that I was trying to punish civilians in the Department. These accusations fed the developing misperception that I cared more about weapons systems than I did about people.

My focus on personnel was not limited to civilian manpower alone. I felt it important to review military personnel operations as well. Over the prior decade, the military services—Army, Air Force, Navy, and Marines—had been the dominant voices in deciding who would move up to become senior generals and admirals. I was given not too subtle hints from senior uniformed officers that the secretary of defense was expected to steer clear of the senior promotion process. My task, as it was suggested to me, was to give pro forma approval to the candidates presented by the services and to duly forward their recommendations to the President. The President's approval was expected to be a similar formality.

The results, predictably, tended to reflect each individual service's interests, which were not always the same as Department-wide interests. The passage of the Goldwater-Nichols Department of Defense Reorganization Act of 1986 imposed requirements for a more joint perspective as a key element for promotion. I sensed that service parochialism remained in the list of officers submitted from the services. I recognized that officers with stars on their shoulders had generally earned them for good reasons. But I felt that special attention was essential in selecting the three- and four-star generals and admirals. They would become the key leaders of the military services and the combatant commands for the twenty-first century.

One crucial aspect to transforming the Department, in my mind, was

* In the end, in October 2009, after labor unions representing federal workers spent many millions of dollars to help elect sympathetic lawmakers, Democratic majorities in both houses of Congress voted to kill the new pay-for-performance system we had put in place.

aggressively carrying out the intent of the Goldwater-Nichols legislation by reducing the redundancies, divisions, incompatibilities, and rivalries among the services—a process referred to as achieving "jointness." Goldwater-Nichols had set the stage for developing joint capabilities that would both reduce costs and allow the services to leverage and capitalize on each other's strengths. I wanted to encourage as much joint planning and as many joint operations among the Army, Navy, Air Force, and Marine Corps as possible. I was convinced that jointness could not be mandated from the top. It had to be inculcated in layers well below the secretary of defense. This required multiple leadership centers and individuals some layers down who shared that conviction and recognized the need for innovation and flexibility within their own services. They needed to be able to work in Washington with other departments and agencies that were out of their well-established comfort zones. And above all, they had to be candid and forthright, willing to disagree in private with me and with the President if their military advice differed from a course being considered.[16] I felt that the only way to ensure that I was recommending those kinds of candidates to the President was to be personally involved in the selection process.

I called on my senior military assistant from my first tour as secretary, Staser Holcomb, a retired vice admiral living on the West Coast. Staser came to Washington and worked with the service chiefs to put together dossiers on their candidates for the key service and joint positions so we could conduct a more than perfunctory review. Knowing that I needed senior input to help with these decisions, I established a four-person committee that included the Department's top two civilian officials and top two military officers: the chairman and vice chairman of the Joint Chiefs, the deputy secretary of defense, and me.

We discussed the tasks that would need to be performed for a specific post and the qualities and experiences that would best qualify an individual. Then we considered the recommendations of the services, secretaries, and chiefs, as well as other candidates. This was not a simple exercise. What may make for an outstanding fighter pilot, for example, is not necessarily the same set of skills needed for success as a combatant commander or service chief. After considering the various candidates, each of the four members of our committee made a point of becoming acquainted with the services' top candidates, well before we needed to make our recommendation to the President. I did not want the prospects who happened to work in the Pentagon to have an undue advantage just because we were more likely to know them. So as I and the others traveled around the country and the world, we made a point of meeting with the top prospects for the senior posts that would soon be vacant.

In my view it was certainly proper that I be involved in senior promotions. Indeed, it was the secretary of defense who had to make the recommendations to the President, and it is the President who makes the nominations to the U.S. Senate. I saw it as an important responsibility. I had had a good relationship with many of the military leaders I worked closely with as secretary under President Ford. I was the one who came to the defense of then chairman of the Joint Chiefs, George Brown, when many were calling for him to be fired. But because my new system represented a major change in how the Department currently operated, it caused considerable contention. Despite the pushback, however, it resulted in an exemplary bench of officers.

I remembered during my first year at Searle that I had ruffled some feathers as I raised questions about the old way of doing business. That was also the case at the Pentagon. It was clear that there were some in the Department who felt I was brusque or asked more questions than made them comfortable. In a large bureaucratic institution, Newton's laws of physics apply: A body at rest tends to remain at rest, and a body in motion tends to remain in motion. I was determined that the Department of Defense accelerate forward.

Then, at President Bush's specific direction, I launched an unprecedented, comprehensive review of America's global defense posture. This was one of the most fascinating, well conceived, and fruitful projects we implemented at the Pentagon. But it too rankled several groups—some in the military, some in foreign governments, and some in the State Department—stirring up a veritable trifecta of harrumphing, protest, and consternation. Admiral Jim Ellis told me what his Naval Academy physics professor had taught him: "If you want traction, you must first have friction." We were generating more than our share of heat.

The way our forces were stationed overseas was so outdated, it was as if they had been frozen in time for the decades since Berlin and Tokyo fell in 1945, the armistice halted the Korean War in 1953, and the Cold War ended in 1991. Of the quarter million troops deployed abroad in 2001, more than one hundred thousand were in Europe, the vast majority stationed in Germany to fend off an invasion by a Soviet Union that no longer existed. An additional one hundred thousand were in East Asia and the western Pacific, vestiges of the occupation of Japan in World War II and the Korean War. Those deployments were obviously not taking into account the twenty-first-century reality that Germany was now one of the wealthier nations in Europe and that Japan and South Korea were among the most capable and self-sufficient in Asia.

Yet the status quo persisted in the Department; senior DoD officials were not questioning those deployments. Some combatant commanders seemed to feel they owned the forces and assets under their commands, and were loath to part with them. I started to pepper officials with what seemed to me obvious questions. Was it still wise to have large numbers of our forces in a defensive posture in western Germany to deter a tank invasion from the Soviet Union? Did we still need so many thousands of troops stationed in South Korea when the Korean people were increasingly irritated by the American troop presence, and given that Korea could well afford to do considerably more to defend its own territory? Was the enormous investment the American taxpayers were making in our military really meeting the challenges and realities of the twenty-first century or of the last century?

I also found it unwise to have large numbers of our troops stationed in countries where we needed to get approval from the host government and even in some cases from their parliaments before the president of the United States could move our forces where needed to defend the American people. It was unfair to the American taxpayer to be paying for one set of forces to defend Europe and another to defend East Asia, but then not to be able to use them elsewhere as might be required to defend our country and our interests.

I asked the policy office at the Pentagon to look at the globe afresh and to consider what our posture would be if we reconfigured it ideally, on the basis of what we might need in the future rather than for the past.[17] The task involved a number of complex questions. Moving troops and their families away from bases Americans had been using for decades meant disrupting a way of life that had been created around some of these large bases—complete with American schools, shopping villages, hospitals, and restaurants. And though some of our deployments seemed outdated, the presence of our forces in Germany had been providing Europeans with a sense of comfort and security. Our presence in South Korea and Japan was a sign of American resolve to defend northeast Asia—an important sector of the globe that lived in the shadow of a burgeoning China and a reckless North Korean dictator.

I believed our troops had to do more than serve as symbols or security blankets for wealthy allied countries. We needed capable, if independent-minded, allies willing to invest in their own defenses. In large part because America was taking on much of the job for them, European defense expenditures were disturbingly low and declining as a percentage of their GDPs. In prosperous South Korea, the government had taken the unfortunate step of shrinking their own army on the assumption that we would maintain our presence and be prepared to bring in additional divisions if North Korea provoked a war.

Keeping in mind our new national security strategy, with its emphasis on the unanticipated, I knew we could no longer assume that we could predict where we might have to conduct military operations. Whether it would be for humanitarian work—earthquake or tsunami relief, for example—or combat operations, our forces needed the flexibility to move rapidly and without requiring the approval of a host country. Further, I wanted our military to be not only where they were needed but also where they were wanted, appreciated, and where we could move them rapidly to deal with whatever contingencies might arise. I questioned the desirability of tying our forces to massive, permanent bases, especially when it created opposition among local populations. Tensions between our military and Okinawan politicians, for example, had been growing for some time.[18] In the country that governed Islam's holiest shrines, Saudi Arabia, the presence of our troops spawned resentments against both the American and Saudi governments. Osama bin Laden propagandized on this point to recruit terrorists and raise money.[19]

No previous U.S. administration had attempted such a major global defense posture review; we aimed to rationalize our facilities, activities, relationships, legal arrangements, and surge capabilities worldwide to fit a strategy intended to look into the future, not reflect the past.* Our work, not surprisingly, stimulated interest and concern. President Bush's political opponents who wanted to come across as more hawkish on defense issues made ridiculous accusations that we were "[pulling] back our forces."[20] This ignored the fact that our posture review increased our capability to project forces rapidly anywhere in the world. The more suspicious wondered why we were in such a rush to get this done. My view was, why wait? We had wasted billions of dollars, and we had been sitting in place across the globe for close to sixty years.

Senior State Department officials initially raised no objections to our review. Secretary of State Powell received periodic updates and seemed content with our analysis. But whatever Powell thought about the defense posture

* In addition to our global posture, I also thought our bases and facilities in the United States should not be off-limits to review. In 2001, on my recommendation, the Bush administration proposed the largest U.S. military base realignment and closure (BRAC) effort in history. We reduced the number of bases across America to streamline DoD, improve its overall effectiveness, and cut costs. By closing bases we no longer needed, we projected that we could save the American taxpayer an estimated $5.5 billion every year. We also ended up earning criticism from a number of members of Congress who represented areas where bases might be closed.

review, others in his department anonymously voiced reservations in the press that echoed the concerns and questions of some of our allies that opposed changing the status quo. From Bosnia to Kosovo to the Sinai peninsula, it seemed that the U.S. military was engaging in new peacekeeping efforts every few years. Those efforts were stretching DoD resources. We either had to increase our capabilities or find ways to pare down our peacekeeping efforts sooner.[21]

When I pushed to reduce the numbers of American military forces supposedly monitoring a two-decade-old truce between Israel and Egypt in the Sinai peninsula, "[s]ome State Department officials [began] to argue that a withdrawal would underscore what is already seen by some in the region as an American retreat from the Middle East."[22] When I learned, for example, that the Pentagon had been spending $225 million every year to maintain our forces in Iceland, I sent a memo to Powell recommending we make a change.[23] I pointed out that our aircraft originally had been stationed in Iceland to track Soviet subs in the North Atlantic. Now that there was no Soviet Union, they were spending their time helping Icelandic fishermen in distress. More than $2 billion had been spent since the end of the Cold War in 1989 to keep our aircraft in Iceland. I believed the $4 billion we would be spending over the next twenty years could be better invested elsewhere. Even so, it took me three years of pressing and prodding—and the resulting loss of another $700 to $800 million to taxpayers—before I could get our military presence in Iceland renegotiated. This was accomplished over the continued opposition of the State Department.[24] Iceland was a wake-up call for me. If it was that hard to change our posture there, changes elsewhere in the world would be even more difficult.

CHAPTER 23

Bears in the Woods

"There's a bear in the woods. For some people, the bear is easy to see. Others don't see it at all. Some people say the bear is tame. Others say it's vicious and dangerous. Since no one can really be sure who's right, isn't it smart to be as strong as the bear? If there is a bear?"

—*Reagan presidential campaign ad, 1984*

Upon arriving at the Pentagon, I made a list of what I saw as the areas of the world that would need to be near the top of our national security priorities. Each needed to be managed deftly. I was particularly focused on our relations with two of America's former rivals—a resurgent Russia and a strengthening China.

Russia, in particular, was an early priority, and I worked hard to establish a productive relationship with my Russian counterpart, Defense Minister Sergei Ivanov. Fortunately, Ivanov was one of the most enjoyable foreign officials I encountered. He was intelligent, quick, well connected in Moscow, and had a sense of humor. Ivanov was a fine conversationalist and spoke excellent English. Unlike some former Soviet diplomats, he didn't engage in long lectures. "I see you get right to the point," I said to him in our first meeting, as we discussed U.S.-Russian relations. "I will try my best to do so as well."[1] Ivanov was an avid basketball player and fan, so I took him to a Washington Wizards game when he was in town for a meeting. Our friendship was genuine, and I think it proved helpful.

But there were limits to how far personal affinity could go. Unsurprisingly, Ivanov would become uncomfortable when in meetings an American official would make a reference to the West's victory in the Cold War and the collapse of the Soviet Union. He was a steady and effective supporter of President Putin's agenda and never allowed daylight between himself and his government's policies.

In 2001 Russia was at a crossroads, and in many ways it remains there even a decade later. Though the Russians retained the nuclear arsenal of a great power, in other respects they were weak. They had lost much of their old empire. Their gross domestic product was small and largely dependent on the extraction and sale of oil and natural gas. Their population was shrinking. They faced security challenges from China and Chechen Muslims.

It was difficult for many in our country to move away from the Cold War mindset that characterized the Russian government as an enemy. For many, the idea of a threatening superpower—what the Reagan campaign famously characterized as a "bear in the woods"—remained deeply ingrained. While I exercised a certain caution when it came to the Russians, I was hopeful that the relationship could change. During the 1990s, I had been a member of a group of American and Russian business leaders who sought ways to encourage the growth of trade, commerce, and industry within the former Soviet Union. The U.S.–Russia Business Council, sponsored by the RAND Corporation, offered me an opportunity to spend time in Moscow, getting to know the country's business leaders in the years following the Soviet collapse. Many Russian businessmen wanted a more liberal economy and increased Western investment. Others who had benefited from the system of corrupt, state-sanctioned monopolies, preferred to see that system perpetuated.

It seemed to me Russia's leaders were considering two options to reclaim their status as a great power. One was to consort with those regimes around the world that were hostile to the West—China, North Korea, Iran, Iraq, Venezuela, and Cuba, for example—and to increase Russia's sway through intimidation of its neighbors. Choosing that path would entail pressuring the former Soviet satellites to respect Russia's "sphere of influence." It also would mean that the Russian government would likely face economic difficulties if foreign corporations consequently decided to invest elsewhere.

As I saw it, Russia had another option. It could become a significant global economic power and a partner with the West. It had vast natural resources. Its population included world-class mathematicians, scientists, and engineers. It had an educated labor force with skills relevant to the world economy. I thought that Russia might be able to accomplish a feat of rebirth similar to Germany's and Japan's following World War II—but with advantages that the Germans and Japanese did not have. The Cold War had not left Russia a scene of physical devastation. The country therefore could conceivably become a focus of international trade and investment if Russian leaders were willing to create an environment hospitable to enterprise.[2] I was reminded of what former President Nixon told me in 1994 after a visit to Russia. "The Cold War is over," said the old cold warrior, "but it is not won."[3] His point was that though communism had failed, freedom was still on trial in Russia. If Russia succeeded in building a free system, Nixon said, it would encourage other totalitarian states to move in the same direction. "But if it fails," he warned, "it will lead to more dictatorships."[4]

I wanted Russia to join the circle of advanced, prosperous societies and would have been pleased to see the country grow in strength as a friend or even a partner of the West. Accordingly, I thought the best path for the United States was to avoid hectoring Russia on imperfect democratic practices, but rather to encourage it along a path toward freer economic and political systems. I tried to put myself in their shoes as I considered how we could best make the case to them about our goals and intentions. "Discussions with Russia ought not to be stove-piped into segments," I wrote in one memo. "What they want is in the political and economic areas—dignity, respect, standing and foreign investment to help their economy."[5] Respect, especially, seemed to be the key. That at least was my perspective when the administration began to discuss one of the prickliest issues in U.S.–Russia relations: missile defense.

We knew Russia's leaders were likely to oppose a system, to some degree. But I hoped that they could see beyond the old Soviet complaints that our program could spark World War III. The objection was wrong on its face. The relatively small scale of our proposal would not make us capable of defending against Russia's massive arsenal of missiles. No well-informed Russian official seriously worried that the United States's missile defense program would protect America against a massive nuclear strike from Russia. I suspected that their real concern might have been that U.S. missile defenses could damage Russia's image as a world power.

A necessary step for implementing an initial missile defense program was to remove the legal barrier to developing the system: the Anti-Ballistic Missile (ABM) Treaty. I believed it was well past time to withdraw from a disadvantageous treaty that, moreover, by 2001 was of dubious legality.* The Bush administration seemed united on this point.

In an effort to help assuage concerns about our missile defense interests, in August 2001 I made a visit to Moscow, my first as Bush's secretary of defense. The last time I'd traveled to Russia as a member of the government was with President Ford to discuss a new Strategic Arms Limitation Treaty with Soviet leader Leonid Brezhnev. Though Vladimir Putin came of age in the Soviet era as a KGB agent, he was no Brezhnev. Putin was savvier with the media and more sophisticated. He exuded a youthful self-assurance, undoubtedly a political asset in a country with an aging population. Putin did, however, begin our meeting in the Kremlin with a Soviet-style monologue, forcefully outlining his positions and commanding rapt attention.

When he was finished, he seemed interested in getting a sense of the approach our new administration would take to Russia and invited an exchange. "Mr. President," I began, "I share your hope for a warmer relationship between our two countries." I noted that I enjoyed working with his defense minister, who had joined us for the meeting.

In fact, I repeated some of the points I had made earlier to Ivanov, appealing to the Russians' self-interest. "As a businessman for almost twenty-five years," I said, "I know that an environment hospitable to enterprise—with the rule of law, a free press, anticorruption efforts, and the like—are vital to attracting foreign investment." I noted that "money is a coward"—that is, when potential investors see instability and uncertainty, they tend to invest their money elsewhere. I told Putin that when businessmen see that Russia's closest associates are Cuba, North Korea, Iran, Libya, and the like, and see corruption and periodic public opposition to American policies, they conclude Russia is an uncertain place and that their investments could be at risk. Those were not welcome conclusions for a Russia that sought to emerge as a world economic power.[6]

Putin and I also talked about the way business executives make decisions on where to build manufacturing plants, where to do research, and, in short, where they decide to conduct business. We discussed how, in a free country, people vote with their feet. Businessmen favor countries that create a competitive business environment.

* The only other signatory to the ABM Treaty, the Soviet Union, had ceased to exist.

On the central issue of my visit—the ABM Treaty—Putin said something that I thought he believed, but which I had not expected him to say. He told me that he was not wedded to the old Cold War doctrine of mutual assured destruction, which sought to use the threat of a nuclear exchange as a deterrent between the superpowers. Putin said he understood that our proposed missile defense system would be small scale, designed to deter and defend against rogue states. He knew well it could be overwhelmed by Russia's arsenal, and that once operational, the system could successfully defend against handfuls, not thousands, of missiles.

But Putin forthrightly admitted he had a political dilemma. He said he might look like a "traitor" to Russia's national security if he allowed the United States to withdraw from the ABM Treaty without protest.

Putin left me with the impression that he was interested in the option of closer ties with NATO and the West. "Russia is being pushed out of the system of civilized Western defense," he observed. He charged that NATO had not been sufficiently receptive to including Russia in its collective defense strategy. There was an explanation for this, of course. Many NATO countries—particularly those close to the Russian border—were wary of the Russians. After all, some of them had only recently been threatened or intimidated by the "big bear." Others had been unwilling Soviet satellite states.

Still, I told Putin that I thought it was conceivable that if Russia continued developing freer political and economic systems and accepted NATO's expansion along its borders, the United States and NATO could welcome Russia into a more stable relationship with the West. I'm not sure my response satisfied him, but I thought it was unrealistic to expect a warm relationship with NATO to blossom overnight, given the attitudes of the Warsaw Pact nations that had so recently joined.

Later that evening, I learned how far America and Russia still had to go to fully understand one another. At a dinner with Ivanov and senior Russian military officials, General Yuri Baluyevsky, then the country's second-ranking military officer, regaled us with a fascinating "fact" I suspect he may have learned from the internet. The brains behind the U.S. missile-defense system, he declared, as if he had unearthed an embarrassing secret, was "an economist named Lyndon LaRouche." LaRouche, of course, was well-known in the United States as a political extremist and conspiracy theorist. He inhabited the murky zone where the far left and far right wings of politics bend toward each other. To my knowledge, his influence on the American missile defense program was nil.

I made an effort to correct the record for the assembled Russians. But the encounter was troubling. It was not in either of our interests that Russian military leaders should lack such basic knowledge about the United States and the ways American officials think and operate.

If Russia loomed large in early discussions in the Bush administration, the rise of the People's Republic of China (PRC) and its implications for American strategy in Asia was perhaps an even greater and more delicate issue. I had some familiarity with the PRC going back to the 1960s. I was not an early admirer. In Congress, I had been a supporter of the Committee of One Million—a bipartisan organization "in opposition to any concessions to Communist China."[7] After Nixon's historic opening, I traveled to China with Henry Kissinger in 1974 to continue normalization talks with the then vice premier, Deng Xiaoping, who later became the country's paramount leader.*

I returned to China in 1999 as part of a delegation of former national security officials sponsored by the American Foreign Policy Council. The occasion was the fiftieth anniversary of Mao Zedong's victory over the nationalist forces of Chiang Kai-Shek and the founding of the PRC. By then, Beijing's streets were more congested, its air much denser with smog than before, as automobiles had largely replaced bicycles. To commemorate the occasion, the Communist Party had set up a series of exhibitions with cultural displays depicting each of China's many diverse provinces. As befit what the Chinese thought of as a "renegade" province, the Taiwan exhibit was light on culture. In the center of the large room was an enormous diorama of Taiwan under siege. Models of Chinese warships and bombers were attacking the island, while Chinese troops stormed its beaches and missiles landed in its cities. Though the tragedy of Tiananmen Square in 1989 had opened the eyes of some in the West to the Communist regime's capacity for ruthlessness, the prevailing sense was that China would not flex its growing muscles for the foreseeable future. After seeing that Taiwan display, I was not so sure.

Unlike many Western policy makers, the Chinese made a practice of thinking several moves ahead while they looked to take advantage of current events. Kissinger once remarked to me that the game the PRC plays is

*In our meeting, Deng was still trying to understand the American democratic system. He wondered how the U.S. Congress could enforce laws on China to reclaim American assets lost in Mao's Communist takeover twenty-five years earlier. "I could explain it," I told him, "but it would take a great deal of mao tai," referring to the Chinese liquor.[8]

neither checkers nor chess. It was something far more complicated—patient and cautious. "It's a totally different game," he said, "and they're good at it."[9] The writings of Sun Tzu were not quaint historical literary contributions in China but principles the Chinese live by to this day. A recurring theme of those writings is long-term strategic thinking. "Be extremely subtle, even to the point of formlessness," Sun Tzu wrote. "Be extremely mysterious, even to the point of soundlessness. Thereby you can be the director of the opponent's fate."[10] Sun Tzu taught that a battle could be won through careful preparation and superior knowledge of the enemy, even before the enemy knows a battle has begun.

I arrived in the George W. Bush administration among the more cautious about China's long-term ambitions. The PRC consistently said it was seeking a comfortable relationship with the United States and the West and took some steps to reinforce that promise. At the same time it was steadily building up its military capabilities, placing hundreds of missiles across the strait from Taiwan and periodically engaging in heavy-handed provocations.[11] I was intent on understanding what the PRC's intentions might be. What implications might their actions have for their neighbors, such as Taiwan, India, Singapore, Mongolia, and Vietnam, and for our close allies in Japan and South Korea? What might it mean for the flow of commerce in the Pacific? Why was there so little transparency about their defense spending and its purposes? Each time I raised such questions in various diplomatic forums, it invariably led to headlines about my "hard-line" approach toward China.

We were fooling ourselves if we believed the Chinese were the "strategic partner" that President Clinton and others had wishfully suggested.[12] When I worked on China issues in the 1990s, I was struck by an old Chinese adage: "Sometimes you have to kill a chicken to frighten the monkeys." It was illustrative of their approach: China would coerce and make an example out of their neighbors, internal dissenters, and internal independence movements (such as the Tibetan and Uighur efforts) for the purpose of bringing others into line.[13]

Whatever my concerns about Chinese intentions, I had a reasonably clear view on what the administration's stance should be. As with the Russians, I tried to put myself in their shoes. Policy making often involves trade-offs. If the administration appeared too accommodating, the Chinese might well interpret that as a sign of weakness, which could encourage more belligerence. Conversely, if we treated China as a threatening rival, our antagonism could encourage the more militant elements in internal Chinese debates to prevail. Soon after my return to government, I put some of these thoughts on paper:

- We ought to avoid unnecessarily working ourselves into problems with China.
- Confronting China with a list of the things we want from them, telling them how to behave, won't work.
- Our goal ought to be to not emphasize them as a threat today, but, rather, see if we can't seize the opportunity to establish a relationship that will be more to our advantage when they do become stronger.[14]

President Bush felt that we had an opportunity to work with China's leaders to try to help shape their country's future by demonstrating firmness, candor, and cooperation. I agreed with that approach. I watched the Chinese carefully to see the extent to which their actions reflected their words. The Chinese were watching us as well. It was not long before we had an opportunity to learn more about each other and, unfortunately, I don't think America emerged from that encounter with the better hand.

In the predawn hours of April 1, 2001, the American crew of the EP-3 flight designated Mission PR32 made its way from Kadena Air Base in Okinawa on a routine mission over the South China Sea.* The American EP-3 was a lumbering, four-engine propeller-driven aircraft outfitted with an impressive array of advanced electronics. It was in international airspace conducting a reconnaissance mission some seventy miles off China's shores and following a long-established flight path that was in full compliance with international agreements.[15] As we were entitled to carry out these routine missions, so too were the Chinese entitled to dispatch aircraft to monitor our activities. But in previous months, China had stepped up its maneuvers around our reconnais-

*In 1956, I learned that one of our close friends and a fellow Navy pilot, Jim Deane, had been shot down while flying a similar reconnaissance mission off the coast of China. Lieutenant Deane's remains were never recovered. There were rumors he might have survived the crash and was being held captive, but we were unable to get any conclusive information. Deane's wife asked her congressman, Gerald R. Ford, for his help in obtaining information. Later, on my 1974 trip to China with Kissinger, I was surprised when Kissinger handed me a memo about Jim Deane, whose fate he planned to raise with the Chinese. When I became secretary of defense in 2001, I tried to gather more information on missing American pilots, including Deane, when I met with Chinese officials. Despite our efforts, the Chinese never budged on the issue and Jim's widow, Beverly Deane Shaver, continues to search for answers.

sance planes, occasionally endangering them and their crews.* The Clinton administration had protested to the PRC about these activities the previous December, but without effect.[17]

As the twenty-four-member crew of the U.S. EP-3 neared the conclusion of their six-hour flight, they were intercepted by two PRC F-8 fighter jets, one of which maneuvered aggressively. After two increasingly dangerous passes, the Chinese pilot apparently miscalculated and flew into one of the EP-3's propellers, delivering a fatal blow to the Chinese F-8 and shearing off our EP-3's nose cone. With the nearest allied air base at least six hundred nautical miles away, the American crew had to make an emergency landing on Hainan Island, entering Chinese airspace.[18] As they descended, the crew attempted to destroy the sensitive information and equipment that was onboard to protect American intelligence-gathering capabilities.

When the EP-3 landed, the Chinese government's greeting was decidedly unfriendly. Armed Chinese soldiers interrogated the crew in the middle of the night and refused to allow them to send word of their fate to American officials.[19] This was the hospitality of a nation whose pilot had almost killed two dozen American service members. The PRC's state-run Xinhua News Agency reported falsely about the incident. Instructing the Chinese people to "denounce U.S. hegemonist act," the government asserted that the EP-3 "rammed and damaged a Chinese jet fighter."† The Chinese government had effectively kidnapped an American crew and then lied to the world about it. Further, the Chinese were demanding that the United States apologize for the entire incident.

As the Chinese held our crew hostage, President Bush and the National Security Council deliberated on how to react. State Department officials considered the crisis a diplomatic matter and proceeded as if the Pentagon need have no role in helping to shape the American response. Though I recognized that the U.S. ambassador in China would handle negotiations to secure the crew's release, it was Defense Department personnel who were being held hostage. Knowing the sensitivity of the situation—China was obviously testing the new American president—I saw the problem not as a matter to

* Of the forty-four Chinese Air Force interceptions of U.S. reconnaissance flights prior to April 1, 2001, six involved Chinese planes coming within thirty feet of U.S. aircraft and two involved Chinese planes coming within ten feet.[16]

† The article went on to say that the U.S. reconnaissance plane had violated Chinese airspace, and in doing so was a "threat to the national security of China." The article "modestly" closed with the demand that "the U.S. side . . . make a prompt explanation to the Chinese government and people about the U.S. plane's ramming of the Chinese jet and its infringement upon China's sovereignty and airspace, apologize to the Chinese side and shoulder all the responsibility arising from the incident."[20]

be worked out by a small circle of State Department officials but one to be decided by the President, with the advice of his NSC, which included the Defense Department. The diplomats' default position was to negotiate a settlement that seemed designed to placate the Chinese government. But for me, after their provocation, keeping the Chinese happy was not a goal that I thought should be at the absolute top of America's priority list.

On the morning of April 2, 2001, a day after the capture of the American crew, Bush called Powell, Rice, and me into the Oval Office. The President asked each of us for our views. Powell and Rice appeared to favor a U.S. apology. Powell told us that State Department officials also favored a suspension of the routine U.S. reconnaissance flights that the Chinese had been periodically intercepting. Powell added that Admiral Dennis Blair, the combatant commander of the U.S. Pacific Command, supported the recommendation to suspend the flights. These views reflected the natural inclination to move quickly to bring the unfortunate incident to an end, even if America had to humble itself to get the crew back as rapidly as possible. American companies were investing many billions of dollars in China. There were significant economic interests in maintaining good relations with the PRC by offering an apology and moving on.

When the President asked me what I thought, I said I did not favor an apology or suspending our reconnaissance flights. The Chinese knew they were in the wrong. Capitulating to their threats and feigned outrage could embolden China's military and political leaders to commit still more provocative acts. I did not believe that America would benefit from being seen as a weak supplicant. Moreover, I thought that there should be some kind of clear penalty for China's dangerous behavior. I recommended that we temporarily suspend our military-to-military contacts with the PRC. I strongly favored these military exchanges in general, but the PRC had been using the contacts as intelligence-gathering missions, and had been denying us truly reciprocal visits of equal value by American military officers. Since the Chinese benefited from these military exchanges, this seemed to be an opportunity to impose a cost on them and to later renegotiate more balanced exchanges. Bush agreed to that proposal but remained undecided on the apology.

The impasse over the EP-3 crew ultimately ended with Bush approving a letter from U.S. Ambassador Joseph Prueher to the Chinese Minister of Foreign Affairs expressing "regret" over China's "missing pilot and aircraft" and for our EP-3 entering China's airspace without "verbal clearance."[21] This language was unfortunate, since the fact was, of course, that our aircraft had entered China's airspace only because the alternative was crashing in the South China Sea. The wording was in effect an apology, and the Chinese played it as one. The twenty-four U.S. crew members were released, though it would be months before we finally got back the EP-3, and then in pieces, after the Chinese had inspected every inch of it.

The April 2001 incident provided an early window into the workings of the Bush administration's "interagency process"—the bureaucratic term for the way the several national security–related departments and agencies interact, advise the president, and carry out his decisions. The vice president, the secretary of state, the secretary of defense, the chairman of the Joint Chiefs of Staff, the director of the CIA, and the national security adviser all had an opportunity to offer their views to President Bush at the height of the crisis. Having considered the options, and the advice we recommended, he decided the course he thought was best. Even though Bush chose a course somewhat different from my recommendations, he made the decision. I thought that was exactly how the NSC should have functioned. Regrettably, that would not always be the case.

CHAPTER 24

The National Security Council

Throughout my decades in public life, I have seen personalities come and go, but some degree of friction in the NSC's processes has remained a constant. In the Nixon administration, I observed then National Security Adviser Henry Kissinger and Secretary of State Bill Rogers differ over foreign policy before Nixon concluded that the solution was for Kissinger to take Rogers' place while keeping his post at the NSC. As White House chief of staff, I saw in the Ford administration how the President had to navigate between Kissinger's détente policy on the one hand and Jim Schlesinger's (and later, my) concerns about it on the other. The media covered clashes between National Security Adviser Zbigniew Brzezinski and Secretary of State Cyrus Vance exhaustively during President Carter's administration. I also observed the differences between Secretary of State George Shultz and Secretary of Defense Cap Weinberger during the Reagan years.

The disagreements were not simply the result of their personalities, though there is generally no shortage of strong views among senior government officials. More often than not, the differences were the almost inevitable result of the differing statutory responsibilities and roles of the various federal departments. Add to those the influences and pressures of the many congressional committees and subcommittees that oversee the executive branch and jealously guard their jurisdictions, interests, and authorities, and friction is created.

Just as there is no single successful model of management in business, there is no single correct model or approach for a president to use to lead his NSC. The optimal system, of course, is the one that works best for each individual president. Some leaders (Ford and Kennedy, for example) preferred to hear discussions and debate personally. Some (Nixon and Reagan) relied somewhat more heavily on memos that set out various options together with arguments pro and con for each suggested approach. Some (Nixon and Clinton) had close relationships with trusted advisers and tended to disfavor larger meetings. Some presidents made a point of staying at the strategic level in policy discussions (Reagan), while others routinely drilled down into minute details (Carter).

Still, there are basic principles and good practices for NSC management that are applicable in most cases. Foremost among these is that the president's senior advisers understand the National Security Council's role as well as their duties as members or advisers. The NSC's task is to mitigate problems that arise from the way our government is organized. Brilliant and farsighted as they were, the Founders of our country created a federal government structure suited to handle eighteenth-century international problems. They established cabinet departments for diplomacy (State), for defense and deterrence (War and Navy), and for finance (Treasury). That was sufficient two centuries ago, when problems in the world generally fell into one of those categories at any given time.

But by the end of World War II, America's interests and activities around the world could not be categorized distinctly as diplomatic or military. Scholars invented the term "national security" to apply to matters that often combined diplomatic, military, financial, intelligence, law enforcement, and other considerations. In 1947, during the Truman administration, Congress approved the National Security Act, which among other things created the Department of Defense (by merging the War and Navy departments), the CIA, and the National Security Council.

The National Security Act, however, did not abolish the basic eighteenth-century structure of the U.S. government. It recognized that the president, before making decisions about world affairs, should hear not only from the secretaries of state or defense, or from the leadership of any other single department, but rather from the heads of all the relevant offices of the government. Though the National Security Act did not knock down the several major "stovepipes" of diplomatic, military, and financial policy in the U.S. government, it did bend them at the top so that the policy thoughts coming from each would come together in a committee known as the National Security Council.

The NSC's purpose was to help ensure that the president would be able to regularly look at all facets of a complex, multidimensional issue.

If anything, problems in the world since the mid-1940s have become even more intertwined. Most major national security challenges—from terrorism, weapons of mass destruction (WMD), arms proliferation, drug trafficking, piracy, ungoverned spaces to cyberwarfare and threats of and ongoing wars in general—represent intricately combined diplomatic, military, intelligence, economic, and other considerations. The State, Defense, Treasury, and Justice departments, with their distinct competencies and separate statutory responsibilities, are in most instances even less well suited to our national security requirements today than they were when the 1947 act was adopted. For American policy to succeed, multiple agencies of the government have to receive strategic guidance from the president and be required to work together to implement that guidance. This puts a premium on timely, clear instructions and continuous management of the government's multiple, separate bureaucracies.

The interagency policy process is understandably bumpy in the early days of an administration. The president can make things better by active engagement and by bringing his own views and approaches to bear. The NSC of George W. Bush confronted many hard questions, especially after the terrorist attacks of September 11, 2001. The NSC did work of which all its members can be proud. Its chief deficiency, in my view, was not that it sometimes produced imperfect approaches to challenging issues, though it sometimes did. That is to be expected. Rather, in my view the President did not always receive, and may not have insisted on, a timely consideration of his options before he made a decision, nor did he always receive effective implementation of the decisions he made.

By statute, there are four members of the National Security Council: the president, the vice president, the secretary of state, and the secretary of defense.[1] Though not a member of the NSC, the national security adviser and the NSC staff have the role of managing the entire process for the president. The chairman of the Joint Chiefs and the director of the CIA also generally serve as advisers to the NSC.* And, of course, at the president's invitation,

* Under the Goldwater-Nichols Act of 1986, the chairman of the Joint Chiefs is the principal military adviser to the president, the National Security Council, and the secretary of defense. Though the chairman is not in the chain of command or a member of the NSC, he generally serves as the communication link for military actions between the national command authorities—the president and the secretary of defense—and the combatant commanders.

others may sit in periodically as well, such as the secretary of the treasury, the attorney general, the director of the FBI, or the White House chief of staff.

During the George W. Bush administration, the NSC generally met in the Situation Room in the basement of the West Wing. We sat at a wood table, with the President presiding; the national security adviser would chair the committee of principals meetings, which included the same participants as the NSC but without the President. At seats along the walls of the Situation Room were senior NSC staff and often staff members supporting the principals at the table, who would take notes, and on occasion provide support for their principals during the discussions. The small room would often be quite full. One NSC meeting was so brimming with staff along the walls that we joked, "Why don't we just have our meeting at Sam's Club?"

George W. Bush conducted NSC meetings without pretension. Though he always demonstrated respect for the office he occupied, he was not formal or officious. He led the discussion, asked questions frequently, sometimes aggressively, often kept his own opinions and views to himself during the discussion, and, when he gave guidance to his team, did so with confidence and authority. He didn't take kindly to latecomers to his meetings, which, at his insistence, began and ended on time.

Presidents often are caricatured in ways that belie their true qualities. In the case of George W. Bush, he was a far more formidable president than his popular image, which was of a somewhat awkward and less than articulate man. That image was shaped by critics and by satirists, but also by his aw-shucks public personality and his periodic self-deprecation, which he engaged in even in private. His willingness to laugh at himself—and especially to poke at his occasional unsuccessful wrestling bouts with the English language—was a sign of inner comfort and confidence. Bush used humor to ease underlying tensions and was effective at it. In our meetings, I found Bush incisive. He showed insight into human character and, I found, often had an impressive read of the nature and intentions of foreign officials. He was firm without being unfriendly. He asked excellent questions and deftly managed the discussion. Still, NSC meetings with the President did not always end with clear conclusions and instructions.

Vice President Cheney was a thoughtful and influential presence—far more influential than other vice presidents I had observed up close. In contrast to other members of the NSC, the embedded power of the office of the vice president is modest at best. A vice president is not bolstered by a large senior staff and bureaucracy. He does not command a major instrument such as the diplomatic corps or the U.S. armed forces. He does not issue formal intelligence analyses and does not control the law enforcement apparatus of the federal government. He cannot award multimillion-dollar contracts. But Dick Cheney was uniquely influential as a vice president because he thought systematically, did his homework, and presented his ideas with skill, credibility, and timeliness.

In general, Cheney tended to keep his counsel during NSC meetings, taking notes quietly. He was the opposite of the often boisterous Nelson Rockefeller and the seemingly disinterested Spiro Agnew. A careful listener, he would sharpen the discussion by asking questions to provide the President and others with additional information or a perspective that had not yet been discussed or possibly considered. His broad experience added considerable value around the conference table.

In meetings, Cheney would not differ with the President, even when he might not have been entirely in agreement. He attached high importance to preserving the President's options. That argued for keeping any difference of view he might have with the President a private matter between the two of them. Dick did not share with me his private conversations with the President. Nor did I ask about them. The combination of keeping his opinions to himself, and yet being influential, gave Cheney an air of mystery. And for people who concluded that they did not like the substance of his views—or concluded they did not like the views attributed to him by others—this could make him seem to be a negative influence.

I realize that it is hard to overcome a personal bias about a friend I've known for more than four decades. But the caricature of Cheney as the man wielding the reins of power, playing his colleagues and even the President as marionettes, is utter nonsense. Perhaps to his detriment, Cheney seemed not to feel a compelling need to rebut the criticism or improve his popularity. In part this was because he was the rare vice president who did not aspire to his boss' job or seek glory for himself. But what he gave up in not clarifying his views or correcting misinterpretations publicly, he made up for with outsized influence. President Bush knew he could trust Cheney to give him advice that wasn't colored with any personal or political ambition.

The third full member of the NSC in George W. Bush's first term was Secretary of State Colin Powell. I had met then Colonel Powell twenty-five years earlier, when as secretary of defense I visited the army base at Fort Campbell, Kentucky. In the early 1970s, the Army's officer corps was overwhelmingly white, and Powell proved himself to be a barrier breaker. His poise, confidence, and leadership skills made him one of the Army's most promising younger officers. I followed his career with interest through the Reagan and George H. W. Bush administrations. Powell was reported to have considered the idea of running for president himself in 1996. By that time, he was admired by a great many Americans. I counted myself among them.*

Because of his popularity, Powell brought political heft to a new administration led by a relatively young and untested president. I felt that Powell, with his stature and bipartisan support, might be in a unique position to lead the State Department to serve the President, as Shultz had for Reagan and Kissinger had for Nixon and Ford.

He got off to a fast start in his remarks in Crawford on December 16, 2000, when Bush named him as his nominee for secretary of state. Powell took clear aim at what I believed was one of the most critical national security issues facing the country: the proliferation and use of weapons of mass destruction.

As much as I applauded Bush's choice of Powell and Powell's comments during their first appearance together that December, there was an uneasy subtext to the announcement. The appointment brought to my mind an event that had occurred twenty-six years earlier. In August 1974, hours after Richard Nixon had told the country he would resign the following day, Vice President Gerald Ford went out on the lawn of his Alexandria, Virginia, home and announced that Henry Kissinger would stay on as secretary of state and national security adviser. Like George W. Bush, Ford was facing questions about who he was, the breadth of his foreign policy experience, and even his legitimacy. In Bush's case, the long circus that was the Florida vote recount had made him the victor of a controversial—and in the eyes of some, an illegitimate—election.

I'm sure Ford and Bush each intended the announcements of their secretaries of state to provide reassurance to the country and to the world. Still, I was concerned that Ford's announcement made him seem as if he might be dependent on Kissinger, who was much better known. I wondered if Bush might have left a similar impression in the manner he had introduced his nominee for secretary of state. Stressing how impressed he was with Powell's

* Powell had an engaging sense of humor and could poke fun at himself and some of the stereotypes of the State Department. On one occasion, Cheney, Rice, and I were at the State Department for one of our regular lunches, which we took turns hosting. The rest of us periodically kidded Powell about the State Department's lavish meals. This time when we arrived, Powell had the table set elegantly with cloth napkins and matching silverware, and at each of our place settings silver platters with matching silver covers awaited. After we all took our seats, hovering waiters in tuxedos pulled off the silver covers simultaneously in a dramatic fashion. Underneath we found brown paper bags with sandwiches in them. Powell grinned, and we roared with laughter.[2]

prominence and prestige, Bush may unintentionally have signaled that he not only wanted Powell, but needed him.

Powell inadvertently reinforced this impression, leading the *New York Times* to report that, "President-elect George W. Bush stood silently by as the general delivered a discourse on what is in store."[3] "Powell seemed to dominate the President-elect," the *Washington Post* observed, "both physically and in the confidence he projected."[4] Columnist Thomas Friedman wrote, "[Powell] so towered over the President-elect, who let him answer every question on foreign policy, that it was impossible to imagine Mr. Bush ever challenging or overruling Mr. Powell on any issue."[5]

This perceived personal dynamic between the President-elect and the Secretary-designate had the effect, intended or otherwise, of reinforcing a deeper institutional dynamic. Throughout the twentieth century, presidents of both political parties have expressed concern that the State Department at times was less than responsive to guidance from the nation's elected leadership. The Foreign Service was so mistrusted by President Nixon that he and Henry Kissinger often worked around it. President Reagan, too, faced resistance from within the State Department—often in the form of press leaks that denigrated Reagan's hard-line and often highly successful policies toward the Soviet Union.[6]

Over time, I observed that Powell's relationship with President Bush had its own unique dynamic. Bush had an easygoing manner as a rule, but it was less so in his dealings with Powell. Powell was valued as an adviser and respected as a man of considerable accomplishments, but his department seemed to remain skeptical about President Bush and less than eager to implement his policies.

Some of Powell's actions fostered an impression that he saw his service in the cabinet as a means of representing the State Department to the President as much as he saw it as representing the President at the State Department. On his first day as secretary of state, Powell announced to the career diplomats of the Foreign Service that he would be their man and representative at the White House.[7] One longtime observer of the interagency process was Peter Rodman, who served with me in the Bush administration Defense Department as an assistant secretary of defense. In his excellent book, *Presidential Command,* he noted, "Where Henry Kissinger and James Baker had come into the building with a determination to impose political direction on the career service, Powell chose to embrace the organization."[8] Though I never saw any firsthand evidence of it in NSC meetings, journalists reported that Powell felt Bush was not sufficiently taking the State Department's positions into account on issues from North Korea to Iran.[9] But, of course, it was also for the State Department, like all executive branch departments and agencies, to take into account the President's views as well. This is a delicate balance for all cabinet officers. As I was learning at the Pentagon, it was much safer to win support within the department by subordinating one's views or the views of the President to career officials than to try to reorient an entire department in line with the President's thinking and his national security priorities.

Powell's approach was welcomed by career foreign service officers and the media. Journalists from time to time duly characterized the Secretary of State as something of a maverick in the Bush administration, a voice of reason who often spoke out at NSC meetings against proposals favored by the President, the Vice President, and me. Many in Congress came to think this as well. I recall one newspaper article in June 2001 in which Joe Biden, then the chairman of the Senate Foreign Relations Committee who worked with the secretary of state, characterized Powell as "the good guy" in the Bush administration and "the only man in America who doesn't understand he's a Democrat." Biden then described me as a "unilateralist" and a "'movement conservative' who stands for everything liberal Democrats abhor." Never sparing with his words, the future vice president declared that if Bush sided with me over Powell, "we're in deep trouble."[10] Still, I could not resist sending Powell the article with a note attached: "You've got a new best friend!"[11]

The media image of Powell battling the forces of unilateralism and conservatism may have been beneficial to Powell in some circles, but it did not jibe with reality.* The reality was that Powell tended not to speak out at NSC or principals meetings in strong opposition to the views of the President or of his colleagues. This was regrettable since Powell had important experience as a leader in both military and civilian capacities, and headed a major element of America's national security apparatus. Though the *Washington Post* among others referred to me as Powell's "nemesis," in fact our relation-

* A particularly egregious example appeared in the *Washington Post* in 2003 entitled "POWELL AND JOINT CHIEFS NUDGED BUSH TOWARD U.N." The article claimed that Powell and Joint Chiefs Chairman Dick Myers overruled a reluctant Bush, Rice, and me about seeking the international community's help in postwar Iraq. It was so utterly untrue that both Myers and Powell took the rare step of publicly disputing it. This was the sort of storyline that continued throughout the administration. Other similar headlines included: "POWELL TRIED TO TALK BUSH OUT OF WAR" and "POWELL'S DOUBTS OVER CIA INTELLIGENCE ON IRAQ PROMPTED HIM TO SET UP SECRET REVIEW."[12]

ship was professional and cordial.[13] Like most cabinet officers, Powell was protective of what he viewed as his department's prerogatives.

Though Powell and the other members of the NSC received numerous policy memos from me, I rarely received memos from him suggesting approaches or providing insights into his thinking.* In preparation for an NSC meeting on a given topic, routine position papers from departments, including State, often would be made available for discussion. But those memos were largely process-oriented and rarely laid out concrete policy recommendations. I believe that the administration would have benefited had State more often proposed strategies for discussion with the President instead of the anonymous hindsight critiques that appeared from time to time in press accounts and books. Powell's associates in the State Department seemed to suggest, in lower-level interagency meetings and in press interviews often attributed to "senior administration officials," that he quite often did not favor the President's course on a given subject.

The differing cultures of the institutions involved in the National Security Council, and the personalities of the heads who represent them, require deft management by the president and the national security adviser. As I see it, there are three main functions of the adviser: to identify where strategic and policy guidance from the president is necessary or desirable; to organize interagency deliberations so the president can make informed decisions and provide the necessary guidance to his administration; and to oversee the implementation of the president's decisions, ensuring that they are carried out effectively. Among the core attendees of NSC meetings, only the national security adviser works in the White House and has routine daily access to the president. In that regard, Condoleezza Rice's closeness to Bush was an asset. She knew the President far better than the rest of us and spent considerably more time with him than all of his other senior advisers on national security combined. Her personal access to and affinity for President Bush gave Rice substantial influence as a national security adviser and an unusually strong voice in matters under the purview of the NSC.

I had been looking forward to working with Rice, having been impressed

* I find that committing a point of view to paper sharpens my thinking. It also permits other participants in the discussion on a given issue to understand my perspective more precisely. This approach, of course, has its drawbacks. Stating one's position in a written document becomes part of history. It makes it hard to claim down the road that one was wiser than might have been the case, and it limits one's ability to wait to see how events unfold before being publicly committed to a specific course of action.

with her for years. As we came to work together in the Bush administration, however, our differing backgrounds became clear. Rice came from academia. She was a polished, poised, and elegant presence. I decidedly was not. One time Rice and I were sitting together in an NSC meeting, and I was wearing a pinstripe suit—one that I very well might have owned since the Ford administration. The suit was so well used that the pinstripes on the right leg above the knee were worn off. Rice noticed this, frowned, and pointed discreetly at my leg.

Looking down at my suit, I noticed for the first time the missing pinstripes. "Gee," I whispered to her with a smile, "maybe Joyce can sew them back on." Condi's eyes widened.

As encouraged as I was that Rice seemed to enjoy Bush's trust and confidence, I knew the burdens of the job of national security adviser were taxing for even the most seasoned foreign policy specialist and could be particularly so for someone with modest experience in the federal government and management. Rice was something of an outlier in the Bush NSC in that she had not served in multiple agencies of the government, and while she had served on the NSC staff in the earlier Bush administration, she had not had senior-level experience. But Rice was intelligent, had good academic credentials, and brought a younger person's perspective to the process. I considered those all qualities from which the administration could benefit.

Rice's first months in office were a learning experience, however, and foreshadowed challenges for the new administration's interagency process. Rice seemed keen on setting new precedents as national security adviser. She and her staff did not seem to understand that they were not in the chain of command and therefore could not issue orders, provide guidance, or give tasks to combatant commanders.[14] Rice also suggested that she be allowed to personally interview candidates for the combatant commands and the chiefs before the President saw them, and that she approve my official travel. I had no objection to Rice's attending the President's interviews with combatant commanders if that was his choice, and I certainly kept the national security adviser and secretary of state informed of my travel plans. I did not, however, accede to either suggestion.

The most notable feature of Rice's management of the interagency policy process was her commitment, whenever possible, to "bridging" differences between the agencies, rather than bringing those differences to the President for decisions. It's possible that Rice had developed this approach from her time as a university administrator—as provost at Stanford

University—where seeking consensus and mollifying faculty members by trying to find a middle ground are not uncommon. Rice seemed to believe that it was a personal shortcoming on her part if she had to ask the President to resolve an interagency difference. She studiously avoided forcing clear-cut decisions that might result in one cabinet officer emerging as a "winner" and another as a "loser." By taking elements from the positions of the different agencies and trying to combine them into one approach, she seemed to think she could make each agency a winner in policy discussions.

It may also be that Rice put a premium on harmony among the principals because her exposure to interagency policy making came during the administration of George H. W. Bush. As vice president, the senior Bush had watched as President Reagan's top national security officials clashed over issues, requiring Reagan to adjudicate their disputes. As president, the senior Bush presided over a smoother interagency process. When she became national security adviser for George W. Bush, I suspect Rice may have been trying to re-create that dynamic.

After a president has made a decision, a senior official has the responsibility to implement it faithfully. The president, after all, has the task of making the call as the elected representative of the American people. If a senior official cannot in good conscience carry out a presidential decision for whatever reason, he or she has the option of resigning.

Lower-level executive branch officials are in a similar situation regarding the heads of their agencies. I expected Defense Department officials to tell me their views, debate with me, and try to persuade me when they believed I might be wrong or misinformed about important matters—right up until a decision was made and it was time to implement. I have always felt that if officials were in the room when substantive issues are discussed, they were there for a reason. I considered it their duty, whether military or civilian, to speak up and voice opinions, even if—especially if—they disagreed with me or with others taking part in the discussion. Even after I made a decision on a matter, I remained open to people in the Department asking me to reconsider, so long as the decision was being implemented in the meantime.

While disharmony is a word that can have a negative connotation, the fact is that a vigorous debate about policy options can be healthy. Out of the occasionally contentious Reagan NSC, for example, came some of the truly important national security decisions produced by a recent U.S. administration. I did not think that any president's decisions should be taken by his cabinet officials as wins or losses. Interagency deliberations were not like a season of baseball, with the various agencies competing as rival teams and individual scores are kept.

I worked to understand Rice's approach and to cooperate in her efforts to resolve differences in the principals committee. On some occasions, however, the management of the interagency process created problems that outweighed any benefits that might have come from a bridging approach. On a number of issues—North Korea, Iran, Iraq, China, Arab-Israeli peace talks, and others—Rice would craft policy briefings for the President that seemed to endorse conceptual points one department had advanced, but also would endorse proposals for the way ahead that came from a different department. In other words, one department might "win" on strategy while another might "win" on tactics. For example, in the wake of the Iraq war, those of us in the Defense Department argued that the best way to get Syria to change its sponsorship of terrorists, pursuit of WMD, and sending jihadists into Iraq was to pressure the regime diplomatically. The President agreed to this recommendation. However, the process and tactics were delegated to the State Department, which organized high-level American delegations to Damascus that had a quite different and less than successful result.

This bridging approach could temporarily mollify the NSC principals, but it also led to discontent, since fundamental differences remained unaddressed and unresolved by the President. Indeed, an unfortunate consequence was that when important and controversial issues did not get resolved in a timely manner, they sometimes ended up being argued in the press by unnamed, unhappy lower-level officials. I doubt this would have been the case had the President been asked to make a clear-cut decision. If given an order from the President, most Department officials would have then saluted and carried it out, even if it had not been their recommendation.

I had other issues with Rice's management of the NSC process. Often meetings were not well organized. Frequent last-minute changes to the times of meetings and to the subject matter made it difficult for the participants to prepare, and even more difficult, with departments of their own to manage, to rearrange their full schedules. The NSC staff often was late in sending participants papers for meetings that set out the issues to be discussed. At the conclusion of NSC meetings when decisions were taken, members of the NSC staff were theoretically supposed to write a summary of conclusions. When I saw them, they were often sketchy and didn't always fit with my recollections. Ever since the Iran-Contra scandal of the Reagan administration, NSC staffs have been sensitive to written notes and records that could implicate a president or his advisers. Rice and her colleagues seemed concerned about avoiding detailed records that others might exploit. This came at the expense of enabling the relevant executive agencies to know precisely what had been discussed and decided at the NSC meetings. Attendees from time to time left meetings with differing views of what was decided and what the next steps should be, which freed CIA, State, or Defense officials to go back and do what they thought best.

In one August 2002 memo to Rice, I raised this lack of resolution. "It sometimes happens that a matter mentioned at a meeting is said to have been 'decided' because it elicited no objection," I wrote. "That is not a good practice. Nothing should be deemed decided unless we expressly agree to decide it."[15] Rice started putting a note at the bottom of draft decision memos: "If no objections are raised by a specific deadline, the memo will be considered approved by the principals." That, too, was impractical. Powell and I were frequently traveling. I did not want to have others assume I agreed with something simply because I missed an arbitrary deadline.[16]

From 2001 to 2005, I sent Rice a series of memos suggesting ways I thought the NSC process might be strengthened.[17] "As we have discussed, the interagency process could be improved to help all of us better manage the high volume of work we have," I wrote to Rice in August 2002. "I've talked with my folks about it to see if we could come up with some ideas that might be helpful."[18] Some of the problems I raised in my memos were administrative and relatively minor but could have resulted in an improvement in efficiency. For example, I noted that we had principals committee meetings on a weekly basis, sometimes two to three meetings a week, at the White House. Unlike the national security adviser, the rest of us—the secretary of state, the director of the CIA, and I—had departments we needed to run. Going to the White House so often was time consuming. If the NSC's performance was improved, many hours of time each week would be freed up, we would be better prepared, and more meetings would end with concrete decisions.*

No one likes to have his or her style of management questioned. Rice was a person whose general performance over the years had undoubtedly been seen as above reproach. She seemed unaccustomed to constructive sugges-

*For example, over one three-month period in 2003, there were thirty-one meetings at the White House scheduled by the NSC staff. We did not receive any papers in advance for these meetings. Further, 48 percent of the meetings were canceled and we received summaries of the conclusions for only 17 percent of the meetings held.[19]

tions, and not much changed for the better. The core problems the NSC faced resulted from the effort to paper over differences of views.

In his book, Peter Rodman wrote: "[I]t is no small task to provide psychological support to the person on whose shoulders rests the heaviest burden of decision in the world."[20] Throughout the Bush administration, Rice was a regular presence at Camp David and in Crawford, and was almost always the last person the President talked to on any given national security issue. She used that proximity and authority to press for action in the President's name. But it was not always clear to me when she had been directed by the President to do something or when she simply believed she was acting in the President's best interest—one could not check every question with the President himself. And one could certainly not fault Rice for being disloyal to the President. I thought it unlikely that Rice was managing the NSC as she did without Bush's awareness and agreement.

Nonetheless, I always found that in one-on-one situations, Bush was perfectly willing to make a decision even when presented with vexing choices. The bridging approach Rice favored did not take advantage of Bush's demonstrated willingness to engage in the candid, open, and fair hearing of views I knew he was fully capable of managing. I believe that kind of engagement would have resulted in a more effective NSC process.

This aversion to decisions in favor of one course of action or another—and sometimes in favor of one department or agency over another—ironically led to more disharmony than would have been the case if the President had had an opportunity to make the decisions himself. Rice's emphasis on bridging and consensus concealed misgivings that were later manifested in leaks to the press. This conveyed to the world an NSC often in less than good order.

Outside observers in the press and partisans have always taken note of and hyped differences within every administration. NSC meetings, some observers wanted to believe, were epic clashes of larger than life characters divided neatly into heroes and villains. Often news stories were reduced to fit the recognizable story line of an opera, a plot with winners and losers, no matter the facts. Our NSC discussions were nothing like what was described by the book chroniclers and so-called experts, none of whom had ever attended an NSC meeting.

In the Bush administration there were some differences over complex, difficult issues, to be sure. This is always how it has been, how it will be, and how it should be. But they were largely substantive differences. Instead of trying to understand the nuances behind the differences, it is considerably easier for nonparticipant observers, pundits, and lower-level staff to try to personalize disagreements that are otherwise abstract and to pigeonhole the cast of characters into a familiar story line. That approach doesn't require much research, time, or thought—just a vivid imagination. But once the conventional wisdom hardens and the characters are defined in the popular press as good or bad, winners or losers, it is nearly impossible to change it.

The personalities were no more pronounced and the debates were no more epic or intractable in the Bush administration than I had seen in previous administrations. Indeed, if anything, the tensions were noticeably less.

Fashioning national security policies, corralling interagency interests, and ensuring that the departments and agencies responsible for implementing President Bush's national security policies had clearly defined missions was not an easy task. Surely any inability to achieve this could be tolerable in times of peace. But, as I periodically wondered, could we be quite so tolerant if the United States again faced serious threats to its security? We would soon find out.

CHAPTER 25

The Agony of Surprise

When I spoke to President Bush in the Oval Office in May 2001, investment in America's national defense, as a percentage of our gross domestic product, was at its lowest level since just before Pearl Harbor. A mismatch was emerging between the President's campaign message about military needs and what was now being approved by his White House. I had recommended a $35 billion increase over the Clinton defense budget of the year before. I would have asked for significantly more if President Bush had not made clear to me that his other initiatives—such as increased federal aid to education and tax relief—were his major priorities.

I knew that the Defense Department's resources had been stretched, but it was not until I arrived at the Pentagon and had an opportunity to survey the landscape that I realized just how bad things actually were. Shipbuilding, for one, was underfunded. In the Reagan years the United States had been planning a 600-ship Navy. After the George H. W. Bush and Clinton administrations we were at 315 ships and dropping. Military aircraft were aging; some planes were going to have to stop flying, and needed replacements were not coming along. Pay was uncompetitive.[1] The spiraling cost of health care in the military further pressured the budget. And this was before considering the costs of meeting the President's transformation agenda. I warned Bush about the approaching budgetary crunch and the impact it would have on the military and their families. "It will not be pleasant," I cautioned.

I urged the President to advise the White House Office of Management and Budget that national security and defense were priorities for his administration. I was concerned that OMB would not approve the increases the Department needed. There were even suggestions at OMB that we cut military force levels.[2]

While the impression was that things were generally calm around the globe, I reminded the President of the intelligence community's reports: Iran was pursuing chemical, biological, and nuclear weapons; North Korea was aggressively pursuing longer-range ballistic missiles and nuclear weapons; the Chinese were increasing their military capabilities across the board. National defense could not be something that came after domestic issues.[3]

The President heard me out, but I soon learned that I had not been persuasive enough. Bush approved an $18 billion increase for the department, about half of what I had recommended. I was disappointed, but others were furious. Some conservatives called Bush's defense spending plan "inadequate and reckless" and urged that I resign in protest.[4]

By late summer I was not gaining the traction necessary to carry out the President's plans. Not only were we not getting the funding we needed, but also a large number of his civilian nominees remained unconfirmed by the U.S. Senate. Then, that August, White House chief of staff Andy Card delivered still more bad news: With a flagging economy, revised projections from the Congressional Budget Office were showing that the deficit would be even higher than had been predicted. Card said it was likely that DoD would get an even lower level of funding than the President had previously approved.

As I encountered the expected opposition to my initiatives within the Pentagon's five walls, there was a palpable sense that inertia was playing a winning hand. Washington turned to its favorite summer pastime: speculating about a cabinet shake-up. "There's been talk on the Hill—generated no doubt by Rumsfeld's detractors, a fairly large generating source up there—that he might be on the way out soon," wrote a columnist in the *Washington Post*. The criticism centered on my plans to transform the U.S. military. The article noted that a "sweepstakes" had already begun on who might succeed me.[5]

I knew how important it was to impart a sense of urgency and seriousness of purpose within the Pentagon. The moment there was any sign that I was backing off the reforms the President had promised, and that I was convinced were needed, they would be doomed. So I upped the ante. I gave a speech directly to the entrenched interests in the Pentagon and in Washington.

"The topic today," I began, "is an adversary that poses a threat, a serious threat, to the security of the United States of America."

> This adversary is one of the world's last bastions of central planning. It governs by dictating five-year plans. From a single capital, it attempts to impose its demands across time zones, continents, oceans, and beyond. With brutal consistency, it stifles free thought and crushes new ideas. It disrupts the defense of the United States and places the lives of men and women in uniform at risk. Perhaps this adversary sounds like the former Soviet Union, but that enemy is gone: Our foes are more subtle and implacable today. You may think I'm describing one of the last decrepit dictators of the world. But their day, too, is almost past, and they cannot match the strength and size of this adversary. The adversary's closer to home. It's the Pentagon bureaucracy. Not the people, but the processes. Not the civilians, but the systems. Not the men and women in uniform, but the uniformity of thought and action that we too often impose on them.[6]

I stated that in the Pentagon, despite an era of scarce resources taxed by mounting threats, money was disappearing into duplicative duties and bloated bureaucracy. This was not because of greed, I said, but because of gridlock. Innovation was stifled not by ill intent but by institutional inertia.

The reception my speech received was polite. I knew some in the audience agreed with me. Others did not. "RUMSFELD DECLARES WAR ON BUREAUCRACY," read some headlines.[7] That was fair enough.

When I delivered that speech, I was worried, but not about my longevity in the office of the secretary of defense. I planned to serve at the pleasure of the President as long as I could be effective and not a day longer. But I was seriously concerned that we had a Department of Defense that was not ready for the challenges coming toward our country. The one thing I knew for sure was that challenges would come, and probably from unexpected sources. "The clearest and most important transformation is from a bipolar Cold War world where threats were visible and predictable to one in which they arise from multiple sources, most of which are difficult to anticipate, and many of which are impossible even to know today," I warned.[8] The date was September 10, 2001.

I arrived at the Pentagon the next morning recalling my time as secretary of defense twenty-five years earlier, when I had to convince skeptics on the need for more investment in the defense budget. Again I found myself trying to persuade reluctant members of Congress to increase funding. At a breakfast for nine members of the House Armed Services Committee, most expressed support for my efforts but doubted if we would be able to get the necessary votes. Republicans feared that supporting a significant defense increase could leave them politically vulnerable.*

"Sometime within the coming period," I said, "an event somewhere in the world will be sufficiently shocking that it will remind the American people and their representatives in Washington how important it is for us to have a strong national defense." Mine was not a particularly original statement, and I'd said a variation of it many times before. Several months earlier, in fact, I had dictated a note to myself that I intended to offer when I was next testifying before Congress. "I do not want to be sitting before this panel in a modern day version of a Pearl Harbor post-mortem as to who didn't do what, when, where and why," I wrote. "None of us would want to have to be back here going through that agony."[9]

I sometimes remarked that the only thing surprising is that we continue to be surprised when a surprise occurs. In 1962, Harvard economist Thomas Schelling wrote a foreword to a book on Pearl Harbor that captured this idea perfectly. "We were so busy thinking through some 'obvious' Japanese moves that we neglected to hedge against the choice that they actually made," he wrote. "There is a tendency in our planning to confuse the unfamiliar with the improbable."[10] I was so taken with his piece that I sent a copy to President Bush during our first month in office as well as to many members of Congress. I expressed the hope that the Senate Armed Services Committee would hold hearings on the subject of surprise.

As my breakfast with the members of Congress was coming to a close that September morning, my senior military assistant, Vice Admiral Edmund

* Democrats were urging that any money from a projected budget surplus be directed to a so-called, nonexistent, Social Security "lockbox." Unlike the internet, the lockbox idea was an Al Gore invention. During the 2000 campaign, Gore and congressional Democrats used the gambit in an attempt to turn any proposal they didn't like—such as cutting taxes to leave more of the American people's hard-earned money with them—into an effort to raid Social Security. The whole debate struck me as absurd. There was no budget surplus for a lockbox (it was only a theoretical projection), and the last people in Congress who tended to be worried about restraining spending were the proponents of the lockbox idea. Moreover, most everyone knew that Social Security needed fundamental reforms that few were willing to confront.

Giambastiani, passed me a note. An aircraft had crashed into one of the World Trade Center's twin towers in New York. It was, I assumed, a tragic accident. I said good-bye to the members of Congress, who returned to Capitol Hill, escaping by only a few minutes the traumatic scene that was about to play out at the Pentagon.

Back in my office, Giambastiani turned on the television to see the video of one of the towers burning. Putting the set on mute but glancing at it from time to time, I received an intelligence briefing from Denny Watson, my regular briefer. Her daily presentations were similar to those provided to the President each morning. Watson was a fine intelligence professional: engaged in the details and willing to pose questions to her fellow analysts. As we reviewed the threat reports from around the world, September 11 seemed to be no more or less different than any other day. From our chairs we could hear airplanes going by the building en route to Washington National Airport's runway; the flight path down the Potomac River was only hundreds of feet from my office window. Aircraft often took off and approached for landing close to the eastern side of the Pentagon.

We were a few minutes into my briefing when the scenes on the television set distracted us. A fireball was erupting from the other World Trade Center tower as a second airliner tore through the upper floors of the building. Within the seventeen minutes between the first and second plane crashes, the world passed from one period of history into another.

I watched, stunned, as the twin towers of the World Trade Center, symbols of America's economic strength, were engulfed in smoke and flames. Hundreds who were on floors above the site of the impact were trapped. As the flames rose the floors filled with asphyxiating smoke. Some people on the upper floors jumped to their deaths rather than wait for the fire to reach them. Years of increasingly brazen terrorist acts against American and Western interests had escalated to the ones that created the disaster now displayed on television screens across the globe. But they were not the last.

I was still in my Pentagon office, absorbing news of the attacks in New York, when I felt the building shake. The tremor lasted no longer than a few seconds, but I knew that only something truly massive could have made hundreds of thousands of tons of concrete shudder. The small, round, wood table at which we were working, once used by General William Tecumseh Sherman, trembled. A legendary Union general who had torched his way through the South to turn the tide of the Civil War, Sherman had famously commented that "war is hell." Hell had descended on the Pentagon.

I could see nothing amiss through my office windows, so I left and moved rapidly along the E Ring, the Pentagon's outer corridor, as far as I could. I soon found myself in heavy smoke, and it was not long before I was forced to a lower floor.

An Air Force lieutenant colonel improbably emerged from a cloud of fumes looking disheveled and uncertain. As the chaos intensified and buffeted those near the scene, all I retained was an image of the horrified look on his face as he cautioned, "You can't go farther."

I headed to a nearby stairwell and down a flight of stairs toward an exit. Outside I found fresh air and a chaotic scene. For the first time I could see the clouds of black smoke rising from the west side of the building. I ran along the Pentagon's perimeter, and then saw the flames.

Hundreds of pieces of metal were scattered across the grass in front of the building. Clouds of debris, flames, and ash rose from a large blackened gash. People were scrambling away from the building, refugees from an inferno that was consuming their colleagues. Those who could ran across the grass away from the building. Those who could not were being helped. Some were wounded and burned.

It had been but a few minutes since the attack. The official first responders—local police and firefighters—had not yet arrived on the scene. A few folks from the Pentagon were there doing what they could to assist the wounded. I saw some in uniform running back into the burning building, hoping to bring more of the injured out.

"We need help over here," I heard someone say. I ran over. One young woman sitting in the grass, wounded, bruised, and a bit bloodied, looked up at me and squinted. Even though she couldn't stand she said, "I can help. I can hold an IV."

As people arrived on-site to assist, I turned back toward my office to gather what additional information I could. On my way I picked up a small, twisted piece of metal from whatever had hit the Pentagon. Minutes later I would learn from an Army officer that he had seen the unmistakable body of a silver American Airlines plane crash into the Pentagon. That piece of the aircraft has served me as a reminder of the day our building became a battleground—of the loss of life, of our country's vulnerability to terrorists, and of our duty to try to prevent more attacks of that kind.

The smoke from the crash site was spreading through the building. The smell of jet fuel and smoke trailed us down the corridor. Upon arriving back in my office, I spoke briefly with the President. He was on Air Force One somewhere over the southeastern United States, having left an appearance at a school in Florida when the second plane hit the World Trade Center. He was anxious to learn what damage had been done by the attack on the Pentagon. I reported what information I had.

In retrospect, catastrophes inevitably raise "what ifs." One was that the disaster could have been even worse. Most of the offices in the area of the building that was hit had recently been closed for renovations. Instead of the nearly ten thousand employees who would normally have been working near the impact site, less than half of that number were present that morning.[11] Further, due to the recent renovations, the new walls of the section were reinforced with steel. It had blast-resistant windows and ballistic cloth to catch shrapnel.[12] It also occurred to me that if the hijacked plane had hit the other side of the building, near the river entrance, a section that had not been renovated, much of the senior civilian and military leadership of the Department would undoubtedly have been killed.

Before long, the smoke in my office became heavy, so along with several staff members I headed to the National Military Command Center in the basement.* A complex of rooms outfitted with televisions, computer terminals, and screens tracking military activities around the world, the NMCC is a well-equipped communications hub. Despite the fires still raging in the Pentagon and sprinklers dousing wires and cables with water, our links to the outside world were functioning, although sporadically.[13] The chairman of the Joint Chiefs, General Hugh Shelton, was en route to Europe. The vice chairman, General Dick Myers, the man the President had recently nominated to be Shelton's successor, had been on Capitol Hill making courtesy calls with members of the Senate Armed Services Committee. Upon learning of the attack, he rushed back to the Pentagon and joined me in the command center.

There were two sides of Dick Myers, and I came to know both well. He looked like the grown-up version of a humble high school football hero from a Norman Rockwell cover of the old *Saturday Evening Post*. But the other side of Dick Myers was one that the public did not see. He had the self-confidence, fire, independent spirit, and tenacity of a fighter pilot tested repeatedly in combat. In his early years he had been frightened of planes because he had witnessed a crash as a child. Yet he came up through the ranks of the Air

*They included: Ed Giambastiani; Jim Haynes, the Department's general counsel; Steve Cambone, the deputy undersecretary of policy; Larry Di Rita, my special assistant; and Torie Clarke, the assistant secretary of defense for public affairs.

Force to the highest position in our armed forces. In our private meetings, the determined, persistent man who had logged over six hundred combat flight hours in Vietnam would often emerge.

Myers and I discussed raising America's threat level to Defcon (Defense Condition) 3, an increased state of alert for the nation's armed forces, two levels short of full-scale war.*

"It's a huge move," Myers said, "but it's appropriate."[14]

General Myers reported that combat air patrols were now in the skies over Washington, D.C.—the first time in history this step had been taken. We also launched two fighters to protect Air Force One and were scrambling more.[15]

I was told that Vice President Cheney was at the White House in the underground communications facility. Colin Powell was traveling in Peru and would be returning to Washington. George Tenet was hurrying back to CIA headquarters after a breakfast meeting. President Bush was en route to Barksdale Air Force Base in Louisiana. The Secret Service, with the support of Vice President Cheney, advised Bush not to return to Washington until the situation was clarified. We were receiving unverified reports of hijacked airliners heading toward U.S. cities. Targeting the White House remained a possibility.

I looked at screens displaying the dozens of aircraft still in the air while the Federal Aviation Administration and NORAD (the North American Aerospace Defense Command) tried to determine which, if any, were hijacked planes and where they might be heading. At some point we received word that an aircraft believed to have been hijacked was down somewhere in Pennsylvania.[16]

Defense Department officials executed our continuity-of-government plans, according to long-established procedures, to ensure that at least some of America's leadership in all branches of the federal government would survive an enemy attack. I had been involved in planning and exercises for continuity-of-government operations during the 1980s, at the request of the Reagan administration. In those days, the plans postulated a nuclear attack by the Soviet Union. Now it was terrorist attacks that had put those plans into use for the first time in our history. The plan called for the secretary of defense to be moved out of the Pentagon rapidly to a secure location outside of Washington. But I was unwilling to be out of touch during the time it would take to relocate me to the safe site. I asked a reluctant Paul Wolfowitz, the deputy secretary of defense, and my special assistant, Larry Di Rita, to leave immediately for Site R, the Pentagon's backup headquarters, which was staffed for such an emergency.

* The last time the Defcon had been raised to that level was in 1973, during the Yom Kippur War, when I was ambassador to NATO.

It was not long before the Vice President reached me by phone. Like the rest of us, he was receiving a jumble of conflicting information. There was a report that there had been an explosion at the State Department and another of a plane crash north of Camp David, both of which proved false. A Korean Airlines aircraft was flying toward the United States with its transponder signaling the code for "hijack." There was a report of an unidentified aircraft from Massachusetts bound for Washington, D.C., which was particularly worrisome because two of the known hijacked flights had originated in Boston.[17]

"There's been at least three instances here where we've had reports of aircraft approaching Washington," said Cheney. "A couple were confirmed hijack. And, pursuant to the President's instructions I gave authorization for them to be taken out," he added.

"Yes, I understand," I replied. "Who did you give that direction to?"

"It was passed from here through the [operations] center at the White House," Cheney answered.

"Has that directive been transmitted to the aircraft?"

"Yes, it has," Cheney replied.

"So we've got a couple of aircraft up there that have those instructions at this present time?" I asked.

"That is correct," Cheney answered. Then he added, "[I]t's my understanding they've already taken a couple of aircraft out."

"We can't confirm that," I told him. We had not received word that any U.S. military pilots had even contemplated engaging and firing on a hijacked aircraft.

"We're told that one aircraft is down," I added, "but we do not have a pilot report. . . ."[18]

As it turned out, the only other aircraft that crashed had not been shot down. It was United Airlines Flight 93, a hijacked plane that went down in a field near Shanksville, Pennsylvania. The plane's passengers had learned in midair through private telephone calls that their hijacking was one of several terrorist operations that day. Courageous men and women onboard then fought with the hijackers and prevented them from completing their mission, which likely was targeting the White House or the Capitol.*

As a former naval aviator, I was concerned about the orders being given

* Each of the other three hijacked aircraft had five al-Qaida terrorists onboard, and the difference between four and five terrorists may have meant the difference between failure and success. In 2002, the individual believed to be the twentieth hijacker—the missing hijacker from United Flight 93—came into U.S. custody in Afghanistan. The detention and interrogation at Guantánamo Bay of the suspected terrorist, Muhammed al-Qahtani, would later become a focal point of controversy.

to the military pilots. There were no rules of engagement on the books about when and how our pilots should handle a situation in which civilian aircraft had been hijacked and might be used as missiles to attack American targets. Myers was troubled too. "I'd hate to be a pilot up there and not know exactly what I should do," I said to him.[19]

Myers observed that even a plane that appeared to be descending toward an airport in the Washington metropolitan area with no prior sign of hostile intent could suddenly veer off and strike any federal building in the D.C. area. By then, he said, "it's too late." Any plane within twenty miles of the White House that did not land on command, he speculated, might have to be shot down.[20] It was a chilling thought. A military pilot in the skies above our nation's capital, likely in his twenties or early thirties, might have to make an excruciatingly tough call. But our pilots, Myers stressed, were well trained. I had no doubt they would follow their orders if necessary, but with a prayer on their lips.

Echoing the earlier instructions from the President, I repeated his orders to Myers: The pilots were "weapons free," which authorized them to shoot down a plane approaching a high-value target.[21]

During an update on the situation in New York, I learned that both towers of the World Trade Center had collapsed. Many hundreds had been incinerated. Throughout lower Manhattan, truck drivers, postal workers, stockbrokers, the elderly, and schoolchildren were scrambling away from the smoke and flame. They were making desperate retreats from the dense clouds of dust and debris of the collapsing towers. Heartsick and fearful, some looked up at the sky over New York Harbor to see if more planes were coming. Families awaited word about loved ones who had gone to work that morning in the World Trade Center and had not been heard from.

As we were working at the Pentagon, smoke from the crash site was seeping into the NMCC. Our eyes became red and our throats itchy. An Arlington County firefighter reported that carbon dioxide had reached dangerous levels in much of the building. The air-conditioning was supposed to have been disabled to avoid circulating the hazardous smoke, but apparently it took some time for it to be shut down.

Myers suggested that I order the evacuation of the command center, and he argued that the staff would feel bound to remain there as long as I stayed in the building. I told him to have all nonessential personnel leave but that I intended to keep working there as long as we were able. Relocating to any of the remote sites would take at least an hour of travel and settling in, precious moments I did not want to lose if we could keep working in the Pentagon. Eventually we moved into a smaller communications center elsewhere in the building known as Cables, which had less smoke. As the day went on, the firefighters stamped out enough of the fire so that the smoke in some portions of the building became tolerable.

Shortly after noon, I received a call from CIA Director George Tenet. From the outset of the Bush administration Tenet and I had discussed the need for a more effective strategy to combat terrorism.[22] We had been preoccupied by the 2000 bombing by Islamist extremists of the USS *Cole* in a Yemeni port, an attack to which the United States had never responded. "George, what do you know that I don't know?" I asked.[23]

The information at this juncture was still uncertain.[24] But Tenet said the National Security Agency (NSA) had intercepted a phone call from an al-Qaida operative in Afghanistan to a phone number in the former Soviet republic of Georgia. The al-Qaida operative stated that he had "heard good news" and indicated that another airplane was about to hit its target.[25]

An hour later I again spoke to the President, who by then had arrived at Barksdale. I briefed him on the steps we had taken and updated him on what we knew about the attack on the Pentagon.[26] American Airlines Flight 77—a Boeing 757—had departed Washington's Dulles airport bound for Los Angeles at 8:20 a.m. On board were fifty-nine passengers and crew. A passenger, Barbara Olson, managed to use her cell phone to call her husband, Ted Olson, the solicitor general of the United States, to tell him that her plane was being hijacked. There were teachers onboard and students going on a field trip. The youngest passenger was a three-year-old girl named Dana Falkenberg.

The jet had come in from the west at a speed of more than five hundred miles per hour, flying precariously low over stunned drivers along Route 27. The plane screamed over the Pentagon parking lot and hit the first floor of the building's western wall. With forty-four thousand pounds of thrust from engines at full throttle, the nose of the aircraft disintegrated as the rest of the plane continued to punch through the walls of the building—the E Ring, the D Ring, and the C Ring—at over seven hundred feet per second, clearing a path for the rest of the aircraft.[27] More than 181,000 pounds of aluminum and steel, jet fuel and humanity had collided with the building. The Pentagon was still standing, but the plane and everyone in it had been obliterated on impact.

Bush, frustrated at being kept so far from where he felt he belonged—in Washington—blurted out what first sprang to mind. "The United States will hunt down and punish those responsible for these cowardly acts," he said, an echo of his father's words shortly after the 1983 bombing in Beirut, Lebanon. I would later offer a suggestion to the President about the word "cowardly." The men who had gripped the controls of the aircraft and flew them into buildings at five hundred miles per hour were many things—evil, ruthless, cruel—but I felt we underestimated and misunderstood the enemy if we considered them cowards. They were Islamist fanatics dedicated to advancing their cause by killing innocents and themselves in the process, and they would not be easily intimidated or frightened, as cowards would be.

I also advised the President in the days following that I believed our nation's response should not primarily be about punishment, retribution, or retaliation. Punishing our enemies didn't describe the range of actions we would need to take if we were to succeed in protecting the United States. The struggle that had been brought to our shores went beyond law enforcement and criminal justice. Our responsibility was to deter and dissuade others from thinking that terrorism against the United States could advance their cause. In my view, our principal motivation was self-defense, not vengeance, retaliation, or punishment. The only effective defense would be to go after the terrorists with a strong offense.

In our initial discussions with the President that day, Myers and I recommended that he order a partial call-up of the Air Force reserves to ease the strain on our pilots, since round-the-clock patrols in the skies above our country would be needed. Bush agreed and asked me to convey his thanks to the Pentagon employees who were still at their posts. He made clear that he would like to act quickly against the perpetrators of the attacks. I said we would get to work on how best to do that. "The ball will soon be in your court," he added.

As I got off the phone, I thought again of the Beirut bombing. Ever since then, a small circle of national security experts, including George Shultz, had worried that it was only a matter of time before Muslim extremists found their way to our shores. "Terrorism is a form of warfare, and must be treated as such," I had said back in 1984, in the aftermath of the U.S. withdrawal. "As with other forms of conflict, weakness invites aggression. Simply standing in a defensive position, absorbing blows, is not enough. Terrorism must be deterred."[28] We could not stop all acts of terrorism or eliminate all casualties. But we could send a message to terrorists and to regimes that sponsored and harbored terrorists that if they continued to do so it would be at a price.

I remember observing to those with me early that afternoon that America's prior history in responding to terrorism had not been effective. I considered our responses to provocations and attacks by our adversaries over the last decade hesitant and, in some cases, feckless, including: letting Libya's Muammar Gaddafi off for his role in the bombing of Pan Am Flight 103; the first World Trade Center attack of 1993; the plotted assassination of George H. W. Bush by Iraqi agents the same year; America's retreat under fire in Mogadishu in 1993; the Khobar Towers bombing in Saudi Arabia in 1996; the East African embassies bombings in 1998; and the 2000 attack on the USS *Cole*. Actions and inactions by previous administrations had left the impression that the United States was leaning back, not forward.[29]

"We can't bluster," I said to my staff. "If you cock your fist, you'd better be ready to throw it."[30]

Time also was important. I remembered that after the terrorist massacre of Marines in Beirut, American support for the Lebanese government and for action against the terrorists waned quickly.

"One week from now," I remarked to Myers, "the willingness to act will be half of what it is now."

Myers thought differently. "I think the country's attention span will last longer this time," he said. If we didn't take the right steps to engage the American people and prepare them for the length of the war ahead, I wasn't so sure.[31]

At 3:30 p.m:, President Bush convened his first National Security Council meeting following the attacks. Joining us via secure video teleconference (SVTC) from Offutt Air Force Base in Nebraska, he began by echoing some of the comments he had made to me on the phone earlier in the day. "No thugs are going to diminish the spirit of the United States," he told us. "No coward is going to hold this government at bay. We're going to find out who did this. We're going to destroy them and their resources." The President discussed what the terrorist attacks might mean for the American people. He speculated about how people would react, especially in the cities struck by the terrorists: Would they go to their jobs the next day? Would children go to school?

During the meeting, a fresh report came in of still another suspicious plane—this one coming from Madrid and scheduled to land in Philadelphia. Over the secure video, the President authorized the use of force if necessary to bring down the airliner.[32]

The President insisted that the government rebound quickly after the attack. I reported that I would have the Pentagon open the following day. Not only did the Department have a great deal of work to do, I felt it was important that the terrorists not be seen as successful in shutting down the U.S. Department of Defense.

Tenet reported that the intelligence community now believed with some confidence that Osama bin Laden's al-Qaida network was responsible for the attacks. The CIA had discovered that two of the hijackers were suspected al-Qaida operatives—including one who had been linked to the 2000 bombing of the USS *Cole*.[33] One month before 9/11, Ramzi bin al-Shibh, a senior al-Qaida lieutenant in close contact with Bin Laden, had discussed the details of the operation with Muhammed Atta, the lead hijacker. Their conversations were in a code in which they pretended to be students talking about various academic fields. What they actually talked about were which targets to hit: "architecture" meant the World Trade Center; "arts" referred to the Pentagon; "law," the Capitol building; and "politics," the White House. As he related this chilling information, Tenet warned of the possibility of additional, copycat attacks.

The State Department reported that it had placed all U.S. embassies on heightened alert. The President said he saw the attacks not as a problem for the United States alone but as a challenge to free nations, and that it was necessary to organize a global campaign against terrorism by enlisting as many countries as possible into a large coalition. He expected help not just from our traditional allies—Britain, Germany, and France had offered immediate assistance—but from new partners. We discussed the fact that our reaction to the attack would need to have many parts, and that some of our partners might want to participate in only some of them.

Later that afternoon I spoke with Russian Defense Minister Sergei Ivanov. He sounded sad as we discussed the casualties. He pledged Russia's cooperation. As it happened, I already had a request to make. The Russian military was conducting an aircraft exercise near Alaska, and our forces were understandably sensitive now about any intrusions into American airspace. I didn't want problems to arise inadvertently between our two countries. So I asked Ivanov if he would have his military stand down. He promptly agreed to halt the exercise.

That evening also offered an opportunity for political rivals in the United States to come together, at least for a time. At the Pentagon, I met with Carl Levin, the chairman of the Senate Armed Services Committee, and John Warner, the ranking Republican. They wanted to come to the Department to express their support.

"We're foursquare with you," Warner said.

"We will be totally arm in arm," Levin seconded, saying he looked forward to my leadership.[34]

I was heading to a press briefing in the Pentagon and the two senators asked to attend to show their support. So at 6:42 p.m., I appeared before the Pentagon press corps with Levin, Warner, and Joint Chiefs Chairman General Hugh Shelton, who had returned from his scheduled trip. As the Pentagon burned—it would continue to burn for several days—I told reporters that the Defense Department would be open in the morning, fulfilling its responsibilities. "The Pentagon's functioning," I said. "It will be in business tomorrow."[35] Asked about how many might have perished in the building, I replied, "It will not be a few."

Senator Levin vowed to support efforts to "track down, root out, and relentlessly pursue terrorists, [and] states that support them and harbor them."[36] When Levin was asked a question about Democratic opposition to increasing the defense budget, he replied that he and the Armed Services Committee now were united in support of the President's defense increase.[37]

On the evening of the attack, nations around the world were voicing support for a robust response. The German chancellor, Gerhard Schroeder, called the attacks "a declaration of war against the entire civilized world." The French newspaper *Le Monde* declared, "We are all Americans."[38]

In the Middle East, friendly and unfriendly regimes were shaken by the attack, unsure of what they should say or, more to the point, unsure about what we might do. The leaders of Iran and Saudi Arabia expressed condolences.[39] Of course, we had yet to test if those nations would be with us when we acted against the terrorists.

Only one regime openly gloated about the attack. "The United States reaps the thorns its rulers have planted in the world," Saddam Hussein declared from Baghdad.[40] Iraq's state-controlled newspaper charged: "The real perpetrators [of 9/11] are within the collapsed buildings."[41] This was truly remarkable. Even the Iranian government sensed that it was bad form to poke the Great Satan in the eye as thousands of American bodies were being recovered from the rubble.

In the aftermath of the attacks, I was sensitive to comments made by foreign leaders. When President Hosni Mubarak of Egypt made a poorly chosen comment about 9/11, for example, I was not happy.[42] I asked my staff to let me know what a government had said about the attacks whenever I met with foreign leaders. If their comments were supportive, I wanted to thank them, but, I added, "If they were harmful, I will remember that, too."[43]

From the Oval Office at 8:30 that evening, President Bush delivered his first formal remarks after the attack to the nation. The presence of the President in Washington was reassuring. "We will make no distinction between the terrorists who committed these acts and those who harbor them," he announced, setting out a new declaratory policy. This was a crucial element of our strategy to do everything we reasonably could to prevent follow-on attacks. Though the President wanted to strike directly at the terrorist groups that had organized the attack, actionable intelligence was scarce. But we did know the location of the states that were instrumental in supporting the international terrorist network—and we also had the means to impose costs on those regimes. Afghanistan's Taliban regime, Syria's Bashar al-Assad, Iraq's Saddam Hussein, and the clerical rulers of Iran were now on notice: Bush had announced that the costs for state support of terrorism had just gone up.

After the speech, President Bush convened a meeting of the National Security Council in the shelter underneath the White House. He reiterated his determination to end the distinction between terrorist groups and their state sponsors. Nations would have to choose, he said, and not try to live in some middle ground between terrorist warfare and respectable state sovereignty. Powell, back from Peru, said that Afghanistan and Pakistan would have to stop providing terrorists sanctuary.

As secretary of defense it was my job to advise the President, but also to interpret his guidance and ensure that it was implemented. I told the President and the NSC that, for the moment at least, the American military was not prepared to take on terrorists. A major military effort, I said, could take as many as several months to assemble. President Bush said he was eager to respond, but he wanted to ensure that our response, when it came, was appropriate and effective.

I also mulled the President's words about attacking terrorists and the territory from which they planned and plotted attacks. Did that mean we should be planning to strike terrorist targets in nations with whom we had friendly relations? I suggested that we think about the problem more broadly. We needed to consider other nations, including Sudan, Libya, Iraq, and Iran, where terrorists had found safe haven over the years and where they might seek refuge if we were to attack al-Qaida's hub in Afghanistan.

We had little specific intelligence to support targeting terrorist operatives themselves, I noted, so we should take action against those parts of the network that we could locate, such as the terrorists' bank accounts and their state sponsors. If we put enough pressure on those states—and this didn't necessarily mean military pressure—they might feel compelled to rein in the terrorist groups they supported. This might enable us to constrain groups that our intelligence agencies couldn't locate.

Much has been written about the Bush administration's focus on Iraq after 9/11. Commentators have suggested that it was strange or obsessive for the President and his advisers to have raised questions about whether Saddam Hussein was somehow behind the attack. I have never understood the controversy. Early on, I had no idea if Iraq was or was not involved, but it would have been irresponsible for any administration not to have asked the question.

The hopes I had when I was serving as President Reagan's Middle East envoy for a more positive relationship between Iraq and the United States obviously had not been realized. It had been many years since I met with Saddam Hussein, and I knew he had not mellowed with age. America had gone to war against Iraq to liberate Kuwait from Saddam's 1990 invasion. Iraqi forces fired at American and British pilots patrolling northern and southern UN no-fly zones almost daily. From 1990 on, Iraq had been on the State Department's list of state sponsors of terrorism. Since I had worked with Paul Wolfowitz in 1998 on the Ballistic Missile Threat Commission, I knew that he had been concerned about the relationships of terrorists with regimes hostile to the United States. His knowledge of the subject of Iraq was encyclopedic. He had pressed intelligence officials about possible links between the 1993 bombing of the World Trade Center and various state sponsors of terror, including the Iraqi government. Though American intelligence analysts in the 1990s generally said that the Islamic terrorists who committed the first World Trade Center bombing were probably working without state involvement, Wolfowitz was not convinced.

I remember one commission briefing in particular, when the name first came up that would become familiar to all Americans after 9/11: a Saudi millionaire named Osama bin Laden. Bin Laden had declared a holy war against the United States, listing what he characterized as a number of "crimes and sins" committed by the U.S. government against Muslims.

"The ruling to kill the Americans and their allies—civilians and military," the fatwa stated, "is an individual duty for every Muslim who can do it in any country in which it is possible to do it." He had laid out al-Qaida's intentions to undermine America's financial and military power and to intimidate our friends and allies. These were not idle threats or the harmless rants of a madman. Al-Qaida had declared war. America had been on notice of that threat for at least three years.

During our work on the Ballistic Missile Threat Commission in the late 1990s, Wolfowitz and former Clinton CIA Director Jim Woolsey questioned CIA analysts about what the United States was doing about al-Qaida. They asked about Bin Laden's bank accounts and whether his funds had been confiscated after the East African embassy bombings. The officials gave the standard nonresponse: They would look into the matter.

As the events of the day—a day that seemed like the longest in my life—drew to a close, I returned to the Pentagon from the White House. The sky was dark but klieg lights illuminated the crash site for the rescue workers who continued to fight the flames and to search for any remaining victims in the wreckage. I called some of my team together in my office to take stock of events. Torie Clarke, the assistant secretary of defense for public affairs and the Pentagon's spokeswoman, had a blunt manner that I appreciated. "Have you called Mrs. R.?" she asked me.

By then it was approaching 11:00 p.m., more than twelve hours since the morning's attack. "No, I haven't," I answered.

Clarke bore in. "You mean you haven't talked to Joyce?"

When the Pentagon was hit, Joyce was at the Defense Intelligence Agency at Bolling Air Force Base for a briefing with the defense attachés and their spouses from around the world. I had been so engaged that day that I hadn't even thought of calling her. After almost forty-seven years of marriage, one takes some things—perhaps too many things—for granted. I had been told Joyce was taken from the meeting and that she had been informed that the Pentagon had been hit.

Clarke looked at me with the stare of a woman who was also a wife. "You son of a bitch," she blurted out.

She had a point.

CHAPTER 26

War President

America awoke the next day a nation at war. Above pictures of the burning World Trade Center, the *Washington Times* had a one-word front-page headline that read, in large, bold, capital letters: "INFAMY."[1] Across the United States, Americans expressed anger and sadness. They also voiced fear of further attacks. Many wondered if they were safe, how their lives might have to change, whether their family members and friends were in danger. Major landmarks considered likely targets were watched with anxiety. Each rumor of another attack set people on edge. Some feared for family members in the military. The financial world was in shock. The stock market suffered one of its biggest drops in history when it reopened six days after 9/11. Hundreds of billions of dollars—property damage, travel revenue, insurance claims, stock market capital—all lost in a single day because nineteen men with a fanatical willingness to die boarded four commercial airliners wielding box cutters.

Throughout the Pentagon, the environment had changed radically. Smoke and the smell of jet fuel lingered. Many of the Pentagon's seventeen miles of usually bustling corridors were quiet. Halls were sealed off with yellow police tape. Armed Air Force jets patrolled the skies overhead.

NATO unanimously invoked Article 5 of the North Atlantic Treaty, which provides that "an armed attack against one . . . shall be considered an attack against them all."[2] The NATO nations sent five AWACS aircraft and crews to help patrol American airspace in the months after 9/11. It was a welcome sign of commitment and support from the alliance, for which I was and remain deeply grateful. NATO was born early in the Cold War, when it was thought that the United States might have to come to the defense of our allies in Western Europe. Despite my many years of association with the alliance, it had never crossed my mind that NATO might someday step up to help defend the United States.

At the Pentagon, I noticed a different look on people's faces as I passed them in the corridors. We had lost members of our Pentagon family and were determined to protect the country and prevent this from happening again. Calling for "a fundamental reassessment of intelligence and defense activities," even the *New York Times* sounded almost unilateralist; they suggested America should be prepared to take the fight to the terrorists, with or without our allies. "When Washington has prepared to act in the past it has often been stymied by faint-hearted allies," the paper's editorial board charged. "Some of America's closest friends have found it more useful to do business with countries that have either supported terrorists on their soil, been indifferent to them or been too afraid to go after them."[3] Members of Congress were working together in ways that promised a truly united approach, with a spirit perhaps not seen since the attack on Pearl Harbor. On September 18, 2001, Congress passed a joint resolution amounting to a declaration of war. It was approved by stunning margins: 420-1 in the House and 98-0 in the Senate. The resolution gave the President the authority to use all "necessary and appropriate force" against those whom he determined "planned, authorized, committed, or aided" the 9/11 attacks and those who "harbored" the terrorists.[4]

No longer were discussions in Washington or the White House focused on the issues that had divided Americans—stem cell research, the Social Security lockbox, or withdrawing from the ABM treaty. Defense of the American people was now the nation's number one priority.

Administrations frequently end up being judged by an event they had not anticipated—the Cuban missile crisis for John F. Kennedy; the invasion of Kuwait for George H. W. Bush; and the terrorist attacks on the Pentagon and World Trade Center for George W. Bush. After the attack, Bush won plaudits for his leadership even from opponents. Critics who had considered him to be an accidental president out of his depth were, for the moment, silenced.

Later controversies tended to obscure Bush's sound stewardship of the country after the 9/11 attacks. But in those critical moments for the country, he was somber, purposeful, and determined to act. He was deeply saddened by the loss of so many lives but not distracted by his sorrow. With his advisers, he probed, questioned, and provided well-considered guidance. In fact, he did better than that. He was both courageous and strategic.

The war against the terrorists would require all of the cabinet departments and agencies to take on new roles. The attorney general would be charged with new legal challenges and developing a new mission in counterterrorism for the FBI. Beginning in the 1970s, civil liberty considerations had resulted in the erection of an information barrier that prevented the FBI and domestic law enforcement agencies from sharing information freely with the CIA and the intelligence community. After 9/11, this theoretical wall was widely considered a dangerous and unnecessary barrier to effective counterterrorism work. The Department of Justice and the CIA had to negotiate a delicate balance, devising new ways to cooperate and exchange intelligence while protecting our civil liberties.

The Treasury Department would be tasked with helping to track terrorist financing. The Department of Energy would have to ensure the safety of American nuclear power plants and work with our allies to make sure their nuclear programs and materials were secure. And still other elements of the government would need to join the effort. The President believed—and over the years that followed frequently underscored—that it would not be enough for the Defense Department and the CIA to be the only departments at war. All elements of our national power would need to step up.

On the morning of September 12, President Bush visited the Pentagon to inspect the damage and thank the rescue workers. He met those who were still pulling body parts from the wreckage. It was impossible for me to get out of my mind the image of the passengers on that doomed plane during their frightful descent. The thought of men and women working quietly in their Pentagon offices and then hearing the deafening roar of the engines or seeing through their windows an unfamiliar shadow about to consume them was equally haunting.

Perhaps noticing my distraction, the President put his arm on my shoulder. "You're carrying a heavy load," Bush said, "and I appreciate it." I was grateful for his thoughtfulness, but I knew his load was even heavier, and that the members of our armed forces and their families would in the end bear the heaviest burdens of all.

Two days later President Bush asked me to open the first cabinet meeting after 9/11 with a prayer. I had never been one to wear my faith on my sleeve, but I valued prayer and the connection to the Almighty. I believed those of us in positions of authority needed to keep in mind that all human beings are prone to error. I felt the need to seek the Lord's guidance as we charted our way forward. I began,

> Ever faithful God, in death we are reminded of the precious birthrights of life and liberty You endowed in Your American people. You have shown once again that these gifts must never be taken for granted. . . We seek Your special blessing today for those who stand as sword and shield, protecting the many from the tyranny of the few. Our enduring prayer is that You shall always guide our labors and that our battles shall always be just.[5]

Looking back on the weeks following 9/11, some accounts suggest an administration that seemed to have a preordained response to the attacks. From my vantage point, however, quite the opposite was the case. It was a time of discovery—of seeking elusive, imperfect solutions for new problems that would not be solved quickly. There was no guidebook or road map for us to follow.

We had discussions at our roundtable meetings in the Pentagon and in the Situation Room at the White House about the best way to characterize the threats our country faced and the nature of the conflict ahead. Early on, President Bush labeled the effort the "war on terror." In one sense, calling the new conflict a war was helpful. It signaled that he believed treating terrorism as a law enforcement matter and terrorists as common criminals would not be adequate. Bush rightly rejected the longstanding practice of treating jihadist terrorist attacks as simple matters of domestic crime. The term also helped drive home the point that our primary goal was not to punish or retaliate, but rather to prevent additional attacks against America and our interests.

However, I became increasingly uncomfortable with labeling the campaign against Islamist extremists a "war on terrorism" or a "war on terror." To me, the word "war" focused people's attention on military action, overemphasizing, in my view, the role of the armed forces. Intelligence, law enforcement, public diplomacy, the private sector, finance, and other instruments of national power were all critically important—not just the military. Fighting the extremists ideologically, I believed, would be a crucial element of our country's campaign against them. The word "war" left the impression that there would be combat waged with bullets and artillery and then a clean end to the conflict with a surrender—a winner and a loser, and closure—such as the signing ceremony on the battleship USS *Missouri* to end World War II. It also led many to believe that the conflict could be won by bullets alone. I knew that would not be the case.

I was also concerned about the other word in the phrases: terrorism, or terror. Terror was not the enemy, but rather a feeling. Terrorism was also not the enemy but a tactic our enemies were using successfully against us. Saying we were in a war on terrorism was like saying we were in a war against bombers or we were waging a war on tanks, as opposed to a war against the people using those weapons.

Striving for appropriate nomenclature is part of sound strategic thinking.[6] If we did not clearly define who exactly we were at war against, it was harder to define the parameters of victory. As I developed these thoughts over the weeks and months following 9/11, I periodically raised them in the Department, with the President, and with the members of the National Security Council. I urged that we find ways to avoid the phrase war on terror and consider other alternatives.[7]

The phenomenon we were up against was not easily delineated in a few words. Sometime later, I tried out the phrase "struggle against violent extremists" in place of war on terror. A struggle suggested that military action alone would not be sufficient. Violent extremists seemed to be more accurate than terror or terrorism, but it was not quite right either, in that it stopped short of noting the central fact that our enemies were Islamists. My attempts to calibrate our administration's terminology eventually gave rise to a minor brouhaha in the press.[8] Ultimately, President Bush settled the issue and decided against my suggestions by reaffirming that we were fighting a global war on terror. I was not able to come up with a perfect alternative.

From the beginning, members of the administration worked gingerly around the obvious truth that our main enemies were Islamic extremists. I didn't think we could fight the crucial ideological aspect of the war if we were too wedded to political correctness to acknowledge the facts honestly. While we certainly were not at war against Islam, we did intend to fight and defeat those distorting their religious beliefs—their Islamic religious beliefs—to murder innocent people. I thought the best term was *Islamist* extremists, which made clear we were not including all Muslims. Islamism is not a religion but a totalitarian political ideology that seeks the destruction of all liberal democratic governments, of our individual rights, and of

Western civilization. The ideology not only excuses but commands violence against the United States, our allies, and other free people. It exalts death and martyrdom. And it is rooted in a radical, minority interpretation of Islam.

The war declared on us was not about any particular policy dispute. Though Bin Laden and others referenced their opposition to the U.S. forces based in Saudi Arabia or our policies with respect to the Arab-Israeli conflict, those were more excuses to rally support, recruits, and financing. The intractable Arab-Israeli dispute in particular was a frequently referenced source of irritation to Arab leaders and was used as an excuse for nearly every setback in the region. But in fact the extremists sought a return to an ancient caliphate that would require blurring boundaries in the Middle East and North Africa and part of Spain, putting the territory all under the rule of one pan-Islamic state, much like the Taliban's rule in Afghanistan.

One of the more complex strategic challenges we faced was how to fight an enemy that was present in numerous countries with which we were not at war. Unlike conventional conflicts, where the enemies were nations and the United States could attack the enemy wherever our forces could find him, we knew that our current enemies, the terrorists, were not just in Afghanistan but could also be in Pakistan, Saudi Arabia, Yemen, and a number of other countries. These were sovereign countries—and in some cases friends and partners—and there were delicate legal and diplomatic issues involved in sending intelligence operatives or special operations forces, even if we discovered that al-Qaida or another terrorist group might have a cell there. If we asked permission, there was a risk that a country would say no or that the information might leak. If they offered to go after them, we knew they did not have the same capabilities as our forces. Senior Bush administration officials understood that to meet the terrorist challenge, we generally would have to reach an understanding with these countries on the nature of the threat—and on the actions that we could take in response.

Eleven days after 9/11, I sent a note to the President suggesting a way to think about working with our friends and allies in response to the attack. "The mission must determine the coalition," I wrote. "The coalition ought not determine the mission."[9] The memo stemmed from a conversation I had in my office the day before with Israel's resolute former prime minister, Benjamin Netanyahu. He cautioned against building any permanent alliance that would restrict our flexibility in the future.

Though I understood the great value of having friends and allies in support of our efforts, I knew that not every country was likely to be willing or able to be helpful in all of the activities. As a result, not every operation would benefit from being tied to the largest coalition possible. I wanted the administration to think through carefully the activities we needed to undertake and then fashion the largest coalition possible for each of the necessary missions.[10]

I respected the well-considered views of America's friends, even when they might differ in some respects from our own. In fact, the several coalitions we would eventually assemble to go after terrorists and their sponsors would evolve over time. Each country had its own perspectives and concerns, I understood also that some nations would want to keep private or downplay their cooperation with a particular mission. I saw that as a fact to be accepted.

No senior administration official ever suggested that the United States would be better off responding to 9/11 alone. To this day I find it surprising that Bush administration critics were so successful in claiming that that was the President's view. The truth was that we solicited and eventually gained the assistance of more than ninety countries in the global coalition against terrorism. An even greater number took part in our Proliferation Security Initiative, a multilateral program designed to interdict the spread of weapons of mass destruction.[11] The unilateralism accusation against Bush was a preposterous charge. That we were so ineffective in countering it was a harbinger of other communication problems to come.

A key element of the administration's policy was that the primary purpose of America's reaction to 9/11 should be prevention of attacks and the defense of the American people, not punishment or retaliation. The only way to protect ourselves is to go after the terrorists wherever they may be.[12] This was a more ambitious goal than the approaches previous presidents had set. It reflected Bush's view, which I shared, that 9/11 was a seminal event, not simply another typical terrorist outrage to which the world had become accustomed. The 9/11 attack showed that our enemies wanted to cause as much harm as possible to the United States—to terrorize our population and to alter the behavior of the American people. No one in the administration, as far as I know, doubted that the men who destroyed the World Trade Center and hit the Pentagon would have gladly killed ten or a hundred times the number they killed on 9/11. They were not constrained by compunction, only by the means to escalate their carnage. This meant that their potential acquisition of weapons of mass destruction—biological, chemical, or nuclear—represented a major strategic danger.

This danger was highlighted dramatically by a Johns Hopkins University simulation of a biological attack on the United States. The report on that work, called "Dark Winter," was published just three months before 9/11. The researchers concluded that an outbreak of smallpox in three cities in the American interior could, within two months, result in approximately three million Americans infected, with one million dead. Such an epidemic could lead governors to try to insulate their states from the disease by shutting down interstate commerce, and lead to the imposition of martial law nationwide.[13] The report, drafted mainly by former officials of Democratic administrations, was widely read and much commented upon within the Bush administration. No responsible president could allow a scenario like that to materialize if there were reasonable steps he could take to avert it.

In the months after 9/11, I urged our Pentagon team and the combatant commanders to go through a mental exercise: I asked that they imagine that three or six months from now a major terrorist attack occurs in the United States. What would you regret not having done in the interim to prevent that attack? I urged them to head off regret. "Ask yourself what it is we must do every day between now and then to prevent that attack if possible, and if not to prevent it, at least to reduce the damage and save American lives. We must get up every morning and know that that is our job."

The President knew that a series of 9/11-type attacks—in conjunction with biological toxins, or suitcase nuclear weapons, or other nightmare combinations—could drastically alter the free and open nature of our society. It wouldn't be enough to rely on the FBI to investigate, indict, and prosecute terrorists in absentia as earlier administrations had done. Nor could we rely on precision air strikes to punish those we suspected were involved. Nor was this struggle simply about apprehending one man—Osama bin Laden—or one organization—al-Qaida. The task we faced was about systematically pressuring, attacking, and disrupting terrorist networks worldwide.

Terrorists had an easier time indoctrinating, recruiting, training, equipping, raising funds, and planning their attacks when they enjoyed a stable base of operations. So I argued that our strategy should be to put them on the defensive—indirectly (through the states that gave them safe havens) and directly (whenever we had actionable intelligence). The emphasis on a global campaign was important, I believed, because striking only al-Qaida in Afghanistan would result in little more than causing the terrorists to shift their base to Pakistan, Somalia, Yemen, Sudan, or elsewhere. To deny them safe havens, we needed to take action so that terrorists would feel unsafe wherever they tried to flee. So, for example, if the United States acted as a hammer against al-Qaida in Afghanistan, our diplomacy should try to ensure that Pakistan would function as the anvil. Also, the United States should conduct maritime interdiction operations to catch al-Qaida and other terrorists who might try to flee from Pakistan to the Arabian Peninsula or East Africa. There would be what I called secondary effects—terrorists would move to wherever there was the least pressure on them.[14] Denied safe havens, terrorist groups would have to scatter, creating inconveniences and vulnerabilities we could capitalize on. If they were continually on the run, worried about detection and capture, they would have less time, less energy, and less ability to plan attacks. Our goal had to be nothing less than making everything hard for them—raising money, traveling, communicating, recruiting, transferring funds, finding safe havens—in short, complicating everything they needed to do to be successful in their attacks.

Aware of the public's impatience, I urged the President to try to adjust the American people's expectations away from quick, decisive results. I stressed that the war on terrorism would be "a marathon, not a sprint."[15]

People commonly talk about the campaign in Afghanistan as if it were the inevitable response to 9/11. Events can often seem to have been obvious in retrospect. But the administration had a range of possible responses, none very attractive. One of the approaches the President considered was to focus on a tailored, retaliatory strike against al-Qaida and its operatives in Afghanistan. That approach would have been similar to our country's earlier responses to terrorist attacks: arrest the terrorists and bring them to justice and launch cruise missiles or drop bombs on their crude training facilities. But that was not going to be good enough this time.

Led by its supreme ruler, Mullah Muhammed Omar, Afghanistan's Taliban regime was one of the most isolated governments in the world. At the time of the 9/11 attack it had diplomatic relations with only three nations: Pakistan, Saudi Arabia, and the United Arab Emirates. The Taliban had broad and longstanding ties to terrorism. Our intelligence agencies were certain that Bin Laden was hiding and operating under their hospitality. Bin Laden had been the Taliban's "guest" since 1996.[16] After he masterminded the 1998 bombings of United States embassies in East Africa, the Clinton administration launched Tomahawk cruise missiles at al-Qaida training camps in Afghanistan. He escaped injury and, as a result, al-Qaida continued to do its work—up to and including killing thousands of Americans on 9/11.

Even though the Taliban regime in Afghanistan had refused a Clinton administration request to hand Bin Laden over to the United States, President Bush decided to give them an additional opportunity. That seemed reasonable to me. After 9/11, the Taliban might have recalculated, deciding that it would be prudent to accommodate this new American president who was backed by an angry, united American people, a large and growing international coalition, and the most powerful military on earth.

Responding to news reporting that the Taliban had aided the 9/11 plotters, Taliban leaders issued a cynical statement. "Mullah Omar condemns this act," it said. "Mullah Omar says Osama is not responsible. We have brought peace to this country and we want peace in all countries."[17] Every sentence was untrue.

On the morning of Saturday, September 15, President Bush assembled his National Security Council at Camp David. The famous presidential retreat was no longer the cluster of rustic log cabins I had known in the early 1970s; Camp David had become a more modern facility, with many of the comforts of the White House, and for me, at least, had lost some of its appeal.

Autumn had arrived in western Maryland, and even as we gathered inside the wood-paneled conference room of Camp David's Laurel Lodge, most of us wore fleece jackets against the chill. The discussions that day began with a briefing from Tenet. He laid out an interesting first cut of a plan that proposed sending small CIA teams to Afghanistan to begin gathering on-site intelligence on al-Qaida and Taliban targets.

General Shelton followed with a presentation on what his staff suggested might be accomplished militarily. Six foot five and built like a tree trunk, Shelton had an unmistakable presence in the halls of the Pentagon. He had been an Army special operations officer who had spent most of his adult life in uniform. He was disappointed that his four-year term as chairman was coming to a close at the end of the month, just as America was entering a conflict in which special operations forces would play a larger role than ever before.

The shock of 9/11 had not provoked much originality or imagination from the Chairman or his staff. It was true that in the ninety-six hours since the attack, Shelton had not had time for substantive discussions with the Joint Chiefs of Staff, General Tommy Franks, the head of Central Command (CENTCOM), or the senior civilian leadership, much less with the CIA, whose support and intelligence would be critical. I alerted Bush that what Shelton would be presenting was not a satisfactory recommendation of the Defense Department but simply some of his preliminary ideas to begin the discussions.

The first option Shelton presented was a cruise missile strike, similar to what the prior administration had executed in response to earlier terrorist attacks during the 1990s. It was obviously inadequate. President Bush made clear he was in no mood for more of the same ineffective half-measures. He told Shelton we needed to "unleash holy hell." "We're not just going to pound sand," he added.

Shelton's second option was a somewhat more muscular version of the first: cruise missile strikes accompanied by American aircraft bombing Afghan targets for several days. To Bush this represented pounding sand a little harder.

A third option was a combination of cruise missile strikes and stealth bomber runs plus what Shelton called "boots on the ground." It was not clear precisely what the missions would be for those troops. There were not many good targets for conventional American ground forces to engage. And, in any case, it would take considerable time to deploy a large force to that remote, landlocked country.

The President said he wanted American military forces on the ground in some fashion as soon as an effective response could be prepared and mounted. Shelton responded that a buildup of conventional ground troops could take months. I was concerned that during those months of preparation al-Qaida could scatter, and that the American people would be at risk of another attack. I decided we would spend the next several days working around-the-clock to develop a more appropriate plan.

Deputy Secretary Wolfowitz helped conceptualize the global war on terrorism as being broader than just Afghanistan. At that Camp David discussion Wolfowitz raised the question of Iraq, but Bush wanted to keep the focus on Afghanistan. Wolfowitz also suggested that wherever we struck first, our special forces should be a part of the military strategy. He had been impressed by the use of special forces to locate and destroy Iraqi Scud missiles during the 1991 Gulf War. Two weeks after 9/11, he wrote in a memo that "In addition to using Special Forces to attack targets associated with Al Qaida or the Taliban, we should consider using those [Special Forces] as a kind of armed liaison with anti-Al-Qaida or anti-Taliban elements in Afghanistan."[18] We believed our special operations forces could establish links with potential allies in Afghanistan, providing us with better intelligence and demonstrating that we were willing to help those who helped us. It was also a way of emphasizing the point that we were not fighting the Afghan people but only those who were supporting terrorism. The various suggestions from those in attendance and others became the nucleus of an audacious military campaign.

Looking back now on 9/11 and the early U.S. response, I see things we should have done differently and things that we might have done better. The administration, for example, should have focused more effectively and earlier on the ideological nature of the Islamist extremist enemies instead of describing the enemy vaguely as terrorism. We should not have shrunk from labeling the challenge Islamist while still properly making clear that we did not view Islam—the religion, as opposed to the totalitarian political ideology—as an enemy.

By the same token, we should have avoided personalizing the war around particular individuals—such as Osama bin Laden and Mullah Omar. Though I was eager to see them in American custody or dead, I knew the war would not end with their capture or their deaths. We needed to go after their networks and their means of operating. Nonetheless, the war's progress was frequently measured by whether Bin Laden was at large or not. He became the face of the enemy, which was likely exactly what he wanted.

We also could have engaged and asked more of the American public in the war effort. One of the common criticisms by Democrats and Republicans was that President Bush did not encourage the American people to make sacrifices in the immediate aftermath of the attacks. A myth arose that Bush simply encouraged citizens to "go shopping." That is not what he said—he was actually urging people to get on with their lives—and I understood his logic. Nonetheless, I sensed that Americans were anxious to do something—to be involved, to help—just as so many did their part for the war effort during World War II, with Victory Gardens, war bonds, and rationing. But the twenty-first century versions of those public contributions were not clear.

The President might instead have pushed for more education and scholarship on Islam and more training in languages like Arabic, Pashtu, and Farsi. The administration might have mounted a serious and sustained effort on alternative sources of energy to reduce America's dependency on foreign oil. We might have more energetically encouraged young people to volunteer in a civilian reserve corps or in the U.S. military and intelligence services. Instead the President said that "one of the great goals of this nation's war is to restore public confidence in the airline industry. It's to tell the traveling public: get onboard. Do your business around the country. Fly and enjoy America's great destination spots . . . Take your families and enjoy life."[19]

Also, in retrospect, I believe we might have put even greater pressure on some key partners, such as Saudi Arabia. Our relationship with the Saudis was a continuing concern for me in the months after 9/11. In memos to Cheney, Powell, and Rice, I urged that we develop a strategy to move that country in a better direction. Noting Saudi support for madrassas—Islamic schools that taught anti-Americanism and encouraged violence—I suggested Powell travel to the country to deal personally with these issues.[20] I also asked my staff "how we would start going after them to get them to behave responsibly, stop supporting terrorism and also to start doing the kinds of things they are going to have to do if they are going [to] survive as a country."[21] The Saudi government eventually made reasonable efforts against al-Qaida and its affiliates, but we might have been able to get them to do more sooner had America intensified its diplomacy in coordination with our allies. There were dangers in pushing friendly governments too hard, but in retrospect I think we may have given those dangers more weight than they merited.

Some critics suggested that the administration overreacted to the 9/11 attack. Their contention was that the terrorism problem and the challenge of radical Islamism were not and are not large enough to have justified a war on terrorism. I disagree. Islamist totalitarian ideology fuels an international movement that considers the United States and the West as enemies—not just of their movement but of God. Adherents to their extremist ideology are passionate, often fanatical, and certain in their conviction that their holy mission is to destroy their enemies utterly and without mercy. They have the advantages of being able to use Western technologies, gain access to international travel, and exploit the openness of liberal democratic societies and free people, all of which enable them to cause us great harm—harm of a magnitude many multiples of what we experienced on 9/11.

Lenin once said, "The purpose of terrorism is to terrorize." By sowing fear, terrorists seek to change our behavior and alter our values. Through their attacks, they trigger defensive reactions that could cause us to make our societies less open, our civil liberties less expansive, and our official practices less democratic—effectively to nudge us closer to the totalitarianism they favor. I thought our priority should be to maintain our free society and our values, and to not be terrorized into altering our free way of life. I had learned in Beirut in 1983 that a terrorist can attack any place and at any time of his choosing, using any conceivable technique. It is not physically possible to defend against terrorists day and night in every location, against every method of attack. In order to maintain our civil liberties and the sense of security Americans take pride in, we needed to go on the offensive.

In a way we made it easier for critics to discount the danger of terrorism, because the administration succeeded in our strategic goal: preventing additional attacks on the United States. There were attempts, but they were foiled. The institutions, laws, and policies that the President initiated contributed to discovering and deterring those attacks. For all the criticism the administration received, some no doubt deserved, one fact remains: Anyone who lived through 9/11 never would have believed that almost a decade later there would not have been another successful attack on our soil. That this was avoided was not the result of good luck. Rather, it was the result of an aggressive, unrelenting offensive against the enemy. The ultimate credit for that belongs to President George W. Bush.

The Taliban had heard demands and complaints from American administrations before. Nothing significant had come of them. "We don't foresee an attack against us," said the Taliban foreign minister, "because there is no reason for it."[22]

Taliban officials undoubtedly believed that Afghanistan's forbidding geography would discourage anything but a cosmetic military effort. After all, they had heard President Clinton declare after a previous Bin Laden attack in 1998 that Afghanistan had "been warned for years to stop harboring and supporting these terrorist groups. But countries that persistently host terrorists have no right to be safe havens. . . . There will be no sanctuary for terrorists."[23]

Things were different now. And if the Taliban believed America was bluffing, they miscalculated.

PART IX

Into the Graveyard of Empires

Afghan-Uzbek Border

FEBRUARY 15, 1989

One after another, Soviet soldiers boarded military convoys. Their final withdrawal from Afghanistan was underway. A few waved good-bye as they looked at that country for the last time. Just across the border, in Uzbekistan, the returning troops received flowers, were serenaded by a military band, and sat at long, linen-draped tables for a banquet in their honor.[1] Though it was likely not lost on any of the soldiers that the Soviet adventure in Afghanistan had ended in failure, their commander, General Boris Gromov, saluted his men for fulfilling their "internationalist duty."[2]

General Gromov had arranged to be taken back into Afghanistan by helicopter so he could be the last member of the Soviet military to depart the country, making a dramatic exit by walking alone across the inaptly named Friendship Bridge that connected Afghanistan to the Soviet Union. "There is not a single Soviet soldier or officer left behind me," he declared. "Our nine-year stay ends with this."[3] The Soviet "stay" in Afghanistan officially came to a close on February 15, 1989, at five minutes before noon local time. Appropriately, the USSR's final act in the war was another miscalculation: Gromov's choreographed departure occurred two hours later than had been planned.[4]

The Soviet Union put a brave face on its humiliation. But it was obvious to people around the world—and to the Soviet people in particular—that Afghanistan was the rock on which the last empire of the twentieth century had foundered. Lasting just less than a decade, the war had claimed the lives of fifteen thousand Soviet soldiers.[5] It disillusioned a generation of young Russians who had been led to believe that the Soviet Army was invincible. Even General Gromov, while distancing his military from the failure, later acknowledged the depth of the calamity, admitting that "the war was a huge and in many respects irreparable political mistake."[6]

The legacy of the decade-long Soviet misadventure would not be erased easily. The Soviets had brutalized the country's people, killing one million and displacing five million more. They had also destroyed much of the land, stripping its forests of trees. The prospects of survival for the puppet regime they left behind in Kabul were exceedingly poor. Once the Soviets withdrew, opposition forces, known collectively as the mujahideen ("holy warriors" in Arabic), quickly closed in on Kabul and seized power.

For most of the 1980s the U.S. government channeled funds and materiel to various mujahideen groups as part of the largest covert operation in CIA history.[7] As the Soviets completed their retreat, the CIA station in Islamabad, Pakistan, cabled the headquarters at Langley, Virginia, two words: "We won."[8]

Not long afterward, American activities in Afghanistan ended. After the disintegration of the Soviet Union, the administrations of George H. W. Bush and Bill Clinton turned their attention away from Cold War preoccupations. In the chaos and civil war that consumed the country after the Soviet departure, the United States embassy in Kabul closed its doors. As America lost interest in Afghanistan, Saudi Arabia and Pakistan poured in millions of dollars to fund roads, clinics, radical Wahhabi madrassas and mosques. The Pakistani government cultivated Afghanistan's Pashtun warlords and, beginning in 1996, supported the regime that became known as the Taliban. None of this caused any noticeable concern at the senior levels of the U.S. government. Few American policy or intelligence officials imagined that they would ever have to concern themselves again with that distant, poor, and abused land.

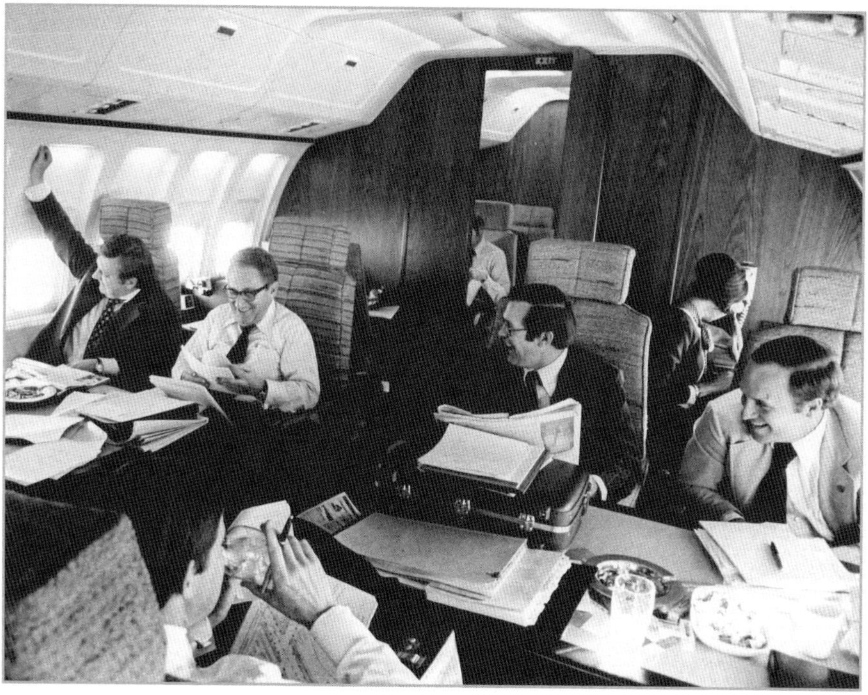

27

On Air Force One with Larry Eagleburger (left), Henry Kissinger (center), and Dick Cheney (right). Serving as White House Chief of Staff was among my most challenging assignments, but it could also be enjoyable.

28

Ford's fine sense of humor kept us all coming back day after day. It appears the President won this tennis match with photographer David Kennerly.

29

President Ford meeting with his advisers on the disastrous economic situation he had inherited (left to right: Bill Simon, Ron Nessen, Dick Cheney, and Alan Greenspan).

30

On his first trip abroad as President, Ford visited Vladivostok in the Soviet Union. His meetings, including this official luncheon with General Secretary Brezhnev and Foreign Minister Gromyko, were held in a former mental health sanitarium.

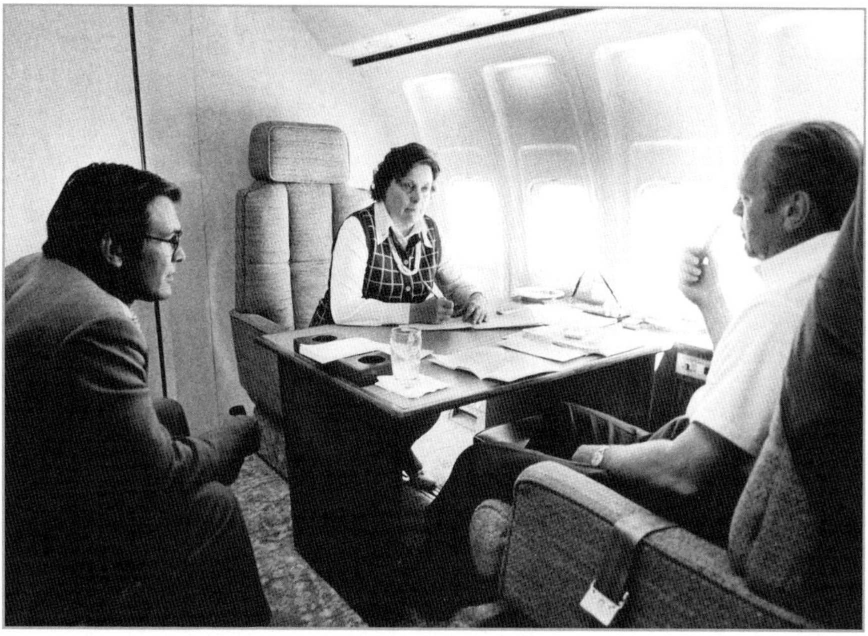

31

Two assassination attempts in September 1975 added to President Ford's challenges. After the attempt by radical Squeaky Fromme, my longtime secretary, Lee Goodell, took down the President's recollections on our return flight to Washington, D.C.

32

During the second assassination attempt, the bullet from Sarah Jane Moore's pistol passed between the President's head and mine, before hitting the wall of the St. Francis Hotel.

33

My mother, Jeannette, with Joyce, Nick, Marcy, and Valerie at my first swearing-in ceremony as secretary of defense. This is a favorite photograph of the special people in my life.

34

Nick, then eight years old, was taken aback by the nineteen-gun salute at the ceremony, but tried hard not to show it.

© RON SACHS/CNP/SYGMA/CORBIS

35

General-turned-statesman Yitzhak Rabin (left center) succeeded Prime Minister Golda Meir in 1974 to become the first Israeli-born leader of the Jewish state. He impressed me with his patriotism, which was tempered by a realistic understanding of the challenges of the Middle East. Tragically, he was assassinated in 1995.

36

In March 1976, President Ford awarded the Department of Defense Distinguished Service Medal to my colleagues from NATO (left to right), Belgian Ambassador André de Staerke and French Ambassador François de Rose, as well as my successor as U.S. ambassador, the noted diplomat David Bruce.

38

It seems that most of what I have done in life has resulted from working closely with bright, energetic, broadly experienced people. As I entered the business world with precious little background, I benefited from the talents of Jim Denny (left) and John Robson (right). I had known John in high school and Jim in college, but it had never occurred to me that we might wind up working together at G. D. Searle in the 1970s and 1980s. It was my great good fortune that we did.

The President's loss to Jimmy Carter in the 1976 election was tough, but the Fords continued to approach life with optimism, confidence, and good humor. It was a privilege to serve in his administration and to receive the Presidential Medal of Freedom in January 1977.

37

39

Serving as President Reagan's Special Envoy for the Law of the Sea Treaty, I met with two old friends in Tokyo: U.S. Ambassador to Japan and former Democratic leader of the Senate Mike Mansfield of Montana and Prime Minister Yasuhiro Nakasone, with whom I had worked when I served as a member of the Japanese-American Parliamentary Exchange fifteen years earlier.

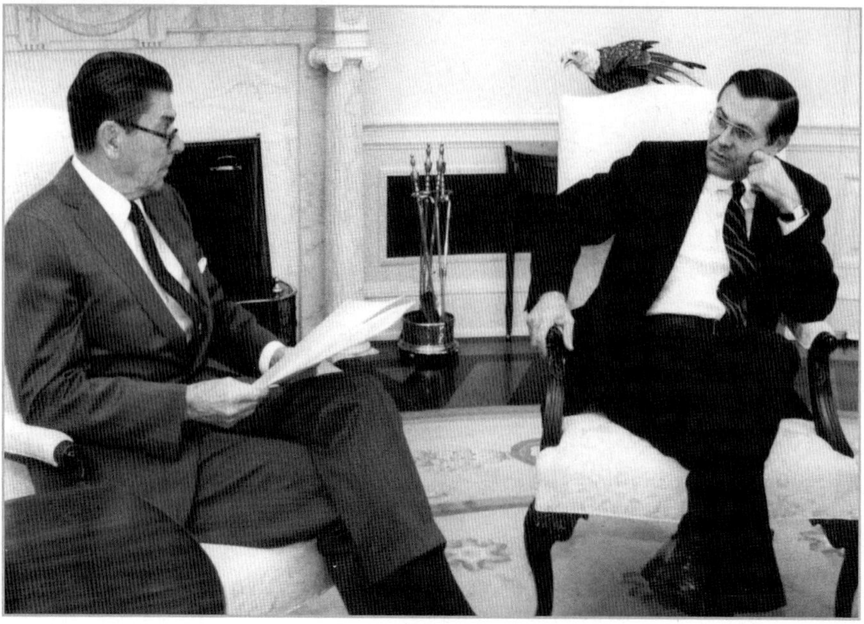

40

President Reagan asked me to serve as his Middle East envoy days after the terrorist attack on the Marine barracks outside Beirut, Lebanon, in October 1983. Reagan was deeply distressed over the loss of American lives. If in the end the problem of Syria, Lebanon, and Israel proved as intractable for his administration as for others, it was not for lack of will on the President's part.

41

With Jack Kemp (left), Howard Baker, and Colin Powell discussing the 1996 presidential campaign. While our candidate, Bob Dole, had long experience in government and a compelling personal story of service, we were never able to challenge the personal charm and easy manner of his opponent, Bill Clinton.

As the year 2000 approached, Joyce and I thought we were moving into our rural period in Taos, New Mexico.

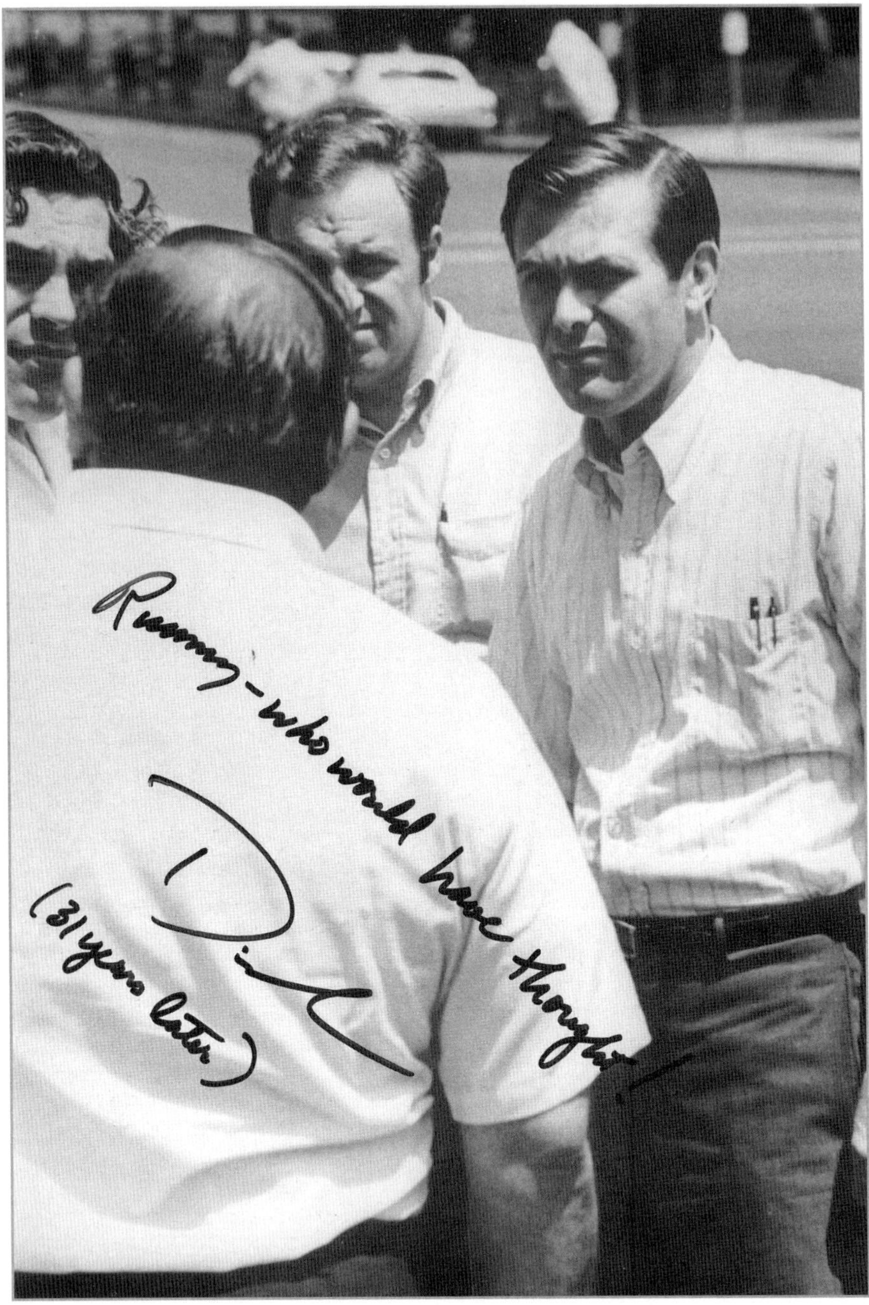
Rummy - who would have thought!
(31 years later)

Dick Cheney and I were both amazed to find ourselves serving together in another administration some three decades after our time together at OEO. Cheney marked the occasion by signing this old photograph.

44

My second swearing-in as secretary of defense, this time with my old friend and colleague Judge Larry Silberman doing the honors.

45

With Colin Powell, Dick Cheney, and Condi Rice at the Pentagon, March 2001. From the beginning of the Bush administration the four of us met weekly for lunch when we were in town, and Colin, Condi, and I had a regular telephone call each morning. I respected them all.

The Pentagon, September 11, 2001.

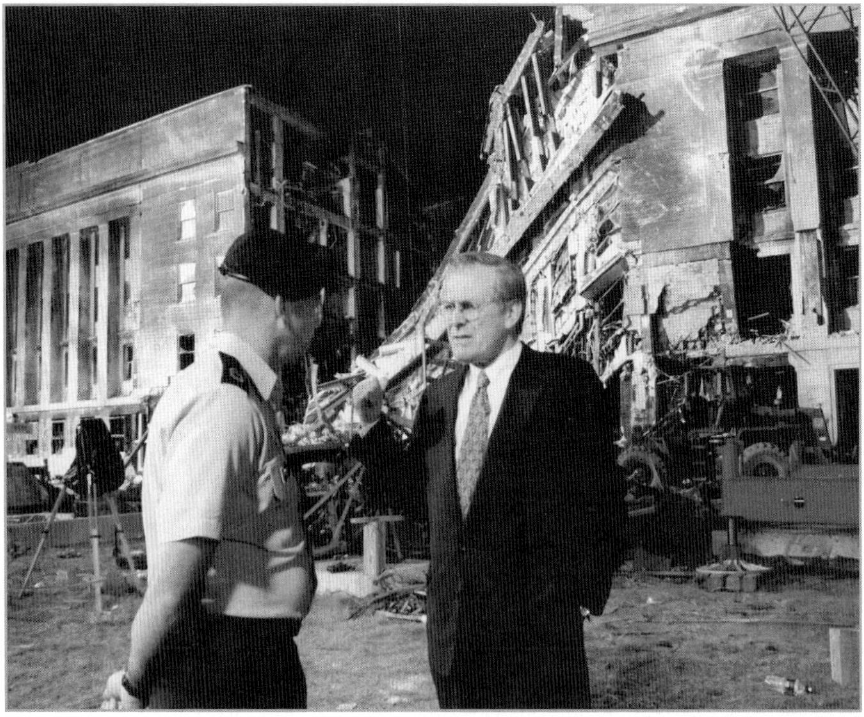

The Pentagon, September 12, 2001.

48

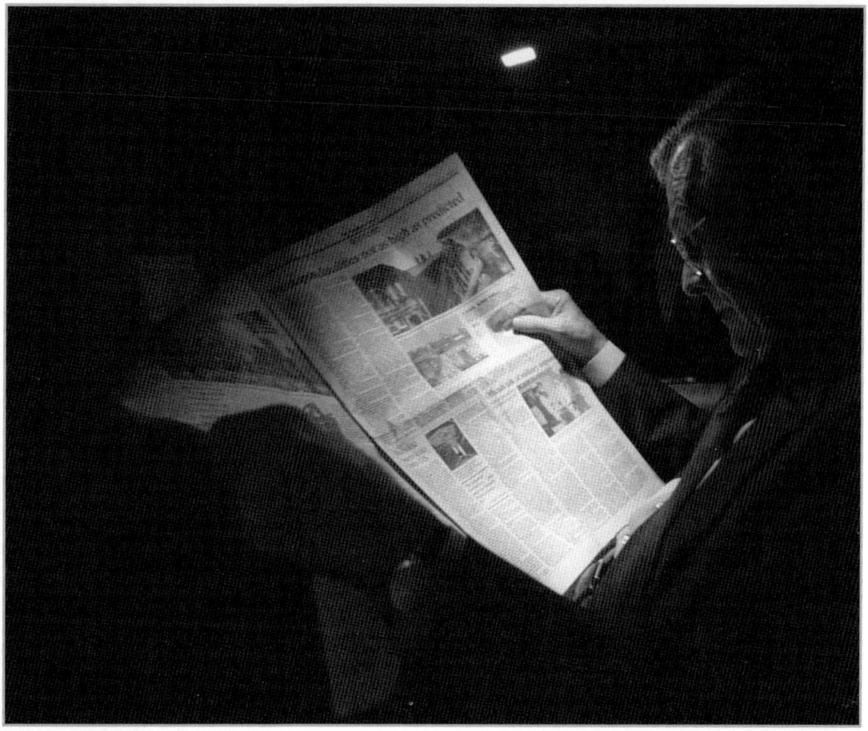

During my early-morning drives to the Pentagon through empty Washington streets in the days after 9/11 I saw how the terrorist attacks gripped the nation and filled the newspapers.

49

(Left to right) Doug Feith, Gen. Jim Jones, President George Bush, Condi Rice, Gordon England, Gen. Hugh Shelton, Gen. Jack Keane, Adm. Vern Clark conferring at the Pentagon the day after 9/11.

Ground Zero, New York City.

51

Meeting with the Pentagon press in the days after 9/11, Gen. Myers and I responded to hundreds of questions about this new and uncertain conflict—the first war of the twenty-first century.

52

With Vice President Cheney while our miniature dachshund Reggie patrolled the area. After 9/11, we were never really off the clock.

53

At a meeting around my stand-up desk in the hours before military action started in Afghanistan with advisers Steve Cambone, Paul Wolfowitz, Larry Di Rita, and Torie Clarke.

CHAPTER 27

Special Operations

When U.S. military action against the Taliban regime and its al-Qaida guests was imminent in late 2001, I mulled over the lessons of the Soviet defeat. The Red Army was only the most recent in a long line of foreign forces that had attempted to secure the country. Afghanistan's tough, martial people and land-locked, mountainous terrain had undone the plans of even the most intrepid invaders. Alexander the Great was nearly killed by the arrow of an Afghan archer. Though Genghis Khan managed to extend his empire into Afghan territory after savage warfare, his successors could not hold it. In 1842, Afghan resistance forced the British military to make an ill-fated retreat from Kabul to its garrison in the city of Jalalabad, a little more than one hundred miles away. Some sixteen thousand British soldiers and camp followers began the trek. Only one man made it to safety.[1] After 9/11, analysts in the United States and abroad wondered aloud if American armed forces would also stumble similarly.[2]

Since President Bush had decided to confront Afghanistan, the challenge was to strike our enemies in such a way that it would shock terrorist networks worldwide. We wanted to not only destroy al-Qaida in Afghanistan, but to cause al-Qaida and its affiliates everywhere to scramble for cover, to coerce their sponsors to sever their ties with them, and to persuade our allies and friends to join us in our efforts. Afghanistan would be the opening salvo—our nation's first major foray into a global, unconventional war aimed at preventing terrorists from launching future attacks against Americans.

By the end of September 2001, we had not yet determined exactly how we could best achieve our goals. Some administration officials at State and the CIA argued in favor of allowing the Taliban to stay in power in the interest of maintaining regional stability. But a question, at least in my mind, was whether this might be a time when the United States had an interest in instability if it might bring about needed changes.

The more we considered a policy toward the Afghan regime, the more persuaded I became that there was little prospect of an acceptable accommodation with them. The Taliban leaders were brutal totalitarians who had imposed an extremist Islamic ideology on the Afghan people. Women could not attend school, could not leave their homes without a male family member, and could not see male doctors, which made medical treatment for them next to impossible. Citizens could be jailed for owning a television. A man could be imprisoned in Afghanistan if his beard were not long enough. It was illegal for youngsters to fly kites. Afghan soccer stadiums were used for public stonings and beheadings. The so-called Ministry of Vice and Virtue patrolled the streets, beating any who violated the Taliban's laws. In an act of deliberate and barbaric vandalism, the Taliban dynamited two monumental, carved Buddhas in Bamiyan in March 2001, turning the magnificent sixth-century statues into rubble.

If the Taliban remained in power, we risked sending a message to other nations that harbored and aided terrorists that they could assist a group like al-Qaida and then negotiate a "grand bargain" with the United States. Indeed, over the years, a number of governments had successfully bargained with terrorist groups in order to keep their own countries from being attacked. But in my view, rewards of security guarantees and aid in return for dubious promises of better behavior in the future were not the best means of deterring more terrorist attacks.

In the weeks after 9/11, work went forward at the Defense Department on an unconventional military campaign. As we began planning, I came to rely on the incoming chairman of the Joint Chiefs of Staff, Dick Myers. As a matter of principle that was informed by my experience in the Ford administration, I felt strongly that the secretary of defense and the chairman of the Joint Chiefs of Staff needed to be closely linked, especially in wartime. And with Myers, it was easy to put that principle into practice. I believe we averaged three or four hours a day together while we held our posts.

Myers and I began working closely with the officer who would lead the military effort in Afghanistan: General Tommy Franks, who had been appointed by President Clinton to head the U.S. Central Command. A big, tall, earthy man with a quick smile, Franks had a colorful manner of speaking—though he could on occasion complete a sentence without an expletive. Born just after the close of World War II, Franks was adopted by a couple in Oklahoma, and the family later moved to Midland, Texas. In 1965, he enlisted in the Army as a private and moved up through the ranks to become a four-star general. He lacked the polish of some of his fellow generals, who had graduated from West Point and spent many years learning the ways of Washington, D.C. But on the battlefield Franks was a leader.

We had worked together very little in the eight months I had been in office; as a result, it took some time for us to get used to each other. My habit of asking probing questions was new to Franks; he needed to become comfortable with my queries and confident of my regard for him. After several weeks of daily contact, and at least one sushi dinner, we developed an effective working relationship.

President Bush took to Franks from the start. Once, when Bush asked him how he was doing, Franks replied, "Mr. President, I'm sharper than a frog hair split four ways."[3] That was the kind of folksy manner they both liked. He and Franks would occasionally joke about how far "two boys from Midland" had come.

Franks knew something about the history of Afghanistan and its long record of defeating outsiders attempting conquest. He also knew that when seeking cooperation from Afghanistan's neighbors in the weeks ahead he would be having many cups of tea with the political and military leaders of the twenty-six countries in CENTCOM's area of operations.

Franks' immediate task was to develop a war plan. Though even the best one off the shelf would have required substantial updating to fit the new realities we faced, the fact was that there was no existing war plan for Afghanistan. Further complicating matters, there was scant current intelligence on the country. Steep and damaging budget cuts to our intelligence community during the 1990s had resulted in American operatives being moved to other matters after the Soviet withdrawal. By 2001, our intelligence personnel did not know the extent to which tribal leaders would tolerate, let alone welcome, American forces into the country. We didn't even have an up-to-date picture of the terrain. In some cases our analysts were working with decades-old

British maps. The early information we did receive was spotty: one site might or might not have been an al-Qaida safe house; another may or may not have been a Taliban weapons facility. In addition, few intelligence operatives and analysts spoke the Afghan languages.

We faced other planning issues. The use of our Navy would be limited in landlocked Afghanistan. The high altitudes and dust would make helicopter operations challenging. Ground forces would have a difficult time trying to operate in the unfamiliar and inhospitable Afghan terrain in the approaching winter months. The United States did not have even modest working relationships with most of Afghanistan's neighbors.* The Department of Defense would need to rapidly organize a campaign—in which it could cooperate with local militias, conduct manhunts, and operate with agility—as the enemy reacted and adapted in an environment it knew far better.

Several days after 9/11, I asked Franks how long he thought it would take CENTCOM to craft a plan for Afghanistan. We both knew he would need considerably more detail than the sketchy options presented by Shelton at Camp David on September 15.

"Two months," Franks responded.

The President was not going to wait patiently for another two months to take action. Daily threat reports provided by the intelligence community cautioned that additional terrorist attacks were likely. Therefore, we needed to begin putting pressure on their networks as rapidly as possible. Additionally, the passes through the towering Afghan mountains would soon be blanketed with snow, rendering them impassable.

"General, I'm afraid we don't have that much time," I told Franks. I asked him to come up with a first cut of a plan in a few days.

On September 21, 2001, Franks and I drove over to the White House to present his initial operational concept. Wanting the meeting to be as confidential as possible, Bush restricted the group to four senior generals—Shelton, Myers, Franks, and Major General Dell Dailey, head of the U.S. Joint Special Operations Command (JSOC). The President also parted from his normal practice of meeting in the Situation Room and had us meet in his private residence on the second floor of the White House.

Bush was informal, his jacket off and his sleeves rolled up. At one point

* Pakistan, Iran, Turkmenistan, Uzbekistan, Tajikistan, and China all share borders with Afghanistan.

he lit a cigar as he listened to Franks and Dailey. The President's black dog, Barney, ambled around the room.

As Franks prepared to outline his initial concept, I reminded President Bush: "You are not going to find this plan completely fulfilling. We don't."

Bush said he understood that this was a work in progress.

Franks and Dailey led the briefing. Bush would need to be working with them closely in the months ahead, and I thought it important that the Commander in Chief get to know them early on.

A key element of Franks' plan involved linking American special forces teams with Afghan forces. This was a departure from the first concept that had been outlined at Camp David, which focused on using conventional U.S. military might. Wolfowitz and I encouraged Franks to take full advantage of our special operators.[4] General Dailey briefed the President on targets that could be handled by the elite squads.

The President asked how soon a campaign could begin. Franks responded that under this type of plan, his forces could begin to attack in the following two weeks.[5]

Bush liked that answer. He ended the meeting saying that he would continue to counsel patience to the American people. We were all aware that passions were running high.

While the imminent operations in Afghanistan would be challenging, we did have some advantages. An active opposition movement—the Northern Alliance—had been trying to liberate the country from the Taliban and al-Qaida for five years. Joining up with these opposition forces would ally us with seasoned local fighters who knew the languages and the terrain. But this approach also had risks. For years these fighters had been unsuccessful. Some intelligence officials, the CIA's station chief in Pakistan in particular, cautioned that if America allied with the Northern Alliance militias, which were dominated by ethnic Tajik, Uzbek, and Hazara fighters, we ran the risk of uniting the ethnic Pashtuns in southern Afghanistan against us and planting the seeds of a north-south civil war. This was one reason some recommended a continuing role for the Taliban in postwar Afghanistan.

Franks and I looked for opportunities to manage those risks. Though we understood well the need to also reach out to anti-Taliban Pashtuns in the south, the Northern Alliance, comprising some twenty thousand Afghans, remained the most credible and best-organized opposition force in the country. At first glance they appeared to be a ragtag band of unsuccessful, poorly armed guerrilla fighters on the verge of defeat. But they were also tough, motivated, and battle hardened.

For years the Northern Alliance had been led by the "Lion of Panjshir," Ahmad Shah Massoud. Through his audacious combat against Soviet forces during the 1980s and his force of personality, Massoud commanded the respect of millions of Afghans, and he had pulled together several ethnic groups under the banner of his leadership. To this day Massoud's image, with his signature woolen pakol hat and checkered scarf, remains emblazoned on posters, tapestries, and murals in homes and public places across much of Afghanistan. Massoud struggled to keep his outnumbered Northern Alliance forces in the fight against the Taliban. He had repeatedly asked Western countries for military and financial support. The United States had been less than forthcoming. As a result, the Northern Alliance had an arsenal that was a small fraction of the Taliban's. During the Clinton administration, CIA officers advised Massoud not to kill Bin Laden if the opportunity arose. "You guys are crazy," Massoud reportedly responded. "You haven't changed a bit."[6]

While Massoud's importance as a leader of the Afghan people was largely lost on Western governments, it was not lost on al-Qaida. The terrorist organization sent operatives into Massoud's camp disguised as reporters. Once in his presence, they detonated explosives hidden in their equipment, killing him. The assassination occurred on September 9, 2001.

As al-Qaida had intended, the death of Massoud left the Northern Alliance forces with a leadership vacuum. But other leaders emerged, including: General Fahim Khan, a Tajik and heir apparent to Massoud; General Abdul Rashid Dostum, an Uzbek; General Ismail Khan from Herat in western Afghanistan; Abdul Karim Khalili of the Hazara minority; Muhammed Mohahqeq; and Muhammed Attah.*

These men were not saints, but saints are in short supply in the world. Though moral considerations in American national security policy are of critical importance, warfare continually poses excruciating moral trade-offs. I recalled Winston Churchill's famous retort to criticism of his alliance with Stalin, an acknowledged butcher of millions, against Nazi Germany. "If Hitler invaded hell," he said, "I would make at least a favorable reference to the devil in the House of Commons."

My willingness for our forces to work with the Northern Alliance was based on my conviction that we would be making a mistake if our military

* He should not be confused with the terrorist who led the nineteen September 11 hijackers, an Egyptian also named Muhammed Atta.

effort appeared to the Afghans as an American invasion aimed at taking control of their country. I concluded it would be far better to position ourselves as the allies of indigenous Afghan forces. I saw this as the best way to avoid the heavy-handed errors of Afghanistan's past invaders and occupiers.

This was one of the lessons of Vietnam for me. I thought the Vietnamization strategy of President Nixon and Secretary of Defense Mel Laird, to push America's South Vietnamese allies to do more for themselves, would have been far more effective, perhaps decisive, if it had been implemented from the outset of the war. In Afghanistan there was at least a possibility that the United States could play a supporting rather than a leading role in the fight against al-Qaida and the Taliban from the beginning.

On September 30, 2001, I outlined our approach for Afghanistan to President Bush as part of a broader framework for the fight against terrorists. Given the scope of al-Qaida's reach, as well as that of other groups in the web of international networks of Islamist extremists, I thought we needed to start thinking early about how this larger campaign might take shape.

I developed this approach during lengthy consultations with Myers, Franks, and the senior civilians in the Pentagon, including Paul Wolfowitz, Doug Feith, and Peter Rodman. The memo setting out this framework was an example of the constructive working relationships at the senior levels of the Department of Defense—military and civilian. We would meet and then circulate draft papers. It started with some preliminary ideas that were then reviewed and polished until we were reasonably satisfied with what was truly a collaborative product, though it came under my signature.

Because the global task that lay ahead was too big, too broad, and too multidimensional for us to think we could rely exclusively on American military forces, I suggested the following to the President:

> The U.S. strategic theme should be aiding local peoples to rid themselves of terrorists and to free themselves of regimes that support terrorism. U.S. Special Operations Forces and intelligence personnel should make allies of Afghanis, Iraqis, Lebanese, Sudanese and others who would use U.S. equipment, training, financial, military and humanitarian support to root out and attack the common enemies.[7]

In the Afghan war's early phases, it was especially important that the United States work with local groups to develop better intelligence before initiating major air strikes, so as to minimize civilian casualties.[8] We did not want our war of self-defense and our fight against extremist regimes, which oppressed their Muslim citizens, to be symbolized by images of Americans killing Muslims. The signal we needed to send, I wrote, was that "our goal is not merely to damage terrorist-supporting regimes but to threaten their regimes by becoming partners with their opponents."[9]

The Northern Alliance was not to be our only support in this campaign. In a matter of weeks, President Bush and the Departments of State and Defense had brought together a coalition of dozens of supportive nations. At CENTCOM headquarters in Tampa, Franks assembled a "coalition village," where representatives from partner nations provided input. Britain, Canada, Germany, and Australia offered infantry, aircraft, naval units, and special operations forces. Japan was prepared to send refueling ships, destroyers, and transport aircraft. France and Italy each offered to deploy an aircraft carrier battle group. In all more than sixty-nine nations would eventually contribute to the coalition effort in Afghanistan.[10]

As CENTCOM finalized the war plan, Myers and I communicated daily with Franks and his deputy, Marine Lieutenant General Mike DeLong. I believed that Washington policy makers should, as a rule, show considerable deference to the professional judgments of the combatant commander. But the plan being developed for Afghanistan was not an off-the-shelf one that had been war-gamed and practiced. We did not have a longstanding doctrine on how to conduct this sort of war. Therefore, the chiefs and DoD civilians helped hone the approach before Franks presented it to the President and the National Security Council. The hard-charging Franks was not always delighted with what he considered to be an overabundance of advice but, in the end, he told me, he felt the results were worth it.

As I had hoped and expected when Franks first briefed the President, the plan he eventually developed was a substantial improvement. It would begin with a major air campaign. Bombs and cruise missiles first would target the Taliban's few radars, limited air-defense systems, and command-and-control facilities, weakening their ability to coordinate a counterattack. Strike fighters from aircraft carriers—the USS *Enterprise* and the USS *Carl Vinson*—off the coast of Pakistan, B-2 stealth bombers flying on seventy-hour sorties from Whiteman Air Force Base in Missouri, and B-52s staging out of Diego Garcia, an island in the Indian Ocean, would hit suspect targets across Afghanistan. Helicopters would insert our special operations teams—over time numbering some two hundred individuals—to link up with anti-Taliban militia commanders. Once embedded, our special operators would call in American air support for Northern Alliance ground operations as well as provide supplies for our new allies. A relatively small contingent—several thousand conventional Army soldiers and Marines—would follow to help deal with remaining enemy fighters that the Northern Alliance and special operations forces had not killed or forced to surrender. Additional forces would be on alert if Franks determined they were needed.

One of the most innovative elements was a merger of the CIA's broad authorities and experienced intelligence operatives with the Defense Department's greater military resources. CIA teams would make first contact with the Northern Alliance elements and lay the groundwork for American military cooperation. The next phase called for the insertion of U.S. Army Special Forces Operational Detachment Alpha (ODA) teams, twelve-man squads trained to work alongside foreign fighters. Together with their special operations counterparts from the other branches—Navy SEALs and Air Force combat air controllers—these men would take on the toughest missions in Afghanistan. Once in country, the ODAs, or A-Teams, as they were called, would link up with friendly Afghan militia commanders.

During the Afghan campaign, I worked as closely with CIA Director George Tenet as I have with any government official. We had lunches most Fridays, during which we worked out any issues or challenges facing the Agency or the Pentagon. Tenet had a brash joviality that I enjoyed. It wasn't hard to work long hours alongside someone like Tenet, who had a way of lightening the mood.

Given the large scale of the planned operation, Tenet and I agreed that operational control of the joint Defense-CIA efforts would migrate over time from the CIA to Defense once our special operators were on the ground with the Afghan anti-Taliban militias. The CIA would have the lead initially, since its personnel would be in Afghanistan first. Command would shift to Franks and CENTCOM, as the campaign took on more of a military character. This was exactly the kind of flexible, cooperative arrangement that was needed. We didn't want to stifle improvisation in the field, but at the same time we could not afford to have confused lines of command.

A few in the CIA apparently objected to the agreement Tenet and I reached and portrayed it as a power grab.[11] I understood the complaints from lower levels at the Agency. There had always been deep-seated anxieties at the CIA about the much larger Defense Department. Though I know Tenet did not feel this way, some at the CIA did not want to be seen as subordinate to the Department of Defense. Tenet and I were conscious of the challenge that all presidents have in getting the various agencies of the government to work jointly. But we both felt that close, visible personal cooperation between the two of us at the top could ease them and encourage a joint approach for those down the chain of command.

In addition to the teamwork of DoD and CIA operators in the field, a second key element of the war plan was the introduction of America's twenty-first-century technology to the relatively primitive operations of the Afghan militias. For years Northern Alliance commanders had managed to survive by building a modest arsenal of AK-47 automatic rifles, rocket-propelled grenades, a few rusty Soviet tanks, and some helicopters that could barely make it off the ground. Once embedded with the Northern Alliance, American special operations forces would upgrade their weaponry, provide supplies, and serve as on-the-ground air controllers to call in precision air strikes. The effort would combine the use of satellite communications, laser designators, GPS capability, and powerful precision munitions with friendly Afghan intelligence, language skills, cultural familiarity, and ground combat manpower.

CIA operatives scrambled to revive long-lapsed relationships with Northern Alliance commanders. This effort was complicated by the Agency's ties with the Pakistani government, which favored the ethnic Pashtuns in southern Afghanistan. In line with the views of the Pakistani government, CIA officials continued to caution President Bush against any military plan that relied heavily on the Northern Alliance.[12] I worried that the views of some intelligence officials seemed colored by Pakistan's interests, which were not necessarily identical to ours.

Powell, Armitage, and other State Department officials also expressed misgivings about the Northern Alliance. Without offering an alternative or explicitly disagreeing with our approach, Powell described the Northern Alliance militias as a "fourth world" fighting force, implying that it could not prevail against the Taliban and al-Qaida. Though I understood those concerns—the Northern Alliance, after all, had been unsuccessful over the preceding years—ultimately I disagreed with them. I believed that with our airpower and special operators, the Afghan opposition could drive the Taliban from power at significantly less risk to our men and women in uniform than a conventional invasion. Myers, Franks, and I concluded that we should continue to base our military strategy on cooperation with the Northern Alliance and opposition militias in the Pashtun south.

Help in developing our linkages with friendly Afghan forces came from an unlikely source. On September 26, I ran into California Congressman Dana Rohrabacher in the Pentagon parking lot. He had worked in President Reagan's White House and developed an interest in the mujahideen's efforts to rid Afghanistan of the Soviet occupiers in the 1980s. The congressman said that he and his staff were in contact by satellite phone with Northern Alliance commanders whom they had known in the 1980s. His contacts reported that Taliban morale was up, and that our allies in the Afghan opposition forces were discouraged by statements made by Bush administration officials that America's goal was not to remove the Taliban but instead to seek a compromise with it.[13] We were sending mixed signals to our enemies and to our friends.

In later years, critics would pose questions as to why we didn't immediately prepare to deploy 50,000, 100,000, or 150,000 American troops to Afghanistan. There were several reasons. If we were going to employ overwhelming force at the outset, we would have needed many months to build a large occupying army. This would have given the Taliban time to prepare for the conflict, and al-Qaida both the incentive and the opportunity to relocate. In addition, we would have risked additional terrorist attacks in the interim, and made it easier for our enemies to portray us as imperialist invaders and occupiers, like the Soviets and others before us. Finally, delay may have eroded popular support at home and abroad for the President's counterterrorism strategy. It is also the case that large numbers of American troops in Afghanistan could have limited our ability to act elsewhere in the world if necessary. We had to keep in mind that other contingencies could arise, particularly if a would-be aggressor believed the United States military was stretched thin. This was Myers', Franks', and my assessment—and ultimately President Bush's.

As such, the emerging war plan did not call for the kind of armored divisions and heavy artillery the Soviets had used in Afghanistan. Rather, it emphasized speed, flexibility, and precision. Air strikes and small helicopter-borne teams were arranged to execute quick responses to the changing circumstances on the ground. U.S. special operations forces would provide the technology necessary for our naval and air-strike aircraft to attack al-Qaida and the Taliban with unprecedented precision firepower.

The Army's Special Forces, the Navy's SEALs, and the Air Force's combat controllers had not been previously entrusted with the lead in such a major mission. The few hundred men who were ready to risk their lives in the service of their country by going after the Taliban and al-Qaida terrorists alongside the Northern Alliance forces were among the most highly trained, best equipped, and most experienced soldiers on the face of the earth. Some were fluent in the local languages and versed in the cultures they would be encountering. They had trained foreign militaries and understood how to get along with those who thought and fought differently. They were experts in the irregular guerrilla warfare that would be critical to success. They were trained in demolition, hand-to-hand combat, and mountain and desert warfare. American special operators would be the sharp tip of the spear in the first war of the twenty-first century.

The military services also found ways to adapt and contribute to our unconventional Afghan campaign. It took a creative, forward-leaning admiral to assist in a country three hundred miles from the nearest ocean. In Admiral Vern Clark, the chief of naval operations, the U.S. Navy had such a leader. Within hours after the 9/11 attack, submarines and Arleigh Burke–class destroyers armed with Tomahawk cruise missiles were speeding toward the Indian Ocean and the Arabian Sea. Clark ordered a refit of the 60,000-ton USS *Kitty Hawk* from a fleet aircraft carrier designed for launching jet aircraft into a "lily pad," a seaborne platform for helicopters carrying special operators. The ship was in the northern Arabian Sea and in position to send the special operations teams into Afghanistan by early October.

With the Soviet disaster still in many people's minds, with winter approaching, and with our faith in a group of haggard yet battle-hardened Afghans, the United States was on the verge of one of the most unorthodox military campaigns in our history.

CHAPTER 28

Little Birds in a Nest

General Franks planned to insert special operations teams into Afghanistan on the evenings of October 6 and 7 using a nontraditional, celestial ally. The moon would rise several hours after sunset, allowing our forces a small window when their helicopters could traverse the vast Afghan mountain ranges in darkness and be less vulnerable to Taliban antiaircraft emplacements.

Knowing military action was coming, I set out in the first week of October to meet with leaders in some of the countries in the region. In Saudi Arabia, Oman, Egypt, Uzbekistan, and Turkey I consulted with government officials on our plans, sought their advice, and learned what support they might be willing to provide. I assured our potential partners of two things: The United States would appreciate whatever public or private support they might offer, and we were going to respond aggressively with force against the terrorist threat on a vastly different scale and level of intensity than in the past. This was a welcome message to most leaders of the region, who did not relish the prospects of emboldened radicals in their backyards.

I generally made a point of refraining from asking for specific types of assistance in meetings with foreign leaders. Nor did I spend a lot of time "transmitting"—giving lengthy presentations on the President's goals and views and trying to push them to see things our way. I listened instead, which was valuable either because the foreign leaders had useful thoughts to convey or simply because those leaders were grateful to be heard out by the American secretary of defense. It is hard to overstate the practical importance of mutually respectful discussions of this kind. I have always found that these exchanges are especially important with smaller nations, and particularly with those that have not had long close relations with the United States.

When foreign leaders offered assistance, as they often did, I expressed our appreciation. I made a practice, however, of not publicly discussing the specifics of our understandings unless they did so themselves. Some nations preferred to support the United States quietly, so as not to inflame their enemies, stir up domestic political opposition, or become a terrorist target. This practice, of course, allowed administration critics to claim we were acting unilaterally, often without knowing the extent of the assistance and cooperation we actually received.

The aides who made official foreign trips with me—I visited seventy-five countries, many of them several times, and traveled 750,000 miles during my second tour as secretary of defense—generally described them as forced marches. We could not afford to waste time. If I could squeeze in stops to two countries on a given day, I did. Three was even better. The combination of constant motion, jet lag, early morning wake-up calls, and difficult, high-stakes work was invigorating. But it could be tough for the staff. On one flight I received a memo from a few long-suffering stalwarts who had dubbed themselves "Rummy's Tube Dwellers." They joked that they had "taken control of the plane, and diverted to the Virgin Islands," unless I agreed to some "non-negotiable demands" such as "frequent flyer miles . . . less diet coke, more martinis . . . For every day spent in a 'stan' [the countries of Central Asia] we get 4 comp days."[1]

On October 4, we arrived in Oman, a country on the eastern tip of the Arabian Peninsula. Sultan Qaboos received us in a large, open tent in the middle of the oppressively hot and humid Omani desert where he regularly camped to meet with his subjects. The tents were brightly colored. Carpets of deep reds and blues covered the sand inside. Those of us in our American contingent, in dark suits and black SUVs, did not cut the image of modern-day Lawrences of Arabia. Every article of clothing we wore was quickly drenched through from the heat. Qaboos, however, seemed unfazed by the temperature as he held forth.

With his immaculately trimmed, strikingly white beard and Bedouin features—skin hardened by sand and sun—Qaboos was much as I had remembered from when I met him in 1983 as President Reagan's Middle East envoy. The Sultan was sympathetic toward the West, having been educated at Sandhurst, the British military academy, and having served in the British army. In his three decades as sultan, Qaboos had opposed Islamist fundamentalism. He skillfully developed Oman—a nation that in 1970 had few diplomatic relations with foreign states, a meager education system, less than ten miles of paved roads, and a draconian legal code—into a modern Middle Eastern country.

Qaboos became emotional when he discussed 9/11. Then he said something that I found striking. He speculated that the attacks might serve an important purpose by awakening America and the world to the dangers of Islamist extremism and the lethality of weapons of mass destruction. He urged a sustained campaign against the terrorists, cautioning that it would take a long time to do it right. Qaboos lamented that the Arab news media promoted the terrorists' point of view. And he said we should suggest to other Muslim friends that their leading clerics speak out against terrorist atrocities to change the moral climate that influences young people. He told me he considered some of the Arab countries "hypocrites" who turned to America when they were in trouble but did little when America needed them.[2] In that assessment he found a sympathetic ear.

Sultan Qaboos also offered important assistance to the Afghan campaign. He said Oman would allow us to base our C-130 aircraft at Masira Island in the Arabian Sea.

"We trust you. We're allies," he said simply. "I have nothing else to add."[3]

From Oman, we headed to Egypt, where I met with President Mubarak. After a career as an air force officer, Mubarak had risen to power in 1981, following the assassination by Islamist extremists of his predecessor, Anwar Sadat. Mubarak, then the vice president, had declared a state of emergency and assumed near dictatorial powers. Usually pragmatic in foreign policy, Mubarak followed Sadat's strategy of cooperation with the United States on issues such as Iraq, counterterrorism, and peace talks with Israel. For decades Egypt had received billions of dollars in American aid annually.

I had first met Mubarak in June 1975 when, as White House chief of staff, I accompanied President Ford to his meetings with President Sadat in Salzburg, Austria. I had worked with Mubarak later when I served as President Reagan's Middle East envoy, in 1983. Little had changed about the man since our first meeting. On a personal level, I found him animated, even ebullient. Sensing that war in Afghanistan was imminent, he wanted to impart some advice. He shared President Bush's concern that simply firing cruise missiles at caves in Afghanistan would not be effective. He urged us to use financial assistance to "buy allies on the ground." He reflexively mentioned the Israeli-Palestinian issue as a root cause of terrorism but did not dwell on it. This was the standard line in the Middle East—everything was Israel's fault, although in truth Arab nations had done little to help the Palestinians.[4]

My next stop was Uzbekistan, the most populous of the Central Asian republics and perhaps the most crucial of my trip. It was an example of a country that was generally ignored by American officials. Central Asia, which includes several former Soviet republics, is a blank slate to many in the West, in contrast to Eastern Europe, which Americans had reached out to after the collapse of the Soviet Union. This was due, in part, to personal familiarity. A major reason Americans were eager to forge close ties with Poland, the Czech Republic, and other Eastern European countries after the Cold War was that many Americans in cities like Chicago, Detroit, and Pittsburgh had relatives there or next-door neighbors of East European descent. It worried me that the countries of Central Asia were not getting similar attention, aid, and encouragement as they tried to move toward freer political and economic systems. Yet because of their location—squeezed between two large nuclear powers, Russia and China, and straddling the legendary East-West corridor through Asia—they were countries of great strategic importance with a potential that remains to this day largely unfulfilled. Well before 9/11, in fact, I made it a personal goal to develop new relationships in Central Asia.* Now suddenly their support was of enormous importance. We needed overflight rights, and fueling and operating stations in countries like Uzbekistan, Tajikistan, Turkmenistan, and Kyrgyzstan. Indeed, U.S. military operations could not begin or be sustained in Afghanistan until we made the necessary arrangements with its neighbors.

The Uzbek president, Islam Karimov, had come to power as a commissar in the waning days of the Soviet Union. He was now attempting a balancing act. He wanted to support America's efforts in Afghanistan but not at the expense of riling his neighbor, Russia. Karimov started our meeting in Soviet style with a thirty-minute statement.[5] I recalled Russian President Putin opening in a similar manner when I first met with him, so it did not surprise me; for many who came of political age in the Communist system, this was their normal approach with foreign leaders. Possibly they saw it as a way to

* At my first meeting of NATO defense ministers in Brussels in June 2001, I made a point of meeting privately with the minister of defense of Uzbekistan, Kodir Gulyamov, which surprised some of our NATO allies.

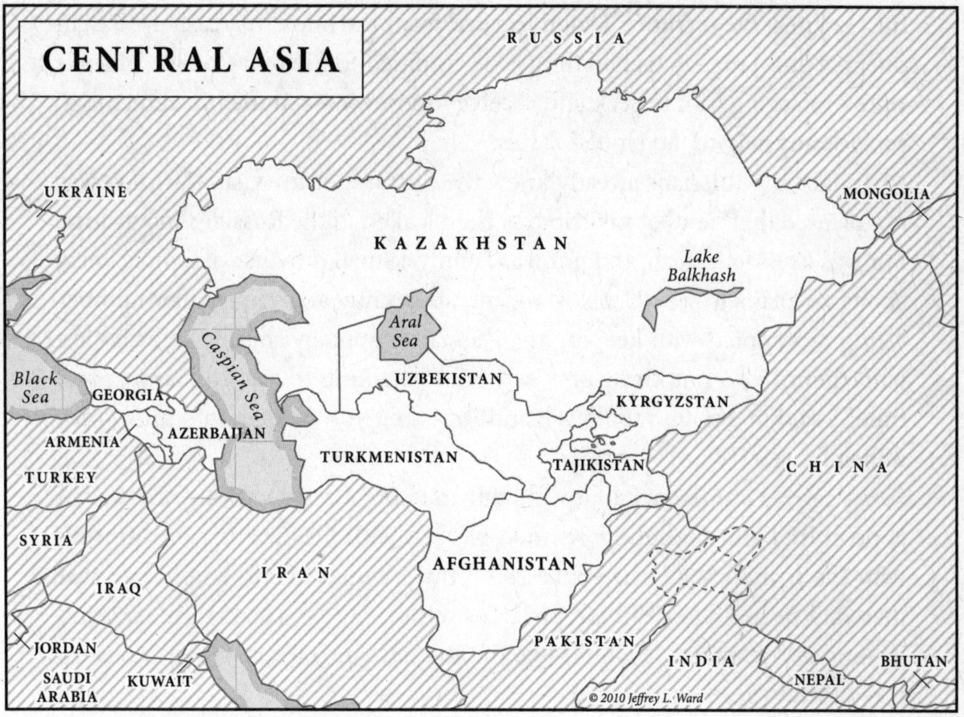

assert authority at the outset of a meeting. In any event, after his formal opening remarks, Karimov became quite cordial.[6]

Usually I did not ask countries for anything specific, but in Uzbekistan's case it was clear what we needed. Karimov agreed to allow our special operators to launch from the decaying Uzbek air base at Karshi Khanabad, known as K-2, conveniently located only 120 miles from the Afghan border. Two decades earlier K-2 had been used by Soviet bombers during their invasion and occupation of Afghanistan. Now the Uzbek base would be used once again, but this time for the liberation of the same troubled people to their south.

Echoing the Egyptian president, Karimov said, "You can buy any warlord and neutralize him. You don't need to persuade him to join the Northern Alliance, just neutralize him." As his translator spoke, I reflected on the differences in English between buying and renting, the latter being more likely for the transactions he was describing. He stressed the importance of putting an Afghan face on the conflict: "In Afghanistan, only Afghans should fight." And he underscored the importance of coupling military force with humanitarian aid to try to win over the population. He was wise in his advice, and helpful. He knew the territory. I soon learned from Karimov that earlier Russian offers of assistance to us had limits: He confided to me that Russian officials were pressuring him to seek and receive Moscow's assent before agreeing to provide any help to the United States.

In fact, the Russians already knew the purpose of my visit. Karimov was not pleased that news of my trip had been leaked to the Russians in advance, nor was President Bush, and nor was I. Only a small universe of people knew about my plans to visit Uzbekistan, and apparently an even smaller number were preoccupied with keeping the Russians happy by sharing information with them. "I do not know precisely who is talking to the Russians in real time," I said in a memo to Powell and Rice, "but you folks should know how unhelpful it is."[7]

At a press conference following our meeting, President Karimov was in good spirits. But though he seemed pleased with his evolving relationship with the United States, he spoke carefully. "I would like to emphasize that there has been no talk of quid pro quos so far," he said. Having little interest in subtlety, he added, "I would like the Russian journalists, in particular, to take this into account."[8]

As I departed Uzbekistan, I was asked by a member of our traveling press corps whether the Taliban might stay in power if we were to target al-Qaida in Afghanistan. Even as late as October, despite the public statements by President Bush that should have ended the administration's internal debate, there were American officials who were still telling journalists that it was in our interest to reach an accommodation with the Taliban.

"Tony Blair said today the Taliban needs to either surrender Bin Laden or surrender power," a reporter told me. "Did he frame that correctly?"

"Well, I guess there are those who think it might be nice if they did both," I answered.[9]

On my last stop, in Ankara, Turkey, its leaders offered assistance with military facilities. They were strong backers of our plan to arm and supply the Northern Alliance. The Turks knew the Taliban threatened the interests of Muslims worldwide. For many years I had considered Turkey a key country for the United States—a West-leaning Muslim democracy and NATO member that could function as a link between East and West. I had always been concerned by the American tendency to favor Greece over Turkey, at least in part because of our large politically active Greek-American population and their representation in Congress. "The U.S. needs to publicly show more support for Turkey," I noted in December 2001, "if we are going to have their help when we need it."[10]

Before I returned to Washington, a videotape from Osama bin Laden was aired on the Arab news channel Al-Jazeera, the Arabic TV station that would regularly provide a platform for terrorist propaganda over the coming years. In this tape, his first since 9/11, Bin Laden prophesied that the United States would fail to oust al-Qaida from Afghanistan and renewed his call for jihad against the West.

We did not help our cause against al-Qaida's propaganda machine when CENTCOM announced that Infinite Justice would be the name for combat operations in Afghanistan. The phrase provoked immediate criticism from Muslims who asserted that infinite justice is reserved for God alone. In light of that early error, I joked with the President that Operation Unilateral Hegemony would have been about as well received. Bush was sympathetic. He had created a similar flap when he referred to the war on terror as a crusade. Christendom's Crusades, of course, hardly symbolized the kind of cooperation with Muslim partners that we knew we needed.

Such missteps focused attention on the pitfalls of waging war against a global network of Muslim extremists whose history, culture, and practices were unfamiliar to most Westerners, myself included. There was an enormous amount about Muslim communities we had to learn if we were to reduce the influence of the extremist ideology that was motivating the terrorists. Soon thereafter, at one of my regular morning meetings in late September, General Dick Myers told us CENTCOM's replacement for the name of the Afghanistan campaign: Operation Enduring Freedom.

As the sun was setting in Afghanistan on October 7, 2001, giving way to a moonless sky, morning broke in Washington, D.C. That Sunday I stood with General Myers in the Pentagon's National Military Command Center awaiting the start of America's operations in Afghanistan. Through Myers, I had sent Franks the execute order signed by the President for Operation Enduring Freedom.

In the command center, the same place where we had worked in the smoke after the Pentagon came under attack, the senior civilian and military leadership gathered to ensure everything was on track. Myers and I sat at the head of a V-shaped, dark wooden table with senior team members arrayed to our left and right. On television monitors in front of us, Franks appeared from

CENTCOM headquarters in Tampa; on other screens were several of his senior officers who were deployed across the Middle East. The video feed was grainy, but we could hear Franks and his officers clearly. Franks informed us that bombs and missiles would begin to strike their targets at 12:30 p.m. Eastern Time, or 9:00 p.m. in Kabul.[11] Oddly, Afghanistan's local time zone differed by thirty minutes from the on-the-hour time zones used by most of the rest of the world. This peculiarity seemed apt for a nation run by men who wanted to turn the clock back to the seventh century.

Each senior officer leading a major component proceeded to report on the readiness of his forces. Each had previously assured the President that he had what was needed to begin and complete the mission. All indicators were green—ready to go.

After the teleconference ended, I called Franks. "General," I said, "the President asked me to extend to you his respect and best wishes, and that we're going to finish what began on September 11."

"God bless America," Franks replied.

That first Sunday of October was less than a month after 9/11. The Pentagon remained scarred, and rubble from the World Trade Center still smoldered. But America was now on the offense. The young Americans who would be risking their lives to defend our country were very much on my mind. Each was a volunteer. In the years that followed I had the privilege of meeting with large numbers of them. Many had signed up for military duty after 9/11 knowing they would likely be sent abroad to fight for their country. I thought about America's last extended military campaign in Vietnam. Large numbers of casualties had increased the pressure on American military and political leaders to bring the war to an early and unsuccessful end. There was, of course, the possibility that the fighting in Afghanistan could produce a similar heartbreaking outcome. Our strategy of putting American forces on the ground—and not conducting the campaign entirely by means of high-altitude bombing, as in the 1999 Kosovo campaign—increased the likelihood of U.S. casualties.[12] We had planned as best we could and prayed for the safety and success of our troops.

An hour after President Bush addressed the nation to announce the start of Operation Enduring Freedom, General Myers and I went to the Pentagon press room to brief on the start of military operations. We outlined the President's goals, which while challenging, were limited: to make absolutely clear to the Taliban and to the world that harboring terrorists carried a price; to acquire intelligence for future operations against al-Qaida and against the

Taliban; to develop relationships with the key groups in Afghanistan that opposed the Taliban and al-Qaida; to make it increasingly difficult for the terrorists to use Afghanistan as a base of operations; to alter the military balance over time by denying the Taliban the offensive systems that hamper the progress of opposition forces; and to provide humanitarian relief to Afghan people suffering under the Taliban.[13]

In the early hours of the Afghan war, I watched video links from aircraft dropping munitions. Among the first targets were the al-Qaida training camps at Tarnak Farms and Duranta. B-52s dropped two-thousand-pound bombs on the tunneled caves of Tora Bora near the Pakistani border. All known Taliban tanks were targeted. Fuel depots, training camps, radars, runways, and the few dubious aircraft in the Taliban air force were hit. Over the course of five nights, every fixed enemy target that American intelligence had identified in Afghanistan was attacked.

Bombs weren't the only things we were dropping on Afghanistan, however. The country had long been suffering from drought and in a number of areas food was in short supply. In the first forty-eight hours alone, American aircraft dropped some 210,000 individual food rations.[14]

After the first wave of air sorties was complete, unmanned Predator aircraft outfitted with high-resolution cameras remained, loitering silently and unobserved above Afghanistan and feeding back images of additional targets. Early on the evening of October 7, Franks called me with urgent information. A Predator drone flown remotely was following a convoy believed to be carrying the leader of the Taliban, Mullah Omar. Franks told me the convoy fit the profile of that used by the Taliban's leadership. It had stopped at what appeared to be a mosque.

In the weeks leading up to the war, Franks briefed me on various targeting categories and the risks of unintended, or, as it is also called, collateral damage to mosques, schools, hospitals, and urban areas. Franks had developed a detailed template for assessing the risk of collateral damage. Each of his target files included a photo and several metrics that gauged the likelihood of injuring civilians at various times of the day, his level of confidence in the intelligence sources, and the various angles at which munitions could be directed at the target. The experts at CENTCOM calibrated the type of weapon, the size, fuse, trajectory, and time of the attack to the circumstances of each target, with the goal of limiting collateral damage. Without question, more effort was devoted to avoiding collateral damage in Afghanistan than in any previous conflict in America's history.

Before making a targeting decision, CENTCOM consulted their legion of lawyers for advice. The concern for civilian casualties was understandable for humanitarian as well as strategic reasons. Every time a civilian was accidentally killed or injured, the loss of innocent life was lamented—and our cause suffered. The United States was held to a much higher standard than the enemy, who did not seek legal counsel before they struck purposefully at civilians.

Still, I wanted commanders making go or no-go decisions on targeting with the advice of lawyers—not the other way around. The legal impulse by nature was to be restrictive and risk averse, which was not always compatible with waging an effective war against vicious fanatics. I had seen how the rules of engagement issued by President Reagan during the Lebanon crisis of the 1980s had been diminished at each layer of command until the result bore little resemblance to what the President had intended. Though I wanted commanders like Franks to benefit from legal advice, he needed to make the calls himself.

I had told the combatant commanders even before 9/11 that I expected them to lean forward. I said that I would be too, and that they could be certain I would back them up on tough calls, even if they did not work out. I was concerned that America's risk aversion in prior years had emboldened terrorists and rogue regimes worldwide.

Immediately after Franks called to inform us of the plan to attack the convoy, I placed a secure call to Bush to inform him of the sketchy facts as we knew them: a likely high-value target, possibly Mullah Omar, was in a building that looked like a mosque. The President gave the green light. I told Franks he was authorized to hit the target. I did not say I had received Bush's authorization, however. If something went awry, I thought it would be better if those down the chain of command believed that only I was responsible for what turned out to be a poor decision.

In the end, the operation was, as Franks put it, "no joy"—meaning that it was unsuccessful. And I got no joy from learning why it failed. To avoid damaging the building, those who controlled the armed Predator decided to fire a Hellfire missile at a vehicle outside the suspected mosque instead of into the compound itself. The vehicle explosion sent men pouring out of the building, scattering for the hills. Presented with a chance to hit a target that might have been the top Taliban leader, we had failed.

In the days after that operation, Franks and I discussed how to accelerate the speed at which he could decide on whether to attack a high-value target. Figures like Osama bin Laden, Mullah Omar, or al-Qaida's number two, Ayman al-Zawahiri, could disappear from our intelligence picture as quickly as they appeared, often keeping themselves in the vicinity of civilians both to deter an attack and to increase the likelihood of civilian casualties if we were to strike.

"The payoff for getting a key leader is high," I said. "Look for a new process—anything to speed it up." We couldn't let precious seconds pass as dozens of people offered their views on whether to hit the target or not.

Franks understood. "I will make the hard calls on collateral damage and not use the need to call you as a reason to slow it up," he said. "I'll take the hit on that."

"I'll be right there with you when you make the call," I assured him.

"We're going to catch these bastards sooner or later," Franks added. "It's just going to take time."[15]

As Air Force bombers and Navy strike aircraft destroyed Afghanistan's limited air defenses, the Taliban offered little effective resistance. We worried that the enemy might have obtained U.S.-built Stinger antiaircraft missiles that had been used to shoot down Soviet helicopters fifteen years earlier. As it turned out, the Taliban had little antiaircraft weaponry. Not a single American aircraft was lost to enemy fire in those early days. Only the hazards of weather, dust, and geography posed a serious threat to our pilots and crews.

Despite the heavy bombing, Taliban forces were holding their lines against the Northern Alliance, which, two weeks into the campaign, still had not achieved a single significant battlefield success. They were not moving forward aggressively to liberate Afghanistan's northern cities.

Meanwhile, allies of the Taliban from the tribal regions of Pakistan poured into Afghanistan, reinforcing the enemy lines. The international news media broadcast images of white pickups with men in black turbans roaming the streets of major cities, sending the message that the Taliban was still in control. Bombs dropped from aircraft could inflict damage to be sure, but they could not liberate a people.

Still, there were some bright spots. In those first days of combat in Afghanistan, the Predator and other unmanned aerial vehicles (UAV) conclusively proved their value to our military and intelligence personnel.* The information UAVs sent to our commanders about troop locations, at no risk to

* Until 2001, UAVs had been used mainly on an experimental basis. When they first had been ready for operations, Defense and CIA officials debated over who would control them and who would pay for their use. In both bureaucracies, some officials were eager to avoid responsibility and preferred not to be burdened with the cost. After 9/11, with coalition operations underway in Afghanistan, George Tenet and I began to sort out Defense-CIA joint Predator operations. We came to an agreement over who owned and paid for the assets, where they would operate, and who would "pull the trigger" on the very few UAVs that were armed at the time.

American lives, was invaluable. But as with all technology, it had to be used for its proper purpose. At some point in the months after 9/11, I was asked whether I wanted to have the video links from Predator drones and other live video images piped directly to my office in the Pentagon. Feeds were being sent to the White House Situation Room and to the operations centers of the military services. Recalling how LBJ picked out bombing targets from the White House, I was uncomfortable with people all over Washington congregating around the screens and second-guessing the decisions of commanders in the field—second-guessing that I suspected would eventually find its way into the press. Those making the life-and-death decisions on whether to destroy a target did not need a raft of onlookers outside the chain of command constantly looking over their shoulders. Nor did I want people treating the feeds as an object of curiosity. War was not a spectator sport or a video game. I declined to have the feeds piped into my office and asked that they be turned off in any offices that had no compelling reason to receive them.

By mid-October, with the air war well underway, some of the many nongovernmental organizations (NGOs) in Afghanistan were complaining about U.S. military actions. Some were quoted in press reports saying that the American bombing campaign was limiting their ability to provide food for needy people and putting their workers at risk. Most of the food aid from the NGOs was coming through Pakistan to southern Afghanistan, where the Taliban was in control. The NGOs, often supported by the American taxpayer through programs run by the U.S. Agency for International Development and the State Department, wanted the United States to help them distribute food in towns and villages that were held by the Taliban. When the Department of Defense declined to help feed the enemy, some NGOs accused us of using food as a weapon.

I had no interest in using food as a weapon, and it was an oft-repeated admonition from President Bush that we should not do so. But it didn't make sense to me that American military personnel should risk their lives so food could be delivered to Taliban strongholds, especially when there were urgent needs for food in areas controlled by our Afghan allies. Some humanitarian organizations further argued that U.S. food aid paid for by U.S. taxpayers should not be identified as coming from the United States. Their contention was that America had a bad reputation and Afghans would react negatively if they knew the source of the food. Again, I disagreed. One purpose of the aid was to build goodwill among ordinary Afghans, so they would support our coalition's effort to liberate their country from the Taliban and al-Qaida. We even took pains to communicate to the Afghans that the food was fit for consumption according to Muslim religious law. I did not believe hungry people would refuse to eat food because it was known to come from the United States. And the humanitarian organizations provided no evidence that that was the case.

Some NGOs tried to ingratiate themselves with Taliban authorities by criticizing the actions of the U.S. military and our coalition partners in the press. But rarely, if ever, did I hear an organization complain publicly about the brutality of the Taliban or al-Qaida. At one point the Taliban raided the offices of a major international humanitarian organization, taking medical supplies and stripping the office bare. The organization did not say a word about it, presumably for fear of retaliation.[16] The same organization freely publicized its complaints about the United States.

Throughout the twelve days of the bombing campaign, members of the Northern Alliance questioned whether we were being effective. Targeting the Taliban and al-Qaida required information and tactics that only our special operations forces could provide for precision air strikes. Without the coordination of our laser targeting against the key Taliban and al-Qaida emplacements, Afghan commanders were reluctant to go on the offensive.

Meanwhile, at the Pentagon, we waited anxiously for CIA and special operations teams to link up with Northern Alliance commanders and the Pashtun opposition leaders in the east and south. At K-2 in Uzbekistan, the Army Special Forces A-Teams under the command of Colonel John Mulholland also waited for the signal to move. The special operators were champing at the bit, ready for their assignment as "the tip of the spear." But the signal to deploy into Afghanistan was not forthcoming.

The press was impatient as well. Once combat operations began, I received variations on the same question from Pentagon reporters: When would American ground forces be deployed? I counseled patience. Wars have their own tempo, I said. "Patience" was a proper theme, and I invoked it sincerely, even though I knew I often lacked that quality myself.[17]

By mid-October, communications by satellite phone had been established with several Northern Alliance commanders, but only one CIA team had managed to connect with them on the ground. Code-named Jawbreaker, the team had linked up with General Fahim Khan, Massoud's successor and the de facto leader of the Northern Alliance. The delays in teaming up with the other Northern Alliance commanders were excruciating for me.

"My goodness, Tommy," I repeatedly said to Franks. "The Department of Defense is many times bigger than the CIA, and yet we are sitting here like little birds in a nest, waiting for someone to drop food in our mouths." It seemed we couldn't do anything until the Agency gave us a morsel of intelligence or established the first links on the ground.

In truth, the frustration extended well beyond Tommy Franks. In the month after 9/11, I had been continually disappointed that the military had been unable to provide the President with military options to strike and disrupt the terrorist networks that were planning still more attacks. In one memo to Chairman Myers and Vice Chairman of the Joint Chiefs, Marine General Peter Pace, I wrote that "for a month, DoD has produced next to no actionable suggestions as to how we can assist in applying the urgently needed pressure other than cruise missiles and bombs." My October 10, 2001, memo continued:

> I am seeing nothing that is thoughtful, creative or actionable. How can that be? . . . The Department of Justice and its counterparts in other nations have arrested hundreds of suspects. The Department of the Treasury and its counterparts in other nations have frozen hundreds of bank accounts totaling hundreds of millions of dollars. The Department of State has organized many dozens of nations in support. But DoD has come up with a goose egg. . . .
>
> You must figure out a way for us to get this job done. You must find out what in the world the problem is and why DoD is such a persistent and unacceptably dry well. . . . We are not doing our jobs. We owe it to the country to get this accomplished—and fast. Your job is to get me military options. It is the [President's and my] job to balance risks and benefits. We cannot do our job unless you do your job. If we delay longer, more Americans could be killed. Let's get it done.[18]

Myers and Pace pushed all of the combatant commanders to come up with more options. In Afghanistan, Franks explained that there were factors outside anyone's control contributing to the delays. Blinding dust storms and white-out conditions in the high mountain passes had forced several teams to turn back. The CIA and CENTCOM were trying to use several older Soviet helicopters, similar to those the Taliban had in its possession, to fool the Taliban. But the old Soviet choppers were unreliable and not well suited for the weather conditions.

After one particularly long day in the first week of October, Franks called. The distress over the delays, expressed by everyone he was talking to in the chain of command from the President on down, was wearing on him. Franks questioned whether I still had confidence in him and asked if I thought the President should select a different commander. I admitted that the waiting was difficult but assured him flat out that he and his operation had our full confidence.

I had to keep reminding myself that we were still only a few days into this campaign. Meanwhile, critics of the administration were plunging into despair. Some in the press, reflecting the concerns they were hearing, resurrected the word "quagmire," an echo of the bitter domestic opposition to the Vietnam War. On September 18, seven days after 9/11 and one month before the first special operations teams would even enter Afghanistan, the Associated Press reported, "Now it may be the United States' turn to try a foray into the Afghan quagmire."[19] A later editorial in the *Dallas Morning News* read, "[A]nother generation of American servicemen may be sucked into a quagmire in a foreign land."[20] "Are we quagmiring ourselves again?" the columnist Maureen Dowd asked two days later.[21] R. W. Apple, a well-respected foreign correspondent, opined on the front page of the *New York Times*, "Like an unwelcome specter from an unhappy past, the ominous word 'quagmire' has begun to haunt conversations among government officials and students of foreign policy, both here and abroad. Could Afghanistan become another Vietnam?"[22]

At one press briefing after another, General Myers and I were asked why the military operations were not progressing faster. I believed it was my job to urge CENTCOM to move forward as quickly as possible, and I did so in private. But much of the public discussion, especially the growing quagmire chorus, lacked restraint and historical perspective.

I usually enjoyed my exchanges with the Pentagon press corps. There were several dozen reporters who were regularly assigned to the Pentagon beat. They had small offices not far from the room where we gave media briefings. Most were knowledgeable, hardworking, and reasonably objective, though often skeptical. Many had been in the Pentagon when American Airlines Flight 77 crashed into the building. I was sympathetic to them. Some periodically said that they had to cope with guidance from their editors, who knew that playing up a potential disaster is what sold. As the saying goes, "If it bleeds, it leads."

I often injected humor into our exchanges with journalists. It's a relief to find occasion to lighten the mood when discussing serious matters. At one point, our press conferences were parodied on the television show *Saturday Night Live*. I remembered the show for its spoofs of President Ford in the 1970s that did him real political damage. Still, I had to admit that the skits of my press conferences—with comedian Darrell Hammond playing my bespectacled self—were amusing.

Over the years I had seen many times what happens in politics when a public figure receives a good deal of media attention. Journalists rely heavily on standard narratives that both conform to and shape the conventional wisdom about government officials. If one starts with "good press," one often gets more and more favorable coverage; early bad stories often spawn additional negative reporting. But journalists also relish dramatic reversals. One memorable observation in this regard was made by World War II general Joseph Stilwell, who warned, "The higher a monkey climbs, the more you see of his behind."

Still, a free nation could not survive without a free press and an open, transparent government. It was what we were fighting for against our enemies.[23] I felt an obligation to explain to the American people in press conferences what the Defense Department sought to achieve in Afghanistan and what was happening on the ground there.

CHAPTER 29

Kabul Falls, Karzai Rises

On October 19, the first of our Special Forces A-Teams made it into Afghanistan, and the twelve men successfully linked up with the ethnic Uzbek warlord General Abdul Rashid Dostum south of Mazar-e-Sharif. Later that day, two hundred U.S. Army Rangers descended onto a dusty airstrip designated Objective Rhino in southern Afghanistan.[1] Franks had learned of the airstrip from Sheikh Muhammed bin Zayed, military chief of staff of the United Arab Emirates, who had outfitted the remote location as a camp for hunting with falcons in the surrounding hills.[2] Rhino was strategically positioned between Kandahar and the Pakistani border—an ideal place from which to attack enemy terrorists trying to flee Afghanistan and seek sanctuary in Pakistan's tribal regions. CENTCOM broadcast to the world the greenish night-vision images of the seizure of Rhino, demonstrating that the U.S. military was moving into Afghanistan.

In the south our forces raided deep into Taliban-controlled territory. Near Kandahar, they launched an attack on one of the compounds of Taliban leader Mullah Omar. They began to call in supplies to be delivered by air—food, medical assistance, and ammunition—as well as the massive firepower of U.S. Air Force and Navy aircraft. Members of the A-Teams served as forward air controllers, using laser range finders and GPS technology to pinpoint targets for devastatingly accurate air strikes. By the beginning of

November the Taliban front lines in the north were being bombarded with two-thousand-pound Joint Direct Attack Munitions (JDAM) and an occasional fifteen-thousand-pound BLU-82 Daisy Cutter, then the most powerful non-nuclear weapon in our arsenal. The Taliban lines were also attacked by U.S. Air Force AC-130 gunships, an aircraft with 105 millimeter howitzers, 40 millimeter cannons, and 25 millimeter Gatling guns able to fire an intimidating eighteen hundred rounds a minute. Intelligence sources reported that the gunships' withering fire was particularly devastating to enemy morale. Our special operations forces were spotting Taliban fighters on ridgelines and calling in close air support to attack them.

On November 5, the forces under Northern Alliance commander General Dostum—outnumbered by the Taliban by eight to one—began their assault on Mazar-e-Sharif, the largest city in northern Afghanistan. Capturing Mazar was a crucial objective because it would open a land bridge from Uzbekistan, which was valuable for resupply efforts, particularly during the critical winter months.[3] At first Mazar's walls protected the Taliban's artillery units and antiaircraft missiles. But from the surrounding hills, special operators spotted major Taliban units and targeted them with air strikes. Four days after the assault began Afghan and American forces, some on horseback, rode into the heart of the city, cutting off the Taliban, capturing Mazar, and sending the first major signal to the Afghan people and the world that the Taliban could be defeated.

Meanwhile, General Fahim Khan's troops moved to seize the northern cities of Taloqan and Kunduz. General Ismail Khan captured Herat in the west. Pashtun forces were marching toward Kandahar. The ingenuity of American special operators and CIA teams, combined with precision U.S. airpower and the grit of Northern Alliance troops, forced Taliban fighters to retreat to the south. The quagmire talk began to die down, at least for the moment.

As the northern cities began to fall, I made another trip to meet with Afghanistan's neighbors.[4] My first stop in Russia attracted the most attention and had the potential to be the most uncomfortable. The country's disastrous decade-long occupation of Afghanistan still rankled. A speedy military victory by American forces would be another embarrassment. Perhaps for this reason President Putin refused to allow the United States to move military equipment through Russian territory and sought to constrain our developing relationships with the neighboring former Soviet republics.

After meeting with Defense Minister Ivanov, reporters pressed him about whether Russians troops were going to join the coalition effort in Afghanistan. "I am asked this every day," Ivanov replied, "and every day I say no."[5] I agreed privately, knowing that Russian troops reentering Afghanistan would not be greeted as liberators.

At the close of the Ivanov meeting, I was escorted to the gilded rooms of the Kremlin for a meeting with President Putin. He spoke without pause for close to ninety minutes. He was, as usual, somewhat of an enigma. Though he denied us tangible assistance for the Afghan effort, he was generous with his advice—which Afghans we could trust, the motives of regional players—right down to military tactics. He also pushed for the United States to buy Russian military equipment for Afghan Northern Alliance commanders. He declared without any sense of irony that the Afghans were very familiar with Russian equipment.

From Russia I traveled to Pakistan and then India. Both nations had had poor relations with the United States prior to the Bush administration. Our military had had next to no contact with Pakistani forces for a decade because of an American law that barred military support or training to Pakistan unless the U.S. government certified that Pakistan was not producing a nuclear weapon. Because of this congressional ban, a generation of Pakistani military officers had no ties to their American counterparts, which had spawned mistrust and bad feelings.

Yet in 9/11's aftermath, the United States was able to develop an increasingly constructive partnership with Pakistan. Powell and his State Department colleagues had begun to persuade President Pervez Musharraf that he needed to cast his lot either with the United States or the Taliban and the Islamist extremists his country had backed for years. When he saw that America intended to act forcefully after 9/11, Musharraf chose the United States. Other Pakistani officials, however, hedged their bets by retaining ties with the Taliban and various terrorist groups that operated against India.

Musharraf was a gracious host. Though he was clearly in charge of his government, he had enough confidence to let his advisers speak freely in meetings—something that was unusual in that region. He was forthright about his domestic constraints, and he warned that the United States needed to do a better job combating enemy propaganda in the Muslim world—a crucial objective that should have been a top priority for the Bush administration over the years to come, but which to our lasting disadvantage was not.

Our country's relations with India also improved dramatically under the Bush administration.[6] The United States had all but shunned India after its 1998 nuclear weapon test.[7] But from the earliest days of the administration, I believed India—the world's most populous democracy—was going to be of strategic importance. I did not think it made any sense for us to be at odds with them. In February 2001, only fourteen days after I took office as secretary of defense, I sought out a bilateral meeting with the Indian national security adviser, Brajesh Mishra, at a security conference in Munich, to make this point. President Bush was ready to make ties with India a priority for his administration.

Despite the cordial welcome, my meetings with Afghanistan's various neighbors left me with misgivings. The region was a maelstrom of suspicion and intrigues. Pakistan distrusted the Northern Alliance. India distrusted Pakistan and vice versa. Russia distrusted our relations with its neighbors. And nearly everyone distrusted the Russians. Each of the countries surrounding Afghanistan—especially the one country I did not visit, Iran—seemed prepared to jockey for influence with whatever government arose and ready to use their longtime connections in that country as proxies. Stability—much less democracy—would be difficult to bring to an impoverished country that had for decades known little more than civil war, occupation, drought, drug trafficking, warlords, and religious extremism.

On the long flight back to the United States, I spoke to President Bush over a secure phone. "Afghanistan risks becoming a swamp for the United States," I told Bush, using the word I once used when I was President Reagan's envoy to the Middle East. "Everyone in Afghanistan has an agenda or two. We're not going to find a lot of straight shooters."

Bush expressed optimism about our efforts there. But I was not optimistic about the country's ethnic groups coming together and sharing power. "It's my view we need to limit our mission to getting the terrorists who find their way to Afghanistan," I advised the President. "We ought not to make a career out of transforming Afghanistan."[8]

Once American special operations forces were on the ground in Afghanistan, territory began to fall to our Afghan allies more quickly than we had imagined possible. By early November, Northern Alliance troops had advanced to the outskirts of Kabul, and were poised to take the capital city. At this point, the months-long discussions within the administration over what to do with the Taliban came to a head. State Department and CIA officials again expressed concern about the prospect of Northern Alliance troops seizing the capital city. Tenet reported that his intelligence experts were concerned that some Pashtun tribes in the south with historic ties to Pakistan and the CIA would be offended if the country's capital was taken and occupied by Northern Alliance forces.

I supported the Northern Alliance's advance into Kabul for a simple reason: It was the only realistic option. The Northern Alliance leaders had no intention of letting their enemies in the Taliban hold on to Kabul while they had the advantage.[9] Furthermore, as a practical matter, the few dozen U.S. special operators embedded with the Northern Alliance probably would not have been able to stop their advance even if we wanted them to.

Even as the issue was still being discussed in the National Security Council, reports surfaced in the press that Powell and Rice were saying the United States was not going to advance on Kabul. Their comments concerned me, given the position I thought the President had set out clearly in speeches about removing the Taliban.* On November 13, I sent a memo to Bush, copying Powell, Rice, and Tenet. "Mr. President, I think it is a mistake for the United States to be saying we are not going to attack Kabul," I wrote. "To do so, tells the Taliban and the Al Qaida that Kabul can be a safe haven for them. The goal in this conflict is to make life complicated for the Taliban and the Al Qaida, not to make it simple." I also made the point that if we wanted to open the routes to the south, where al-Qaida and the Taliban still roamed with relative ease, we would need to control the capital city. "It is one thing to not take Kabul," I added. "It is quite another to announce to the world that we are not going to take Kabul. I have read that Condi and Colin have both been saying this. I don't believe anyone talked to me or Tommy Franks about the concept of doing that. I think it is a bad idea."[11]

Not waiting for Washington to decide, the Northern Alliance forces marched on Kabul on their own initiative. In a desperate broadcast to his fleeing troops, Taliban leader Mullah Omar reportedly warned them to stop "behaving like chickens." It was to no avail. When Northern Alliance forces first set foot in the city, on November 13, 2001, they met little resistance. All that remained of the Taliban's defenders in their former seat of power was a group of a dozen or so fighters hiding out in a city park. Just five weeks after

* Powell remarked, "All of the countries in the region—the United States, Russia and, as you heard, Pakistan, through Musharraf last evening—say, it's better that they not enter Kabul. There's too many uncertainties as to what might happen." Secretary Powell went on to say, "Entering a city is a difficult thing. You put people in close quarters, they are of different tribal loyalties. We have seen what has happened previously when you had an uncontrolled situation and two forces arriving in Kabul at the same time not meaning each well."[10]

our air strikes had begun, Afghanistan's capital city was under the control of Northern Alliance forces. I was relieved. When I conveyed the news to the President, he was eager to see the offensive continue.

Soon anti-Taliban forces gained control of many areas in eastern Afghanistan, including the city of Jalalabad that straddled the important route leading to the Khyber Pass and Pakistan. Al-Qaida leader Mohammad Atef, a deputy to Bin Laden, was killed in an air strike. The remaining Taliban forces were being driven farther and farther south, toward Kandahar, a city of some three hundred thousand people that had become a way station for the most hardcore enemy fighters. There the Taliban would make its stand. A small contingent of U.S. Marines, under the command of a gruff and brilliant warrior, Brigadier General James Mattis, bolstered our presence in southern Afghanistan. The focus of the campaign now turned to an Afghan fighter who would be charged with taking Kandahar.

Though he had the demeanor of a polished, urbane, and scholarly gentleman, Hamid Karzai was tough and tenacious and seemed to command respect from diverse quarters of Afghan society. The day after the American bombing of the Taliban began, he crossed the border into Afghanistan from Pakistan on a motorcycle, where he helped organize anti-Taliban forces in the country's south. A Pashtun tribal leader from a prestigious clan, he commanded a small cadre of Pashtun troops.* In an early skirmish, a bomb dropped from a B-52 had sent shrapnel and debris in his direction, slightly wounding him in the face.[12] Karzai and his forces reached Kandahar on December 7. Contrary to expectations, the city fell quickly. The Taliban apparently knew that they could not win, so they had decided to regroup to fight another day.

By early December, two months to the day since the start of our combat operations, the Taliban had been pushed out of every major city in Afghanistan. By any measure, it was an impressive military success. Estimates varied, but likely some eight thousand to twelve thousand Taliban and al-Qaida fighters were killed—and hundreds more were captured. Eleven U.S. servicemen had given their lives, and another thirty-five had been wounded in this initial campaign against al-Qaida and the Taliban.

* Early on, Karzai emerged as a possible candidate for a national leadership post. As such, we wanted him protected. At one point during the fighting against a much larger Taliban force, Karzai was evacuated briefly to Pakistan. In talking with Pentagon reporters, I mentioned Karzai's evacuation. Though my remarks were accurate, I did not want to give a false impression that Karzai had sought to retreat, which he most certainly had not. Karzai, understandably, didn't want it known that he had been taken out of Afghanistan, even for a short period. I later apologized to Karzai. He responded graciously.

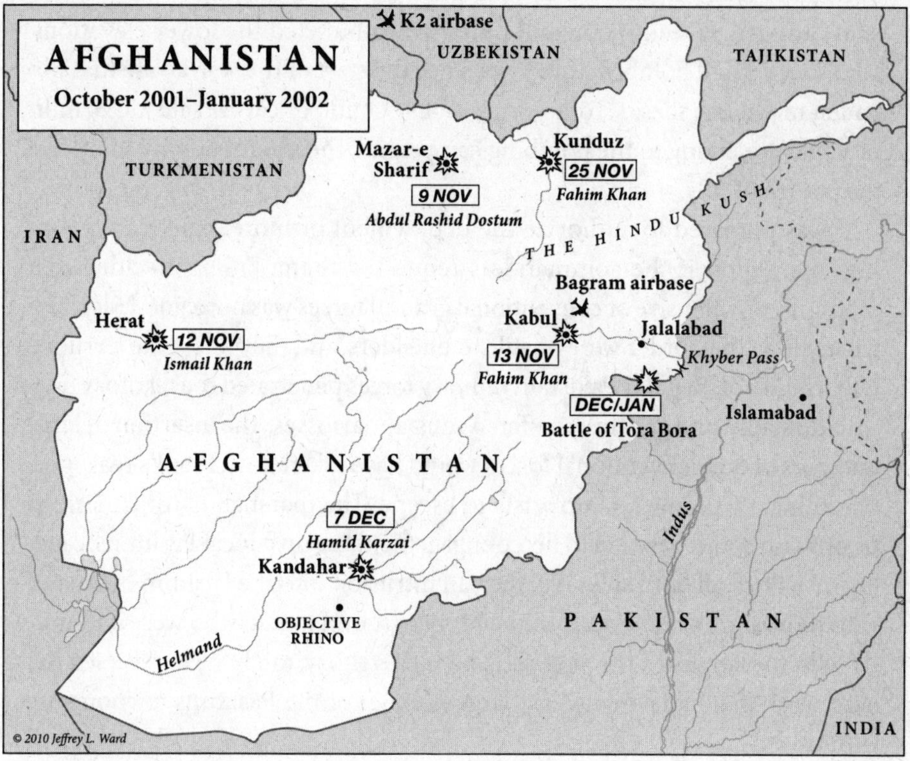

Most Taliban and al-Qaida forces had been neutralized, at least for the moment, with one important exception: the holdouts in the mountainous area along the border with Pakistan known as Tora Bora, meaning "black dust." The peaks of the White Mountains are among the highest in the world with altitudes of fifteen thousand feet. The eastern reaches of the mountain range include the legendary Khyber Pass, the notch through which armies had made their way onto the Indian subcontinent for thousands of years.

Tora Bora and its surrounding valleys were so treacherous to armies—any army—that much of the territory was out of the control of both the Afghan and the Pakistan governments. Local Pashtun tribal chiefs had been the only authorities there for centuries. They recognized no national boundaries and no earthly laws but their own. During their fight against the Soviet Union, many of the Afghan mujahideen found refuge in Tora Bora's intricate labyrinth of caves. Now an unknown number of al-Qaida fighters sought shelter there. Among them, some speculated, was Osama bin Laden.

When Franks and CENTCOM were contemplating military options in the border between Afghanistan and Pakistan, the peaks were already covered in snow and ice. Freezing rain and bitter winds buffeted the lower elevations. CENTCOM had bombed Tora Bora since the start of the war, aware that Bin Laden might flee there. "Tora Bora is a busy chunk of earth," said a U.S. military pilot, referring to the bombing campaign. "The mountains are lit up like the Fourth of July."[13]

I was prepared to authorize the deployment of more American troops into the region if the commanders requested them. Franks decided that mounting an offensive of conventional ground forces was not a good idea. The tribes along the border were hostile to outsiders, and they knew the territory. Others did not. Regular Pakistani military forces penetrated the territory only with difficulty, and generally suffered substantial losses. The insertion of large numbers of our conventional forces would have taken time, Franks reasoned, providing a window for terrorists to escape. The marshalling of American troops also could have led to fierce engagements against local Pashtuns, causing casualties on both sides. Further, an intrusion into the Pashtun heartland with thousands of American conventional ground forces, who were unfamiliar with the language, the cultures, and the territory, might have reversed the hard work that had convinced a large number of the Pashtuns to cooperate with us.

I believed a decision of this nature, which hinged on numerous operational details, was best made by the military commander in charge. Franks had to determine whether attempting to apprehend one man on the run, whose whereabouts were not known with certainty, was worth the risks inherent in such a venture. It was not an easy call. Though a number of people, including some at the CIA, suspected that Bin Laden might have taken refuge in the Tora Bora area, no one knew that for certain. Earlier in the war we had received several reports of supposed sightings of both Mullah Omar and Bin Laden, which all proved to be false.*

When the President said he was going to get Bin Laden "dead or alive," I noted that I had my preference.[14] Still, the emphasis on Bin Laden concerned

* At one point I watched a Predator video feed of a tall, lanky man wearing a turban and white robes and surrounded by what looked like an entourage of bodyguards. Our military command center was abuzz with anticipation. There was not a doubt in anyone's mind that the image on the screen in front of us was Osama bin Laden. As they made final preparations to take out the target, something spooked the man we were observing, perhaps an intelligence tip or someone catching sight of our Predator UAV above. He took off, running like a gazelle over rocky, rugged terrain. He couldn't have been more than twenty years old. Bin Laden was in his midforties in 2001. Intelligence later corroborated that the man we all were absolutely convinced was Bin Laden was not.

me. To my mind, the justification for our military operations in Afghanistan was not the capture or killing of one person. Our country's primary purpose was to try to prevent terrorists from attacking us again. There was far more to the threat posed by Islamist extremism than one man. I also suspect that if we had added a large conventional force and U.S. casualties rose in Tora Bora, the same people who faulted the decision to keep the troop presence small would have blamed us for causing needless American deaths.

Instead of a large American invasion of Tora Bora, the CIA and special forces recruited a Pashtun coalition, known as the Eastern Alliance and led by General Hazrat Ali, to provide the bulk of the manpower. Though not publicized, U.S. special operators joined the Eastern Alliance's advance, traveling from ridgeline to ridgeline and taking fire from al-Qaida positions. While Eastern Alliance forces were gaining control of more of the ridges around Tora Bora each day, each evening at sundown they would leave their positions and return to their villages in the valleys to break their fasts for Ramadan. Learning of this, I began to rethink the question of whether we needed to insert more U.S. forces.

On December 20, I sent a memo to CIA Director George Tenet saying that we might be missing an opportunity in Tora Bora, and perhaps we should reconsider the earlier decision against bringing in more U.S. forces. "How do we get Ali to get his forces to move?" I asked Tenet. "It seems to me we have to get a full court press on it, or else we are going to have to use some of our own."[15] I made it clear to Franks that if he believed he needed more troops, he would get them as quickly as possible. As I told him, I wanted to know "whether or not we should have had more people on the ground to avoid having so many people get away."[16]

Much later, I learned that a CIA operative on the ground had requested some Rangers to help with Tora Bora.[17] He even wrote a book on the subject.[18] I never received such a request from either Franks or Tenet and cannot imagine denying it if I had. If someone thought Bin Laden was cornered, as later claimed, I found it surprising that Tenet had never called me to urge Franks to support their operation. I can only presume that either their chain of command was not engaged or that they failed to convince Tenet of the quality of their information. Another explanation is that their recollections may be imperfect.

Throughout the campaign in Afghanistan, officials at the State Department and the CIA deliberated over who they thought might best run the eventual post-Taliban government. I had doubts about the ability of Americans to make that kind of a decision. We did not want to repeat the Soviet mistake of installing a government that would be widely seen as a puppet regime. I favored putting in motion a process that would allow Afghans to select their own leadership.

I was pleased when our administration worked with the United Nations to help enable Afghanistan's various ethnic and political groups to deliberate on their path ahead. Over eight days of negotiations in Bonn, Germany, assisted by Zalmay Khalilzad (a future U.S. ambassador to the country), the Afghans came to agreement.[19] They named Hamid Karzai as the head of an interim administration. Karzai had been seen as a likely candidate in part because he did not have a large military force and seemed willing to work across tribal and ethnic lines. The interim administration would oversee the convening of something that I, and I suspect most Americans, had never heard of: a loya jirga, or a traditional Afghan tribal council. The first loya jirga would establish a transitional governing authority. A second loya jirga would lead to the drafting of a constitution. The Afghans followed through with these agreements and implemented a form of representative rule in a part of the world that had little tradition of democracy.

On December 16, 2001, I made my first visit of many to a liberated Afghanistan. It was also the first visit to the country by a senior American official in a quarter of a century. We landed at Bagram Airfield, a decaying facility built by the Soviet Union. Our plane was parked on a runway surrounded by land mines. MiG fighter jets, battered and unusable, lay scattered across the tarmac, vestiges of the Soviet occupation. Parked alongside them were American C-130 transport planes, AC-130 gunships, Black Hawk and Chinook helicopters, and rows and rows of supplies. I was struck at seeing symbols of these two different eras side-by-side—one of failed conquest, the other of a successful liberation, at least thus far.

As I stepped off the military aircraft, I was greeted by an Afghan honor guard of Northern Alliance fighters standing along the side of the taxiway. American special operators stood with them, sun-drenched and bearded. One of the Americans came forward to greet me, with pride in his voice. "Welcome to Afghanistan, sir," he said.

"No air of triumphalism marked [Rumsfeld's] visit," the *New York Times* noted.[20] That was deliberate on my part. I made a conscious decision to arrive in the country in a manner that acknowledged a coalition victory but also that our work was far from done. It was certainly true that al-Qaida terrorists no longer enjoyed the support of a host government in the country, but they still posed a lethal threat. The Taliban had been driven from power, but they were not likely to give up altogether. "It's going to take time and energy and effort and people will be killed in the process of trying to find them and capture them," I cautioned.[21]

I met with the incoming leaders of Afghanistan, including Karzai and General Fahim Khan, in a battle-scarred hangar at Bagram. The windows had been blown out. Camouflage netting adorned the walls while Afghan carpets covered the floor—a juxtaposition with which I suspected these hardened leaders of the resistance against the Taliban were familiar.

Karzai wore the lambskin hat that would become a trademark for him. As we sat on folding chairs drinking tea, we began a conversation that would continue for years. From the outset Karzai demonstrated political savvy. One of his first comments referred to the slain Northern Alliance leader, Ahmad Massoud, as "our very fine commander" and a "martyred man."[22] It suggested that Karzai wanted to be seen as an Afghan, not a Pashtun, and he wanted us to know that. He praised the United States military. "You liberated Afghanistan," he declared warmly, calling this an opportunity Afghans had long awaited.[23]

One of my final meetings that day—one that was particularly memorable—was with a group of war-worn Americans. The men were part of the Special Forces teams that had been among the first troops to arrive on the ground in Afghanistan. The commanding officer of ODA 555, "Triple Nickel," presented me with a faded and tattered Taliban flag that had been flying over Kabul when they arrived. Their A-Team had linked up with Northern Alliance commander Fahim Khan and was the first U.S. Special Forces team to enter the Afghan capital.[24]

The approach that Franks, Myers, Wolfowitz, Tenet, and I had favored, putting special operations teams in the thick of the fighting with the Northern Alliance, had worked well. I listened as the team recounted their operations—the stuff of heroic literature but told in a plainspoken manner. Some had taken part in raids against senior al-Qaida and Taliban personnel. It was as admirable a group of young men as any I had ever met.

Their work was a demonstration of the kind of defense transformation that the President envisioned—a mentality of eyes-wide-open situational awareness, can-do determination, and creative adaptability. The U.S. military had not undertaken cavalry charges on horses for many decades, but during the campaign fifty-year-old B-52 bombers were dropping bombs guided by GPS and lasers directed by a small team of Americans on horseback. Some had helped guide one-ton bombs to hit targets a long touchdown's throw from their positions. They were working alongside Afghans who they had never met before, let alone trained with, but along with our Naval and Air Force precision bombing, they had toppled the Taliban in a matter of weeks. Through trial and error, these men tailored tactics, techniques, and procedures to fit the unusual circumstance they faced—bringing devastating force to bear with relatively little American manpower on the ground.

As we talked about their cavalry charge, I asked how many had ever ridden a horse before they arrived in Afghanistan. Only a few hands went up. The rest had had to learn in the most dangerous circumstances imaginable—and, at first, on uncomfortable wooden saddles.*

"Tell me what else you need," I asked them. They had all they needed, they responded. It was the make do with what you have attitude that permeated their ranks.

I appreciated their toughness, but I pressed them. "Tell me what we could do better in the future," I asked.

Looking ahead, they said they needed to be on the ground sooner, before combat operations began. They needed more time to get into towns and villages and get to know the local populations. They were convinced of the value of enlisting local populations in the fight.

For his first several months as chairman of Afghanistan's interim government, Karzai was widely viewed as exercising little real authority, and only within a severely restricted sphere. He was deprecated by some as the "mayor of Kabul."[25] Early on, Pacha Khan Zadran, a Pashtun warlord from the eastern city of Gardez, decided to test the new Afghan leader's mettle. Demanding recognition as a provincial governor, Pacha Khan threatened to ignite a civil war against Karzai's fledgling government with his militia forces. It was a crucial moment for Karzai, and a test of his ability to lead.

* One soldier confided that they had encountered a phenomenon largely unknown to them until that point: saddle sores. The problem had become so severe, in fact, that they found it difficult to ride. Some tried Vaseline to make it more comfortable, but the conditions were so windy and dusty that the sand turned the Vaseline into a scratchy paste. Then some clever mind came up with a different solution: pantyhose. It was another example of the often unexpected challenges our forces had had to meet and overcome.

In April 2002, Karzai told Pacha Khan to surrender or be annihilated. This was a rather bold ultimatum, since Karzai originally had no large militia of his own that he could rely on. Karzai expressed a desire to have American forces available to him if his new government's military, amassed from the militias of other allied warlords, could not defeat Pacha Khan's militia. He believed he wouldn't actually need the assistance, since he was confident Pacha Khan would back down if he merely threatened that American forces would intervene. I told Karzai I'd get back to him after I consulted with my colleagues.

This led to animated discussions in the National Security Council over whether Karzai should be allowed, in effect, to threaten the use of the United States military against an uncooperative and potentially threatening Afghan leader. Powell and Rice seemed to support Karzai's position, as did Vice President Cheney. They argued accurately that Karzai was vulnerable and might need American assistance if Afghanistan were to remain under the control of a central government. I felt a bigger principle was at stake. As I pointed out in a May 10, 2002 memo to the President, the current moment was "of unusual importance" and perhaps "the most significant war-related call to be made since forces were sent into Afghanistan in October 2001." "The issue," I wrote, "is whether the Afghan government will be required to take responsibility for its actions—political and military—or whether it will be allowed to become dependent on US forces to stay in power."[26]

I was concerned that giving Karzai the ability to threaten the use of American military force could make him seem to be exactly what some of his rivals said he was—a pawn of the United States. If Karzai could not prevail against local forces without American military assistance, I felt he could not survive politically anyway. A second point, I told the President, was that "it is not in the interest of the US or Karzai for us to make it easier for Karzai to rely on force, rather than political methods, to resolve [his] problems with regional leaders."

It was not a perfect analogy, but I was convinced Karzai needed to learn to govern the Chicago way. In the 1960s, Mayor Richard J. Daley ruled Chicago—a city of many diverse and powerful elements—using maneuver, guile, money, patronage, and services to keep the city's fractious leaders from rebelling against his authority. In parts of Chicago, where officials threatened the mayor's authority, potholes were left untended and other services were neglected. In areas where local officials cooperated with the mayor, Daley brought the services of the city government to bear and was generous in his patronage. My point was that instead of giving Karzai the freedom to throw around the weight of the U.S. military, he should learn to use patronage and political incentives and disincentives to get the local Afghan warlords, governors, and cabinet officials in line. "A Karzai tempted to overreach could drag us into re-living the British and Soviet experiences of trying to use outside force to impose centralized rule on the fractious people of Afghanistan," I concluded in my memo to President Bush.[27]

Even if it meant getting some things wrong in his first months in office, Karzai would need to learn the tough lessons of governing. I knew Karzai would be unlikely to develop those skills if all he needed to do to settle the inevitable differences was to invoke American military power.

President Bush agreed with my recommendation, and I told Karzai he would have to resolve the dispute without the promise of rescue by the American military. In short, Karzai was not authorized to threaten the use of American military force. It was a gamble, but in the end, Karzai and Pacha Khan resolved their differences as I had hoped, through negotiation. Pacha Khan eventually sought a role in the Afghan parliament, and Karzai did not stand in his way.[28]

Our military was justly proud of what it had accomplished in Afghanistan. The creative and constructive way the CIA and the Defense Department worked together showed that America was not a superpower capable of only massive applications of brute force. The United States, still a young nation, had operated strategically and skillfully in Afghanistan, an ancient land in which many great empires had stumbled badly over the millennia. Our country, at least for the moment, had avoided becoming the latest corpse in Afghanistan's graveyard.

At the outset, expectations were low, but when major military operations in Afghanistan ended in five weeks, expectations heightened dramatically. Typical was the well-meaning comment of a 10th Mountain Division soldier reported in the *Washington Post*: "We got hit three months ago and in less than three months we've toppled this regime. And within a week from now, we've got an interim government that's stepping in. What more can you ask for than a splendid little war over here?"[29]

The sentiment was understandable, but I did not think the long struggle against terrorism could or should be viewed as a series of quick, relatively painless, "splendid little wars." I was convinced that that was not going to be the case. Though the deep-seated pessimism at the outset of the war proved to be misplaced, I knew too that the buoyant optimism after the Taliban was toppled would prove to be just as mistaken. Ending the Taliban's rule over Afghanistan would be only the opening of a long, sustained campaign that would require patience and grit. Taking the fight to the terrorists would mean our military men and women would have to be deployed elsewhere. To keep the pressure on, we would need to continue to pursue the terrorists wherever they took refuge and isolate the regimes that harbored them and could give them the weapons of mass destruction they desperately sought. The President had told me privately what he had in mind.

PART X

Saddam's Miscalculation

Washington, D.C.

JANUARY 16, 1991

In a televised address from the Oval Office, President Bush announced the start of military operations in Iraq. He set forth the reasons for his decision to go to war. It was a long list. He and the national security officials in his administration—Dick Cheney, Colin Powell, and Paul Wolfowitz among them—believed that the United States and its allies had exhausted all reasonable diplomatic efforts to force Saddam Hussein's regime to comply with its obligations to the UN Security Council and, further, the UN's economic sanctions were not accomplishing their objectives. According to American intelligence officials, Saddam was working to add a nuclear bomb to Iraq's arsenal, which the CIA judged already contained chemical weapons.[1] "Saddam Hussein started this cruel war," the President said. "Tonight, the battle has been joined."[2]

The date was January 16, 1991. And the president was George Herbert Walker Bush.

During that first Gulf War, I had been out of government for nearly fifteen years and living back home in Chicago. I watched the war from afar. I was impressed with the combination of air power and tank warfare in the southern Iraqi desert that decimated Saddam's army. Television images showed the wreckage of Iraqi tanks, armored personnel carriers, and trucks littering what became known as the highway of death.

With Saddam's forces on the run, the Bush team faced a crucial decision, one that would have lasting consequences. The war's initial goal had been achieved: Saddam's forces had been driven from Kuwait. The question then was whether the United States should end the conflict or move to Baghdad to topple Saddam Hussein's regime.

"I remember very clearly Colin Powell saying that this thing was turning into a massacre," Robert Gates, then the deputy national security adviser, later recalled. "And that to continue it beyond a certain point would be un-American, and he even used the word unchivalrous."[3] Others in the administration, including Secretary of State James Baker, said they believed Saddam had suffered such a thorough defeat that he would not be able to retain power.[4] Bush agreed, and drew the war to a quick close. Before the war ended, President Bush had urged Iraqis to "take matters into their own hands" when it came to the weakened dictator. With the administration's encouragement, pro-democracy elements in Iraq twice rose up in an effort to topple Saddam's regime.*

As part of the U.S.-Iraqi cease-fire agreement, General Norman Schwarzkopf allowed the Iraqis to operate helicopters, supposedly for the purpose of withdrawing their troops. Saddam proceeded to use his helicopter gunships to put down both of the revolts against his regime, massacring tens of thousands of Shia in the south and Kurdish Iraqis in the north. In Washington, some in the administration, including Wolfowitz, urged the Bush national security team to intervene and stop the massacres. The President decided otherwise. "[I]t was not clear what purpose would have been achieved by getting ourselves mixed up in the middle of that," said Powell, then chairman of the Joint Chiefs of Staff.[5] The rebels were quickly crushed by Saddam's forces in the spring of 1991, creating among many Iraqi dissidents a lasting sense of betrayal and distrust.

For his part, Saddam Hussein came to believe that the United States lacked the commitment to follow through on its rhetoric. He saw America as unwilling to take the risks necessary for an invasion of Iraq. As he would explain to his interrogators after his capture in December 2003, Saddam had concluded that America was a paper tiger. He interpreted the first Bush administration's decision not to march into Baghdad as proof that he had triumphed in what he called the "mother of all battles" against the mightiest military power in world history. Looking back, an opportunity to take care of the problem before it turned into a larger crisis was missed and the tyrant was emboldened.

By 1992, a U.S. presidential election year, Bill Clinton, the politically astute young governor of Arkansas, accused President George H. W. Bush and his predecessor, Ronald Reagan, of being "soft" on Iraq. I was interested in this debate, as I had played a role in the drama when I met with Saddam Hussein as President Ronald Reagan's Middle East envoy. Clinton may have been looking to burnish his national security credentials by trying to appear tougher in foreign policy than the Bush administration. Clinton's running mate, Tennessee Senator Albert Gore, Jr., went even further than Clinton, accusing President

* Some of the leaflets dropped from U.S. aircraft encouraged Iraqi army units and civilians to rebel. CIA-sponsored radio broadcasts spread the same message.

George H. W. Bush of deliberately concealing the extent of Saddam's ties to terrorism, his attacks on U.S. interests, and his efforts to develop a nuclear weapon.[6] Clinton and Gore pledged that their administration would be under no illusions when it came to dealing with Saddam. Supporters of the 1992 Democratic presidential ticket exploited the poor economic news of the day by distributing a bumper sticker that read: SADDAM HUSSEIN STILL HAS HIS JOB. DO YOU?

A campaign to take Baghdad and oust Saddam was a daunting notion. Saddam had options if U.S. forces had marched to Baghdad in 1991, including the use of chemical or biological weapons against our forces. The senior Bush also pointed out that regime change in Baghdad had not been among the U.S. goals when the pledge to liberate Kuwait was first made. The administration felt it would not have full coalition support if it decided to continue on to Baghdad.

Others I respected had a different view. While still British Prime Minister, Margaret Thatcher had famously warned President George H. W. Bush not to "go wobbly" after Iraq's invasion of Kuwait. But the formidable Thatcher had reluctantly resigned before the war was concluded. She seemed unhappy with the result in Iraq. "There is the aggressor, Saddam Hussein, still in power," she later observed. Contrasting his fate to Bush's and hers, she noted, "There is the President of the United States, no longer in power. There is the Prime Minister of Britain, who did quite a lot to get things there, no longer in power. I wonder who won?"[7]

Colin Powell, who had played such a prominent role in the decision not to attempt regime change, responded to the criticism. "[I]n due course, Saddam Hussein will not be there," he predicted. "And when that happens, all this interesting second-guessing will seem quite irrelevant."[8]

CHAPTER 30

Out of the Box

In the first Gulf War's aftermath, Iraq remained a festering problem. Though its army had been defeated in Kuwait, the regime remained intact. In an attempt to keep Saddam Hussein in check, and to pressure him to comply with demands by the United Nations, the Security Council imposed economic sanctions banning trade with Iraq, including in oil. The United States, Britain, and France imposed UN-sanctioned no-fly zones over the Kurdish-populated areas in northern Iraq and the Shiite-populated region in southern Iraq. American, British, and—initially—French aircraft patrolled the zones regularly.*

Undeterred, Saddam continued to use brutality on a massive scale. After suppressing the Shiite and Kurdish uprisings in 1991, Saddam drained the marshlands of southern Iraq, turning the region into a salt-encrusted desert. His purpose was to punish the "marsh Arabs" for their support of the rebellion against him. He drove some 150,000 Iraqis from their homes. His intelligence services were merciless in torturing suspected opponents. Arbitrary arrests and unexplained disappearances were commonplace. He built rape rooms to bring "dishonor" to the female members of families

* The French ended their participation in the no-fly zones in 1998.[1]

suspected of opposition to him.* And before long the Iraqi military began a near daily routine of firing on coalition aircraft patrolling the no-fly zones.

Saddam's regime claimed it had destroyed its arsenals of proscribed weapons, but the United Nations weapons inspectors were skeptical. Iraqi officials spied on the inspectors, sanitized suspect sites before the teams arrived, and barred them from examining Saddam's vast palace complexes. He reorganized his biological weapons program creatively by closing his military-run weapons facilities while creating dual-use plants capable of making products for both civilian and military use.[2] Facilities that produced fertilizer and antibiotics, for example, could be retooled quickly to create chemical and biological weapons. By 1998, Saddam had stopped cooperating with the UN inspectors altogether, effectively forcing them out of the country and ending even a pretense of complying with the UN Security Council's demands. In response, the UN adopted still more resolutions expressing outrage at Saddam's "totally unacceptable" actions.[3] But few nations, other than the United States and Great Britain, appeared willing to do much, if anything, to enforce the UN resolutions.

In January 1998, I joined a group of former national security officials in signing a letter to President Clinton that called for stronger action against Saddam's regime.[4] "The only acceptable strategy," our letter read, "is one that eliminates the possibility that Iraq will be able to use or threaten to use weapons of mass destruction." For the short term, we endorsed military strikes on suspected weapons facilities. For the long term, we called for removing Saddam and his regime.[5]

Later in 1998, large bipartisan majorities in each house of the U.S. Congress generally endorsed the policies recommended in our letter to Clinton. The Iraq Liberation Act declared that the goal of U.S. policy should be "to remove the regime headed by Saddam Hussein from power." The U.S. House of Representatives approved that legislation by a vote of 360 to 38.† It passed the Senate without a single dissenting vote. Clinton signed the legislation into law. Regime change in Iraq was now the official policy of the United States.

Even as Clinton endorsed regime change, some administration officials

* In the days after the liberation of Iraq in 2003, I was given a video that U.S. Army soldiers had found. It was a twelve-minute film Saddam's internal security services had put together. The video documented various methods of torture that his regime used, including beatings, limb and tongue amputations, and beheadings. Men were thrown off three-story buildings. Some were forced to hold out their arms to have them broken by lead pipes. Saddam's men proudly videotaped their atrocities to terrorize others.

† Republicans voted 202 to 9 and Democrats voted 157 to 29 in favor of the bill.

contended that the existing UN economic sanctions had kept Saddam reasonably under control—"in a box," as Clinton's Secretary of State, Madeleine Albright, put it.[6] However, the sanctions administered through the UN's Oil-for-Food program had loopholes big enough to drive trucks through. The UN was generating billions of dollars in illicit, unrestricted funds for Saddam Hussein, who used the cash to finance, among other things, his dual-use weapons facilities.[7] The so-called Oil-for-Food program became one of the greatest scams perpetrated in the six decades of the United Nation's existence.[8] When the second Bush administration came into office in January 2001, the Iraqi "containment" policy was in tatters.

Various commentators asserted that Clinton's successor, George W. Bush, was intent on "fixing" his father's error of leaving Saddam in power.[9] From what I saw, that was not the case. Before his inauguration, when I met with the President-elect in Austin, Texas to discuss defense policy, the subject of Iraq did not even come up. The first person I remember mentioning the issue to me in 2001 was Clinton's outgoing Secretary of Defense, Bill Cohen. He and the senior military officers in the Clinton administration were fully aware of the dangers our aircraft crews faced in the skies over Iraq. Despite the risks, Cohen believed that discontinuing our patrols of the no-fly zones was not an option. It would be a victory for Saddam and further erode an already fraying coalition of nations committed to containment of his brutal regime.

Iraq's repeated efforts to shoot down our aircraft weighed heavily on my mind. Iraq was the only nation in the world that was attacking the U.S. military on a daily basis—in fact, more than two thousand times from January 2000 to September 2002.[10] I was concerned, as were the CENTCOM commander and the Joint Chiefs, that one of our aircraft would soon be shot down and its crew killed or captured.* In my first months back at the Pentagon, I asked General Hugh Shelton, chairman of the Joint Chiefs, to brief me on CENTCOM's plans in the event Iraq successfully brought down one of our planes. The plan, code-named Desert Badger, was seriously limited. Its goal was to rescue the crew of a downed aircraft—but it had no component to inflict any damage or to send any kind of message to Saddam Hussein that such provocations were

*On the dangers posed by Iraq, General Jim Jones, then commandant of the Marine Corps, was among the most vocal. He was concerned that our operations over Iraq were, as he put it, "a high risk strategy without clear objectives or a discernible end state." "I am working [on] the problem and certainly agree with your concern," I wrote back on September 10, 2001.[11]

unacceptable. Our friends in the region had criticized previous American responses to Iraqi aggression as weak and indecisive and had advised us that our enemies had taken comfort from America's timidity. The Desert Badger plan was clear evidence of that problem. I asked Shelton and General Franks to have their planners come up with a range of other options the President could consider. If an aircraft was downed, I wanted to be sure we had ideas for the President that would enable him to inflict a memorable cost. The new proposals I ordered included attacks on Iraq's air defense systems and their command-and-control facilities to enable us to cripple the regime's abilities to attack our planes.

Several weeks into the administration we had reason to signal to Baghdad that the days of mild and ineffective U.S. responses to their repeated provocations were coming to a close. Iraq was working to strengthen its air defense and radar capabilities in the no-fly zones by installing fiber-optic cables to make it more difficult for us to monitor their communications. The network was a direct challenge to the UN no-fly zones. On February 16, 2001, after Iraqi ground units had again targeted our aircraft, twenty-four American and British aircraft launched a coordinated attack on five Iraqi air defense sites, destroying them.*

Though Iraq was discussed occasionally at the senior levels of the administration, by the summer of 2001, U.S. policy remained essentially what it had been at the end of the Clinton administration—adrift. I decided to bring my questions about our inherited Iraq strategy to the members of the National Security Council to seek some clarity and presidential guidance.

In July, I sent a memo to Cheney, Powell, and Rice asking that we hold a principals committee meeting to discuss Iraq. In the document I raised two scenarios that could have the effect of forcing the President to make a decision on Iraq under unfavorable circumstances. The first involved its neighbor Iran obtaining a nuclear weapon, which would dramatically change the balance in the region and possibly spark a regionwide arms buildup. Second was the possibility that "Somebody, whether Iran, Iraq, or Usama Bin Laden, could take out the royal family in one or more of the Gulf states and change

* When the strike took place, President Bush was on a state visit to Mexico. He and I had both approved the strikes, but neither of us was informed of their timing. So when reporters asked the President about them at the joint press conference he was having with Mexican President Vicente Fox, Bush was caught by surprise. Keeping the Commander in Chief in the dark about the timing of a strike was not the preferred course of action. But, one month into the new term, I was the only Senate-confirmed Bush-nominated official in the Department of Defense. We were still missing the entire layer of senior civilians who would coordinate communication with the White House and other members of the National Security Council.

the regime and the balance, perhaps inviting Iranian or Iraqi troops in to protect them." I also noted that some event totally unforeseen by us and out of our control could force a U.S. decision on Iraq. I argued that we would be better off developing a policy well ahead of events that could overtake us. On the broader subject of Iraq, I outlined a range of possibilities for consideration:

> We can publicly acknowledge that sanctions don't work over extended periods and stop the pretense of having a policy that is keeping Saddam "in the box . . ."
>
> A second option would be to go to our moderate Arab friends, have a reappraisal and see whether they are willing to engage in a more robust policy. We would have to assert strong leadership and convince them that we will see the project through and not leave them later to face a provoked, but still incumbent, Saddam. The risks of a serious regime-change policy must be weighed against the certainty of the danger of an increasingly bold and nuclear-armed Saddam in the near future.
>
> A third possibility perhaps is to take a crack at initiating contact with Saddam Hussein. He has his own interests. It may be that, for whatever reason, at his stage in life he might prefer to not have the hostility of the United States and the West and might be willing to make some accommodation. Opening a dialogue with Saddam would be an astonishing departure for the USG, [U.S. government] although I did it for President Reagan [in] the mid-1980s. It would win praise from certain quarters, but might cause friends, especially those in the region, to question our strength, steadiness and judgment. And the likelihood of Saddam making and respecting an acceptable accommodation of our interests over a long period may be small.[12]

I thought a diplomatic overture on Iraq from the Bush administration—a "Nixon goes to China" approach—was worth suggesting to the President. As I wrote in my memo to the NSC principals, echoing my thoughts of some twenty years earlier when I visited Baghdad, "There ought to be a way for the U.S. to not be at loggerheads with both of the two most powerful nations in the Gulf—Iran and Iraq." Though the Iran-Iraq War had ended more than a decade earlier, the regimes in Tehran and Baghdad still viewed each other with hostility. Despite that animosity, both still had poor relations with the United States. I wondered if the right combination of blandishments and pressures might lead or compel Saddam Hussein toward an improved arrangement with America.* While a long shot, it was not out of the question.

The National Security Council never organized the comprehensive review of U.S.-Iraq policy I requested in the summer of 2001. We can't know how the Bush administration's Iraq policy might have evolved if 9/11 had not occurred, but that event compelled our government to make terrorism a focus of intense attention. It demanded that American officials reexamine national security policy comprehensively in light of the vulnerabilities the attack exposed. It forced the still new administration to recognize the special danger posed by nations that both supported terrorist groups and possessed or pursued weapons of mass destruction.

Though intelligence did not report that Saddam was tightly connected to al-Qaida or that he was involved in the 9/11 attack, Iraq was included in almost any analysis of state supporters of terrorism. Iraq had been on the State Department's list of state sponsors of terror since 1990. The regime's links to individual terrorists and terrorist groups earned Iraq its place on the "axis of evil" list.[14]

When I was queried by reporters on links between Iraq and terrorists, I referred to an unclassified written statement I had requested of George Tenet and that was subsequently prepared by the CIA. The paper was taken directly from Tenet's unclassified conclusions provided to Congress, which stated:

- We have solid reporting of senior level contacts between Iraq and al-Qa'ida going back a decade.
- Credible information indicates that Iraq and al-Qa'ida have discussed safe haven and reciprocal non-aggression.
- Since Operation Enduring Freedom, we have solid evidence of the presence in Iraq of al-Qa'ida members, including some that have been in Baghdad.
- We have credible reporting that al-Qa'ida leaders sought contacts in Iraq who could help them acquire WMD capabilities. The reporting also stated that Iraq has provided training to al-Qa'ida members in the areas of poisons and gases and making conventional bombs.[15]

* After his capture in Iraq by the American military in 2003, Saddam told an FBI interviewer he was interested in pursuing a "security agreement with the United States to protect [Iraq] from threats in the region" before the invasion occurred. For someone supposedly interested in cultivating a new relationship with the United States, Saddam had an odd way of showing it: firing on American pilots, praising and rewarding terrorists, and applauding the 9/11 attacks.[13]

Tenet, the CIA, and members of the Bush administration were certainly not the only ones thinking about possible linkages. A few hours after the 9/11 attack, James Woolsey, CIA director under President Clinton, raised the question of whether Saddam was involved.[16] ABC News, the *Guardian* newspaper, and other media outlets floated similar questions prominently. Their queries were not unreasonable. At the time Saddam was offering twenty-five-thousand-dollar bonuses to the families of suicide bombers to encourage them to attack Israel. He allowed terrorist groups such as the Mujahedin-e-Khalq, the Kurdistan Workers' Party (PKK), the Palestine Liberation Front, the Popular Front for the Liberation of Palestine, and the Arab Liberation Front to operate within Iraq's borders.[17] During the 1990s, terrorists supported by Saddam struck in Rome and Vienna, killing Americans and Israelis. Saddam gave refuge to terrorists on the run, like Abu Nidal, whose group was responsible for some nine hundred deaths and casualties, including a number of Americans, in attacks in more than twenty countries.[18] Abu Abbas, who hijacked the cruise liner *Achille Lauro* and murdered an American citizen, Leon Klinghoffer, was living openly and safely in Baghdad.

Documents discovered after the coalition's invasion of Iraq in 2003 shed more light on the depth of the regime's linkages with terrorism. As far back as January 1993, for example, Saddam had ordered the formation of "a group to start hunting Americans present on Arab soil; especially Somalia."[19] Saddam used his paramilitary group, the Fedayeen Saddam, to train thousands of terrorists to be deployed both inside and outside of Iraq's borders.[20] While the idea of Iraq working with al-Qaida to inflict harm on the United States did not seem to be much of a stretch, in my public remarks I stayed close to the CIA's official assessment.

My concerns about Iraq went beyond Saddam's support of terrorism or any involvement with al-Qaida. It went beyond his savage oppression and genocidal acts against his own people. My view rested on the fact that previous attempts to reduce the risks Saddam posed had failed. The UN sanctions that had checked Iraqi ambitions in the 1990s were crumbling. Further, the sanctions were punishing the Iraqi people more than they were disadvantaging Saddam Hussein and, as a result, international support for the sanctions had waned. Saddam's belligerence was one of the main reasons we had kept U.S. troops in Saudi Arabia, which had fueled Bin Laden's propaganda. Saddam's long record of aggression and regional ambition were not in doubt, and there were no indications that he had changed. If anything,

Saddam seemed emboldened by a decade of UN and American acquiescence. It was increasingly clear that Iraq's continued defiance of the United Nations would further weaken that institution and encourage other dangerous regimes to follow suit.

In the aftermath of 9/11 and our changed global environment, I wanted updated thinking about U.S. interests and options. I asked Douglas Feith, the undersecretary of defense for policy, to consider the broader principles involved, not just Iraq's history under Saddam. Among other questions, I asked: What steps should the United States consider taking—when, and with whom? Is it proper to act alone? What about the argument that we should try to obtain approval from the UN Security Council? When is it reasonable to conclude that all means short of war have been tried and have failed? Is preemptive action to forestall the threat then justified?

Feith was the right person for the assignment. He listened carefully to views contrary to his own and could reformulate them and present them respectfully and accurately. He advised that even those friendly to the United States and sensitive to our security interests worried about a world in which the American president could decide to bring about regime change by force in country after country. I understood that concern. The Bush doctrine of preemption, or more precisely, anticipatory self-defense, could not be seen as a license for an American president to exercise unchecked military power on a whim. After all, the Founding Fathers saw unchecked power as the greatest danger to human liberty. Our Constitution created a system of checks and balances in the hope of ensuring that no president, legislative body, or court could accrue enough power to overwhelm the others. Feith and his policy team formulated these thoughts in a 2002 memo titled "Sovereignty and Anticipatory Self-Defense."[21]

In the twenty-first century, the idea that countries could be left alone unless and until they actually launched an aggressive war had to have exceptions. The lethality of modern weapons and the stated intent of terrorists to use them made it difficult to sustain that traditional view. Regimes with records of aggression and dishonesty, and which had or were working toward WMD capabilities, could inflict far more massive damage than ever before. An Iranian nuclear strike on the small state of Israel, for example, could destroy so much of the nation that Israel might be unable to survive as a viable state. Could a responsible Israeli prime minister allow that to occur by waiting until after a nuclear missile was launched? Nuclear or biological material covertly passed to a terrorist organization could be detonated or released in one or more of our cities, killing millions, bringing our economy to a halt, and effectively suspending our country's cherished civil liberties. Could an American president sit back, wait, and take that risk?

In our system of governance, U.S. presidents, even when invoking preemption, are still accountable to the American people and subject to the internal checks inherent in the American political system. A president has to make decisions with an eye to the powers of the Congress and the courts, as well as the increasingly large role of the media, the internet, and other nongovernmental actors.[22] Most importantly, a U.S. president must face public opinion and the consequences that come with elections. Preemptive military action or anticipatory self-defense undertaken by the United States also requires allies—including bases, overflight rights, transit routes, shared intelligence, and logistical support. While not legal checks, these were practical checks we all needed to keep in mind.

A secretary of defense and senior military officials in the chain of command are often considered by outsiders to be the most vocal advocates of the use of military force. I've found that more often the opposite is true. Since those in a position of responsibility for the troops understand well the costs of war, they can often be reluctant war fighters. I supported military action against al-Qaida and the Taliban because they had left us no alternative. Saddam, to my mind, was different. I thought we might be able to find other ways of bringing about regime change in Iraq.

On September 21, 2001, I wrote myself a note. "At the right moment," I stated, "we may want to give Saddam Hussein a way out for his family to live in comfort."[23] I thought an aggressive diplomatic effort, coupled by a threat of military force, just might convince Saddam and those around him to seek exile. By 2002, the Iraqi regime had seen what we were able to do in Afghanistan. If there were enough rational individuals around Saddam, they might be convinced that George W. Bush was not bluffing and was committed to the disarmament of Saddam Hussein. I hoped the world could stand united in that message. That hope was doomed to disappointment.

CHAPTER 31

The Case for Regime Change

Fifteen days after 9/11, the President asked me to join him in the Oval Office alone. Our meetings almost always included some combination of the vice president, the chairman of the Joint Chiefs of Staff, the secretary of state, the national security adviser, or the White House chief of staff—but not on the morning of September 26.

The President leaned back in the black leather chair behind his desk. He asked that I take a look at the shape of our military plans on Iraq. He knew the Joint Chiefs and I were concerned about Saddam Hussein's attacks on our aircraft in the northern and southern no-fly zones, but two weeks after the worst terrorist attack in our nation's history, those of us in the Department of Defense were fully occupied.

He wanted the options to be "creative," which I took to mean that he wanted something different from the massive land force assembled during the 1991 Gulf War. I certainly did not get the impression the President had made up his mind on the merits of toppling Saddam Hussein's regime. In fact, at the September 15 NSC meeting at Camp David days earlier when Iraq had been raised, he had specifically kept the focus on Afghanistan.

I told him I would review CENTCOM's existing Iraq plan and speak to General Franks about updating it.

There was another matter President Bush wanted to discuss with me that morning. "Dick told me about your son," he said. "Are you and Joyce doing okay?"

Although Nick had been in recovery from drug addiction at the time of Bush's inauguration, his condition had been fragile, and he had relapsed. He had tried several times to turn his life around, but by the late summer of 2001, he was bottoming out again. He would disappear for periods, turning up occasionally in various towns across the West. Joyce and I had left Washington at the end of August to spend Labor Day weekend in New Mexico. After being out of touch for weeks, Nick reappeared in Taos while we were there.

In a long, painful visit, we again tried to convince him to seek treatment. My inclination was to do whatever it took to get him clean, even if it was against his wishes. Joyce understood better than I did that addiction was a disease that people eventually have to overcome on their own. As parents we could only offer support, encouragement, and a direction. Nick was weighing heavily on my mind when I returned to Washington in early September. One part of me was always thinking of him and the terrible state he was in. But in the days after 9/11, being distracted wasn't an option.

On September 18, a week before my meeting with President Bush, Nick had called Joyce from Taos. "Happy birthday, Mom," he said. He then told her he was leaving to check into a treatment center. Valerie's husband, our son-in-law Paul Richard, and a friend of ours in Taos had agreed to take him. Nick said they had convinced him, and he was ready.

I had shared the information on Nick with Cheney, who had apparently passed it on to Bush. Because I knew the President had a great deal confronting him, I was surprised that he was mentioning our son, but he spoke with such concern that my family troubles seemed to be the only thing on his mind.

I told the President the activity surrounding 9/11 had not given me much time to think about our situation. But Joyce and I desperately wanted Nick's treatment to be successful this time.

"I love Nick so much," I said.

"You have my full support and prayers," Bush said.

What had happened to Nick—coupled with the wounds to our country and the Pentagon—all started to hit me. At that moment, I couldn't speak. And I was unable to hold back the emotions that until then I had shared only with Joyce. I had not imagined I might choke up in a meeting with the President of the United States, but at that moment George W. Bush wasn't just the

President. He was a compassionate human being who had a sense of what Joyce and I were going through.

Bush rose from his chair, walked around his desk, and put his arm around me.*

Because I had been reviewing the various war plans regularly, I knew no one would think it out of the ordinary for me to request a briefing on our existing options on Iraq. As a precaution, however, I asked for briefings to cover several contingencies in various parts of the world.

As the CENTCOM briefers moved through their PowerPoint slides on the on-the-shelf Iraq war plan, it quickly became clear that it was only a slightly modified version of the one used during the first Gulf War. It called for roughly the same number of forces used then—nearly half a million U.S. troops to be marshaled into the region over many months. They were to invade through Iraq's southern desert, much as they had in 1991. Because the firepower and precision of U.S. forces had increased substantially since then, the plan would represent a vastly more lethal force in 2003.† Someone in the briefing described the plan, appropriately I thought, as "Desert Storm on Steroids."

This was not what the Commander in Chief had told me he was looking for. It was a stale, slow-building, and dated plan that Iraqi forces would expect. A decade had come and gone since the Gulf War, yet the war plan seemed to have been frozen in time. Everyone in the briefing recognized that CENTCOM and Joint Staff planners would need to do a major overhaul.

I did not hear any more about Iraq for two months. Then, on November 21, 2001, a week after coalition forces had driven the Taliban from Kabul, the President called me aside at the end of an NSC meeting. He led me into a small, unoccupied office a few feet from the Situation Room, closed the door, and sat down.

"Where do we stand on the Iraq planning?" he asked.

I told him I had been briefed on the existing plan, and that it was very much like one for the Gulf War a decade ago. As I expected, it was not what the President was seeking. "To make progress," I said, "I need to engage others in the Pentagon and at CENTCOM to update the Iraq plan. It will need a good deal of work."

* Since he admitted himself into treatment in September 2001, Nick has lived a drug-free life with the support of his wife, Anne.

† In Desert Storm, 10 percent of U.S. weapons were precision guided. By 2001, a decade later, some 70 percent of U.S. air-delivered weapons were guided by lasers or GPS with devastating accuracy.

"That's fine," Bush replied. I told him that CENTCOM could update it in the normal order of things, but that they would need to work with intelligence officials as well. The latest intelligence on Iraqi military capabilities, suspected WMD sites, and other targets would shape how CENTCOM refashioned the plan. That meant I would need to talk to Tenet, and senior military officials would need to have discussions with their counterparts at the Agency.

The President said he didn't want me to communicate with people outside of DoD for the time being, and that he would personally talk to Tenet and others at the right moment.

Back at the Pentagon, I asked Myers to stop by my office. I knew his focus at the time was almost exclusively on Afghanistan. Once we were alone, I told him about our new guidance: "Dick, the President wants to know what kind of operations plan we have for Iraq."[1]

Myers showed no surprise. This was a request from the Commander in Chief, and the General's instinct was to get to work. Myers had been with me when I had been briefed on the existing Iraq plan. He agreed it needed a thorough reworking. We both knew that CENTCOM's planners were already taxed, given their ongoing work on Afghanistan. Nonetheless, I told him we should have Franks and CENTCOM bring the plan in line with the current capabilities of our military and with the latest intelligence on Iraq.

After receiving his new assignment from Myers, Franks took a look at the current Iraq war plan and confirmed our opinion that it was seriously out-of-date. In fact, I knew of no military officials who believed that the "Desert Storm on Steroids" war plan would be appropriate for the current circumstances. Saddam's overall military capability had eroded since Desert Storm. At the same time, American military capabilities in precision-guided weapons had improved substantially. Also in my mind was the fact that in the 1991 Gulf War, enormous quantities of equipment and other materiel sent to the Gulf were never used.*

One thing that was clear was that Iraq would require a great many more troops on the ground than CENTCOM had marshaled in Afghanistan. Saddam's forces, unlike the Taliban's, were sizable. The Republican Guard contained formidable, well-trained armored divisions. And in Iraq, with the exception of the Kurds who kept to the north, there were no effective anti-regime forces like the Afghan Northern Alliance and Pashtun militias ready

* In 1990 and 1991, the military had shipped some four hundred thousand short tons of ammunition into the Iraq theater. More than 80 percent was returned to the United States untouched.[2]

to help topple Saddam. By and large, the Iraqi opposition was disarmed, in exile, or dead—the last being Saddam's preference.

By Christmas 2001, Franks was ready to brief the President on an initial cut. Bush invited us to his ranch in Crawford, Texas, on December 28. With the President's permission, I opted to join them by video teleconference and have Franks travel to the ranch alone. The President and Franks rarely had a chance to talk to each other one-on-one. I wanted this visit to be an opportunity for them to do just that.

When Myers and I joined the teleconference, the President and Franks seemed to be getting along well. Bush's respect for him was bolstered by Franks' quick and successful military campaign in Afghanistan. It also was clear that Franks' experience in the Afghan campaign had honed his capabilities and built up his confidence.

I often thought of Dwight D. Eisenhower's insightful observation that "plans are worthless, but planning is everything," which I had adopted in my collection of Rumsfeld's Rules. With the first contact with the enemy, elements of any plan generally have to be tossed aside. Split-second improvisation, experience, and leadership take over. Still, careful preparation is invaluable. Becoming acquainted with facts, terrain, people, capabilities, and possibilities helps military leaders cope and adapt, as they must, when new circumstances inevitably arise and it becomes necessary to adjust, recalibrate, or even discard the original plan.

I suggested that Franks start by focusing on the key assumptions underlying his plan—that is, what he expected to be happening inside and outside Iraq if war came. I believed that key assumptions needed to be the foundation of any contingency plan, but I had found that military planners did not always cite them or give them the probing, intense consideration they merited. In meetings at the Pentagon, I emphasized that failing to examine the assumptions on which a plan is based can start a planning process based on incorrect premises, and then proceed perfectly logically to incorrect conclusions.[3]

I was particularly concerned, for example, when I was shown the contingency plan for a possible conflict on the Korean Peninsula. By then our intelligence community's assessment was that the North Korean regime had at least one or several nuclear weapons, yet the old war plan did not factor that absolutely essential assumption into its calculus.

Similarly, I urged the military planners to think carefully about the range of possible Iraqi responses to possible U.S. military actions. This iterative process was also happening at levels well below ours. Franks was getting input from State Department advisers and CIA analysts present at CENTCOM. With a continually evolving diplomatic and intelligence landscape, the Iraq plan was never fixed. Planning would take place until President Bush actually made his final decision and signed an order to execute, and on every day thereafter as new circumstances evolved.

In Texas, Franks went through each of his key assumptions, giving the President an opportunity to consider them and comment. As was usually the case, many of the major assumptions CENTCOM relied on in the political-military sphere came from the intelligence community. Military planners are not necessarily experts in the language, culture, history, and politics of the people in the Defense Department's wide and varied spheres of operation. One assumption was that Iraq possessed WMD, and that advancing U.S. troops could come under chemical or biological attack. Another of Franks' considerations was that Saddam's most loyal forces might turn the capital into "Fortress Baghdad," leading to a long and bloody standoff with substantial risk to both the city's civilian population and to American troops fighting in the urban environment. Other assumptions in the plan included: some countries in the region would give cooperation and basing rights; Iraq could attack Israel in the event of a conflict; forces would need to number at least 100,000 before combat operations could begin; and regional threats like Syria and Iran would not become directly involved.

It was also an assumption that anti-Saddam opposition groups inside and outside of Iraq would favor a U.S. and coalition military effort. Though they were unlikely to be able to offer tangible military assistance, as the Northern Alliance had in Afghanistan, the opposition, with help from the Department of State, could form part of a provisional government, much as the Bonn process had led to a broad-based interim government in Afghanistan. Myers and I directed CENTCOM planners to begin thinking through a postwar plan, even in the preliminary phases.

On the operations side, Franks' plan called for an invasion force buildup of 145,000 troops over six months, which would be increased to 275,000 if and as needed. The President, the Joint Chiefs, and I stood ready to muster whatever number of troops Franks determined would be necessary to get the job done. He believed that Operation Enduring Freedom in Afghanistan and U.S. operations elsewhere could provide a degree of cover to allow him to bring forces forward and arrange them around the Middle East without creating a major stir. To counter the concern about a possible Fortress

Baghdad scenario, Franks emphasized speed as one of his most important priorities once war began. If U.S. forces could begin an attack with an element of surprise and race to Baghdad, Saddam's forces might not have time to reinforce and arm their defensive positions there. A swift campaign would also help satisfy our Muslim friends in the region, who were concerned about domestic unrest if major combat operations against another Muslim nation were prolonged.

I thought Franks' December 2001 briefing was a solid early cut, considering the relatively short time he had had to prepare. Bush seemed satisfied as well. The President expressed the hope I shared that diplomacy would persuade the Iraqis to comply with UN Security Council resolutions. Franks, Myers, and I would happily throw many thousands of hours of work into the shredder if it meant the men and women of the U.S. military would not have to go to war. Nonetheless, we all believed, as the President did, that the intelligence about Iraq and Saddam's documented history of aggression and deception were too unsettling to not at least be ready for a military confrontation if diplomacy were to fail.

Though the intelligence failures surrounding Iraq are now well-known, recent history is abundant with examples of flawed intelligence that have affected key national security decisions and contingency planning. They include, for example: the poor quality of the intelligence gathered on the ground in Vietnam; the underestimates of the scale of the Soviet Union's military efforts during the Cold War; a lack of awareness about the brewing Iranian revolution that forced the Shah, an American ally, to flee the country; the failure to detect preparations for India's nuclear test; and consistently underestimating the number of missiles that China had deployed along the Taiwan Straits. For Iraq, there was a similar pattern of intelligence estimates that had dangerously miscalculated Saddam's capabilities. In 1991, experts actually underestimated Saddam Hussein's nuclear capability. After the Gulf War, UN weapons inspectors were surprised to discover that Iraq had been no more than a year or two away from having enough fissile material to produce a nuclear bomb.*

Less than perfect intelligence reports are, of course, a fact of life for national security decision makers. Intelligence officials have some of the most difficult

* David Kay, the chief UN weapons inspector in 1991, believed it would have been only twelve to eighteen months until the regime reached "regular industrial-scale production of fissile material," or enriched uranium, that could be used in an atomic bomb.[4]

jobs in the world. Uncertainty, gaps in knowledge, and outright errors are inevitable. Targets are hostile and working to deceive and conceal the very information that is most sought after. Closed, repressive regimes and their terrorist allies can make their decisions in small, tightly controlled cliques without regard to public opinion, parliaments, or media scrutiny, making it particularly difficult to discover their intentions.

It wasn't only our enemies that compounded the intelligence community's challenges. Budget cuts during the 1990s amounting to 10 percent of the intelligence community's budget were a costly self-inflicted wound that weakened our capabilities for years, particularly in the area of human intelligence. I had worked with our intelligence agencies off and on over some three decades, and intensely when I chaired the Ballistic Missile Threat Commission in 1998. That experience was sobering. Compartmentalization hampered intelligence analysis. Policy makers did not engage sufficiently with intelligence professionals in setting intelligence priorities and asking informed questions about their analyses and conclusions.* In a unanimous letter to CIA Director Tenet, our bipartisan commission members shared our concerns about the quality of the intelligence community's products. In the letter we wrote:

> Unless and until senior users take time to engage analysts, question their assumptions and methods, seek from them what they know, what they don't know and ask them their opinions—and do so without penalizing the analysts when their opinions differ from those of the user—senior users cannot have a substantial impact in improving the intelligence product they receive.[5]

What was unique about Iraq was that the intelligence community reported near total confidence in their conclusions. Their assessments appeared to be unusually consistent. In August 2002, Deputy CIA Director John McLaughlin presented to the principals committee the intelligence community's judgments about Iraq's WMD activities. McLaughlin, a serious and measured

* I considered it my responsibility to ask questions and seek needed information from briefers. In my experience, the good briefers and analysts did not show discomfort when I engaged them. In fact, they tended to enjoy the give-and-take and seemed appreciative of the interest of a senior official. Some commented that the interchanges helped them do their work better and provided useful input for their colleagues. After a few in the CIA alleged that some policy officials had "politicized intelligence," in 2004 I asked not to receive my daily oral briefings from the CIA. If questions were going to be reported as efforts to distort rather than to better understand or clarify the information we were receiving, it not only wasn't worth taking time to receive the briefings, it had risks. As a result, I began simply reading the CIA briefing materials and asking the undersecretary of defense for intelligence to pose any questions I might have.

career intelligence professional, described the situation in stark terms. According to my notes, his briefing concluded that:

- Iraq had reconstituted its facilities for biological and chemical weapons.
- There were 3,200 tons of chemical weapons the regime previously had that remained unaccounted for.
- Saddam had a mobile biological warfare capability, and a variety of means to deliver them, likely including UAVs.
- Saddam had retained many of the same experts who had developed nuclear weapons prior to the Gulf War.
- There was construction at old nuclear facilities, and Iraq was "clearly working" on fissile material, which meant that Saddam could have a nuclear weapon within one year.[6]

McLaughlin's briefing covered many of the same points that were emphasized in the intelligence community's analyses of Iraq's WMD programs, and later in Secretary of State Colin Powell's presentation to the UN. As McLaughlin gave the Agency's official and authoritative briefing, I wrote a note to myself. It said "caution—strong case," but I added, "could be wrong."[7] There were few qualifiers in the briefing. In the run-up to the war in Iraq, we heard a great deal about what our intelligence community knew or thought they knew, but not enough about what they knew they didn't know.

Two months after McLaughlin's briefing, in October 2002, the National Intelligence Council (NIC), the coordinating body for the U.S. intelligence community's analytical products, issued the authoritative National Intelligence Estimate (NIE) on Iraq. The NIE, which is now declassified, was an alarming report on Iraq's weapons systems. The report included the following:

- We judge that Iraq has continued its weapons of mass destruction (WMD) programs in defiance of UN resolutions and restrictions. Baghdad has chemical and biological weapons as well as missiles with ranges in excess of UN restrictions; if left unchecked, it probably will have a nuclear weapon during this decade.
- Iraq has largely rebuilt missile and biological weapons facilities damaged

during Operation Desert Fox and has expanded its chemical and biological infrastructure under the cover of civilian production.

- Although we assess that Saddam does not yet have nuclear weapons or sufficient material to make any, he remains intent on acquiring them. Most agencies assess that Baghdad started reconstituting its nuclear program about the time that [UN] inspectors departed—December 1998.
- If Baghdad acquires sufficient fissile material from abroad it could make a nuclear weapon within several months to a year.
- Baghdad has mobile facilities for producing bacterial and toxin BW agents; these facilities can evade detection and are highly survivable. Within three to six months these units probably could produce an amount of agent equal to the total that Iraq produced in the years prior to the Gulf war.
- Saddam, if sufficiently desperate, might decide that only an organization such as al-Qa'ida—with worldwide reach and extensive terrorist infrastructure, and already engaged in a life-or-death struggle against the United States—could perpetrate the type of terrorist attack that he would hope to conduct.
- In such circumstances, he might decide that the extreme step of assisting the Islamist terrorists in conducting a CBW [chemical or biological weapon] attack against the United States would be his last chance to exact vengeance by taking a large number of victims with him.[8]

American intelligence officials were joined in many of these startling assessments by intelligence services from other nations—Britain, Australia, Spain, Italy, and Poland among them—all of whom judged that Saddam's regime possessed WMD and was expanding its capabilities. Even Russia, China, Germany, and France, then skeptical of any military action against Iraq, agreed. "There is a problem—the probable possession of weapons of mass destruction by an uncontrollable country, Iraq," said French President Jacques Chirac. He added, "The international community is right . . . in having decided Iraq should be disarmed."[9] On the subject of Iraq's nuclear weapons program, the German chief of intelligence actually held a grimmer view than the U.S. intelligence community: "It is our estimate that Iraq will have an atomic bomb in three years."[10] Egyptian President Hosni Mubarak cautioned General Franks that Saddam had biological weapons and would use them on American forces.[11] A multitude of specific, seemingly credible reports, some even illustrated with satellite photographs, provided supporting evidence.

Early in the war, while major combat operations were still underway, I was asked on a news program if I was concerned about the failure to find WMD in Iraq. I had always tried to speak with reserve and precision on intelligence matters, but on this occasion, I made a misstatement. Recalling the CIA's designation of various "suspect" WMD sites in Iraq, I replied, "We know where they are. They're in the area around Tikrit and Baghdad."[12] I should have used the phrase "suspect sites." My words have been quoted many times by critics of the war as an example of how the Bush administration misled the public.

One of the challenges for historians is distinguishing the essential from the inessential, the predominant from the marginal, the characteristic from the exceptional. Promoters of the frequently repeated "Bush lied, people died" line have scoured a voluminous record of official statements on Iraqi WMD to compile a small string of comments—ill chosen or otherwise deficient—to try to depict the administration as purposefully misrepresenting the intelligence. While I made a few misstatements—in particular the one mentioned above—they were not common and certainly not characteristic. Other senior administration officials also did a reasonably good job of representing the intelligence community's assessments accurately in their public comments about Iraqi WMD, despite some occasionally imperfect formulations.

Intelligence evidence about WMD had a way of taking pride of place in the litany of reasons for going to war. In fact, that should have been only one of the many reasons. There was a long list of other charges against Saddam Hussein's regime—its support for terrorism, its attacks on American pilots in the no-fly zones, its violation of the United Nations Security Council resolutions, its history of aggression, and its crimes against its people. At one point I cautioned Torie Clarke, the assistant secretary of defense for public affairs, that the administration's spokespeople were not using all of the many arguments that had been presented against Iraq.[13] Obviously the focus on WMD to the exclusion of almost all else was a public relations error that cost the administration dearly.

In October 2002, Congress passed the Authorization for Use of Military

Force Against Iraq. This often overlooked but significant congressional action reflected a strong, broad, and bipartisan view that Saddam Hussein's regime would need to be toppled by force to protect the United States and international peace and security. Rather than focusing solely on WMD programs, the legislation listed twenty-three separate indictments against the regime. The points included:

- violating resolution of the United Nations Security Council by continuing to engage in brutal repression of its civilian population . . .
- attempting in 1993 to assassinate former President Bush . . .
- firing on many thousands of occasions on United States and Coalition Armed Forces engaged in enforcing the resolutions of the United Nations Security Council; . . .
- members of al Qaida, an organization bearing responsibility for attacks on the United States, its citizens, and interests, including the attacks that occurred on September 11, 2001, are known to be in Iraq; . . .
- Iraq continues to aid and harbor other international terrorist organizations, including organizations that threaten the lives and safety of United States citizens.[14]

The House of Representatives passed that authorization by a margin of 297 to 133. The legislation, in fact, garnered 47 more votes of support in the House than the congressional authorization of the 1991 Gulf War. The Senate vote—77 to 23—was similarly lopsided. In later years, when things got tough, some who supported the military force authorization tried to explain away their votes. They claimed they were hoodwinked and misled on the intelligence or that they didn't think the legislation had actually authorized military action. In the military there is a phrase accorded to people like that: You wouldn't want to be in a foxhole with them.

The views of a number of prominent legislators were in fact quite different before the war began than their later statements.

"We have no choice but to eliminate the threat," Senator Joe Biden said in August 2002. "This is a guy who is an extreme danger to the world."[15]

"In the four years since the inspectors," Senator Hillary Clinton stated, "intelligence reports show that Saddam Hussein has worked to rebuild his chemical and biological weapons stock, his missile delivery capability, and his nuclear program." Stepping into what would become a controversial issue, Clinton volunteered that Saddam "has also given aid, comfort, and sanctuary to terrorists, including al-Qaida members."[16]

"When I vote to give the President of the United States the authority to use force, if necessary, to disarm Saddam Hussein, it is because I believe that a deadly arsenal of weapons of mass destruction in his hands is a threat, and a grave threat, to our security and that of our allies in the Persian Gulf region," said Massachusetts Senator John Kerry, who later adopted a quite different tone as the Democratic Party's presidential standard-bearer in 2004.[17]

"Iraq's search for weapons of mass destruction has proven impossible to completely deter," said former vice president and 2000 Democratic presidential candidate Al Gore, "and we should assume that it will continue for as long as Saddam is in power."[18]

Three of the Democratic front-runners for president—from the 2000, 2004, and 2008 campaigns—made absolutely clear their conviction that Saddam Hussein was a threat to our country. Yet when opposing the Bush administration's efforts in Iraq became politically convenient, they acted as if they had never said any such thing.

Throughout 2002, General Franks briefed the National Security Council numerous times on the evolving war plan. The latest version of the plan called for a force of up to 450,000 U.S. troops for a ground invasion. During the plan's development, CENTCOM planners had come up with the idea of "on ramps" and "off ramps" that would allow Franks to increase or slow the flow of troops into Iraq depending on circumstances. Franks believed that speed was the key to success in Iraq, as it had proved to be in Afghanistan.

Before an NSC meeting at Camp David, on September 7, 2002, Colin Powell called Franks to say he intended to ask a question about troop levels for the initial invasion. I thought calling Franks beforehand was a thoughtful thing for Powell to do, so Franks would not be caught off guard.

Franks told me about Powell's phone call, and I told him to respond directly to every point that Powell or anyone else on the NSC might raise. If Powell had concerns, Franks and I wanted him to lay them out in front of everyone for a serious discussion.[19] Powell was not only secretary of state, he was also a former chairman of the Joint Chiefs of Staff who knew a good deal about invading Iraq.

Powell had long been a proponent of the doctrine of "overwhelming force," known variously as the Weinberger or Powell Doctrine. This approach sought to correct the problems created by President Lyndon Johnson's gradual escalation policy in Vietnam during the 1960s and the deployments of small contingents of troops to places like Lebanon and Grenada in the 1980s. I appreciated the merits of overwhelming force, but complex operations in the real world often don't adhere to hard-and-fast rules. I have found that there often seem to be exceptions even to the wisest doctrines. It is appealing to seek simplicity and relief from the burdens and risks of continually having to make difficult judgment calls. Faced with major decisions, senior officials—military and civilian—need to be careful not to follow doctrine mechanically instead of engaging their judgments.

At Camp David, despite his call to Franks, Powell did not raise any questions about troop levels, the war plan, or the numbers of troops in a postwar environment though press stories, to my great surprise, reported that Powell later indicated that he had.[20] Instead, he expressed the thought that "long supply lines" might slow down the invasion.*

After everyone had an opportunity to comment, I surveyed the officials in the room from the Vice President to the Secretary of State to the National Security Adviser to the White House Chief of Staff to the Director of the CIA, and finally to the President. "I want all of you to be comfortable with this plan," I said. No one dissented. No reservations were voiced.

In addition to the 450,000 forces made available for deployment to the theater, the Iraq war plan, designated OPLAN 1003 Victor, authorized commanders to draw on thousands more U.S. forces in neighboring nations for support in logistics, intelligence, and communications. The plan called for 150,000 troops to be deployed immediately and an additional 300,000 kept in the pipeline as CENTCOM deemed necessary. Other troops would be supporting the ground forces from the air and sea. Additionally, we could count on support ranging from ground troops to overflight rights from forty-eight other nations.[22] With nearly half a million ground troops available if necessary, this was not the "light footprint" war plan some critics would later claim it was.[23]

In the autumn of 2002, as troops and supplies were moved to the region,

* I have no knowledge of what Powell may have said to individuals when not in my presence—such as news reporters. But in the National Security Council meetings I attended, this was the only time I heard Secretary Powell discuss the issue. A few years later, when that issue started to surface in the press, I asked both Rice and the President if they had any memory of Powell ever suggesting a need for more troops. Bush said Powell might have said something to him, but was uncertain. Rice said she was at all the meetings between Powell and the President and had no memory of Powell raising the issue.[21]

Franks, Myers, and I discussed a system called the Time-Phased Force and Deployment Data (TPFDD, pronounced "tip-fid") to manage deployments. It produced highly detailed plans for how and when specific units would be needed on overseas missions. Figuring out which reserve and active units and what supplies—literally hundreds of thousands of tons—were required for combat is an exceedingly complex task. Reserve units would have to be called up.* For every combat soldier—"the teeth" of the operation—there were large numbers of personnel needed for the support—"the tail." The TPFDD, as it existed, was an all-on or an all-off plan, with little flexibility in between. The problem was that we needed more than an on or off switch. We needed a rheostat that could ratchet up the American military presence in a way that complemented President Bush's diplomatic efforts. Our hope was that coordinated military and diplomatic pressure would persuade Saddam to back down and war could be avoided.

On November 26, 2002, two days before Thanksgiving, Franks came to Myers and me with what he called the "mother of all deployment orders." It would have authorized the flow of 450,000 troops to the Persian Gulf region as envisioned by the TPFDD. Franks' proposal would have put the switch to full "on." The problem was that from a diplomatic standpoint, the timing was not good. The next day, UN inspectors were reentering Iraq for another round of inspections. This was a critical component of the President's diplomatic approach. If I approved sending several hundred thousand U.S. troops to the Gulf at that moment, Bush would be accused of being intent on war no matter the result of the inspections. Though it might help convince Saddam Hussein of the President's seriousness of purpose, it could rattle potential allies.

Another consideration was the effect of the proposed deployments on military families, active duty and reserves, as we moved into the Christmas holiday season. I was concerned about having tens of thousands of our soldiers shipping out and leaving their families right before Christmas and New Year's Day if there was no need to do so, which at that moment there was not.†

*In the wake of the Vietnam War, the Army organization structure was changed so that the Army Reserves would have to be called up in the event of war. "They're not taking us to war again without calling up the reserves," General Creighton Abrams remarked. The TPFDD was a legacy of the military's post-Vietnam mindset.[24]

† At a commander's conference in February 2003, a midlevel officer stood up and, in his question, informed me for the first time that the Army was giving only five days' notice for National Guard and Reserve call-ups. It was a strikingly and unacceptably short lead time, given that members of the Guard and Reserves had full-time jobs and lives outside of that in the uniform. I felt they needed and deserved at least thirty days' notice of a possible call-up, if at all possible. And, in this case, it was possible, and in short order we managed to get the Army to fix its system.

I asked Franks if the plan could be adjusted to enable him to send troops to the region more selectively. This would help the troops and their families and be more supportive of the pace of the President's diplomatic efforts. It fell to General John Handy, the commander of U.S. Transportation Command, to improvise, by breaking up the TPFDD into smaller pieces and flowing the forces in at a more measured pace. Handy recognized the problem and deftly managed the task. Redesigning the flow of forces, rather than simply turning on the TPFDD, had its costs. Some logisticians complained about having their hard work scrapped in favor of a different flow. I could understand their frustrations. There was an important lesson to be learned, though: Military deployments not only needed to be more sensitive to the lives of those being called up, but they also needed to be more flexible so as to combine military considerations with presidential diplomatic initiatives.

To gain broader international support if the President were to decide in favor of military action against Iraq, he knew it would be desirable to have the backing of the United Nations Security Council. Though the irony was missed by most people, it was the Security Council's own resolutions on Iraq that the supposedly unilateralist Bush administration and its allies were seeking to enforce. As diplomatically and politically useful as a Security Council use-of-force resolution might have been, it was not a necessary precursor to military action. American-led coalitions had used our military abroad without the UN Security Council's approval on many occasions under both Democratic and Republican presidents dating back to the 1948 Berlin airlift.*

There was little doubt that at least some of the nations on the UN Security Council would not take part in an effort to dislodge Saddam. Russia and China, in particular, were often opposed to American proposals. France sometimes joined them.[25] Saddam's agents actively worked to cultivate their friends in Paris, Berlin, and Moscow by offering lucrative oil and other contracts. The French had an especially close, longstanding relationship with him. "France in particular," as Saddam put it when I met with him in 1983, "understood the Iraqi view."[26] French leaders in industry, and perhaps some in politics, not only "understood" Iraq; they came to profit handsomely from it. President Jacques Chirac, for one, seemed comfortable with Saddam,

* Other instances of military action without UN Security Council approval are: Vietnam War (1959–75); the liberation of Grenada (1983); the liberation of Haiti (1994–95); NATO's bombing of Bosnia and Herzegovina (1995); the U.S.-UK bombing of Iraq (1998); and NATO's bombing of Yugoslavia (1999).

whom he had shown around French nuclear power facilities in the 1970s. He had also negotiated an agreement to sell Iraq a nuclear reactor. In the decades that followed, France sold some $1.5 billion of military equipment to Iraq.[27] I don't doubt that Iraq's intransigence in defying the United Nations had been at least in part a result of Saddam's belief that the UN Security Council was ineffective, and that his friends there would continue to give him political cover. He was right—almost.

By the end of 2002, the United Nations had reached a new low. The organization's members seemed to have abandoned judgment and elected Libya, one of the world's most backward dictatorships, to chair the UN Commission on Human Rights. To top that, the UN made Iraq the chair of the UN Disarmament Commission. This put Saddam in the driver's seat of a body responsible for examining whether he was complying with disarmament obligations to the UN. And when it came to Iraq, the UN Oil-for-Food program had become a sad story of corruption and lies, as a later independent investigation established.*

As frustrating as the organization could be, it was not in America's interests to see the United Nations follow the path of its predecessor, the League of Nations, the organization that watched as Italy's Fascist forces invaded Abyssinia in 1935. President Bush wanted to rally the United Nations to support a U.S.-led effort to enforce the Security Council's resolutions on Iraq. British Prime Minister Tony Blair, a persuasive advocate, buttressed Bush's efforts. Bush and Blair, Powell and British Foreign Secretary Jack Straw coaxed and cajoled the members of the UN Security Council on the matter. Finally, on November 8, 2002, the Security Council voted 15-0 to support Resolution 1441. The resolution condemned Iraq's weapons programs, demanded that Iraq reopen suspected weapons facilities for inspection, and threatened "serious consequences" if Iraq failed to provide the UN a comprehensive list of the WMD it retained. The resolution stated that this was Iraq's "final opportunity" to comply with the international community.[29]

There had been no fewer than seventeen UN resolutions demanding that Saddam comply with various requirements since 1991. They specified that his regime demonstrate that it had: destroyed its WMD arsenal; ended support for international terrorists; stopped threatening neighbors; and ceased oppressing Kurds and Shiites. Because nothing seemed to result from their

* According to the Volcker report, "[D]ifferences among member states impeded decision-making, tolerated large-scale smuggling, and aided and abetted grievous weaknesses in administrative practices within the Secretariat. . . . As a result, serious questions have emerged about the United Nations' ability to live up to its ideals."[28]

noncompliance with the earlier resolutions, Iraq concluded, not unreasonably, that it could safely respond to this latest, UN Resolution 1441, with still another shrug.

Weeks later Saddam Hussein's regime produced a contemptuously incomplete declaration of their weapons programs. In December 2002, President Bush concluded that Iraq was in "material breach" of UN Resolution 1441.[30] United Nations weapons inspector Hans Blix reported to the UN that "Iraq appears not to have come to a genuine acceptance, not even today, of the disarmament which was demanded of it and which it needs to carry out to win the confidence of the world and to live in peace." Blix also said that based on an Iraqi Air Force document and Iraq's former claims, one thousand tons of toxic nerve gas, one of the most lethal chemical weapons, remained "unaccounted for." Since Iraq had actually used nerve gas before in the Iran-Iraq War, there was every reason to believe the regime still possessed it.[31]

Though Resolution 1441 was written as Iraq's last chance to come into compliance with its obligations to the United Nations—the tip-off to most people was the phrase "final opportunity"—some members of the Security Council proceeded to insist that there needed to be still another vote on an additional "this time we really mean it" resolution before they would sign onto any military action. Prime Minister Blair seemed to believe that it might be possible to obtain such a resolution and, along with it, additional international support, most notably from France and Germany. The other way to look at it—and perhaps the way Saddam did—was that this was an opportunity to further drag out the process.

Seeing the disappointing state of play, at one point Bush told me with a rueful smile, "This is a quagmire of my own making." In fact the diplomatic efforts surrounding the final months before combat operations began proved to not be anyone's finest hour.

CHAPTER 32

A Failure of Diplomacy

"War is a failure of diplomacy."
—source unknown

President Bush believed that the key to successful diplomacy with Saddam was a credible threat of military action. We hoped that the process of moving an increasing number of American forces into a position where they could attack Iraq might convince the Iraqis to end their defiance. On January 11, 2003, I approved the deployment of an additional thirty-five thousand troops, with aircraft and warships, to the Gulf region, sending still another signal that the time for cooperation was dwindling.

For a year, officials from both France and Germany had said they were looking for a diplomatic compromise with the United States that would open the way for them to support the use of force in Iraq, if it proved necessary. On January 22, President Chirac and German Chancellor Gerhard Schroeder announced that they would oppose ousting the regime.

It was a regrettable position for two longtime U.S. allies, not to mention historic rivals themselves, to oppose America's diplomatic and possible military effort as strongly as they did. In the United States critics used France and Germany to claim that "Europe" was opposed to the administration's stance on Iraq. That, of course, was not true. A large majority of European countries were supportive. More troubling, the French and Germans were, intentionally or not, giving Saddam's regime the impression that they could stop a military confrontation. By giving Saddam a false sense of security, and thereby reducing the incentive for him to comply with the UN's demands, the French and Germans undoubtedly made a war more likely, not less.

Hours after the French and German declaration, I traveled to the Foreign Press Center for a scheduled briefing of foreign reporters. One questioner asserted that the attitudes of the French and Germans were representative of "the mood among European allies."

"[Y]ou're thinking of Europe as Germany and France," I replied. "I don't. I think that's old Europe." I pointed out that if the reporters looked at the entire composition of NATO today, the center of gravity had shifted east with its new members. Those countries, I asserted, were "not with France and Germany on this. They're with the United States."[1]

I had no sense that anything I had said was anything other than blindingly obvious. But I soon learned that my "old Europe" comment had touched a raw nerve. It caused an uproar, especially from those who felt they were on the receiving end of my remark. The French Finance Minister called the comment "deeply irritating."[2]

Ironically, my comment was unintentional. I had meant to say France and Germany represented "old NATO" not "old Europe." As a former ambassador to NATO, I had been thinking of the alliance that existed when I served in Brussels. In the 1970s, when there were fifteen countries in the alliance, France and Germany played a large role. But after the Cold War's end, NATO extended membership to a dozen Eastern European nations, changing its size and outlook. While serving as secretary of defense in the Bush administration, I took a particular interest in visiting Eastern Europe and its leaders. I was comfortable with those countries, since Chicago has a large representation of Eastern Europeans.* This shift in the center of gravity of NATO eastward naturally reduced the role of France and Germany. Having been liberated from the Soviet Union only a short time earlier, the nations of Eastern Europe had a recent understanding of the nature of dictators, whether a Stalin, a Ceauşescu, or a Saddam Hussein.†

* I was reminded of that fact during a meeting in Vilnius with Lithuanian President Valdas Adamkus. "Secretary Rumsfeld," he said, "I remember you when you first ran for Congress in Illinois in 1962." Adamkus had lived in the Chicago area for a number of years. He told me that he ran on the Republican ticket for sanitary district trustee in Cook County at the same time I was running for Congress. "You won your race and I lost mine," he added. "But you're now a president," I replied. "I'd say you've made out all right for yourself."

† "If Americans had listened to some European leaders during the past 50 years," the President of Latvia told me, "we [Latvia] would still be in the Soviet Union."[3]

Shortly after my "old Europe" comment, and to counter France and Germany's negative position on Iraq, ten Eastern European nations jointly declared their support for military action. "Our countries understand the dangers posed by tyranny and the special responsibility of democracies to defend our shared values," their leaders declared jointly. "[W]e are prepared to contribute to an international coalition to enforce [UN Resolution 1441] and the disarmament of Iraq."[4]

In any event, the phrase "old Europe" entered the vernacular. The segment of Americans that preferred calling french fries "freedom fries" loved it. The elites in Paris and Bonn who thought themselves the guardians of a sophisticated, new world order did not. All in all I was amused by the ruckus.

Nearly fifty nations would join the American and British–led coalition willing to change the regime in Iraq—with thirty members committed to concrete, visible support and the others preferring to provide assistance more discreetly. As far as everyone on the NSC was concerned, the more nations involved in the invasion and in the postwar period, the better. It would mean less burden would fall on the United States and, in particular, on our military. I agreed with Churchill's formulation. "There is at least one thing worse than fighting with allies," he observed, "and that is to fight without them."

Yet even this impressive achievement did not prevent critics from accusing Bush of "acting alone." It was harmful, to say the least, when Senator John Kerry publicly denigrated the forty-five nations that were supporting the coalition effort in Iraq. He acidly referred to them as members of the "coalition of the coerced and the bribed."[5] This was an especially peculiar charge for two reasons. The first was that Kerry, like most of the Democrats in the Senate, had supported the decision to go to war—at least, when things seemed to be going well. Second, he presented himself as an internationalist, yet he was insulting our friends and allies and purposefully harming our coalition, simply to score a domestic political point.

The deeper irony was that his charge was perfectly misdirected. It was true that some nations in the coalition provided only a little help, but in some cases that was all they could afford to offer. Others, particularly the British, Polish, Spanish, and Australians, extended substantial help, in the form of military and civilian personnel and materiel. Given all we now know about the deep corruption in the Oil-for-Food program, if any nations might have been charged with having been bribed or coerced to take a position on the war in Iraq, it should have been some of the nations that opposed military action, not those that supported it.

In February 2003, to further rally international support and increase pressure on Saddam, President Bush decided that the United States would make a major presentation to the UN Security Council on the threat Iraq posed and its defiance of UN resolutions. The point person for that presentation was an obvious choice. Secretary of State Colin Powell was not only America's senior foreign policy official, he also carried substantial credibility at home and abroad.

As he prepared to make his case for military action against Saddam, Powell worked closely with Tenet and other senior CIA officials, traveling to CIA headquarters, meeting with analysts over several days, and working late into the night. Powell went over his presentation extensively with Condoleezza Rice to be certain they had analyzed all of the facts and information, and had raised every conceivable question, to hone America's case. Powell and his aides considered how to achieve an Adlai Stevenson moment—a reprise of the UN ambassador's forceful 1962 presentation to the UN during the Cuban Missile Crisis, which turned the tables on the Soviet Union.[6]

On February 3, two days before Powell was to go to New York, he sketched out his briefing to the President at an NSC meeting. "We have sources for everything," Powell confidently told the President. If Powell felt duped or misled about any aspect of his presentation, as some would later claim, there was no sign of it two days before he delivered it.[7]

Powell would touch on Iraq's links to terrorists and mention the small Kurdish town of Khurmal, which, the CIA had been reporting since early 2002 housed an underground facility for testing chemical weapons, including ricin and cyanide.[8] The site was operated by Ansar al-Islam, a Sunni extremist group with ties to Abu Musab al-Zarqawi, a Jordanian member of al-Qaida. A number of al-Qaida terrorists, including Zarqawi, were believed to be present at the Khurmal facility, having recently fled from combat in Afghanistan.[9] Some in the intelligence community believed elements of Ansar al-Islam were funded by al-Qaida and could be colluding with Saddam's regime. The reach of the Iraqi intelligence services was extensive in the country, with a vast network of informants, so it was not unreasonable to conclude that the Iraqi government knew of this fairly sizable terrorist operation.*

Many months before the February NSC meeting, Chairman Myers, General Pace, the vice chairman of the Joint Staff, and CENTCOM planners, in close coordination with the CIA, had developed a range of options to attack

* As the CIA noted at the time, "[I]t would be difficult for al-Qaida to maintain an active, long-term presence in Iraq without alerting the authorities or obtaining their acquiescence."[10]

Khurmal. They included a ground assault using CIA operatives, U.S. special operations forces, and Kurdish militia fighters known as the peshmerga. Another way was to destroy the facilities using cruise missiles and air strikes. The ground option had the advantage of collecting better evidence on the WMD operation, but given how well defended the site was, it was almost certain to entail casualties.

We were aware that the intelligence about the facility, though extensive, could not be considered conclusive. But taking all the risks into account, Myers and I were convinced that the intelligence was sufficiently persuasive to warrant military action. The members of the Joint Chiefs of Staff were also unanimous in their recommendation to strike.[11] We believed that hundreds of suspected terrorists, including Ansar al-Islam's senior leadership, suspected al-Qaida members, and an active chemical weapons facility were in our sights. With a military strike, we thought we would gain more clarity on the CIA's reporting on Iraqi WMD programs in short order. Myers, Tenet, and I went back to the President and the NSC several times in 2002 to urge an attack on the facility. Each time we were unpersuasive. Powell and Rice were concerned that a U.S. strike within Iraq's borders could cause Saddam to take action against the Kurds and make America's diplomatic initiatives in building a coalition and gaining support at the UN more challenging. Bush agreed with them.

In February 2003, as Powell briefed the National Security Council on his upcoming UN speech, I spoke up once again on Khurmal. If we were ever going to hit the facility and have a favorable result, we would have to do it at the same time, or preferably just before, Powell spoke, since he would be telling the world that we knew about the WMD facility. Once the terrorists learned from Powell's speech that we were aware of their presence, they would flee.

Before the NSC meeting ended, I offered my recommendation for the last time: "We should hit Khurmal during the speech," I said, "given that Colin will talk about it."

Powell objected. "That would wipe out my briefing," he said, adding, "We're going to get Khurmal in a few weeks anyway."[12]

In his dramatic address before the UN Security Council on February 5, 2003, Powell presented recordings, satellite photographs, and documents that he argued proved that Iraq was engaged in WMD activities in defiance of the UN. "My colleagues, every statement I make today is backed up by sources, solid sources," Powell told the Security Council. "These are not assertions.

What we are giving you are facts and conclusions based on solid intelligence."[13]

On the subject of nuclear weapons, Powell left no room for doubt about his convictions about Saddam's intentions. "[W]e have more than a decade of proof that he remains determined to acquire nuclear weapons," Powell said, with the authority of his years of military and diplomatic service. "Saddam Hussein is determined to get his hands on a nuclear bomb." He echoed the Agency's estimates about linkages between the Iraqi regime and al-Qaida. "[W]hat I want to bring to your attention today," he said, "is the potentially much more sinister nexus between Iraq and the al-Qaida terrorist network, a nexus that combines classic terrorist organizations and modern methods of murder."[14] Powell went on to finger Khurmal. "[T]he Zarqawi network," he said, "helped establish another poison and explosive training center camp . . . and this camp is located in northeastern Iraq."[15]

As expected, shortly after Powell's speech was delivered, many of the terrorists fled Khurmal. When our troops and intelligence operatives eventually arrived there in March 2003, days after the war in Iraq began, they engaged in a firefight with the terrorists remaining.[16] By then, much of the facility had been destroyed by cruise missile strikes and fighting on the ground, but clear signs of chemical weapons production were found, including chemical hazard suits, manuals to make chemical weapons in Arabic, and traces of the deadly toxins cyanide, ricin, and potassium chloride.[17] For whatever reason, the administration never made public these facts about an active WMD production facility run by terrorists in Iraq. Members of Ansar al-Islam would later become part of the insurgency. Ironically, had Powell not objected to the DoD and CIA proposal to attack the Khurmal site before he gave his presentation to the UN, we might have been able to gather the conclusive evidence of an active WMD facility, that he said existed in his UN speech.

As we now know, portions of Powell's presentation about Iraq's WMD programs proved not to be accurate, but something interesting happened over the years that followed. Here was a briefing, personally developed by the Secretary of State, with the close assistance of the National Security Adviser, the CIA Director and the intelligence community. It was consistent with strong statements of congressional support for military action, including those from many prominent Democrats, as well as with the assessments of several foreign intelligence agencies. And yet, over time, a narrative developed that Powell was somehow innocently misled into making a false declaration to the

Security Council and the world. Powell himself later contended, in defense of his participation, "There were some people in the intelligence community who knew at that time that some of these sources were not good, and shouldn't be relied upon, and they didn't speak up. That devastated me."[18] When asked why these people did not speak up, he replied, "I can't answer that."[19]

Powell had spent decades in uniform and had become the most senior military officer in our country, and at every level he had spent long hours dealing with intelligence. As President Reagan's national security adviser, he routinely had been exposed to reporting and analysis from the intelligence community. As secretary of state, his department's own intelligence agency reported to him. There was no one else in the administration who had even a fraction of his experience in intelligence matters, including CIA Director Tenet. Powell was not duped or misled by anybody, nor did he lie about Saddam's suspected WMD stockpiles. The President did not lie. The Vice President did not lie. Tenet did not lie. Rice did not lie. I did not lie. The Congress did not lie. The far less dramatic truth is that we were wrong.

Whatever those in old Europe may have thought, Iraq's neighbors took a different view of the prospect of military action. In meeting after meeting in Washington and in the region, Arab leaders confided to us that Saddam was a danger in their part of the world. Some believed he was irrational, citing reports that he had taken to writing out the verses of the Koran in his own blood. They made clear that they would be better off if Saddam were gone, though some were uneasy about publicly supporting the idea of a U.S. military invasion. They noted that the last time they had supported military action against Iraq, Saddam remained in power—angry, dangerous, and still threatening. I suspect that that must have made subsequent gatherings of the Arab League somewhat awkward.

In my visits with leaders from other countries in the Gulf and North Africa, I received another oft-repeated message: If you go after Saddam, do it quickly. The leaders were worried about the "Arab street" erupting in anger at the West's invasion of a Muslim country. I was skeptical of the idea that a monolithic Arab street existed. My experiences suggested that each Arab country was different, but I did understand that popular discontent could cause them difficulties.

During my time in the Bush administration, I went to Vice President Cheney's office only occasionally. Our positions were such that we were not working together daily, as we had thirty years earlier in the Nixon and Ford administrations. So it was somewhat unusual when Cheney asked me to come over to the White House for a confidential meeting on January 11, 2003.

Joining us were Myers, and Cheney's guest: Prince Bandar, the Saudi ambassador to the United States. No voice in the region tended to be as crucial when it came to U.S. interests as Saudi Arabia. At ease in American culture—Bandar smoked, rooted for the Dallas Cowboys, and cited the Founding Fathers—he still retained the ear of the Saudi elite. Bandar's diplomatic credibility was burnished by a colorful background that included service as a Saudi Air Force pilot.

"The President has made the decision to go after Saddam Hussein," Cheney told the Prince. Of course Bush would not irrevocably decide on war until he signed the execute order for Operation Iraqi Freedom—that would come only hours before the first military actions commenced—but this was the first time I had heard a senior administration official speak with such certainty about imminent military action. The President had apparently asked Cheney to alert the Saudis that the United States was serious and would request their cooperation. The United States needed several military facilities in Saudi Arabia to accommodate coalition forces that would be taking part in the invasion.

Though Bandar did not seem surprised, the Ambassador was leery. "Let's not repeat the mistake of the President's father," he said, referring to the decision in 1991 to stop short of taking Baghdad and removing Saddam Hussein. The unfortunate impression that the United States might retreat after sustaining some casualties was apparently not shared only by Saddam Hussein and Osama bin Laden. Bandar thought Saudi support was "doable," but with caveats. The Saudi people would not support a long period of combat operations in a neighboring Arab country. He emphasized the importance of having a small American footprint in the kingdom and in Iraq once our troops toppled Saddam.[20]

The Saudis' position, echoed by other Arab states, was that the U.S.-led invasion should be quick and decisive, and that the U.S. troop presence in Iraq should be small and reduced rapidly. General Franks had consulted with many leaders in the region and had received similar messages.

U.S. diplomatic efforts with another key ally in the region were foundering. Despite optimistic assurances from our diplomatic corps, the United States was having trouble persuading Turkey to permit transit across their country, from the north into Iraq. In the months leading up to the critical vote of Turkey's parliament, the administration had confidence that they would grant us the approval we sought. No one had anticipated that the vote might fail. I remembered thinking in the early months of Bush's presidency that it was important for us to work closely with the Turks, because we might need their cooperation.[21] That day had come. But the Turkish parliament did not approve the U.S. transit request, by a razor-thin margin.*

The lack of support by a key NATO ally in the region was a serious operational setback, as well as a political embarrassment—and very likely an avoidable one. Powell might have aided our efforts by traveling to Ankara to make our case personally. I also might have visited Turkey in those crucial weeks, or encouraged President Bush or Vice President Cheney to make a personal appeal to the Turkish leadership.

Without a threat to Saddam's forces in the north and west from U.S.troops advancing from Turkish soil, enemy fighters would have an opportunity to escape to the north and operate in the Sunni-dominated provinces where there would be no coalition presence early on. Our inability to invade Iraq from Turkey may well have been a key factor in the rise of a Sunni-backed insurgency after major combat operations ended. Turkey's decision made it essential that Franks find other ways to get coalition forces to Baghdad and the north of Iraq as quickly as possible, to close off the Iraqi military's escape routes.

As harmful as all of this was, there was a modest upside. In the summer of 2002, I received word that a *New York Times* reporter had detailed information about a version of CENTCOM's classified war plan for Iraq, and that his paper was going to run a story on it. I asked General Pace to call the *Times* to urge the paper to not run the story. We did not want Saddam's forces to be better prepared against us and put more American lives at risk. Pace made the call, but the *Times* published the story anyway, though with some modifications.[22] At the time I dictated a note to myself. "It would be wonderful if everyone who likes to leak memos and everyone who likes to publish classified material had a daughter or son in the advanced party of every military operation," I said. "I suspect it would get their attention."[23]

The newspaper reported that CENTCOM's plan was to send American

* A majority of the Turkish lawmakers voted in favor of the law allowing our forces to pass through Turkey on the way to Iraq, but the 264 to 251 vote failed to meet a parliamentary rule that required a majority of those present to vote in favor. Because there were 19 abstentions, three more votes in favor of the resolution were needed for it to pass.

forces into Iraq from the north and west through Turkey, and to use another invasion force that would enter Iraq from the south, thereby creating a vise around Baghdad that might trigger a quick Iraqi surrender. Even though on the eve of military action, the Iraqis knew, like everyone else, that Turkey had voted against helping our military effort, the *New York Times* had said otherwise. Because of that article, Saddam's generals prepared to repel an attack from the north anyway. Apparently they had not yet learned that you can't believe everything you read in the press.

A major story line about the invasion of Iraq has been the debate about troop levels—whether the U.S. invasion force or stabilization force should have been larger.[24] In realify, there was full debate and discussion, but there was no disagreement among those of us responsible for the planning. The officer in charge of preparing the Iraq war plan was General Franks. The chief military adviser to the President and the NSC was General Myers. Among Myers, Franks, and me, there was no conflict whatsoever regarding force levels. If anyone suggested to Franks or Myers that the war plan lacked sufficient troops, they never informed me. Moreover, if anyone did do so, they were unsuccessful, since they did not dissuade Franks from his view, nor Myers from his, nor, to my knowledge, any of the chiefs from theirs.

In December 2002, the *Washington Post* made headlines with a story that two members of the Joint Chiefs of Staff were opposed to the war in Iraq and to the war plan they had participated in developing, and had approved. "[A]spects of the plan, which appear riskier than usual U.S. military practice, worry the chief of the Army, Gen. Eric Shinseki, and the commandant of the Marine Corps, Gen. James L. Jones, defense officials said" the paper declared.[25]

I was astounded by the report, which, if true, deserved the headline it generated. It would be most unusual, to say the least, for sitting members of the Joint Chiefs to publicly oppose the Commander in Chief, the Secretary of Defense, the responsible combatant commander, as well as the Chairman of the Joint Chiefs of Staff on the eve of a potential war. Both Jones and Shinseki had been invited to, and for the most part attended, the many deliberations on the Iraq war plan in "the Tank"—the Joint Chiefs' conference room—with Franks. They had each taken part in a number of meetings with the President, with Myers, and with me.[26] Neither Jones nor Shinseki raised concerns, either about the wisdom of President Bush's intention to go to war if diplomacy failed or of Franks' war plan on how to fight it.[27]

The day the story appeared I called each of them on the phone, reaching Jones first. "General Jones," I said, after referencing the *Post* article, "you have had every opportunity to talk and you haven't."

"You're right," Jones responded.[28] A seasoned insider known for his skill in navigating the Washington political scene, Jones knew well the effect of appearing in the press criticizing a war plan, particularly when he hadn't raised a single criticism of it on the inside. He said it wouldn't happen again. He told me explicitly that he wanted me to know he was "on board with the plan." To my knowledge, Jones never corrected the record with the *Washington Post*.

Though Jones seemed to take responsibility for the remarks attributed to him, Shinseki was a different matter. When I raised the article with him, he indicated that the story was not true, and that he had not expressed doubts to anyone.

"Who do you believe?" Shinseki asked. "The *Washington Post* or me?"[29]

When he put it that way, I was not inclined to believe a press report over what a four-star general said to me personally. Even though Shinseki was adamant that the *Post* had the story wrong, no correction from Shinseki found its way into the paper either.

The incident reveals much about how Washington works. Neither general was directly quoted in the story saying he was skeptical, yet on the front page of the *Washington Post* they were so portrayed. Each denied the central element of the story. Still, the story ran, was never corrected or retracted, and as a result, Shinseki and Jones gained reputations as war skeptics and heroes to war critics. I respect both Shinseki and Jones for their service to our country, but I cannot explain their failure to correct the public record.*

Six weeks after the article appeared, President Bush invited the senior military officials to the White House to give them still another opportunity to review and offer their comments on the war plan. I accompanied the combatant commanders and the Joint Chiefs of Staff to the cabinet room on January 30, 2003. Once we were gathered, the President went around the long table. Looking each of them squarely in the eye, Bush asked the four-star officers in uniform, one at a time, to offer their views and to raise any questions or issues they might have. This was one more chance for the most senior officers of the United States military to express any reservations they might have directly to the President, the Chairman of the Joint Chiefs, General Franks—the responsible combatant commander—and me. No one in the room—not

*Both generals went on to serve in the Obama administration: Shinseki as secretary of veterans affairs and Jones as national security adviser.

General Shinseki, not General Jones, nor anyone else—raised an objection. These were all decorated, experienced senior officers, not wilting wallflowers. I assumed and expected that they would speak up if they had reservations—indeed, it was their duty to do so. They did not.

It was not long before Shinseki, I believe unintentionally, would again be catapulted into the public spotlight. That February, after having been called to testify to Congress about the impending war, the soft-spoken general became one of the most famous members of the Joint Chiefs of Staff in recent history—a poster child, even a martyr, for opponents of the war.

The popular version of the General's now famous February 2003 testimony is that Shinseki testified to members of Congress that far more troops would be needed in Iraq than were provided for in the war plan. Because he had supposedly spoken truth to power, the *New York Times* claimed he was later "vilified, then marginalized" by members of the Bush administration, including me.[30] Both assertions were false.

It is undoubtedly too late to correct the literally hundreds of misstatements that were repeated in what Jamie McIntyre, the Pentagon reporter for CNN, described as a media-generated myth elevated to "the level of Scripture."[31]

General Shinseki appeared before the Senate Armed Services Committee on February 25, 2003, before the war started. During his testimony, he was asked a question by Senator Levin of Michigan, the ranking Democrat on the committee.

> LEVIN: General Shinseki, could you give us some idea as to the magnitude of the Army's force requirement for an occupation of Iraq following a successful completion of the war?
>
> SHINSEKI: In specific numbers, I would have to rely on combatant commanders' exact requirements. But I think . . .
>
> LEVIN: How about a range?
>
> SHINSEKI: I would say that what's been mobilized to this point—something on the order of several hundred thousand soldiers are probably, you know, a figure that would be required. We're talking about posthostilities control over a piece of geography that's fairly significant, with the kinds of ethnic tensions that could lead to other problems. And so it takes a significant ground-force presence . . .[32]

It remains a mystery why Levin would decide it was in our country's interest to publicize in an open hearing Franks' planned number of troops four weeks before the war began, but it was not Levin's unusual question that received attention. Shinseki's response began a media firestorm that sought to pit what some journalists and war critics characterized as his lone, courageous voice against an administration bent on war.

Reflecting on his actual comments, what Shinseki said was unremarkable. He noted that the forces mobilized in the region to that point were probably enough. He also said he deferred to the combatant commander, General Franks, for the exact requirements. When asked by journalists about Shinseki's comment, I should have known better than to respond to a quote that I had not heard myself, but I took the bait. So did Paul Wolfowitz, who characterized Shinseki's answer as "wildly off the mark." We were focused on avoiding any signals to the enemy about how many troops Franks had in mind. Bush's political opponents inflated Shinseki's comments into a grand confrontation with the administration he served, though, in fact, there was no clash at all.

It was later claimed that, in retaliation for Shinseki's comment, I authorized a leak of the name of his supposed replacement, Army Vice Chief of Staff General Jack Keane, a year before Shinseki was slated to retire. I did not talk to the press about Shinseki's successor, nor did I ask anyone else to do so. Neither the President nor I had decided on Shinseki's replacement. Furthermore, when the dust settled it was not Keane at all but General Pete Schoomaker, and only after Shinseki had completed every day of his full four-year term as chief of staff and retired with full honors.

Shinseki was not dismissed early or otherwise rushed out the door. Yet literally hundreds of news reports in the press and on television falsely declared that General Shinseki was fired for insubordination and "shunted aside."[33] Critics of the administration explained Shinseki's silence during the war—he declined to respond to press requests or correct the record—as the result of the alleged shunning he supposedly had suffered at the hands of senior Department officials. This hardened into a myth that he was punished for telling the truth about the war. Its promoters cite as evidence that I did not attend Shinseki's retirement ceremony. The truth is that Shinseki did not invite me, despite the fact that several senior officers urged him to do so.

As Shinseki was departing in June 2003, he addressed the controversy that journalists had inflated into a major crisis in civilian-military relations in a private end-of-tour memorandum. "During the February testimony, I didn't believe there was a 'right' answer on the number of forces required to stabilize Iraq," he wrote. Shinseki said that his testimony was "misinterpreted."[34]

He saw that his testimony had been distorted for political purposes. Perhaps someday he will publicly correct the gross and repeated mischaracterizations in the media.

The Shinseki myth did harm to civilian-military relations. It became widely believed among the military's active and retired communities, which came to resent the bad treatment I supposedly inflicted on a general officer. The myth also bolstered the allegation that I was intolerant of views that challenged my own and that I punished those who put them forward.

In fact, the opposite was the case. I welcomed and made a point of encouraging different views, dissent, and challenges. It was a constant refrain of mine at meetings that all proposals and plans are based on assumptions, that those assumptions should be spelled out clearly, examined skeptically, and reexamined routinely—and that applied also, indeed especially, to my own. Everyone makes errors in judgment, and the higher the official, the worse the consequences can be. So it was a principle with me that subordinates should speak up.

In 2002, for example, I sent a snowflake to a representative of the CIA who sat in on some of my Pentagon meetings:

> When I told you I want you to speak up, I meant it. You know a whale of a lot about this subject, and every once in a while I see you in the back of the room looking reticent. That doesn't help me at all! I need you to step up and say, "Have you thought about this?" or "What about that?" or "I think differently." I am very comfortable with that. You may not want to do it to some of the other principals, but I am delighted to have you do it to me.[35]

As I believe in being challenged, I also made a practice of challenging my challengers. I wanted to make sure people disagreeing knew what they were talking about. When a challenger failed to support his views, I did not pretend to be impressed. But, in my view, no professional, let alone a three- or four-star military officer, should be intimidated into silence by a boss who asks questions and expects sensible answers, even honest answers as simple as an "I don't know, but I'll get back to you."

While the President and I had many discussions about the war preparations, I do not recall his ever asking me if I thought going to war with Iraq was the right decision. The President was the one charged with the tough choice to commit U.S. forces. I did not speculate on the thought process that brought him to his ultimate, necessarily lonely decision. We were all hearing the same things in briefing after briefing, and one NSC meeting after another, mulling over what we knew of the Iraqi regime and what the intelligence community believed about its capabilities and intentions. Though there were differences among us, they were not differences at the substantive or strategic levels of whether or not to allow Saddam Hussein's regime to remain in power. Not one person in NSC meetings at which I was present stated or hinted that they were opposed to, or even hesitant, about the President's decision. I took it that Bush assumed, as I did, that each of us had reached the same conclusion.

The process toward war had been incremental. Up until the very minute the President authorized the first strike, there was no moment when I felt with razor-sharp certainty that Bush had fully decided. Like the rest of us in the chain of command, Bush was reluctant to use force and invite the serious challenges it entailed. This came through in his dogged attempts to bring the UN onboard to enforce their own sanctions and his ongoing diplomatic initiatives to stave off armed conflict. It seemed to me Bush was balancing a growing imperative to take military action and a natural reluctance to commit American troops and our nation to such a struggle.

Wars, it has been correctly said, are failures of diplomacy. And in the run-up to the war with Iraq, institutions, nations, and individuals failed. The United Nations failed to live up to its charter by not enforcing its resolutions. France, Germany, and Russia contributed to the failure by allowing Saddam to believe they would forestall action and he did not need to comply with the UN resolutions. For our part, we as an administration and as individuals failed to persuade Saddam or his top generals that we were prepared to take down his regime if necessary.

I wondered if we worked hard enough through intermediaries to encourage him to find another way out.* I thought, or at least hoped, to the very end that he might decide at the last minute that he would prefer a comfortable exile to the risk of capture and death. Other dictators, such as Haiti's Jean-Claude "Baby Doc" Duvalier and Uganda's Idi Amin, had made similar choices to save their lives. Why not Saddam Hussein? If Saddam actually believed we were serious, I thought that his instinct for survival might work to our advantage. It would not be easy to stomach Saddam sipping Campari on the coast

*On September 30, 2002, for example, I dictated a note: "I want to talk to the Vice President about getting Tenet active in getting Arabs in states to help offer Saddam a way out."[36]

of southern France, but if his comfortable exile meant sparing the world—and thousands of American men and women in uniform—a war, I was all for it.

On March 17, 2003, President Bush made yet another effort to avert war by offering Iraq's ruling family one last chance to avoid an invasion. It was an overture I urged and supported fully. "Saddam Hussein and his sons must leave Iraq within forty-eight hours," Bush said in a primetime address from the White House. "Their refusal to do so will result in military conflict commenced at a time of our choosing."[37]

Unmoved, the Iraqi leader was shown on Iraq's state television in full military uniform chairing a meeting of his ruling Baath Party and his top generals. Saddam's eldest son, Uday Hussein, even issued an ultimatum of his own, urging President Bush to "give up power in America with his family."[38] Saddam Hussein was defiant—for the last time.

CHAPTER 33

Exit the Butcher of Baghdad

Only a few hours before the forty-eight-hour deadline for Saddam to leave Iraq for a life in exile expired, George Tenet called me from CIA headquarters in Langley. He said he had an urgent matter to discuss and would be coming to the Pentagon immediately.

The CIA had developed a network of informants across Iraq who reported tips on Saddam's activities. In my office, Tenet informed General Myers and me that two of the Agency's sources had information that Saddam Hussein and possibly his sons, Uday and Qusay, were en route to a family compound called Dora Farms, south of Baghdad. We knew there was a possibility that the informants could be compromised, or in error. Saddam constantly tested the loyalty of those around him. If the dictator had penetrated the CIA's network of informants, he could be using the sources to encourage us to strike a false target, possibly one where American bombs might kill innocents. The campaign might therefore begin amid charges of American war crimes against Iraqi civilians.

If Bush authorized a strike, it might have to take place before the public deadline set for Saddam to resign expired. Though we had no indication that Saddam might comply, Bush would be accused of going back on his word. Tenet and I agreed that the issue needed to be brought to the President, so we drove across the bridge over the Potomac to the White House.

By mid-afternoon Bush had hastily assembled the NSC in his small dining room just off the Oval Office. Tenet repeated what he had told me. "How solid are your sources on this?" Bush asked. Tenet expressed his high level of confidence.

We discussed the possible outcomes if a strike were ordered, the risk of action as well as the risk of inaction. Suppose it turned out that Saddam was meeting at the compound to comply with the President's ultimatum to resign and leave Iraq? What if it turned out to be a civilian target? What if our aircraft accidentally killed innocent Iraqis and Saddam got away?

As we contemplated these risks, Tenet left the room to speak by secure phone to Agency officials who were in touch with their source on the ground in Iraq. He came back with another promising report: Saddam had just arrived at the site in a taxi. The Iraqi dictator was known to use cars painted like taxis to move around the country inconspicuously. The Agency's contacts also reported that Saddam's whereabouts had been verified by a sophisticated electronic tracking system used by his bodyguards. Tenet believed the intel was as solid as it could be.

The President went around the room asking each of us if we favored a strike. Cheney, Powell, Myers, Tenet, and Rice all said yes, as did I. I felt Saddam had made his choice. He was not going to stand down. Removing him and his sons with an early air strike would eliminate the top of the Iraqi military command structure with a single blow. That might lead to a large-scale surrender of Iraqi military forces, saving many American and Iraqi lives. Any chance to avert a broader war had to be seriously considered. The President agreed. But keeping his word, he ordered that the attack commence after his forty-eight-hour deadline expired.

In the early morning hours of March 20—only ninety minutes after the deadline—two U.S. Air Force F-117 stealth fighters flew undetected into Iraqi airspace and released four one-ton bunker-busting bombs onto the Dora Farms complex. The war in Iraq had begun.

As we awaited confirmation that the attack had hit the target, early reports were promising. An eyewitness reported that Saddam Hussein had been brought out of the rubble on a respirator. Then the story started to change. Despite the multiple sources, at least one eyewitness, and the sophisticated tracking devices, Saddam was not, as it turned out, at Dora Farms. Neither were his sons. This first salvo in the war with Iraq foreshadowed the various intelligence failures that would later come to light.

Forty-five minutes after U.S. aircraft had dropped the first bombs targeting Saddam, President Bush appeared on television from the White House to inform the country that the war in Iraq had begun. Saddam responded with a broadcast to the Iraqi people, claiming that Americans would soon lose "patience" with the war effort.[1] He ended his message with language characteristic of Islamists: "Long live jihad and long live Palestine."[2] It was a notably unsubtle message—one that made clear the allies he sought.

General Franks had realized that it was not possible to achieve strategic surprise against Saddam's forces given the purposefully ill-disguised fact that our military had been building up in the region over several months. Nonetheless, Franks thought he might still gain an advantage through tactical surprise. In the 1991 Gulf War, and in our recent operations in Afghanistan, coalition forces conducted a long air campaign before the ground invasion. This was undoubtedly what Saddam and his generals expected to happen again, which would give the Iraqis time to lobby leaders in the Muslim world and Saddam's supporters at the United Nations to come to his aid before our tanks started rumbling across the desert. Instead, Franks decided to order the air and ground offensives to start simultaneously.

Franks was concerned that a delayed ground invasion might expose American forces staging in Kuwait and elsewhere in the Gulf to the risk of chemical or biological attack. Intelligence and military officials warned that once Saddam judged that our forces were on the march and approaching Baghdad to remove his regime, he would have nothing left to lose and would likely use WMD against the coalition forces. Based on the intelligence, Franks ordered American soldiers and Marines advancing into Iraq to be outfitted with the bulky and uncomfortable chemical and biological protective suits.

The initial coalition push toward Baghdad from the south had two thrusts. The first was spearheaded by the Army's 3rd Infantry Division, and the second by the 1st Marine Expeditionary Force (I MEF) and Task Force Tarawa. At the same time, a contingent of Marines took their objectives in the southern Rumaila oilfields to prevent Saddam from sabotaging the Iraqi people's most valuable natural resource, as he did during the first Gulf War. While British forces successfully took the southern city of Basra, American forces moved rapidly toward Baghdad, engaging the enemy along the way only as necessary.

There was less fighting in the south than had been expected. Many of Saddam's conscript forces, fearing the fate they would meet against coalition armor and airpower, deserted their positions, removed their uniforms, and fled to their homes.

During the first nights of the campaign, some American special operations

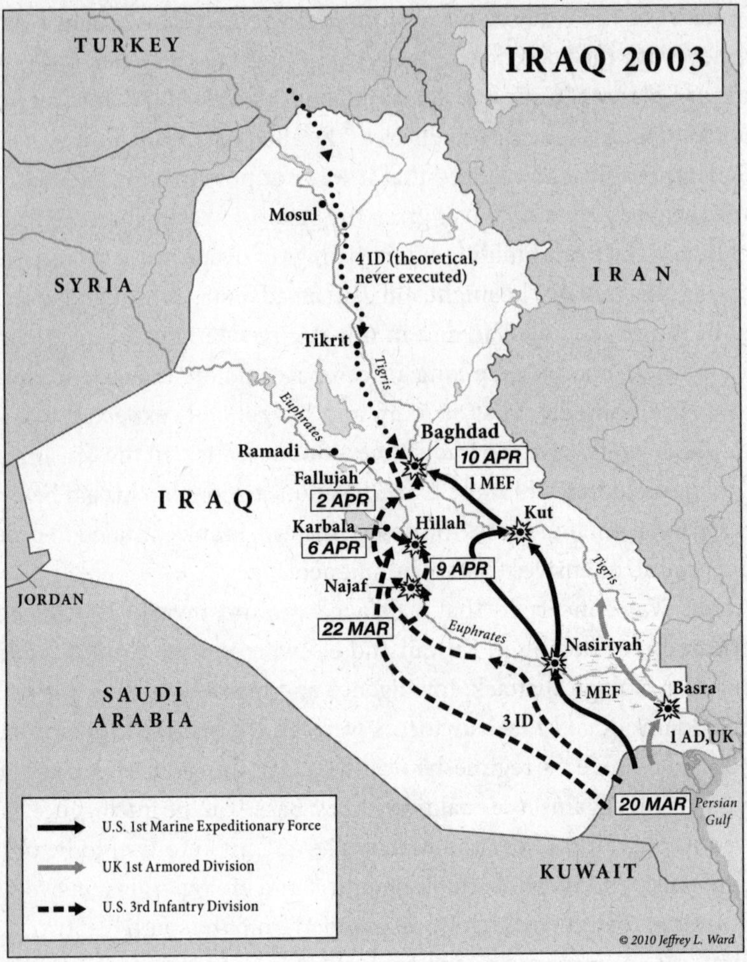

commandos dropped into northern Iraq while others stalked the western deserts. As in Afghanistan, they used night vision and handheld laser devices to identify Saddam's forces, which American aircraft proceeded to attack with pinpoint accuracy.

Coalition forces met their first sustained challenge when they advanced on the city of Nasiriyah, a key strategic target because it commanded crossings over the Euphrates River. Given the city's importance, American forces expected resistance from the Iraqi army. Instead, the enemy took the form of hundreds of Fedayeen irregular forces that had arrived in trucks, buses, and taxis. Eleven U.S. troops were killed in the fighting. A nineteen-year-old private named Jessica Lynch was captured by the enemy and extravagant reports about her resistance to capture flooded the media.* In hindsight, the real story out of Nasiriyah was the role of the Fedayeen Saddam and the magnitude of the threat they posed. Our intelligence community had not anticipated the kind of enemy that coalition forces eventually faced in Iraq—or the kind of irregular operations by Saddam's paramilitary forces that foreshadowed the insurgency. Not until our forces were on the ground did we learn the extent to which the Fedayeen Saddam had stockpiled weapons and ammunition in nearly every city, town, and village in the country to help quell any uprising against Saddam. The Fedayeen were trained in counterinsurgency and capable of promptly and ruthlessly suppressing revolts against him.

The Fedayeen soon emerged as the core of an irregular enemy that attracted hundreds, and eventually thousands, of foreign fighters from across the Muslim world looking to fight the West. American forces routinely found a variety of foreign passports on the bodies of enemies they captured or killed in battle. Most of the passports documented that their bearers had crossed into Iraq from Syria. These non-Iraqi jihadists tended to be poorly armed with Kalashnikov rifles and rocket-propelled grenades, but they had the ability to blend in well with the Iraqi civilian population, and they fought with the fervor of fanatics.

As it turned out, weeks before the war began, Saddam's ministry of defense had made efforts to integrate Arab jihadists into Iraqi training camps.[3] Captured documents describe legions of Muslim fighters from Syria, Libya, Bulgaria, Turkey, Tunisia, Egypt, United Arab Emirates, and the Palestinian territories.[4] One, dated March 27, 2003, describes an Iraqi intelligence official's conversation with the leader of Hamas in Gaza in which "[h]e requested us [the Iraqi government] to open the checkpoints at the border to let the volunteer fighters participate in the war."[5] The report continued, "Hamas is willing to carry out demonstrations and suicide attacks to support Iraq." Captured log records also documented the steady stream of foreign fighters into Iraq during this period.[6] Saddam ordered that Arab Fedayeen volunteers receive the same salaries and benefits as Iraq's Special Forces.[7]

It soon became clear that the gaps in our intelligence about the Fedayeen Saddam were signs of a broader problem. For years there had been an

*The reality was different from the media storyline. In the fog of war, Lynch's unit had become lost after taking a wrong turn, and in a firefight she had been wounded and captured. Lynch's captors took her to a local hospital, where a courageous Iraqi reported her whereabouts to U.S. forces. After her rescue, Lynch reportedly remembered little about the ordeal, but like most American troops who had volunteered to serve their country, she was brave and dedicated.

overreliance on reconnaissance from aircraft and satellites rather than on-the-ground human intelligence. The problem was not endemic only to the CIA. Intelligence agencies within the Defense Department, such as the Defense Intelligence Agency, also failed to assess correctly the threat posed by the Fedayeen. While the attraction of foreign jihadists to the conflict in Iraq was possible given their hatred of America, the fact is that our intelligence agencies failed to warn of the possibility, and, as a result, our forces were not well prepared for it.

We would discover more gaps in U.S. intelligence. We would find that the reality on the ground ran counter to the prewar intelligence reporting that had informed CENTCOM's planning. It turned out that Iraqi infrastructure was not in serviceable condition; most of it was ramshackle and disintegrating. It turned out that the Iraqi army did not remain in whole units capable of being used for reconstruction after liberation; it dissolved itself. It turned out that the Iraqi police was not a trustworthy, professional force capable of securing the country after the invasion; they would have to be recruited and trained from scratch.

This intelligence failure on the existence and capabilities of the Fedayeen and foreign jihadists to wage an asymmetric war against our troops posed daunting consequences for the coalition effort. American forces that were prepared to fight more conventional forces had to adapt to an enemy that hid among civilians and fought by means of ambushes, car bombs, and improvised explosive devices (IEDs). The Fedayeen and foreign jihadists fighting our troops in March and April 2003 would form the core of an insurgency that would engulf Iraq later in the year.

The coalition force's advance toward Baghdad coincided with a *shamal*, a massive sandstorm that turned the skies over Iraq orange. In some places, the sand mixed with rain and became an unpleasant mud. Though the shamal slowed the U.S. drive northward, it did not stop it. Nor did it turn into the advantage for the Iraqi army that many thought it might.[8] Iraqi forces around Baghdad believed the clouds of sand would give them cover. But our Joint Surveillance and Target Attack Radar System (JSTARS) aircraft in the sky above were able to penetrate the dust clouds with infrared cameras that could see the Iraqi forces below as they repositioned their armor. The Iraqis were stunned as American bombs, with demoralizing precision, broke through the clouds of dust and sand to destroy the Iraqi tanks.

One week after the invasion began, General James Conway, commanding general of the I MEF, and General William Wallace of the Army's V Corps ordered a seventy-two-hour pause to resupply their troops. I understood the reason for the pause, given the logistical challenges involved with the movement of tens of thousands of troops, thousands of pieces of armor, trucks, and humvees, and supplies. The pause, however, led to news reports that U.S. forces were "bogged down," this time in an Iraqi quagmire.[9]

Despite concerns about the accuracy of some of the press coverage, we decided to give news reporters unprecedented access to real-time information as the war was underway. During the planning phase, the Pentagon's assistant secretary for public affairs, Torie Clarke, approached me with the creative concept of embedding reporters with American forces from the outset of the war. Clarke was aggressively engaged in making the Pentagon responsive to a continuously evolving media environment.

Myers and I weighed the pros and cons of Clarke's proposal and came to the conclusion that embedding reporters was worth the risk. We believed it would give them a firsthand understanding of the courage and the professionalism of the men and women in our armed forces. Some seven hundred reporters and photographers were embedded with American forces when the war in Iraq began.[10] The process created new burdens for our forces, since they had to provide the journalists with food, shelter, transport, and, importantly, be responsible for their safety. No single element of the invasion force had the whole picture. But we concluded they could do a better job presenting the reality of the conflict than they would pool reporting from coalition headquarters.

The program posed risks for the journalists. From 2003 to 2009, seven embedded reporters were killed in Iraq, and several others were wounded.[11] The embedded reporters' bravery was a proud chapter in American journalism. Despite the dangers, many journalists acknowledged the success of the embedding experiment. Some of the best reporting from the war and the postwar period came from these reporters. The *New York Times'* John Burns and Dexter Filkins had some of the most compelling coverage from the field with stories that hewed closely to the facts. To my surprise and disappointment, the program eventually became controversial within the press corps. One reporter told me that continuing to embed with U.S. troops meant being ostracized by other reporters who contended that a close linkage with the military could compromise their objectivity.

There was a flip side to the media coverage in Iraq that I also found telling. A month after Saddam's regime was toppled, the chief news executive at

CNN, Eason Jordan, wrote an op-ed in the *New York Times* titled "The News We Kept to Ourselves." He belatedly described some of the horrific crimes committed by Saddam Hussein's regime against Iraqis suspected of being too cooperative with reporters, including an instance in which the secret police beat a woman every day for two months and forced her father to watch. Jordan revealed that the Iraqis smashed her skull and tore her body apart limb by limb. CNN knew about these acts of barbarism for over a decade but had reported not a word of it out of fear the Iraqi government might eject them from their Baghdad news bureau.

"I felt awful having these stories bottled up inside me," Jordan confessed. "Now that Saddam Hussein's regime is gone, I suspect we will hear many, many more gut-wrenching tales from Iraqis about the decades of torment. At last, these stories can be told freely," he added.[12]

During major combat operations in Iraq, the Pentagon adopted what the military calls a "battle rhythm." For many in the Department, long days grew even longer. Saturdays and Sundays became like any other day of the week. For me, a typical day began at 6:45 a.m. when Powell, Rice, and I talked over the phone. We needed to keep each other apprised of what had occurred overnight (daytime in Iraq and Afghanistan) and what we expected might happen over the coming twenty-four hours. Powell would give diplomatic updates and Rice would pass on any questions or concerns the President might have. That call would typically be followed by a thirty-minute secure videoconference at 7:25 a.m. with General Franks and his senior commanders, as well as the senior civilian and military leaders at the Pentagon, including the Chairman and the Joint Chiefs. Using slides and statistics, Franks would report on the progress of his operations. I would call the President if there was anything I needed to report immediately. And it was not unusual for Bush to call me with a question about a report or a news story he had seen or if he was concerned about some aspect of the campaign. The day would be interspersed with NSC and principal committee meetings at the White House and more operational updates, as well as meetings with members of Congress and our coalition partners.

As the advance on Baghdad resumed after the sandstorm and subsequent pause for resupply, the 82nd and 101st Airborne Divisions entered the war. Two brigades of the 101st Screaming Eagles, under the command of Major General David Petraeus, were airlifted outside of the holy city of Najaf, the site of the revered Imam Ali Mosque. Block by block, the 101st cleared the city of enemy fighters, and then advanced toward Hillah, where the Hammurabi Division of the Iraqi Republican Guard blocked the way to Baghdad. Hillah was one of the relatively few places where conventional Iraqi forces directly engaged our forces. Petraeus' troops reduced the Hammurabi Division to wreckage. The last obstacle before Baghdad having been cleared, nothing stood between our forces and the southern outskirts of Iraq's capital city.

Media analysis suggested that the battle for Baghdad might be like the brutal siege of Stalingrad during World War II.[13] There were reports that Saddam Hussein had seen the movie *Black Hawk Down*, about the ill-fated U.S. involvement in Somalia.[14] The lesson he and other enemies had taken away was that American forces could be defeated in urban conflict because our tolerance for casualties was judged to be low. Some in the White House also feared that Saddam could turn Baghdad into an urban nightmare for American and coalition troops by using the city neighborhoods as death traps. This was by far the most urgent concern of Rice and White House Chief of Staff Andy Card, who, before the war began, had asked for numerous briefings on the subject. Franks grew impatient with the number of times he was asked to brief on Fortress Baghdad at the White House.

After pushing through the Karbala Gap on the outskirts of Baghdad and securing the river crossings into the capital, U.S. forces were poised to take the

DICK WRIGHT, TRIBUNE MEDIA

city. Some of the fiercest fighting took place around Baghdad International Airport.* Intelligence was reporting that Fedayeen, regular army and Republican Guard units had massed in central Baghdad. U.S. troops launched what became known as thunder runs into the heart of the city to test the strength of the resistance.

As columns of U.S. tanks and armored vehicles sped through Baghdad, the world was introduced to an unconventional celebrity. He was a figure who not only provided comic relief in a time of war, but also offered a disturbing insight into the delusional world that was the Saddam Hussein regime. The Iraqi minister of information, Muhammed Saeed al-Sahhaf, popularly known as Baghdad Bob, had a special talent for either ignoring unwelcome facts or lying about them shamelessly.

After U.S. forces seized the Baghdad airport, he claimed: "We butchered the forces present at the airport. We have retaken the airport! There are no Americans there!" But as Baghdad Bob was making his wild pronouncements on television, just around the corner American forces seized Saddam's parade ground downtown. Confronted with this evidence, he was impressively undaunted. "There you can see," Baghdad Bob said. "There is nothing going on."[15]

Despite Baghdad Bob's protestations to the contrary, the U.S. military's thunder runs into Baghdad damaged the Iraqi forces' morale and killed large numbers of Iraqi and foreign fighters. U.S. forces encountered not the Special Republican Guard divisions they expected but instead legions of jihadists on the streets of Baghdad. Saddam knew his Republican Guard tank divisions were no match for the American military, but the fanatics armed with small weapons and craving martyrdom proved to be formidable foes.

On April 9, 2003, the Marines reached Firdos Square in the heart of Baghdad. "The midget Bush and that Rumsfeld deserve only to be beaten with shoes by freedom-loving people everywhere," Baghdad Bob declared, as American troops fixed a rope around the neck of the larger than life statue of Saddam that dominated the square, much as his likeness populated the rest of the capital city and the entire country.[16]

*One mile east of the airport, Army Sergeant First Class Paul Ray Smith and the soldiers of the 3rd Infantry Division were clearing a position to hold enemy prisoners of war. Without warning, Republican Guard troops began firing from a nearby watchtower, and nearly one hundred Iraqi troops threatened to overrun his position and an aid station where dozens of wounded American soldiers were receiving medical attention. Smith manned a machine gun and led a counterattack from an exposed position. Though he would not survive the battle, Smith prevented Saddam's men from attacking the aid station, saving the lives of over a hundred American soldiers. For his courage, Paul Ray Smith became the first to receive the Congressional Medal of Honor in the wars that began after September 11, 2001.

Our forces were understandably exhilarated by the prospects of the liberation of Baghdad they had made possible. As the statue of Saddam was pulled down by Iraqis and Marines, one Marine draped an American flag over the statue's head. I remember General Myers expressing concern and calling someone at CENTCOM to fix the problem. Whether Myers' message got through or not, the American flag was removed. As the statue came down, a crowd of Iraqis began to beat Saddam's likeness with their shoes—an Arab expression of disrespect. Critics of the war would belittle those who claimed the Iraqis would greet the Americans as liberators—and to be sure not all Iraqis did—but in Firdos Square that day, the sentiment was clearly one of liberation.

Saddam's regime collapsed twenty-one days after the war began. The invasion was accomplished with skill, precision, and speed—and a minimum of casualties—by Franks, his team at CENTCOM, and the men and women volunteers in uniform. It was a heady moment. Less than two years after 9/11, the U.S. military had changed the regimes in Afghanistan and Iraq, two of the world's leading sponsors of terrorism.

PART XI

The Occupation of Iraq

Baghdad, Iraq

APRIL 9, 2003

As cheering Iraqis in the heart of the capital brought down the over life-sized statue of Saddam Hussein, a scene decidedly less euphoric was occurring in a Sunni neighborhood just across the Euphrates. More than one hundred armed Iraqi soldiers, many wearing civilian clothing, entered the National Museum of Iraq. They took up sniper positions to contest the final advance of American soldiers and Marines into Baghdad and tried to turn the museum into a fortress.

A custodian of Iraq's long and rich history, the Iraqi National Museum housed a peerless collection that illuminated the beginnings of civilization. The importance of this heritage was lost on no one, least of all the American military. CENTCOM planners had put the National Museum of Iraq high on the coalition's "no-strike" list.*

Immediately after the regime collapsed in early April 2003, Iraqis across the country released pent-up grievances against the tyranny that had smothered them and impoverished their country for over thirty years by looting from government buildings. Looters ransacked and stripped Saddam's palaces bare of furniture and decorations. Faucets and toilets in many public buildings disappeared, and wires were pulled from walls to salvage the copper. Stealing back property that was considered stolen from the Iraqi people struck them, evidently, as justified.

The looting made it appear that postwar Iraq was descending into chaos. A camera caught an Iraqi taking a vase out of a building in Baghdad—and that scene was replayed over and over across the world. This was accompanied by images of coalition troops standing by in tanks. The implication? America was fiddling while Baghdad burned.

A flood of disaster stories gushed forth. News organizations wildly asserted that nearly all of the museum's collection had been looted.[1] "[I]t took only

*The list also included hospitals, mosques, and schools.

48 hours for the museum to be destroyed," the *New York Times* reported, "with at least 170,000 artifacts carried away by looters."[2] But the news stories tended not to blame the Iraqi fighters for breaking into the museum, turning it into a combat zone, and putting its collections at risk. "American troops were but a few hundred yards away as the country's heritage was stripped bare," National Public Radio claimed.[3] Some even accused American servicemen of participating in the reported heists.[4] "You'd have to go back centuries, to the Mongol invasion of Baghdad of 1258, to find looting on this scale," said one British archaeologist.[5]

Across the world, officials, especially those opposed to the war, made a great complaint. United Nations Secretary General Kofi Annan piled on, issuing a statement "deplor[ing] the catastrophic losses."[6] French President Jacques Chirac, a man of bottomless cynicism whose anti-Americanism had become reflexive, called the alleged museum looting "a veritable crime against humanity."[7] As if the ill-grounded comments of foreign officials were not enough, I then had the experience of turning on the television and seeing my colleague, Secretary of State Powell, in Washington issuing what was in essence a public apology on behalf of the U.S. government about the museum looting, with a promise to recover what was lost.[8]

Iraq and Afghanistan were the first wars of the twenty-first century—the first where operations were reported in real time on blogs, talk radio, and twenty-four-hour news channels. The public was hearing all kinds of allegations and one-sided, sensational reports. It took a while for the facts to catch up. Contrary to early reports, coalition forces had moved rapidly toward the museum to secure it. When American troops arrived, there were no visible looters. The advance on the building was halted, however, when our troops came under a barrage of sniper fire and rocket-propelled grenades from inside. The American commander on the ground faced a vexing choice. If his troops engaged further with the enemy forces in the museum, he risked destroying portions of the building, including whatever artifacts were within.[9] Because the rest of Baghdad was rapidly falling under coalition control, the commander decided to hold back, expecting that enemy forces in the building soon would disperse.

I thought the looting being reported was tragic, but I did not fault our troops. Iraq is the size of the state of California. Unfortunately, it would have been impossible to gather a force large enough to stop it all. In addition, General Franks had a long list of priorities for his troops that were as important, if not more so. They had to defeat remaining enemy units. They had to search the suspected WMD sites identified by the CIA. They had to secure large caches of weapons that had been placed all over the country. They had to locate, seize, and secure government documents that Iraqi officials were no doubt busily shredding. They had to find Saddam Hussein and other senior Iraqi officials, to bring an earlier end to the war. They had to act as local police, since the Iraqi army and police force had unexpectedly disappeared.*

It had been only days since coalition forces had ended Saddam Hussein's regime in a military campaign prosecuted faster and more successfully than most had predicted. Meanwhile, critics of the administration had made error after error—calling the campaign in Afghanistan a quagmire just days before the overthrow of the Taliban government, calling the advance on Baghdad a quagmire just days before American forces overthrew the Saddam Hussein regime—yet they never seemed to lose credibility. Now critics were once again selling the public and the world a bill of goods about the alleged looting of the national museum and the alleged indifference of American forces to this supposed rape of Iraq's cultural heritage, which also proved not to be the case. The irresponsible reporting was harmful to our troops just as they were trying to build relationships with Iraqi citizens.

At the same time these unsettling allegations were being made, my family was undergoing a personal crisis. In the first week of April, Joyce became extremely ill. It was increasingly clear something was terribly wrong. It turned out that she was suffering from a ruptured appendix. The problem had gone undiagnosed for some days. Our daughter Valerie flew in to be with Joyce at the hospital. At the time, I was spending more than fifteen hours a day at the Pentagon. I would visit Joyce in the hospital in the early morning and then again in the late evening hours. At one point she looked so pale and weak that she reminded me of how her wonderful mother, Marion, looked just before she died at age ninety.

Though Joyce would eventually and thankfully make a full recovery, all of this weighed heavily on my mind when I was preparing for a Pentagon press briefing on April 11, 2003 as the looting furor continued. I intended

*At one point, I commented to General John Abizaid and General Myers: "The history books suggest that the way they stopped looting in earlier era[s] in Iraq was to get the tribes to provide security for things like electric power lines and oil wells." I asked, "Have we considered talking to some of the tribes about providing that security and paying them for it, like we would police, and having them be responsible?" It would be precisely these tribes that would prove critical to achieving a level of security in the country three years later.[10]

to remind the press and the American people about the success our forces had just achieved. I wanted to put events in context and defend our troops. I thought I could tamp down the controversy. Unintentionally, I wound up fueling it. A reporter asked me if I thought the words "anarchy" and "lawlessness" were ill chosen to describe the situation in Iraq. "Absolutely," I responded. I expressed my frustration that reporters insisted on highlighting the negative aspects of Saddam's ouster, which was a positive, albeit complex event.

"Given how predictable the lack of law and order was, as you said, from past conflicts," another queried, "was there part of General Franks' plan to deal with it?"

In fact, military planners had expected a difficult transition period. CENTCOM had prepared plans to institute martial law if the commanders thought it necessary.[11] CENTCOM's public order plan hinged on a key intelligence assumption that proved to be inaccurate: The existing Iraqi police could be helpful in keeping order.* The military had experienced what Generals Myers and Franks and I ironically called "catastrophic success." Because Saddam's forces had crumbled so rapidly, our troops were able to liberate Baghdad even faster than anticipated. "Freedom's untidy," I said. "Free people are free to make mistakes and commit crimes and do bad things. They're also free to live their lives and do wonderful things, and that's what's going to happen here."[13] Then I vented some annoyance by uttering a few ill-chosen words: "Think what's happened in our cities when we've had riots, and problems, and looting. Stuff happens!" I was thinking back to the riots in American cities after the assassination of Martin Luther King, Jr., when whole blocks of Washington, D.C. were set aflame.

I had uttered more than a thousand words at that press conference before I said "stuff happens," but they were the only two words that seemed to matter. My point was that in all wars, bad things happen. During World War II, cities across Germany suffered from looting and chaos soon after Allied troops entered. The northern city of Bremen was, as one shocked onlooker described it, "probably among the most debauched places on the face of God's earth" as liberated Germans looted stores, museums, and government buildings.[14] Liberated Iraqis were doing the same thing, filling the temporary vacuum that

*The intelligence community assessed that the Iraqi "police and justice personnel appear to have extensive professional training," as one brief provided to the NSC principals asserted. This proved to be off the mark. To a great many Iraqis, the police force was equated with the abuses of Saddam's regimes. The police lacked legitimacy and thus authority, posing a major problem for the coalition as an insurgency took root.[12]

existed between the old order and the new. What I said was characterized as callous and indifferent. Once I saw how my comments were being interpreted in the media, I realized I had made a mistake.

As it happened, most of what the media had reported about the museum looting—that monstrous "crime against humanity"—turned out to be false. After reports about the looting of the Iraq National Museum first surfaced, CENTCOM's director of operations, Major General Gene Renuart, dispatched Marine Colonel Matthew Bogdanos to Baghdad to investigate. Though press reports commonly reported 170,000 items stolen, Bogdanos discovered that only a tiny fraction of that was actually looted.[15] Somewhere between 3,000 and 15,000 items were later proved missing from the museum collections.[16] Those numbers included the state-sanctioned looting, theft, and forgery that Saddam Hussein's regime had used as a source of revenue for some years.[17] The press claims that had become an international sensation, Bogdanos concluded, were "intentionally false, a fiction perpetuated first by some museum staff, and then repeated by the press."[18]

I also received firsthand information about the museum from an unusual source. Our informant was a spy who had been in Baghdad prior to the invasion. Days before coalition bombs began falling on regime targets in the capital, he had visited the already closed national museum. He peered through the museum's windows and found none of the museum's antiquities on display. Well before the war started, it appeared, the museum curators had put tens of thousands of pieces in safe vaults or taken them out of Baghdad.* This same plan had been used in the Iran-Iraq War and during the first Gulf War. The museum staff also left doors unlocked, which suggested that the director, a Baathist and Saddam ally, intended for the fighters and looters to move about freely in the compound.

A few media outlets belatedly issued some corrections, but not with anything approaching the prominence of their original false reports of extensive looting.† "Officials at the National Museum of Iraq have blamed shoddy reporting amid the 'fog of war' for creating the impression that the majority of the institution's 170,000 items were looted in the aftermath of the fall of Baghdad," noted the *Daily Telegraph* one month later.[20] One museum official

*Today the Baghdad Museum is open and thousands of ancient Near Eastern artifacts have been moved back into their displays.

†The situation brought to mind a quote I had read: "The power of the media is willful and dangerous because it dramatically affects Western policy while bearing no responsibility for the outcome. Indeed, the media's moral perfectionism is possible only because it is politically unaccountable."[19]

tried to explain the confusion: "I said there were 170,000 pieces in the entire museum collection . . . not 170,000 pieces stolen. . . . No, no, no. That would be every single object we have!"[21]

Those in the press who created and spread the grossly false and harmful stories about the museum looting took no responsibility for the negative pall that quickly engulfed the coalition's efforts. It was as if the news media had shrugged its collective shoulders and said "stuff happens."

CHAPTER 34

Catastrophic Success

Before the war, officials in the Department of Defense spent many months analyzing contingencies and risks—both the risks of war and the risks of leaving Saddam Hussein in power. We knew the United States could defeat Iraq's forces in a reasonable period of time, but the more difficult challenge came after the end of major combat operations. Our military was well organized, trained, and equipped to win wars. Winning the peace after an enemy regime has been removed is quite another matter. There were many difficulties still ahead when the statue of Saddam Hussein was pulled down in Firdos Square on April 9, 2003, but it was not the absence of postwar contingency planning that caused them.

Some who might have been in a position to know better suggested that the Iraq war would be a "cakewalk" and that the risks were few.[1] That was not the view of those who would be ordering the men and women of our military into combat—not President Bush, not me, and not any of those I worked closely with at the Pentagon. In fact, the members of our Defense Department team were thinking long and hard about potential problems in post-Saddam Iraq.

No war has ever gone according to plan, but that did not absolve any of the President's advisers of their duty to prepare carefully and consider the possible perils that our forces might face. Because of the public controversy and divided opinions over the impending war, I believed it was important to give the President a full set of things to consider, especially those arguing against military conflict.

In the autumn of 2002, during a National Security Council meeting on Iraq, I departed from the agenda to read a handwritten list of possible problems, later referred to as the "Parade of Horribles," that I believed could result from an invasion. Sitting at the table in the Situation Room, with Bush, Cheney, Powell, Rice, Tenet, and the others in attendance, I went through the items one by one. The list was meant to generate serious, early thinking about the potential risks and what might be done to assess and reduce them. I also hoped to encourage others on the NSC to raise their concerns. That discussion was brief.

Because I considered the topic so important, when I returned to the Pentagon I used my notes to draft a memo, which I sent to a few of the Department's senior civilian and military advisers for comment. The DoD policy shop and dozens of military planners at CENTCOM and on the Joint Staff had been working long hours on contingencies in the event of war. Taking their suggestions into account, I expanded my original list and submitted it as a memo to the President and the members of the NSC. "It is offered simply as a checklist," I noted, "so that they are part of the deliberations."[2]

With regard to the risks of an invasion, my memo listed a number of problems that were worth thinking about in case they materialized, though they ultimately did not:

- While the US is engaged in Iraq, another rogue state could take advantage of US preoccupation—North Korea, Iran, PRC in the Taiwan Straits, other?
- There could be higher than expected US and coalition deaths from Iraq's use of weapons of mass destruction against coalition forces in Iraq, Kuwait and/or Israel.
- Fortress Baghdad could prove to be long and unpleasant for all.[3]

My memo to the NSC also directed attention to some serious risks that did in fact materialize, in whole or in part:

- US could fail to find WMD on the ground in Iraq and be unpersuasive to the world.

- US could fail to manage post–Saddam Hussein Iraq successfully, with the result that it could fracture into two or three pieces, to the detriment of the Middle East and the benefit of Iran.

- Rather than having the post-Saddam effort require 2 to 4 years, it could take 8 to 10 years, thereby absorbing US leadership, military and financial resources.

- Iraq could experience ethnic strife among Sunni, Shia and Kurds.

- World reaction against "pre-emption" or "anticipatory self-defense" could inhibit US ability to engage [with other countries in order to deal with problems of common concern] in the future. [4]

To take just one for example, I understood that if WMD were not found, the administration's credibility would be undermined. That was why I felt we needed to make sure everyone understood that WMD was only one of the many reasons underlying the decision to remove Saddam. If we had had a full discussion of this possibility then, it might have made an important difference in the administration's communications strategy. It also might have tempered the WMD-focused briefing Powell would make to the UN Security Council several months later in February 2003.

My memo did not argue for or against military action in Iraq. That was not the intent. Indeed, at the end, I noted that "it is possible of course to prepare a similar illustrative list of all the potential problems that need to be considered if there is no regime change in Iraq."[5] I wrote the memo because I was uneasy that, as a government, we had not yet fully examined a broad enough spectrum of possibilities. Unfortunately, though the Department of Defense prepared for these contingencies in our areas of responsibility, there was never a systematic review of my list to the NSC.

To analyze what an American presence in postwar Iraq might look like, we needed to know with precision what the desired objective was—what were America's goals. In March 2001, six months before 9/11, I had written a short paper titled "Guidelines When Considering Committing U.S. Forces" that summarized what I believed the commander in chief should consider before ordering combat operations.[6] The memo was intended to help the administration establish a framework for when and how military force should be applied, and under what circumstances. I had seen over the years that there often was pressure on presidents to use military force without clearly achievable military objectives.

When it came to the administration's goals in Iraq, my views were straightforward. They were to help the Iraqis put in place a government that did not threaten Iraq's neighbors, did not support terrorism, was respectful to the diverse elements of Iraqi society, and did not proliferate weapons of mass destruction. Period. The aim was not to bestow on it an American-style democracy, a capitalist economy, or a world-class military force. If Iraqis wanted to adapt their government to reflect the liberal democratic traditions espoused by Thomas Jefferson and Adam Smith, we could start them on their way and then wish them well.

As soon as we had set in motion a process, I thought it important that we reduce the American military role in reconstruction and increase assistance from the United Nations and other willing coalition countries. Any U.S. troops remaining in Iraq would focus on capturing and killing terrorists and leftover supporters of the old regime that were still fighting.

I questioned the way earlier administrations had used the military in post-conflict activities. When we took office in 2001, more than twelve thousand forces remained in the Balkans performing tasks that might have been turned over to local security forces earlier.[7] Throughout my tenure, I focused on reducing the American military presence in Bosnia and Kosovo and assigning security responsibilities to local security forces or international peacekeepers from countries more directly affected by potential instability in the area.*

I recognized the Yankee can-do attitude by which American forces took on tasks that locals would be better off doing themselves. I did not think resolving other countries' internal political disputes, paving roads, erecting power lines, policing streets, building stock markets, and organizing democratic governmental bodies were missions for our men and women in uniform. Equally worrisome, locals could grow accustomed to the unnatural presence of foreign forces acting as their de facto government and making decisions for them. The risk was that these nations could become wards of the United States.

My experience in Lebanon during the Reagan administration also demonstrated the problem of dependency on U.S. forces in countries facing internal strife and violence. By late 1983, the Marine presence in Beirut was just

*In the 2000 campaign, candidate George W. Bush had indicated that he was similarly ill disposed to sending American troops to take on "nation-building" missions. "I don't think our troops ought to be used for what's called nation-building," Bush said.[8]

about the only thing keeping the country from either descending into a civil war or falling under Syrian domination. When President Reagan, spurred by the Congress, withdrew the Marines, Lebanon quickly succumbed to Syria.

One of the guidelines in my memo on putting American forces at risk was that a proposed action needed to be "achievable—at acceptable risk." "We need to understand our limitations," I wrote. "The record is clear [that] there are some things the U.S. simply cannot accomplish."[9] Thus, at the Department of Defense, postwar planning for Iraq had begun with the generally accepted recognition that recent efforts to rebuild nations had been flawed. We had tried to avoid those mistakes in Afghanistan by emphasizing the importance of building up indigenous security forces, both army and police, and promptly establishing a new, independent government under the leadership the Afghans selected. But unfortunately the U.S. military seemed to be doing most of the postcombat stabilization and reconstruction work on its own. Despite tireless efforts by the Defense Department's comptroller, Dov Zakheim, to solicit funds and assistance from friends and allies for reconstruction, their contributions were minimal.[10] At the Bonn conference in 2001, the United Nations had treated Afghanistan's reconstruction like Solomon's baby, but without Solomon's wisdom. Reconstruction activities had been divided among different coalition nations—training the police and border guards (Germany), rebuilding a judiciary (Italy), counternarcotics (Britain), disarming militias (Japan)—without any realistic assessment of their ability to deliver. Afghanistan's reconstruction proved largely to be a series of unfulfilled pledges by well-intentioned but poorly equipped coalition partners. So too the contributions of the civilian departments and agencies of our government were modest.

I understood that there were times when the United States would not be able to escape some nation-building responsibilities, particularly in countries where we had been engaged militarily. It would take many years to rebuild societies shattered by war and tyranny. Though we would do what we could to assist, we ultimately couldn't do it for them. My view was that the Iraqis and Afghans would have to govern themselves in ways that worked for them. I believed that political institutions should grow naturally out of local soil; not every successful principle or mechanism from one country could be transplanted in another.

As early as the summer of 2002, well before the Iraq war, the Pentagon policy team, led by Doug Feith, was developing an approach that would allow Iraqi opposition elements—including the Kurds of semiautonomous northern Iraq and the sizable exile community—to participate in an interim governing body. A key member of our policy team, Assistant Secretary of Defense Peter Rodman, sketched out some of the imperatives we needed to consider.*

The post–World War II German and Japanese models of reconstruction, Rodman contended, were the wrong analogies. Rather, he suggested we look to postwar France, where Roosevelt and Churchill planned an Allied military occupation because they did not think Charles de Gaulle commanded the respect of the French people. When De Gaulle returned to France after D-Day and millions came to greet him, however, Allied military planners, led by Eisenhower, reconsidered. Rodman observed that if the Allies had gone ahead with the plan for occupation, the Communists, who were then the backbone of the French anti-Nazi resistance, "would have taken over the countryside while the allies sat in Paris imagining that they were running the country."[11]

Rodman's point was that we didn't want Americans holed up in Baghdad deluding themselves that they were actually controlling the country. There were "bad guys all over Iraq—radical Shia, Communists, Wahhabis, al-Qaeda—who will strive to fill the political vacuum," Rodman presciently warned. To prevent a vacuum, the U.S. government should begin preparing moderate Iraqis to take over their country. I agreed with Rodman's analysis.

Feith and Rodman alerted me that in the interagency discussions at the deputies committee level and below, the State Department had different ideas.† Officials at State favored what they called a Transitional Civil Authority, led by the United States, that would govern post-Saddam Iraq for a multiyear period. State's idea, as Rodman wrote, "is that (1) the Iraqi opposition is too divided to fill the vacuum on its own, and (2) the U.S. will want to control what happens with Iraqi WMD, oil, etc."[12]

On July 1, 2002, I forwarded Rodman's assessment to Cheney, Powell, Tenet, and Rice, in the hope that they might be similarly persuaded that an American occupation would be a mistake:

*Rodman had come of age as a protégé of Henry Kissinger during the Nixon and Ford administrations. Like Kissinger, he was a strategist who thought long term, the kind of adviser I favored. Rodman was a quiet presence in Department meetings. When he spoke, it was with unusual precision and insight.

†The deputies committee was the most senior interagency forum below the cabinet level. Departments were represented by the deputy secretaries or under secretaries in the meetings.

> Organizing the Iraqi Opposition to assist with regime change is needed for two reasons: to ensure legitimacy, particularly in the eyes of other regional players, and to make sure the wrong people don't fill the vacuum created by the end of the Saddam regime. Regional leaders have argued that it is important for Iraqis to be seen participating in the liberation of their country. . . . An attempt to run Iraqi affairs by ourselves *without* a pre-cooked umbrella group of Iraqi Opposition leaders could backfire seriously. . . . In Iraq, there are many undesirable opposition elements—a Communist faction, Sunni fundamentalists, and radical Sh'ia—all with presumably some support around the country and in some institutions. Organizing the democratic opposition groups that we favor into a real political-military force is essential to preempt these groups, avoid a political vacuum, and avoid a chaotic post-Saddam free–for-all.[13]

A chaotic post-Saddam free-for-all was the last thing we wanted if President Bush decided to go into Iraq. I was reasonably certain that the memo was read, but it did not lead to any resolution on a postwar strategy by the NSC.

At CENTCOM headquarters in Tampa, General Franks and his staff prepared the Iraq war plan in its four required parts: Phase I, preparations for a possible invasion; Phase II, shaping the battle space with the start of air operations; Phase III, decisive offensive and major combat operations; and Phase IV, posthostilities stabilization and reconstruction. In the summer and fall of 2002, Franks and his team had a lot on their plates. In addition to Iraq war planning, they were still engaged in counterterrorism operations in Afghanistan and maritime interdiction operations off the Horn of Africa.

Recognizing the burdens on CENTCOM, Myers expressed concern that it might not be paying sufficient attention to Phase IV.[14] Franks admittedly had little enthusiasm for setting up a postcombat government or dealing with the related tangle of bureaucratic and interagency issues. As the general noted in his memoir, "I'm a war fighter, not a manager."[15] Myers advised me that he had decided to establish a new group to help CENTCOM plan for postcombat operations. He asked Franks to stand up Combined Joint Task Force 4, which would work in Franks' Tampa operation on Phase IV.

Outside of the Pentagon, teams at the United States Agency for International Development, the NSC, and the State Department also were working on plans for the postwar period. Among these initiatives was the Future of Iraq project at State, which consisted of a series of documents addressing aspects of postwar Iraq.[16] Later, the State Department effort was dubbed in the press as "the earliest and most comprehensive planning undertaken by the U.S. government for a post-Saddam Iraq."[17] Some of the participants in the project later mischaracterized that work as a State Department plan that Pentagon officials ignored. "Many senior State Department officials are still bitter about what they see as the Pentagon's failure to take seriously their planning efforts, particularly in the 'Future of Iraq' project," the *Washington Post* wrote some years later.[18]

In fact, senior DoD officials did review and consult those papers, finding some of them to be helpful. But the Future of Iraq project—outlining broad concepts—did not constitute postwar planning in any sense of the word. There were no operational steps outlined in them nor any detailed suggestions about how to handle various problems. One State Department official, Ryan Crocker, a future ambassador to Iraq, was heavily involved in the project and he later acknowledged, "It was never intended as a post-war plan."[19] If it had been, it could at least have given us a blueprint to discuss and consider.

The Future of Iraq papers were likely circulated at lower levels within the government, as is often the case with concepts and proposals. But I was not aware of an effort by any senior official at State to present these papers for interagency review or evaluation, as would certainly have been needed had they been intended as a plan. The notion that a few in the State Department may have alerted people to potential problems in postwar Iraq—even if quite helpfully—was not on its face a seminal achievement. I had listed problems that might arise in postwar Iraq in my "Parade of Horribles" memo. That does not mean my memo was a plan or a solution.

Further complicating matters prior to the war was an undercurrent of concern about the wisdom of even conducting large-scale planning. This could signal that America considered war inevitable and derail President Bush's diplomatic efforts, which continued almost until the day the war began.

In discussions of postwar Iraq, the toughest challenge was the tension between two different strategic approaches. The debate between them was legitimate, but it remained just that—a debate. It was never hashed out at the NSC and never finally resolved. Right up until the handover of sovereignty to the Iraqis in 2004, the basic difference was between speed—how quickly we could turn over authority—and what was called legitimacy—exactly what political and constitutional processes needed to be in place prior to turning the reins over. The Pentagon leaned to the former, the State Department to the latter.

Postwar planning for Iraq lacked effective interagency coordination, clear lines of responsibility, and the deadlines and accountability associated with a rigorous process. I suspect that the failure to fashion a deliberate, systematic approach by which the President could establish U.S. policy on the political transition in post-Saddam Iraq was among the more consequential of the administration. Trying to achieve a bridge or compromise between the two different approaches was not a solution.

The postwar planning for Iraq exposed a gap in the way the United States government is organized. No template exists for the kind of postwar planning that proved necessary in Afghanistan, Iraq, and, for that matter, in Kosovo, Bosnia, and elsewhere. There was no single office that could take charge of the military and civilian elements of postwar reconstruction.* That left the Department of Defense, with its expertise in war-oriented planning—but not in postwar reconstruction—as the only practical option.

In the fall of 2002, President Bush and I considered the advantages of unity of command and effort in postwar reconstruction. Dividing responsibilities between security and reconstruction, as had been the case in Bosnia and Afghanistan, was not an encouraging model.[20] The President agreed. When the President issued National Security Presidential Directive 24 (NSPD 24) on January 20, 2003, directing the Defense Department to coordinate postwar planning and assume the lead for postwar reconstruction, some critics grumbled about a Defense power grab.[21] I don't know of anyone at the Pentagon, myself included, who was looking for more assignments. The Department of Defense was engaged enough in the military aspects of the global effort against terrorists, including in Afghanistan, the Horn of Africa, and Asia.

With the President's decision, in January 2003 the Department of Defense created the Office of Reconstruction and Humanitarian Assistance (ORHA). The office's mission was to help CENTCOM manage the transition to the postwar phase in Iraq.[22] To run the organization, I recruited Jay Garner, a barrel-chested retired lieutenant general who had spent nearly four decades in the U.S. Army. I had met him when we served together on the Space Commission in 2000. General Garner knew Secretary Powell and had fought in Iraq

*In late 2003, when this deficiency became apparent, Doug Feith and I joined White House officials in urging the State Department to undertake the responsibility of creating an office of stabilization and reconstruction and a civilian reserve corps that could deploy as our military reserves did. Powell agreed eventually on the condition that it would be "small scale." He was understandably concerned about State being assigned additional missions without increasing its budget, personnel, and resources. Such an office came into being only in 2004, but with less authority and a smaller mandate than it merits.

during the 1991 Gulf War, when Powell was chairman of the Joint Chiefs of Staff. In what was called Operation Provide Comfort, Garner had led twenty thousand troops to assist Iraqi Kurds battered by Saddam's regime. He helped to secure an autonomous Kurdish enclave in northern Iraq. When U.S. troops withdrew from Kurdistan and the American flag was lowered in July 1991, Garner was the last American to cross into Turkey. Thousands of Kurds delayed his departure by lifting him on their shoulders in celebration of his work.[23]

I saw Garner's military background as a valuable asset. I knew the civilian reconstruction effort in Iraq would have to be done in close cooperation with CENTCOM's military personnel—the unity of effort envisioned in the President's directive. Once on the ground in the Gulf region, Garner's office would become an element of CENTCOM, reporting to Franks, and thereby assuring unity of command. I believed a retired general, one who knew many CENTCOM officers and understood military culture, would have the best chance of avoiding friction with the military personnel. I also thought that Garner's prior association with Colin Powell would foster good relations between the reconstruction office and the State Department.

Garner believed, as I did, in empowering local populations to do things for themselves. "We're notorious for telling people what to do," he said. Garner thought American heavy-handedness had been a mistake in Vietnam, one he didn't want to repeat in Iraq.[24] Once the military had toppled Saddam's regime, I thought it was strategically important to put the United States in a supporting role to the Iraqis as soon as possible. This was the Pentagon's and—at least as I understood it—the President's vision.

Months before the war began in Iraq, we encountered strong resistance from State and the CIA to the idea of working with Iraqi expatriates. I couldn't quite understand why the idea was controversial. One of the first things we did in Afghanistan, after all, was develop relationships with the Northern Alliance and Afghan exiles. Hamid Karzai, in fact, had lived for years abroad. I thought it made sense to do something similar in Iraq: reach out to the anti-Saddam elements (largely confined to the autonomous areas of Kurdistan) and to the Iraqi exiles who had been advocating the liberation of their country for many years.* These Iraqi "externals," many living in the

*The State Department and CIA had also not favored having the Northern Alliance advance on Kabul for fear the Afghans might not be able to settle disputes among Afghanistan's ethnic divisions. Their view seemed to be that the United States needed to orchestrate the takeover of the Afghan capital and set up a balance of power for them.

United States or London, included some highly educated and skilled professionals. Some clearly had ambition. While by no means monolithic in their politics or their views, they shared an interest in Iraq's freedom and success. I thought the diversity of views among them was not only natural, but healthy. Why, I wondered, wouldn't we want them involved in a post-Saddam Iraq early, rather than late or never?

Key officials at State and in the CIA, including at senior levels, viewed the externals in general as untrustworthy, however. Particular animus was directed against Ahmed Chalabi, a secular Shiite from a wealthy Baghdad family who lived abroad. Chalabi had worked with the CIA in the 1990s to promote resistance to the Iraqi regime. The relationship soured after the CIA and Chalabi quarreled over responsibility for a failed operation in northern Iraq that led to the murder and exile of many hundreds of anti-Saddam Iraqis. Despite his differences with State and the CIA, Chalabi retained bipartisan support among elements of the U.S. Congress, having been a strong proponent for the 1998 Iraq Liberation Act.

Some concocted a myth that the Pentagon was engaged, as CIA Director Tenet put it in his book, in "thinly veiled efforts to put Chalabi in charge of post-invasion Iraq."[25] Chalabi knew a number of administration officials, including but not exclusively some at the Pentagon. I had met him once or twice at meetings set up for the Iraqi exiles. He struck me as one of a number of bright Iraqis looking to do what they could for their country. However, no one in the Department of Defense urged that Chalabi be "anointed" as the ruler of post-Saddam Iraq, although some officials admired his skills. Robert Blackwill, who served as Rice's director for Iraq and was previously U.S. ambassador to India, once remarked that Chalabi was the "Michael Jordan of Iraq." I assumed Chalabi would participate in an interim government, but I had no idea who would emerge as its head. That was for the Iraqis to decide.

The State Department's and CIA's desire to ensure that Chalabi not have a leadership role in postwar Iraq may have led both organizations to oppose the exiles generally. For example, CIA officials opposed our efforts to constitute a force of Iraqi exiles to fight and act as interpreters and translators alongside our troops in the invasion. Tenet was cool to the idea. When "Agency officers suggested to DoD that they scrap the idea of a fighting force of Iraqi exiles . . . [w]e were scoffed at once again," he wrote.[26] While not large in size, I believed the Free Iraqi Forces, as they were called, could be a useful corrective to the perception that the United States was invading Iraq to occupy the country rather than liberate it.[27] At least in part because of a lack of cooperation from the State Department and the CIA, we were unable to recruit and train enough Free Iraqi Forces to show that Iraqis were involved in the military campaign to rid their country of Saddam.[28]

State Department and CIA officials instead argued that the United States should assist Iraqis from inside the country to emerge as the new leaders. I had no problem with that approach—in theory. But in reality it would take a long time to assemble a team of acceptable and capable candidates within Iraq after Saddam's ouster. His Iraq was hardly a training ground for aspiring leaders. Visible political opponents tended not to have long lives. Regrettably, because of State Department wariness of the Iraqi externals, the United States did little to include them in planning for the postwar period until after Saddam's regime had fallen.*

Instead of putting an Iraqi face on postwar Iraq as soon as possible, the State Department proposed an American-led civil authority for an indefinite period.[29] On March 1, 2003, Powell sent a memo from the State Department historian labeled "informative." The paper argued that any occupation would take "time." That apparently was Colin Powell's position on the matter.[30]

At a principals meeting in the White House on March 7, 2003, two weeks before war would begin, we discussed whether to put Iraqis in charge of the post-Saddam government sooner rather than later. In Powell's absence—he was in New York at the United Nations—Richard Armitage represented the State Department.

In late 2002, I had proposed that after Saddam's regime was toppled, we should promptly announce a provisional council, the Iraqi Interim Authority (IIA). This Interim Authority, designed as an Iraqi variation on the one in Afghanistan, was intended to bring Iraqis from all parts of the country, plus externals, and all political factions into a temporary national governing coalition. Its immediate but limited responsibilities would include supervising the drafting of a constitution, playing a significant role in the conduct of Iraq's foreign policy, and administering selected departments of the government. Membership would include representatives from Iraq's Kurdish, Sunni, and Shiite populations. For several months, the deputies and the interagency

*More than a year before the war began, in January 2002, Pentagon officials were pushing for a U.S. government-sponsored conference for all the external groups to show a united front against the Saddam regime. Deputy Secretary of State Armitage generated a series of bureaucratic impediments to stop or delay the meeting. Eventually, in December 2002, the administration organized a conference in London. By then, nearly a year had passed, to the detriment of our country's planning efforts. Even then, State and CIA remained skeptical of the Iraqi externals, and voiced doubts about the Iraqis' ability to come together to build a new country.

coordinating committees discussed, debated, and refined the concept. The State Department had been uncomfortable with the proposal.

"Don't rush this," Armitage urged in our NSC meeting. "We'll sacrifice legitimacy."

Vice President Cheney countered that no one, least of all him, was pushing for a few Iraqis with Washington connections to fly in and take the reins of a nation of twenty-five million people. But he noted, "We can't leave the government to chance." Cheney indicated that without Iraqis transitioning into positions of responsibility quickly, there would need to be a prolonged American occupation.

I continued to feel that doing little to cultivate a cadre of Iraqi leaders, as Armitage seemed to be suggesting, would be a mistake. "I believe legitimacy comes because the Iraqi Interim Authority is temporary," I said. "How well it works will determine its legitimacy." Nobody at the table was going to be able to determine in advance whether or not an interim Iraqi government would be seen as legitimate by the Iraqi people.

"We should take two or three months to consult all Iraqis before we appoint an Interim Authority," responded Armitage. This too was a consistent message from State: delay.

"So you wouldn't have an Interim Authority at all?" Cheney asked. The reason for the Iraqi Interim Authority was that it would serve for a short time—probably no more than several months. But if it were substantially delayed, there would be no point in establishing an Interim Authority at all. The meeting ended without resolution.

On March 10, 2003, we met again to discuss the same issue—this time at the National Security Council level with President Bush chairing the meeting.

The President agreed with the framework of the Iraqi Interim Authority proposal. Though we had provided a detailed plan for implementation, the exact execution and timing were left to be worked out in consultation with the Iraqis, who would start by leading smaller ministries and in later stages take control of the more important ones.[31] Only after those on the Interim Authority had developed and demonstrated their leadership capability would they take over key government ministries such as the Ministry of Defense, the Ministry of Interior, and the Ministry of Oil. But it was not clear if this would be in days, weeks, or months.

The following day I went to see the President. I was concerned about unresolved issues in this planning and the lack of policy resolution. Even though Bush had decided in favor of the Interim Authority, it still was not certain whether State would support quickly transitioning power to the Iraqis as I favored and—I thought—the President had decided.

Because the Defense Department would have to implement whatever plans for postwar Iraq the President finally approved, I wanted to be sure we would have the necessary resources in place. I told the President I thought I should go to Iraq for two weeks after major combat operations to oversee the beginning of the Phase IV plan. I said I would work with General Garner to help ensure that we do whatever was necessary to allow the Iraqis to take leadership of their country.

President Bush didn't cotton to the idea. "What if we had a problem with North Korea?" he asked.

It was a fair question. As we were preparing for war in Iraq, North Korean dictator Kim Jong Il was increasing pressure on the Korean Peninsula by flagrantly violating previous diplomatic agreements to end its WMD programs. The President was concerned that Kim Jong Il might view an Iraq war as an occasion to increase his troublemaking in the region.

"Well, Mr. President, if that happened," I replied, "I would come home immediately."

The President thought about that for a moment. Then he shook his head. "No, Don," he replied. "You need to be here."[32]

I should have pressed the point harder. It was clearly important to establish order in Iraq after Saddam was gone—after coalition forces would end three decades of Baathist rule. We would have to fill the resulting political vacuum with a mechanism by which sectarian and ethnic groups could join to govern in a peaceful way. The tensions from State officials pulling in one direction, toward a more lengthy U.S.-run occupation and the Defense Department in another direction, would have to be managed carefully. A top-level administration official in Baghdad might have made a difference in those early days. There would have been someone able to decide firmly in favor of one option over the other and extract additional guidance from Washington as required. I did not have a full understanding at the time, however, just how badly that was going to be needed.

CHAPTER 35

Mission Accomplished?

In the weeks after Iraq's liberation, the Department of Defense was still pushing for an Iraqi Interim Authority with some independence. With Saddam's forces defeated, the Iraqi people were wondering what would come next. Given the region's pathologies and the propaganda aired on Al-Jazeera, I was concerned that people across the Muslim world would believe that the United States sought to establish a colonial-type occupation for the purpose of taking Iraq's oil. We needed to put forward a group of Iraqis as the core of a new interim government in order to avoid that perception. We were losing valuable time.

On April 1, I sent a memorandum to the President and the members of the National Security Council saying that the time for trying to craft "the perfect plan" was over. "We have got to get moving on this," I wrote. "This is now a matter of operational importance—it is not too much to say that time can cost lives."[1] It wasn't often that I wrote the President in such unequivocal terms, but I felt interagency deliberation needed to come to an end. Absent "a fundamental objection," I wrote, I was going to have General Franks announce the first steps to create the Iraqi Interim Authority as soon as possible.[2]

State Department officials again objected. They argued that establishing the IIA so soon after the war would complicate things. They also contended that the situation in Iraq was different from Afghanistan, which is a poor country with little infrastructure in place, and therefore a new government could be established more readily. They believed that we needed to take some time to ensure we did it the right way.

An unequivocal order from the President resolving the differences was not forthcoming, so those of us in the Defense Department resigned ourselves to what we thought might be a delay of a month or two. Rice was pushing for a senior diplomat to head up the reconstruction effort, so I understood that it might make sense to wait until he was chosen and had a chance to assess the situation. As I would learn, a delay of a month or two was not what Powell and his colleagues had in mind.

At the end of April I traveled to the Gulf region. As I wrote to the President in a report summarizing my meetings, the leaders I met with unanimously believed that a quick transition to Iraqis would "help ease the apprehension of their people of a long-term U.S. occupation." It was, I added, a good reason for us to move forward on the Interim Authority.[3] I noted the remarkable consensus among our Arab partners of the threats posed by that perennial irritant in the Middle East, Syria. That regime's behavior had not changed since I met with Syrian leaders in the 1980s. They were still aiding terrorists and still causing trouble.

The liberation of Iraq engendered a feeling uncharacteristic for the Syrian regime—fear. Their leaders appeared to be rattled by America's ouster of Saddam Hussein. They might have been wondering if they would be next. When I arrived in Kuwait, the foreign minister said that a Syrian official had asked him to pass word to me that they were not harboring terrorists or facilitating the entry of jihadists into Iraq—the very things we knew they were doing. "We need to keep up the pressure," I wrote the President.[4]

On April 28, I took off from Kuwait International Airport and in fifteen minutes was over newly liberated Iraq. Only eighty miles of arid desert and some of the densest oil fields in the world separate Kuwait City from the southern Iraqi city of Basra. But in another sense the two countries seemed a universe apart. Moving from Kuwait to Iraq reminded me of leaving democratic West Germany and entering totalitarian Eastern Europe back in the 1970s. The modern Kuwaiti cityscape gave way to dusty, one-story buildings barely discernible from the thousands of square miles of sand that surrounded the Euphrates and Tigris river valleys.

Saddam's legacy to the Iraqi people was an economic system that combined the worst elements of Stalinist central planning with organized crime–style enrichment for the fortunate few. Iraq had billions of barrels of oil and one of the Arab world's most educated populations. Yet the dictator had cut off the Iraqi people from the rest of the world, brutalized them, eviscerated their sense of trust in one another, and denied them the fruits of economic progress.

It had been just over nineteen years since I was last on Iraqi soil. The regime I had visited back then had been swept away: Saddam and his top lieutenants were on the run.

On my first stop, in Basra, I thanked the British forces who had once again proven the value of America's special relationship with the United Kingdom. The government of Prime Minister Tony Blair had been one of the first to lend support to America after the 9/11 attacks. When the President delivered his historic speech to a joint session of Congress on September 20, 2001, Blair had flown to Washington from London to express his country's solidarity. Blair and his secretary of state for defense, Geoffrey Hoon, had sent more than forty thousand troops to help topple Saddam's regime and to secure southern Iraq. I found Blair to be the most eloquent public voice explaining the rationale and sense of urgency for the coalition effort. Though he endured relentless domestic criticism, he stuck by his decision.

The British had engaged in difficult close combat with the Fedayeen Saddam in the cities of the south. Some Fedayeen had climbed onto the advancing British tanks and had to be removed with bayonets in hand-to-hand fighting. The job of the American forces would have been infinitely harder without them. The British had the correct perspective about the postwar situation we faced. As the commander of the British 1st Armored Division told me, "There is no humanitarian crisis, except the one the regime caused by turning off the electricity and water."[5] The surprise and speed achieved by our invasion forces prevented the environmental and humanitarian catastrophes we had feared.

Coalition commanders had declared southern Iraq "permissive," meaning that the enemy forces had been rooted out. Farther north, and in and around Baghdad, there was still resistance. For much of our C-130 flight into the capital, as we traced the path inscribed by the Euphrates and Tigris rivers, we flew low over the riverbanks to reduce the risk from surface-to-air missiles.

In the polished marble rooms of one of Saddam's many palaces, I met with General Jay Garner and his staff for a briefing on the activities of the Office of Reconstruction and Humanitarian Assistance. Garner was optimistic about the progress being made and hopeful for Iraq's future. As we drove through liberated Baghdad in the late afternoon traffic, cars raced forward to pull alongside and honk and wave. In one car the driver gave us the thumbs-up, but a passenger in the backseat gave a thumbs-down. I mused that in Iraq only Saddam won 100 percent approval.

At a power plant in southern Baghdad, Iraqi and American military engineers briefed us on the sorry state of the country's infrastructure. The power grid, manufacturing base, water and sewer systems, and oil drilling and refining capacity all were on the verge of collapse. Pipes and wires in many facilities were literally being held together by duct tape and string. The Department of Defense had expected that there would be a need to fix what might be destroyed in the war, but our intelligence had not prepared CENTCOM and interagency planners for an entire infrastructure that was crumbling at its foundation from years of underinvestment and neglect. It was clear from those earliest days that it would take many hundreds of millions of dollars to reestablish basic services.

The Iraqis who were in charge of the Baghdad power plant, and those in the facilities and ministries, were Baathists; they had been privileged under Saddam Hussein. Retaining these professionals could be problematic, because many others were reluctant to work with anyone who had received favors from the regime. Ideally, senior Baathists would not be allowed to stay in place. But we did not have the luxury of being doctrinaire. The coalition and the Interim Authority that followed would need many skilled people to keep a dysfunctional country running, even if they were Baathists. With regard to the technocrats, at least, I wrote to the President, it would be best to find a way to work with them.[6]

My visit offered a sobering look at the challenges ahead. As I warned our troops at a meeting in a huge hangar at Baghdad Airport:

> We still have to find and deal with the remaining elements of the former regime. We have to root out and eliminate terrorist networks operating in this country. We have to help Iraqis restore their basic services. And we have to help provide conditions of stability and security so that the Iraqi people can form an interim authority—an interim government—and then ultimately a free Iraqi government based on political freedom, individual liberty, and the rule of law.[7]

At General Franks' request, President Bush would formally declare the end of major combat operations the following day, on May 1, 2003. This would mark the beginning of Phase IV—posthostilities stabilization and reconstruction. Franks had hoped that announcing the end of combat operations would encourage those of our allies who preferred not to be part of the invasion to now feel comfortable enough to support reconstruction.[8] He had notified me in a cable that, after the President's declaration, Army Lieutenant General David McKiernan would be the senior commander in Iraq for ninety days.[9] McKiernan and the senior officers at his headquarters, dubbed "the dream team" in some Army circles, would be tasked with the command of the many thousands of American troops.

On my flight heading back to Kuwait City I was startled to see McKiernan onboard the C-130 aircraft. I asked him where he was going.

"To my headquarters back in Kuwait," he said.

"Well, aren't you in charge of what's going on in Iraq?" I asked.

McKiernan told me he went in and out of Iraq once, sometimes twice a week to check on things. It struck me that in the crucial weeks following the fall of Saddam, McKiernan did not seem to think of himself as the commander in charge of the ground operations, and didn't seem to be preparing to take over command of all coalition forces in the country, as Franks had indicated in his cable. That meant that the senior American military leadership in the country consisted of Army and Marine division commanders. To be sure, these were some of America's most talented war fighters: Army Major Generals Ray Odierno and David Petraeus and Marine Major General James Mattis. They each reported to General McKiernan, but McKiernan seemed to have removed himself from the critical daily responsibilities in the country.

The following day—May 1, 2003—President Bush flew in a U.S. Navy S-3B Viking onto the deck of the USS *Abraham Lincoln*. He stood under a sign that said "MISSION ACCOMPLISHED" and announced that "major combat operations in Iraq have ended."[10] Bush was correct, but those in charge of his public affairs team did not appreciate the sizable difference between the end of major combat operations and "mission accomplished." The phrase would haunt his presidency until the day it ended.

I had seen an early draft of the President's speech while flying to the Gulf. It seemed too optimistic to me.[11] As I discussed my thoughts with Bush over the phone, I suggested edits to tone down any triumphalist rhetoric. He was receptive to my concerns. From the transcript I read of the delivered remarks, it was clear the speech had been muted. It was not the words in the President's speech that left the public perplexed when tough fighting in Iraq continued, but the unforgettable banner behind him.

The next day, when asked about the President's speech, I tried to strike a note of caution:

> [I]t would be a terrible mistake to think that Iraq is a fully secure, fully pacified environment. It is not. It is dangerous. There are people who are rolling hand grenades into compounds. There are people that are shooting people. And it's not finished. So we ought not to leave the world with the impression that it is.[12]

I had another issue with the President's remarks. "The transition from dictatorship to democracy will take time, but it is worth every effort," Bush had said. "Our coalition will stay until our work is done." That was not the way I understood our plan. A nation that had suffered under decades of dictatorial rule was unlikely to quickly reorganize itself into a stable, modern, democratic state. Deep sectarian and ethnic divisions, concealed by a culture of repression and forced submission to Saddam, lurked just below the surface of Iraqi society.

I hoped Iraq would turn toward some form of representative government, but I thought we needed to be clear-eyed about democracy's prospects in the country. Even the United States, though it had been the heir of hundreds of years of British democratic political development, did not evolve smoothly or quickly into the liberal democracy that we benefit from today. Millions of African Americans were considered property for more than seventy-five years after our country's founding. Women couldn't vote until nearly one hundred and fifty years after independence from England. I was concerned that the President's remarks suggested that the United States might remain until Iraq had achieved democratic self-sufficiency which might take decades. I doubted whether the American people would have the patience for a protracted, multiyear occupation as Iraqis fumbled their way along the road toward something approximating a free, nondictatorial government. And I assumed the Iraqi people would be even less willing to put up with a long American occupation, which could become a rallying point for rebellion.

Senator Daniel Patrick Moynihan once said, "[T]he central conservative truth is that it is culture, not politics, that determines the success of a society."[13] A millennia-old culture dating to the very beginnings of civilization would have to work its way toward adopting practices we considered democratic gradually. The art of compromise, which is central to a successful democracy, is not something that people learn overnight. If we hurried to create Iraqi democracy through quick elections, before key institutions—a free press, private property rights, political parties, an independent judiciary—began to develop organically, we "could end up with a permanent mistake—one vote, one time—and another Iran-like theocracy," as I wrote in a May 2003 memo.[14]

I conveyed these thoughts to the President and to Rice, suggesting the administration soften the democracy rhetoric. I proposed that we talk more about freedom and less about democracy, lest the Iraqis and other countries in the region think we intended to impose our own political system on them, rather than their developing one better suited to their history and culture.[15]

I wondered as well how we would define democracy if that became our goal. If Iraq never created an American-style system of government, would that mean that our mission had been a failure or that the troops would have to stay indefinitely? Emphasis on Iraqi democracy invited critics of the war to find the innumerable instances in which Iraq would inevitably fall short. Further, Iraq's neighbors, our regional partners, who would be important to our efforts to stabilize post-Saddam Iraq, were less than enthusiastic about our emerging posture. In fact, the reason so many countries supported us, and the reason two successive U.S. presidents and the Congress of the United States supported regime change in Iraq, was because of the consistent emphasis on the security threat posed by Saddam Hussein. Bringing democracy to Iraq had not been among the primary rationales.

It was hard to know exactly where the President's far-reaching language about democracy originated. It was not a large part of his original calculus in toppling Saddam's regime, at least from what I gleaned in private conversations and NSC meetings. I didn't hear rhetoric about democracy from Colin Powell or State Department officials. I know it did not come from those of us in the Department of Defense. Condoleezza Rice seemed to be the one top adviser who spoke that way, but it was not clear to me whether she was encouraging the President to use rhetoric about democracy or whether it was originating with the President.

Bush often expressed his belief that freedom was the gift of the Almighty. He seemed to feel almost duty-bound to help expand the frontiers of freedom in the Middle East. I certainly sympathized with his desire to see free systems of government spread around the globe. I had met and greatly admired Natan

Sharansky, a former Soviet dissident, whose ideas on democracy had deeply influenced Bush. As much as I agreed with both Sharansky and Bush that we would all be better off if the world had more democracies, I thought we needed to be careful about how we pursued it. I believed in expanding the frontiers of freedom where possible, but that goal had to be tempered by our limited ability to achieve it.

As the unsuccessful search for WMD stockpiles dragged on, the administration's communications strategy seemed to shift further toward democracy as a reason for America's presence in Iraq. This intensified during the 2004 presidential campaign. Instead of explaining the WMD failure within the context of imperfect intelligence, and emphasizing Saddam's intent and ability to restart his WMD programs if given the chance, as the Iraq Survey Group, led by former UN weapons inspector Charles Duelfer, had definitively concluded, the shift to democracy seemed to some as a way to change the subject.[16]

My concerns about the military's management of Iraq in the first days of the critical postwar period were abated somewhat when I learned that there finally would be a full-time military commander. Lieutenant General Ricardo Sanchez assumed command of ground forces in June 2003. The child of a Mexican American family, Sanchez had grown up along the Texas side of the Rio Grande in a one-bedroom house without plumbing. The future three-star Army general earned his commission in the early 1970s through ROTC. Sanchez had an admirable record of performance in the 1990s in the Balkans, where he had demonstrated the blend of military professionalism and political sensitivity that is needed when commanding coalition forces in another country. He had glowing recommendations from the Army leadership, particularly Chief of Staff Eric Shinseki, who had taken an interest in Sanchez's advancement. Sanchez had been serving in Germany as a two-star division commander and had deployed into Iraq with his division after most major combat operations were over. His was an important assignment, involving command of some fifteen thousand troops. However, as commander of all coalition forces in Iraq, Sanchez would have to lead a force more than ten times that size, work with numerous coalition nations, and command a headquarters that he had never been trained or prepared to assume.

The reality—which should have been clear to the senior Army leadership, CENTCOM, and to the Joint Chiefs of Staff—was that Sanchez was not only the most junior three-star general in Iraq, but the most junior three-star in the entire U.S. Army. I can only speculate that part of the logic behind an otherwise inexplicable selection was that CENTCOM and the Army staff believed that with the emergence of an Iraqi Interim Authority and a reconstitution of Iraqi security forces, we could begin a drawdown of coalition forces. This would have left Sanchez commanding significantly fewer than the 170,000 coalition troops there in mid-2003. It may also have been assumed that Sanchez would be operating in a postwar environment, in which an international peacekeeping force could maintain security if needed.

Whatever the rationale behind the decision, it later became clear that Sanchez had been put in a terrible position. The establishment of a government, the long-term care of detainees, the training and equipping of security forces, and, ultimately, the engagement of an increasingly deadly terrorist threat called for a senior military official with far more experience. That the Army leadership, with the agreement or acquiescence of CENTCOM and the Joint Staff, slotted him for the top command post was a serious misassessment. Further, the assignment required a large, fully staffed supporting headquarters that the U.S. Army, CENTCOM, and the Joint Chiefs of Staff in Washington failed to provide Sanchez with for months. I later learned that Sanchez was operating with well less than half—37 percent—of the staff he required for his headquarters. "It seems to me we have a real problem," I wrote to General Myers when in 2004 I first discovered the scope of the failure to properly staff Sanchez's headquarters. These deficiencies were brought to light by investigations into the abuse at Abu Ghraib prison. "A combatant commander asks for something. The Joint Staff agrees to it. You recommend it to me. Then the Services never fulfill it."[17]

I do not recall being made aware of the Army's decision to move General Sanchez into the top position. He had been assigned to Iraq during ongoing force rotations that took place in the aftermath of major combat operations. During this time, divisions and other units that had deployed as part of the force buildup as early as late 2002 were being rotated out, and new units were being rotated in. As a component of those changes, the Army and CENTCOM developed the structure for the command elements. To my recollection, the chief of staff of the Army and CENTCOM leadership did not bring the relevant plans to my attention. But even as the situation in Iraq deteriorated, and Sanchez and his minimal staff were becoming overwhelmed, no senior official in the Army, CENTCOM, or the Joint Staff recommended a change. The problem of the McKiernan to Sanchez transition caused me to change the nature of my involvement in assigning officers to senior positions. Previously, the chairman and the vice chairman of the Joint Chiefs, the deputy, and I had been principally involved in promotions at the four-star level. Now we decided to increase our involvement in decisions regarding key service appointments.

In my view, much of the blame that later fell on Sanchez was misplaced. To be sure, there were failures on his watch, but much of the responsibility belonged to his superiors in the Army and the senior leadership of the Department.

In late April 2003, we also faced an unexpected personnel move at CENTCOM headquarters: General Franks announced his plans to retire. For the past two of his three years at the post, Franks had spent his days and nights planning two demanding military campaigns, and he was anxious to step down. I asked him to stay to oversee the transition of power to an Iraqi authority, but he insisted on departing. I was disappointed to have a leadership transition at such a critical time.

Franks' position as combatant commander at CENTCOM was assumed by his deputy, General John Abizaid. The son of an Arab American Navy veteran of World War II, Abizaid graduated from West Point, earned a scholarship that allowed him to study Arabic in Jordan, and later completed a master's degree in Middle Eastern studies at Harvard. Cerebral in demeanor and strategic in thinking, Abizaid embodied military, regional, and linguistic expertise.

As commander of CENTCOM, Franks had established and assumed responsibility for the Coalition Provisional Authority (CPA), with Jay Garner reporting to him. I had advised Garner before he took the post at ORHA that, as circumstances evolved, the top civilian post in Iraq would likely be assumed by a senior official from the State Department.

In early May, the President announced the selection of former Ambassador L. Paul "Jerry" Bremer to replace Garner. Though Garner was disappointed that his tour was ending sooner than expected, he had done his job well and had formed a good working relationship with emerging Iraqi leaders, who he had assured would soon be leading the Iraqi Interim Authority.*

*I recommended to President Bush that Garner be appointed ambassador to Afghanistan soon after he returned to the United States, but without success. I believed he could inject a sense of urgency into the State Department mission in Kabul.[18]

Garner was pushing for a swift transition to the Iraqis—a policy I agreed with but about which Rice and perhaps the President himself seemed to have developed second thoughts. The interdepartmental policy differences that had not been decisively resolved came to the surface. The way the Bremer selection was handled added another layer of difficulty.

"The choice of Mr. Bremer is a victory for the State Department over the Pentagon," the *New York Times* promptly announced.[19] "Some administration officials were so concerned that the move not look like a setback for Defense Secretary Donald H. Rumsfeld that they were considering having him announce it upon his return from Baghdad on Friday night, to make it look like a Pentagon initiative."[20]

I didn't know who "some administration officials" were, but from the Pentagon it looked like Deputy Secretary of State Armitage was again feeding the press his version of events. His leaks were so brazen that I finally mentioned them to Powell. "Colin, we have a problem," I said in one such conversation on March 31, 2003. "Rich Armitage has been badmouthing the Pentagon all over town. It's been going on for some time and it's only gotten worse."[21]

I asked Powell to try to manage his deputy. The President was facing rearguard disloyalty from a small band of "senior State Department officials" who were attacking the administration and the effort in Iraq in the press as anonymous sources.*

"I don't know what the hell is in Armitage's craw," I told Powell, "but I'm tired of it."[23] Powell told me he would look into it. He expressed concerns about Wolfowitz, whom Powell claimed was leaking against him. I didn't believe that was true. I made a point of repeatedly telling those I worked with at the Pentagon not to speak to the press against State, the CIA, the White House, or any members of the administration—no matter how strong the temptation. "If you've got a problem," I told senior Pentagon staff, "come and see me."[24]

Several months later the subject of leaking came up in a meeting with the President and White House Chief of Staff Andy Card in the Oval Office. Most of it was routine business—senior military nominations, an update on

*The failure to take responsibility for leaks that threatened to damage the administration ultimately belonged to the White House. In April 2003, a few weeks after my phone conversation with Powell, I assembled a package of news articles quoting officials from the State Department, including Armitage, that revealed damaging assertions against the administration, and sent the memo to Card. The articles, I noted, "reflect a hemorrhaging in the administration. It is clearly not disciplined." Though it was seldom noted, Armitage also leaked CIA operative Valerie Plame's name to the press, causing further damage.[22]

operations in Iraq, and preparations for our meeting later that morning with Colombian President Alvaro Uribe. As the meeting closed, Bush raised the issues between the State and Defense Departments that were being leaked to the media.

"The controversy between DoD and State is hurting. It needs to stop," the President said.[25] I couldn't have agreed more. It was what I had been counseling for over a year. The problem was that he was talking to the wrong person.

"Mr. President, I have repeatedly told my folks never to leak or trash their colleagues. All the evidence suggests that it is State that is trashing us. If anyone has any information that my folks at DoD are leaking anything or trashing anyone, tell me."

Card interjected, "That's what they say at State."

"Look Andy, if it's going both ways, I need to see evidence," I responded.

The meeting left a sour taste in my mouth. The truth was that there weren't stories in the newspapers about Defense officials anonymously criticizing their counterparts in the State Department.

The next day the President called me. "I've got great confidence in you and what your team at DoD is doing. I didn't mean to send the wrong signal. You're doing a fabulous job."

"I appreciate the call, Mr. President. I may have taken yesterday's meeting amiss, but if you feel there's a war between the State and Defense Departments, it takes two to fight, and DoD isn't fighting. What is happening is hurting you. If it gets to a point where the solution is for me to leave, I will do so in a second."

"That's a crappy solution," Bush responded.

"It's certainly not my first choice, but we need you in the White House, and if my leaving would help, I'm ready."

Then Bush added, "I'm working hard on Powell and Armitage. I've seen the recent articles and I know what's going on."[26]

In fact, the selection of Bremer was not a triumph of State over Defense. I believe I may have been one of the first to include his name on a list of possible candidates for the post.* Bremer came to my attention for a possible

*After a brief talk with Bremer, I told Card that "I think he is the man" to head the CPA. Tenet said he had heard good things about Bremer, and Powell said he thought well of Bremer but wanted to "run a couple of traps" before he could say he was comfortable. I later learned a slightly different version of the story of the Bremer selection. Apparently when I mentioned Bremer, Powell was delighted, because Bremer had close links to the State Department.[27]

senior diplomatic job in a discussion I had with George Shultz soon after I returned to the Pentagon in 2001. He recommended Bremer along with several others for presidential envoy slots, if and when the need arose, in much the same way Shultz had recommended me to President Reagan as an envoy on the Law of the Sea Treaty and later to the Middle East. I liked the idea of having the presidential envoy in Iraq be one with ties to the State Department, since State's involvement was badly needed. The Defense Department could not perform all or even most of the nonmilitary tasks that needed to be done. For postwar stabilization and reconstruction to be successful, it would take leadership and resources from State and other cabinet departments, as well as from coalition nations. I also liked that Bremer was considered an action-oriented executive, able to get things done.

Because Bush had placed the Defense Department in charge of Bremer and postcombat stability operations, Bremer met with me prior to his departure to discuss a rough road map and guidelines. Our discussion was based on a DoD memo titled "Principles for Iraq—Policy Guidelines," which had twenty-six guidelines I had vetted with others in the Pentagon, the State Department, and the NSC. Our May 13 memo did not lay out the details or exact timing of the way forward. I understood that Bremer would need flexibility to respond to the circumstances he found. But I had no reason to think that Bremer had any doubts about the advisability of the policy that President Bush had approved before the war: the development of the Iraqi Interim Authority, with the goal that it would exercise substantial authority as soon as possible.

Bremer's mandate was to make the memo's twenty-six principles operational. We had no illusions that the coalition would be able to withdraw if Iraq collapsed into chaos. "Without security for the Iraqi people," I wrote, "none of their goals will be achievable." But, I stressed the importance of handing over responsibilities to the Iraqis.

> In staffing ministries and positioning Iraqis in ways that will increase their influence, the Coalition will work to have acceptable Iraqis involved as early as possible, so Iraqi voices can explain the goals and direction to the Iraqi people. Only if Iraqis are seen as being engaged in, responsible for, and explaining and leading their fellow citizens will broad public support develop that is essential for security.[28]

At the Department of Defense we recognized that some of the aspiring Iraqi leaders would fail to meet our standards for good governance and efficiency. There were precious few Mr. Smiths (as in the Jimmy Stewart movie) in the world. But it was of paramount importance that U.S. officials should take advantage of every opportunity to increase the influence of well-intentioned Iraqi leaders and begin to give them control of their country.

Bremer and I discussed the need to work closely together. I had decided I would give him considerable latitude for decision making, since he was the man on the ground. Bremer, however, had a robust definition of the term "latitude." When I was a special envoy for President Reagan, I only reported through Secretary of State Shultz. It seemed appropriate that I report directly through the cabinet officer who had the day-to-day responsibility to manage the issues on which I was focused. Even with the title of "presidential" envoy, I never sought and rarely had direct interactions with the President. It did not occur to me to try to bypass the secretary of state and go directly to President Reagan, nor would I deal directly with any other cabinet officials without first engaging my direct supervisor, who, in my case, was Shultz.

Bremer had a totally different approach. He assumed that he had direct access to President Bush from the start. The President and Rice both not only accepted but facilitated Bremer's unfiltered contact with them. On the same day that Bush announced Bremer's appointment, May 6, 2003, they had a private lunch. I made a note to myself at the time: "POTUS had lunch with him alone—shouldn't have done so. POTUS linked him to the White House instead of to DoD or DoS [State]."[29]

The President could of course have lunch with whomever he wanted. But in Bremer's case, such actions contributed to a confused chain of command. This imprecision damaged Washington's communications with the CPA throughout the period of Bremer's tenure.

It became clear that Bremer intended to not be exclusively connected to any cabinet official. Bremer later wrote that after one of his private meetings with President Bush, "[Bush's] message was clear. I was neither Rumsfeld's nor Powell's man. I was the president's man."[30] He quickly established active relationships with Rice, Powell, and, as a career Foreign Service officer, his former colleagues in the State Department. Certainly it was desirable that the CPA have good ties to the political and diplomatic apparatus of the Bush administration, given the nature of its responsibilities in Iraq. I did not discourage that. What developed, though, was something I had not anticipated. Bremer was able to pick and choose the members of the NSC he would deal with on any particular issue, the result often being that the other members were left in the dark. The muddled lines of authority meant that there was no single individual in control of or responsible for Bremer's work. There were far too many hands on the steering wheel, which, in my view, was a formula for running the truck into a ditch.

CHAPTER 36

Too Many Hands on the Steering Wheel

Upon his arrival in Baghdad on May 11, the press labeled Ambassador Bremer as America's "viceroy" in Iraq. He seemed to embrace the idea with relish. Bremer believed, as he wrote in his memoir, that his assignment "combine[d] some of the vice-regal responsibilities of General Douglas MacArthur, de facto ruler of Imperial Japan after World War II, and of General Lucius Clay, who led the American occupation of defeated Nazi Germany." The difference, Bremer contended, was that his job was even more challenging than theirs had been.* I had no idea that he would see himself this way. It certainly was not a mindset conducive to working with proud and wary Iraqis or with the large American military contingent in the country. Perhaps unavoidable but adding to the unfortunate imagery was the fact that Bremer's offices were in one of Saddam's grand palaces. Its many marble rooms, filled with opulent murals and statues, offered a grotesque glimpse of the Iraqi dictatorship. Paintings and inscriptions glorified the Iraqi regime. At least one of the sayings etched in Arabic on the ceiling was of dubious provenance: "Ask not what your country can do for you but what you can do for your country—Saddam Hussein."[2]

Though I would have entered Iraq with a notably different mindset had I been in Bremer's shoes, I wasn't in his shoes. To his credit, he put his own

*Bremer quotes himself as saying, "I'd settle for MacArthur's problems."[1]

life on hold to work long days in punishing heat. Every day Coalition Provisional Authority officials went to work on behalf of their country. That took courage and a sense of duty. In later years, Bremer and his team, along with the Department of Defense, would be subjected to criticism for employing young, seemingly underqualified staffers in jobs critical to helping establish a postwar Iraqi society. What is often neglected in those critiques, however, was that the CPA was chronically short of staff. There was not a long line of seasoned volunteers to take on the challenges and frustrations that Bremer and the others withstood.

At the Pentagon, I established a special office, headed by former Wall Street banker Reuben Jeffery and retired Army colonel Jim O'Beirne, to support Bremer and reduce the paperwork and logistics challenges that would otherwise consume the CPA's time. A large number of Pentagon officials—military and civilian—volunteered to go over to Iraq to help. Unfortunately that esprit de corps was not widely found in other cabinet departments. The Department of State, outfitted with large numbers of experts in diplomacy and foreign affairs, provided two hundred names of would-be recruits. But when Jeffery and his team began contacting them, most demurred, many saying that their spouses or families didn't want them going to Iraq.[3] Overall, the State Department was filling less than 40 percent of the slots it was slated to fill on the governance teams.[4] One State official later admitted their attitude: "Let's see what impediments we can put in their way. Let's see how long we can be in delivering this particular commodity or individual or amount of expertise. Let's see how long we can stiff 'em."[5] I asked the director of administration at the Pentagon, Raymond DuBois, to coordinate financial and personnel support to the CPA. He became so frustrated with State's lack of cooperation that he personally canvassed the retired Foreign Service officer community for volunteers.[6]

In order to get up to speed, I encouraged Bremer to work closely with Garner. I hoped he could take advantage of Garner's knowledge of Iraq and its emerging leadership. I had also asked my special assistant, Larry Di Rita, whom I had sent to Kuwait to help Garner stand up ORHA several months earlier, to stay on in Baghdad to help bring Bremer up to speed. A sharp and gregarious formal naval officer, Di Rita could help to impose structure and order into what was bound to be a challenging start for the CPA. But Bremer seemed not to want much assistance from those who had been engaged in Iraq before he arrived. He was eager to send Garner back to America and excluded him from key meetings during their transition.

Bremer's relationship with Sanchez was also apparently strained from the start, perhaps because Bremer thought he needed to establish control of Iraq and not yield authority to the military.* I was concerned that Bremer refused to meet with the four-star commander of Joint Forces Command, Admiral Ed Giambastiani, when he was in Iraq working on a lessons-learned project, which proved to be a valuable assessment of what actually took place in the days after Saddam's ouster.[7]

Most troubling was that Bremer proved reluctant to cede any significant authority to the Iraqis. In his memoir he noted that several weeks before he arrived in Baghdad he heard on the radio that "Jay Garner had announced his intention to appoint an Iraqi government by May 15." Upon hearing the news, Bremer wrote, "I almost drove off the George Washington Parkway."[8] Garner's plan, in fact, would have consisted of a group of Iraqis advising the CPA, not a total handover of authority. Through political conferences in the Iraqi cities of Nasiriyah and Baghdad, Garner had skillfully cultivated leaders for the new Iraq, among internals as well as externals. He also had ensured there was an Iraqi presence in each of the country's twenty-three ministries.[9] When Bremer departed for Baghdad, I believed he would work with Garner to build on his momentum by creating an Iraqi transitional government. It took months before I realized that this was not what Bremer had in mind.

At the State Department's insistence, I reluctantly had agreed to a month or so delay in implementing the Iraqi Interim Authority when the policy was established in March. I agreed that Bremer needed a chance to find his footing in Baghdad. But Bremer wanted to delay implementation of the IIA and the creation of an independent Iraqi government possibly by years, and seemed to think he had the President's support to do so. Bremer later wrote, "[T]he President's instructions to me . . . when I had lunch with him alone on May 6th, were that we're going to take our time to get it right. . . . The President had effectively, though perhaps not formally, changed his position on the question of a short or long occupation, having before the war been in favor of a short occupation. By the time I came in, that was gone."[10] That would have been news to me, and I suspect it would also have come as news to the President. Bush, at least in my presence, never wavered in his desire to turn power over to the Iraqis as quickly as possible. Then again, he never firmly resisted the State Department's efforts to slow the timeline either. This ambiguity may have been just enough for Bremer to decide he had Bush's support for delay.

*When I met with the two of them on my visits to Iraq, their body language signaled a lack of rapport. By the end of their tours in mid-2004, I received reports that they were barely speaking.

In any event, Bremer certainly never discussed with me his perception that the President had decided on a significant reversal in his policy toward Iraq.

For at least the first month of his tenure, in fact, Bremer continued to report back to me and Defense officials that he was implementing the President's plan to create an interim Iraqi government as soon as possible. In a June 2, 2003 memo, he wrote to me that in a meeting with Iraqi political leaders he "laid out our vision for establishing an interim administration (IA) in the next five to six weeks."[11] Seven days later I responded with a memo expressing my agreement with his plan and "the need to move quickly to create a leadership council for the Interim Administration." I noted we were running out of time to put an Iraqi face on the CPA:

> Indications are that Iraqi political/ethnic groups are restless. Standing still may lead to unraveling. Progress toward an IIA may be essential to retard centrifugal forces. . . . Regime remnants are coalescing to some degree and stepping up sabotage. Their dream is a guerrilla insurgency. But guerrilla insurgencies depend on popular support. Progress toward an IIA will help neutralize if not dry up that popular support.[12]

Patience among Iraqis was wearing thin, and an insurgency was gaining momentum. Bremer gave no indication to me that he disagreed with my analysis that the best way to avert an escalating insurgency was to give Iraqis the opportunity to govern themselves.

By July, however, Bremer, echoing Colin Powell, apparently had concluded that a power-sharing arrangement between the coalition and Iraqis would not work. He asserted that there could only be one government at a time—the CPA or an Iraqi one, but not both.[13] Bremer then announced he would appoint an advisory "political council" of thirty-five Iraqis called the Iraqi Governing Council (IGC) and indicated that he would be making all the decisions.[14]

Even as mere advisers, the Iraqis on the council seemed to irritate Bremer. He frequently complained about their leadership abilities. "Those people couldn't organize a parade, let alone run the country," he wrote later.[15] From my perspective, the leaders could not be judged on their administrative skills when they were not given real authority to administer anything. If the CPA had treated the governing council as something resembling an embryonic Iraqi government, the members might have been motivated to work more energetically and productively. Indeed, I thought one of the most important roles these leaders could play was to put an Iraqi face on the postwar administration, rather than an American one. I suggested to Bremer that the Iraqi Governing Council send someone approximating an ambassador to the United States: "It seems to me it could help our cause if there were a talented, articulate Iraqi available for the media every day explaining the views of the Iraqis who favor freedom and self-government."[16] This was typical of my guidance to Bremer. Contrary to popular perception, I was not inclined to issue direct, detailed, not to be questioned orders to those who work for me. I have found that people at senior levels generally do better when given broad guidance and the leeway to exercise their judgment as changing circumstances arise. In Bremer's case, he had too much leeway.

I wondered if it would have been better for the CPA to promote self-government first and foremost at the local level, and to diffuse power out of Baghdad's insular Green Zone complex. Our military division commanders across Iraq were tailoring their operations to the unique circumstances in their parts of the country. General David Petraeus, for example, held local elections in the northern city of Mosul soon after liberation. That was an action-oriented, aggressive approach that worked in that part of Iraq but may or may not have worked in other areas. I believed that one template was unlikely to fit the whole country. Iraq was too ethnically and geographically diverse for a nationwide model. But the CPA was a Baghdad-centric organization that too often handed down decrees for the whole country without regard for the differences from province to province.

When a U.S. Marine commander recommended holding local elections in June 2003 in Najaf, a city they judged was ready for an elected town council, Bremer objected.[17] He did not seem to favor organic political development at the local level. It wasn't until April 2004 that Bremer approved an order on the operations of provincial and local councils. He also seemed to see little value in engaging Iraq's tribes, which I considered key forces for stability in Iraqi history.

I learned much later from Admiral Giambastiani that Bremer was uncomfortable with the Commander's Emergency Response Program (CERP). CERP was an enormously valuable way to allow American military commanders across Iraq to help fund small-scale development projects in their area of responsibility (AOR).[18] The local military commanders knew which projects were needed to earn local support to make headway against the insurgency. Our military commanders were convinced the funds were often more valuable than bullets, but Bremer refused to allocate CERP money to the military from the Saddam government's seized assets.

In July 2003, Bremer announced a new program for the CPA called "Achieving the Vision to Restore Full Sovereignty to the Iraqi People." The document listed as the primary goal the "early restoration of full sovereignty to the Iraqi people" and added that the CPA "will not leave until we have succeeded in carrying out the President's [Bush's] and Prime Minister's [Tony Blair's] vision."[19] Bremer's interpretation of that vision included improving water resource management, improving health care services, reforming the tax system, building a welfare safety net, improving education and housing, and creating a vibrant civil society.[20] I was struck by the reality that our own country was still working on some of those areas two centuries after our independence.

Bremer's ambitions went far beyond the limited role for the United States that the Department of Defense and the interagency process had planned for and well beyond the role that had been resourced. CENTCOM had planned to liberate Iraq and set up the rough framework for the country to govern itself. The military had not planned to occupy every corner of Iraq with an American soldier or to try to impose a Western-style democracy on the country. The result was that the CPA and Iraq ended up with the downsides of an occupation strategy and few of the benefits—and without the resources that might have allowed some mitigation. The means were not well linked to the ends. It would be several months before those of us in Washington fully recognized that such a shift in policy had occurred.

It was natural, perhaps inevitable, that there would be missteps in the aftermath of liberation in so unfamiliar a country. But in those critical early days, the ambiguities in fundamental strategy were harmful. Bremer's arrival marked an unfortunate psychological change in Iraq—from a sense of liberation, with gratitude owed to the American military and our allies, to a growing sense of frustration and resentment that Iraq had come under the rule of an American occupation authority.*

The failure to establish an Iraqi interim government quickly was not the cause of every problem we faced in post-Saddam Iraq. The legacy of tyranny, the harmful actions of ill-intentioned neighbors, the catastrophic state of its infrastructure, the mistrust of foreigners, the ethnic and sectarian tensions, and the political vacuum all contributed to the instability. Nonethe-

*A subtle but important semantic misstep was that the administration allowed the United Nations to label the United States "an occupying power" in Security Council Resolution 1483. The unanimous May 2003 resolution signaled broad international approval for the coalition's efforts in a liberated Iraq, but it gave credence to the propaganda of our enemies that we were "occupying" Iraq.

less, I am persuaded that many of these difficulties became worse as a result of the delay in ceding authority to the Iraqis. The CPA's top-down approach inadvertently stoked nationalist resentments and fanned the embers of what would become the Iraqi insurgency. Many Iraqis associated the CPA with imperiousness and heavy-handedness. In his book *War and Decision*, Doug Feith argues that the main problem with the CPA was not the commonly cited decisions on de-Baathification or the disbanding of the Iraqi army that gave rise to an insurgency. He suggests that the CPA's policies and methods fueled the insurgency in other, more subtle ways.[21] The broader impression of an overbearing U.S. authority issuing edicts to the Iraqi people buttressed the anticoalition arguments of militants like Muqtada al-Sadr and Abu Musab al-Zarqawi. This played well into propaganda that the United States was trying to dominate and exploit Iraq rather than liberate it and return it promptly to Iraqi control.

Bremer issued two important orders soon after he arrived in Baghdad. In subsequent years both orders became characterized as the two original sins of the occupation and the cause of the difficulties in the years that followed. At the time, however, they were greeted with approval by a great many Iraqis and were put into place with the best of intentions.

CPA Order Number 1 concerned the policy of de-Baathification—the removal from the government of officials in the top layers of Baath Party.[22] Many were minority Sunni Arabs who had run Iraq for three decades. The Baath Party was less of a political party than a symbol of the state, much like the Communist Party in the Soviet Union or the Nazis in Germany. As such, it had become a widely hated vestige of Saddam's regime. Bremer, rightly in my view, thought it was important to make clear to Iraqis that the Baathists who had served a regime that had terrorized the citizenry, deployed the secret police, murdered regime opponents, and authorized torture chambers and rape rooms were not going to return to power.

But we knew that many thousands of Iraqis had been forced into the Baath Party and were members in name only. Under Saddam, almost anyone who wanted to advance professionally had to join, including schoolteachers, doctors, and engineers. There was no desire or intention to punish everyone in the system. As I had noted immediately after my trip to Baghdad at the end of April 2003, in certain sectors Baathists were keeping the fragile Iraqi infrastructure from collapsing.[23] The goal of de-Baathification was to target those at the top of the party, the ones who were so closely linked with the former regime that they could not be trusted to serve in the post-Saddam government. The de-Baathification policy in fact was akin to the Allies' de-Nazification policy in Germany after World War II, which barred some 2.5 percent of the German population from postwar government service. In Iraq, by contrast, DoD officials intended the policy to cover only one tenth of 1 percent of the population.[24]

Though the policy later found few defenders at the top level of the administration, de-Baathification initially had broad support among the relevant cabinet departments and agencies. The approach was promoted in the State Department's Future of Iraq Project that, as noted, later became touted in the media as the neglected plan for postwar Iraq.[25] Two weeks before the war began, an NSC staff member briefed the President on the policy. He explained that there were 1.5 million members of the Baath Party in Iraq but proposed removing only the 1 to 2 percent who were what he called "active and full members." All told, there were some twenty-five thousand people who could lose their government jobs. There were no objections from any of the principals present at the NSC meeting. However, the President did express some skepticism. "It's hard to imagine punishing twenty-five thousand people," Bush said. He then asked the critical question: "Who will do the vetting?"[26] The President understood that there was a good deal of pent-up rage against the ruling Sunnis by Iraq's Shia and Kurdish populations. In the wrong hands, it would be easy for de-Baathification to be an ax rather than a scalpel.

After Bremer announced the policy in May, he appointed Ahmad Chalabi, a member of the Iraqi Shia majority, to administer it. With Chalabi in charge, just as the President had feared, de-Baathification gained a reputation for score settling. Stories circulated about schoolteachers who were fired, former Baathist officials who were beaten in the streets, and even murders—acts that the CPA had not authorized, condoned, or had even minimal control over.

De-Baathification inflamed the minority Sunnis, who saw it as an act of vengeance against them as a group. Sunnis justifiably argued that while many of them had been forced to participate in the Baathist government, they were not all complicit in Saddam's crimes. The policy, and how it was administered, led some Sunnis to become embittered against the American presence in Iraq.

CPA Order Number 2—the decision to disband the Iraqi army—has since become one of the most criticized decisions of the war. Of the dozens of important decisions made during that week in May 2003, it was not one that stuck out with unique prominence at the time. But in hindsight, its importance is unmistakable.

Disbanding the army was not my instinct. Everything I wanted to do in Iraq was tied to the thought that we should have the Iraqis doing as much for themselves as possible. If we disbanded the army, it would mean that as many as four hundred thousand young Iraqi men would be put out of jobs and onto the streets. Some were armed, had military training, and could become susceptible to calls for resistance against the United States, coalition forces, and the new Iraqi government.

Before the war I had agreed it would be wise to keep the Iraqi army as a reconstruction corps—something loosely resembling FDR's Civilian Conservation Corps. In January 2003, Feith and his staff, working with the Joint Staff, drafted a briefing called "Rebuilding the Iraqi Military" that recommended retaining the regular army.[27] One month later, at a February 26 meeting, Pentagon representatives briefed the NSC principals on the DoD plans for what they called "the reintegration of the regular army." Under the plan, those structures of the military that were tainted with the crimes of the Baath regime—the Republican Guard and secret police among them—would be dissolved, but the regular army would be retained to assist in keeping security. The proposal would use the army "as a national reconstruction force during the transition phase."[28] The assumption was that they had structure and manpower as well as skills and equipment that could be valuable assets. By March, the brief was updated with the recommendation that following combat operations in Iraq, the army "should 'maintain its current status in assembly areas and permanent garrisons.'"[29] In short, the Iraqi army would be retrained and used as an instrument of defense of the new Iraqi state.

But I was aware that there were some downsides to keeping it in the form we found it. Controlled by Sunni officers loyal to Saddam, the army had been an instrument of terror against many Shia and Kurds. It was bloated with senior officers—eleven thousand generals, almost all of them Sunnis.[30] (By comparison, the U.S. Army, about the same size as Saddam's, had about three hundred generals.) Corruption was deeply ingrained. The Kurds and Shia, together composing 80 percent of Iraq's population, would also vehemently oppose any attempt to retain Saddam's army. We had to ask whether it made sense to risk alienating the vast majority of Iraqis by trying to keep and reconstitute the army. I concluded that the benefits outweighed the risks, and that we would keep it intact to help with security and reconstruction.

The calculus changed, however, as coalition troops drove north to Baghdad. Faced with the prospects of death or capture if they engaged our coalition forces, many members of the Iraqi army removed their uniforms and deserted. Undoubtedly, large numbers of the army's conscript soldiers—most of them Shia—had never wanted to serve the Saddam regime in the first place and didn't plan to stay any longer than necessary. CENTCOM was operating on the U.S. intelligence community's judgment that the Iraqi army would remain intact after the invasion, and that the largely Shia conscripts at lower levels of the military would be available to actively work with coalition forces to secure and reconstruct the country.* That judgment turned out to be incorrect.

The Iraqi army, in Bremer's words, "disbanded itself."[32] The evolving situation called to mind the John Maynard Keynes quote, "When the facts change, I change my mind. What do you do, sir?" Few, if any, of the arguments in favor of using the army continued to be applicable, while most of the reasons against using it remained. Bremer recommended a change of course.[33] He made the decision in close coordination with his senior adviser on defense issues, Walter Slocombe, who had served as undersecretary of defense for policy in the Clinton administration and who at my request had agreed to assist the CPA.

Bremer and Slocombe championed a proposal to create an entirely new Iraqi army. The training and equipping of the army would fall under the control of the CPA and not, as commonly assumed, under the United States military. Bremer briefed me and several other Defense officials about the outlines of the plan on May 19, 2003 and then other members of the National Security Council three days later. His decision, particularly its specifics, did not receive the full interagency discussion it merited.[34] We were told that each of the soldiers was to receive a stipend while the army was reorganized, so that they would not be aimless, unemployed, and on the streets.[35] Unfortunately, there was a month delay before Bremer's office announced the payments and another month before the CPA could issue them.[36] Many members of the Iraqi army became embittered. The initial pace of training the new army was also excruciatingly slow.[37]

Later I revived the question of whether it might be desirable or possible to reassemble units of the old Iraqi army and bring them into service in some

*It's difficult to penetrate the fog of war even after the fact, but in the years that followed, some senior military officers who were on the ground now believe there were at least some Iraqi units that might have been called back to duty. Some believe that as many as three Iraqi divisions might have been available for use. "The idea," Lieutenant General McKiernan later said, "was to bring in the Iraqi soldiers and their officers, put them on a roster, and sort out the bad guys as we went." If McKiernan had been acting as the senior commander in Iraq on the ground, as I believed he was supposed to be, his view might have prevailed.[31]

form.[38] I asked General Abizaid for an assessment. But Bremer strenuously objected to this idea, apparently on the grounds that Iraqis would not want any remnants of the old army reconstituted.[39] Whether or not disbanding the Iraqi army was ultimately a good idea, the failure to reform and reconstitute it quickly was costly.

Bremer's plan for a new Iraqi army focused on defending Iraq from an external threat rather than on using it for internal security.* This decision stemmed from his certain view that the Iraqi people would never trust or tolerate any version of Saddam's army patrolling their streets. Yet the far greater threat to Iraqis was not from outside invaders but from the insurgency being waged from within. The army was being trained to fight the wrong war.

For nearly a year Abizaid made efforts to get the training of the Iraqi army transferred from the CPA to the military, which had vastly more experience. Bremer finally relented in the spring of 2004. In the meantime, Abizaid and Sanchez had built up the Iraqi Civil Defense Corps, a force of military units that remained in their communities, but the size of Iraq's national security forces was still too small to deal with the insurgency.

It is fair to ask why differences between the CPA and CENTCOM, and more broadly between State and Defense, were not better resolved. I have asked it myself as I look back. The fact was that Bremer's views on Iraqi governance and occupation reflected those of the State Department. Those key differences were never clearly or firmly resolved in the NSC. Only the President could do so.

As time went on, Bremer's pride of ownership in his policy concerning the Iraqi army wavered. In 2005, Bremer said the decision had been his, calling it "the most important decision I made, and it had the effect of avoiding a civil war in Iraq."[40] However, by September 2007, as criticism of his decision intensified, Bremer wrote an op-ed in the *New York Times* entitled, "How I Didn't Dismantle Iraq's Army."[41]

Apparently Bremer felt he was blamed unfairly for the decision, and in truth, it wasn't all Bremer's fault. Many shared responsibility for the policy. I was told of Bremer's decision and possibly could have stopped it.[42] Members of the NSC had been informed of his decision before Bremer announced it, and not one participant registered an objection.[43] My impression was that President Bush wanted Bremer to have considerable freedom of action. However, it is now clear that the NSC should have deliberated the decision more

*The CPA called the proposed new army the New Iraqi Corps. Though it had been done unwittingly, the acronym NIC was a particularly foul word in Arabic.

fully. We should have had more clarity about the critical details of implementation, ensuring that the stipend payments and the size, purpose, and timeline for it were well understood and agreed to beforehand.

There is no mistaking that the decision to dissolve the Iraqi army had consequences, but as time has gone on we may be finding it has had some advantages as well.[44] Perhaps because much effort was poured into building a new force from scratch, it is emerging as one of Iraq's more effective institutions. By way of contrast, its police force suffers from lack of training and discipline, sectarianism, and corruption. As in Afghanistan, the State Department was, by U.S. law, placed in charge of police training in Iraq. However, State sent very few qualified people to either country.[45] In the case of Iraq, for reasons still unclear, the training program was delayed for six months. As a result, the country was without any sort of internal security force for a critical period following the war.

Defense officials repeatedly urged State and its representatives at the CPA to improve police training and devote more resources to the task.[46] But just as he had with regard to the training of the army, Bremer argued against having the U.S. military take over Iraqi police training. "I do not agree with placing the Iraqi police program under the military command," Bremer wrote me in February 2004, after I informed him that DoD would be assuming responsibility for police training. He said the transfer would "convey to the Iraqis the opposite of the principle of civilian standards, rules and accountability for the police."[47] This would have been a compelling argument if Iraq were Nebraska. But it wasn't. It was a war zone that was suffering from a vicious insurgency. We needed a capable police force to bring law and order and gather intelligence to stop the insurgency from metastasizing further, and we needed it fast. Too much time had been wasted already. The whole process had cost us a year—and done incalculable harm to our country's mission in Iraq in the interim.

The early months of the Iraq occupation—throughout the summer of 2003—saw the stirrings of an Iraqi insurgency. In August, the illustrious United Nations envoy to Iraq, Sergio Vieira de Mello, was killed when a flatbed truck filled with explosives barreled into the UN headquarters in Baghdad. Twenty-two other UN officials were also killed. The attack sent a chilling message to nations and organizations that were then considering joining the stabilization and reconstruction efforts. From that point on, our efforts to persuade countries to contribute became considerably more difficult.

Military commanders told me that before the attack they had warned UN officials several times that cement revetments and gates were needed to protect the UN compound. In declining to heed those warnings, they explained to our commanders, "That would make us too much like you." After the bombing, the United Nations closed its mission and withdrew from Iraq.

When the signs of a resistance movement emerged that summer—grenade attacks, small-arms fire, the occasional suicide bomber, or car bomb—we tried to identify who and what was fueling the movement. At first, the insurgency consisted of former regime figures and common criminals. On the eve of the invasion, Saddam had released one hundred thousand prisoners who contributed to the lawlessness.[48] Eventually the insurgency extended to groups like al-Qaida, which tapped into popular Sunni hostility against the Shia as well as the resentment that many Sunnis felt at the loss of their political privileges. Though the Sunni resistance initially seemed to lack organization and strength, its forces were soon being augmented by foreign fighters, jihadists who began pouring across Iraq's borders from Syria and Saudi Arabia.

The resistance was centered in Iraq's western Sunni provinces. Because the 4th Infantry Division had been denied access to Iraq's north through Turkey, most of the Sunni territory was not covered by U.S. troops in the early days of the war. Major combat operations were over by the time U.S. troops reached those strongholds. This meant that cities like Fallujah, Tikrit, and Ramadi never experienced major battles with U.S. troops and became safe havens for insurgents.

In the list of intelligence shortcomings, the failure to highlight the dangers of an insurgency was among the more serious. Intelligence reports occasionally discussed the possibility of postwar disorder and instability, but I don't recall seeing a briefing that anticipated the likelihood of a sustained guerrilla campaign against the coalition.* Our intelligence community lacked an appreciation for the Baathist regime's ability to finance, command, and control an insurgency after Saddam's overthrow. They repeatedly asserted that ideological conflicts between the secular Baathists and the jihadist religious

*In 2004, after the fact, the Senate Intelligence Committee's report could highlight only one small section at the end of a thirty-eight-page National Intelligence Council document suggesting that the CIA cautioned of an insurgency: "[R]ogue ex-regime elements could forge an alliance with existing terrorist organizations or act independently to wage guerrilla warfare against the new government or Coalition forces." This point was not included in the executive summary at the front of the document. Though press reports and opportunistic politicians seized on this line years later, CIA Director Tenet, to his considerable credit, came forward and put it into proper perspective in his memoirs: "It's tempting to cite this information and say, 'See, we predicted many of the difficulties that later ensued'—but doing so would be disingenuous. . . . Had we felt strongly that these were likely outcomes, we should have shouted our conclusions."[49]

extremists of al-Qaida precluded strategic cooperation between them—yet such cooperation became the heart and soul of the insurgency.

Out of the dozens of intelligence and military briefings on what might be expected from a war in Iraq, the first time I had heard of the possibility of "protracted guerrilla war" came from someone removed from the intelligence community. In April 2003, as our troops raced northward through Iraq, a retired Marine colonel named Gary Anderson wrote an op-ed on the possibility of a guerrilla war. Anderson had served in Somalia and Lebanon and was steeped in the lessons of asymmetric warfare. "Many observers of the war with Iraq are focused on the looming battle for Baghdad in anticipation that it will be the culminating event of the conflict . . . ," he wrote in the *Washington Post* several days before the fall of Baghdad. "But in the view of the Iraqi leadership, it may be only the end of a first stage in a greater Iraqi plan." He warned about the rise of "a protracted guerrilla war against the 'occupation,' which the American-British coalition bills as liberation."[50] He even raised the specter that the new phase of the war could be managed by Saddam himself. After reading Anderson's article, I decided it should be of interest to Bremer and Abizaid. Because I found it different from what we were being told, I also sent it to Myers, Wolfowitz, and Feith and asked them to give it some thought.[51]

Senior DoD officials discussed what we should label this resistance movement in July 2003. I did not want to label the enemy inaccurately or give it legitimacy that it didn't deserve. As the new CENTCOM commander, Abizaid did an initial assessment of the problem. In one of his first press briefings as CENTCOM commander, he called it "a classical guerrilla-type campaign against us."[52] Guerrillas can have positive connotations in many parts of the world. Many saw guerrillas as the brave vanguard of an outmatched force committed to bringing down a government through asymmetric means. I was also cautious about using the word "insurgency" at first. Insurgency struck me as an organized effort with a central command and control committed to the overthrow of a government. DoD's official definition of the term supported this interpretation.* In summer 2003, Iraq didn't have its own government and, moreover, the attacks seemed to lack central coordination. I told senior DoD officials that we had "to do a better job of using words that

*According to the official Defense Department dictionary, guerrilla warfare was defined as "military and paramilitary operations conducted in enemy-held or hostile territory by irregular, predominantly indigenous forces." An insurgency was defined as "an organized movement aimed at the overthrow of a constituted government through use of subversion and armed conflict."[53]

are well thought through and calculated to express exactly what we mean."[54] I didn't want to end up with another label like "war on terror" that we might regret down the road.

Abizaid didn't back down. In response to my queries, he gave the reasons why he believed it was a guerrilla war: The resistance had some public support; the attacks were sustained and asymmetric; and it was beginning to demonstrate some organization. The growing momentum of the attacks, particularly in western, Sunni-populated areas, proved Abizaid's point. He had done what I expected of all those who served in the U.S. military: When questioned by the Secretary of Defense, he marshaled the facts and arguments to support his position. He convinced me that we were indeed facing an insurgency. In November 2003, I asked for information and briefings on historical insurgencies and what the lessons learned of Britain's successful counterinsurgency in Malaya (now Malaysia) during the 1950s were.[55] There was no mistaking that there was a gaping blind spot where our government and intelligence community might have anticipated the possibility of an insurgency in Iraq.

As the months went on, it was clear that when I made suggestions to Bremer, he did not take them well. His formal direction from the President to report through me was being ignored. He was receiving guidance directly from many in the administration—the President, Rice, Powell—and choosing which guidance he preferred. After four months of what looked to me to be a series of unfortunate decisions, I felt a need to intervene.

I was onboard a military plane returning to the United States after a four-day trip to Iraq and Afghanistan on September 8, 2003, when I scanned the Pentagon's "Early Bird," a compilation of the top national security–related stories in major newspapers. One item that caught my attention was an op-ed by Bremer in the *Washington Post* entitled, "Iraq's Path to Sovereignty." This was the first I'd heard of the article's existence. In fact, I had just spent two days in Baghdad with Bremer, and he had mentioned nothing about it, nor had he even hinted at the startling news it contained.

"[H]ow can we get Iraqis back in charge of Iraq?" Bremer asked in his article. "Elections are the obvious solution to restoring sovereignty to the Iraqi people. But at the present elections are simply not possible."[56] He outlined seven steps that Iraq would have to take on its path to self-government, including economic progress, ratification of a constitution, and then elections. Only after the completion of these steps, Bremer wrote, would the CPA relinquish control of the country. I thought to myself that a turnover could take years under Bremer's policy—and if there were a stalemate at any step, it could take longer. This was quite a departure from our approach in Afghanistan. Afghans had had a sovereign interim government operating before their new constitution was drafted, let alone ratified, as a number of increasingly frustrated Iraqis noted.

I recognized, of course, that the plan Bremer was now outlining was similar to the approach long favored by the State Department, in which Iraq would regain sovereign power only after a multiyear period of U.S. administration. Indeed, Secretary Powell, at Bremer's request, flew to Baghdad to insist that this plan was the only way to ensure a successful and stable Iraq.[57] Bremer recounts Powell declaring to a meeting of the Iraqi Governing Council in Baghdad that giving sovereignty to the Iraqi leaders at that time was "entirely unacceptable."[58] Bremer's decision to publish his op-ed without informing me—and his apparent decision to follow the State Department's view—ended even the pretense that he reported through the Department of Defense, or that I was in any way in Bremer's line of authority.

Yet I was astonished to learn much later that Bremer had approached the President about moving out from under his theoretical reporting relationship through me, citing my "micromanagement." "Don terrifies his civilian subordinates," Bremer reportedly told the President. "I can rarely get any decisions out of anyone but him. This works all right, but isn't ideal."[59] The micromanagement charge was ironic coming from Bremer, of all people. Over the previous months I had worked to try to develop a good working relationship with him. I commended him for his work and made a point of noting whenever he seemed to be on the right track.[60] I still had considerable sympathy for the challenges he faced. He was in a tough job and getting criticism and advice from all sides. The Iraqis were pressing for more authority. The insurgency was blossoming. But Bremer and his CPA suffered not from too much oversight on my part but from too little. That needed to change. Bremer's op-ed reflected the still unresolved internal conflicts in the administration's Iraq policy. I decided it was worth a last-ditch effort to get it back on track.

CHAPTER 37

Liberation from the Occupation

Beginning in September 2003, after Bremer's article was published, I assembled a review group on Iraq policy, headed by Doug Feith and Lieutenant General Walter "Skip" Sharp, the director of plans on the Joint Staff. I hoped to bring resolution to the unresolved debate about our strategy for when to hand over authority to Iraqis. With input from Generals Myers, Pace, and Abizaid, we reformulated the five principal U.S. strategic goals for an Iraqi government: renouncing terrorism, abandoning WMD and long-range missile programs, seeking peace with its neighbors, remaining a unified country, and developing the Iraqi economy.[1]

Our plan called for the prompt assembly of a group of Iraqis to select an interim prime minister, help draft a constitution, and pave the way for elections. We also called for a date certain for the transfer of full sovereign authority: no later than the middle of 2004. I wanted to give Iraqis concrete assurance that the occupation of their country was going to end—and soon.[2]

I asked Bremer and Abizaid to fly to Washington to discuss it with us at the Pentagon. My hope was to sit down with Bremer and have him offer ideas and input, with the ultimate goal of getting him to buy in to our plan. I had a sense that our effort might prove successful.

Prominent Iraqis had protested Bremer's views as set forth in his op-ed. They were not pleased with his assertion that Iraqis would be taking on substantive roles later rather than sooner. Their significant outcry seemed to have put Bremer in a more cooperative mood. In fact, I thought he might be ready to accept a dignified way for him to drop his plan altogether.

I cleared much of my calendar for the two days Bremer and Abizaid would be in Washington. Over the course of our hours-long meetings, we showed them our strategic review and solicited their thoughts.[3] As I had hoped, Bremer was receptive. By the close of our discussions, he had reversed his position that the Coalition Provisional Authority could not be dismantled until after elections were held.

On October 29, 2003, with Bremer's acquiescence, I presented the agreed-upon proposal to the President and the members of the National Security Council. As he heard our timetable, Powell again expressed reservations, calling the turnover plan "exceptionally ambitious."[4] The President liked it, however, which was not surprising since it was in line with what I thought he had preferred to do all along. Bush soon set June 30, 2004, as the deadline for turning over sovereign power to the Iraqis. The occupation now had a foreseeable end.

As this was going on in October 2003, there was a curious development. A number of news outlets began to report that there had been a shake-up in the administration's Iraq policy—but it was not the one that actually had just occurred. "President Bush is giving his national security adviser, Condoleezza Rice, the authority to manage postwar Iraq and the rebuilding of Afghanistan," *USA Today* reported.[5] In what the *New York Times* called "a major reorganization" of the postwar effort, it quoted a senior administration official as saying that "[t]his puts accountability right into the White House."[6]

The news stories surrounding Rice's announcement reported that she had established something called the "Iraqi Stabilization Group," with undetermined responsibilities. CNN reported that it "will be responsible for handling the day-to-day administration of Iraq."[7] One newspaper ran a cartoon of Rice pulling down a statue of me in front of the Pentagon, as Saddam's statue had been pulled down in Firdos Square.

I thought it would have been terrific if Rice and her staff had the interest and skill to manage all U.S. efforts in Iraq and improve the situation. But they did not. In fact, the lack of resolution on issues relating to the administration's Iraq strategy at the NSC level had been a major contributing factor to the problems in the first place. Years later I learned that Bremer had been having a daily phone call with Rice at 6:00 a.m., Washington time. She had had ample opportunity to offer Bremer and the CPA management advice. After the press began speculating about the new powers of Rice's group—and the supposed coup against the Pentagon—Rice tried to clarify the situation. Publicly she said she had consulted

CONDI RICE OBSERVES
THE SIX MONTH
ANNIVERSARY OF THE
FALL OF THE SADDAM
STATUE...
RUMSFELD
IRAQ POLICY

I sent the cartoon to Rice with a note saying she should keep it for her scrapbook.[8]

on the establishment of the group with various officials, including me. That was not the case. I was informed of the new group's existence as a fait accompli, but not consulted about whether it was desirable, necessary, or appropriate.

The news stories about Rice's new management plan also repeated the widely believed canard that the State Department had been cut out of postwar planning.[9] The stories bore the unmistakable fingerprints of Powell's top aides.

I had been eager for the State Department to accept more responsibility in Iraq and would have been the last person to shut them out. When we asked the State Department to send experts to Iraq, they failed to meet their quotas.[10] When we asked for support for reconstruction teams in Afghanistan and Iraq, they struggled to fill them. When the State Department was in charge of training the Iraqi police, it did not get the job done. Powell was in National Security Council meetings and principals meetings on Iraq and shared in every major decision. It was a mystery as to what these State Department officials felt they were not involved in. I was skeptical that either the National Security Council or the State Department truly wanted to be accountable for the administration's Iraq policy, and I was all too aware that Rice and the NSC were not able to manage it.

On October 6, 2003, I sent a memo to the President with copies to Cheney and Andy Card. "In Monday's paper," I wrote, "Condi, in effect, announced that the President is concerned about the post-war Iraq stabilization efforts and that, as a result, he has asked Condi Rice and the National Security Council to assume responsibility for post-war Iraq."[11] I recommended that Bremer's reporting relationship be formally moved from Defense to the NSC or to State:

> At this point there is a certain logic to [the] transfer. We all understand and agreed that at some point the stabilization responsibilities would move out of DoD.
>
> Next, increasingly, Jerry Bremer has been reporting directly to Colin, Condi and you, as well as to DoD, so the effect of the change should not be major.
>
> Third, the responsibilities that Jerry is currently wrestling with are increasingly non-DoD type activities—they are increasingly political and economic.
>
> Finally, Condi, in effect has . . . announced that that is the case. To not make the transfer now will cause confusion as to where the responsibility resides.[12]

I further noted that I had told Bremer months earlier that I would prefer to have him report to the President, Rice, or Powell. "[H]e is fully aware of my willingness to have this reporting relationship adjusted now that the circumstances there have matured," I wrote.[13] No one took up my offer. In fact, Rice shortly thereafter reversed herself, apparently at the President's insistence, and informed the press that, contrary to her previous announcement, nothing about the administration's Iraq policy had changed.

One week later, after a principals meeting on October 14, 2003, Rice asked to see me privately. She apologized for the flap over Iraq and said that she was doing everything to correct it.

I interjected, "You're failing. You could have said something in the NSC meeting in front of the President and the principals."

"Don, you've made mistakes in your long career," she replied.

"Yes, but I've tried to clean them up."[14]

Over the first four years of the administration, I had repeated discussions with Rice and Card suggesting a series of reforms to the NSC process. Mindful of my own admonitions that complaints without tangible recommendations for solutions were generally unhelpful, I had sent a number of memos to Rice and Card proposing that they institute changes to improve the

President's most important national security body. But there had been little or no improvement.[15] It was not pleasant to see these problems up close, knowing how they undermined our nation's policies.

On December 6, 2003, I went to Iraq to assess the situation on the ground and made another attempt to clarify Bremer's chain of authority. Meeting him at the Baghdad airport, we moved into the lounge, where I took him aside. "Jerry," I began, "it is clear to me now that you are reporting to the President and to Condi." My view was that he should report to Powell at the State Department, not to Rice at the NSC, and that State should take on the responsibility for the civilian aspects of reconstruction in Iraq.

"I will keep my hand in on security," I said, "and I will try to be as helpful to you as I can, but I don't want four hands on the steering wheel."

I also said I didn't think the NSC was doing its job well, and that Rice's taking on an operational role in Iraq was a grievous mistake. When the NSC staff engaged in operations abroad in the Reagan administration, I noted, they wound up overseeing a trade of arms for hostages in Iran and brought the Iran-Contra scandal down on the President's head.

Bremer told me that he shared my concerns about the NSC, and that he didn't disagree with or object to anything I said. I wished him well. At that meeting, as far as I was concerned, any lingering pretense that I oversaw his activities came to an end.[16]

By the time I arrived in Baghdad that December, military officials told me they were beginning to believe they might finally have Saddam—officially dubbed High Value Target Number One—in their sights. But reports of Saddam sightings were as frequent as they were unreliable. Even as a deposed dictator, he remained skillfully elusive. He had a number of hideouts and body doubles. He reportedly slept in a different place every night.

I put a high priority on Saddam's capture and considered it a critical step in giving Iraqis confidence that the old tyranny was gone and would never come back. Even after Saddam's overthrow, many Iraqis feared that the war was not over—and that the Baathists might be heard from again. They had lived in terror of the midnight knock on the door from regime agents for so long that they had difficulty moving past the worry that conceivably one day Saddam Hussein might return to power. Saddam had worked for decades to build his cult of personality. Suddenly turning himself into an amateur genealogist, he even declared he was a direct descendant of the prophet Muhammed. His picture was in all public buildings, on billboards, in homes, and in restaurants, reinforcing the idea in Iraqis' minds that he was everywhere and everything. Saddam had survived several wars, an earlier U.S. invasion, coups, and uprisings. Iraqis asked themselves, with justification, whether he might pull off such a feat again.

Even the deaths that July of Saddam's vicious sons, Uday and Qusay, had not been enough to overcome the fear that a Hussein regime could return in some form. Active participants in the regime's crimes, Saddam's sons long had been his heirs apparent and were rumored to be even more sadistic than their father. If Saddam died, Iraq under their leadership was likely to be even more oppressive and hostile to Western interests than it had been under Saddam. After the invasion, Uday and Qusay had gone into hiding. When coalition authorities tracked them to a building in Mosul, they became engaged in a fierce firefight, seemingly determined not to be taken alive. Their wish was granted.[17]

After his sons were killed, there was an intelligence report that Saddam Hussein was paying $60 million for his agents to target the President's two daughters and my two daughters for reprisal attacks. That threat report was brought up at an NSC meeting in October 2003. I acknowledged it, but went on with our discussion.

"You need to take this seriously," Bush said. He had received word that pictures of his daughters had been found in Uday Hussein's palace.

Tenet broke in, reinforcing the President's concern. "You took out Saddam's sons. They might well go after your daughters." Needless to say, I was concerned about my family, but there was little I could do about it other than encourage them to take precautions.

On December 6, 2003, I visited Kirkuk in northern Iraq, where I met with Major General Ray Odierno. At a hulking six foot five inches, Odierno looked like a superhero in a movie. As commander of the Fourth Infantry Division in the Sunni areas to the north and west of Baghdad, he was leading the hunt for Saddam Hussein. I asked a number of questions about how close we were getting to him and what intelligence methods Odierno was using—human intelligence, signals intelligence—and how many suspects he was rounding up. Odierno made no promises but indicated that the trail was getting warmer.

Exactly one week later, in the late afternoon of Saturday, December 13, I had just left the Pentagon and arrived at General Myers' house for a brief stop at a holiday party he was hosting when I was summoned for an urgent call from CENTCOM. The many reporters present were curious when I had to quickly end my conversation and go upstairs to Myers' private office. Abizaid told me over the secure line that our military had finally captured Saddam Hussein. Through an operation code-named Red Dawn, U.S. military personnel had rounded up a host of people judged likely to be hiding Saddam, or at least knowledgeable of his whereabouts, including former bodyguards, palace officials, and tribal leaders. One of these informants directed our forces to a farmhouse near Tikrit, Saddam's ancestral home. There they found a trapdoor concealed by dirt and rubble. As one soldier prepared to lob a grenade into the hole, another noticed that there was a man inside.

As he was hauled up into the light, the man looked disoriented. He was carrying a pistol but made no effort to use it.

"My name is Saddam Hussein," he announced. "I am the President of Iraq and I want to negotiate." The Butcher of Baghdad was pulled from the small, dirty "spider hole" at 8:30 p.m. Baghdad time.[18]

I immediately telephoned the President, who was at Camp David. In light of a number of prior false alarms, I didn't want to say anything too definitive.

"Mr. President," I began as soon as he picked up my phone call, "first reports are not always accurate, but—"

"This sounds like it's going to be good news," Bush interrupted.

I told him I had been advised by Abizaid that our troops believed they had captured Saddam Hussein. Bush too expressed caution. He asked why we thought it was him. My answer was that U.S. military officials had identified a bullet hole in his left leg and distinctive tattoos on his body; I added, however, that I wasn't necessarily persuaded by that. Saddam's body doubles could easily have been given similar identifying marks. I told him I was more impressed that our troops had found a sizable amount of money with him. I did not think it likely that a body double would be carrying some $750,000 in U.S. currency.

I assumed that our military would announce Saddam's capture. Sanchez and Odierno were the ones who had been hunting him and had successfully tracked and captured him. Their dogged work had led to a major achievement. I thought it also would have been logical for them to have some senior Iraqi official participate in the announcement, to give it added credence. Instead, Bremer strode to the microphones at his Green Zone headquarters in Baghdad the following morning. "We got him," he announced. Bremer was beaming. I was not.

Shortly after his capture, Iraqi officials displayed Saddam on television. The Iraqi people needed to see him for themselves, so they could be convinced that their resilient and elusive former leader was really in hand. As I saw this bedraggled figure, my mind flashed back to my meeting with

BY PERMISSION OF MIKE LUCKOVICH AND CREATORS SYNDICATE, INC.

him, the grand potentate. Twenty years later, Saddam Hussein was under arrest. The capture led to jubilation throughout much of Baghdad. There was a noticeable uptick in Iraqis' interest in cooperating with coalition authorities, and, it seemed, an increasing optimism.

It was tempting for me to meet with Saddam in jail, as Bremer and members of the Iraqi leadership had done. However, I was actually more interested in seeing Tariq Aziz, who had been captured months before. I knew that nice guys didn't last long in criminal regimes, but he lacked the obvious hard edges that many of his fellow Baathist bigwigs displayed. He had a manner that could obscure the underlying evil of the regime he represented—a paradox I had always found interesting whenever I sat across from him and engaged in the friendly conversations we had. I would have been interested in hearing Tariq Aziz's version of events—how things had gone so wrong for him since our visits together in Iraq and in Washington in the 1980s. I wanted to know why Saddam had refused to comply with seventeen UN resolutions, and why they didn't leave the country when President Bush had given them a chance in the days before the war. I wanted to understand the tortured logic behind the regime's serial deception on its WMD programs and why their warped bluff had invited the very thing they hoped to deter. Ultimately, I decided there was no way to talk with my old acquaintance without creating a spectacle.

It was a mistake not to make the separation between the Department of Defense and Bremer official and publicly visible. Had I successfully done so, the Department might have been spared some of the criticism for another of the CPA's decisions, relating to a violent event in the city of Fallujah.

Known as the "City of Mosques," Fallujah by the spring of 2004 had become a haven for militants operating against the coalition. Baathists, al-Qaida terrorists, marginalized Sunnis, and criminals looking to make easy money planting roadside bombs had turned the city into a nest of killers. Car bomb factories and terrorist safe houses were scattered throughout the area. Many of the city's two hundred mosques had become nodes of the disparate resistance movements.

On March 31, 2004, Iraqi insurgents ambushed four Blackwater contractors. They were pulled from their convoy and dragged through the city streets. Their murdered bodies were hanged over a Euphrates River bridge. Photographs and videos of the carnage promptly flashed around the world.

These crimes were monstrous—everyone understood that. But what many also did not seem to realize was that this act had a sinister and calculated purpose. The insurgents knew that they couldn't hold off an American assault with arms alone. Instead, they had a sophisticated propaganda effort designed to intimidate and make Americans question whether their effort was worth the cost. The shocking images of bloodied and charred American corpses dangling from a bridge was a public relations victory for them. Increasingly, people questioned why Iraq seemed to be chaotic, violent, and out of control after its liberation.

All of us on the National Security Council recognized that we could not allow an Iraqi city to become a sanctuary for murderers and terrorists. My impulse was not only to find the enemies who had committed the atrocity, but also to send a message across the country that anyone who engaged in acts of terror would face the might of the U.S. military.

With the situation appearing to worsen that spring, General Myers and I approved Abizaid's request to extend the tours of twenty thousand of our forces. Abizaid had earlier hoped that we might be able to gradually begin reducing troop levels. But that now seemed less likely.

On April 6, 2004, the Marines began an offensive to secure Fallujah, the largest combat mission in the eleven months since the end of major combat operations. Through no fault of the Marines, Operation Vigilant Resolve proved to be neither vigilant nor resolute. After three days of intense fighting, the Marines commanded a quarter of the city. But the gains came amid controversy, as the enemy's savage tactics, combined with their successful propaganda effort, had their desired effect.

Insurgents took over public buildings, notably mosques and hospitals, and used them as bases from which to attack the advancing Marines. When an American air strike destroyed a mosque, it led to a public outcry fueled by false news stories on Al-Jazeera that trumpeted civilian casualties and carnage.* It was asymmetric war in its purest form. The insurgents of course were violating the laws of war: using civilians as human shields; firing on Marines from houses in Iraqi neighborhoods, daring the Marines to fire back; and storing their weapon caches in mosques, schools, and hospitals. The enemy sought to convince the world that America's use of force was indiscriminate, disproportionate, and reckless.

Sunni members of the Iraqi Governing Council, who were anxious to assume control of their government as the June deadline for Iraq sovereignty approached, expressed outrage at the U.S. attack on Fallujah and pressed Bremer for a cease-fire.

On April 9, Bremer, Abizaid, and Sanchez participated in an NSC meeting via secure video from Baghdad. I joined the President, Powell, and Rice in the Situation Room. "We have a real threat with the top Sunni members of the Iraqi Governing Council," Bremer told the President. He said they were threatening resignation and the dissolution of the council. "I've agreed to a twenty-four-hour cessation of operations," Bremer said, adding, "This is not a cease-fire."

It sounded exactly like a cease-fire—even a capitulation—to me. The Iraqi Governing Council wanted time to negotiate, but I doubted any real concessions would be extracted from an army of fanatics who had vowed to attack the new Iraqi government. I wanted to continue the operation.

"What do we do when the Iraqi Council asks for an extension?" I asked.[19]

"I recommend we don't grant it," Abizaid answered quickly.

*We learned that several Al-Jazeera correspondents were embedded with the terrorists. They knew when and where attacks against Iraqi and coalition forces would take place, and they videotaped the attacks showing our troops being killed.

"I tend to agree," Bremer interjected, "but we can't rule it out, and we shouldn't answer hypothetically." His reluctance indicated to me an extension of the twenty-four-hour so-called cessation of hostilities was all but certain.

I knew Bush's instinct was to take the enemy out, but he also had to consider the diplomatic aspects. "How long do the Marines need to conclude their operations in Fallujah?" he asked.

"Three to four days," Abizaid replied.

"Well, tell 'em we'll quit in four days," Bush said.

As the Iraqi Governing Council engaged in discussions, our Marines, still taking fire from the enemy, held their positions but halted their advance. As the twenty-four-hour cessation of hostilities expired, just as I had anticipated, Bremer was reluctant to continue the offensive. He said he feared uprisings in Iraq and a "collapse of the entire political process" if the Marines continued.[20] It was not an unreasonable concern, but for me an even greater worry was the insurgent attacks that were continuing against our troops. I felt our military was being tested, and we needed to push back against the challenge.

Bush seemed to share that view. At the NSC meeting the next day, on April 10, the President worried that there would be consequences if people thought, as he put it, that "we've been whipped."[21] But the President did not issue an order for the Marines to continue.

The President decided that extending or canceling the cease-fire was an operational decision—one that belonged to the senior officials on the ground. Directly countermanding the recommendations of the two most senior commanders responsible, Abizaid and Sanchez, in addition to Bremer, was not in the cards. The Commander in Chief made the call to let them proceed as they saw fit.

There was logic in deferring to Bremer and Abizaid in that they had made some real progress elsewhere in Iraq. The military's efforts and arrests of senior members of the regime gave the Iraqi people an opportunity to close the book on their recent past and bring the criminals to account. By October 2003 the country's electricity generation was higher than prewar levels, though in the years that followed it would ebb and flow with the pace of attacks.* With help from Undersecretary of the Treasury John Taylor, they rapidly created and distributed new Iraqi currency and curbed inflation.

*The often cited statistics about electricity generation did not give a full picture. After insurgent attacks on the power grid began taking a toll on production, Iraqis began to figure out the best solution for themselves. They bought generators for their homes and businesses that were far less susceptible to attacks than the large, vulnerable, and expensive power plants, lines, and transformers that made up the national grid.

Real Iraqi GDP growth during the CPA period was 46.5 percent.[22] The stock market opened, as did schools and hospitals across the country. In March 2004, Bremer and CPA officials drafted an interim constitution known as the Transitional Administrative Law that protected human rights, asserted the freedom of religion, and established the basic structure of a representative Iraqi government.[23] It left a lasting imprint on Iraqi society. These were important signs of progress that received relatively little recognition.

The first battle of Fallujah, in April 2004, however, was not among the triumphs of that period. The cease-fire stalled the momentum the Marines had gained. The Iraqi Governing Council again said they would resign if our forces pressed on. Eventually our coalition allies began to urge us to call off the attack. They were seeing the same images as many across the Arab world: wounded Iraqis, damaged mosques, and interviews with Fallujans describing supposed crimes by Marines targeting schools and hospitals. The widely disseminated propaganda increased the sense that the situation was one misstep away from a total, nationwide revolt against coalition forces. The Iraqi Governing Council tried to persuade the insurgents to lay down their arms and abandon the city. Bush was unhappy with the situation as was I. It was doubtful that a cease-fire would be productive.[24] I knew that sooner or later, we would have to return to the enemy's stronghold.

Given a growing insurgency and the existence of sanctuaries like Fallujah where insurgents received support from the local population, it was clear that we needed to find a way to involve the Sunnis in the new Iraq. Only a small percentage of them were directly engaged in the insurgency or linked to groups like al-Qaida, but many others sympathized with the resistance and the sense that their country was being occupied by forces hostile to them. It was easy to appreciate why many Sunnis—who were once accorded all of the privileges in Iraqi society—might see the future without Saddam and his largesse as bleak. Around the time of the Fallujah standoff, General Abizaid and I were discussing a Sunni outreach strategy. He thought there could be a way to peel off the disaffected Sunnis from the Islamist extremists and hard-core Baathists. There were intelligence reports about former Iraqi generals and other senior Baathists who had fled Iraq but had connections with insurgents who were ready to negotiate.* A large payment of cash by us could

*Two of the most promising leads were from two Sunni former army generals, Abdul Razaq Sultan al-Jibouri and Talal al-Gaood, who had reached out to the U.S. military in late 2003 and offered to help negotiate peace with Sunni tribes in Anbar province.

buy a change of allegiance, they informed us. We needed to determine if their offers were in good faith. Abizaid persuaded me of the merits of a determined outreach effort.[25]

In April 2004, I suggested to Bremer that he put together a strategy designed to "change the mindset of disenfranchisement and hopelessness" among the Sunnis.[26] Senior military officers and I had been concerned for over a year that the Sunni tribes were being neglected, but we had found a less than receptive ear in the CPA.[27] The Sunni outreach I outlined included easing up on de-Baathification efforts by moving Ahmad Chalabi out of the process.* I urged Bremer to focus on "labor-intensive projects in Sunni areas" and those near moderate Sunni mosques. I also asked him to build ties to Iraq's Sunni tribes through regular visits with their leaders. We could contract with members, as Saddam did, to provide essential services, such as protecting the electrical grid from sabotage. The tribes and their leaders—in Shia and Kurdish communities as well as Sunni areas—were the backbone of Iraqi society. Not engaging them was unwise. Tribal leaders, I suggested, also could help us recruit for the security forces and put pressure on members of their tribes who helped the insurgency.

But Bremer was not inclined to work through the tribes. Despite his agreement to turn over sovereignty by June, it remained difficult to get him to accept the idea that Iraq belonged to the Iraqis, and that the Iraqis were entitled to their own culture and institutions.

In the spring of 2004, we faced the danger of a two-front insurgency. Sunni insurgents were gaining ground and establishing sanctuaries in Iraq's west, in places like Fallujah. Meanwhile, Shia militias, under Muqtada al-Sadr, were threatening rebellion in the south. The son of a revered ayatollah who was murdered by Saddam's lieutenants, Sadr demonstrated little of his father's intellectual prowess. As a failing seminary student, he had earned the nickname "Mullah Atari" in recognition of his fondness for video games. Yet he developed a following and became a powerful and violent leader of opposition to the American occupation. His angry sermons drew flocks of young men from Shia slums, enabling him to establish a militia that gained influence through a combination of social services and mob terror. Sadr

*DoD's willingness to remove Ahmad Chalabi from a governance role in de-Baathification if he continued to be too stringent seemed not to register with those critics who argued that DoD officials were somehow fixated on making Chalabi the leader of Iraq.

intimidated other Iraqis by being able to put thousands of thugs and young males on the street. These mobs, called the Mahdi Army (though it was in no sense an army), were a potent force for disruption, demonstrations, and terror.

That April, long-simmering tensions with Sadr came to a head in Najaf, Iraq's holiest Shia city. Taking advantage of the Fallujah flare-up, Shia gangs heeded Sadr's call, televised on Al-Jazeera, to attack coalition forces throughout southern Iraq.[28] Sadr had established his own Islamic courts and prisons in Najaf—the heart of the Shiite clerical establishment—where eyewitness accounts reported torture in the style of Saddam's regime.[29]

There were several discussions in the National Security Council about whether, and if so when, our forces should take Sadr into custody. As early as August 2003 I had recommended that Abizaid and Bremer begin to think through "what we are going to do if red lines are crossed."[30] When Sadr began calling the coalition "the enemy," I felt he had crossed the line.[31] If he wanted to define us as his enemy, my view was that we should treat him as one. He had evidently ordered the murder of one of Iraq's most respected moderate Shia leaders, Abdul Majid al-Khoei. I felt it was important to establish the principle that no one—not even a cleric with the loyalty of tens of thousands of Shia—should be above the law. In January 2004, I recommended that the CPA arrest Sadr to demonstrate "that the rule of law applies to Shi'a as well as Sunni."[32]

But there was another legitimate consideration that preoccupied us. Arresting Sadr risked making him even more popular, and could further inflame tensions with the Shia majority, possibly triggering an outright civil war. When Sadr was holed up in the holy city of Najaf, for example, several senior clerics who opposed him nonetheless argued strongly against storming the city to arrest him. They feared it would aggravate sectarian tensions and damage holy sites.[33] Still, my view was to arrest the demagogue.

Since this was a decision that could have a significant impact on the relationship between the coalition and our Iraqi allies, the President concluded that Bremer had to decide the best course to take. As coalition forces surrounded Najaf, Bremer and Sanchez decided to let the Iraqis take action on their own to deal with Sadr and his so-called Mahdi Army.[34] I understood the reluctance to storm the city. But the idea that the Iraqi clerics or politicians would take on Sadr seemed unrealistic.

To my amazement, Bremer has since claimed that he wanted to go after

Sadr but "[W]e got word that Rumsfeld had given instructions not to execute the plan to arrest Muqtada until 'further notice.'"* That was not the case. It is possible that others on the NSC with whom Bremer regularly communicated might have opposed arresting Sadr, but I did not. In fact, I was so taken aback by Bremer's suggestion that I later asked Pentagon officials to examine the issue and find out if anyone else at the Defense Department might have led Bremer to think we had wanted him to refrain from acting. The conclusion was that no one had done any such thing.[36] Again, through no fault of their own, our military appeared ineffective, not only against the terrorists in Fallujah but also against the vocal cleric looking to cause trouble.

There was another cleric who was in many ways Sadr's polar opposite—sage and learned, modest, moderate, and, above all, restrained. Grand Ayatollah Ali al-Sistani kept his distance from Americans, declining to meet with U.S. officials—military or civilian. At critical points he calmed passions among the millions of Shia who revered him. He encouraged them to accept the separation between religion and the state in a constitutional democracy, rejecting Iran's form of clerical rule. In the face of consistent provocations by al-Qaida and Sunni insurgent groups against Shia people, shrines, and mosques, and the rebellions urged by Sadr, Sistani counseled calm and patience. Without him, I have no doubt that Iraq would be very different today—and not for the better. His leadership, along with many others who truly wanted a better life for their people, offered hope as we moved toward finally giving them the sovereignty they desired.

Though a latecomer to relinquishing power to the Iraqis, Bremer worked to organize the transition once the decision was made. He planned a timetable with the Iraqi Governing Council that set out dates for writing an interim constitution and setting up a transitional national assembly. With the CPA's assistance, they drafted their interim constitution in March 2004. Though based in part on principles from our Constitution, it was by no means an American document, but appropriately an Iraqi document. It protected the rights of minority Sunnis, Kurds, and Christians and gave the long beleaguered majority Shia a full role in their government. Bremer and

*I wanted to make sure the details of a move to arrest Sadr had been properly considered before action was taken. With this in mind, at one point in 2003, I dictated a series of questions for Bremer and CPA security officials to consider before they moved against him. Bremer writes in his book that these "exasperating" questions were tantamount to my opposition to the plan. Asking questions about the operation and how it would be done was basic prudence. It was a mistake not to have asked similar "exasperating" questions about some of Bremer's other decisions.[35]

the Coalition Provisional Authority deserve credit for helping Iraqis craft the most representative constitution in the history of the Arab world.

In May 2004, following the recommendations that the Defense Department's policy shop and the Joint Staff had developed, Iraqis on the governing council met to select an interim prime minister. Ayad Allawi, a medical doctor by training, became the first Iraqi leader to assume power since Saddam Hussein. He was a symbol of opposition to Saddam. In years past Allawi, along with some of Saddam's generals, had attempted to overthrow the Iraqi regime. He fled to London, where Saddam's hit-men broke into his residence and attacked him with an ax as he slept, wounding him in the head and chest. Miraculously, he survived and remained resolute in his opposition to the regime. Though a secular Shia, Allawi had launched the Iraqi National Accord in 1990—a group comprising many Sunni, Baathist military officers who had become disaffected with the Saddam Hussein regime. The Iraqi Governing Council selected him unanimously as prime minister.

The approach of the June 30 handover date proved an irresistible draw for terrorists and insurgents. They staged several bloody suicide bombings, which seemed designed to intimidate the Iraqis and cast doubt on whether they would be able to lead. The enemy understood well that attacks against a sovereign government would not be nearly as popular or as widely supported as attacks against coalition "occupiers."

After several of these bombings, doubts resurfaced within and outside of the U.S. government about whether the Iraqis truly were ready to govern themselves. Reporters frequently asked Bremer and others if the date for the transfer was still on track. Bremer defended the plan steadily.[37] I did as well. I had no doubt that the turnover was the right thing to do.

As June 30 approached, intelligence reports warned that enemy fighters were planning an ugly reception for the new government, in the form of massive attacks across the country. Bremer wisely decided to outmaneuver them by moving the date of the handover forward by two days.

At the time, I was in Istanbul with President Bush at a historic NATO summit meeting. The alliance was going to admit seven new members, all formerly part of the Warsaw Pact. Three were former republics of the Soviet Union. The alliance had fifteen members when I served as U.S. ambassador there in the early 1970s. It would now have twenty-six. The meeting in Istanbul, in fact, would be the largest gathering of NATO heads of state ever assembled. I felt a great sense of satisfaction seeing the leaders of those once communist nations free to chart their own courses and voluntarily, indeed

eagerly, join the NATO alliance. It was a vindication of the tough, nerve-racking, long-sustained, costly, and high-minded half-century struggle by the allied countries, with bipartisan U.S. leadership, to contain and eventually defeat Soviet communism.

As I surveyed the large, circular table and the representatives of our alliance partners, I thought about Iraq. I wondered if decades from now Americans might look back on the liberation of those long repressed Iraqis with the same kind of satisfaction that we felt about our liberation of Europe from Nazism and Soviet communism.

I was sitting with the U.S. delegation when an aide passed a cable from Iraq to Condi Rice. In a ceremony with little fanfare—certainly less than when he had arrived in Iraq a year earlier—Bremer presented Prime Minister Allawi with a letter from President Bush affirming the dissolution of the Coalition Provisional Authority.[38] Rice penned a note on the cable and passed it to me.

"Mr. President, Iraq is sovereign," the note read, marking the historic day of June 28, 2004. "Letter was passed from Bremer at 10:26AM, Iraq time." I handed the note to the President. He had been concentrating on the NATO discussion but looked down long enough to read it. He then took out his pen and wrote "Let Freedom Reign!" before turning to the British Prime Minister, Tony Blair, seated to his right, and whispering the good news. The two leaders smiled at one another and shook hands.

The U.S. and coalition occupation was over. Not a moment too soon, I said to myself. For me the question was whether it was too late. We were still trying to regain the trust of the Iraqi people—a task that had been made more difficult not only by a long and heavy-handed occupation but by the crimes of a few military guards at a prison called Abu Ghraib.

PART XII

Wartime Detention

Washington, D.C.

APRIL 28, 2004

Two months before Iraqis assumed control of their country, the world was shocked by images of U.S. soldiers taunting naked Iraqi prisoners at Abu Ghraib prison. The digital photos, taken by the soldiers in acts of pornographic self-indulgence, documented the sadistic abuse and torment they were inflicting on prisoners in their charge. The acts were inexcusable. The photographs threatened to weaken public support and call into question the legitimacy of our ongoing efforts on the eve of the transition to Iraqi sovereignty.

Prior to the public release of the images, I was shown a portion of them. Many depicted military guards performing humiliating acts on Iraqi prisoners—forcing them into what appeared to be a human pyramid, with naked detainees piled on top of one another. In some photos, the guards were shown pointing, laughing, or giving a thumbs-up.

A number of other photographs were not released to the public at the time. They showed soldiers engaged in similarly disturbing sexual, sadistic acts—but with each other: Americans on Americans. Had all of the pictures been released at once, the public might have drawn more quickly the conclusions that I drew: These acts could not conceivably have been authorized by anyone in the chain of command, nor could they have been any part of an intelligence-gathering or interrogation effort. Rather, they were the senseless crimes of a small group of prison guards who ran amok in the absence of adequate supervision.*

To my knowledge, no one in the Pentagon had forewarning of the issues that gave rise to the abuses at Abu Ghraib, but that was beside the point. Unacceptable acts had been visited upon human beings in U.S. charge. The ramifications were so great that, as the head of this department of three million people, I felt compelled to step forward to take responsibility for the

*Not all of the photos were released to avoid inflaming the situation on the ground in Iraq and other places where American servicemen and -women were at risk.

institutional failure.[1] As I began to come to terms with what had happened at Abu Ghraib, the events left me feeling punched in the gut.

It was the U.S. military command in Iraq that first announced publicly that it was conducting an investigation into instances of abuse of Iraqi detainees in January 2004. At the time there was little media interest in the story, but once it was accompanied by photographs three months later, that changed dramatically. In another unique feature of war in the twenty-first century, the photographs made their way across the world within minutes, inviting a reaction that was as angry as it was swift. Leaders of nations across the world issued condemnations. The Vatican's foreign minister, invoking the word "torture," called Abu Ghraib "a more serious blow to the United States than September 11."[2]

I shared the sense of outrage, but the reaction to Abu Ghraib in some instances seemed to be exacerbated by motivations other than simply getting to the bottom of what had transpired and bringing to justice those who had engaged in the illegal acts. The shameful abuse at Abu Ghraib would be exploited by many: America's enemies, of course, who skillfully used the outcry for their propaganda purposes; Arab governments that had an interest in making their populations think of the Iraqi liberation as dangerous and chaotic; opponents of the war, who used the abuse to justify their position that the efforts in Iraq were immoral; and, most obviously, political opponents of President Bush seven months before the 2004 election. In some quarters, the reaction quickly veered into overstatement.

"We're not going to recover from this damage," Congressman John Murtha announced. "This one incident destroyed our credibility in Iraq and in all the Arab world."[3] "Shamefully, we now learn that Saddam's torture chambers reopened under new management—U.S. management," Senator Ted Kennedy declared on the floor of the United States Senate.[4] For a senior senator to equate the perverted escapades of a handful of guards on the midnight shift with the routine practices of rape, torture, and murder in Saddam's prisons was appalling, even by the low standards of a political season. I was surprised when my colleague Colin Powell mentioned Abu Ghraib in the same context as the My Lai massacre—an appalling episode from the Vietnam War that involved the cold-blooded murder of hundreds of civilians. "I don't know what to make of it," Powell said. "I'm shocked. I mean, I was in a unit that was responsible for My Lai."[5]

Also lost in the melee was any recognition that the military command in Iraq first brought these abuses to light. A soldier discovered the photos and handed them to senior military officials. A prompt investigation began, leading to the suspension of seventeen personnel.

Critics nonetheless expanded their attacks by taking the inexcusable acts at the Abu Ghraib prison as the basis of a systematic critique of the Bush administration's war policies. An article in *The New Yorker*, citing anonymous sources, asserted that the abuses were part of official and systematic coercive interrogation methods.[6] Those false charges were widely disseminated and repeated by people who could and should have known better. "What happened at the prison, it is now clear, was not the result of random acts by a few bad apples," stated Al Gore. "It was the natural consequence of the Bush administration policy."[7]

The Economist placed a picture of a detainee on its cover under the headline "RESIGN, RUMSFELD." Similar calls came from the *New York Times*, the *Boston Globe*, and Democratic members of Congress. Though I didn't often find myself in agreement with them, I was quickly coming to the same conclusion, although for quite different reasons. I believed my resignation as secretary might demonstrate accountability on the part of the U.S. government. I thought that my resignation might also allow the administration and the Iraqi people to move beyond the scandal.

On May 5, at 10:00 in the morning, one week after the photos became public, I walked into the Oval Office with a handwritten note. "Mr. President," it said, "I want you to know that you have my resignation as Secretary of Defense any time you feel it would be helpful to you."[8] I told him that if the controversy over the abuse kept growing, I might not be effective in managing the Department. I also said that I believed someone needed to be held accountable.

Bush had been deeply affected by the photographs. He shared my view on the importance of accountability.

"Don, someone's head has to roll on this one," he said. I told the President he had my resignation, and I thought he should accept it. However, I left our meeting without a decision.

That evening, Bush called me at the Pentagon. He said he had thought the matter over. "Your leaving is a terrible idea," he said. "I don't accept your resignation."

He asked if there was anyone else he should hold accountable by firing them, and he raised General Myers as a possibility. "Mr. President," I replied, "you would be firing the wrong person."

There was a rationale for firing a senior official. I understood and shared the President's need to hold someone at the top accountable for what had happened. But it would have been unjust to fire General Myers, who as chairman of the Joint Chiefs of Staff was not in the chain of command and had no direct line of responsibility in the abuse at Abu Ghraib.

I too wanted to demonstrate accountability by removing those at senior levels who were ultimately responsible for the lack of training, supervision, discipline, and professionalism that led to the inexcusable actions at the prison. As I discovered in the weeks after the abuse came to light, responsibility was diffuse.

Complicating matters was the fact that there were two lines of responsibility: the operational chain of command through CENTCOM, and the administrative chain of command through the Army. The operational chain of command started with the Commander in Chief and ran through me to the CENTCOM combatant commander to the U.S. commander in Iraq down to military officials at Abu Ghraib prison. The administrative chain of command started with me and ran through the secretary and chief of staff of the Army. I hoped that each chain of command quickly would identify where the primary responsibility lay and that we could hold accountable the appropriate senior officers.* That is not what happened. To help put the matter behind the Defense Department, I determined that President Bush deserved an option, and that left nobody but me.

On May 7, 2004, I crossed the Potomac and headed up Independence Avenue to Capitol Hill to testify on the abuses. In Washington there was speculation as to whether I might resign on the spot. There were also suggestions that more members of Congress might personally demand my resignation at the hearing. As I made my way to the Capitol, protesters lined the entrances to the Senate and House office buildings, some carrying signs accusing me, the President, and the military of war crimes.

In my testimony and subsequent press conferences on Abu Ghraib, I

*Another problem was that those at CENTCOM and the Army who had been in positions of responsibility and partly responsible for the circumstances that preceded the abuses at Abu Ghraib had already left their positions. By the spring of 2004, most of those still in the relevant posts had been in there for relatively short periods of time. On the operational side, General Abizaid had been on the job for only several months when the abuse occurred. Under him, General Sanchez was the officer directly overseeing operations in Iraq and, therefore, the officer most likely to be fired. But in my view the Army administrative chain had thrust Sanchez into a position he never should have been in, and proceeded to deny Sanchez the staff and support he required and requested and that I had authorized. The Army's leadership had also been in flux. I had already fired Secretary of the Army Tom White in April 2003 for other reasons. Les Brownlee was an acting secretary when Abu Ghraib occurred. The Army chief of staff, General Shinseki, who had been in charge when the original deficiencies in training, selection of senior personnel, and establishing Sanchez's headquarters occurred, had retired after his full four-year term in June 2003. The new Army chief of staff, Pete Schoomaker, had been in his position for only several months when the abuse occurred.

wanted to express my deep feelings of disgust and outrage at these indefensible acts. But there was a legal limit on what I could say publicly. The servicemen and -women depicted in the photos were awaiting trial by courts-martial. In the military justice system, the judge, jury, and prosecutor are all members of the Defense Department, and any comment made by an official in the chain of command—military or civilian—risks exerting what is called "unlawful command influence" on the outcome of the trial. If I had expressed my strongly held opinion on the guilt of those involved, it could have made it impossible to hold them accountable by law. My public statements on Abu Ghraib were carefully calibrated with legal advice. Most Americans were understandably outraged at those who had committed these acts, and they wanted to know that President Bush and I were outraged as well. Unfortunately, because both of us were at the top of the chain of command, we had to take care that our words were properly measured.

In seven hours of testimony to the Senate and House Armed Services committees alongside General Myers and Army officials, I explained what we knew about the Abu Ghraib abuse and that we were determined to do our best to make sure it never happened again.* I opened my testimony by raising the question of who bore responsibility for what had taken place. "These events occurred on my watch," I said. "As Secretary of Defense, I am accountable for them. I take full responsibility."[9]

On behalf of the Department, I apologized to the President, the Congress, the country, and the Iraqi detainees who were in military custody. Promising a full investigation, I regretted that those of us at the Pentagon had not known about the abuse—and had not seen the pictures—earlier. I stressed the importance of a full, open airing of what had taken place at Abu Ghraib and of a transparent system to punish the illegal acts. "[H]owever terrible the setback," I said, "this is also an occasion to demonstrate to the world the difference between those who believe in democracy and human rights and those who believe in rule by the terrorist code."[10] I ended with an appeal to the members of Congress, to Americans, and to the world. "Judge us by our actions," I said. "[W]atch how a democracy deals with wrongdoing and scandal and the pain of acknowledging and correcting our own mistakes and weaknesses."[11]

During my testimony, Senator Evan Bayh, a Democrat from Indiana, asked me if my resignation would help undo some of the damage to our reputation.

*Myers and I were accompanied by Les Brownlee, Acting Secretary of the Army; General Peter Schoomaker, Chief of Staff, United States Army; Lieutenant General Lance L. Smith, Deputy Commander, CENTCOM.

"That's possible," I responded. I did not volunteer that I had already submitted it to the President.

Though Bush told me I should not resign, the matter still was not settled in my mind. The previous week had been excruciating because the scandal was so damaging to our armed forces and the country. I generally thrived under pressure, but I wasn't thriving now. Abu Ghraib was threatening to consume the Defense Department, eclipsing the fine work thousands of servicemen and -women did every day. The Democratic National Committee was already using Abu Ghraib to raise funds for its campaigns.

That Sunday—Mother's Day—our children called and told me they were with me no matter what I decided. Vice President Cheney said that with Iraq in such a difficult condition, the President wanted me at the Defense Department. "You have to stay," he urged in a phone call.

I was later reminded of an episode more than a half century earlier. In April 1952, when I was studying naval science in college, the U.S. Navy destroyer USS *Hobson* struck the aircraft carrier USS *Wasp* in the dark of night. The *Hobson* sank to the Atlantic seafloor with 176 men aboard.[12] The commanding officer, Lieutenant Commander W. J. Tierney, went down with the vessel. A Navy board of inquiry ultimately concluded that Tierney was to be held responsible for the incident. It could not have been easy to demand accountability from a commanding officer who lost his life. Nevertheless, there is a tradition on the sea and in our Navy that with authority comes responsibility and accountability. The Navy's venerable tradition regrettably seemed not to have taken hold to the same extent in the other military services. The case of the *Hobson* said a lot about leadership—and its consequences.

On May 10, 2004, President Bush came to the Pentagon for a briefing on Iraq. At the end of the briefing, I asked the President if I could see him alone. As we sat at the round table in my office overlooking the Pentagon's River Entrance, I handed him a second letter of resignation.[13] "By this letter I am resigning as Secretary of Defense," it read. "I have concluded that the damage from the acts of abuse that happened on my watch, by individuals for whose conduct I am ultimately responsible, can best be responded to by my resignation." As he read my letter, Bush was quiet.

"Mr. President, the Department of Defense will be better off if I resign," I insisted.

"That's not true," he responded, tossing the letter across the table back to me.

I told the President my mind was made up. Nonetheless, he insisted that he wanted some time to think about it and to consult with others. The next day, Vice President Cheney came to the Pentagon. "Don, thirty-five years ago this week, I went to work for you," he said, "and on this one you're wrong."

In the end, Bush refused to accept my resignation. He had concluded that my departure would not make Abu Ghraib go away, and that he preferred to have me stay to manage the problem and the Department. For some in the United States and around the world, Abu Ghraib was a metaphor. The pictures from the prison had come to symbolize the war many had come to oppose. The President may have felt that my resignation might embolden the critics of the war effort, who would frame it as an indication of the administration's guilt and argue that it proved the Iraq war was hopeless.

As much as I believed I was right to resign, I eventually accepted the President's decision and agreed to stay and continue to manage the scandal, while working to keep the Pentagon, two wars, and our major transformation efforts moving forward. I now believe that this was a misjudgment on my part. Abu Ghraib and its follow-on effects, including the continued drumbeat of "torture" maintained by partisan critics of the war and the President, became a damaging distraction.* More than anything else I have failed to do, and even amid my pride in the many important things we did accomplish, I regret that I did not leave at that point.

Hundreds of individuals inside the Defense Department and on independent panels outside spent thousands of hours looking into the reasons that the abuse at Abu Ghraib occurred. One thing that became clear was that the crimes had nothing whatsoever to do with interrogation or intelligence gathering. The U.S. soldiers shown in the photographs were not interrogators, nor were they involved in collecting intelligence from those detainees. Further, the individuals they were abusing were not intelligence targets undergoing interrogations. The guards were not following any guidelines or policies approved at any level. They were a small group of disturbed individuals abusing the Iraqis they were in charge of guarding.

Part of the cause of Abu Ghraib was a lack of training. Part of it was a lack of discipline and supervision. And part of it was the failure from the outset of the Department of the Army and Joint Staff to provide the appropriate

*The magnitude of the scandal naturally tempted charlatans to come forth to capitalize on the outrage. In March 2006, the *New York Times* profiled Ali Shalal Qaissi, the founder of the Association of Victims of American Occupation Prisons. Qaissi claimed to be the hooded prisoner made famous by Abu Ghraib guards who placed a prisoner on a box with wires attached to his hands. Qaissi handed out business cards with the silhouette of the image on it. The newspaper, among other media outlets, accepted the story without skepticism. It later was exposed as a lie.[14]

and agreed-upon staff and support to General Sanchez's headquarters in Iraq, which made it difficult, if not impossible, for his busy command to oversee adequately the growing population of Iraqi detainees in prisons like Abu Ghraib.

I directed officials at the Pentagon to cooperate fully with the numerous investigations underway—some of which I ordered. Vice Admiral Albert Church, a cousin of the crusading Senator Frank Church who led the Senate's intelligence investigations in the 1970s, conducted one of them. "One point is clear," he concluded. "[W]e found no direct (or even indirect) link between interrogation policy and detainee abuse."* A nonpartisan investigation led by two former Secretaries of Defense, James Schlesinger and Harold Brown, which included the late Congresswoman Tillie Fowler and retired General Charles Horner, found that "There is no evidence of a policy of abuse promulgated by senior officials or military authorities."[16] After twelve nonpartisan, independent reviews and investigations of Defense Department detainee policies,[17] not one found evidence that abuse had been encouraged or condoned by senior officials in the Defense Department—military or civilian.†

On May 29, 2004, at the height of the controversy, I attended the dedication of the World War II Memorial on the Washington Mall. A number of people came up to me to offer encouragement. The most unusual was a gray-haired former president and husband of the junior senator from New York who was castigating the administration over the scandal at the same time.

Bill Clinton walked across the large reception tent and shook my hand. He said something to the effect of "Mr. Secretary, no one with an ounce of sense thinks you had any way in the world to know about the abuse taking place that night in Iraq." He added, "You'll get through this."[18] I appreciated the gracious gesture.

The abuse at Abu Ghraib and illegal acts committed elsewhere in U.S. military detention facilities are part of the story of detention operations in wartime, to be sure. But they are only part of the story. Between 2001

*The Church Report concluded: "[N]one of the pictured abuses . . . bear any resemblance to approved policies at any level, in any theater. . . . [N]o approved interrogation techniques at GTMO are even remotely related to the events depicted in the infamous photographs of Abu Ghraib abuses. . . . If an MP ever did receive an order to abuse a detainee in the manner depicted in any of the photographs, it should have been obvious to that MP that this was an illegal order that could not be followed. . . . We found, without exception, that the [Defense Department] officials and senior military commanders responsible for the formulation of interrogation policy evidenced the intent to treat detainees humanely."[15]

†A report by Senator Carl Levin in 2008 disregarded all of these findings and claimed that "senior officials in the United States government solicited information on how to use aggressive techniques, redefined the law to create the appearance of their legality, and authorized their use against detainees."

and 2006, more than eighty thousand captured personnel passed through Defense Department custody. Of those, there were only a small number of documented cases of abuse. Each time there was an allegation of wrongdoing, it was promptly investigated and prosecuted when appropriate. The rare instances of abuse should not blind the world to the professionalism and skill of the tens of thousands of Americans in uniform who were entrusted with detainee operations.

CHAPTER 38

The Least Worst Place

"At the top there are no easy choices."
—*Dean Acheson,* Present at the Creation

In the heat of war, human frailty can undermine discipline and corrupt behavior even among well-trained soldiers. World War II, for example, saw instances of war crimes committed against captured soldiers on both sides of the conflict.* Detention operations in war have also suffered from misjudgments. President Franklin D. Roosevelt authorized the internment of more than one hundred thousand Japanese Americans in desolate camps across the western United States although they were not enemies.

Even in nonmilitary, peacetime situations, detention is a difficult task, as the staggering statistics of murder, rape, and abuse in federal, state, and local prisons across the United States attest.† Whenever and wherever abuse of prisoners occurs—from Bagram to San Quentin—it is an evil deed and a shameful disservice to our country, our society, and the huge majority of

*In 1943 American troops executed fifty to seventy unarmed Italian and German prisoners of war in the Sicilian town of Biscari. At the liberated concentration camp at Dachau, U.S. troops shot and killed Nazi SS guards who had already surrendered. A lengthy investigation and military cover-up of the murders followed.[1]

†More than sixty thousand inmates are sexually abused every year in American prisons and jails. A September 2009 Justice Department report shows that out of ninety-three federal prisons, ninety-two reported instances of prison employees sexually abusing prisoners.[2]

civilian and military guards who perform their difficult duties with professionalism.

When it came to captured terrorists, I knew that housing and interrogating them would require close attention and inevitably arouse controversy. Each step of the way toward crafting a coherent policy, we confronted complicated legal and policy dilemmas. Some critics cast these issues as simple questions of right and wrong. On matter after matter, however, we found ourselves facing decisions for which the options available were all imperfect.

We were dealing with individuals capable of horrific acts of murder and destruction. Yet they were human beings in the custody of a nation that properly holds itself to high standards. Belief in human dignity is the underpinning of Western civilization and one of the chief differences between Americans and our enemy. I knew our government had to create a legal architecture that afforded detainees due process while protecting our national security. I also believed that we needed to reinforce the incentives embodied in the Geneva Conventions. The Conventions are treaties with the broad purpose of protecting innocent life by deterring violations of the laws of the war, such as targeting civilians, not just for ensuring the proper treatment of prisoners of war.

In the months and years following 9/11, most detainees in American custody were categorized as unlawful enemy combatants. They were enemies who had ignored the long-established rules of warfare and, as a result, effectively waived the privileges accorded to regular soldiers. Some of these captured detainees were terrorists and insurgents who had attacked—and, in many cases, killed—American and coalition forces. Inevitably, others would be in our custody by mistake, as is also the case in our domestic criminal justice system.

We also knew that some detainees possessed potentially time-sensitive information that could prevent future attacks and save American lives. But while it was important to obtain that information, it was also imperative to put rules and safeguards in place to govern interrogations. In keeping with my oath of office, it was my duty to help protect the country and the American people from all enemies, and to preserve and defend the Constitution. We had a responsibility to protect innocent civilians. I was among those obligated to see to the effective and proper interrogation and detention of those captured in the war against terrorists.

Since 9/11, our primary responsibility was to prevent another attack on our people. On a near daily basis we were receiving fragmentary pieces of intelligence on a range of threats. Terrorists could use suitcase radiation weapons, or vials of anthrax or smallpox, that could spread widely and quickly, devastating the populations of major American cities. The questioning of those in Department of Defense custody provided information that saved innocent American lives. I make no apology for that.

From the outset of the global war on terror, one of the Defense Department's tasks was to fashion a process for deciding whom to hold and whom to release. I pressed military commanders and intelligence officials with a number of questions: How many detainees should we plan to hold? For how long? At what locations? For what purposes?

This was a war that could be long and have no definitive end. We were fighting irregular forces—al-Qaida and other terrorists—not military personnel of a nation that upheld the laws of war. Our enemies were extremists motivated by an ideology in which it is perfectly acceptable, indeed in their minds a sacred obligation, to kill ordinary civilians—men, women, and children.

The longer America held detainees, the more problems we would have. The guidance I gave to the Department was to be highly selective, so that we would hold as few detainees as possible. I wanted procedures in place for promptly evaluating those captured on the battlefield, to release as many as possible without compromising American lives, and to transfer as many others as possible to the custody of their home countries. As I frequently told the President and others, the last thing we wanted was for the United States, let alone the Department of Defense, to become "the world's jailer."[3]

On November 13, 2001, the day Kabul was taken by the Northern Alliance, President Bush issued a military order formally appointing the secretary of defense as the "detention authority" for captured prisoners and for establishing the outlines of a justice system to try them.[4] The order was the product of a series of discussions between White House and Justice Department lawyers.

The President's order required that the Defense Department establish facilities to house suspected terrorists and conduct "military commissions to sit at any time and any place, consistent with such guidance regarding time and place as the Secretary of Defense may provide."[5] The order was based directly on decisions that had been made by presidents of both political parties during wartime, most recently by Franklin Roosevelt during World War II. Indeed, much of the language was taken verbatim from Roosevelt's order establishing military commissions in 1942, which had been upheld unanimously by the Supreme Court of the United States.[6]

The relevant sentences of the President's order were brief, but the tasks they set out were colossal. They would require the work of thousands of people for hundreds of thousands of hours. Bush was delegating wartime responsibilities to the Department of Defense that had not been used by our government in more than half a century.

I agreed with the President's decision to shift from a peacetime approach, which treated terrorist acts as law enforcement problems, to a wartime footing, which deemed terrorism as an act of war. This fundamental change in philosophy was challenged by some who preferred trying terrorists in civilian courts of law after the fact and treating them as common criminals. The reality was that America had tried that approach for decades, and it had proven inadequate for stopping terrorist attacks before they occurred. Treating the conflict as a war—coupled with Congress' September 18, 2001 authorization of the use of all "necessary and appropriate force" in the fight against terrorists—was the proper way to move beyond a reactive policy of retaliation and achieve the President's goal of establishing proactive measures to prevent terrorist attacks against America.

Still I questioned whether our military was the appropriate institution to hold captured enemy combatants. From World War II through Korea and Vietnam to the first Gulf War, it was true that the military had shouldered the responsibility for the detention of captured enemy forces. But as I saw it, this unconventional conflict—against an amorphous enemy and with no finite duration—did not fit neatly within the laws of war pertaining to conventional conflicts. When it came to detention, our military had been schooled in holding enemies of regular armed forces—that is, lawful combatants entitled to prisoner of war (POW) status. Our armed forces did not have experience or established procedures for dealing with captured terrorists who, under the laws of war, were not entitled to the privileges of POWs.

What the President directed us to undertake required the advice of attorneys familiar with U.S. statutes and our international agreements. One of the notable changes I had observed from my service in the Pentagon in the 1970s was the prevalence of lawyers—in almost every office and in nearly every meeting. By the time I returned as secretary in 2001, there were a breathtaking ten thousand lawyers, military and civilian, involved at nearly every level of the chain of command across the globe. That the Department of Defense could function at all with ten thousand lawyers parsing its every move is astounding.

The number of laws and regulations relevant to the Defense Department had exploded correspondingly. Most elements of warfare in the twenty-first century were governed by complex legal requirements, from tactical rules of engagement to strategic issues involving negotiations over the Anti-Ballistic

Missile Treaty. It was a considerably bigger challenge than two and a half decades earlier, but we needed to ensure that the Department was always in compliance with the law.

Many fine attorneys worked on detainee affairs, including Harvard law graduate and former Army Captain William "Jim" Haynes II, who as general counsel was the Pentagon's chief legal adviser. Haynes spared no effort to protect the interests of the armed forces while ensuring the Department's activities were respectful of our nation's laws. He and his large staff seized the nettle of detention issues from the outset. Haynes was aided by Dan Dell'Orto, a talented career civil servant and retired Army lawyer who had served in the Pentagon during the Clinton administration. The breadth and complexity of the issues Haynes, Dell'Orto, and the general counsel's staff dealt with on any given day—personnel, procurement, courts-martial, promotions, intelligence, contracting, international law, and treaties—rivaled the workload of any government legal office.

The President's November 13 order required that the Defense Department establish new rules for wartime detention. The guidance handed down by the President was that all detainees in U.S. custody were to be treated humanely, regardless of their legal status.[7] In a separate Department of Defense order to the combatant commanders on January 19, 2002, I echoed the President's order and directed all personnel to "treat [al-Qaida and Taliban detainees] humanely" and "in a manner consistent with the principles of the Geneva Conventions."[8]

Though isolated cases of abuse and mistreatment of detainees have occurred in every war, American military forces have a long record of restraint and professionalism when it comes to holding captured enemies. After his army's success on the frozen fields outside Princeton, New Jersey, George Washington issued unequivocal orders on the treatment of captured British soldiers: "Treat them with humanity, and Let them have no reason to Complain of our Copying the brutal example of the British army in their Treatment of our unfortunate brethren."[9] Chairman of the Joint Chiefs Dick Myers and I wanted to make sure that the military upheld this high tradition. Even while fighting an enemy whose use of brutality was the norm, we insisted on aligning our military's conduct with the humane principles on which our Republic was founded.

In November 2001, a violent rebellion of Taliban and al-Qaida detainees in northern Afghanistan brought into focus the dangers and difficulties of managing fanatical killers in custody. General Rashid Dostum, an ethnic

Uzbek Northern Alliance commander, as well as a powerful and tough warlord, held several hundred Taliban and al-Qaida foot soldiers in Qala-i-Jangi, a nineteenth-century mud-and-brick fortress near Mazar-e-Sharif.* Among the Qala-i-Jangi prisoners that November was an English-speaking man who looked out of place. His name was John Walker Lindh, and he would become known as "the American Taliban."

During the questioning of Lindh and his fellow prisoners, two CIA agents asked him about his background and the circumstances of his capture on the battlefield among the al-Qaida and Taliban fighters. In the middle of the interrogation, a detainee leaped toward the two American intelligence operatives, touching off a prisonwide rebellion. The ensuing battle pitted Dostum's few Northern Alliance guards, a handful of British Special Air Service (SAS) troops, U.S. Special Forces, and the two CIA agents against several hundred Taliban and al-Qaida, many committed to fighting to the death. The battle raged for three days. The prisoners managed to capture a Northern Alliance cache of weapons—including AK-47s, rocket launchers, mortars, and grenades.[10] U.S. AC-130s and Black Hawk helicopters came to support the pinned-down coalition forces while Taliban and al-Qaida fighters held out in the basement of Qala-i-Jangi.[11] Only when they were flushed out of the fortress with water did the fighting end. Before the battle there had been three hundred al-Qaida and Taliban prisoners, but only eighty-six emerged to surrender.[12]

The battle led to the deaths of some forty Northern Alliance soldiers, while another two hundred were injured.[13] U.S. and British Special Forces also had taken casualties. Johnny Micheal Spann, one of the two CIA officers at Qala-i-Jangi prison that weekend, was killed in action in the first minutes of the battle, becoming the first American to die in combat operations in Afghanistan.[14] His body was booby-trapped with a hidden grenade by the al-Qaida and Taliban prisoners so those recovering his remains would be wounded or killed. The episode was another reminder that many of those detained were there for a reason—they were violent, vicious, and would not hesitate to kill again.

After the toppling of the Taliban, there was no central government in

*In early 2002 there were reports that some al-Qaida and Taliban prisoners in Dostum's custody might have died in shipping containers near the northern Afghan town of Dasht-e-Leili. Dostum insisted that the deaths had been accidental, the result of suffocation, combat injuries, and sickness. The scope of what exactly occurred—whether negligence or malfeasance, as some later alleged—was never determined. What was clear was that U.S. Special Forces had not seen, taken part in, or condoned the action. Dostum, a leader respected by a large number of Afghans, particularly ethnic Uzbeks, was a valuable ally to the Northern Alliance and to our Special Forces in defeating the Taliban and al-Qaida; he also later was a member of the country's freely elected government. Like many complex figures and phenomena in Afghanistan, he was a fact of life.

Afghanistan and no functioning criminal justice or prison systems. As coalition forces eliminated pockets of resistance in the early weeks of January 2002, the Northern Alliance was holding hundreds of suspected al-Qaida and Taliban prisoners—including the survivors of the battle at Qala-i-Jangi prison. Most detainees were vetted informally and sent home; others were permitted to join the Northern Alliance. As U.S. forces established a few large bases in Afghanistan, a growing number of detainees began to accumulate in military custody.

Some detainees were supporters of the Taliban who had joined the fight against the Northern Alliance and coalition as foot soldiers. Others were senior Taliban leaders. Still others were foreigners, many affiliated with al-Qaida. They had come to Afghanistan from various corners of the world—the Middle East, Europe, Southeast Asia, and Africa—to conduct jihad against the West and to kill Americans. The origins and records of some of the Northern Alliance prisoners were unclear. These men had been picked up in bad company, and some were terrorists or the terrorists' allies. But others may have been innocent people who happened to be in the wrong place at the wrong time. While we couldn't afford to release dangerous men with important intelligence information in their heads, we certainly didn't want to hold mere bystanders.

In analyzing the legal status of the detainees, government lawyers examined the Geneva Conventions. Updated and refashioned in 1949, the modern Geneva Conventions reflected the fact that Axis powers had committed horrific crimes against noncombatants during World War II. The premise of the 1949 Geneva Conventions is that a civilized and responsible nation, even while fighting and killing enemy soldiers, should abide by humane rules and mitigate the brutality of war. The Conventions regulate the way parties to Geneva are to treat enemy prisoners, setting up a system of incentives to encourage combatants to obey the laws of war and discourage the loss of innocent life.

The architects of the modern Geneva Conventions also envisioned and assumed a degree of reciprocity and mutuality of interest among the warring parties. The Conventions' drafters knew about irregular warfare, such as that of the French anti-Nazi resistance, but they did not have in mind or prescribe rules for asymmetric warfare that deliberately targets civilians—like al-Qaida's large-scale use of suicide "martyrs." Al-Qaida's videos of beheadings publicly celebrate cruelty, proving beyond a doubt that al-Qaida does not treat detainees humanely, especially Americans.

George W. Bush was not the first president to face the issue of whether terrorists should be granted the protections of the Geneva Conventions. During the Cold War, the Soviet Union and its proxies pushed for adding rules to the Geneva Conventions that would grant such privileges to, and therefore legitimize, Soviet-backed guerrillas. President Ronald Reagan stood firmly against those revisions.[15] He said the amendments giving irregular combatants the full protection of the Geneva Conventions would "undermine humanitarian law and endanger civilians in war."[16] The Reagan administration also was convinced that rewarding irregular combatants with the full rights and privileges of lawful combatants would not only make a mockery of the Geneva Conventions, but would undermine one of their key purposes, which was to protect civilians.

At that time, the *Washington Post* lauded President Reagan's position in an editorial entitled, "Hijacking the Geneva Conventions."[17] The *Post* approvingly quoted Reagan: "[W]e must not, and need not, give recognition and protection to terrorist groups as a price for progress in humanitarian law." The *New York Times* editorial board agreed, calling the proposal "a shield for terrorists." It added:

> President Reagan has faced more important but probably no tougher decisions than whether to seek ratification of revisions to the 1949 Geneva Conventions. If he said yes, that would improve protection for prisoners of war and civilians in wartime, but at the price of new legal protection for guerrillas and possible terrorists. He decided to say no, a judgment that deserves support.[18]

By 2002, both the *New York Times* and the *Washington Post* editorial boards had swung a full 180 degrees in the opposite direction.[19]

Consistent with the Reagan administration precedent, there was broad consensus in the Bush administration and, at least initially, among legal experts across the political spectrum, that the Geneva Conventions did not apply to al-Qaida terrorists in U.S. custody.* The logic was simple: Al-Qaida was not a nation-state and was not a party to the Geneva Conventions.† Its

*In a 2002 interview, Clinton Justice Department official and future attorney general in the Obama administration Eric Holder said, "It seems to me that given the way in which they have conducted themselves, however, that they are not, in fact, people entitled to the protection of the Geneva Convention [sic]. They are not prisoners of war. If, for instance, Muhammed Atta had survived the attack on the World Trade Center, would we now be calling him a prisoner of war? I think not. Should Zacarias Moussaoui be called a prisoner of war? Again, I think not."[20]

†Only nation-states—not groups or individual actors—may ratify treaties.

fighters also did not meet the four fundamental requirements for lawful combatant and prisoner of war status in the Third Geneva Convention: operating with a responsible command structure; wearing identifiable uniforms; carrying their arms openly; and obeying the laws of war. Al-Qaida terrorists, by contrast, bombed marketplaces posing as merchants and shop-goers—with explosives under their clothes, in their car trunks, or hidden on children. The nineteen 9/11 hijackers posed as businessmen in suits and commandeered civilian airliners to attack civilians, killing three thousand Americans and citizens from ninety other nations. Such deliberate, surprise attacks on civilian targets demonstrated nothing but contempt for the Geneva Conventions.

I agreed that if the United States automatically accorded the privileges of POW status to every individual captured on the battlefield (or more privileges, such as the right to appeal their detention in U.S. courts), regardless of their compliance with the Geneva Conventions, there would no longer be any incentive whatsoever for enemies to abide by the Geneva rules. Terrorists could have the best of both worlds: all of the advantages of being irregular, unlawful combatants but without any of the consequences. If accorded POW status, terrorists would not be required to give up any intelligence they possessed. Under the Third Geneva Convention, POWs are only obligated to provide name, rank, serial number, and date of birth—the most basic information—when questioned.* That means that even a number of the interrogation methods used every day in police stations across the United States are forbidden. The Geneva Conventions also require that POWs be given access to athletic uniforms, musical instruments, alcohol, tobacco, and the military justice system used by the detaining force.†

Because neither Taliban forces nor al-Qaida terrorists met the unambiguous requirements for POW status, they were not entitled to its special protections. This determination was not "abandoning" or "bypassing" the Geneva Conventions as many have erroneously alleged.[23] It was, in fact, adhering to the letter and spirit of the Conventions. President Bush directed that as a matter of policy the treatment of al-Qaida and Taliban detainees would meet

*"Every prisoner of war, when questioned on the subject, is bound to give only his surname, first names and rank, date of birth, and army, regimental, personal or serial number, or failing this, equivalent information."[21]

†POWs must also be held "under conditions as favorable as those for the forces of the Detaining Power who are billeted in the same area." Put a different way, housing POWs in individual cells—even with the luxuries of cable TV and individual bathrooms, as is done in many minimum security prisons across the United States—could be a violation of the Geneva Conventions. They must be housed as soldiers, in open barracks under the same conditions as U.S. forces and are entitled to wear their uniforms and badges of rank.[22]

a high standard. He saw this not so much as a legal obligation, but as simply the right thing to do.

The plain words of the Geneva Conventions support the position he ordered, as did the written words of his most prominent administration officials. Indeed, in February 2002, William Taft IV, the senior legal adviser to Secretary of State Powell, advised White House Counsel Alberto Gonzales: "The lawyers all agree that al Qaeda or Taliban soldiers are presumptively not POWs."[24] Powell apparently felt strongly enough in this case to put his thoughts in writing. His preferred option, he wrote, entailed announcing "publicly" that "members of al Qaeda as a group and the Taliban individually or as a group are not entitled to Prisoner of War status under the Convention."[25]

Though it was clear that the privileges of the Geneva Conventions did not apply to terrorists, there was serious debate about whether the Geneva Conventions applied in any way to America's conflict with the Taliban regime. The Taliban were the de facto government of Afghanistan, a country that was a party to the Geneva Conventions. However, officials and lawyers in the Justice Department concluded that even though Afghanistan had ratified the Geneva Conventions some years before, the Taliban had not been recognized as that country's government, either by the United States or by most other countries, nor did they actually control a viable nation-state. Because Afghanistan was deemed a "failed state," Attorney General John Ashcroft and Justice Department officials maintained that the President was not required by law to apply the Geneva Conventions to America's war against the Taliban.[26]

Those of us in the Defense Department did not address Justice's legal position, but we had a different view as a matter of policy, perhaps none more strenuously than the Chairman of the Joint Chiefs of Staff. One day in late January 2002, General Myers strode purposefully into my office with a concerned look on his face. Several days before, White House legal memos leaked to the press had given the impression that President Bush might be considering not applying the Geneva Conventions at all in Afghanistan, based on the Department of Justice's legal opinion.[27] Myers felt strongly that it would be a mistake not to apply the Conventions to the Taliban. We couldn't risk the perception that we were discarding long-established rules of international law and our treaty obligations.

I concluded that Myers was correct. Knowing that administration lawyers were weighing in, I wanted to make sure President Bush heard the Chairman's and the Defense Department's views.[28] I asked Rice to set up an NSC meeting on the subject so that we could make the Department's case.

At the NSC meeting on February 4, 2002, Myers and Doug Feith presented our position, which was based on the language and purposes of the Geneva Conventions. We contended that the U.S. government should not use a legal argument to avoid applying the Geneva Conventions to the conflict in Afghanistan. The memo we brought to the meeting set out our position:

- A "pro-Convention" position reinforces [the US Government]'s key themes in the war on terrorism.
- The essence of the Convention is the distinction between soldiers and civilians (i.e., between combatants and non-combatants).
- Terrorists are reprehensible precisely because they negate that distinction by purposefully targeting civilians.
- The Convention aims to protect civilians by requiring soldiers to wear uniforms and otherwise distinguish themselves from civilians.
- The Convention creates an incentive system for good behavior. The key incentive is that soldiers who play by the rules get POW status if they [are] captured.
- The US can apply the Convention to the Taliban (and al-Qaida) detainees as a matter of policy without having to give them POW status because none of the detainees remaining in US hands played by the rules.[29]

The DoD memo concluded by summing up what we thought the U.S. position should be:

- Humane treatment for all detainees.
- US is applying the Convention. All detainees are getting the treatment they are (or would be) entitled to under the Convention.
- US supports the Convention and promotes universal respect for it.
- The Convention does not squarely address circumstances that we are confronting in this new global war against terrorism, but while we work

through the legal questions, we are upholding the principle of universal applicability of the Convention.[30]

Though the Justice Department offered its well-considered legal view, we noted that the Taliban was effectively the government of a country that was a party to Geneva. Our position was that it was "[h]ighly dangerous if countries make application of [the] Convention hinge on subjective or moral judgments as to the quality or decency of the enemy's government."[31] Powell's position, as outlined in his January 25 memorandum, was in line with ours.[32] The discussion was the sort of thing that I thought would have done the drafters of the Geneva Conventions proud. Justice Department officials were doing their jobs: defining the President's flexibility within the law. And the policy makers in the Department of Defense were doing theirs: making clear that while it is mandatory to stay within the law, not everything that is lawful is necessarily the best policy.

President Bush was apparently persuaded by Myers and Feith's arguments, and on February 7, he set forth his conclusions in a memo.[33] While he didn't challenge the Justice Department's legal reasoning, he seemed to feel that it risked putting the administration in a position where it could be criticized for not respecting the Geneva Conventions. Ironically, of course, the Bush administration came under exactly that unfair criticism, notwithstanding the fact that the President had explicitly decided that his administration would take a pro–Geneva Conventions stance.

In a conventional war, detention issues would have fallen under the responsibility of the military commanders in each theater of operations. But CENTCOM commander Franks was reluctant to have hundreds of those captured remain in the theater as his command's responsibility. There were no existing satisfactory Afghan prisons that he could use, nor were there easily discernible front lines behind which detainees could be safely held. The rebellion at the Qala-i-Jangi prison demonstrated the challenge vividly. Additionally, Franks and I agreed that frontline American troops would be better used for counterterrorism missions than as prison guards or interrogators.

I thought it preferable to have Afghanistan take on the responsibility of holding detainees captured on its soil. Then, with our assistance, Afghans could begin to seek the swift transfer of non-Afghans to their countries of origin for detention there.[34] If a limited number of detainees were going to have to be in U.S. custody, I preferred to hand over major detention responsibilities to another department or agency. Suffice it to say that there were no departments of the government eagerly coming forward to assist. Another possibility I considered was to create an entirely new entity with the explicit purpose of administering detention policy and operations, running tribunals and trial proceedings, negotiating with other countries around the world for the further detention of individuals, and coordinating competing interagency interests. There was no enthusiasm for this approach either, and DoD was selected.

President Bush's November 2001 military order provided for the detention of enemy combatants "at an appropriate location designated by the Secretary of Defense outside or within the United States." To comply with the order, a number of locations were discussed, including some in the United States. The crumbling federal prison on Alcatraz Island or the maximum security Disciplinary Barracks at Fort Leavenworth, Kansas, were considered. So were other possibilities—such as a ship that could be permanently stationed in the Arabian Sea and island military bases in the Pacific and Indian oceans.[35] Attention then turned to the U.S. military facility near the southeastern tip of Cuba.

Christopher Columbus sailed into the narrow stretch of bay named Guantánamo on his second trip to the New World in 1494. In the wake of the Spanish-American War, President Theodore Roosevelt signed a treaty with the Cuban government establishing the U.S. Navy base on Cuban soil, and leasing the land for two thousand dollars annually. I traveled to the sleepy base twice in the 1950s, as a midshipman aboard U.S. Navy battleships, and later as a naval aviator for training. With palm trees and beaches, the U.S. Naval Station at Guantánamo Bay, or "Gitmo" as it was called, was a low-key facility used to refuel and resupply Navy ships and aircraft patrolling the Caribbean.

When asked by journalists why Gitmo was chosen to house detainees, I described it as "the least worst place."[36] Grammar aside, the phrase conveyed my uneasy feelings about the entire detainee dilemma. We had made the best possible choice among a number of unattractive options. It was chosen because it was far from the ever-shifting battlefield in Afghanistan, where U.S. troops had to guard against the possibility of enemy assaults and attempted escapes. It was controlled entirely by the United States military, even though it was not then subject to American legal jurisdiction. It had some existing infrastructure, including a naval hospital. Its use would not further complicate diplomatic relations with a host nation, since our relations with Fidel Castro's Cuba were poor at best.

Additionally, Guantánamo had a history of use as a detention facility dating back to the Carter years, when it was first used to house Cuban and Haitian refugees. The Carter administration and its successors through the Clinton administration did not afford the refugees the same legal rights as Americans because they were neither on U.S. soil nor U.S. citizens. In 2001, Bush administration lawyers determined that foreign nationals held at Gitmo would not have automatic access to U.S. courts, which had also been the case for the refugees that had been held there by several previous administrations of both political parties.

On January 11, 2002, al-Qaida and Taliban detainees began arriving at Guantánamo Bay. Initially, they were housed at Camp X-Ray, an existing facility built during the Clinton administration for illegal immigrants. We intended this arrangement to be temporary, pending construction of appropriate, modern facilities, which were completed within a few months. Soon after the first detainees arrived, we suffered a costly self-inflicted wound. Intending to demonstrate openness to the press, and to showcase the humane treatment of the detainees, the Pentagon public affairs office released photographs taken while the detainees were still in temporary quarters at Camp X-Ray. The photographs showed prisoners wearing orange jumpsuits behind chain-link and barbed-wire fences. Some wore blacked-out goggles and had their hands tied behind their backs during transfers, so that they could not attack their guards. The photographs, with primitive facilities and conditions, became enduring images of Guantánamo. They were repeatedly referred to by critics of the Bush administration long after the permanent, state-of-the-art facilities were completed. It was another example of how little was understood about war in the information age.

Contrary to the notions suggested by those early photos, the detainees at Gitmo had warm showers, toiletries, water, clean clothes, blankets, culturally appropriate meals, prayer mats, Korans, modern medical attention equal to that provided to our troops, exercise, writing materials, and regular visits by the International Committee of the Red Cross.

In early 2002, the U.S. military's Southern Command (SOUTHCOM) sent up, through the Pentagon's Joint Staff, a construction proposal for a permanent detention facility at Guantánamo Bay. The proposal, presented to me through General Pete Pace, the vice chairman of the Joint Chiefs and a former SOUTHCOM commander, envisioned a costly and seemingly permanent two-thousand-bed facility. Given the battlefield pressures to move detainees out of the areas of operations, military commanders wanted to move as many as possible as quickly as possible to Guantánamo Bay.

Government organizations tend to use whatever resources are available to them. I knew that if I approved such a large facility, our forces would almost certainly ship enough prisoners to fill it. I wanted to preempt that tendency. I told General Pace that I thought we would be better off with a considerably smaller facility, and that I wanted to generate downward pressure on the number of inmates to be sent to Gitmo. I said I wanted transfers of detainees to Guantánamo Bay to be kept to a minimum—to only individuals of high interest for interrogation who posed a threat to our nation's security. Pace came back with revised proposals several times. On each go-round, the size of the proposed expansion of the facility became smaller and more specialized, to handle only the toughest and most dangerous cases. It was not an easy process for General Pace, who had to balance the pressures from CENTCOM's battlefield commanders with pressures from a secretary of defense who was dead set against making it easier for them to avoid tough choices by simply sending all questionable cases off to Gitmo. Pace was getting squeezed, but typically he handled the situation with good humor. At one point, when he was preparing to present yet another version of the proposal, he showed up for our meeting wearing a flak jacket, a helmet, and a grin. Finally I agreed to build a facility that could house several hundred inmates, not the two thousand originally proposed. The facility was designed so it could be expanded, but only if I became convinced in the future that there were sound reasons to house additional terrorists there.

I instructed our commanders to develop a selection process to winnow down the number of detainees to be held for long periods. I wanted captured enemies to first be sorted out in the field according to predetermined intelligence and safety criteria rather than just being sent to Guantánamo. For all but a few of the most important and dangerous detainees, I wanted them to stay in the country and have the new Afghan government begin to exercise responsibility for them.[37] I urged Powell and the State Department to encourage Afghans (and later Iraqis) to take on the responsibility for holding lower-level detainees captured in their country.[38]

I also called for an ongoing evaluation of the detainees. I knew we ran the risk of mistakenly releasing some people who might attack us in the future, just as is the case in our civilian prison system, but I saw this as a risk we had to take. Otherwise we risked alienating populations whose assistance we needed and do an injustice to individuals who were not actually involved in terrorism.

As the number of detainees at Gitmo rose, I pushed and prodded senior Pentagon officials on almost a weekly basis as to when and how detainees could be transferred to their home countries. "You have to get your arms around this detainee thing," I wrote in one snowflake.[39] "We need to get rid of more detainees," I told Doug Feith five days later. "How do we do it?"[40] And three months later I urgently wrote again, "I do want some people out of Guantánamo sent to their own countries. I really mean it. I want that done. I would like a report every two days on what is happening on this."[41]

I repeatedly urged the State Department to try to persuade the detainees' countries of origin to take responsibility for captured combatants under sensible conditions as soon as detainees began arriving in 2002.[42] In the first several years the Guantánamo Bay detention facility was open, State Department officials had little success in pressing foreign governments on the matter. Most foreign governments did not want to take suspected terrorists any more than we wanted to hold them.* Despite my efforts to keep numbers down, Gitmo's detainee population ballooned beyond 650 in its first two years.†

One of my biggest disappointments as secretary of defense was my inability to marshal the resources within our government to help persuade America and the world of the truth about Gitmo: The most heavily scrutinized detention facility in the world was also one of the most professionally run in history. Irresponsible charges leveled by human rights groups, by editorial pages, and, most shamefully, by members of the U.S. Congress who had every opportunity and reason to know better, unfairly tarnished Guantánamo's reputation—and the reputations of our country and of the men and women of the American military who served at the facility. Even worse, the inaccurate allegations were exploited by terrorists to improve their fundraising and recruitment. This, in fact, was a component of the enemy's propaganda strategy. In one al-Qaida training manual, the so-called Manchester document, the first lesson if captured was to "insist on proving that torture was inflicted on them by State Security before the judge."[43] Its second lesson

* If we transferred detainees to governments that were tolerant of terrorists, they might well return to fight against us. Some nations were unable to give us the necessary human rights assurances and might turn the detainees over to security forces, from which they might receive treatment unacceptable by our standards. Other nations would not agree to allow U.S. officials to visit with transferred detainees to ensure their humane treatment or interview them to obtain additional intelligence. Still, I didn't want to allow these issues to become excuses for not working the problem aggressively.

† Over the next three years we were able to reduce the number by a third, mostly by moving detainees to other nations. By the end of the Bush administration more than five hundred detainees had been moved out of detention at Guantánamo Bay.

was to "complain of mistreatment while in prison."[44] The hope, of course, was that some gullible people in the West would believe their repeated fabrications. Because of the stigma that clung to Gitmo, the terrorists found it an easy case to make.

In May 2005, *Newsweek* magazine wrote that U.S. guards at Gitmo had flushed a Koran down a toilet "in an attempt to rattle suspects" for interrogation purposes.[45] Unnamed sources, *Newsweek* said, had verified the allegation. The story set off a firestorm of protest in a number of Muslim cities. Commentators denounced the troops serving at Gitmo. Demonstrations and riots erupted around the world. In Afghanistan, seventeen people died in the rioting.

After a thorough examination by the Defense Department, the individual believed to have made the original allegation recanted. We then asked *Newsweek* to withdraw its story, but its editor would only express "regret that we got any part of our story wrong, and [we] extend our sympathies to victims of the violence and to the U.S. soldiers caught in its midst."[46] A number of those to whom *Newsweek* extended its sympathies were already dead. And the reputations of those military personnel serving at Gitmo had been besmirched again, as was the reputation of our country—to the benefit of the terrorists.

It was a grim irony. We deliberately made the facility transparent, which made the repeated inaccuracies all the more irresponsible. Almost from its inception, the Defense Department arranged for regular and well-attended visits by members of Congress, representatives of news organizations, opinion leaders, and other visitors and observers from around the world. In the five years after detainees began to arrive, some 145 members of Congress, Democrats and Republicans, took advantage of the Department's open invitation to visit Gitmo. There were representatives from across the executive branch—the State Department, the CIA, the FBI, the Department of Justice, and a whole host of DoD agencies and organizations—stationed there. Over time, more than one thousand U.S. and international journalists visited. We arranged for high-level European parliamentary groups to visit. Hundreds of lawyers were given access to the detainees there, as was the International Committee of the Red Cross on a regular basis.

Nearly every observer who visited Gitmo recognized that it was safer, better, cleaner, and more professionally run than most American federal, state, and local prisons, and certainly better than most foreign prisons. A senior Belgian government official said after visiting Gitmo, "At the level of the detention facilities, it is a model prison, where people are better treated than in Belgian prisons."[47] More money was spent on religiously sensitive meals for detainees at Gitmo than on meals for the American troops stationed there. The average weight gain per detainee was twenty pounds. Detainees were given Korans in their native languages. Five times each day the Muslim call to prayer sounded across the facility, and numerous arrows indicated the direction of Mecca. Detainees had access to a basketball and volleyball court, ping-pong tables, and board games. Some detainees chose to take classes in Pashtu, Arabic, and English. There were even movie nights, featuring popular Hollywood fare (which I suppose could raise a host of troubling questions). They watched sports events like the World Cup. The library had thirty-five hundred volumes available in thirteen languages (Harry Potter was the most requested). They received medical, dental, psychiatric, and optometric care—health care equal to that provided to our troops.[48]

Critics nonetheless continued to denounce Guantánamo as a "law-free zone" and "legal black hole."[49] Amnesty International called it "the gulag of our times."[50] The number-two Democratic leader in the U.S. Senate, Dick Durbin, compared American behavior at Guantánamo Bay to that of "Nazis, Soviets in their gulags, or some mad regime—Pol Pot or others—that had no concern for human beings."[51] It would have been a disgraceful comment from someone who hadn't known better, but coming from a senior congressional leader speaking on the Senate floor, it was particularly damaging and inexcusable.

As the issue of detainees became increasingly politicized, even some senior administration officials, including ones who had been involved in the discussions that led to the administration's detention and interrogation policies and the establishment of Gitmo, were less than supportive.[52] They were anonymously cited in news reports "on background" concurring with President Bush's opponents that Guantánamo was a stain on America's reputation and should be closed.[53] In late 2003, I wrote a memo to Secretary of State Powell, Attorney General Ashcroft, and National Security Adviser Rice saying:

> [T]here continues to be static concerning the handling of the detainees at Guantánamo. I suggest that: If an agency is dissatisfied with the Administration's policy, they propose a change to the policy to the NSC [or if] an agency doesn't like a particular result from the interagency process (for example, a decision on a specific detainee), they elevate their concern to the NSC and propose an alternative.[54]

Precious few were stepping forth to defend the President's policy and rationale. "Administration policy on detainees in GTMO is clearly an issue about which there is not unanimous agreement—in the Administration, in the Congress, in the country or in the world," I wrote in my December 2003 memo, adding:

> That being the case, and since, nonetheless, it is our Administration's policy, it would help if all agencies would help defend the Administration's policy and explain the reasons for it to the Congress, to the country and to the world. I don't think DoD is the best communicator of the Administration's policy on detainees, since it is seen as a legal matter. Nonetheless, we are supporting it energetically. It would be appreciated if all agencies would pitch in and help carry the message.[55]

I was perfectly willing to shutter the facility if a better alternative could have been found that would be as effective at obtaining intelligence and preventing terrorists from returning to the fight. But no alternative to Gitmo was proposed. Nor did I receive any replies to my memo. Meanwhile, the public drumbeat against Guantánamo Bay intensified.

Gitmo, though damned across the political spectrum, offered a solution—however imperfect—to the problem of keeping high-risk detainees out of circulation. What was the alternative—letting them go and then hoping to catch them as they were committing their next terrorist attack against the American people? Dedicated men and women of the U.S. armed forces performed an enormously valuable service in running a first-rate detention and interrogation operation at Guantánamo. The base has logged a proud record of professionalism and success. Detainees routinely attacked the military guards there—kicking, biting, head butting, and throwing "cocktails" of feces and urine.[56] The prisoners demonstrated remarkable resourcefulness in turning personal items into deadly weapons: blankets into garrotes, sinks into bludgeons, and wires into daggers. The guards demonstrated impressive restraint. In those few cases where the military guards were goaded by detainees and crossed the line, disciplinary action was taken.

To date, not a single prisoner has escaped from Guantánamo, and hundreds of terrorists have been kept from returning to the fight. At Gitmo, intelligence officials have uncovered information that has helped prevent terrorist attacks—information about al-Qaida's leadership, the identities of operatives, terrorist communication methods, training programs, travel patterns, funding mechanisms, and plans to attack the United States and our allies. Detainees have provided information on bank accounts, al-Qaida front companies, improvised explosive devices, and tactics.[57] Coalition intelligence officials and our forces on the ground in Afghanistan and Iraq have used this information to help protect the American people.

Despite the more than $500 million that U.S. taxpayers have invested in state-of-the-art facilities at Gitmo, and in operations there since 9/11, both of the 2008 presidential candidates, John McCain and Barack Obama, pandered to popular misconceptions by promising to shut it down.[58] On his second full day in office, President Obama vowed to close the facility "promptly."[59] Years later, however, Guantánamo remains open, undoubtedly because the Obama administration, despite its promises, has not found a practical alternative. Eventually it may be closed, but it will be closed at great financial cost. More important, the problems Guantánamo was established to address will remain.

CHAPTER 39

The Twentieth Hijacker

Though hundreds of thousands of vacationers and business travelers passed through Orlando International Airport every year, there was something unsettling about the man who had just arrived from London on Virgin Atlantic Flight 15. As he approached immigration control, Muhammed al-Qahtani presented a Saudi passport. When questioned by customs agents he revealed that he did not have a return ticket or a hotel reservation, and he refused to give the identity of the individual he said was picking him up. Though he carried nearly twenty-eight hundred dollars in cash, he had no credit cards. Qahtani did not seem the type to visit Disney World.

"He gave me the creeps," a suspicious Immigration and Naturalization official later testified to the 9/11 Commission, saying that he had the bearing of "a hit man."[1] Before long Qahtani felt he had entertained enough questioning about his travel plans. He withdrew his application for entry and caught the next flight back to London, then to Dubai, on August 4, 2001. He left the INS agent with an ominous three words: "I'll be back."[2]

That December, as winter closed in on the mountain passes along the Pakistan-Afghanistan border, Qahtani made his way to the al-Qaida nest in Tora Bora. As U.S. and Northern Alliance forces stepped up their pummeling of the cave complexes, its murderous denizens, including Qahtani, fled to Pakistan's tribal areas. But along with some two dozen other terrorist suspects, he was captured by Pakistani forces, who handed him over to our military on the Afghanistan side of the border.

As he was questioned by American military interrogators and intelligence officials, Qahtani claimed he had traveled to Afghanistan to "practice falconry"—a fiction that he was later forced to abandon when he couldn't provide any details about the sport.[3] Military interrogators judged him to be a high threat to our troops there and a possible threat for more terrorist attacks in the United States. Suspected of ties to senior al-Qaida figures, Qahtani was designated detainee number 063 and transported to Guantánamo Bay in February 2002.

At Guantánamo, the pieces began to fall together. Qahtani, investigators learned, had trained at the al-Faruq training camp near Kandahar "for the purpose of participating in jihad, which he deemed a religious obligation."[4] He was trained to fire small arms and rocket-propelled grenades. Intelligence officials then discovered Qahtani's failed attempt to enter the United States at the Orlando airport shortly before 9/11. They learned that the man who had been waiting to meet him there was Muhammed Attah, ringleader of the 9/11 attacks.[5] Investigators also uncovered that Qahtani had placed several phone calls with a calling card associated with Muhammed Attah, to another Saudi, Mustafa al-Hawsawi, a financier of the attacks.[6] Hawsawi had dropped Qahtani off at the airport in Dubai.[7]

American intelligence officials came to believe Qahtani had been trained to become a weapon himself—as the fifth and final "muscle" hijacker on United Flight 93.[8] Through the courage and heroism of the passengers who attacked the hijackers onboard—and possibly in part because that team of terrorists was one man short—Flight 93 crashed into a field in Shanksville, Pennsylvania, rather than its likely objective of the White House or the U.S. Capitol building. Had the immigration officer not been sharp enough to dissuade Qahtani from entering the United States just weeks before, the Flight 93 hijacking might have succeeded in finding its target.

Qahtani's story is a vivid example of the complex moral questions that we faced in developing interrogation policies for prisoners in U.S. custody. A senior al-Qaida operative implicated in the worst terrorist attack in history was in DoD custody. Qahtani potentially possessed a treasure trove of intelligence information, including perhaps facts about future attacks planned against Americans. But like many senior al-Qaida officials, he was proving resistant to questioning. The issue ultimately made its way to my office.

By the late fall of 2002, the first anniversary of 9/11 had come and gone without another act of terrorism on American soil—a fact that in itself was a marvel, and in my view a result of President Bush's effort to go on offense against the enemy. Still intelligence sources around the world were warning of new attacks. Ayman al-Zawahiri, Bin Laden's top deputy, released a tape recording in which he pledged to "continue targeting the keys of the American economy."[9] Al-Qaida terrorists launched attacks in Tunisia and Pakistan over the summer. In September, FBI agents outside of Buffalo, New York, arrested a group of Yemeni Americans, soon called the Lackawanna Six, who were later convicted of providing material support to al-Qaida. In October, bombs tore through nightclubs in Bali, killing 202 and injuring hundreds more. In the Washington, D.C., area, the so-called D.C. snipers terrorized the region; for three weeks no one knew whether or not their attacks were connected in some way to overseas terror groups. The system, in the parlance of the intelligence community, was "blinking red." But little intelligence was being obtained from military detainees.

The Defense Department was neither organized nor trained to elicit information from terror suspects. During the decade of lean defense budgets in the 1990s our government had not only cut combat forces, it also had furloughed military interrogators and experts in human intelligence. Because of the urgency and importance of obtaining information from detainees to help us prevent future 9/11s, the task was to develop interrogation guidelines, clarify rules and regulations, and improve our human intelligence-gathering capabilities to fit the unconventional and protracted first war of the twenty-first century.

Military interrogators at Guantánamo first used traditional interrogation methods honed in conventional conflicts and designed for use with POWs protected by the Third Geneva Convention. Since the privileges of Geneva POW status did not apply to unlawful combatants such as war on terrorism detainees, interrogators had more flexibility.

Army Field Manual 34–52 prescribed guidelines and broad doctrines governing interrogation but did not prescribe specific techniques. It gave broad latitude for interrogators in some areas—arguably too much—while little in others. The American military's approach for decades was to try to build trust with enemy prisoners. Military interrogators were trained in a combination of rapport-building techniques through which the prisoners might eventually choose of their own free will to provide useful information. By early

2002, however, it became clear that rapport-building techniques were not succeeding with key al-Qaida terrorists. "We saw firsthand in Afghanistan how ineffective schoolhouse methods were in getting prisoners to talk," two military interrogators concluded.[10] Some of the detainees had clearly undergone interrogation-resistance training. Al-Qaida fighters by and large scoffed at the efforts of Americans to promote rapport, except if they could use those efforts for deception.

Al-Qaida operatives also knew that the barbaric methods they employed—burning victims with cigarettes, electrocution, and cutting off people's heads with knives—were not employed by the United States. Thus, there was little incentive for detained terrorists to provide useful information to us, and every reason for them to stonewall and delay.

But delay held risks for us in the post-9/11 environment. The American intelligence community's ability to collect reliable information through interrogations of captured enemies could be the difference between success and failure in preventing more attacks and defeating our Islamist extremist enemies. Interrogations led to some of the most impressive successes in the war on terror, including: the capture of Saddam Hussein; the capture of two dozen terrorists in Germany who were plotting an attack against Ramstein Air Base; and the death of the leader of al-Qaida in Iraq, Abu Musab al-Zarqawi. A revelation by a single detainee could be the key to preventing multiple attacks against the United States and our allies.

On October 11, 2002, the interrogators assigned to Joint Task Force 170 at Guantánamo Bay sent up, through every level in their chain of command, a request to use some techniques they believed were lawful and humane but which would go beyond the Army Field Manual. Their focus was on one individual in particular—Muhammed al-Qahtani.

Qahtani was more than simply brawn. He appeared to have known about the planning of the 9/11 operation. He was familiar with the inner workings and high-level personalities of al-Qaida. He was also a determined liar. Like many al-Qaida members and Taliban personnel captured early in the conflict, he pretended to be an inoffensive bad-luck guy indiscriminately swept up by U.S. forces in the fog of war. But an innocent bystander he was not. Qahtani aspired to the glory of jihad against America, and it was possible he held the key to saving a great many American lives from future jihadist operations. U.S. military commanders at Guantánamo had a responsibility to try to gather that information.

For months, FBI agents made no headway using law enforcement interview methods with Qahtani. According to a DoJ inspector general report, the FBI agents exceeded their own traditional rules and policy guidelines by isolating and threatening him.[11]

The military interrogators and their commanding officer, Major General Michael Dunlavey, put together a list of techniques they thought might be effective in inducing Qahtani to cooperate. Their request moved up the chain of command to the four-star SOUTHCOM combatant commander, Army General James T. Hill. On October 25, 2002, General Hill forwarded the request to General Myers.

"[D]espite our best efforts," Hill wrote, "some detainees have tenaciously resisted our current interrogation methods."[12] He requested consideration of interrogation methods that went beyond the Army Field Manual, but which might still be implemented in ways that were legal and humane. A combatant commander with initiative, General Hill wanted to provide his interrogators with all the tools that were lawful and appropriate. Hill was leaning forward. He wasn't to be faulted for that. He flagged the fact that there were complexities here, and accordingly he was seeking clarification up his chain of command.

The additional techniques proposed by the Guantánamo interrogators fell into three categories. The techniques ranged from yelling in Category I, to deprivation of light and sound and other measures that would cause a temporary sense of isolation and disorientation in Category II. One technique included changing the detainee's regular hot meals to standard MREs (meals ready to eat).[13] I found it strange that serving detainees the same meals our soldiers ate could be called an enhanced interrogation procedure. Category III involved more aggressive and controversial techniques, which SOUTHCOM proposed only for Muhammed al-Qahtani. The techniques included making the detainee believe that he, or a family member, might suffer death or severe pain if he failed to cooperate, exposure to cold, and the "[u]se of mild, non-injurious physical contact such as grabbing, poking in the chest with the finger, and light pushing."[14] Category III also included the "[u]se of a wet towel and dripping water to induce the misperception of suffocation."[15] This latter practice became known as waterboarding. Each of the Category II and III techniques proposed by SOUTHCOM would require explicit review and permission at senior military levels before they were employed by the interrogators.

I did not believe it would be appropriate for anyone in Defense Department custody to be waterboarded or stripped and subjected to cold temperatures, and I rejected those techniques.[16] Military interrogators were not trained to do those things. There were important military traditions of restraint that I intended to preserve. I was deeply uncomfortable with nudity and any techniques that had a tinge of sexual humiliation. As I remarked in meetings when the treatment of detainees was discussed, I believed the American people would not approve of anything of that sort. When the SOUTHCOM interrogators suggested removal of comfort items or clothing, I read that not as referring to nudity but as part of a set of measures to make a recalcitrant interrogation subject feel disconnected from familiar items that gave him comfort and stability, such as particular books or favored items of apparel. Changes in sleeping and other ordinary daily scheduling could also cause a captured terrorist combatant to let down his guard.

General Hill's October 25 request for additional techniques went through several weeks of policy and legal review at various levels, both civilian and military, before it arrived on my desk. On November 27, Jim Haynes, the Department's general counsel, sent a memo to me with his recommendations. "I have discussed this with the Deputy [Paul Wolfowitz], Doug Feith and General Myers," Haynes wrote, adding: "I believe that all join in my recommendation that, as a matter of policy, you authorize the Commander of USSOUTHCOM to employ, in his discretion, only Categories I and II and the fourth technique listed in Category III ('Use of mild, non-injurious physical contact such as grabbing, poking in the chest with the finger, and light pushing')." Haynes concluded, "Our Armed Forces are trained to a standard of interrogation that reflects a tradition of restraint."[17] He recommended against other Category III proposals put forward by SOUTHCOM, including creating fear of death or severe pain, exposure to cold, and waterboarding.

I agreed and approved the recommendations. At the bottom of the Haynes memo I scrawled a note that referred to the Category II technique that could require a detainee under certain circumstances to stand for four hours while interrogators questioned him.

"However, I stand for 8–10 hours a day," I wrote. "Why is standing limited to 4 hours?"[18] My offhand comment was a statement of fact. I used a stand-up desk and spent much of the day on my feet. The note received enormous attention when detainee abuse became a major public issue. It was a mistake to make that personal observation to my general counsel. It certainly was not a signal to the Department that it would be okay to stretch the rules, as some have suggested.[19]

Pentagon lawyers had determined that the interrogation methods I approved in that memo were both legal and humane. I believed then—and I believe today—that they were. However, the application of any interrogation technique requires care and the supervision of experts. Any technique that is legal and humane on its own could conceivably be applied in ways that are not legal and not humane if, for example, it is done repeatedly, over long periods of time or used in an inappropriate combination with other techniques. That is why detailed interrogation plans have to be approved at the appropriate levels of military command. Plan specifics were devised, as they should have been, by experienced interrogators and their commanders at Gitmo, not by officials in Washington far removed from day-to-day management of the interrogation operations.

Moreover, I understood that the techniques I authorized were intended for use only with one key individual. General Hill advised that Muhammed al-Qahtani had information that could save American lives. He and others in the chain of command believed additional techniques were warranted. Any proposals to use these methods on others would have to come back up the chain of command for review.*

Many claims have been made about the usefulness of various interrogation strategies and methods. In the case of Qahtani, the reports from the interrogators say the approved techniques yielded important information. Qahtani ultimately acknowledged that he was an al-Qaida member and had met with Bin Laden. He admitted he knew the 9/11 terrorists and was sent to the United States by Khalid Sheikh Muhammed, the chief planner of the attacks.[20] Qahtani acknowledged he knew Richard Reid, the terrorist who plotted to blow up an airliner with explosives in his shoes, and also knew Jose Padilla, who was thought to have plans to bomb apartment buildings in Chicago.[21] Qahtani provided useful information about al-Qaida's planning for 9/11, its methods of cross-border infiltration, and information about Bin Laden's bodyguards. Much of the information from Qahtani's interrogations remains classified, but the Schlesinger and Brown panel concluded that the interrogation was critical in "gaining important and time-urgent infor-

*I approved interrogation techniques beyond the traditional Army Field Manual for one other detainee, Muhammed Ould Slahi, in August 2003, in accordance with an April 2003 working group proposal that had been approved by senior military and civilian DoD officials. Slahi had recruited some of the 9/11 al-Qaida pilots and been a key facilitator in the 2000 Millennium Plot. He tenaciously resisted questioning. After he was isolated from other detainees and interrogated, Slahi became one of the most valuable intelligence assets giving information on al-Qaida. Within weeks intelligence reports indicated that he began cooperating as a result of the interrogation plan and was providing large amounts of useful intelligence.

mation."[22] One military report by two general officers found that Qahtani "ultimately provided extremely valuable intelligence."[23]

Qahtani's interrogation did not lead, as some critics have alleged, to the abuse at Abu Ghraib, or anywhere else for that matter. "We found no link between approved interrogation techniques and detainee abuse," Vice Admiral Albert Church concluded from his independent investigation of detainee operations.* He noted that "the Office of the Secretary of Defense was a moderating force that cut back on the number and types of techniques under consideration."[25] The Church report stated of Guantánamo Bay:

> [D]etainees were more likely to suffer injury from playing soccer or volleyball during recreational periods than they were from interactions with interrogators or guards. . . . In our view, the extremely low rate of abuse at GTMO is largely due to strong command oversight, effective leadership, and adequate training on detainee handling and treatment.[26]

At the time, my approval of Haynes' December 2002 cover memo, in response to SOUTHCOM's request for additional interrogation techniques for Qahtani, was uncontroversial. My decision to accept the DoD general counsel's recommendations, approving some interrogation strategies sought by General Hill but rejecting others, was done with the concurrence of senior Defense Department officials, both military and civilian.

It was not until January 10, 2003, thirty-nine days after I had approved a limited number of the proposed techniques, that Haynes informed me that some military lawyers had expressed concern and suggested that Qahtani's interrogation plan might be construed as mistreatment. As urgent as it was to obtain terrorism-related intelligence, I was not willing to allow the use of methods that could be reasonably challenged as improper. It made no sense to fight terrorists in a way that might raise questions about our respect for the law and that could ultimately undermine our efforts. When I learned of the concerns, I promptly suspended my prior approval of the additional interrogation techniques.[27]

I then instructed Haynes to assemble a team to review the interrogation guidelines. I wanted the team to include any and all of those military or

* Admiral Church has said, "I thought going in that I was going to find something different. I thought I was going to find the dots connecting. . . . You had pictures of Abu Ghraib. You had leaks beginning to show up about harsh interrogation techniques approved by fairly high levels in the office of the Secretary of Defense. And so . . . it occurred to me there's probably some pretty close linkage there. But the facts didn't bear that out. In fact, most of the abuse that we found had no relation to interrogation at all. . . . So I thought there would be a linkage, I didn't see it in terms of the abuse."[24]

civilian personnel who were concerned about them or the interrogation plan: intelligence officials, defense policy experts, and lawyers from every military service. When I met with the group one weekend in February or March 2003, I told them that I wanted their honest views. They seemed to appreciate that they had been brought into the process, and gave me the clear impression that if they had any concerns, they were being resolved.

In April 2003 the review group we had impaneled reached its conclusions. Their report identified thirty-five techniques that they believed could be used legally for key al-Qaida members under proper interrogation plans.[28] After reviewing their report, I authorized only twenty-four of the thirty-five techniques they had recommended. Each of the techniques I approved, I was told, had been unanimously supported by the members of the legal review team, as well as by each of the service secretaries and each of the members of the Joint Chiefs of Staff involved in the process.*

I was informed that several senior military officials participating in the review expressed concern that my decision was too restrictive, that we might be risking American lives by authorizing only limited interrogation methods and excluding other techniques. Some officials were especially dismayed by my suspension of the methods being employed in the Qahtani case, because they thought they were on the verge of an intelligence breakthrough. However, I wanted an approach that would reflect the best judgment of all of the relevant components of the Department of Defense, military and civilian. The techniques I approved after receiving the April 2003 conclusions did just that.

The subsequent politicized public debate about this subject has obscured a fact of great importance: None of the authorized interrogation methods—either those approved in December 2002 and used on one detainee until I rescinded them, or those that I later approved in April 2003—involved physical or mental pain. None were inhumane. None met any reasonable person's definition of torture. From start to finish, my goal in interrogation matters was to balance the nation's need for intelligence against considerations of military tradition and morale. Like all solutions that balance complex and weighty issues, Qahtani's interrogation was imperfect and not without controversy, but as soon as concerns were raised, I addressed them immediately.

* In April 2003 the service secretaries were: Thomas White, secretary of the Army; Hansford Johnson, acting secretary of the Navy; and James Roche, secretary of the Air Force. The members of the Joint Chiefs of Staff were: General Eric Shinseki (Army); General Michael Hagee (Marine Corps); Admiral Vern Clark (Navy); and General John Jumper (Air Force), plus the chairman, Dick Myers, and the vice chairman, Pete Pace.

Some two and a half years later, I learned what had happened to Muhammed al-Qahtani during his interrogation.[29] I was surprised and troubled. Some of what took place sounded to me as if the interrogation plan may have gone beyond the techniques I had approved. Apparently Qahtani was exposed to cold temperatures at some point, which I had rejected in my authorization. It appears he was stripped and humiliated. The combination and frequency of techniques interrogators had used with Qahtani called into question their appropriateness, at least in my mind. They may not have been in keeping with the intent of my January 2002 order that all detainees in the custody of the Defense Department were to be treated humanely.[30]

If Qahtani's true identity had been known at the time of his capture, before he came into DoD custody, it is highly likely the CIA would have assumed responsibility for him, rather than DoD. The Defense Department's detention operations often are confused with those undertaken by the CIA, but they were two separate sets of activities. At some point in the months after 9/11, the CIA established an interrogation program for high-level al-Qaida operatives captured around the world. Their highly classified program apparently began after Pakistani forces captured senior Bin Laden lieutenant Abu Zubaydah in a March 2002 gun battle.[31] Over the next year, the Agency successfully collected intelligence from Zubaydah and captured and interrogated other senior al-Qaida lieutenants, which eventually led to the capture of the mastermind of 9/11, Khalid Sheikh Muhammed.*

As a member of the National Security Council, I was made aware of the Agency's interrogation program—but as I now understand it, it was not until well after it had been initiated, and well after the senior members of the congressional intelligence committees in Congress, including future Speaker of the House Nancy Pelosi and others had been briefed.† Along with my colleagues on the NSC I learned that the CIA had developed a series of enhanced techniques to achieve Zubaydah's cooperation. The CIA's program employed some of the interrogation methods that I had rejected for use in the Defense Department. We were told the Justice Department had determined that the interrogation techniques the CIA was using—up to and including waterboarding—were legal.

* For a full discussion of the CIA's interrogation program, see Marc Thiessen's treatment of this issue in his book, *Courting Disaster.*

† According to an April 2009 Senate Select Committee on Intelligence report prepared by Democratic Senator Jay Rockefeller, and consistent with my recollection, Colin Powell and I were informed of the enhanced interrogation techniques on September 16, 2003—a year after members of Congress had received extensive briefings.[32]

Though the CIA utilized waterboarding and other techniques that I rejected in the Department of Defense, I saw no contradiction. Some techniques that might be appropriate for a very small number of high-value terrorists by a highly trained and professional group of CIA interrogators in a controlled environment were not appropriate for use by military personnel. It would have been unwise to blur the difference between two distinct institutions. Tight limits on interrogation, such as those contained in the Army Field Manual, are appropriate for the U.S. military. Tens of thousands of detainees passed through U.S military custody in Afghanistan and Iraq. Conversely, the CIA was dealing with a small number of key terrorist leaders believed to be senior al-Qaida operatives. CIA personnel were trained to use enhanced interrogation tactics in carefully monitored situations. We didn't want young military personnel making decisions on interrogating high-level al-Qaida terrorists.[33]

It was for precisely this reason—the difference between the CIA interrogation program and the military's detention operations at Guantánamo Bay and in Iraq and Afghanistan—that in the summer of 2006 I became a thorn in the administration's side. By then the *Washington Post* had published the news, obtained by a leak, that the CIA was holding senior al-Qaida terrorists in secret prisons around the world.[34] In response to the disclosures and the resulting press furor, the CIA and the President's White House staff wanted to announce that the al-Qaida terrorists were being sent to Gitmo. I argued strongly against the proposed transfer.

There was some logic to the idea of the move. The CIA would be able to close the prisons it had operated in friendly countries abroad—countries that were less than enthusiastic that their cooperation might become public. Increasing pressure from the federal courts and evolving interpretations of international law also threatened the CIA program if it remained in the shadows, a legal limbo that understandably made many in intelligence agencies uncomfortable. And finally, the CIA had no better place to put them.

Still, I believed the Defense Department was in the worst possible position to deal with the public aspects of the CIA's handling of high-value al-Qaida detainees. We had not been involved in their detention program and would not be able to defend it with the persuasiveness required. Further, the Defense Department was particularly ill suited to take on another burden after the abuse at the Abu Ghraib prison in Iraq. The military men and women at Guantánamo Bay already were being criticized in the media and in Congress for allegations of abuse (most of which were proven false). I was convinced the military would be damaged further by allegations of detainee mistreatment if the CIA program became conflated with the Department of Defense's detention operations.

I asked Steve Cambone, the Defense Department's undersecretary for intelligence, to be the bearer of the news the White House did not want to hear. It was one of many thankless tasks I assigned to Cambone. Steve had an air of reserved intelligence that, when combined with his physical height, could make him seem intimidating to those who did not know his ready wit and warm personal loyalty. But for a problem like this one, it wasn't a bad thing to have a representative from DoD whom people took seriously. We argued that there needed to be clear lines between the CIA program and the Defense Department program. Critics would ignore the important differences if both the military and CIA detainees were located at Guantánamo.

But the momentum behind the decision was too strong to overcome, even for someone as persistent as Cambone. Though he held the line for months, by late summer it became clear the President favored the transfer. On September 6, 2006, Bush announced that fourteen high-value CIA detainees were on their way to Guantánamo Bay, where they would be confined on the military base run by the Defense Department. In the years that followed, the controversy over the treatment of the CIA detainees only escalated. So did confusion about the many differences between the legal authorities, standards, and operations of the CIA and the Defense Department.

If you ask most Americans how many detainees were waterboarded at Guantánamo, the likely answers range from three to hundreds. The correct answer is zero. When military interrogators at Guantánamo Bay sent up their chain of command a request to use waterboarding in late 2002, I rejected it. To my knowledge, no U.S. military personnel involved in interrogations waterboarded any detainees—not at Guantánamo Bay, or anywhere else in the world.

There is no doubt in my mind that I made the right decision when it came to rejecting the use of waterboarding by U.S. military personnel. Reasonable people can disagree whether it crosses the line into dubious territory.*

*In a June 2004 Judiciary Committee hearing, Democratic New York Senator Chuck Schumer put it much more starkly: "There are times when we all get in high dudgeon. We ought to be reasonable about this. I think there are probably very few people in this room or in America who would say that torture should never, ever be used, particularly if thousands of lives are at stake. Take the hypothetical: If we knew that there was a nuclear bomb hidden in an American city, and we believed that some kind of torture, fairly severe maybe, would give us a chance of finding that bomb before it went off, my guess is most Americans and most senators, maybe all, would say, Do what you have to do. So it is easy to sit back in the armchair and say that torture can never be used. But when you are in the foxhole, it is a very different deal. And I respect—I think we all respect—the fact that the president is in the foxhole every day."

It is one thing to argue against coercive interrogation techniques on moral grounds—that they are contrary to America's values and therefore should never be employed. It is quite another to argue against those techniques on practical grounds—that they do not and will not work. While it may make a convenient plank for critics' arguments against the CIA's interrogation program, there are inconvenient facts to the contrary that must also be taken into account.*

The men and women of the CIA were given a challenging assignment to interrogate senior al-Qaida operatives. I saw the challenges up close when we discovered that the likely twentieth hijacker of the 9/11 attacks was in Defense Department custody. Administration lawyers fully vetted and approved the CIA's program, giving them the green light to proceed. The men and women of the Central Intelligence Agency who elicited critical information from well-connected al-Qaida members, deserve our respect, not condemnation. They are patriots, not criminals.

* I was not told precisely about the intelligence gained through the CIA program, but I believe General Michael Hayden, a four-star Air Force general who had been director of the National Security Agency, and in 2006 led the CIA. Hayden was not a partisan or a bomb thrower. He did not have to defend boldly and publicly a program that he had inherited. After a careful review, Hayden concluded, "I was convinced enough that I believed that we needed to keep this tool available." Hayden, along with former federal judge and U.S. Attorney General Michael Mukasey, wrote that: "[F]ully half of the government's knowledge about the structure and activities of al Qaeda came from those interrogations."[35]

CHAPTER 40

Law in a Time of War

Before 9/11, our nation had tried treating terrorists as common criminals to be investigated by U.S. law enforcement agencies and tried in U.S courts of law. Our country's counterterrorism strategy hinged on hopes that the FBI or local police would get lucky and stop an attack, and then use American courts to try to bring the culprits to justice.

The law enforcement approach not only failed to prevent terrorist attacks from the first World Trade Center bombing in 1993 to the attempted sinking of the USS *Cole* in 2000, it made it even more difficult to track down the enemy. For example, in 1998, within days after documents made public in court revealed that the United States could intercept Osama bin Laden's cell phone and his GPS location, Bin Laden stopped using mobile devices.* If it wasn't clear enough already, the deaths of nearly three thousand American citizens painfully drove home the inescapable conclusion that the U.S. law enforcement approach to terrorism had failed miserably and inflicted a great

* The court proceedings against the so-called Blind Sheikh, Omar Abdel Rahman, who conspired to destroy the World Trade Center in 1993, revealed almost all the U.S. government knew about al-Qaida at the time. To comply with standard criminal procedures in U.S. courts, Andrew McCarthy, the chief prosecutor on that case, was required to turn over to defense attorneys a list of two hundred possible coconspirators. This told al-Qaida which of its members had been compromised and indicated where U.S. intelligence had gleaned its information. Bin Laden reportedly was reading the list several weeks later in Sudan. He must have been shaking his head in contemptuous wonder at how effectively the United States was assisting him in his deadly jihad.[1]

cost on our nation. President Bush decided America could not afford to keep making the same mistakes.

In mid-November 2001, the President announced that trials for terrorist detainees would be held by specially designed military commissions—not ordinary civilian courts and not military tribunals under the Uniform Code of Military Justice. Terrorists were enemies in wartime, no longer domestic criminals. His order of November 13 specified, "Any individual subject to this order shall, when tried, be tried by military commission for any and all offenses triable by military commission that such individual is alleged to have committed, and may be punished in accordance with the penalties provided under applicable law, including life imprisonment or death."[2]

President Bush based this order on longstanding American legal precedents. Military commissions, designed to provide due process but specially suited to the circumstances of the conflict at the time, have been used by the United States in many of its wars since the founding of the Republic.* They were established to provide fair trials for enemies accused of war crimes and other offenses. The military commission's procedures have differed from those of existing tribunals—that is, from civilian courts as well as from military courts-martial—otherwise there would have been no point in creating the commissions.

The best-known military commission was created in 1942 by President Franklin Roosevelt to try eight Nazi saboteurs. All of them had lived in the United States at some time prior to the outbreak of World War II, and at least one was an American citizen. They planned to come ashore from German submarines, blend into the population, and bomb American manufacturing facilities. The conspirators made it onto beaches in Florida and Long Island with large sums of cash and explosives, but no farther.

The eight saboteurs were promptly rounded up. There were demands in the press for their swift execution, which FDR favored. He wrote to his attorney general that "[s]urely they are as guilty as it is possible to be and it seems to me that the death penalty is almost obligatory."[4] In three days, FDR's military commission—meeting in secrecy on the Justice Department's fifth floor in downtown Washington—tried, convicted, and sentenced the eight to death. A total of six weeks elapsed between the capture of the saboteurs and their execution.

* In 1780, George Washington tried a spy linked to Benedict Arnold before a board of inquiry that was essentially a military commission. The use of military commissions by the United States government continued through the Indian Wars and the Mexican-American War. During the Civil War, military commissions tried more than two thousand cases. During World War II and the months after, thousands of prisoners were tried before commissions in Germany and Japan for "terrorism, subversive activity, and violation of the laws of war."[3]

Critics characterized the President's November 2001 military order as vague and sweeping. Given the uncertainties of the time, it was perhaps inevitable that aspects of the President's order were imprecise.[5] Its purpose was to establish only the framework of the military commissions, which led some critics to assume the worst. My longtime friend and *New York Times* columnist Bill Safire criticized the proposed tribunals as "kangaroo courts."[6] I was determined to prove this criticism wrong and to see that the military commissions were fair and would be a credit to America.

Believing in the value of tapping into the expertise, judgment, and experience of experts outside the government, I assembled nine distinguished legal minds from across the political and philosophical spectrum to serve as an outside advisory group to the Defense Department. Government experts are helpful and needed, but it's important to hedge against insularity. I thought the outside group could help fashion rules and procedures for the military commissions and to address the arguments fair-minded critics might raise against them.

We came to refer to this outside group, in shorthand, as the Wise Men. Though they were all wise, they were not all men. They included: Lloyd Cutler, White House counsel to Presidents Carter and Clinton, who had been a junior member of the 1942 team that prosecuted the Nazi saboteurs before FDR's military commission; Bill Coleman, President Ford's transportation secretary, a civil rights hero who was the first black law clerk at the U.S. Supreme Court; Bernard Meltzer, a renowned University of Chicago legal scholar, who served as one of the prosecutors at the Nuremburg war crimes trials; Griffin Bell, attorney general for President Carter; Newt Minow, a distinguished Chicago attorney, who had served as President Kennedy's chairman of the Federal Communications Commission; Martin Hoffmann, a former DoD general counsel and former secretary of the Army; Terry O'Donnell, a veteran Washington attorney and former Air Force judge advocate general; Bill Webster, who had been director of the CIA and director of the FBI; and Ruth Wedgwood, a former federal prosecutor and law professor at Yale and the Johns Hopkins School of Advanced International Studies.

This bipartisan group was not of a mind to rubber-stamp any proposal sent their direction. They were individuals of independent judgment who often disagreed among themselves. They worked closely with Pentagon lawyers to consider precedents, review the legal basis for the commissions, advise on the rules of evidence and procedure for the trials and appeals, and offer comments and criticism regarding all aspects of these complex issues. We were determined to create a process considerably more protective of the rights of the accused than any previous military commission in our nation's history.

Standing together with the Wise Men, I announced Military Commission Order Number One on March 21, 2002. Among the protections provided for defendants were: the defendant was presumed innocent; the defendant had rights to counsel and to a public trial; and guilt had to be proven "beyond a reasonable doubt"; a two-thirds vote of a military commission was required to issue a guilty verdict, just as in military courts-martial under the Uniform Code of Military Justice; and a death sentence would require the unanimous agreement of the members of a commission.[7]

The first reviews were favorable. "The regulations announced yesterday by the Pentagon incorporate the advice of outside experts and respond to important issues raised by legal and constitutional scholars," the *New York Times* acknowledged on its editorial page. "When President Bush first issued the order establishing the tribunals last November, critics, this page included, were concerned about potentially secret trials, inadequate legal representation, verdicts based on flimsy evidence and death sentences imposed by divided panels. The regulations issued yesterday dispel many of these fears."[8] Bill Safire also wrote that he was "somewhat reassured by Defense Secretary Don Rumsfeld's 'refinement' of the hasty order."[9]

I asked Deputy Secretary Wolfowitz to spearhead the effort to make the military commissions operable, but it took another year—until April 30, 2003—for lawyers to agree on the crimes that could be tried before military commissions. Everyone involved wanted to do things right—not fast—but President Bush and I found the lengthy delays disturbing. Whenever we expressed dismay at the excruciatingly slow pace, however, we were reminded by lawyers that we risked exerting "undue and improper command influence," thereby corrupting the military commission process.

Despite the great care we took, some were uncomfortable with the military commissions system. It did not resemble the military's courts-martial system with which military lawyers were familiar. Nor did it resemble the civilian courts with which most Americans were familiar. But the fact was the terrorists we were detaining were not American uniformed personnel to be tried under the Uniform Code of Military Justice. Nor were they garden variety criminals to be tried in American civilian courts. The fact that the detainees were different was exactly the reason the military commissions were different. The lawyers of the captured al-Qaida suspects, along with various groups critical of the war in Afghanistan (and later in Iraq) and of President Bush,

54

Arriving at Bagram Air Base outside Kabul, Afghanistan, in December 2001, we were greeted by a band of haggard but courageous Northern Alliance fighters who had just toppled the Taliban—and by the abandoned wreckage of Soviet-made aircraft.

55

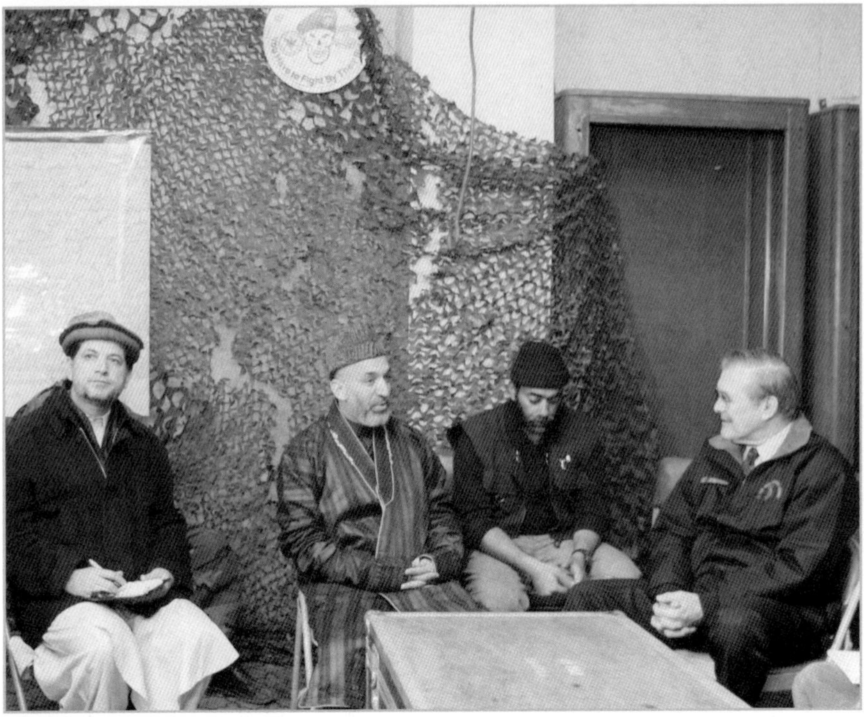

56

During my first visit to Afghanistan I met with the determined leader Hamid Karzai in an abandoned hangar at Bagram Air Base.

57

One of Karzai's challenges was to integrate former Northern Alliance generals such as Ismail Khan into the new Afghanistan. With the assistance of our Afghan-born diplomat Zal Khalilzad he was able to do so, and Khan became an influential provincial governor.

58

During the Afghanistan and Iraq campaigns, those of us meeting in the situation room of the White House could communicate by secure video with commanders around the globe—here President Bush and I prepare for an update from Gen. Tommy Franks.

59

Arriving at Mazar-e-Sharif, Afghanistan, in 2003. Our country benefited from the close partnership between the then U.S. ambassador to Afghanistan, Zal Khalilzad, and our military commander Lt. Gen. David Barno. They understood the importance of linking American diplomatic and military efforts. Their effective model of cooperation was regrettably not always followed by their successors.

60

In the lead-up to the war in Iraq, President Bush made an effort to invite his combatant commanders along with members of the Joint Chiefs of Staff to the White House cabinet room for face-to-face meetings with their Commander in Chief.

61

At a town hall meeting at Camp Buehring, Kuwait. I welcomed the opportunity to meet with our troops overseas. They were a constant source of inspiration.

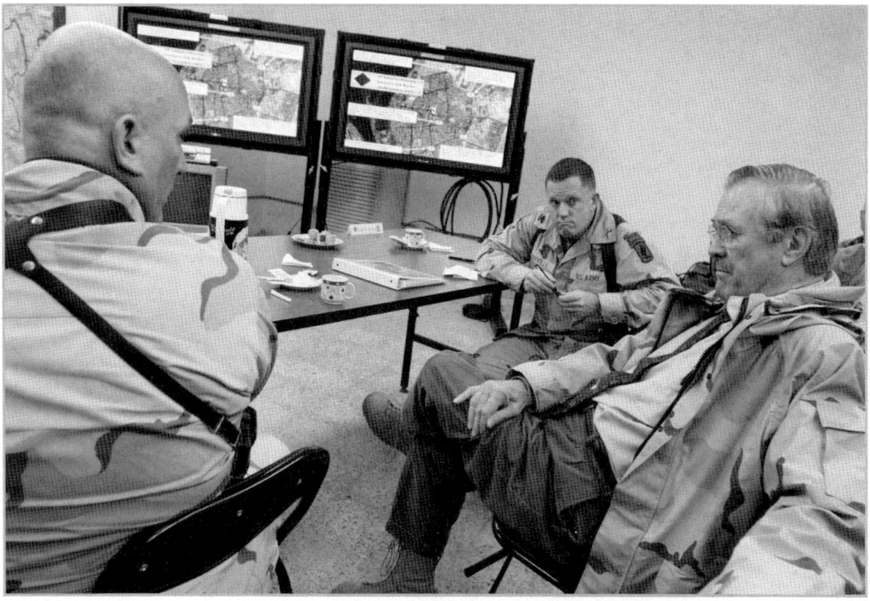

65

With Maj. Gen. Ray Odierno (left) in Kirkuk, Iraq, in December 2003, discussing the hunt for High Value Target Number One: Saddam Hussein.

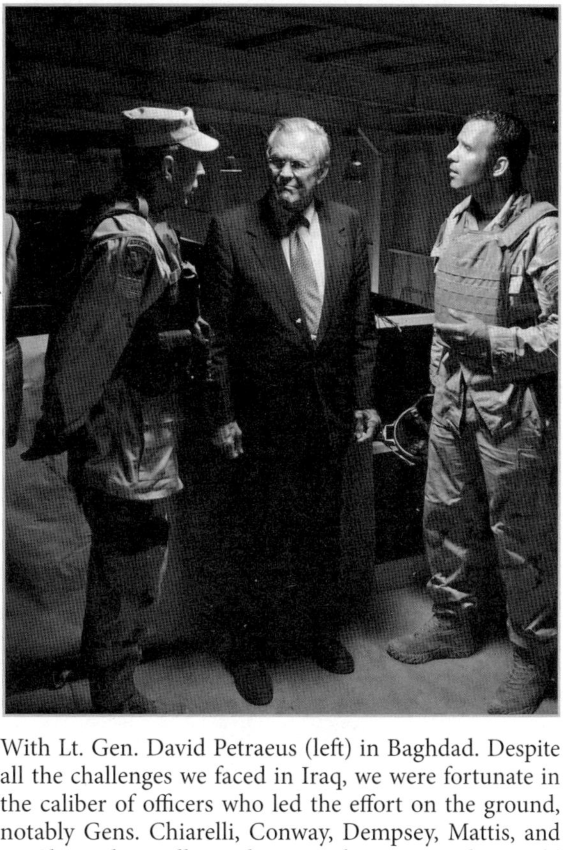

66

With Lt. Gen. David Petraeus (left) in Baghdad. Despite all the challenges we faced in Iraq, we were fortunate in the caliber of officers who led the effort on the ground, notably Gens. Chiarelli, Conway, Dempsey, Mattis, and McChrystal as well as Odierno and Petraeus, who would go on to play pivotal roles in the surge and beyond.

67

Travel to remote corners of the globe was sometimes tiring but always enlightening. Onboard a C-17 cargo plane headed into Uzbekistan with (clockwise from bottom left) Torie Clarke, Marc Thiessen, Doug Feith, Vice Adm. Ed Giambastiani, and my administrative assistant Delonnie Henry.

68

Sultan Qaboos of Oman was one of the most impressive observers of the Middle East. I benefited from his counsel after the Beirut barracks bombing in 1983 and again soon after the 9/11 attacks.

69

With Kazakh officials in Astana. What I had not admitted was that the ceremonial robe they had presented me was covering up a large hole in my old pair of suit pants that had virtually disintegrated as I got out of the car to join the meeting.

70

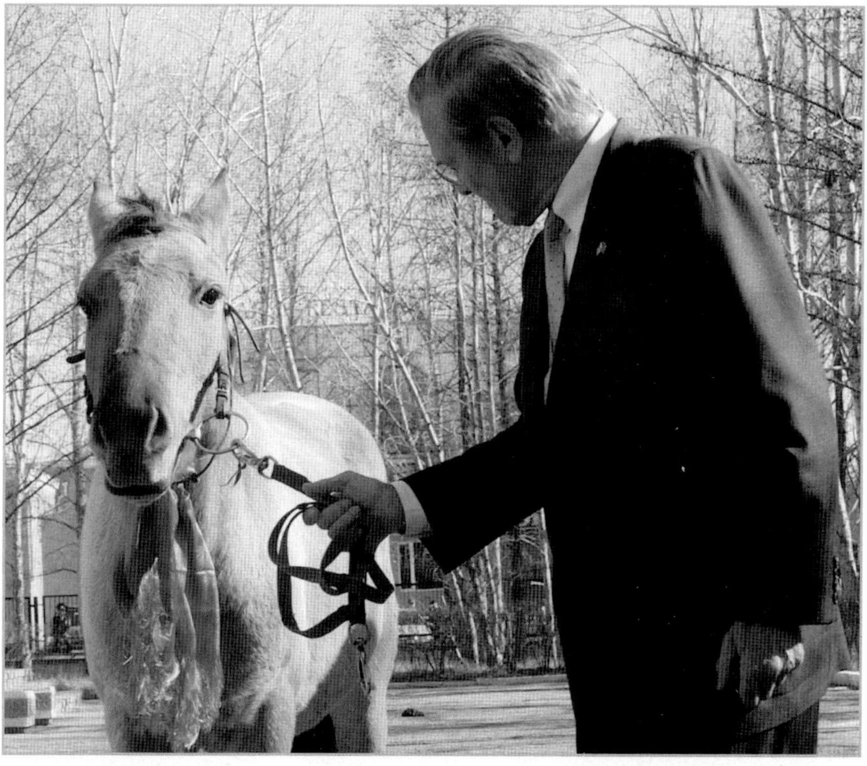

This handsome horse was a symbolic gift from the Mongolian Minister of Defense in 2005. I named him "Montana" because the surrounding steppe looked much like the big sky landscape of Joyce's home state. When President Bush visited Mongolia the following year, he jokingly told his hosts that he had come to see how "Rumsfeld's horse" was doing.

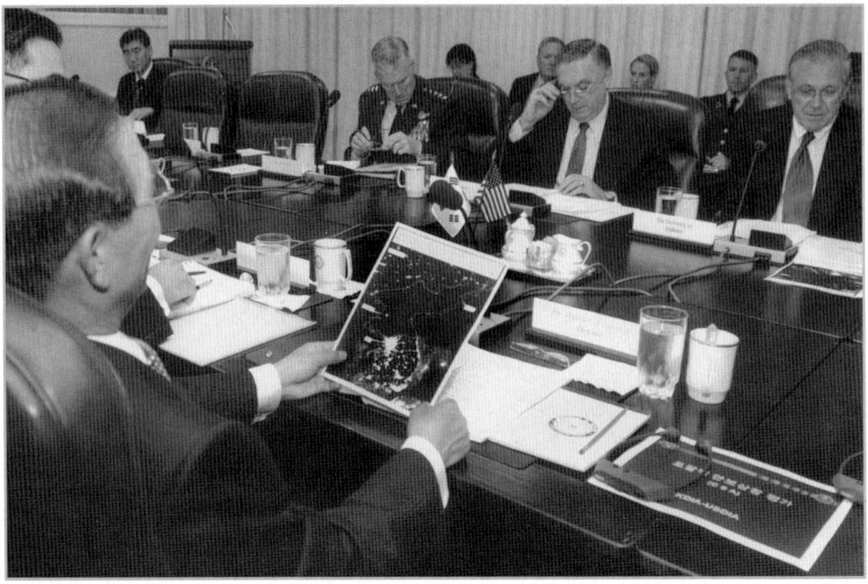

71

(Center to right) With Gen. Dick Myers and Deputy Assistant Secretary of Defense Richard Lawless, I showed my favorite satellite photograph to South Korea's Minister of Defense. The image of the Korean peninsula at night illuminates more vividly than any words the power of freedom.

72

When my colleague Russian Minister of Defense Sergei Ivanov saw the photograph of a young Rumsfeld with former President Dwight Eisenhower in a Pentagon display, he mused, "That would be like me in a photo with Stalin." I laughed and thought, "Not quite."

73 

(Top to right) With my senior assistant Robert Rangel, Assistant Secretary of Defense Peter Rodman, and Lt. Gen. Gene Renuart at a Pentagon meeting with Chinese Vice Foreign Minister Dai Bingguo in 2005. In the years after the 2001 EP-3 incident, relations between China and the United States went from strained to somewhat more cordial.

74 

It was an honor to welcome Lady Margaret Thatcher to the Pentagon in 2006 and to show her one of the ballots from the first free Afghan elections.

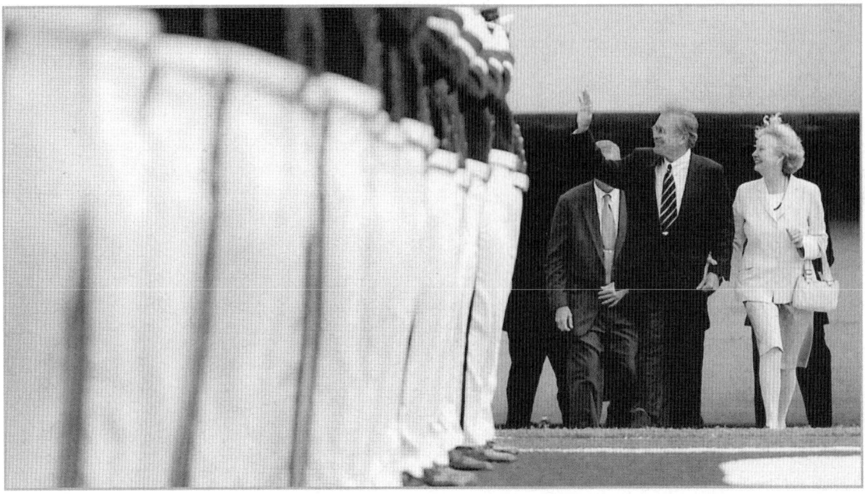

75

With Joyce at the Air Force Academy's 2006 commencement. Through all the challenges of my second tour as Secretary of Defense, Joyce was at my side. At my farewell ceremony in December 2006, Gen. Pete Pace presented Joyce with the DoD Distinguished Public Servant Award. He said the *Reader's Digest* version of the tribute was "We love you, thank you."

76

Joyce skied with the wounded troops in Vail, Colorado, and then enjoyed a barbecue hosted by local firemen. They cheered at what they had never seen before: a seventy-year-old woman sliding down a fire pole.

77

With Joyce at our surprise fiftieth wedding anniversary party in 2004.

Waiting to see the President with the chairman of the Joint Chiefs of Staff Gen. Pete Pace just outside the Oval Office, I paused to shine his shoes so he would look his best. It was an example of civil-military relations at their finest.

79

Thanking World War II veterans at the sixtieth anniversary commemoration of V-J Day in Coronado, California, August 30, 2005. On that day six decades before, I had been selling newspapers where the San Diego ferry docked nearby.

80

The world saw its share of natural disasters in 2005, requiring DoD relief, including Hurricane Katrina and the earthquake in Pakistan. Lt. Gen. Russel Honoré (left) led the Katrina effort with Maj. Gen. Bill Caldwell (center) and Adm. Tim Keating (far right).

81

In the fall of 2006, Joyce suggested we go to the Washington restaurant Old Europe for what we expected to be our last dinner with the combatant commanders.

82

With President George Bush, Vice President Dick Cheney, and chairman of the Joint Chiefs of Staff Gen. Pete Pace at my farewell ceremony at the Pentagon on December 15, 2006. After my remarks, I sat down. As the applause continued, the President turned to me and, using an analogy from his favorite sport, said, "Don, they're calling you out of the dugout."

83

With Joyce and our children, Nick, Valerie, and Marcy, the day of my farewell ceremony. We were ready.

84

Our granddaughters Mia, Sophia, and Rachel with our daughter Valerie looking at my new Pentagon portrait in June 2010.

mounted volleys of attacks, even before the commission rules were completed. As a result, the commissions came under a broad and sustained assault in the courts, in the Congress, and in the press. Yet no preferable alternative has been established almost a decade later.

As Secretary of Defense, I found myself named in a number of lawsuits. Many were frivolous.* Others dealt with some of the thorniest issues in constitutional law and reached the Supreme Court of the United States.

One of those cases was decided on Thursday, June 29, 2006. I arrived at the Pentagon shortly after 6:30 that morning, as usual. In those quiet early hours, when the building's hallways were not yet buzzing with the twenty-five thousand men and women who worked there daily, I could take some time to try to catch up on the mountain of work and reading materials that flowed through the office. Prime Minister Junichiro Koizumi of Japan, an ebullient leader with a flamboyant persona and a passion for all things Elvis Presley, was arriving in town for meetings with President Bush. I liked Koizumi, as did the President. At 9:00 a.m. Joyce met me at the White House for the arrival ceremony for the prime minister on the South Lawn. Afterward, I joined the President in the Oval Office for the two-hour meeting with Koizumi on a range of issues in one of America's most important bilateral relationships.

Meanwhile, a block east of the Capitol building, TV cameras and reporters were gathering to receive the latest set of Supreme Court opinions. At 10:15 a.m., the court chambers fell silent as Justice John Paul Stevens began to read the holding in *Hamdan v. Rumsfeld.*[10] His opinion had split the court 5 to 3. The case, involving a Yemeni detainee at Guantánamo Bay named Salim Hamdan, had worked its way through federal district and appellate courts and had reached the Supreme Court.† Though some journalists and others tried to belittle Hamdan's

* One of the dubious privileges of serving in government in the information age is the increasing number of lawsuits in which public officials are named. Many are from folks looking to make a name or some money for themselves. One lawsuit alleged that the 9/11 attacks were a carefully orchestrated plot hatched at the highest levels of the U.S. government. It claimed that because I supposedly had foreknowledge that a plane was going to hit the Pentagon, I was legally liable for not ordering the evacuation of the building earlier. The many dozens of lawsuits are as ludicrous as they are time consuming and expensive.

† Future Chief Justice John Roberts was on the U.S. Court of Appeals for the District of Columbia Circuit when Hamdan's case came to the appellate level in July 2005. He and the two other judges on a three-judge panel (one a Clinton appointee) unanimously had held that military commissions were legitimate forums to try enemy combatants, because they were authorized by Congress as part of the Articles of War, which are now part of the Uniform Code of Military Justice. Moreover, the court also noted that al-Qaida and its members were not covered under the terms of the Geneva Conventions, and that even if they were, Hamdan could not as an individual enforce the treaty in U.S. courts. Roberts had to recuse himself in the Supreme Court decision because of his earlier involvement in the case. Five—a bare majority—of the members of the Court he would lead voted to overturn Roberts' earlier decision.

importance by referring to him as "Bin Laden's driver," intelligence officials considered him much more than that. He was thought to be a significant facilitator for senior al-Qaida leadership and an arms trafficker. Hamdan was caught in Afghanistan with a surface-to-air missile in his car trunk—odd cargo for a mere chauffeur of little importance. Hamdan had filed a habeas corpus petition, the means by which a prisoner can challenge the basis of his incarceration. Given that Hamdan was neither an American citizen nor apprehended on U.S. soil, I thought his was a creative filing to say the least. In his lawsuit, Hamdan had identified several officials as defendants in addition to me, including President Bush and the military commander at Guantánamo, Brigadier General Jay Hood. As the first named defendant, I earned the dubious distinction of being identified in the shorthand title of the case: *Hamdan v. Rumsfeld.*

The Bush administration's decisions to hold detainees without automatic access to the U.S. court system, to classify them as unlawful or unprivileged enemy combatants (not legally entitled to the POW privileges of lawful combatants), and to use military commissions were based on more than two centuries of American precedents. One was the 1942 case that upheld the constitutionality of FDR's use of military commissions.[11] It made clear that individuals engaged in armed hostilities against the United States and who do not themselves obey the laws of war with respect to uniforms, command structure, and the targeting of civilians, are "unlawful combatants" who can be tried and punished in military—rather than civilian—courts.[12] In another case, the Supreme Court held that German nationals who were tried abroad by military commissions were not entitled to American judicial review.[13] The Court concluded that it did not have jurisdiction to consider claims by alien enemies not held on U.S. soil.

But as we soon learned, that long-established and well-regarded legal foundation could not withstand the startling earthquake produced when American federal courts began to shift the legal ground regarding detainees and the laws of war. In 2004, the Supreme Court began handing down its first war on terror decisions.* They were not total defeats for the government's

*That first case, *Hamdi v. Rumsfeld*, was brought on behalf of Yaser Esam Hamdi, a Saudi national born in Louisiana and, therefore, an American citizen. After his capture in Afghanistan he was transferred to the Navy brig in Norfolk, Virginia. His lawyers challenged the government's right to hold him as an enemy combatant without a civilian criminal charge. The Supreme Court upheld that right, but ruled that he must be given an administrative process to enable him to contest his designation as an enemy combatant. On the same day the Supreme Court decided Hamdi's case, it also issued a ruling in *Rasul v. Bush*. In *Rasul*, the Supreme Court overturned prior precedents and determined that the detainees in Guantánamo were in fact entitled access to American courts. Though we were not required to release any of the detainees because of these cases, the writing on the wall indicated that the Supreme Court would, for the first time, assert judicial authority over the Guantánamo base and the men held there, despite the facts that they were not U.S. citizens and that they were being held outside the United States.

positions, but they reflected a new and unprecedented judicial willingness to reverse a president's wartime detention judgments.

As we departed the President's meeting with Prime Minister Koizumi that June morning in 2006, an aide told me that the U.S. government had lost its argument in *Hamdan*. No one seemed to be able to explain what exactly that meant, but it was clear it wasn't good. To me it sounded like I would be the first secretary of defense in history to lose a case in the Supreme Court of the United States to a terrorist. As we later learned, six of the nine justices issued separate written opinions on the case.[14] After several senior attorneys had sorted through the main opinion, the two concurring and the three dissenting opinions, they concluded that the case amounted to a staggering blow to the military commission system, as well as to the administration's legal positions on which wartime detention operations depended.

In one of the stranger portions of the *Hamdan* opinion, a majority of justices also concluded that Common Article 3 of the Geneva Conventions applied to the conflict with al-Qaida. Common Article 3 established rules for detainees in armed conflicts "not of an international character."[15] I was informed that the phrase had long been understood to refer to civil wars fought within the territory of a single state. In early 2002, administration lawyers had advised the President that Common Article 3 did not apply to the global conflict with al-Qaida. Now, Common Article 3 was deemed by the Supreme Court to apply to that conflict, even though al-Qaida is an organization, not a state, and was not a party to the Geneva Conventions, and even though the conflict is of an international character.

Though I didn't follow the novel reasoning of the Supreme Court majority in *Hamdan*, I agreed fully that there should be a proper standard of care for all detained enemy combatants, even those not technically entitled to POW privileges. Had a standard beyond humane treatment, such as Common Article 3, been established as a matter of policy earlier, the administration might have avoided the sweeping setback that *Hamdan* represented. It is possible that we would have come to a better outcome had we approached the issue as a policy matter to be decided by policy makers with legal advice, rather than viewing it as a legal matter to be determined by lawyers.

I had already begun to reorganize the Defense Department to reflect this concern after the abuse at Abu Ghraib came to light, by creating a senior policy position and a unit on the Joint Staff solely responsible for detainee affairs. I also asked a former Democratic congressman from Texas and future secretary of the Army, Pete Geren, and Army Lieutenant General Michael

Maples to head up a task force to ensure we were better prepared to handle detainee issues moving forward. They carefully reviewed the reforms and recommendations suggested in twelve independent reports on detention operations, and the Department proceeded to implement over four hundred of them. After the *Hamdan* decision, the Defense Department informed all military personnel that Common Article 3 would apply to the country's war against terrorist organizations. We issued Defense Department Directive 2310.01E, which incorporated Common Article 3 of the Geneva Conventions verbatim.[16] The Army Field Manual on interrogation was rewritten to ensure that the standards were compliant with the Geneva Conventions. I knew how important the field manual was and insisted that senior officials in the Department read it carefully and submit edits where they didn't agree.[17] The results were evidently good enough for it to become a gold standard; it was even passed into law by Congress.

The Supreme Court's invalidation of the military commission system necessitated congressional action. Some four months after the *Hamdan* decision, Congress passed the Military Commissions Act of 2006. The legislation, signed into law by the President, included a statutory definition of "unlawful enemy combatant," established military commissions to try foreign nationals who met that definition, set forth processes and procedures for the commissions, and created various avenues for judicial review.*

American courts had been historically reluctant to second-guess the President and the Congress regarding the use of military force—even during controversial conflicts. Throughout America's involvement in Vietnam, for example, the Supreme Court refused to consider challenges to the war's constitutionality. The Supreme Court had been especially cautious when it came to the detention and trial of foreign enemies overseas. In the 1950 case of the Germans tried by military commission, Justice Robert Jackson, who had served as Franklin Roosevelt's attorney general and as the chief prosecutor at the Nuremburg trials, explained the reasons for this sensible policy. Jackson wrote that extending to our enemies the right to judicial review in American courts of law "would hamper the war effort and bring aid and comfort to the enemy." Such trials, Justice Jackson presciently asserted,

* Despite Congress's effort to limit the courts' role in prosecuting the war on terror with the Military Commissions Act (MCA), the courts again would not agree, rejecting the Congress's right even to set practical limits on the enemy's access to courts in wartime. In the 2008 case of *Boumediene v. Bush*, the Supreme Court's majority invalidated much of the MCA—after the Court had suggested the administration and the Congress pass such a bill two years earlier in *Hamdan*. Dissenting Chief Justice Roberts aptly called the perplexing *Boumediene* decision a "constitutional bait and switch."[18]

> ... would diminish the prestige of our commanders, not only with enemies but with wavering neutrals. It would be difficult to devise more effective fettering of a field commander than to allow the very enemies he is ordered to reduce to submission to call him to account in his own civil courts and divert his efforts and attention from the military offensive abroad to the legal defensive at home. Nor is it unlikely that the result of such enemy litigiousness would be a conflict between judicial and military opinion highly comforting to enemies of the United States. Moreover, we could expect no reciprocity for placing the litigation weapon in unrestrained enemy hands.[19]

Jackson's reasoning, which prevailed in 1950, reflected what I believed. But by 2008, Jackson's thoughtful predictions were brushed aside by judges and an almost hysterical campaign by NGOs, detainee lawyers, and academics. Their arguments are impractical as a security matter, inverted as a moral matter, and unprecedented as a legal matter. By proving persuasive to many, even to some members of Congress and some judges, including a bare majority of the Supreme Court, these activists have successfully placed "the litigation weapon" in the hands of our enemies.

As never before in history, today lawyers and legal considerations pervade every aspect of U.S. military operations. Besides contending with enemy bullets and bombs, the men and women in our nation's military and intelligence services must also navigate legal traps set by our enemies, by some of our fellow citizens, by some foreigners, and even by some members of Congress and officials at international institutions such as the United Nations. The rules, regulations, and consequences in legal venues have to be and are taken into account on every corner of the battlefield. American military personnel have found themselves named in lawsuits across Europe and in the United States. The mere threat of lawsuits and legal charges effectively bullies American decision makers, alters their actions, intimidates our security forces, and limits our country's ability to gather intelligence and defend the American people. This is a new kind of asymmetric war waged by our enemies—"lawfare."

Lawfare uses international and domestic legal claims, regardless of their factual basis, to win public support to harass American officials—military and civilian—and to score ideological victories.[20] Each legal action is a thread. The cumulative effect binds the American Gulliver. Enemies who cannot score military victories can nevertheless impair our defenses by litigating warfare.

Lawfare is particularly effective against the United States, because it exploits America's laudable reverence for the law and uses our own finest instincts and institutions—our very respect for law—to make us vulnerable to enemies who have nothing but contempt for those very instincts and institutions.

We cannot yet know what the full consequences of lawfare will be, but the trend is troubling. At home, judges—not elected representatives in Congress or in the executive branch—increasingly determine how a president can operate during wartime against our nation's enemies. Terrorists have been given legal privileges and protections they are not entitled to by any standard. They violate nearly every law of war, yet our courts now perversely award terrorists more rights than any of our traditional military enemies have had throughout our country's history. As a result, whenever and wherever American military personnel capture suspected terrorists, they must assemble evidence and facts to be ready to defend their actions, not only up the military chain of command but in courts of law, in addition to defending themselves in combat.

I received my first lesson in lawfare from a friend who had several close encounters with its spear point. In 2001, Henry Kissinger told me that when he traveled abroad he still faced threats of legal action for his work as secretary of state in the Nixon and Ford administrations three decades after the fact. Various critics have alleged he was complicit in war crimes and other offenses from Southeast Asia to South America.[21] This dedicated public servant and Nobel laureate has had to live with periodic threats of arrest resulting from the action of some rogue magistrate or grandstanding prosecutor—not in the nations of America's enemies, but in Europe, in countries with whom the United States is allied.

I came to appreciate keenly the dangers of lawfare during my second tenure as secretary of defense. In the spring of 2003, General Franks was named in a lawsuit brought before a Belgian court for his role in the Iraq war. The Belgian parliament had passed a law in the 1990s giving their nation's courts the jurisdiction to try war crimes, genocide, and other crimes against humanity wherever they were committed in the world. This concept of universal jurisdiction asserts that any court, anywhere in the world, could put American citizens—military and civilian—on trial if the alleged offense is described as a violation of international law.* But we knew that what was claimed as

* In 1998, a Spanish magistrate sought the extradition from Britain of Augusto Pinochet, Chile's former dictator, on charges of committing torture. Pinochet was visiting London for medical treatment. The underlying rationale was that Chile, though a modern, advanced democracy, was incapable of holding its own former officials to account, so therefore a random foreign court (which happened to be in Spain) could do so. Appallingly, Britain's House of Lords bowed to this notion of universal

international law was sometimes nothing other than the assertion of a hostile foreign critic perched on a judicial bench, or at a university, or within an activist political organization.*

Someone like General Franks, even after he retired from uniform, could be arrested and hauled into a Belgian court at any time. I realized something else as troubling: Any American on Belgian soil was vulnerable to criminal prosecutions—prosecutions that easily could be motivated by nothing more than opposition to U.S. government policy. Hundreds of U.S. military personnel were stationed at NATO headquarters, including the American supreme allied commander and his staff. Thousands more American servicemen and -women transit through Belgium every year, making them ripe candidates for those wishing to harass them with lawsuits and arrest warrants alleging war crimes.

It was one thing if the Belgian government wished to express opposition to the war; it was quite another for their judges to be able to haul American military personnel into their courts for what would amount to little more than political show trials. Belgium's power to do this infringed on American democracy, by subordinating our government—our officials and our country's policies—to a foreign government or organization that is unaccountable to the American people. The more I considered the Belgian law, the angrier I became.

At a NATO defense ministers meeting on June 12, 2003, I made my views known. I walked up to Belgium's minister of defense, Andre Flahaut, and asked to see him in a side room.

"I need to speak with you for a moment," I said.

Flahaut, a Socialist member of the Belgian parliament, and his left-leaning government were frequent critics of the United States. It was impossible to imagine them being overly concerned about grandstanding Belgian lawyers lodging suits against American military personnel and officials.

In language that diplomats might describe as a "frank and full exchange," I raised my concerns about the Belgian law. I told Flahaut that I believed it would be used by judges to target U.S. intelligence and military personnel, not dictators guilty of actual war crimes. I didn't recall the Belgians making any effort, for example, to arrest and try Saddam Hussein.

---

jurisdiction and approved Pinochet's transfer to Spain to stand trial. But before the transfer to Spain occurred, British officials allowed Pinochet to return to Chile to attend to his frail health.

* For example, according to one UN investigator, unmanned air strikes "may well violate international humanitarian law and international human rights law"—including strikes that reportedly have been personally approved by President Obama.[22]

The urgency in my tone was unmistakable, especially when I made what seemed an obvious point. The Belgian government was justifiably proud of serving as the headquarters of NATO, the world's oldest military alliance. But it was worth noting that the reason NATO was located in Brussels was because French President Charles De Gaulle had forced the alliance out of France in 1966. If Belgium was going to enforce a law that made its own territory similarly inhospitable to Americans, I asserted, there was no reason why we could not move NATO's headquarters again.

"It's perfectly possible to meet elsewhere," I said to Flahaut and, later that day, to the press.[23] There were plenty of other cities between Washington and Ankara.

Flahaut was counting on U.S. funding for a new NATO headquarters in Brussels. I added that American support would evaporate instantly absent a prompt shift in the Belgian government's position.

The difference in style between a Chicago-born American and a member of the European diplomatic corps was on full display in that conversation. From his demeanor I could tell he fully understood my point. Within two months of that conversation, the Belgian government repealed its law.

Belgium was not alone in threatening American sovereignty with lawfare. The International Criminal Court (ICC) was proposed in the 1990s as a court for crimes against humanity, genocide, and systematic war crimes. By 2003, the ICC was being discussed as a possible forum to try U.S. military and civilian personnel involved in the Iraq war. The American military had objected strongly to the ICC treaty for these reasons in the 1990s, and the Clinton administration, as a result, refused to sign it until the last days of the President's term. Even after he signed it, Clinton did not submit it to the Senate, where its prospects for ratification—necessary for the treaty to become U.S. law—were bleak.

In the Defense Department we saw the International Criminal Court as a potential lawfare weapon against the United States. One aspect of the treaty that made the court so objectionable was that it would create offices for prosecutors who were effectively unaccountable—even if they acted politically or otherwise improperly—who could prosecute Americans without respecting their rights under the U.S. Constitution. With some State Department officials less than enthusiastic about the idea, I pushed for the U.S. government to "unsign" the treaty. In May 2002, a State official who agreed with our position on the issue, the tenacious undersecretary for arms control and international security John Bolton, formally announced that the United States would not ratify the treaty.

Even with Bolton's support, I was concerned that our government was not paying enough attention to this issue. With the help of Jack Goldsmith,* an expert on international law then working in the Defense Department general counsel's office, we prepared a memo in April 2003 that I sent to Cheney, Powell, Ashcroft, Rice, Card, and Gonzales, observing:

> Last August I urged us to address several disturbing trends in international law, including the ICC, universal jurisdiction prosecutions, and the broader judicialization [*sic*] of international politics and warfare.
>
> I am concerned that this deliberation is not proceeding with appropriate urgency.
>
> There may be a sense that this is "just Henry Kissinger's problem." This is a serious miscalculation. Universal jurisdiction prosecutions are expanding in Europe and elsewhere. The purported content of international criminal law is growing in various unfavorable ways. Just a few weeks ago, a complaint was filed in Belgium against senior U.S. officials growing out of Operation Desert Storm. It is only a matter of time before there is an attempted prosecution of a U.S. official.
>
> There may be a sense that these issues should be shelved during the Iraq matter. On the contrary, the prospect of controversial war should alert us to what all U.S. officials may face.
>
> Our strategy with respect to the ICC seems to be getting nowhere. We have only a handful of Article 98 agreements, and no realistic prospect for significantly more in the near future. Meanwhile, the ICC proceeds apace.
>
> I believe we must quickly develop a campaign to discredit and counter these trends. Attached is a proposal for a more robust strategy to deal with these issues. I suggest we discuss the matter soon.[24]

The fact that the United States was not a party to the treaty and had unsigned it was not enough to protect American servicemen and -women.

* After serving in the Department of Defense general counsel's office, Jack Goldsmith moved to the Justice Department, where he became assistant attorney general of the Office of Legal Counsel (OLC)—the attorney who advises the U.S. government as to what is lawful and what is not. He went on to write *The Terror Presidency: Law and Judgment Inside the Bush Administration,* a valuable history of the unprecedented legal challenges that faced the Bush administration.

I had launched a global campaign to obtain commitments—in the form of what were called Article 98 agreements—from over one hundred nations that they would agree to never surrender Americans into ICC custody.* Defending those who have volunteered to serve our country in uniform and in our intelligence services is not only the right thing to do in principle, it is necessary to protect America's sovereignty—our nation's right to self-governance.

I think of sovereignty in concrete terms. It is a matter of freedom and autonomy. It means that we Americans control our destiny and are not ruled from abroad by officials we did not elect and courts we cannot hold accountable. Sovereignty is integrally tied to democracy, the right of Americans to choose their own leaders, to make their own laws, to limit the powers of government, and to enjoy due process of law.

If unchecked, the growing international judicial encroachments on our sovereignty will encourage an unfortunate and harmful trend toward American isolationism. If U.S. troops and officials can increasingly be tried in foreign courts, many Americans may well decide that sending our military on humanitarian missions, aiding allies, or defending our interests abroad is not worth the risk. Victims of tsunamis and earthquakes overseas could no longer depend on American assistance. Would-be aggressors could take advantage of our reluctance to use our military forces. Lawfare's greatest casualty will likely not be any one American official or serviceman. The greatest casualty will be the loss of America's willingness to use our military as a force for good around the world.

*Article 98 refers to part of the Rome Statute, which established the International Criminal Court. The article allows those nations that are members of the ICC to enter into separate bilateral agreements with other nations that do not want their citizens subject to the ICC.

CHAPTER 41

The Road Not Traveled

"The only exact science known to man is hindsight," John Reid, the British secretary of state for defense, commented in September 2005. He had a good point, though I might suggest that not even hindsight is an exact science, as demonstrated by any number of memoirs and books that explain the same events so differently. I found this myself when I started to subject my own memories to rigorous fact-checking in the process of writing this book.

Looking back, I see there are things the administration could have done differently and better with respect to wartime detention. As the administration grappled with these difficult questions, there were remarkably few interagency meetings devoted to detainee policy. In previous administrations the deputies committee, the highest subcabinet interagency forum on national security matters, regularly helped iron out differences of views among agencies. The principals committee, the members of the National Security Council, excepting the President, could then meet and prepare matters—including any unresolved interagency issues—for his consideration. I suggested without success that National Security Adviser Rice chair deputies meetings on important subjects to give the group some heft and direction. Deputy Secretary Wolfowitz eventually encouraged a group of senior officials from across the government to hold ad hoc deputies-level meetings to address detainee-related questions outside the formal NSC system.

When principals committee meetings were held on detainee policy, little, if anything, was resolved. Instead, the meetings became opportunities to discuss the negative media coverage, such as that about Guantánamo, rather than to propose constructive alternatives and move issues up to the President for decision.[1]

The Defense Department was largely left to deal with the barrage of negative press on its own. With the exceptions of President Bush and Vice President Cheney, others showed scant interest in helping defend the administration detention policy. We needed assistance but received little from the White House communications team. The gap between the reality of our policies and the mythology about them yawned wider and wider in the absence of a concerted effort to confront major untruths as they were continuously repeated.

It was not until January 2005—one year after CENTCOM brought the abuses at Abu Ghraib to light, and more than three years after the President had signed his November 2001 military order assigning the detainee mission to the Defense Department—that the National Security Council staff began to treat the subject of detainees as an administration issue. By that time the President had been reelected and had realigned his National Security Council.

During the President's first term, one problem that resulted from the lack of interagency policy review on this issue was that key policy makers saw detainee questions as essentially legal issues rather than policy matters. Perhaps somewhat paradoxically, given my reluctance to cede control to lawyers over policies such as rules of engagement, I too was guilty of thinking that the legal questions were preeminent. From the first days of combat operations in Afghanistan, I tended to treat detainee matters as something to be sorted out among knowledgeable executive branch lawyers, with little involvement from the policy makers, including me.

The military commissions and other detainee-management matters would have benefited from greater consideration of policy, politics, and diplomacy. That was less likely to happen if the issues were handled as legal matters in interagency meetings of lawyers, who were often not accompanied by policy officials. Legal advice is critical in defining boundaries, to be sure, but it should not be determinative, in that within the legal boundaries there is often a range of possible policy options.

The overly legal focus on wartime detention issues had consequences outside of the executive branch. I now believe that if we had directly engaged Congress from the outset and solicited its public involvement in crafting wartime detention legislation, we might have had a richer debate, and then implemented policies that would have commanded greater support at home and abroad. Of course, Congress, at its initiative, also could have become involved in these discussions from the outset, but the relevant players declined to do so.

Though early legislation on wartime detention would probably not have headed off all the problems, it might have helped. I say this even though I doubt the practices devised in partnership with Congress would have been notably different from those that the administration actually adopted and implemented. But by involving Congress, the administration might have taken into account a broader array of considerations, and at least been inoculated against the charge that it was acting in an unchecked and unlawful fashion. At the minimum, it would have built some defenses against many of the rhetorical attacks directed at essential efforts in the struggle against Islamist extremists. It would have also made clearer that the detainees are not just the Pentagon's problem or the President's problem, but the country's problem—indeed, a problem for the civilized world.

The way the administration reached decisions on detainee policy was generally consistent with a predisposition to protect the historic powers of the presidency. There was good reason to be concerned about preserving the commander in chief's constitutional national security and war powers. After 9/11, calls for greater security through prompt action came from every quarter of the country. By constitutional design, Congress is intended to be slow—to promote deliberation and the weeding out of ideas that may be popular for a moment, but imprudent. Congress was not intended or organized to meet the demands of operational decision making in a crisis. America's founding fathers knew what they were doing when they put the powers to conduct war in the hands of a single commander in chief, not those of a committee composed of the 535 members of the national legislature.

With these thoughts in mind, the administration—especially the lawyers—did not favor asking for legislation in areas in which the president already had robust constitutional authorities because it would set precedents that permanently limited the authority of future presidents. I shared that concern, but it may not have taken fully into account the broader picture—the complete set of strategic considerations of a president fighting a protracted, unprecedented, and unfamiliar war for which he would need sustained domestic and international support.

Vice President Cheney appreciated the importance of preserving the President's powers as commander in chief, especially when they were under assault for short-term political reasons. Cheney and his chief legal counsel and later chief of staff, David Addington, supported by senior lawyers from around the government, helped guard presidential authority as a matter of principle. Looking back, it is possible that the weight given to it may have contributed to an outcome the administration hoped to avoid: encroachment on the president's powers as commander in chief by the Congress and, particularly, by the judiciary.[2] Both the Congress and the judiciary now arrogate to themselves more rights to supervise the president's national security decisions than ever before in our country's history.

The tension among the three branches of our federal government goes back to the founding days of the Republic, when Alexander Hamilton and James Madison argued out the merits of a "vigorous Executive" in the Federalist Papers.[3] The debate has come up time and again—for example, during the Civil War and World War II as Presidents Lincoln and Roosevelt put the nation on war footings by exercising their powers as commander in chief expansively.

Cheney and I had witnessed the era of Vietnam and Watergate, during the fevered debate over the so-called imperial presidency. Late in the Vietnam War, Congress passed the 1973 War Powers Resolution, which declared that American presidents could no longer send U.S. forces into combat without express authorization by Congress, except in exigent circumstances. Cheney and I dealt with this congressional backlash in the Ford White House. In the early days of the Ford administration, Bryce Harlow, the savvy White House liaison to Congress, former Eisenhower aide, and a friend, told me—and I am paraphrasing from memory:

> The steady pressure by Congress and the courts is to reduce executive authority. It is inexorable, inevitable, and historical. Resolve that when you leave the White House, leave it with the same authorities it had when you came. Do not contribute to the erosion of presidential power on your watch.

Harlow's words left an impression on me, and, I suspect, on Cheney.

The executive branch lawyers' view of presidential prerogatives in national security, with a proper concern about congressional and judicial infringement, may well be consistent with the Founding Fathers' intentions. Nonetheless, the role of the federal judiciary has changed significantly over the past fifty years. Since World War II, federal courts have become involved in policy issues ranging from abortion and major league baseball to gun rights and campaign financing. In World War II, the United States detained four hundred thousand German and Italian prisoners of war in camps across the country without any judicial review. Out of the handful of habeas corpus petitions from those POWs, no court in the United States granted a single one. But as Jim Haynes pointed out in 2008, "Today, we have less than 300 unlawful combatants detained at Guantánamo Bay, Cuba, and 246 ongoing habeas cases to go with them."[4]

If it weren't obvious in 2001 that long-established legal precedents, even from the Supreme Court, were no longer reliable guideposts in times of legal activism, it should be sufficiently clear now. One of the finest legal minds in the nation, Solicitor General Ted Olson, advised White House lawyers in the early years of the George W. Bush administration that their view of executive power might not fare well with the twenty-first-century Supreme Court. Had the administration heeded that caution and worked with Congress early on to craft acceptable legislation governing twenty-first-century detainee policies, the courts might—and I stress might—have been somewhat less inclined to assume the role that they now have seized—and presidential powers in wartime might as a result be stronger than they are today.

While the legal justifications behind the decisions and policies we made on detainee affairs were sound and firmly rooted in precedent, there is little doubt that they grew increasingly out of sync with the mood of the country. The intense emotions of 9/11—insecurity and fear, offset by outrage and a resolve to confront the terrorists—eased. Increasingly distant memories of that day were overtaken by new, skewed images of detention—photographs from Abu Ghraib and an avalanche of largely unrebutted misinformation about Guantánamo Bay. Detainees came to be viewed by some in Congress, the news media, and the public less as dangerous terrorists caught on the battlefield and possible sources of lifesaving information about our enemies, but more as victims of abuse deprived of their legal rights.

When the President invoked wartime powers, some questioned

whether we were really in fact at war. As I freely admitted and made a point of saying publicly in the early days after 9/11, the challenge we faced from violent Islamist extremists was profoundly different from the wars Americans had fought in the past. It wasn't a war in the traditional way most Americans understood the concept. The struggle against the terrorists could not be discussed in terms familiar to Americans: battles and fronts, advances and surrenders. The war did not have a distinct beginning and it would not have a clear ending. We knew there would be no peace treaty that would bring the conflict to a ceremonious close. The war's duration was indefinite.

I knew that holding people indefinitely would become increasingly controversial, especially when indefinitely looked like forever to some people. I didn't want our country to hold a single detainee one day longer than necessary. I knew of no good alternative, except to keep moving each individual detainee's case toward resolution by military commission or transfer to their home nations, while examining and reexamining why we were holding them. The American people would need to understand the complexities of the problem and why neither our domestic criminal justice system nor the Uniform Code of Military Justice was adequate for the new challenges.

Our nation's campaign against Islamist extremists would be, as I wrote to the President in a memo only days after 9/11, "a marathon, not a sprint."[5] We were under no illusions that the terrorists would surrender after a few days of bombing in Afghanistan. If the war was going to be the work of a generation, that argued for developing broad and sustainable national and congressional support through a skillful public communications effort, consultation, and a proactive legislative strategy. There was at least temporary bipartisanship at work in the immediate aftermath of 9/11, which might have been leveraged better. Members of both parties were demanding in unison that the President take all the actions necessary to prevent another attack. Congress worked cooperatively—and reasonably quickly—with the President on wartime spending, the creation of new governmental organizations and posts, the Patriot Act, and other matters.* But on wartime detention, that was not the case—it took

*However, it should be noted that even the Patriot Act, which passed with bipartisan support in Congress in 2001, became controversial as time went on. An increasing number of legislators seemed to see it and other national security subjects as potent political issues. It is not unreasonable to imagine that the same could well have happened with detainee legislation.

a series of Supreme Court decisions five years into the Bush administration to provoke interest in the issue.

As a former member of Congress, I might have been better attuned to the need for congressional buy in on such potentially difficult and controversial matters. More than a year before the Supreme Court's decision in *Hamdan* forced the administration to go to Congress for detainee legislation, I pushed the Defense Department to reach out to Congress. In March 2005, I sent a memo to Jim Haynes and the incoming deputy secretary of defense, Gordon England—who was replacing Paul Wolfowitz, then leaving to head the World Bank. England brought with him a management background from business and as secretary of the Navy and then deputy secretary at the Department of Homeland Security. England also had good political instincts. He believed, as I did, that our detention policies would be subject to further scrutiny and criticism absent congressional involvement. As I wrote to Haynes and England in my memo:

> I wonder if we ought to consider proposing to the White House that they propose legislation to try to untangle all of these court decisions relating to unlawful combatants and detainees. It seems to me that getting the Congress involved might help put a lot of clarity into it, give them a role, and keep the confusion resulting from disparate court decisions to a minimum.[6]

Although Congress was not calling for a larger role, we might have sought their input and worked to pin down their support more formally. Because we did not do so, members of Congress felt free to abandon their support for administration policies when we hit bumps in the road.

Partisans in Congress, self-styled human rights advocates, anti-Bush journalists, lawyers of suspected terrorists, and others have argued relentlessly that the war on terrorism detainees at Guantánamo Bay and elsewhere should be viewed not as detainees held off the battlefield pending the end of the conflict, but rather as domestic criminal defendants presumed to be innocent and entitled to a speedy trial in civil courts or immediate release.[7] Because those arguments were not countered effectively, they prevailed in the public debate. Half truths, distortions, and outright lies were too often met with little or no rebuttal. There is plenty of blame to share for the failures in communication. The responsibility was first and foremost with those of us who served as the senior officials in the administration. War is more than secret intelligence, combat, and military operations. To use a military phrase, the center of gravity in a long war shifts from battlefields overseas to the home front. In a democracy, a war can be lost in Congress and in the news media at home, even if battles are won abroad. On the important issue of communicating and formulating detainee policy, we did not confront with sufficient energy or skill the political challenge represented by those who argued for using our own courts and legal system against us.

When it came to detainee policies, it proved easy for outsiders to criticize the Bush administration's perceived mistakes, sometimes in unusually harsh terms. When Barack Obama, for example, assumed the responsibilities of commander in chief in 2009, he found that making policy was much different from making speeches. To the disappointment of some of the President's supporters, his administration has kept in place the most contentious and widely derided Bush administration policies. Terrorists are still not accorded POW status under the Geneva Conventions. Guantánamo Bay—the so-called "gulag of our times"—remains in operation as the best available facility for holding dangerous terrorists. After flirting with trying captured terrorists in civilian courts of law, and even bringing Khalid Sheikh Muhammed to a courthouse in lower Manhattan, the administration changed course in response to a growing public outcry. As a result, military commissions—patterned on those established under the Bush administration—continue to be used to try terrorists. The Army Field Manual on interrogation developed by the Bush Department of Defense in 2006 has been embraced (though unwisely imposed on the CIA). The electronic surveillance of suspected terrorists, once roundly denounced by civil libertarians and by then Senator Barack Obama, continues. Risking allegations of war crimes by international law advocates, the administration has continued UAV (unmanned aerial vehicles) attacks against suspected terrorists, reportedly even targeting U.S. citizens. It is worth noting that killing these individuals by drone missile attacks affords them fewer legal rights than the military commissions President Obama opposed for years.

These decisions by the Obama administration, in my mind, are the correct ones. They undoubtedly were made after careful scrutiny, an examination of the possible alternatives, and with the sure knowledge that our country remains vulnerable to terrorist attack. There is one difference, however: President Obama had the benefit of succeeding a president who in the chaotic weeks after 9/11 had to put all these plans in place quickly, withstanding bitter partisan criticism and unpopularity for having done what he believed was best for the country. President Obama's latter-day support of these decisions is evidence that on most of the big questions regarding our enemies, George W. Bush and his administration got it right.

PART XIII

Pulling On Our Boots: Challenges and Controversies Beyond the War Zones

Annapolis, Maryland

JULY 4, 2006

I was expecting fireworks on Independence Day, but not at 2:30 in the afternoon and not from a despot in North Korea. The multistage Taepo-Dong 2 missile had been on its pad in the northeast corner of the ironically named Democratic People's Republic of Korea for several days. Overhead reconnaissance indicated it was being fueled and possibly prepared for ignition. Smaller, medium-range missiles were in place at other launch sites. We couldn't be sure where any of them were aimed, when they might be launched, what types of warheads they were equipped with, or exactly how far they could go. Military and intelligence officials judged Alaska and Hawaii to be almost certainly within striking distance of North Korea's long-range ballistic missiles.

The leaders of the so-called Hermit Kingdom had a penchant for rattling sabers around American holidays. In the weeks running up to July 4 there had been some speculation that the North Korean regime might fire a long-range missile. No one was certain of its intentions, but the possibilities included a simple test, a demonstration firing, or a launch to place an object in space. The North Koreans could do something even more provocative, and our allies in South Korea and Japan didn't want to be ill prepared in case missiles were aimed toward their territory. The erratic Kim Jong Il might even swing for the fences and attempt to hit our country.

President Bush came into office vowing not to put our country at risk of blackmail by ballistic missiles tipped with nuclear, biological, chemical, or conventional warheads. Since late 2001, when America withdrew from the ABM Treaty and began installing a missile defense system, we had made solid strides in putting a developmental system in place. More than a dozen interceptors were in the ground in Alaska and California that could be launched at a moment's notice. Though critics continued to downplay the capability of our system—some said it was like "hitting a bullet with a bullet"—the program wasn't science fiction anymore.[1] Tests had proven that our interceptors could locate, track, hit, and destroy incoming ballistic missiles.[2]

The President and I were pleased with the progress that had been made. We had overcome the legal obstacles of the ABM Treaty by withdrawing. We had overcome the diplomatic obstacles by offering assurances to allies that we were no longer developing a national missile defense system but one that could be fashioned to deter and defend them as well. We had overcome the technical obstacles and consistent assertions from critics that it couldn't be done by continuing research and development after it was installed; though it wouldn't be a perfect system, it could continue to be improved and calibrated through testing over time.

One of the more challenging obstacles was figuring out the arrangements to actually issue the order—the first in history—to launch an interceptor to destroy an incoming intercontinental ballistic missile. President Bush and I had had many discussions about the precise procedures and delegations of authority for how, when, and by whom the trigger could be pulled. We both appreciated that launching an interceptor in a real-world situation could have grave or unexpected consequences. If the interceptors missed or were launched too late or not at all, an incoming missile could destroy an American city. If the interceptor did hit an incoming missile, deadly debris could spread out over a large area. Given the short time available to make such decisions—every second would be critical after an enemy missile was launched—the President and I concluded that it made sense for him to delegate the launch authority to the secretary of defense.

I had been spending that July Fourth holiday weekend in St. Michaels, Maryland, some seventy miles outside of Washington. Joyce had wisely insisted we find a place outside the capital so I would be away from the Pentagon on some weekends, which would give the staff a respite from the grueling twelve-hours-per-day, seven-days-a-week schedule I had established after 9/11. Joyce and I—with our two miniature dachshunds, Reggie and Chester—had found the old redbrick house on a small branch off the Chesapeake Bay a welcome haven.

But it was not a haven that weekend, as the probability of a North Korean missile launch left a long shadow over the holiday. I was receiving frequent updates over a secure phone on the latest developments. I had with me a Defense Department communications officer—someone able to put me in touch over a secure line with the President and combatant commanders anywhere in the world. He was never more than yards away in times of high alert. At night a security agent with the secure line waited in a car in our driveway, prepared to sprint inside if NORTHCOM—the combatant command for missile defense for the United States—needed me to make the decision on whether to launch our interceptors.

After lunch on Sunday, July 4, Joyce and I left St. Michaels to go to a holiday party. We drove northwest along Route 50, our three-car convoy making good time toward the Chesapeake Bay Bridge. Just after crossing it, we pulled over to the shoulder. The communications officer had Admiral Tim Keating at U.S. Northern Command and Marine General James "Hoss" Cartwright at U.S. Strategic Command on the line. They advised that a long-range Taepo-Dong 2 missile had just been launched from its pad. If it appeared to be on a trajectory toward the United States, I was prepared to give the order to launch our interceptors, which were on high alert. We understood that such an action could invite retaliatory moves from North Korea.

As it turned out, I didn't have to fire that day. The North Korean ballistic missile failed forty-two seconds after launch and fell back on North Korean territory. Later in the afternoon North Korea fired a half-dozen shorter-range missiles, which splashed into the Pacific. Though I did not have to make the call to send our interceptors into space to destroy an incoming ballistic missile, the United States was the first nation in the world to have the ability to make that decision.

The uncertain situation with North Korea was one in a series of challenges that faced the Department of Defense, even as it was engaged in difficult wars in Afghanistan and Iraq. Some of those challenges were easy to foresee, while others came with much shorter notice, such as an ominous gathering of winds off the shores of New Orleans.

CHAPTER 42

Katrina and the Challenge of New Institutions

"A lie will go round the world while the truth is pulling its boots on."

—*As quoted in Rumsfeld's Rules*

Tropical storm Katrina intensified to a category 5 hurricane on August 28, 2005, while it was still several hundred miles out in the Gulf of Mexico. Expecting landfall in the next forty-eight hours, the new NORTHCOM commander, Admiral Tim Keating, began issuing orders and alerts to military units across the United States.* He deployed an advance headquarters to Camp Shelby, Mississippi, and created a staging area for the Federal Emergency Management Agency (FEMA) at Barksdale Air Force Base in Louisiana. The Department of Defense activated a hurricane operations cell in the Pentagon to monitor developments. Search-and-rescue aircrews were alerted that they might soon be needed. Navy ships with relief capabilities were ordered to proceed to the area.[1] Lieutenant General H. Steven Blum, chief of the National Guard, began alerting state Guard forces.

Katrina thundered into Louisiana and Mississippi just before dawn on the

*In response to 9/11, I had worked with Congress to create the U.S. military's Northern Command as a headquarters in Colorado Springs to defend the American homeland. NORTHCOM's first combatant commander, Air Force General Ralph "Ed" Eberhart, stood up the command hub to assist in responding to security threats in the northern hemisphere. At the time it was established, we were most concerned about defending against terrorist attacks, but we also had anticipated the need to respond to natural disasters. With Katrina, the new headquarters faced its first major test.

following day. As the storm's fiercest wind gusts—approaching 150 miles per hour—died down, Army National Guard and Coast Guard helicopters began rescue operations. Available DoD assets were pushed toward the Gulf Coast. Hundreds of active-duty troops and thousands of National Guardsmen began arriving in Louisiana and Mississippi.

Because the Department of Defense is by law a supporting department, not the lead agency in the case of a catastrophic domestic event, the U.S. military was not in charge of coordinating the federal response.[2] Instead, the responsibility for managing the federal government's response rested with the massive new Department of Homeland Security (DHS).[3]

DHS was established with little, if any, input from anyone outside a small circle of White House aides and congressional staffers. The first I heard of the plan was in a phone call from White House Chief of Staff Andy Card in early 2002, the night before it was announced publicly.

Card said officials at the White House—he didn't say who—had quietly worked with key members of Congress to establish a new department and that the President would be making the announcement the next day. DHS promised to be a sizable organization and would absorb a number of components of existing departments and agencies, including, I was told, several from the Department of Defense. This would be among the most extensive reorganizations of the federal government since the National Security Act of 1947.

Card was not asking for my views. He was informing me of the plan on the eve of the announcement. I was surprised. Clearly a decision had been made to put the proposal on the fast track. Because DHS was created in secrecy and haste, there were bound to be unforeseen consequences. I knew how slowly the federal bureaucracy moved, even on a good day. A new cabinet department would need its own facilities and thousands of personnel. It would have to manage relations with labor unions, weed through a thicket of federal regulations, and incorporate a host of agencies that had long been accustomed to different rules, regulations, and modes of operation. These changes would take a long time—likely years, not weeks or months. I also knew that despite its charter, the new department would not have the resources to meet its new statutory responsibilities in the case of a truly catastrophic natural disaster. As I had written in a memo more than a year before Hurricane Katrina struck:

> DoD currently will not be called until all of the first responders—sheriffs, police, FEMA, FBI, Homeland Security, Transportation Security

> Administration, etc.—have tried and failed. . . . Then and only then will the phone ring at the Department of Defense. . . . We know that DoD, whatever its ultimate role in homeland security, will always be called in late, [and] will be imperfectly equipped. . . .[4]

These would prove to be the foreseeable results of the creation of a new federal institution made up of a patchwork of existing organizations from other departments and agencies. Good intentions had abounded. Wisdom had been in shorter supply.

Many perceived the response to Katrina as a slow train wreck. Most of the blame for the shortcomings was quickly placed on Washington. The most powerful nation in the world seemed unable to cope with high winds and floodwaters. While some of the unfolding criticism was warranted, much of it was not.

On the day the storm came ashore, I was in San Diego attending ceremonies commemorating the sixtieth anniversary of V-J Day, but I left before noon to return to Washington. Over the next few days, we had numerous meetings. President Bush was deeply engaged in the federal response. As usual, he peppered the relevant officials, including Homeland Security Secretary Michael Chertoff and FEMA personnel, with detailed questions. Chertoff was a capable cabinet secretary, but it was painfully clear that his department's resources were limited. Understaffed and underequipped, DHS was heavily dependent on hiring private-sector contractors to perform urgent tasks such as restoring electricity and establishing communications. But in a disaster of this magnitude, private contractors were quickly overwhelmed.

Some state and local officials, notably in Louisiana, did not help matters. Governor Kathleen Blanco was reluctant to relinquish command of the thousands of National Guardsmen in her state, as President Bush had urged her to do. Her actions led to an unnecessary delay in the crucial early hours over the issue of who could organize and direct the Guardsmen. The U.S. military knew how to mount a humanitarian operation with precision, speed, and efficiency. It was increasingly clear that the governor of Louisiana did not.

In light of Governor Blanco's unwillingness to cede control of the National Guard, President Bush was faced with two difficult choices: first, whether to federalize the Guardsmen, which would take away Blanco's authority over them, and, second, whether to invoke the Insurrection Act, which would suspend posse comitatus—the longstanding American law that bars federal military forces from conducting law and order missions on U.S. soil. These steps had not been taken over the objections of a state governor since the civil rights movement, when federal troops were deployed to the South to restore order and enforce desegregation. Confronted with images of civil disorder and media reports depicting chaos in New Orleans, White House officials discussed whether Bush should take those steps.

As troubling as Blanco's leadership was, I was concerned that invoking the Insurrection Act and federalizing the National Guard in the Gulf states against the Governor's will could set an unfortunate precedent. The practical consequences were also worrisome. If the President invoked the Insurrection Act and ordered the Defense Department to use active-duty forces for law enforcement missions, we could have nineteen-year-old Marine lance corporals trained to fight in Iraq patrolling the streets of New Orleans as policemen. Because DHS, not DoD, was authorized by statute to deal with domestic problems, our military had not been organized, trained, or equipped to conduct law enforcement in American cities. A mistake or two could make a bad situation worse.

I sensed it was a close call for the President. He ultimately decided against invoking the act and against federalizing the National Guard. Though he was never much of a second-guesser, in the weeks and months after Katrina, he may well have wondered whether he should have taken those measures. From my vantage point, President Bush made the right call.

Without formally stripping Blanco of her authorities, the President had us send as many troops as rapidly as we could to the region to assist DHS. We sent forty-five hundred active-duty troops from the 82nd Airborne and Marines from the First and Second Marine Expeditionary Forces. General Blum effectively worked around state officials to restore order with National Guard troops. Instead of overruling the law on posse comitatus by performing law enforcement missions, thousands of active-duty troops could support the National Guard by delivering humanitarian aid and rescuing stranded victims.[5] Their very presence had the effect of reducing crime and disorder.

From a military standpoint, the response to Katrina was considerably swifter than any previous response to a hurricane, and probably to any natural disaster in American history. During the Hurricane Andrew disaster in 1992, for example, it had taken five days to deploy roughly sixty-eight hundred troops. But within five days of Katrina's landfall, more than thirty-four thousand ground forces from the Guard and active-duty were assisting in rescue efforts.[6] At the peak of our operations, we had some forty-six thousand National Guard troops—citizen soldiers who in many cases were policemen, firefighters, emergency medical technicians, engineers, and municipal workers in their civilian jobs—on the scene.[7] An additional twenty thousand active-duty forces were there as well. There were 350 helicopters and 21 ships conducting round-the-clock operations.[8] Men and women in uniform were rescuing and evacuating thousands of displaced residents and assisting FEMA in reestablishing order in the hurricane's aftermath.[9] They helped to evacuate eighty-eight thousand Gulf Coast residents and rescued another fifteen thousand. Hundreds of Coast Guard helicopter and boat rescue teams provided critical assistance in the effort.

From a headquarters in the New Orleans Superdome, the National Guard launched what amounted to the biggest rescue operation in American history. An active-duty Army three-star officer and gruff Cajun with ties to the region, Lieutenant General Russel Honoré, took charge of the active-duty forces in the region, bringing leadership, discipline, efficiency, and confidence to the effort.

Back at the Pentagon, Assistant Secretary of Defense for Homeland Defense Paul McHale, a former Democratic congressman from Pennsylvania and a colonel in the Marine Corps Reserves, skillfully coordinated DoD's response from the outset, working closely with DHS, FEMA, and the White House.* Because of DHS' lack of resources, McHale anticipated the DoD assets DHS would need and helped their officials prepare the necessary requests for support. McHale had me approve these requests even before DHS had submitted them to expedite the process.

On September 4, 2005, I visited New Orleans. The devastation was terrible. Water had risen to the heights of roofs. Whole neighborhoods were underwater. U.S. military and Coast Guard helicopters were rescuing people stranded on top of their houses. We flew over the Seventeenth Street Canal levee that had been topped, allowing the swollen waters of Lake Pontchartrain to flood one of America's great cities.

As the federal government mobilized to assist Katrina victims, its performance was overshadowed by media coverage of the wrenching drama that had unfolded on the ground. Along with more than eighteen hundred lives,

* With congressional approval, I had created the new position of Assistant Secretary of Defense for Homeland Defense shortly after 9/11 for the purpose of managing the DoD response in the event of a similar terrorist attack or a catastrophic natural disaster in the United States.

the storm had torn away the veneer of civilization in some places. The state and local governments that had kept a lid on anarchy, crime, and violence had dissolved. There were reports of murder and gang rapes. Reflecting the panic on the ground, some reporters and their anchors in the studios became advocates, sharing in the harsh condemnation of the emergency aid workers, the federal government, state and local leaders, in fact, anyone who might bear any responsibility. This chain reaction in the media left a damaging impression that the officials coping with the disaster didn't care and that our government was incapable of mounting an effective response.[10]

Eight months after Katrina I wrote a memo to the President: "The charge of 'incompetence' against the U.S. Government should be easy to rebut, were people to understand the extent to which the current system of government makes competence next to impossible."[11] After five years back in government, wrestling with natural and man-made disasters as well as two wars, it became clear to me that our government institutions were proving inadequate to the challenges of the twenty-first century and the information age. Efforts after 9/11 to refashion and create institutions such as DHS and the director of national intelligence (DNI) had led to suboptimal results: new layers of bureaucracy with the underlying challenges not well addressed.*

We needed to refashion our government institutions and develop new capabilities to respond to the challenge posed by terrorism and other nonconventional threats. For example, we were losing, or at least not winning, the battle of ideas against Islamist extremists. The State Department and other departments and agencies were not fulfilling their promises of political and economic support for reconstruction in places like Iraq and Afghanistan for a variety of reasons, including a lack of both funds and deployable personnel. The threads of national power—military, financial, intelligence, civic, communications—were sometimes working at cross-purposes, much as the Army,

*I thought a better approach to strengthening the intelligence community was not to create a duplicative bureaucracy in the DNI, as the 9/11 Commission had recommended, but to give the CIA director more authorities and support as the coordinating head of the U.S. intelligence community. In October 2004, Congressman Duncan Hunter asked chairman of the Joint Chiefs Dick Myers his opinion on the DNI. As a military officer who had obligations to Congress to give his independent views when asked, even if they differed from the administration's, Myers gave his opinion that the proposed DNI authorities over DoD-related intelligence agencies were problematic. When Andy Card found out about Myers' response, he called me and said, "General Myers' letter on the intel bill is going to cost the President the election." His comment reflected a lack of understanding of senior military officers' obligations. It also reflected a lack of understanding of the political landscape: President Bush won reelection by a comfortable margin just two weeks later.[12]

Navy, Marines, and Air Force had in the era before the Goldwater-Nichols legislation in 1986 mandated the creation of a joint force.[13]

The idea that our government might not be up to the new challenges had preoccupied my thoughts for some time.[14] Just what to do about it occurred to me in an unlikely place from an unlikely source: a Democrat who had inherited the U.S. presidency in 1945.

In the spring of 2006, I visited the Harry S. Truman presidential library outside Kansas City, Missouri, to deliver a speech comparing our struggle against violent extremists to the decades-long challenges of the Cold War.[15] Before my remarks, I spent some time touring the library. It was a treasured opportunity for someone who admired the blunt, no-nonsense midwesterner. I was taken into his private office, which was largely untouched since his death. Inside I glimpsed a wall of books, many of which he'd received from friends and contemporaries, including Winston Churchill. Hanging not far from his office was a large copy of an invitation to his inauguration. The invitation had inadvertently been extended to the President himself. Scrawled at the bottom was Truman's RSVP: "Weather permitting, I hope to attend. HST."

I was a junior in college when President Truman left office. He was deeply unpopular. Truman was a fierce partisan and rather cantankerous man. But what I have come to understand—and what came back vividly to me during my visit—was how central a role he and his administration had in the international challenges of the second half of the twentieth century.

As World War II ended and America entered the Cold War, it fell to the Truman administration to fashion an entirely new construct for an uncertain era. Largely overlooked and certainly underappreciated at the time, his administration crafted many of the institutions and policies that proved crucial to fighting and prevailing in the long conflict against the Soviet Union. The Marshall Plan, for example, provided needed resources to the war-ravaged economies of Western Europe and helped to keep them from sliding into the Soviet Union's sphere of influence. The containment strategy was pursued over many decades. Many Truman-era international institutions, designed to buttress the democracies of the world and encourage the rise of others, are still with us today: the World Bank, NATO, the United Nations, the International Monetary Fund, and the Organization of American States, among them. At home, the Truman administration created the NSC, the CIA, and the U.S. Information Agency, and merged the Navy and War departments into the

Department of Defense. All of that occurred at the inflection point at the end of World War II and the beginning of the Cold War. The George H. W. Bush, Clinton, and George W. Bush administrations had similar opportunities to fashion new policies and institutions for a new era: The inflection point at the end of the Cold War and the twenty-first-century challenges of the information age.

When I returned to Washington I put these thoughts together in a memorandum for President Bush: "Today the world requires new international organizations tailored to our new circumstances."[16] I noted that many of the most pressing threats we faced were global and transnational in scope—terrorism, proliferation, cybercrime, narcotics, piracy, hostage taking, and criminal gangs. By their nature, they could not be dealt with successfully by any one nation—not even the United States—and, as such, required the cooperation of many nations.

I believed that in important ways, existing international institutions—including some whose origins dated back to the days of FDR and Truman—were proving inadequate to the times. The World Bank and International Monetary Fund (IMF) were working to bring development funds to impoverished countries, but a nontrivial portion failed to reach the intended people because of inefficiency and corruption. I was also thinking of the United Nations, which was heavy on anti-American and anti-Israel diatribes and comparatively light on accomplishments. NATO, too, had its shortcomings. Because it was designed as a European defense organization against the Soviets, the North Atlantic Treaty Organization did not have linkages with some of the world's important democracies outside of Europe, such as Japan, South Korea, Israel, and Australia. NATO also required unanimity among twenty-eight member nations that included some occasionally contrarian members, making it difficult to deal with new challenges. The demographics of Western Europe—with aging populations and declining investments in their militaries—did not promise a robust alliance.

I suggested that new international organizations might be needed to bring competence in areas where existing organizations proved to be less well suited to the twenty-first century—areas such as developing and utilizing quick-reaction forces, assisting in military and military police training in foreign countries, counterproliferation, capacity building for the rule of law, and helping to strengthen domestic government ministries. Too often the United States was called on to do the work alone that other countries could, and should, help with. Because ours was the only military in the world that could deal with a serious crisis rapidly, America relieved the pressure on other countries to step forward, which left our forces burdened with the responsibility.[17]

I proposed that the President start a national discussion on this subject and offered a few suggestions of initiatives. The list included such things as a peacekeeping and governance corps that would have a standing capability to respond rapidly to problems abroad before they spun out of control. That could have been useful to handle unrest in Liberia and Haiti, possibly heading off civil strife before it began. Civilian teams could also bolster our military's expanding humanitarian efforts, such as when the massive tsunami struck coasts in the Indian Ocean in December 2004, killing 230,000, and when a 7.6 magnitude earthquake in October 2005 left the Pakistani region of Kashmir devastated, with 80,000 dead and nearly 3 million homeless.

Our humanitarian assistance efforts brought about a noticeable transformation of opinion within those important parts of the Muslim world. We did well for America by doing good. After Defense Department tsunami relief efforts, polls in Indonesia showed that 65 percent of its citizens had a more favorable impression of the United States. Osama bin Laden's approval ratings in Indonesia—the largest Muslim nation in the world—dropped from 58 percent before the disaster to 23 percent afterward.[18] In Pakistan, a country not known for its favorable views toward America, our rescue operations in the wake of their earthquake changed many minds. By November 2005, more than 46 percent of Pakistanis had a favorable view of the United States—more than double the percentage that had held that view six months earlier.[19] The favorite toy among Pakistani children quickly became small models of the American Chinook helicopters that had been so visible in delivering American relief supplies to those left homeless. The Chinooks were referred to in the Pashtun dialect as "Angels of Mercy."

I also recommended some form of maritime organization to which countries with significant naval forces, such as India and Japan, could contribute to combating piracy on the high seas. Because strong and growing economies tended to stem the rise of violent extremism, I suggested that the President consider a new market-oriented institution to provide grants and support to entrepreneurs in developing countries in Africa, Central Asia, and Latin America that would bypass the government level, where waste and corruption in poor countries were often a serious problem. I thought it might be useful to conduct a reassessment of how our country disperses foreign aid—perhaps using microfinance to promote individual entrepreneurship instead of massive block grants to governments, often for large construction projects.

I suggested consideration of a Middle East security initiative to bolster moderate states in the region and to help shield them from threats posed by nations like Iran, as well as consideration of an Asian security organization—in a sense, an organization with some of the attributes of NATO—to engage the United States in building stronger partnerships with our friends and allies in that region. I thought we needed to expand free trade agreements beyond our immediate neighbors to friends and allies around the world.

Here at home, I proposed a review of the executive and legislative branch institutions that were organized and arranged for an earlier era. We needed adjustments so that agencies and departments could function with the speed and agility the new century and the information age demanded. The compartmentalized organization of the executive branch, with its separate elements and the lack of a coordination mechanism, was equally true in Congress, with its separate committees and subcommittees. It was and remains exceedingly difficult to pull all the strands of American power through a single needle eye to create coherent national policy.

I suggested consideration of a new U.S. agency for global communication that could serve as a channel to inform, educate, and compete worldwide in the battle for ideas. We found ourselves engaged in the first protracted war in an era of e-mail, Twitter, blogs, phone cameras, a global internet with no inhibitions, cell phones, handheld video cameras, talk radio, twenty-four-hour news broadcasts, and satellite television.[20] By 2006, it was clear that our government's efforts to counter extremist ideology through public diplomacy and strategic communications were proving an abject failure. We didn't have global communications agencies to engage in a strategic effort to counter the ideology and propaganda of Islamists, as institutions such as the U.S. Information Agency and Radio Free Europe had combated Communist ideology.

Meanwhile, our enemies were successfully hammering home their messages via the internet and satellite television. With media relations committees that met to discuss ways to achieve their violent objectives, terrorist groups such as al-Qaida had proven effective at persuading many credulous observers—Muslims and non-Muslims alike—that they were the exasperated victims of Western oppression rather than the stormtroopers of a totalitarian political movement with a brutal will to power. Our enemies had skillfully adapted to fighting wars in the twenty-first-century media age. But the U.S. government and the West remained—and still remains—pitifully far behind.*

As I wrote my memo, I realized that the many suggestions I was proposing to President Bush were long-term strategic ideas that would require deliberation and discussion, perhaps even trial and error. They would take political capital, which by 2006 was in short supply. What I was proposing transcended any one department. To examine some of these recommendations and conduct a wholesale review of our government's organization, I proposed a bipartisan presidential commission of distinguished officials modeled on the Hoover Commission of 1947. After I handed the President my memorandum, he told me the ideas were worth discussing. However, to my knowledge, there was never a high-level meeting on my proposals. That was not surprising in an administration that at that point was fighting two wars and was under siege by the Congress and the press. Nonetheless, I believed we missed a significant opportunity. Perhaps they were ideas whose time had not yet come.

*The Defense Department made some well-intentioned but ill-fated attempts to compete in this arena. CENTCOM, for example, working closely with the Iraqi government and the U.S. embassy, sought to provide accurate information to the Iraqi people in the face of an aggressive campaign of disinformation by providing accurate news stories for local Iraqi papers. Yet when it was reported that the Pentagon had hired a contractor who in turn compensated our Iraqi allies for printing truthful stories, critics and the press portrayed this as inappropriate government propaganda. The program was immediately brought to a halt.

CHAPTER 43

Gardening

"The way to keep weeds from overwhelming you is to deal with them constantly and in their early stages."
—*George Shultz,* Turmoil and Triumph

While Afghanistan and Iraq commanded the focus of national security officials, there were 190 other countries that also needed monitoring and attention. Some of those nations, of course, were friendly to the United States, some less so, but all had daily interaction with our government at some level. Even officials from international pariahs such as Iran and North Korea were meeting with lower-level American diplomatic and intelligence officials and our intermediaries.

With our various economic and trade relationships and diplomatic and military reach, America does not have the luxury of pursuing policies of isolationism or neglect. We had to keep our attention on the world's many significant activities, meeting constantly with foreign leaders, forging diplomatic and trade agreements, and standing firm and responding as necessary when unfriendly nations provoked our country. George Shultz referred to this kind of daily maintenance with foreign governments as "gardening."[1] Throughout the Bush administration, while waging two wars and being on guard for another attack on our shores, many in the administration worked hard to be effective "gardeners"—with varying degrees of success.

When it came to personal diplomacy, George W. Bush was an active and productive, if publicly underestimated, asset. His decidedly informal brand of diplomacy was novel for some foreign leaders. What he chose to dispense with in polish, he made up for in persistence and reliability. In meeting after meeting, I saw the President put his foreign interlocutors at ease. This personal rapport paid dividends with leaders as diverse as Spain's Prime Minister José María Aznar, Jordan's King Abdullah, and Australia's John Howard. His relationships translated into closer ties between our countries and tangible support for initiatives like the ninety-country Proliferation Security Initiative and on-the-ground assistance in Iraq and Afghanistan.

One of the administration's important strategic successes was in our own hemisphere: helping to keep a democracy of forty-five million people from succumbing to the longest-running, best-financed, and most violent insurgency in Latin America. For more than a decade, the United States had been waging a war against drugs in Colombia. I thought that stopping the flow of drugs into our country, while important, was fated to be unsuccessful as long as the powerful demand for illegal drugs persisted. The Colombian government could spray coca fields and interdict drug runners, but as long as there were millions addicted to drugs around the world, people would find a way to produce and sell what the market demanded. Since the late 1990s, the Clinton administration's $5 billion Plan Colombia had been a bipartisan antidrug initiative demonstrating that our government was doing something about the drug problem.

By 2001, Colombia was teetering on the edge of becoming a failed state, a refuge for drugs and terrorists. The instability was fueled by the narcotics trade and Marxist guerrillas known as the FARC. The guerrillas controlled an area of Colombia larger than Switzerland. It was a safe haven for coca cultivation, kidnapping, murder, extortion, and Communist-inspired terrorism. Many had written off the Colombian government's war against the insurgency as a doomed effort. Some 60 percent of Colombians believed that the FARC would win. If that proved true, a stalwart democracy to our south would be replaced by a narco-terrorist dictatorship.

As part of the response to 9/11, I recommended to President Bush that, in addition to authorizing strikes in Afghanistan, he consider a plan to provide military assistance to Colombia's efforts against the insurgents—not just the drug traffickers. Visibly assisting Colombia, I argued, would reflect the truth that the campaign against terrorists was global, and that we were not targeting only Islamist extremists.

There was, however, an Islamist terrorist element even in Latin America. Islamist extremists, many affiliated with Hezbollah and other terrorist groups, were taking advantage of ungoverned areas in several locations in the region to operate and raise money. If a government would not or could not govern its own territory, that was an invitation for adventurers of various types—terrorists, political revolutionaries, drug dealers, and other criminals—to enter and take advantage of the vacuum. Such weeds thrive where the atmosphere of authority is thin, and they can spread aggressively.

President Bush was eager to assist Colombia. Our efforts received an unexpected boost in 2002, when Alvaro Uribe was elected president. FARC rebels had killed his father and attempted to kill Uribe on no less than fifteen different occasions over his political career. As a presidential candidate he campaigned fearlessly against the FARC and vowed to reclaim Colombian territory from the drug lords. After his election he kept track of what he considered the key measures of his war's success, including the numbers of monthly kidnappings, homicides, acres of land taken back from the FARC, and even the number of kilometers Colombians traveled on their holidays, since for many years traveling on some roads was a death sentence. When I met with Uribe, he would invariably have a yellow note card in his jacket pocket, listing his benchmarks.

In our first visit in June 2002, weeks after the Colombian elections, I told Uribe we might be willing to lend a hand by offering assistance in an integrated counterinsurgency campaign that strategically combined American and Colombian political, intelligence, economic, and military assets. If we were going to do more than just focus on trying to intercept drug shipments and spraying coca fields, there was one major hurdle: the U.S. Congress. Fearing direct American involvement in a guerrilla war in Latin America, Congress had imposed strict limits on intelligence sharing and military activities with the Colombians. The only authorized missions were those designed to reduce drug production, and there was even a congressionally imposed limit on the number of American military personnel to be allowed in Colombia at any given time.

Working with policy officials Doug Feith, Peter Rodman, and Roger Pardo-Maurer, we were able to reorient our assistance to Colombia toward counterterrorism and targeting the FARC guerrillas. The Congress agreed to change our authorities to allow for more than just the narrow focus on drugs. Our goal was to help the government of Colombia assert control—effective sovereignty, as we called it—over its entire territory.

In President Alvaro Uribe, we had the most skillful partner we could have hoped for. Unassuming and slight in build, Uribe was unafraid to take on the FARC and reclaim Colombian territory (he also commanded the overwhelming support of the Colombian people, reaching a 91 percent approval rating at one point).[2] With expanded authorities and intelligence cooperation, we could take the fight to the enemy. An energetic Army Reserve Special Forces noncommissioned officer who had fought alongside the Nicaraguan Contras in the 1980s, Pardo-Maurer aggressively sought interagency and bipartisan support. Without adding a dollar to our budget, we made our aid far more effective than it had been before. Drug production decreased, and hundreds of thousands of acres of land were taken back from the FARC. The campaign to win back Colombia from the terrorists proved to be a major success.

Another significant success involved one of the most worrisome nations in the world—the Libya of Colonel Muammar Gaddafi. The State Department had long listed Libya as a leading sponsor of international terrorism. Libya was also notorious for its multiyear pursuit of weapons of mass destruction. The Gaddafi regime was responsible for the 1988 terrorist bombing of Pan Am Flight 103 over Scotland, which killed 270 people, including 189 Americans.

After 9/11, the Bush administration had a rare opportunity to persuade Libya—and perhaps some other terrorist-supporting or WMD-pursuing regimes—to choose a different path. I believed that if we put sufficient pressure on Afghanistan and Iraq, other countries might recognize that their interests in self-preservation meant that they too needed to end their support for terrorism and their WMD programs. This was the case with Gaddafi, who, after we invaded Iraq, reportedly told Italian Prime Minister Silvio Berlusconi that he did not want to become the next Saddam Hussein. It was not mere coincidence that only a few days after Hussein was plucked in such a degraded state from his subterranean spider hole and imprisoned in Iraq, Libya's dictator acknowledged and agreed to dismantle his country's long-running nuclear and chemical weapons programs.[3]

Though our activities elsewhere in the Middle East were gaining few headlines—we wanted it that way—the United States and its partners were also capturing and killing terrorists outside of Afghanistan and Iraq. Sensitive operations involving the CIA and U.S. special operations forces were ongoing in the Horn of Africa, Northern Africa, Pakistan, and Yemen, where terrorists had fled after we put pressure on them in their former sanctuaries in Afghanistan and Iraq. By developing relationships and establishing a presence in those countries beforehand, we made it harder for fleeing terrorists to find refuge there.[4] Since 9/11 we had made manhunting and the skills needed to track (find), isolate (fix), and capture or kill (finish) individuals a priority for our military. By 2006, we had become quite successful using highly classified intelligence operations to track down our enemies in countries around the world. These counterterrorism efforts in ungoverned areas required not only careful military preparation and training, but skillful diplomatic support.

Our administration's gardening record was not perfect, however. Certainly my "old Europe" comment was not a model of deft alliance management. And in other cases too, our stewardship in foreign affairs left something to be desired, especially in Bush's second term.

Shortly after his reelection, President Bush rearranged his national security team. Colin Powell departed as secretary of state. National Security Adviser Condi Rice took over Powell's post. Her longtime deputy, Steve Hadley, moved up to become national security adviser. CIA Director George Tenet had departed the administration several months earlier and had been replaced by Florida Congressman Porter Goss.

I hoped that these changes might improve the way interagency meetings were planned and run and the way decisions were summarized and implemented. I also hoped that State's new leadership would make the department more supportive of the President's policies. I thought the quiet competence of Steve Hadley might help the interagency process by providing Bush with clear options and ensuring his decisions were carried out. If so, Hadley would be less inclined to seek the forced consensus or bridging approach that I found ineffective in the first term. I hoped he would be more willing to move contentious issues up to the President for decision, where they belonged. I was particularly encouraged by his choice of a deputy, J. D. Crouch, who had served in the Defense Department before becoming the ambassador to Romania.

I thought Rice could be a good secretary of state in that she was close and loyal to the President. To get the benefit of the skills and resources of the State Department, a president needs someone to lead it who is intent on having that often independent-minded agency follow his strategic guidance. I was confident Rice would be inclined and might even be able to do just that; she had an opportunity to become a secretary of state in the mold of Henry Kissinger and George Shultz by bringing the President's agenda to the State Department rather than the world's agenda, as reflected through our diplomats, to the President. Yet despite the realignment inside the Bush administration, 2005 and 2006 witnessed some diplomatic failures.

On the steps of the U.S. Capitol at his second inauguration, President Bush proclaimed an ambitious goal for the nation: "ending tyranny in our world." The State Department's interpretation of the President's conviction about the benefits of democracy led to complications with nations we needed as friends and partners. Promoting democracy and human rights in closed societies is laudable, and often serves U.S. interests. But sometimes the rhetoric came across as lecturing, and it could on occasion hurt our friends without actually improving human rights. I made a practice of asking whether the United States had any real leverage that might persuade foreign rulers to follow a different course to establish freer political and economic systems. Sometimes berating countries feels good to the beraters and wins domestic political points, but scolding them can often come at the expense of losing critical cooperation and alienating foreigners who see the United States as a bully.

Instead of labeling countries as good or bad—democratic or nondemocratic, pro–human rights or anti–human rights—I thought a better way of categorizing countries was to consider the direction in which they were heading. If a country that had been a longtime abuser of human rights and a foe of democracy was making steps toward freer political and economic systems, I believed we should calculate whether continued progress in the right direction was likelier to be achieved by encouraging rather than publicly chiding its leadership. I recognized the U.S. interest—practical as well as moral—in having other countries respect basic human rights and function democratically. But I saw that interest of ours as one of several that needed to be considered in the making of U.S. policy. It was not the sole interest, and it did not necessarily trump all others.

After Rice became secretary of state in 2005, she made it a priority to push Pakistani President Pervez Musharraf toward more democratic practices.

Rice publicly called for Musharraf, the senior army officer, to seek democratic elections and relinquish his military uniform—a symbolic step designed to promote civilian rather than military leadership in Pakistan.[5] Musharraf was trying to hold together a weak government, filled with elements that did not share his affinity for the United States. We were dependent on Pakistan's logistic support for our efforts in Afghanistan; the country also had a formidable arsenal of nuclear weapons that could fall into the wrong hands if Musharraf's government fell to a radical Islamist element. I questioned whether it was for U.S. officials to dictate what clothes Musharraf wore to work. I was disappointed but not surprised when only months after he complied with Rice's request, he could no longer assert control over the military and was forced by various political forces to step down. The alternatives to Musharraf were, in my view, not likely to be better, and that has proven to be the case.

A similar situation presented itself in Uzbekistan. In the days after 9/11, Uzbekistan had provided important cooperation for our activities in Afghanistan. From 2001 to 2006, I traveled there several times and met with Uzbek officials elsewhere. By his own admission, President Islam Karimov was not an American-style democrat—there were few if any in the region—but he had shown no hostility toward U.S. interests. In fact, to Russia's displeasure, he had allowed U.S. forces to use his Karshi-Khanabad (K2) airfield, a key link by which many tens of thousands of tons of supplies and aid, as well as our military forces poured into Afghanistan. We were working closely with the Uzbek military and their helpful minister of defense, Kodir Gulyamov. He was a physicist by training and the first civilian minister of defense in the former Soviet Union. In the spring of 2005, all of that changed, and it led to what I thought was one of the most unfortunate, if unnoticed, foreign policy mistakes of our administration, one that was aided and abetted by a bipartisan group in Congress.

The facts as best as can be determined are these: In the early morning hours of May 13, 2005, in the eastern Uzbek city of Andijan, heavily armed men stormed the town prison. It appeared that the goal of the assault was to release members of an Islamic extremist group accused of seeking to establish an Islamic state, a caliphate, in eastern Uzbekistan.[6] The rebels attacked the town's government center and took officials hostage, killing some of them.[7] Before long, Uzbek government forces massed to put an end to the situation. A firefight between the insurgents and government forces ensued, and innocent bystanders, including human shields used by the rebels, were caught in the crossfire.[8] The U.S. Defense Intelligence Agency speculated that "[s]ecurity forces probably lost control of the situation and fired on noncombatants."[9] But information remained sketchy.

Self-proclaimed human rights advocates with longstanding records of opposition to the Uzbek government quickly got into the act. By 2001, "human rights" had become a sizable global industry. For some it was a cause, for some a profession. Many seemed interested in embarrassing the United States and Israel while ignoring human rights abuses by oppressive regimes such as Cuba and Zimbabwe. The facts were often mangled in the process. In spite of the fact that video filmed at the time showed the attackers in Uzbekistan to be heavily armed, the group Human Rights Watch declared them peaceful "protesters" who had come under attack by government forces for being "especially pious" Muslims.* In the Western press, estimates of the number killed by the government ranged from 175 to well over 1,000. Comparisons were made to the massacre of Chinese citizens in Tiananmen Square, and stories circulated of a deliberate massacre of civilians peacefully demonstrating in the street.[11] The Uzbek government—which was not accustomed to the demands of a free press—didn't exactly help its case by refusing to provide much information about its side of events.

Some members of Congress began a campaign of condemnation of the Uzbek government. Two weeks after the events in Andijan, Republican Senators John McCain and Lindsey Graham traveled to the capital of Tashkent to deliver a public rebuke. "[H]istory shows that continued repression of human rights leads to tragedies such as the one that just took place," McCain lectured.[12] Around the same time, I received a letter from McCain, cosigned by five other senators, insisting that America not pay the $23 million we owed the government from our military's use of the Uzbek air base at K2. "[G]overnment security forces in the city of Andijan massacred hundreds of peaceful demonstrators," they wrote. "We strongly object to making a payment to Uzbekistan at this time."[13]

I replied to the senators, "The bills we have from the Uzbeks are for services rendered in the war on terrorism. Our national policy, as a general rule, is to pay legitimate bills presented for goods and services by other nations."[14] Paying our bills, though occasionally politically difficult, was

* Human Rights Watch reported that "Uzbek government forces killed hundreds of unarmed people who participated in a massive public protest in the eastern Uzbek city of Andijan. The scale of this killing was so extensive, and its nature was so indiscriminate and disproportionate, that it can best be described as a massacre. . . . One group of fleeing protesters was literally mowed down by government gunfire." Amnesty International called the uprising a "mass killing of civilians" and denounced the Uzbek government's "indiscriminate and disproportionate use of force."[10]

the right thing to do.[15] What's more, failing to pay for the services we had requested and received and the goods we consumed would send a harmful message to all of the other nations helping us that the United States could not be relied on.[16]

After the facts were uncovered and eyewitness reporting was gathered, it was clear that Uzbek authorities had confronted an effort intended to overthrow the local government. The government's security forces and public affairs officials functioned poorly, but this was not a simple case of soldiers slaughtering innocents, as had been widely alleged and misreported. At a principals meeting in the middle of the crisis, I argued for a more measured handling of Uzbekistan, to encourage Uzbek leaders to move in the right direction, toward freer political and economic policies. I did not favor berating them and shoving them back in the wrong direction—particularly when we lacked a clear understanding of what actually had taken place.[17] Before calling for draconian sanctions and making public statements criticizing the government, I thought we needed to first find out the facts and then balance our clear interests in promoting freer political systems and human rights with national security interests. I argued further that if we handled the human rights issue incorrectly and damaged our relationship with Uzbekistan, we could make their human rights situation even worse, as the Uzbek regime would likely clamp down against those who had been closest to the United States and the West.* Any incentives Karimov once had to move toward a more open society would be undermined. Further, I knew that it would seriously damage our efforts in Afghanistan.

My arguments did not prevail. At an NSC meeting, Condi Rice responded to me by declaring, "Human rights trump security." I wondered if she had really thought that through. She seemed to be saying that if a country didn't behave as we did or as we expected, it would be shunned, even if turning it away from us took a toll on our nation's security, and to make matters worse, it arrested their progress on human rights. If we took such a good and evil view of the world, we wouldn't be able to count on support from any non-democratic country. "We made a clear choice, and that was to stand on the side of human rights," senior State Department official Nick Burns echoed in the press.[18]

*Indeed, this is exactly what happened. The Uzbek minister of defense, who had helped forge military-to-military ties with our country since 2001, was put on trial and kept under house arrest. Gulyamov had been a staunch representative of Uzbek interests, but he was also a cooperative partner in America's efforts in Afghanistan.

Karimov didn't appreciate the recitation of complaints he heard in meetings with U.S. officials. Uzbek government officials also asserted that the State Department ignored their requests to renegotiate the base lease for the U.S. air base at K2, the critically important lifeline into Afghanistan. On July 29, 2005, two months after the riots at Andijan, the Uzbek Ministry of Foreign Affairs delivered a letter to the U.S. embassy in Tashkent, indicating that we were no longer going to be able to use the air base.[19] The Karimov government gave us six months to pack up, which left those of us in the Defense Department scrambling to try to come up with alternatives, all of which were considerably more expensive. Our eviction from Uzbekistan came at a critical time, just when it appeared that the Taliban was mounting a renewed offensive after three years of relative calm. American-Uzbek military-to-military relations were cut off abruptly, ending a relationship that, beginning in 2001, had exposed Uzbeks to democratic values and principles, such as freedom of speech and civilian control of the military.

Uzbek leaders then began to strengthen ties with nations that would not berate them regarding democracy and human rights—such as Russia and China. Karimov signed a formal treaty of friendship with Russia in November 2005, a marked reversal in attitude from when I had met with him four years earlier.

"Russia was and remains for us the most reliable bulwark and ally," Karimov noted at the signing ceremony.[20] The treaty, he added, "demonstrates with whose interests our interests converge and with whom we intend to build our future."[21]

In July 2006, I wrote Hadley, "We are getting run out of Central Asia by the Russians. They are doing a considerably better job at bullying those countries [than] the U.S. is doing to counter their bullying."[22] We were effectively taking ourselves out of the region, and in the process reversing their progress toward freer systems as well as damaging our national security interests. "We need an Administration policy for Central Asia, and we need the NSC to see that our agreed policy—once we have one—remains in balance," my memo to Hadley continued.[23] I saw our administration's knee-jerk response as shortsighted and misguided. Human rights had not trumped security. The truth was that human rights and our country's security had both suffered.

Ironically, while we were lecturing and chastising our friends and partners in the name of democracy, administration officials were reaching out to some of the most brutal and undemocratic regimes in the world, lending them the legitimacy they sought. In the weeks after major combat operations had ended in Iraq, intelligence had indicated that the regimes in Syria, Iran, and North Korea were nervous, since Saddam's regime had toppled in just three weeks. But by 2006, their worries had been eased. Bush's first-term initiatives to isolate regimes that pursued weapons of mass destruction and sponsored terrorists were dropped to pursue negotiations with them in the second term. Unambiguous records of deception, provocative behavior, and broken promises stretching back decades were set aside in the hope of obtaining reversals from countries such as Iran, Syria, and North Korea through diplomatic engagement. A risk, of course, was that our apparent eagerness could send the wrong signal and make the situation worse.

One of the finest qualities of Americans is our optimism. We tend to believe that people of goodwill anywhere can find solutions to most problems. But there are limits to diplomacy, just as there are limits to goodwill. Some problems cannot be solved through negotiations. Some despotic governments take advantage of international negotiations to achieve prestige, which is political capital for them. Some regimes use terrorism and WMD programs as bargaining chips to extract concessions from other countries. These regimes, and sometimes members of the world's diplomatic corps, see negotiations and engagement as useful ends in themselves.

I remembered from my time as Middle East envoy for President Reagan how unproductive the many meetings with the Syrians had been. Because they had little incentive to make concessions, our diplomatic efforts appeared to them as signs of weakness that they could exploit. At the same time, there were occasions when I did see advantages to meeting with adversaries, such as Saddam Hussein, when there seemed to be reasons to believe that we might find some common interests. We had to be clear-eyed as to precisely what our goals were before sitting down at the negotiating table. We needed to understand what our interests were, what the other nation's interests were, and in what ways they might coincide, if at all. We also needed to know what our leverage was and what the other side's leverage might be.

Since 1979, Iran has considered itself at war with the United States, which it calls the Great Satan. Iran has taken the Soviet Union's place in the Middle East, forming the core of a resistance bloc that is ready to ally with any state or organization at odds with the United States, the West, and our Sunni Arab friends in Jordan, Egypt, and the Gulf.

Since the radical Islamist regime came to power there, no other nation in the world has been responsible for as many deaths to U.S. troops as Iran. The 1983 attack against the U.S. Marine barracks in Lebanon was organized by Iran. Beginning in 2004, Iran began supplying Iraqi insurgents with explosively formed penetrators (EFPs), especially deadly improvised explosive devices. Iran was training Shia insurgent groups in Iraq to use them. "If we know so much about what Iran is doing in Iraq, why don't we do something about it?" read one of my November memos to the Chairman of the Joint Chiefs.[24] But a country strained by two wars and an administration battling criticism and declining public approval was not ready to be firm with Iran. The prospect of another confrontation left many searching for other options.

With nearly two hundred thousand U.S. troops in two countries bordering Iran, the regime could not discount the strength we had in the region. Since Iranian Revolutionary Guard members and its elite branch, the Quds Force, were training and arming Iraqi militants to kill Americans, I thought we could pursue them within Iraq with special operations raids. We also could seek stricter sanctions—especially on gasoline, which Iran lacked the capacity to refine—putting pressure on the regime and further isolating it from the international community. The possibilities of military pressure and diplomatic engagement were not mutually exclusive. Rather, the task was to closely link the two.

To change the Iranian regime's behavior, I believed one of our best options was to aid the freedom movement inside Iran. Supporting those locked away in Iranian prisons might eventually lead to something like the Soviet Union's downfall, which Ronald Reagan, Margaret Thatcher, and Pope John Paul II hastened by supporting Soviet dissidents. Millions of Iranians chafed at the rule of the ayatollahs. This became clear after protesters in the Green movement took to the streets in the wake of fraudulent elections in June 2009. DoD policy officials wrote a number of memos suggesting ways to reach out to the Iranian opposition movement: bringing their leaders to the White House, supporting them financially, providing them with technology to communicate with one another and to the outside world, and more forcefully speaking about the nature of the evil regime they were opposing.

Ultimately, the President decided that negotiations were the best way to try to deal with Iran. Every American administration since the Iranian revolution has participated in some form of diplomatic engagement with them; publicly, privately, or both. Beginning with Ambassador Zalmay Khalilzad in December 2001, the Bush administration also authorized American diplomats to hold discussions of one type or another with representatives from Iran, but nothing as substantial as the policy of engagement the State Department began to pursue in 2006. In an April 2006 memo I wrote of the proposed U.S.-Iran talks with the so-called EU Three (France, Germany, and Britain): "I think they are a disaster. We are stepping on a rake."[25] The negotiations yielded no significant concessions. To the contrary, Tehran seemed to have accelerated its illegal weapons programs, continued to fund Hezbollah in Lebanon, crushed its domestic dissidents, threatened to erase Israel from the map in another Holocaust, and escalated their attacks against American servicemen in Iraq.

For decades, Syria has been considered a prized quarry for optimistic American diplomats. After my efforts to engage the Syrians in the early 1980s, George H. W. Bush's secretary of state, James Baker, traveled to Damascus no fewer than twelve times. Warren Christopher and Madeleine Albright made more than forty trips between them during the Clinton administration. American secretaries of state spent hours in the Syrian president's waiting room cooling their heels as they awaited an audience. The Syrian state press played up these meetings with foreign officials, especially from the United States, as signs of Syria's clout in the world. Although for some time after 9/11, President Bush had carefully denied Syria such injections of prestige, the State Department's eagerness for engagement eventually resurfaced, with Powell and Armitage both making trips there, hoping for a diplomatic breakthrough that never came.

That hope was not solely the province of diplomats, however. CENTCOM military commander John Abizaid was a proponent of trying to peel off Syria from Iran, encouraging them to forge a historic peace with Israel and thus help to end the Israeli-Palestinian conflict. Many in our military as well as in the State Department had long thought the stalemate over the Palestinian territories to be an underlying cause of violence in the region. I was skeptical, and even more skeptical of bringing in Syria from the cold. Nonetheless, I forwarded Abizaid's arguments to the President, thinking it was important that he know his CENTCOM commander's views on the matter.[26]

Peace with Israel and an accommodation with the United States were not high on the priority list of the Syrian regime—not unless there was something major in it for them. Hafez al-Assad and his son Bashar (who took the reins after his father's death in June 2000) hailed from a small Muslim sect, the Alawites. To maintain power in a nation with a Sunni majority, they burnished their pan-Arab credentials by working against Israel and making a not too hidden effort to oppose American forces in Iraq; they became the hub for gathering suicide bombers and jihadists to travel south across their border.

Throughout the 1990s, Syria built increasingly close ties with Iran and was heavily reliant on it for arms and funding. This alliance was more than just a marriage of convenience, as some have characterized it. The two nations had fashioned a de facto Hezbollah state in southern Lebanon. In exchange for funding and supplies, the terrorist organization Hezbollah worked to advance Syrian and Iranian policies in the region. With weekly flights from Tehran and Damascus shuttling in thousands of small arms and rockets, Hezbollah had amassed a military force to be reckoned with.

In February 2005, former Lebanese Prime Minister Rafik Hariri was assassinated by a massive car bomb in front of the St. George Hotel in Beirut. Hariri was a symbol of Lebanese independence, and as such a threat to the Syria-Hezbollah occupation of his country. Unsurprisingly, evidence that Syria and Hezbollah had their hands in the assassination was abundant, though both denied the claims.[27]

President Bush announced that America supported an international investigation of the murder and would advocate enforcement of UN resolutions calling for the withdrawal of Syria's nearly fifteen thousand troops from Lebanon, as well as its many hundreds of intelligence officials. He recalled our ambassador to Syria.

Hariri's death helped spark the so-called Cedar Revolution, a Lebanese popular movement against Syrian occupation and meddling, changing the dynamic in the region and at least temporarily stalling the U.S. efforts to win over Syria.* My old acquaintance, Walid Jumblatt, the wily leader of the Druze community in Lebanon, reversed his longstanding truce with Syria. I asked Jumblatt on one of his later visits to Washington how he had happened to switch sides. Recalling our strained relations during the Reagan administration, I said, "You were firing mortars and artillery at us back in 1984."

*The Cedar Revolution occurred contemporaneously with other pro-democratic changes in the world. In the months after the felling of Saddam Hussein, so-called color revolutions brought reform-minded, pro-Western leaders to power in Ukraine, Georgia, and Kyrgyzstan. These democratic changes demonstrated the practical and moral value of President Bush's efforts to spread freedom. Still, as I saw it, democracy and human rights promotion were among several important interests we had to consider in our foreign policy.

"Yes," Jumblatt replied, "but I'm with you now." These encouraging signs proved fleeting.

I thought the administration's early policy of pressure and isolation, despite occasionally mixed signals from State Department representatives, had worked reasonably well in making the Syrian regime uneasy and willing to make important concessions, such as withdrawing its military from Lebanon. In Bush's second term, however, there was a change of course and the administration reengaged with Syria. The Department of State proposed relieving Syria's diplomatic isolation and reverting to the practice of sending high-level U.S. officials to Damascus for meetings.

This policy of engagement, combined with our worsening difficulties in Iraq that were at least partly the result of Syria's actions, sent a signal of weakness to Assad that he was quick to exploit. He reverted to his earlier policies of greater hostility toward America and our interests. Yet even in 2007, the State Department invited Syria back to the negotiating table in pursuit of Middle East peace between Israel and the Palestinians. Seeing that the United States was again the supplicant, and with the ill feelings about their assassination of a democratic Lebanese leader seemingly having been forgotten, if not forgiven, the Syrians reverted to their tried-and-true ways: obfuscation and delay at the negotiating table and active support for terrorism and covert pursuit of illegal weapons programs. Proof enough of their true intentions came with the discovery—and later destruction by Israeli aircraft—of a curious facility in eastern Syria: an illegal nuclear reactor nearly identical to one in North Korea. Regrettably, U.S. diplomatic efforts may have emboldened, rather than deterred, one of the world's most dangerous regimes.

By July 2006, well over a decade of U.S. negotiations with North Korea and its erratic leadership had yielded little of benefit to the United States. North Korea continued to test and launch ballistic missiles, bluster about attacking South Korea, and develop nuclear weapons, detonating what intelligence professionals believed was a low-yield bomb in October 2006. We had confronted North Korean officials in 2002 with the fact that we knew about their clandestine uranium-enrichment effort, in violation of the Clinton administration's "Agreed Framework." As I wrote at the time in a memo to the NSC principals,

> We should continue to deny Kim Jong Il the kind of attention he craves and has become accustomed to receiving in response to provocative

> behavior. . . . Getting us to the table is the trophy that Pyongyang seeks; for us to grant it in response to the latest nuclear provocations would only reinforce Pyongyang's weak hand and prove that bad behavior pays.[28]

As long as Kim Jong Il was in power, I thought we had little prospect of inducing his regime to abandon its nuclear weapons program. Every day Kim and his officials focused on ways to consolidate and protect their dictatorship. Their disastrous policies spawned famine, torture, and oppression. The inhumane leadership of North Korea seemed to believe that the surest hold on power was the pursuit of weapons programs.

I thought it worthwhile to try to get China to work diplomatically to persuade North Korea to change its nuclear weapons policy, based on the view that our countries shared an interest in keeping the Korean peninsula free of nuclear weapons. Unfortunately, China seemed more interested in blocking U.S. efforts against North Korea than in keeping the Korean peninsula nuclear weapons–free.* The outcome the Chinese seemed to fear most was a collapse of their neighbor.[29] Then they would be forced to deal with refugees and a failed Korean state on their border. As long as Kim Jong Il had China as a patron of sorts, I was not optimistic that the negotiations with North Korea involving the Chinese, known as the six-party talks, would succeed.

Instead of offering inducements of financial aid and heating oil, I thought there might be a remote possibility that if we put enough diplomatic and financial pressure on the country, some of its senior generals might overthrow Kim Jong Il. By 2006, Rice and the State Department envoy to North Korea, Christopher Hill, made clear that North Korea was the State Department's issue alone, and that the views of the Defense Department would carry little weight. Rice and Hill seemed to believe they could obtain an agreement with North Korea to end its WMD programs. Deputy Undersecretary of Defense for Asian and Pacific Affairs Richard Lawless, a veteran expert on the region with years in the CIA, was no longer included in discussions.

On my desk at the Pentagon I kept a satellite picture of the Korean Peninsula taken at night to remind me of all the Americans who were fighting for

* China may one day regret its position if Japan, South Korea, or Taiwan decides to pursue nuclear weapons to counter the North Korean threat.

the freedom of Iraqis, Afghans, and, most important, for the safety and freedom of our own citizens. The photo shows that south of a distinct line—the demilitarized zone—is a free nation illuminated by the countless bright lights of a successful economy, the world's thirteenth largest. To the north is virtually total darkness, in which only one small pinprick of light shows, marking the North Korean capital of Pyongyang. The two countries have the same people and the same resources, and yet one country is full of light, and the other is dark, hungry, and poor.

The lesson can sometimes be lost on any who take their freedom for granted. I found that younger South Koreans, in particular, needed to be reminded that the reason they weren't locked in the prison state of North Korea was because so many young Americans and allied forces had fought in the so-called forgotten war of the 1950s. Indeed, younger generations of South Koreans seemed to forget that the regime in the north still sought to unify all of the Korean Peninsula under its totalitarian rule.

In November 2003, I encountered this historical amnesia on a visit to Seoul. At an event on the top floor of a skyscraper downtown, a young Korean reporter approached me. The South Korean parliament was then debating whether or not to send troops to assist our coalition forces in Iraq, which had been liberated seven months earlier.

"Why should Koreans send their young men and women halfway around the globe to be killed or wounded in Iraq?" she asked me.

The question struck a deep chord. My close friend Dick O'Keefe had served in the Korean War fifty years earlier. He had been a wrestling teammate of mine at New Trier High School and had gone to Korea during the last year of the war. For the final three weeks that cease-fire negotiations sought to bring the war to an end, both sides engaged in bloody battles as they tried to claim more land before an armistice was finally signed. In the twenty days the negotiations took place, U.S. and allied forces suffered 17,000 casualties, with 3,333 killed.[30] In the last days of the war, O'Keefe was killed.

I had seen O'Keefe's name earlier that day on a wall with the names of all Americans killed in the conflict. I placed a wreath at the war memorial. The legacy of his sacrifice, and the other 36,500 Americans who lost their lives on the battlefields of the Korean peninsula, is that some fifty million Koreans are free today—including that young reporter who asked me her question.

I thought of Dick O'Keefe as I answered her question. "Why," I countered, "should Americans have sent their young men and women halfway around the world to Korea some fifty years ago?"

We stood overlooking Seoul's skyline of bright and tall skyscrapers, a testament to the skills and industriousness of the free Korean people. This had come to the people of South Korea through the courage and sacrifice of others.

Pointing out the window at the lively, free, and prosperous city, I said, "There's the answer."

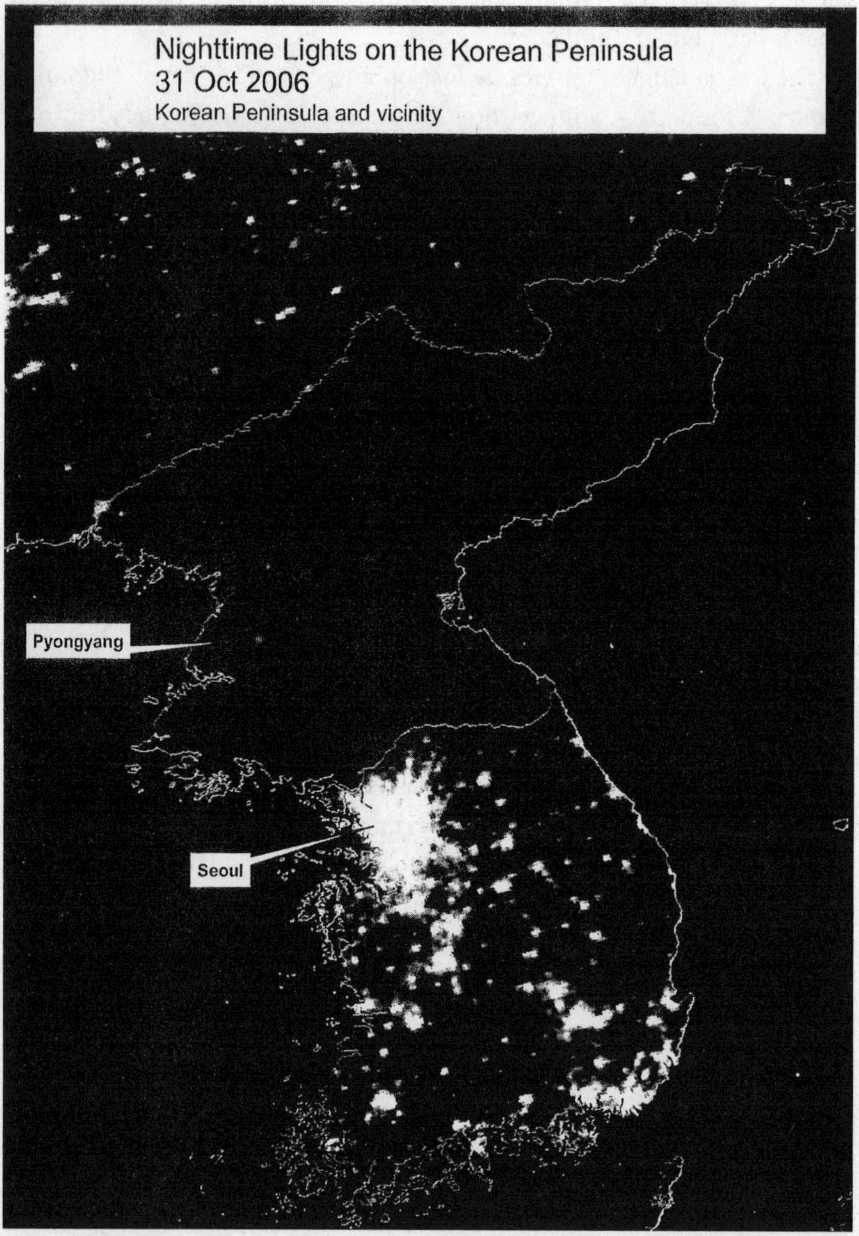

CHAPTER 44

The Army We Had

"You go to war with the Army you have—
not the Army you might want or wish
to have at a later time."

—December 8, 2004

At Camp Buehring, a staging area in Kuwait for U.S. troops headed into Iraq, I held a meeting for some who would soon be deploying northward into a difficult fight against Iraqi insurgents. As I did dozens of times during my six years as secretary of defense, I gave the troops a chance to ask me any question they wished with the media there. After two questions from the audience, a soldier from the Tennessee National Guard raised his hand to ask the next one.

"Our soldiers have been fighting in Iraq for coming up on three years," he began. "A lot of us are getting ready to move north relatively soon. Our vehicles are not armored. We're digging pieces of rusted scrap metal and compromised ballistic glass that's already been shot up, dropped, busted, picking the best out of this scrap to put on our vehicles to take into combat. We do not have proper armament vehicles to carry with us north."[1]

He was raising a serious issue, one that was of concern to the troops and the Army—as evidenced when some of the members of the audience applauded.* I thought the question deserved a careful explanation, and I saw it as an opportunity to provide an overview of the steps the Army was taking to correct the problems they were experiencing. I responded at length:

> I talked to the general [Steven Whitcomb] coming out here about the pace at which the vehicles are being armored. They have been brought from all over the world, wherever they're not needed, to a place here where they are needed. I'm told that they are being—the Army is—I think it's something like four hundred a month are being done. And it's essentially a matter of physics; it isn't a matter of money. It isn't a matter on the part of the Army of desire. It's a matter of production and capability of doing it.
>
> As you know, you go to war with the Army you have—not the Army you might want or wish to have at a later time. Since the Iraq conflict began, the Army has been pressing ahead to produce the armor necessary at a rate that they believe—it's a greatly expanded rate from what existed previously—but a rate that they believe is the rate that is all that can be accomplished at this moment.
>
> I can assure you that General Schoomaker and the leadership in the Army, and certainly General Whitcomb, are sensitive to the fact that not every vehicle has the degree of armor that would be desirable for it to have, but that they're working at it at a good clip. . . . [T]he goal we have is to have as many of those vehicles as is humanly possible with the appropriate level of armor available for the troops. And that is what the Army has been working on.[2]

Lieutenant General Steven Whitcomb, commander of Army forces in the Persian Gulf, came forward to follow my answer by explaining that any delays were "not a matter of money or desire." He added, "It is a matter of the logistics, of being able to produce [the armor]."[3]

The exchange might have seemed straightforward to most of the people at the base. It seemed that way to me. But unfortunately only a few words of my extensive answer—"As you know, you go to war with the Army you have—not the Army you might want or wish to have at a later time"—ended up being isolated in print and as a seemingly endless loop on cable television. The comment was characterized by some critics, and particularly their contacts in the press, as

* I later was told that the soldier's question had been planted by a Tennessee news reporter who had been embedded with the unit. The source of the question was of little importance—it was a critical issue regarding the safety of our troops, and I did my best to answer it fully.

an example of insensitivity.[4] I did not see my remarks that way, and I still don't. My statement carefully laid out the reality of the armed forces that existed when President Bush took office. Any president and any secretary of defense has available the military that their predecessors bequeath to them. The B-1 bomber I approved as secretary of defense in 1976 was being used in Afghanistan in 2001, just as the M-1 Abrams tank I had approved back then was the mainstay of the U.S. Army when I returned to the Pentagon a quarter of a century later. In turn, the number of up-armored vehicles available in 2004 were the consequences of decisions made years before President Bush or I took office in 2001.

My response also told a simple truth about warfare: As a conflict evolves, both sides adapt to the reality of the battlefield. The emergence of improvised explosive devices as the Iraq conflict wore on necessitated a shift to more armored vehicles that the Army had not acquired. It also necessitated a change by the commanders on the ground in their tactics, techniques, and procedures to make the troops less vulnerable. It took time to put up-armored vehicles in the field, and the Army, which has the responsibility to organize, train, and equip the troops, had not been arranged in an optimal way to accomplish that.

Commanders had been grappling with the problem of lethal improvised explosive devices since 2003, when they first began appearing. The favored IED was the roadside bomb. Made with garage door openers, egg timers, toy car radio controls, or washing machine parts, the bombs were inexpensive to assemble and crude in design. They were, however, remarkably effective in killing American and coalition troops.[5] Among the most vulnerable to the roadside bombs were the thousands of humvees—lightly armored trucks—that were often used by our forces to move around in Iraq.

Once ground commanders experienced the first attacks by IEDs in the summer of 2003, they began to adjust. But so did the enemy. Our troops began using jammers to block the signal of remote-controlled bombs—until the enemy shifted to using wires, pressure plates, and heat sensors to activate the bombs. Once our troops became adept at deciphering the telltale signs of IEDs buried under roads, the enemy put explosives in piles of trash, the carcasses of animals, and, most savagely, in the corpses of murdered Iraqis. Our commanders changed their operating tactics as well, and began stopping three hundred yards before suspected roadside bombs. This led the enemy to plant second bombs at places where the convoys were likely to stop. Next, commanders began to position snipers on frequently bombed routes to kill those who planted IEDs, with the result that the enemy began planting IEDs elsewhere. The bombs themselves became increasingly sophisticated.[6] Houses were rigged to explode when Iraqi or coalition troops entered to search them. In Fallujah and other cities, factories churned out massive car bombs that could take out a city block.

By 2004, IED attacks had risen to nearly one hundred per week, becoming the most deadly weapon our troops faced.[7] General Abizaid and I regularly discussed the severity of the problem with General Casey. Abizaid urged that we mount a Manhattan Project–style effort to find a solution to IEDs, and in June 2004 we created the Joint IED Defeat Task Force with a budget of $1.3 billion and a mandate to find ways to counter the threat.[8] I urged that anything and everything be tried. I was told that the task force we assembled had even tried using honeybees to detect IEDs with their keen sense of smell. Hair dryers were mounted on the fronts of vehicles to trigger the bombs' heat sensors.[9]

Coalition troops were increasingly coming under attack from explosively formed penetrators. EFPs use a copper disc that becomes a semimolten slug capable of piercing even the strongest armor. The first EFPs in Iraq were in Shia areas not far from the Iranian border. The chemical composition of their explosive charges had telltale signs of Iranian weapons manufacturers.[10]

We weren't moving fast enough. In December 2004, I again expressed my continued frustration in a note to Myers and Pace. "I am very uncomfortable with the pace at which this is going. We know that vehicles are vulnerable and we know they are less vulnerable with armor. We have known it for some time."[11] And then, "My suggestion is this: until the Services can organize, [train] and equip the forces in a way that fits the tactics and strategies being used by the Combatant Commanders, the Combatant Commanders need to call a halt to what they are doing."[12] If the U.S. Army could not provide enough armor for humvees, the commanders in theater would have to change the ways they fought. I ordered Abizaid and Casey to forbid all vehicles that had not been up-armored from leaving protected bases in Iraq.[13] I told them we would fly in welders with armor and take as many airplanes as needed to get them and the required armor into Iraq. Within a matter of weeks, no unarmored vehicles were allowed outside of protected compounds.

By late 2005, the several billion dollars we had invested in the IED problem had resulted in progress. Casualties were down, even though the number of attacks had spiraled upward. Still, I wanted a more focused senior Army leadership, so I called another general out of retirement and back to duty: four-star General Montgomery C. Meigs. Meigs focused the Joint IED Defeat Organization on the people making the bombs and the enemy networks that sustained them. Armor continued to arrive in the theater, including the first prototypes of the

Mine Resistant Ambush Protected (MRAP) V-hulled vehicles that afforded more protection to the troops. Increased local cooperation and better intelligence about the insurgent networks led to more coalition operations against those who were making the weapons. The IED challenge—and the amount of time it took to equip the force and adjust to the enemy's tactics—highlighted again the need to accelerate the transformation of our military.

I steadily pushed each service to become more agile, more deployable, and better prepared to confront new, previously unanticipated threats.[14] We redirected the Air Force's energies and resources toward fielding more unmanned aerial vehicles, which by 2008 numbered over five thousand—a twenty-five-fold increase since 9/11.[15] Under the leadership of Admiral Vern Clark, the Navy developed a new Fleet Response Plan to double its efficiency and the number of carrier strike groups available for global deployment at any given time. I encouraged the Marines to develop a special operations contingent.

The Army faced the biggest challenges. It has a proud and storied history dating back to the Continental Army of 1775. Under such legendary generals as Grant and Sherman, it preserved the Union in a tough-fought civil war. Under Pershing and Eisenhower it liberated Europe in two world wars. The Army manned the front lines of the Cold War flashpoints, its heavy tanks and artillery acting as a deterrent against a Soviet ground advance in Central Europe. For decades the Army had been organized for large land battles between sovereign states, symbolized by the service's prized seventy-ton M-1 Abrams tank. The immediate challenges we confronted by 2001 though were not from massed enemy forces. By then our adversaries had learned that confronting the United States in a conventional war of massed force was a bad idea. As a result, America was unlikely to soon face the major land, sea, and air battles for which our military had organized, trained, and equipped over many decades. Instead, we needed a military that could quickly deploy in enough numbers to bring decisive lethality to bear, could leverage our country's technological advantages, such as precision, communications, and stealth, and—most important—could quickly adapt to changing circumstances in a given conflict and prevail.

Despite the unquestionable improvements made over the years—in many cases as the result of the lessons learned from the unconventional conflicts of the 1980s and 1990s—the Army was the most resistant to adapting to the new challenges and accelerating its transformation away from its Cold War posture of large, difficult to deploy, heavy divisions.

The small-scale unconventional conflicts of the Cold War, in Panama, El Salvador, Grenada, Lebanon, and elsewhere, were seen almost as distractions and diversions from what the Army was supposed to do and how it was supposed to do it. In fact, the painful experience in Lebanon had led Cap Weinberger, Reagan's secretary of defense, to codify the aversion to smaller-scale conflicts as a matter of doctrine—what became known as the Weinberger Doctrine (his senior military assistant, General Colin Powell, would later adopt a version of it as the Powell Doctrine). The idea was that U.S. troops should only be committed as a "last resort" in support of clearly defined goals, with a clear "exit strategy" and "overwhelming force" to get in and get out.[16]

In the twenty-first century, however, the task was not to "overwhelm" nations and people who were not our enemies. The enemy was not the local population but the terrorists and insurgents living, training, and fighting among them. This came to be the case in the post-9/11 conflicts we were fighting, including the counterinsurgency campaigns that evolved in Iraq and Afghanistan. These required measured application of military power to minimize civilian casualties and encourage local cooperation.

It also struck me that the new realities of warfare meant that our military should be prepared to be used earlier in order to avoid full-scale conflicts altogether. Merely by their presence abroad or the ability to deploy rapidly, our troops could reassure allies and, in some instances, deter aggression from hostile nations or nonstate actors. They could train foreign forces, as they have in Colombia, Georgia, Jordan, and Kenya, so that the militaries of our friends and allies would be better able to take up the fight against mutual threats—instead of leaving it to our men and women in uniform, who carry more than their share of the burden. They could provide critical intelligence to stop terrorist attacks. They could lend a hand in natural disasters around the world, earning valuable goodwill for the United States by their actions, as we did in the aftermath of the Indian Ocean tsunami and the Pakistan earthquakes.

There were officers in the Army who understood the importance of deployability and speed, and who had taken aboard the lessons of previous unconventional conflicts. During the first Gulf War, there had been flashes of brilliance in the ground campaign that suggested that agility, mobility, and speed had their place in the Army. Throughout the 1990s the Army tried to resolve the tension between advocates for greater change and those who were reluctant to push too hard because of the momentum behind existing programs and weapons systems—momentum that would have to be shifted significantly if true transformation were to occur. During the late 1990s, Army chief of staff Eric Shinseki had wisely challenged the Army with the adage that "if you don't like change, you'll like irrelevance a lot less."

Early on, it became apparent to those of us urging the Army to change that transforming it would be a contentious process. We would need to cancel some major Cold War–era weapon-development programs and encourage unconventional thinkers in the leadership who could help to move the institution.

After thorough reviews by the Army, the Pentagon's program analysis and evaluation (PA&E) office, and Deputy Secretary Paul Wolfowitz, I announced in May 2002 that I was cancelling the $11 billion Crusader artillery system.[17] Beyond its stunningly ill-conceived name, the program was an anachronism that typified the challenges we faced. A forty-ton, 155 millimeter howitzer, the Crusader could launch a shell from the Washington Mall and hit Camden Yards in Baltimore. But it was the antithesis of agility and deployability. The Crusader required two large cargo aircraft to deploy just one system with its ammunition and equipment, and it required considerable time and effort to assemble it on arrival. It wasn't clear what role it could play in mountainous, land-locked Afghanistan, for example. I decided instead to use the $9 billion that had not yet been spent on it to invest in precision-guided weapon systems.

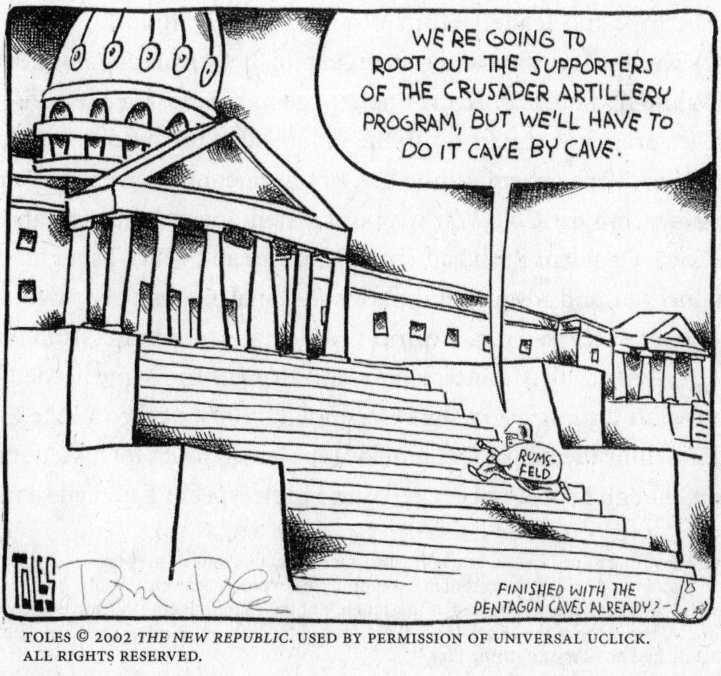

As with the M-1 Abrams tank issue in the Ford administration, my decision on the Crusader provoked near rebellion in the Army establishment, as well as hostility in the iron triangle: Congress, the defense contractors, and the DoD bureaucracy. The artillery community was angry. The defense contractors were apoplectic. Some in Congress were enraged. Some retired Army officers (including a few linked to contractors) were furious at what they characterized as institutional disrespect. Their thoughts were illustrated on the cover of the June 2002 *Armed Forces Journal* featuring my photo and the headline "DOES HE REALLY HATE THE ARMY?"[18]

Some in the Army took actions that in my view bordered on insubordination. The Army's Congressional Affairs office, for example, sent talking points to allies on Capitol Hill arguing that my "decision to kill Crusader puts soldiers at risk" and would cost lives.[19] Ending the Crusader was "[r]eminiscent of unpreparedness in [the] late 1930s," the talking points alleged. "OSD [Office of the Secretary of Defense] is looking for a quick kill to demonstrate their political prowess," they continued. The talking points concluded that "[a] decision to kill Crusader puts the relevance of land power, hence the Army, in question."[20] A colonel on the Army staff called up my military assistant. "Now your boss is going to get what's coming to him," the colonel said. "We've got Congress on our side. We're going to stick it up where the sun don't shine and break it off."

The Army's top leaders, Tom White and Eric Shinseki, were visibly unhappy with my decision and also unhelpful. Before his appointment, Secretary White had been an Army one-star general who, after retiring, was a senior vice president at Enron.* In the months that followed my decision to cancel the artillery system, White had not been cooperative in moving the Army away from the Cold War weapons system toward the agile and more mobile force President Bush had campaigned for and which I sought. White's narrow focus on and advocacy for the institutional interests of a single service was no longer acceptable in a world that demanded jointness and integration of the Army with Marines, sailors, and airmen. The Army needed better, more forward-leaning leadership. On April 25, 2003, I called White into my office for a chilly meeting. I told him I was prepared to accept his letter of resignation, though he had not drafted one. In retrospect I had made a mistake

* Shortly after White joined the Bush administration, Enron filed one of the biggest bankruptcies in American history and became a symbol of corruption in corporate America. White became a target by some who thought he had benefited at the expense of the shareholders and employees who were left penniless. Throughout the controversy I had fended off calls for White to be fired, since to my knowledge he had not done anything illegal.

in putting a retired Army general in as the secretary—at least one who was so unwilling to upset the entrenched bureaucracy and help lead the Army into the new century.

Eventually Congress and the Army supported my decision on the Crusader, but it came at a high cost to me in frayed relationships with a few influential members of Congress and a number in the retired Army community. What I knew was that our nation needed the Army to be relevant for the twenty-first century, and that canceling the Crusader was the right decision for the U.S. Army, the Department of Defense, and, most important, for our country. Now, almost a decade later, no one is clamoring to reinstate the Crusader.

One year after the Crusader dustup, I added to the tensions with my recommendation of a retired four-star Special Forces general, Pete Schoomaker, to be the new Army chief of staff when General Shinseki completed his tour. Some took the decision to bring him out of retirement as a vote of no confidence in the senior Army leadership. In fact, I'd first proposed the job to Shinseki's vice chief, General Jack Keane, seeing institutional benefit to continuing to promote from within the active-duty force. Keane declined for family reasons. While there were certainly other active-duty Army general officers at the three- and four-star level who had proven themselves, I recognized that the next chief would face significant internal resistance to the changes we needed to effect. I decided I wanted someone at the top of the Army who had the ability and desire to jar the institution and transform it into the expeditionary force our country needed. For many hardened Army traditionalists who came of age in a time of a fixed, defensive force designed to repel an assault from Soviet armored divisions in Central Europe, my recommendation to the President of a retired Special Forces officer was the last straw.

Many conventional Army officers considered the Special Forces to be undisciplined cowboys. It was not uncommon in military circles to hear them described as "hotdogs" who took too many risks, got into trouble, and needed to be rescued. General Shinseki, a combat infantry officer who had been wounded in Vietnam, made it clear to me he was not enthusiastic about the Special Forces and their capabilities. "No Special Forces soldier ever pulled me off the battlefield," he once said to me.

The mistrust ran both ways, and the Special Forces folks were less than enthusiastic about Shinseki. For years Army Special Forces had been distinguished by their traditional green berets, which became their nickname. In a break from the past, Shinseki had insisted on requiring all Army personnel to wear berets. His decision was seen by many in the Special Forces and Army Rangers as devaluing their proud symbol.

Since 2001, I had made a priority of increasing the size, capabilities, equipment, and authorities of the special operations forces. By 2006, we had boosted their funding over 107 percent, doubled the number of recruits, and improved their equipment substantially.[21] I authorized the Special Operations Command (SOCOM) as a lead command for war on terror planning and missions. We provided the CENTCOM combatant commander the authority to transfer special ops units anywhere he deemed necessary in his area of responsibility. We shifted some of the tasks that Special Forces had historically been responsible for, such as training foreign militaries, to allow regular forces to do them as well. This freed up special operators for more upper-tier tasks—reconnaissance and direct-action missions. I also urged the Marines to create a special operations contingent, and in 2005 we established the Marine Corps' Special Operations Command (MARSOC).[22] Even though these were historic changes for the armed forces, they were resented by those wedded to the conventional, traditional Army.

Pete Schoomaker was bright, tough, and impatient. In addition to expanding special operations, he decided to implement an idea that had been kicking around for some time but, at least until he arrived on the scene, had met resistance. Schoomaker and I wanted to convert the Army from a force of ten active divisions (of fifteen thousand to twenty thousand troops each) into a force of forty highly capable brigade combat teams (of three thousand to five thousand troops each), with additional combat brigades in the National Guard.[23] Divisions had been part of a centuries-long Army tradition—commemorated with proud banners and songs, each with its own culture, history, and ethos. Divisions also tended to be organized around a central purpose—light infantry or artillery, for example. Often our country's need was for only a portion of the sizable capability of an entire division. It was for readily deployable, smaller, more agile units rather than the full division strength. But the way Army divisions were organized, a small cadre of troops deployed from a division left the rest of the division inoperable. Despite the respect that properly existed for the proud histories of the divisions, modern warfare often calls for relatively more deployable fighting units of a smaller scale.

The successful transition to the modular Army that exists today and that Schoomaker and a new generation of Army officers championed has made a truly historic difference in its capability. The changes created self-contained and interchangeable brigades with their own organic elements such as artillery and infantry. The brigades can be deployed rapidly and work effectively alongside the other services. Sustained deployment of ground forces in Afghanistan and Iraq has been made possible by this innovation. The successful conversion of the central Army maneuver unit from division to brigade has been described by defense analyst Robert Kaplan as "one of the most significant shifts in Army organization since the Napoleonic era."[24]

Canceling the Crusader, dismissing the Army secretary, expanding special operations forces, bringing a four-star officer out of retirement to lead the Army, and a Special Forces officer to boot, encouraging war planning that takes into account speed, precision, agility, and deployability, and shifting from divisions to brigade combat teams—all were decisions that triggered fierce disagreement, and even resentment. I knew that change is hard. But I was always heartened when I met with the troops, because they seemed to appreciate that I was willing to do what it took to get the job done.

PART XIV

The Long, Hard Slog

"It is pretty clear that the coalition can win in Afghanistan and Iraq in one way or another, but it will be a long, hard slog."

—*Memorandum to senior Pentagon officials, October 16, 2003*

Samarra, Iraq

FEBRUARY 22, 2006

In war, fortunes can change rapidly. We saw this in the chaotic days after the rapid overthrow of Saddam Hussein. We saw it again nearly three years later, when the limits of American power became painfully obvious, demanding of a war-weary nation new assessments, approaches, and most of all, resolve.

In the early morning hours of February 22, 2006, Sunni extremists linked to al-Qaida entered the al-Askari Golden Mosque, a major Shia holy site with a dome two hundred feet high that dominated the landscape in the city of Samarra. The extremists overpowered the mosque's guards, laid explosives throughout the building, and then detonated the explosives remotely. The blasts reduced the mosque's famous, venerated golden dome to rubble.

The United States had the most formidable military in the world. We had put men on the moon. Yet as many Iraqis no doubt wondered, why couldn't we stop a handful of thugs armed with small weapons and a few pounds of high explosives?

No one was killed or wounded in the attack, but the bombing of the Samarra mosque was the most strategically significant terrorist attack in Iraq since liberation, seemingly designed by al-Qaida to trigger an all-out Sunni-Shia civil war. Based on the restraint shown by the Shia up to that point and field reporting from commanders that the country was relatively stable and calm following the bombing, we had expectations that the al-Qaida plan would not succeed. As I reported at a press conference, "From what I've seen thus far, much of the reporting in the U.S. and abroad has exaggerated the situation, according to General Casey."[1]

Nonetheless, hours after the bombing, I asked General Pace, who in October 2005 had succeeded Dick Myers as the first Marine chairman of the Joint Chiefs, and Eric Edelman, the new undersecretary for policy, what kind of immediate response we could mount to mitigate the damage of the Samarra mosque bombing.[2] Though some press accounts may have been exaggerated, looking back, it is now clear that the effect of the bombing proved a game changer in Iraq. The event marked the ascendance of Shia militia and a new stage of sectarian conflict focused in Baghdad. The militias, loyal to various Shia political leaders and parties, had existed since the first days of post-Saddam Iraq. They had infiltrated the Iraqi police and army units that we had made a priority to train and equip. In the wake of Samarra, the Shia militias began a campaign of ruthless ethnic cleansing.

Since the end of the Coalition Provisional Authority in 2004, our recalibrated strategy had centered on moving responsibility to the Iraqi security forces as quickly as possible. I believed it was the right approach and would work given time and sufficient patience by the American people. And prior to the Samarra bombing, it had seemed promising. The Iraqis had held successful elections amid a period of declining violence. Through 2005, more and more Sunnis had participated in voting, leading to the smooth and successful government elections in December. Declining attacks against Iraqi civilians and coalition forces would trend lower for months before sudden spikes of violence would seem to erase the recent gains. There had been the hope that we might begin to reduce troop levels in a gradual withdrawal. No longer.

CHAPTER 45

Hands Off the Bicycle Seat

He wasn't on the road to Damascus, but Ambassador Bremer did appear to have had a sudden conversion on his way out of Baghdad. On May 21, 2004, one month before his departure as head of the Coalition Provisional Authority and thirteen months after the end of major combat operations against Saddam, he handed a letter to my military aide, Colonel Steve Bucci, and asked him to deliver the letter to me personally when he arrived back at the Pentagon. Bucci had organized a group of senior staff officers to go to Baghdad in the first months of the CPA to strengthen the organization's management. We were determined to contribute our most capable to the CPA effort.

Bremer's letter recommended a review of troop levels in Iraq. In particular, he asked that we consider deploying an additional division, consisting of 25,000 to 30,000 troops, which would bring the total number of U.S. troops to over 160,000.[1]

Two years later, Bremer cited his letter as proof that he always thought U.S. troop levels in Iraq were too low to enable CPA's mission to succeed. As head of the CPA, Bremer had had ample opportunity to express his opinions, and he had commented favorably on existing troop-level decisions on several occasions. In July 2003, for example, he expressed support for the proposal by CENTCOM's General Abizaid to "reconfigure our troop profile . . . [to] get away from heavy forces towards lighter more mobile force, forces which have

Special Operation skills."[2] That same month Bremer appeared on the television program *Meet the Press*, and host Tim Russert tried to pin him down on the troop-level issue.

"Have you asked Secretary of Defense Rumsfeld for more American troops?" Russert inquired.

"No, I have not," Bremer replied. "I expressed—"

"Do we need more?" Russert pressed.

"I do not believe we do," Bremer replied. "I think the military commanders are confident we have enough troops on the ground, and I accept that analysis."[3]

I was not pleased that Bremer was recommending more troops for the first time as he was on his way out of Baghdad and not in person to provide his reasoning.* Nevertheless, I treated his recommendation as a serious matter meriting the prompt attention of our most senior military officials.† Immediately after receiving it, I sent it to the chairman of the Joint Chiefs of Staff, General Myers, with a memo.

"Questions have been raised about whether US, Coalition and Iraqi force levels in Iraq are adequate," I wrote to Myers, noting that the issue had been raised by some members of Congress, by some retired generals, and now by Bremer.[6] I directed Myers to have General Abizaid and the Joint Chiefs of Staff review Bremer's letter and report back to me. I also asked Myers to assess possible force requirements over the next six months.

Myers' formal response on July 13, 2004 noted that General Abizaid "constantly evaluates the number of forces required to be successful in Iraq" and that he "believes forces in theater are adequate to perform the current tasks."[7] Myers wrote that CENTCOM's plan anticipated a reduction of a brigade of troops by August 2004. The Chairman also noted that "a more optimistic forecast" from CENTCOM envisioned a transition to Iraqi control of security beginning in January 2005, and after which only seven U.S. brigades (the equivalent of some thirty thousand U.S. troops) would be required.[8]

Myers, Abizaid, and the Joint Chiefs anticipated that more troops might

* To my knowledge, Bremer had raised the question of U.S. troop levels only once before. In May 2003, before he even arrived in Baghdad, he sent me a copy of a study that reviewed the numbers of forces deployed in previous postwar conflicts. Bremer later backed off his claim that his May 2003 memo was as emphatic on the need for higher troop levels as had been advertised. Bremer admitted, "What I said was I think this is an interesting report and you ought to take it into account. I didn't ask for more troops. I hadn't even been to Iraq."[4]

† Bremer's memory of the exchange is different than my records. "I did not hear back from him," Bremer wrote in his memoir. I did in fact send Bremer a response, dated May 24, 2004. "I received your memo and I thank you," I wrote. "Attached is a classified copy of the memo I sent to Dick Myers as a follow-up to your thoughts."[5]

be needed "should the current environment change." Myers' memo listed "potential triggers" for such a force increase request: large-scale violent demonstrations, large-scale rioting and looting, a significant increase in attacks on coalition forces, and a general uprising in two major population areas at once.[9] In fact, several months later, CENTCOM did request, and I approved, an increase of more than 20,000 troops to help provide security for the January 2005 elections.

This wasn't the first time I had asked the generals whether troop levels were adequate; I raised the question of whether we had appropriate resources when I visited Iraq and in regular conversations with Myers and Abizaid. Nor was Bremer the first person to suggest that more troops might be needed; there wasn't a day that went by without some member of Congress or retired military officer on television calling for more troops. We were all well aware of the issue. I raised the possibility with our commanders in theater and with senior Defense Department officials that the critics may have a valid point.

At the time of the invasion in March 2003, I believed we made the right call with approximately 150,000 U.S. and 20,000 coalition troops on the ground and the option to deploy up to 450,000 U.S. troops if General Franks judged them necessary. If anything, troop levels were high for the fight our forces initially encountered. Saddam's regime fell more quickly than had been anticipated, and the resistance from Iraqi army units was relatively modest. Our Arab friends had consistently urged us to leave Iraq as soon as possible if war came. Riots and demonstrations might break out if the war dragged on, especially if we were seen as occupiers. That argument seemed reasonable to me. I know it also registered with Abizaid, Franks, and, I believe, with President Bush.

After major combat operations against Saddam's forces came to an end in April 2003, I discussed the issue of troop levels with senior commanders and the chairman and vice chairman of the Joint Chiefs on a near weekly basis. The arguments against substantially increasing troop levels continued to seem persuasive. More troops do not necessarily mean a greater chance for success. In fact, too many troops could hurt our ability to win Iraqi confidence, and it could translate into more casualties, because more troops would mean more targets for our enemies. To my thinking, even more important than the number of forces on the ground were the types of missions they were undertaking. We could send hundreds of thousands of troops to Iraq, and if they didn't have the right operational approach and tactics, they weren't likely to achieve our goals.

The potential benefit of deploying more troops was a continuous preoccupation for me and the commanders over the next three years. Could Iraq's early troubles have been reduced by increasing our force levels? In retrospect, it's possible there may have been times when more troops could have been helpful. General Franks told me in 2008 that, in hindsight, his recommendation to stop the flow of additional troops into Iraq by holding the 1st Armored Division and the 1st Cavalry Division might have been a mistake. However, I know of no senior officials, military or civilian, who expressed disagreement with the decision at the time. Certainly I did not.

In the early spring of 2003, when the decision was made, the possibility of an organized insurgency had not been included in CENTCOM's assumptions. On my April 30 trip to Basra and Baghdad, I was briefed by military commanders and intelligence officials. Except for sporadic skirmishes, the country seemed increasingly pacified. The worst of the looting that had swept parts of Iraq in the first weeks of April appeared to be over. It is conceivable that several thousand more troops in Baghdad, where most of the media was located, might have at least kept the capital from appearing so chaotic, a perception that proved damaging throughout our country and the world.

As the situation in Iraq worsened with insurgent attacks increasing through late 2003 and early 2004, we actively weighed the merits of deploying additional troops. On February 23, 2004, three months before Bremer sent his departure memo, I had an encounter on the issue with CENTCOM commander John Abizaid. En route to Baghdad, we met in the Kuwaiti government's guesthouse for foreign officials. The flight from Washington had been long. I was tired and had a lot of questions.

Abizaid had flown up from CENTCOM headquarters in Qatar to join me for the flight into Iraq the following day. I asked to meet with him along with Bill Luti, the Department's senior policy adviser on Iraq. A former Navy captain, Luti had a sharp mind coupled with an irreverence and pugnacity I found appealing. Despite his usual knack for lightening the mood in meetings, even Luti couldn't ease my sense that things weren't going well in Iraq.

Abizaid and Luti joined me in the office attached to my room. I asked them to close the door.

"Damn it, General," I said. "We're getting pounded back in Washington over troop levels." We appeared to be making little headway against the insurgency. Media pundits, members of Congress, and retired generals were insisting that additional forces were the answer. I needed to know whether Abizaid shared those concerns. If he didn't, I needed to know why he had confidence in maintaining the troop levels he was recommending.

I asked him directly if we needed more. It was not a rhetorical question. I wanted to hear his professional military advice. I made it clear to all senior military officials that they owed me their best advice not only when I asked for it but whenever they had something to recommend.[10] Abizaid replied somewhat wearily that if he thought we needed more troops, he'd tell me so. It was certainly not the first time he had considered the question, and I suspected the constant queries from all quarters were becoming irritating to him. He then listed the reasons he didn't think more troops were needed. He stressed that we were in an asymmetric war that would be won or lost on intelligence. The need was not to get more Americans in uniform on the ground. The need was to get more intelligence professionals on the ground recruiting local informants. We were fighting an enemy in an Arab land where guests were welcome, but Americans who overstayed their welcome would not be. If Iraq wanted to regain the pride and honor so important in its society, Iraqis would need to take on the fight. We couldn't do it for them. We needed more of an "Iraqi face" on the coalition effort in Iraq, not more American troops.

Over the years that followed, I prodded many in the Department to give me their personal views on the issue of troop levels in Iraq (and in Afghanistan, for that matter). When I raised questions as to whether other operational approaches might be considered, such as an even greater focus on training and advising Iraqi security forces or securing the population, they told me their area commanders were tailoring their tactics and techniques to fit the different conditions across Iraq. It wasn't that things were perfect; they did say repeatedly that they needed more civilian experts, better intelligence, and, most of all, more Iraqi troops. There also undoubtedly were areas within Iraq where additional forces were needed due to a request from a local commander. But the overall force level for the country was a different matter, and the view I consistently heard was that the top-line number was sufficient.

I knew that general agreement could be a sign that we were not challenging our own assumptions as rigorously as we might. A comment I made often in meetings, paraphrasing Pat Moynihan, was that in unanimity one often found a lack of rigorous thinking. That's why I periodically sent memos asking for views that differed from whatever seemed to be the broad consensus. I wrote Generals Myers and Pace, saying, "I would like to know what the general officers, and possibly some key colonels, in Iraq think about the various options we face."[11] I followed up the next day: "I don't need to know names, but it would be helpful for me to have a sense of what the commanders at various levels think on these issues. Please include minority opinions and their reasoning."[12] The memo continued:

> For example, I would be interested in knowing whether or not they believe the US and the coalition
>
> 1. Are doing about the right things overall, and with about the right number of troops in their respective areas of operation (specify their AORs).
> 2. Need more troops and, if so, where and for what purposes.
> 3. Would be better off with fewer US troops (where) and doing less of what types of activities.
> 4. Would be better off with the same (larger or smaller) number of troops, but refocusing coalition efforts to put X% (i.e., 10%? 50? 90%?) of our forces on the tasks of organizing, training, equipping, and mentoring Iraqi Security forces.
> 5. Should cut back dramatically on US-only patrols and focus most of their efforts on joint patrols and/or mentoring Iraqi Security forces.
> 6. Put more coalition forces [on] Iraq's borders (with Syria? Iran? and/or [in] Baghdad? Mosul? other?), but remain available to conduct raids throughout the country as required.
> 7. Should establish a larger presence in the relatively secure North and South, and less coalition presence in the Sunni Triangle.
> 8. Other.[13]

I wanted candor, which is why I was willing to accept anonymous responses in case less senior officers might be hesitant to express views that differed from their immediate superiors. The lives of our troops and the success of the war were at stake, so mine was as serious an inquiry as one could make. I wanted to reach down the chain of command to find what more junior officers were thinking. I did not receive any responses that they wanted more forces or that they disagreed with the strategy.

I also had in mind my recollections of the U.S. involvements in Vietnam and Lebanon. In both cases I had observed that local populations, if permitted, would lean more and more on Americans to solve their problems. In the end, the South Vietnamese and the people of Lebanon were left vulnerable and relatively defenseless when American public support for these missions eroded and the United States pulled out.

I was concerned that U.S. and coalition forces might inadvertently discourage Iraqis from taking on increased responsibility for bringing order to their country. Having the United States as a crutch might delay the hard work required for them to build a safe and stable society appropriate to their circumstances. I sometimes used the analogy of teaching someone how to ride a bicycle. After you run down the street steadying the bicycle by holding the seat, you eventually have to take your hand off the seat. The person may fall once or twice, but it's the way he learns. If you're not willing to take your hand off the bicycle seat, the person will never learn to ride.

Never much of a handwringer, I don't spend a lot of time in recriminations, looking back or second-guessing decisions made in real time with imperfect information by myself or others. In my press conferences I did not always conceal my lack of regard for hindsight "wisdom." While in office, I resisted answering the frequently asked, breezy, politically loaded questions, along the lines of "What do you regret most?" or "What do you wish you had done differently?" or "Was this or that a mistake?"

A secretary of defense has to be careful about what he says in public. His comments can affect troop morale or limit the president's options in the future. Nonetheless, officials need to periodically reexamine their own views and judgments. Human beings are fallible, and the information policy makers use to make their judgments is always incomplete, imperfect, and ever changing. The assumptions that underlie strategy can become stale or even proved wrong to begin with. It sometimes requires exquisite balancing skills to be properly skeptical and yet open to criticism in internal deliberations, while not suggesting to allies or enemies abroad that one is adrift or lacking confidence in a policy.

The senior Department advisers were accustomed to receiving skeptical "big think" snowflakes from me. I did this periodically—for the campaigns in Afghanistan and Iraq, the global defense posture realignment, major alliance management issues, transformation, and other significant activities. When one of these internal memos urging a reassessment of our strategy in the war on terror was leaked to the press, however, it made headlines. The front page of the October 22, 2003, *USA Today* read "DEFENSE MEMO: A GRIM OUTLOOK—RUMSFELD SPELLS OUT DOUBTS ON IRAQ, TERROR." "Despite upbeat statements by the Bush administration, the memo to Rumsfeld's top staff reveals significant doubts about progress in the struggle against terrorists," the paper reported, adding: "The memo, which diverges sharply from Rumsfeld's mostly positive public comments, offers one of the most candid and sobering assessments to date of how top administration officials view the 2-year-old war on terrorism."[14] Even though I had limited the addressees to Myers, Pace, Wolfowitz, and Feith, the memo had leaked when it was more broadly distributed to their staffs.

In my meetings with the combatant commanders I had solicited their thoughts on where the United States was doing well and where we needed to do better. This memo was my way of prodding top Pentagon officials to think about the war on terror comprehensively, not one slice at a time. The memo centered on three key questions: First, how do we know if we are winning or losing the global war on terror? Second, is the U.S. government organized properly to prosecute the war? And third, how can the United States do better in countering the enemy ideologically—that is, not just in capturing or killing terrorists, but in preventing young people from becoming our murderous enemies in the first place?

I questioned whether the Defense Department, and the U.S. government in general, were changing fast enough to do what was necessary to win. I assessed the "mixed results" of our efforts against al-Qaida. Many terrorists remained at large. I pointed out that we had done a good job in reorienting the Defense Department to take the offensive in the war with Islamist extremists, but I wondered: "Are the changes we have and are making too modest and incremental?" My memo continued:

> My impression is that we have not yet made truly bold moves. . . . [W]e lack metrics to know if we are winning or losing the global war on terror. Are we capturing, killing or deterring and dissuading more terrorists every day than the madrassas and the radical clerics are recruiting, training and deploying against us?
>
> Does the US need to fashion a broad, integrated plan to stop the next generation of terrorists? The US is putting relatively little effort into a long-range plan, but we are putting a great deal of effort into trying to stop terrorists. The cost-benefit ratio is against us! Our cost is billions against the terrorists' costs of millions.
>
> Do we need a new organization?

How do we stop those who are financing the radical madrassa schools?

Is our current situation such that "the harder we work, the behinder we get"?

It is pretty clear that the coalition can win in Afghanistan and Iraq in one way or another, but it will be a long, hard slog.

Does CIA need a new finding [a presidential authorization for covert activity]?

Should we create a private foundation to entice radical madradssas [*sic*] to a more moderate course?

What else should we be considering?[15]

This document, which became known as the "Long, Hard Slog" memo, was cast by some as a rebuke of the Bush administration's strategy. It was not a sign of doubt, much less of disapproval. Rather, it was my view of what a senior official needed to do to ensure that we were not operating on autopilot—that we did not become complacent or closed-minded.

I was concerned that if the United States focused too narrowly on military means to defeat the terrorist threat posed by al-Qaida and other Islamist extremists, we could end up doing more harm than good over the long term. Even as early as October 2003, it was clear that bullets alone would not win the wars in Iraq or Afghanistan. And in the much broader war against Islamist terrorism, without a serious and sustained ideological campaign to discredit radical Islamism, our enemies were going to be able to recruit and indoctrinate far more terrorists than we could capture or kill—and they'd be able to exploit our counterterrorism measures to feed anti-American resentment.

I also worried that an exclusive concentration of resources on fighting terrorism might invite other powers—perhaps North Korea or Iran—to challenge us by means other than terrorism. Terrorists and insurgents had become a serious threat, but there was no telling what kind of conflicts we might need to deter or defend against down the road a few years or decades hence. In short, we needed to give appropriate priority to other aspects of our national security strategy as well.

My October 2003 memo launched a useful recalibration of the administration's strategy in the war on terror, which resulted in a somewhat greater emphasis on the nonmilitary instruments of national power. We conducted a strategic review of the global war on terror and presented several important thoughts to President Bush, including a proposal for a new U.S. information agency and a civilian reserve corps at the State Department to provide civilian partners for our military in performing stabilization missions. The key elements of our strategic review were incorporated into formal presidential directives. They became the foundation of the 2005–2006 National Military Strategic Plan for the war on terror and helped shape the administration's 2006 National Security Strategy.[16]

One phrase in my October 2003 memo gained special attention: "long, hard slog." For some it evoked the Vietnam War and images of quagmire.[17] I hadn't intended the unflattering comparison, but I did feel we needed to caution ourselves and the American people that the broader war against Islamist extremists might last many years like the Cold War.

We had done much work we could be proud of. We were putting the pressure on al-Qaida and other Islamist terrorist groups around the world. While there had not been another attack on our country, we knew that our enemies were reorganizing as decentralized terrorist cells and as insurgent groups. They would take advantage of our troop presence in Iraq and Afghanistan, using the fighting there to train their next generation of terrorists. And they would use support from Syria and Iran to arm themselves. They would launch headline-grabbing attacks to try to convince the American public that our fight with them was futile, much as the Tet Offensive in Vietnam had. Theirs was a waiting game. They knew that they didn't have to win; they simply had to outlast us.

CHAPTER 46

The Dead Enders

In June 2004, Lieutenant General Ricardo Sanchez ended his tour as commander of American forces in Iraq and was replaced by George Casey, a four-star Army general. Casey began his military career in the late 1960s in the ROTC at Georgetown University. Though Casey had planned to stay for only two years in the military before heading to law school, he felt compelled to stay in the Army as the war in Vietnam raged. The decision was a weighty one for him. His father, a major general, had been killed in a helicopter crash in Vietnam shortly after Casey was commissioned. Throughout his time in Iraq, Casey wore one of his dad's medals around his neck as a reminder of the sacrifice.

After Sanchez's difficult tenure, the appointment of the calm, low-key, and analytical Casey was welcomed. "Boring is good, General Casey, and I applaud you on that," Senator Hillary Clinton told him at his confirmation hearing. "Clearly, you're a master at it. And it goes to the heart of your success."[1]

I had recommended Casey to the President at Abizaid's urging. Casey and his superior at CENTCOM were close personally and saw the Iraq war in similar terms. They emphasized transferring responsibility to the Iraqi government and training and equipping Iraqi forces so that American forces could begin to leave in an orderly fashion. With the end of the CPA, we had returned to our original emphasis on more modest goals—keeping the nation reasonably secure and enabling the Iraqis to defeat the insurgency over time.

In contrast to the strained relationship that characterized the Bremer and Sanchez pairing, Casey worked well with the first U.S. ambassador to a free Iraq, John Negroponte. Measured and calm, Negroponte was a forceful advocate for the United States. His approach was vastly more collaborative with our military commanders in Iraq than Bremer's had been. Casey and Negroponte established their offices next to each other in Baghdad, as I had urged them to do before they left for Iraq. Together they created a joint campaign plan that for the first time in the conflict fully unified the military, economic, and diplomatic strands of the American effort toward common goals.

There was no shortage of work to be done in regaining the momentum toward Iraqi control that had slipped during the occupation. We had lost almost a year in training Iraq's army and police forces because of bureaucratic differences and misplaced priorities. After reorienting the emphasis toward internal security, Abizaid and I made a priority of increasing the number of Iraqi security forces. Consistent with this goal, Ambassador Negroponte shifted substantial reconstruction funds away from infrastructure projects toward the training of Iraqi army and police forces.

I also pushed for more coalition forces to be involved in Iraq to lessen the burden on our troops. We could continue to bear the brunt of the difficult work, such as clearing and holding Iraqi neighborhoods, but other countries could pick up some of the slack by providing force protection at military bases and working at logistic hubs in Kuwait. If deploying troops to Iraq was politically too sensitive, I suggested that some countries replace American troops in places like the Sinai, Kosovo, and Bosnia, so we could focus more of our resources in Iraq and Afghanistan.[2] I had pushed hard for a Muslim military contingent to go to Iraq to belie the propaganda aired on Al-Jazeera that America was waging a war against Islam.[3] Turkey's parliament had at one point agreed to deploy two divisions of troops. But suspicious of their neighboring countries, Iraqi leaders rejected the idea—to the detriment of Iraq's security and to U.S.-Turkey relations.

Some critics contended we were using Iraqis interchangeably with our own forces, as if we thought a recently trained Iraqi soldier was as capable as a U.S. Marine or Army soldier.[4] That was not so; we never envisioned the Iraqi security forces becoming the equivalent of the U.S. military. I did think we could aim for a competent, capable Iraqi force that, over time, could earn the respect and support of the Iraqi people. I believed that training and equipping

Iraqis to secure their own country was the best strategy to achieve a government reasonably capable of dealing with the challenges it faced.*

Unlike most twentieth-century counterinsurgencies, such as that waged by the French in Algeria, the goal of the United States wasn't an Iraq that was disarmed and unable to resist occupation. To the contrary, we wanted an Iraq that we could leave behind fully independent and capable of defending itself with a well-trained and well-armed police force and army. We had a major interest in ensuring the Iraqis were successful. But ultimately we knew that we couldn't succeed for them. If more Iraqis didn't stop insurgents from taking refuge in their neighborhoods, building car bombs in their garages, and destroying power lines and reconstruction projects, and start providing more intelligence tips to Iraqi security forces, then the Iraqi people were doomed to live in a destroyed, violence-engulfed country.[6]

After some difficult months under a two-star general whose efforts resulted in only modest progress, we needed a three-star general who could aggressively accelerate the development of local forces. To reorient the Iraqi Security Forces (ISF) and make their training and equipping a top priority, I settled on an Army general who had excelled as a division commander during the major combat operations stage.

David Petraeus began his career at West Point, where he would later return as a professor armed with a Princeton Ph.D. He was by many accounts ambitious and driven. His experience with low-intensity conflict and peacekeeping in Haiti and Bosnia had served him well during his first tour in Iraq, where he commanded the 101st Airborne Division. He demonstrated inventiveness in Mosul through engagement with the population and a willingness to improvise.[7] He held local elections for a town council and undertook reconstruction projects at his division's level, even as he had to cope with some CPA officials who were cool to initiatives coming from outside the Green Zone.

I'd had limited exposure to Petraeus at the time, so before settling on him I asked other senior officers for their assessments. The consensus was that he was cerebral, and savvy with the press. His personal public relations abilities were so good that the views of some of his colleagues were mixed. But despite some reservations by senior uniformed officials, I decided Petraeus would be

* Having Iraqis defend Iraqis was not only the right strategic course, it was a far more efficient option than using U.S. forces. I had the Defense Department's comptroller, Tina Jonas, calculate the costs of recruiting, training, equipping, and deploying an American, an Iraqi, and an Afghan soldier. She reported that the cost of training and deploying one American soldier, approximately $107,000 per year, equaled the cost of training and deploying fifty-nine Afghan soldiers at $1,800 each or sixteen Iraqis at $6,500 each.[5]

a good fit for a mission in need of strong leadership.* In June 2004, Petraeus deployed on his second tour to Iraq and took charge of training and equipping the Iraqi security forces, with a mandate to make sure they could assume more responsibility fighting the insurgency.[8]

Generals Abizaid and Casey and I agreed that putting Iraqis forward to take the fight to the enemy and assume leadership of their country was our best weapon against the insurgency and the surest way to avoid more U.S. casualties that would eventually sap the political will for America's effort in Iraq. We hoped that as Iraqis gained control of their destiny, the terrorists and regime remnants would no longer be seen as standing in opposition to Americans or coalition occupiers. Instead, the insurgents would be seen for what they were—opponents of the legitimate, elected Iraqi government.

When asked by reporters about the first signs of a sustained and organized resistance in April 2004 following the flare-up in Fallujah, I said, "Thugs and assassins and former Saddam henchmen will not be allowed to carve out portions of that city and to oppose peace and freedom. The dead enders, threatened by Iraq's progress to self-government, may believe they can drive the coalition out through terror and intimidation, and foment civil war among Sunnis and Shias, or block the path to Iraqi self-rule, but they're badly mistaken."[9] Some in the media mistook my use of the phrase "dead enders" to mean I was suggesting that victory was imminent, that the enemy would soon be defeated.[10] In fact, my meaning was exactly the opposite—namely that our forces were locked in a bloody struggle with an enemy that would fight to the bitter end, to their deaths. Rather than dismissing the insurgents, I was saying that because they would fight to the end, our work against them would be difficult.[11]

In its early months the insurgency was dominated by former Baathist regime holdouts. Later, evidence was discovered that suggested that Saddam had planned to mount an insurgency if his conventional forces were unable to turn back a U.S.-led invasion. Saddam's intelligence service disseminated messages to its members to organize a resistance by forming cells and training terrorists in the event of the regime's collapse.[12] General Izzat Ibrahim al-Douri, one of Saddam's close associates and later a leader of the insurgency,

* Petraeus was not the only general officer our team of four would recommend to the President for promotion who would go on to have successful careers. Generals Dave Barno, Stan McChrystal, Pete Chiarelli, Thomas Metz, Martin Dempsey, and Ray Odierno would all have a lasting imprint on the U.S. military.

led a secret program to launch a guerrilla war under the Unified Mujahedeen Command.[13] Baathists, whose ideology is secular, nevertheless tapped into the potent force of jihadism, attracting devout fanatics to their cause.

The Baathist-jihadist axis, at least in its early phases, was less of an insurgency—an armed political movement that arose organically from the general population—and more a counterrevolution. It consisted mainly of Baathists seeking a return of their dictatorial power. When CENTCOM produced a list of the thirty-nine top leaders in the insurgency in the fall of 2004, almost all were connected to the old regime of Saddam. Indeed, early on one prominent insurgent group called itself "the Party of the Return."[14]

The insurgency began primarily as an effort to reclaim Sunni supremacy over Iraq's Kurds and Shia. But by 2004 it had grown, bolstered by the support of a larger, more diverse group, not just of committed Baathists but of a number of non-Baathist Iraqi nationalists as well. Former Baathists exploited Islamist ideology to expand the conflict and attract recruits from all across the Muslim world. To anyone outside this privileged circle of Saddam regime loyalists, creating a new Islamic caliphate in Baghdad was far more appealing than reinstating Saddam and his ilk to power. The insurgency soon became dominated by foreign fighters and terrorists; predominant among them was a group calling itself al-Qaida in Iraq.

Al-Qaida's followers infiltrated Iraq and took advantage of the Sunnis' sense of disenfranchisement and alienation. Though only comprising approximately 20 percent of the population, Sunni Arabs had been the ruling class in Iraq since the British Mandate of Mesopotamia after World War I. But nearly overnight following Saddam's fall, the Sunnis had become a mere minority in a country with a new Shia-led government. Neighboring Sunni governments in Saudi Arabia, Jordan, and Syria were unhappy and worried about the new order in Iraq. Iraqi Sunnis feared they might become targets of reprisals for past grievances, and al-Qaida capitalized on this insecurity. While our intelligence community's prewar view was that secular Baathists and al-Qaida's religious extremists would not cooperate, it had become obvious by 2004 that al-Qaida in Iraq had formed bases in Sunni populations throughout much of the country, using a combination of security promises, persistent recruitment efforts, and brutal intimidation.

At first this may have seemed an attractive alliance to the Sunnis, but al-Qaida was not interested in helping the Baathists return to power. Al-Qaida forces seized control of neighborhoods and villages. They labeled as traitors those Iraqis who cooperated with the Iraqi government or with the Americans.

We received reports of terrorists who murdered children or booby-trapped dead bodies so that families would be killed when they tried to retrieve their loved ones. In Fallujah, those who refused to collaborate with the terrorists who controlled the city were beheaded and tossed into the Euphrates River.[15]

In November 2004, we recognized that our troops had to return to Fallujah. It was a sanctuary for al-Qaida in Iraq and much of the insurgency. Fifteen thousand U.S. Marines and soldiers along with two thousand Iraqi troops encircled the city. In the early morning hours of November 8, they swept northward through the city, block by block, engaging in the toughest urban fighting of the Iraq war. It also proved to be the bloodiest, with ninety-five American troops killed in combat. Though hard won, it was a key victory over the insurgents.[16] Fallujah was cleared of the terrorists who had taken refuge there, and the city has never reverted to the enemy.

We had a priceless advantage in an ideological struggle against the enemy. We could offer the Iraqis a future the majority of Iraqis wanted—a future of self-government and national pride. We could also finally disprove the notion that the Americans were occupiers there to steal their oil. Elections would be a critical step toward that goal.

Holding an election during such a fragile period in a war-torn country carried significant risks. There was the obvious danger that terrorists could launch devastating attacks on Iraqi citizens on election day, setting back any political progress. We also had to keep in mind that if we rushed to national elections, we could end up with an antidemocratic result. Groups that were already well organized would have a major advantage if elections were held too soon. Those groups tended to be bankrolled by the Iranian regime and were deeply sectarian. If they emerged the ultimate winners, the long-term survival prospects of a free society in Iraq capable of resisting foreign influences would be slim. In the worst-case scenario, we could end up with leaders in power who rivaled Saddam in their lust for violence and support for terrorism.

Al-Qaida understood that the fight to establish a free, self-governing Iraq in the heart of the Arab world would be a critical threat to their cause. For some time prior to the elections, enemies of a free Iraq led by al-Qaida put up posters with messages such as "YOU VOTE. YOU DIE." Abu Musab al-Zarqawi, the Jordanian militant who had proclaimed himself leader of al-Qaida in Iraq, declared "a fierce war on this evil principle of democracy." He called the elections a sham meant to deceive the Iraqi people and subjugate them to American puppets. "Anyone who tries to help set up this system is part of it," he warned.[17] Zarqawi claimed that anyone participating in elections was an apostate. The insurgents knew what a powerful threat the elections posed to their cause.

We set an ambitious schedule for three elections in 2005. The first election, which if successful promised to be a watershed event in the Arab world, was scheduled for January. Iraqis would vote to fill 275 seats in their national legislature. The legislature would then draft an Iraqi constitution. In the second vote, the Iraqi people would approve or reject the constitution in a referendum. And finally, the Iraqi people would elect a free Iraqi government under their new constitution.

As the first elections approached in January 2005, commentators across the world predicted disaster.[18] Foreign affairs specialists called for postponement of the elections in light of the terrorists' threats.[19] There was a possibility that many voters, fearing for their lives and the lives of their families, would not show up at polling places. Brent Scowcroft, who had been national security adviser for President Ford and later for President George H. W. Bush, as well as chairman of President George W. Bush's Foreign Intelligence Advisory Board, warned that the elections had "the great potential for deepening the conflict" in Iraq.[20] Others worried that the lack of participation by minority Sunnis, who threatened to boycott the election, would undermine its legitimacy.

Like President Bush, I was determined that the elections go forward. I was under no illusions that free elections would quickly solve all of Iraq's problems, but delaying the vote because of the intimidation of the terrorists would give them a major psychological victory and set back our efforts to help the Iraqis create a representative, sovereign government for themselves.

Iraq's first election day was on Sunday, January 30, 2005, ten days after President Bush's second inauguration. How many, I wondered, would show up at polling stations despite knowing they were risking their lives by voting? With Baghdad seven hours ahead of our time, preliminary reports were already coming in when I turned on the cable news early that Sunday morning.

There was no need for detailed expert analysis to understand the historical consequence of what was taking place across Iraq. The televised images said it all. There were long lines at polling places. Iraqi men dressed in their best clothes were standing proudly as they waited to cast their votes. Some brought their children to watch a piece of history unfold. Voters had to dip their index finger in indelible purple ink to assure that no one voted more than once—and these purple fingers became a proud symbol of participation in a free and fair election. No doubt citizens were emboldened by the highly visible presence of the Iraqi security forces that American forces had trained and equipped. They stayed at their posts and held their ground. Iraqi and coalition forces had imposed extensive security measures to try to prevent terrorist attacks, and their efforts were largely successful.

Over the course of the day, fear gave way to elation. Men and women danced in the streets and waved their purple fingers in the air.[21] "It's like a wedding. I swear to God, it's a wedding for all of Iraq," the director of one polling station in a Sunni neighborhood in Baghdad rejoiced. "No one has ever witnessed this before. For a half-century, no one has seen anything like it. And we did it ourselves."[22]

Nearly 60 percent of registered Iraqis had cast their ballots in defiance of al-Qaida threats and attempts at intimidation. Many Sunnis had not turned out, but they soon came to regret it, as they realized they would have little say in the formation of their new government. They resolved to participate in greater numbers next time.

Nine months later, Iraqis overwhelmingly approved the national constitution their elected representatives had drafted. The successful referendum belied the proposal that Iraq should be split into separate Sunni, Shia, and Kurd autonomous zones, an unhelpful idea some in Congress, Senator Joe Biden prominent among them, had been advocating.[23]

In the late autumn of 2005, we approached the third free election in Iraq, one that would establish a permanent Iraqi government. President Bush held an NSC meeting on November 2 to discuss the security strategy for the election and the perennial issue of U.S. troop levels. Did we need more? In the White House Situation Room, President Bush held forth, with General Casey and others joining on the secure video screen from Baghdad. We discussed ramping up troop levels with additional brigades to secure polling stations for the elections and to deal with any instability in the weeks after. We planned to increase troops to 160,000 and were considering sending two more brigades, as many as 10,000 additional troops.

"My recommendation is don't deploy these two brigades," General Casey said. "None of my commanders believe we need the force."[24]

Casey and Abizaid would not fail to let their superiors in the chain of command know when and if they believed they needed to increase troop levels. They knew well that having too few troops could result in violence that might have been deterred. But like them, I was aware that if we added more troops at the wrong time and in the wrong places, we could weaken Iraqi leadership and stunt the development of a sovereign nation still in its formative stages. It was not a simple issue.

"We need to avoid dependency syndrome," I added, supporting Abizaid and Casey's view. "We need to take our hand off the bicycle seat."

President Bush replied, "Drawdown is the right thing. The announcement before the election is the problem." The President had put his finger on the crux of the issue: If we signaled a drawdown before the December 2005 Iraqi elections, it might discourage people from coming out to vote for a new parliament. Ultimately, Bush decided to hold back one of the two brigades we were considering sending and to deploy the other only as far as Kuwait, to stand by in reserve in case violence in Iraq spiked during the election period.

On December 15, 2005, more than twelve million Iraqis voted for their national legislature, as provided for by the constitution the Iraqi people had ratified. The 70 percent turnout included many Sunnis. A quarter of those elected were female, as mandated by the new Iraqi constitution.

I had sent a memo to President Bush in November 2005 listing some signs of progress in Iraq. The Iraqi Security Forces were beginning to show signs of promise. The Iraqis had a new constitution they had written and approved, and were forming their own governmental institutions. There were tentative, early, and still modest efforts to bring Sunnis, Shia, and Kurds together. In the memo, I also called the President's attention to some of the remaining difficulties: "bursts of violence, including assassinations and attempts to intimidate Iraqi leaders; Iran and Syria continue to be unhelpful, and US casualties." I concluded that there was cause to be somewhat optimistic. "The central question is whether the U.S. will be safer by succeeding in Iraq or by precipitously withdrawing. The answer is clear. Quitting is not an exit strategy. Victory is the only acceptable exit strategy."[25]

The Iraqis were moving forward toward a free, self-governed future. The majority of them showed they were willing to defy the insurgents. But the foreign fighters were not ready to give up. More terrorists continued to flow in from outside, most from Syria and Iran. They continued to stage bloody attacks and inflame sectarian tensions.

Though it was not clear at the time, the Samarra Golden Mosque bombing on February 22, 2006, touched off a new phase of the war. In the wake of the bombing, just ten weeks after the election of a national legislature, Shia militias and death squads, some loyal to Muqtada al-Sadr, joined in the violence.[26] The ranks of Muqtada al-Sadr's Mahdi militia swelled with new recruits. Baghdad witnessed pitched battles, as sectarian militias savaged each other, with civilians often caught in the middle. Shia militias roamed the capital city with handguns and power drills exacting revenge for anyone suspected of cooperating with Sunnis. The death squads' victims were often innocents who happened to have Sunni-sounding names. Many Sunnis, in turn, supported the attacks waged by al-Qaida. Iraqis fled mixed neighborhoods or risked becoming victimized by the militias.

The Golden Mosque bombing also jeopardized ongoing discussions over the seating of a new Iraqi government. It derailed Generals Abizaid and Casey's plans to turn over more responsibility to the Iraqi Security Forces month by month and to reduce U.S. troop levels gradually. The situation was now too precarious to contemplate that shift. Casey recommended doubling the number of troops in Baghdad. If large swaths of neighborhoods in the capital city were engulfed in violence, there could be little progress elsewhere. It would be difficult for national politicians to reconcile and forge a countrywide consensus as long as sectarian militias rampaged within earshot of the seat of their national government. And the Western media, based in Baghdad, would focus on the violence in their immediate area and report that the situation in the country was in decline.

CHAPTER 47

Eyes on Afghanistan

On December 7, 2004, I had arrived in Kabul as a member of the U.S. delegation led by Vice President Cheney for President Karzai's inauguration. The frigid Afghan air was no match for the warmth shared by millions that day as they celebrated their first democratically elected leader in the country's long history. In a repudiation of the restrictive, repressive Taliban rule, Afghan women were given prominent roles in the ceremony. They were even allowed to sing again. Some choked back tears as they did so. A stirring sight that day was children flying kites—a practice that had been banned by the Taliban. It was a wonderful moment, filled with promise and potential, justifying what our forces had fought for.

Three months earlier, in the country's first-ever free national election, Afghans had turned out at polling stations to vote for their nation's president. There were reports that women in Bamiyan province awoke at 3:00 a.m. the day of voting. Because the Taliban had threatened to kill any women who cast ballots, they began their day with a ritual wash and cleansing as if they were preparing to die. In Konar province, the Taliban launched an attack on election day. Although it was one hundred yards from the polling place, the Afghan voters stayed in line. Not one person left.

I thought that the initial success could be attributed to the modesty of our goals. The strategy was based on the idea of letting Afghans solve Afghan problems, assisting them and amplifying their successes where we could—such as helping to build a national army and train a police force—and executing light footprint counterinsurgency operations to protect strategic towns from Taliban influence. There were fewer than fifteen thousand American troops in the country until 2004 and fewer than twenty-five thousand through 2006.[1]

Afghanistan experienced relatively few incidents of violence until the summer of 2005. Intelligence collected from around the country indicated that after the October 2004 elections, the successful vote had so demoralized the enemy that many Taliban were prepared to give up the fight. Aside from a few major engagements, such as Operation Anaconda in the spring of 2002, coalition troops skirmished with Taliban forces only occasionally. There was a visible Afghan government in place early and quickly, led by Hamid Karzai. He persuaded many former warlords to put down their arms and join his government in pursuit of an agenda of peace.[2] Afghan technocrats, many of them Western educated, advised the nation's leaders. We accelerated the buildup of the Afghan National Army (ANA) and the police force, knowing that ultimately they would need to be the ones securing their nation.[3] We encouraged the Karzai government to consolidate and build its country's institutions while recognizing that ultimately much of the state's power would be wielded by tribal leaders and power brokers at the provincial and local levels, as it had been for centuries.[4]

My position was that we were not in Afghanistan to transform a deeply conservative Islamic culture into a model of liberal modernity. We were not there to eradicate corruption or to end poppy cultivation. We were not there to take ownership of Afghanistan's problems, tempting though it was for many Americans of goodwill. Instead, Afghans would need to take charge of their own fate. Afghans would build their society the way they wanted. With our coalition allies we would assist them within reason where we were able.

Some political opponents of the administration claimed that the war in Iraq "distracted" the Bush administration from what was referred to as the "good" and "right" war in Afghanistan.[5] Yet it was precisely during the toughest period in the Iraq war that Afghanistan, with coalition help, took some of its most promising steps toward a free and better future. In my visits to the country every few months, I felt a palpable energy and excitement. Women were beginning to claim their place in society: starting businesses, serving in the parliament, and once again receiving education and medical aid. Afghan presidential and parliamentary elections in October 2004 and

September 2005 took place essentially without incident and were heralded as free and fair. A vibrant media—many dozens of radio and television stations and newspapers—was free to comment on and criticize the coalition presence and Afghanistan's new leaders. By 2006, nearly four million Afghan refugees had returned to their homeland.[6]

An Afghan "face" on the effort was enormously beneficial. Though most of the participant nations had failed to deliver fully on reconstruction pledges made at the 2001 Bonn conference, members of the international community were finding it harder to ignore the pleas of a legitimate Afghan government they had earlier offered to support. Levels of violence remained relatively low, in part because would-be insurgents seemed reluctant to challenge the popularly supported Afghan government. I did not think Afghanistan had suddenly shed centuries of ethnic strife and endemic corruption, but it did seem Afghans might be finding their way to managing their problems without our permanent assistance.

If some later contended that we never had a plan for full-fledged nation building or that we under-resourced such a plan, they were certainly correct. We did not go there to try to bring prosperity to every corner of Afghanistan. I believed—and continue to believe—that such a goal would have amounted to a fool's errand. It struck me that sending U.S. servicemen and -women in pursuit of an effort to remake Afghanistan into a prosperous American-style nation-state or to try to bring our standard of security to each of that nation's far-flung villages would be unwise, well beyond our capability, and unworthy of our troops' sacrifice.

Our more modest goal was to rid Afghanistan of al-Qaida and replace their Taliban hosts with a government that would not harbor terrorists. We were willing to let Afghan traditions and processes determine the political outcomes. Our objectives reflected a healthy sense of the limitations of what we could achieve in a country suspicious of foreign influence.

I also did not see more U.S. troops as the solution to Afghanistan's many challenges. "I am persuaded that the critical problem in Afghanistan is not really a security problem," I wrote President Bush in August 2002. "Rather, the problem that needs to be addressed is the slow progress that is being made on the civil side."[7] Hamid Karzai's government needed help building his country's institutions so he could show the Afghan people that a life of freedom offered more prosperity and security than life under the Taliban. With the exception of Afghanistan's national army, building these institutions required first and foremost assistance from the non-military departments and agencies of the

U.S. government and the coalition countries.[8] Sending more troops to the villages and valleys of Afghanistan would not resolve the country's long-term problems. In fact, they could exacerbate them by fostering resentment among a proud population and providing more targets for our enemies to attack.

The interim government of Hamid Karzai had to deal with a fundamental question of what role the nation's former warlords, the titans who had dominated Afghan politics and effectively ruled different parts of the country since the 1970s, would have in his government and in Afghanistan's future. The warlords commanded sizable militias and patronage networks that could be used in the service of an Afghan state; their considerable resources could just as well be used to tear the country apart if they decided it was in their interests to return to the civil strife of the 1980s and 1990s. A government dominated by warlords risked alienating the Afghan people, the majority of whom did not want a reprise of the lawlessness, factionalism, and brutality that had marked the previous two decades. On the other hand, Karzai could neither confront them militarily nor ignore them altogether. The result would be more internal conflict and very likely the fall of Karzai's government.

To assist the fledgling Afghan leadership, it helped that we had outstanding American leadership on the ground from 2003 to 2005, led by Ambassador Zal Khalilzad and General David Barno. Khalilzad had a charm, confidence, and casualness about him that was appealing and effective. He was a tenacious negotiator and loyal to the presidents he served. Lieutenant General Barno was the widely respected commander of the American military forces in Afghanistan. When he arrived there, Barno moved his office into the U.S. embassy in Kabul and lived in a trailer on the compound, eschewing more official trappings. Every morning Khalilzad and Barno held a country-team meeting with their senior advisers to ensure the closest possible coordination of civil and military activities across Afghanistan. This tight linkage between the State and Defense Departments was a model of how civil-military relations should work.

Khalilzad and Barno worked with Karzai to enlist the warlords' support for the central government and reached out to Afghan tribal leaders to bring security to the country's far-flung provinces. The tribes had contributed greatly to stability throughout Afghanistan's history. Most of the country was too remote and ethnically diverse to be effectively controlled by a centralized government. Though it was much different than our American notions of government, Afghanistan's tribes had been the ribcage of governance at the local level for millennia. This was one Afghan practice the United States wasn't going to change.

The agreed-upon warlord strategy called for building up the capacity of Afghan national institutions, such as the army and police. Karzai managed to rebalance his government through the selection of new personnel for key positions, broadening popular support. That strategy was successful in bringing about the disarmament and demobilization of the warlord militias and in promoting conciliation with some lower-level Taliban fighters. Karzai brought in Tajik leader Fahim Khan to head the new Ministry of Defense and Uzbek warlord Rashid Dostum as the military's chief of staff. I argued that we should train as many Afghans as we could so they could begin to take over the security responsibilities for their country.* By late 2003, there were more recruits from every ethnic group and every corner of Afghanistan signing up for spots in the Afghan National Army than there were slots to fill.

As in Iraq, there was a glaring deficiency in our training of local security forces: the police.[10] Germany had agreed to train Afghanistan's police in early 2002 at the Bonn conference. It sent forty police advisers to Kabul, which was enough to train only several hundred for the capital city.[11] In light of the modest efforts by our coalition partner, the State Department took over the effort a year later. State's Bureau of International Narcotics and Law Enforcement Affairs (INL) had the statutory responsibility for police training by the United States. Unfortunately, they lacked the resources and expertise to fulfill it and so sought help from contractors. Their eight-week basic training course did not include weapons training, and only thirty-nine hundred of the thirty-four thousand "trained" police officers had even been through the eight weeks of training.[12]

I tried to have the police training responsibilities transferred from State to Defense, where the crucial mission could be given the attention, resources, and focus it needed, and where our trainers had backgrounds in training for counterinsurgency.[13] I had worked out an agreement with Colin Powell in 2004, only to have his turf-conscious deputy scuttle it with the Senate Foreign Relations Committee.[14] Without a viable Afghan police force, U.S. forces

*There were persuasive arguments in 2002 and 2003 that the total number of the Afghan National Army be kept below seventy thousand, in that estimates indicated that the Afghan government would not be able to pay the annual costs for an army of a larger size. There was also little violence across the country.[9]

would be taking on the policing duties at an inordinately high cost in taxpayer dollars and American lives.[15] I wrote to NSC Adviser Steve Hadley:

> It is costing the US taxpayers a fortune as long as the US, instead of the Afghans, continues to provide for Afghan security. . . . I don't think it is responsible to the American taxpayers to leave it like it is. We need a way forward. I've worked on it and worked on it. I am about to conclude that it is not possible for the US Government bureaucracy to do the only sensible thing. If anyone has an idea as to what can be done about it, I'd like to hear it. I'm ready to toss in the towel. The only solution I can see is to fashion an old-time decision memo and have the President decide it. If that is necessary, please draft the memo; or, if you prefer not to do it, tell me and I'll do it.[16]

Months later, I was finally able to get permission for the Defense Department to assume responsibility for the police training. Over the next two years, we invested more than $1.5 billion in the mission.[17] An institutional fix to the underlying problem took even longer—over the continued objections of some in the State Department bureaucracy and members of congressional oversight committees who did not want to relinquish budgetary control over their failing State Department foreign police training programs.[18] It was not until January 2006 that we managed to realign our country's authorities for training foreign forces when Congress passed Section 1206 of the National Defense Authorization Act.*

On the military side of our coalition effort, General Barno and Ambassador Khalilzad recommended shifting the strategic emphasis from counterterrorism to counterinsurgency, since most of the remaining al-Qaida and Taliban had fled into the tribal areas of Pakistan.[20] Our forces would still pursue terrorists when and where they found them, but coalition forces would move to strategically located outposts in key population centers outside of Kabul and the main base at Bagram airfield to help to defend the population from enemy infiltration and intimidation. This approach to counterinsurgency didn't require tens of thousands of U.S. troops. It used Afghan army and police to bolster the small American presence and the twenty-two Provincial Reconstruction Teams (PRT) we had established, supposedly com-

*Though initially section 1206 was granted as a "special contingency authority" and a "pilot program," the Obama administration and Defense Secretary Robert Gates have continued to support and defend the law, although some continue to fight a rearguard action against it.[19]

prised of experts from different agencies and bureaus of the U.S. government. The PRT was a well-conceived idea. It was a decentralized way of enabling Americans to work with local Afghan (and Iraqi) leaders on reconstruction projects—but the teams proved difficult to staff with the needed non-military experts able to help Afghans in agriculture, education, civil society, and building local government institutions. Ninety-eight percent of the U.S. contingent in our PRTs ended up being military personnel.*

In June 2005, the tours of Khalilzad and Barno were over. Khalilzad was sent to Baghdad to become the new U.S. ambassador there. Five months before Khalilizad's departure, I had asked the President that I be involved in the decision on his replacement. Typically deciding on diplomatic representation was a matter between the White House and the State Department, but to my thinking, Afghanistan was a different matter given the Defense Department's deep involvement there. "We suffered not getting Zal in earlier than we did," I wrote, referring to the unfortunate selection of Khalilzad's predecessor, a career Foreign Service officer who had had little success in advancing the political process for much of 2002 and 2003. "We need to have someone who can carry [Khalilzad's] level of representation forward without a hitch."[22]

For forty-five days after Khalilzad left Kabul for Baghdad, the United States was without an ambassador in Afghanistan. Rice and the State Department eventually announced the selection of Ronald Neumann, a career Foreign Service officer, to replace Khalilzad, without any discussion with the Defense Department. I expressed my displeasure to Steve Hadley.[23] In the months after Khalilzad's departure, ominous signs began to appear on the horizon.

By early 2006, a reorganized Taliban insurgency had emerged in Afghanistan's east and south. Increasing numbers of Taliban fighters traveled into Afghanistan from Pakistan and retreated back across the border whenever coalition forces tried to engage them. It was likely the Taliban would be mounting an offensive in the summer months of 2006 against coalition and Afghan forces.

Disturbed, I asked Dr. Marin Strmecki, an erudite and longtime student of Afghanistan whose previous analysis in the Pentagon's policy shop had impressed me, to return to the country on a fact-finding mission in early spring and report back to me.[24] That August, Strmecki briefed me. He didn't sugarcoat anything. The bottom line, he told me, was we faced a "deteriorating

* By August 2006, after a major effort, the percentage of non-military personnel in the Afghan PRTs had increased from 2 percent to a disappointing 3 percent.[21]

security situation" caused by a Taliban escalation and weak or bad governance in southern Afghanistan that created "a vacuum of power into which the enemy moved."[25] The Taliban had in fact created a shadow government in towns across southern Afghanistan. If we did nothing, it was possible that the southern city of Kandahar could return to Taliban control.

I made an effort to get Strmecki's report circulated around the administration and encouraged my colleagues to get his briefing. As I noted in a memo to Vice President Cheney and Steve Hadley, "Given the new level of the insurgency there, [Strmecki] has a new strategy for Afghanistan, which I think merits our careful thought and attention."[26] After four years of relative dormancy, the Taliban was poised to mount a serious offensive. Strmecki's recommendation was that if we were to meet the Taliban's escalation, we needed to mount a counterescalation. It would "not require more U.S. or international military forces but does require new diplomatic initiatives vis-à-vis Pakistan, renewed energy and urgency in shaping the U.S. partnership with the Afghan government, and more resources for security and development programs," Strmecki advised.[27]

The central problem was the sanctuary Pakistan provided for the insurgents. I had repeatedly pressed Pakistani President Pervez Musharraf on the issue. Pakistan's largely autonomous western regions were home to many Islamist radicals, some influential in its government's intelligence organization—the ISI—and the military. The thought of Pakistan's nuclear arsenal falling under the control of Islamist extremists or their terrorist allies was nightmarish.

We were also still working to dispel the suspicions that many Pakistanis and their leaders had about the United States, after our Congress had imposed damaging sanctions on their country in the 1990s. Our job was to rebuild the relationships between our two countries to win Pakistani cooperation against al-Qaida and Islamist terrorists and help reduce their nuclear tensions with India.

We had seen some hopeful signs. We successfully pressured Pakistan to shut down its nuclear proliferation operation run by A. Q. Khan, widely regarded as the father of the Pakistani nuclear bomb. Musharraf's government had been helpful in providing intelligence on senior al-Qaida operatives. With Pakistani intelligence, we often mounted sensitive special operations missions into their territory and conducted UAV drone strikes against terrorist targets. Musharraf had ordered Pakistani forces into western Pakistan to attack Taliban and al-Qaida strongholds and, as a result, lost hundreds of his soldiers.

To be sure, Pakistan was less forthcoming with intelligence on the Taliban networks in the country. Some in the Pakistani intelligence services believed they needed to fund and train the Taliban as a hedge against Indian influence in Afghanistan. Musharraf had made some unhelpful truces and arrangements with governors in western Pakistan, which had the effect of allowing the Taliban to regroup. It was clear by 2006 that the Taliban sanctuaries in Pakistan were directly contributing to an insurgency and the destabilization of neighboring Afghanistan.

To blunt the insurgency, I had concluded we needed to expand and accelerate the Afghan National Army well beyond the seventy thousand troops originally planned. Lieutenant General Karl Eikenberry, the commander who had replaced David Barno, had recommended we cut back the size of the ANA to fifty thousand in the fall of 2005, but we soon reversed the decision. I was disappointed to learn that Eikenberry had moved his military headquarters out of the U.S. embassy in Kabul, reversing the close civil-military linkage that Barno and Khalilzad had forged.

Strmecki recommended we develop a "multi-year COIN [counterinsurgency] plan" utilizing Afghan troops to defend key towns and villages against Taliban infiltration.[28] "While the past three years have seen progressive improvements in the counterinsurgency techniques of the Coalition, there are opportunities to undertake additional innovations," Strmecki wrote.[29] Without deploying tens of thousands of U.S. military forces, we could use a parallel structure of civil, nonmilitary support teams to help Afghans stabilize their towns and villages, offering viable livelihoods rather than succumbing to the Taliban. This of course would require yet another effort, building on our earlier attempts, to get other departments and agencies of our federal government to send support teams of civilian experts.

I had sought to increase the NATO alliance's involvement in Afghanistan to lessen the burden on our troops as well. Eventually all of the alliance's forces were placed under one command—the International Security Assistance Force (ISAF) led by an American general—to achieve an integrated effort.[30] It was a major step for NATO that promised a new relevance for the Alliance in the twenty-first century.

Giving NATO a leading role in Afghanistan was not without its challenges. One was that NATO, though a military alliance, operates as a committee by consensus, and it's difficult to conduct a war by committee. The command arrangements between NATO headquarters in Brussels, ISAF headquarters in Kabul, and the different commanders across the country were complex. NATO military forces were also under widely differing instructions from their home governments. If fired on, some forces could only engage in defensive maneuvers. Though I had hoped that NATO's involvement would bring in more international contributions for Afghan reconstruction, it became a pattern for President Karzai to be promised more assistance than he received from the international community.

Most Afghan ministries were not getting the experts and staff support they needed from the State Department and other U.S. agencies.[31] While I respected those who did volunteer to deploy, the staff at the embassy tended to be junior in both age and experience. Moreover, their tours were often too short for them to learn enough to make a substantial contribution. For example, four of the nine political and economic positions in the embassy during Khalilzad's tenure in Afghanistan were left vacant.[32]

In cabinet meetings I asked all of the departments to expedite sending the people we needed. While there were never enough civilian experts, those who did go to Afghanistan and Iraq contributed greatly to the coalition effort. Nonetheless, military officials complained frequently that other government departments were letting them down. On one occasion, when lawmakers came to the White House to meet with President Bush and the NSC, they inquired about the modest numbers of Foreign Service officers being sent to Iraq and Afghanistan. Rice responded that she did not have the power to compel Foreign Service officers to serve in Iraq and Afghanistan. The Secretary of State technically does have the authority to send Foreign Service officers wherever the President deems necessary. However, as Rice pointed out, there was considerable opposition within the career ranks against her using that authority. Military officers expected to be deployed to war zones, which was not the case in our civilian departments or agencies. It was disturbing that we were spending billions of dollars to provide security, but we could not properly staff the U.S. embassy with the needed civilian advisers.

In a meeting on May 26, 2006, President Bush called the NSC together to try to increase civilian support for our efforts in Iraq and Afghanistan. Rice updated us on the numbers of Foreign Service officers who were going to Iraq. The number was below what had been expected and well below what had been promised. General Casey, speaking from Iraq on secure video, remarked that the number of diplomats was inadequate.[33]

Rice, who was unaccustomed to being questioned in front of the President, took issue. "You're out of line, General!" she snapped.[34] This was the first time in the nearly six years I had been in the Bush administration that this type of underlying tension between State and Defense had boiled to the surface in an NSC meeting. I told Rice that if she thought a general officer needed calibration, she should tell me and I would attend to it if I agreed.

In the Situation Room, discussion would often turn to which needed to come first: security or the diplomatic and economic tracks. Defense officials sought more political and economic progress. Officials from State would express concerns about the security situation. The reality was that all three—security, diplomacy, and the economy—had to be closely linked. If progress was absent in one, the others would be hindered. But from the Defense Department's standpoint, we knew that while our military would not lose a battle, it was also true that we could not win strategic success by military means alone, particularly in irregular warfare and counterinsurgency.[35] Because of the various committee and subcommittee jurisdictions, Congress hampered our ability to engage more non-military support in Iraq and Afghanistan. Our non-military institutions were bound by outdated regulations and statutes, slowed by bureaucratic inertia, and in large measure kept away from the action by a government culture that did not promote and reward individuals willing to deploy abroad.

There were encouraging signs of progress alongside harbingers that the real fight for Afghanistan's future was yet to come. With an elected government under Karzai, the Afghan people were taking charge of their destiny. NATO was involved with thousands of troops on peacekeeping, security, and reconstruction missions.

At the same time, there was a growing awareness of a threat to the nascent stability we had strived to create. The Taliban had established strongholds in Pakistan. They were quietly infiltrating Afghan towns and villages along the border. Still, my efforts to turn the NSC's attention to Afghanistan in 2006 were only marginally successful, as Afghanistan still seemed to be going reasonably well—at least in contrast to Iraq—and was gaining far less notice in the media.[36] Nonetheless, I was concerned that we were missing opportunities to consolidate the successes that had been achieved—missed opportunities that could prove costly later. If left unchallenged, the Taliban could threaten the stability of the region and again welcome terrorists into areas under their control. Given our country's inability to adequately staff the embassy and the civilian support teams to buttress any fragile victories over a new, aggressive Taliban enemy, the glass was looking half empty. As daunting as our challenges in Afghanistan were, by the spring of 2006 Iraq teetered on the edge of something even darker.

CHAPTER 48

Iraq's Summer of Violence

By the spring of 2006, al-Qaida had seized the initiative in Iraq. Iraqis were not yet ready to stanch the sectarian bloodshed that the Golden Dome mosque bombing had instigated. Terrorists and death squads had gained an advantage in a number of cities. Some 80 percent of terrorist attacks were concentrated in five of the country's eighteen provinces, with a particular focus on Baghdad.[1] Insurgents coerced children to don suicide vests and detonate themselves in marketplaces. Uncooperative tribal sheikhs would find their relatives beheaded. Spectacular attacks dominated newscasts across the world. War-weary Iraqis, understandably anxious about their future, expressed frustration with coalition efforts and with the quality of their own political leadership.

Grim stories of violence were prominent in the American media and cast a pall across our country—a pall made all the darker by increasing U.S. casualties. By July 2006, two thousand members of our military had been killed in attacks by the enemy in Iraq—IEDs, ambushes, sniper fire among the most deadly. Another nineteen thousand had suffered combat-related injuries. There was a widespread, if inaccurate, perception in America and around the world that the United States had lost Iraq. A growing number in Congress called for a full-scale reassessment of our strategy in Iraq. Some were trying to end the war by cutting off funds for the troops. Others were moving toward a policy they misleadingly called a "redeployment of forces." I had heard that euphemism before about Lebanon in 1984. It meant retreat.

Abu Musab al-Zarqawi, the top al-Qaida leader in Iraq, released a series of audiotapes hoping to rally Muslims to his cause. He castigated the United States and Israel. On one tape he claimed credit for the 2003 murder of the UN envoy to Iraq, Sergio Vieira de Mello.[2] It was widely believed that he had personally beheaded two Americans who fell into al-Qaida's custody—Nicholas Berg and Eugene Armstrong. The U.S. offered $25 million for information leading to his capture, equal to the price being offered for the capture of Bin Laden. Zarqawi had become public enemy number one in Iraq.

When there was every reason for pessimism, it was the determination and commitment of the troops that convinced me that Iraq was not lost to the forces of extremism. Even in the days after the Golden Mosque bombing in Samarra, the troops saw opportunity where many outside observers saw defeat. Samarra forced us to challenge our assumptions about the path we were on. Over the next months, we redoubled our efforts to stabilize the situation and counter the impression our forces might have to withdraw in defeat.

Like the troops under his command, President Bush was not one to quit. His doggedness sometimes could be mistaken for stubbornness, but that tenacity almost singlehandedly avoided the perils associated with the United States losing a major war for a second time in our history. Bush knew time was running out for a successful resolution in Iraq—the American people were losing patience. In one poll, only 44 percent had confidence that we could leave behind a stable Iraqi government. More than 80 percent believed Iraq was engulfed in a civil war.[3]

Bush was not looking for some face-saving gesture that would allow America to bow out gracefully, as some in the administration were recommending. He did not want to "play for a tie" in Iraq, as he told us periodically. A tie would mean defeat in the long run.

In one of Zarqawi's blustering audio tapes, the al-Qaida in Iraq leader vowed that "Bush will not enjoy peace of mind and that his army will not have a good life as long as our hearts are beating."[4] In another tape in April 2006, two months after the Samarra mosque bombing, Zarqawi confidently predicted, "The enemy is failing."[5]

Six weeks later, the United States military begged to differ.

On June 7, I was in Brussels for NATO ministerial meetings when I was summoned by an aide for a secure call with General Casey. My first thought was to brace myself for more bad news from Iraq. As I sat in a small communications tent that kept conversations secure, Casey told me that the terrorist we had sought more than anyone else in Iraq was dead.

Two U.S. Air Force F-16s had dropped five-hundred-pound bombs on an al-Qaida safe house near Baqubah. Through a combination of special operations raids, a highly classified signals intelligence operation, and successful interrogations, our Special Forces had zeroed in on the leader of al-Qaida in Iraq.[6] We had been closing in on Zarqawi for weeks, and over the previous year had kept the President apprised of the latest developments in our hunt for him.[7] Lieutenant General Stan McChrystal, the commander of our special operations forces in Iraq, personally went into the bombed-out building to verify that Zarqawi had in fact been killed.[8] McChrystal saw the mortally wounded Zarqawi pulled out of the rubble before he died a short time later. My senior military assistant Vice Admiral Jim Stavridis informed me that we had confirmation of the kill through fingerprinting at the scene.

Zarqawi's death coincided with another piece of good news. After five months of frustrating delays, the Iraqi government of Prime Minister Nouri al-Maliki had finally selected a minister of defense and a minister of the interior, the two most important cabinet posts. Zarqawi, perhaps more than anyone, had kept Iraqis from progressing toward a civil society. It was fitting that upon his death the new Iraqi political leadership had taken another key step forward.

With its leader now dead, al-Qaida in Iraq was thrown into a period of confusion as its lieutenants struggled to fill the empty leadership mantle. Attacks seemed to have come to a temporary lull, though we were not under the illusion that the insurgency had permanently abated.

On June 12, the President summoned members of the National Security Council to Camp David to discuss the Iraq strategy for the period ahead. He would be departing for meetings in Baghdad the next day. He properly projected determination in his public statements, but in his private meetings Bush was questioning and probing. It was clear he was concerned about the trend lines in Iraq. So was I.

We were joined in a secure videoconference by the new ambassador to Iraq, Zalmay Khalilzad, who had succeeded John Negroponte in Baghdad. While we sorely missed his leadership in Afghanistan, I was pleased to have him in Iraq, where he forged an effective partnership with Casey. In regular videoconferences, Khalilzad kept us apprised of the coalescing government that would be our partner against the insurgency. In our private meetings, however, one could see that Khalilzad and Casey—two individuals not prone to pessimism—were growing weary. The daily cajoling and coaxing of Iraqi officials to take action as their capital city became the epicenter of what was approaching a campaign of ethnic cleansing had taken its toll. The new Iraqi leaders were not feckless or unconcerned about their country—they would agree to approve coalition military actions and robust security measures if prodded. But they weren't George Washingtons either.

A senior public official confronts a test when presented with setbacks in a war. I had seen unconvincing overconfidence from Lyndon Johnson when the Vietnam War started to turn in 1966, and we certainly didn't want to repeat that performance. The President and I saw it as our jobs to balance our concerns with what progress we saw, but without sounding like Pollyanna. If a broad majority in a democracy loses faith in the effort—and there was no mistaking in 2006 that Americans were losing confidence—it cannot be sustained.

As we gathered at Camp David for the June 12 NSC meeting, it was increasingly clear that despite Zarqawi's death, the sectarian strife had not abated and insurgents seemed determined to wage more spectacular attacks. In light of this and the weakening support at home, Bush wanted to discuss any and all available alternatives. I supported that fully.

Abizaid and Casey argued to continue a steady drawdown of our forces. Even after a rise of violence in Iraq that year, their aim was to continue reducing American forces as Iraqi security forces stood up. I too was reluctant to place still more of the burdens in Iraq on Americans rather than on the Iraqis themselves.

Another option discussed at Camp David was the State Department's proposal to draw forces out of Baghdad and major cities, and in effect out of conflict. The idea amounted to letting the sectarian bloodshed work itself out on the theory that American soldiers should not be drawn into an Iraqi civil war. Rice advocated this approach on the grounds that sectarian violence was an Iraqi problem and the Iraqis had to confront it. There was some logic to it, but the State Department approach seemed to be a path toward a staged withdrawal not dissimilar from our departure from Vietnam. There was one important difference: The ascendant Viet Cong and North Vietnamese would not follow us home. If we left Iraq to al-Qaida, we would be certain to have consequences at home with a greater likelihood of terrorist attacks in our cities.

There was another possibility: a counterinsurgency strategy that would put Iraqis in the lead. At the Camp David meeting, we discussed a proposal suggested by Michael Vickers, a former Army Special Forces officer. Vickers had worked for the CIA where he had played a role in arming the Afghan resistance to the Soviet Union.* Prior to the Camp David meeting, Vickers had prepared a memo for the President. "One of the many paradoxes of modern counterinsurgency," Vickers wrote, "is that less is often more." He argued, as Abizaid had, that a successful strategy emphasized intelligence, the "discriminate use of force," a focus on building popular support for the government, protecting the local population, and placing an emphasis on political reconciliation—including amnesty and rehabilitation for insurgents. In contrast, he argued that counterinsurgency strategies that focused on "large-scale sweep and kill-capture operations" without emphasizing building up indigenous capacity to fight the enemy tended to be unsuccessful.

Noting that insurgencies are "protracted contests of wills," Vickers' paper stated that the problem we had faced over the most recent three years in Iraq was that "we have pursued a direct approach to counterinsurgency that has eroded American public support for the war (our center of gravity) more than it has reduced Iraqi support for the insurgency (our enemy's center of gravity)." As a result, he noted, the insurgency had grown. Increasing force levels, he argued to the President, was "highly unlikely to be decisive." Insurgents would still control the initiative, and could always temporarily decline to fight. Instead, he considered it "imperative" to shift to an indirect approach, requiring that we "begin and continue the drawdown of U.S. forces while the insurgency is still raging." Our emphasis, instead, should be on providing "additional resources for Iraqi security forces," including an increase in U.S. advisers.[9]

I found the Vickers proposal to be persuasive, including his emphasis on accelerating the pace at which we put Iraqis in the lead. When I had visited with Iraqi officials over the previous months, they told me that the presence of American forces in Iraqi cities had not been helpful and they should be reduced.[10]

* Some weeks later I recruited Vickers to come to the Pentagon as the assistant secretary of defense for special operations and low-intensity conflict; he remained in the post and became undersecretary of defense for intelligence during the Obama administration.

I sent the Vickers memorandum around the Department of Defense to gauge the reactions of key personnel.[11] The response was positive. Abizaid expressed a note of caution on troop drawdowns, saying that "the art in all of this is to reduce US forces at a rate that is neither too fast nor too slow." I forwarded Abizaid's memorandum to the President.[12]

After the Camp David discussions that June, the President didn't indicate which way he was inclined to go on Iraq. A month later, as sectarian violence increased again, we had another NSC meeting, this time in the White House Roosevelt Room. The mood was downbeat. Khalilzad and Casey had ugly statistics to report.

"The violence is now focused on civilians," Khalilzad said.

"Death squads were responsible for 230 deaths last week, with 200 in Baghdad alone. The Iraqi government is not enforcing the law against the militias," Casey added. Over the past month, sixteen hundred bodies, 90 percent believed to be from executions, had been taken to the Baghdad coroner's office.[13] Iraqi Prime Minister Nouri al-Maliki was seen as giving tacit support to the Shia death squads. Maliki was even lobbying for some of Muqtada al-Sadr's captured lieutenants, known to be responsible for the death squads, to be released from U.S. custody. We declined his request and in fact had directed McChrystal to have U.S. special operations forces target and capture the facilitators of the death squads, some of whom had ties to Iran.

Maliki would be making his first visit to the United States the following week, and it would be a chance for all of us to make clear the gravity of the situation. He needed to understand that if he failed to root out the Shia sectarians that had infiltrated the security forces and upper levels of his government and did not pursue reconciliation with alienated Sunnis, his country would continue to burn. His countrymen had not selected him to watch the country descend into a civil war. History—and the Iraqi electorate—would not be kind to a leader who appeared oblivious to the plight of his people.

President Bush responded, "Last week Maliki was claiming that he wanted to crack down but that U.S. military forces wouldn't let him. If Maliki tries to lay this off on us, it will be an unpleasant visit for him."[14] Maliki knew his claims were untrue. Casey and Abizaid had made clear their desire to pursue the sectarian militias. The obstacle was Maliki's government, which was even considering bringing some of the rogue militias directly into the Iraqi security forces.[15]

Three days later I talked with Khalilzad, Abizaid, and Casey by a secure videoconference. Our military operations seemed to be having little impact on the growing sectarian violence. "Are we at an inflection point?" I asked. "If we are, it's helpful to consider the alternatives." I raised a number of ideas that might change the worsening dynamics that appeared to be approaching a tipping point. Could we just let Iraqis separate themselves and stand aside? Could we "side" with the Iraqi Sunnis or Shia instead of being caught in the middle? Could we deploy an additional number of U.S. forces? Would they be able to stanch the sectarian bloodletting?

Abizaid responded, "The level of violence isn't the measure of success. We have to make this point."[16] He didn't want the enemy dictating the terms of battle. They could easily increase their savagery. He thought there were better ways to measure progress: The intelligence cooperation we were getting from local Iraqis, electricity production, the number of Iraqi troops and police we were training, the number of provinces turned over to Iraqi control, and the like.[17]

In August 2006, Casey told General Pace and me that he thought we needed to put more troops into Baghdad in an attempt to curb the sectarian killings. He thought the best way to increase troops temporarily was to not only deploy new units to Iraq, but to extend the yearlong tour of the 172nd Stryker Brigade by three or four months. Strykers are armored patrol vehicles, light enough to conduct operations in cities and armored enough to defend against gunfire and some roadside bombs. The four thousand men and women of the 172nd had done a superb job in securing Mosul. General Casey now needed them in Baghdad.*

I decided to fly to Fort Wainwright in Fairbanks, Alaska, where the 172nd Stryker Brigade was based. My unpleasant task was to explain to the spouses why their loved ones would not be coming home from Iraq when they had been scheduled to. They had been due back in mere days. Some members of the unit had already returned to prepare for the brigade's homecoming and were themselves now going back to Iraq.

Before I had left for Alaska, I was told by senior Army officials that they

*I let General Casey know that "the late request to keep the Stryker Brigade in Iraq has been unfortunate. . . . We have to do a better job looking around corners to the extent it is humanly possible." Casey responded that he agreed. "As I mentioned to you on the VTC, I tried very hard not to extend them," Casey continued. "But as the security situation in Baghdad continued to deteriorate, it became apparent to us in our planning that the Iraqi Security Forces and Government did not have the ability to make a decisive impact on the Baghdad situation in the near term without more help from us. Extending the Strykers became an opportunity to make a decisive impact in Baghdad at a critical point for the new government and in our mission."[18]

had talked with the families and explained the situation to them. As I learned when I arrived, that was not the case. They had only talked by video teleconference to a few of the senior officers' spouses. In fact, I would be the first Pentagon official to meet personally with these understandably disappointed and in some cases angry family members. As I headed to the base from the airport, "WELCOME HOME" signs dotted the road—signs that now were sadly premature. I then went to meet some eight hundred family members who were gathered in a gymnasium.

I explained the reasons behind the rare extension. General Casey had told me he needed more troops in Iraq at this time. "It's something we don't want to do, but in this case we had to," I told them. One woman asked me to wear a green bracelet she had braided until her husband came home. I kept it on my left wrist until that December, when the last of the 172nd Stryker Brigade finally made it home to Alaska.[19] I still have it to this day.

After brief remarks I opened it up for questions from the audience. Some emotionally expressed their deep disappointment that their family members would not be coming home when they had been told; most were polite, surprisingly so. I knew it was a terrible disappointment for all of them. Everyone in the large gymnasium had endured a year of waiting and praying for the safe return of their loved ones.

After taking questions, I stayed for a long time visiting personally with the military families. As I was about to leave, a woman from behind me whispered in my ear, "You have to have big brass ones to come in here and face this crowd." Amused, I turned and saw she was smiling, too.

In September 2006, a sensational press report fueled the calls for withdrawal from Iraq. Citing an August 2006 Marine intelligence report, an article in the *Washington Post* claimed that the Iraqi province of Anbar, a Sunni-majority area on Iraq's western border, was "lost" to the enemy. "[T]he prospects for securing that country's western Anbar province are dim. . . . There is almost nothing the U.S. military can do to improve the political and social situation there," it concluded.[20] The notion that terrorists had won a part of Iraq was the psychological equivalent of reporting that parts of postwar Germany were lost and would remain under the control of the Nazis.

What the author of the misguided article ignored was that the report the article cited was being overtaken by events on the ground. The Sunnis in Anbar province were turning against the Baathist-jihadist axis and seeking a new way forward for Iraq's Sunni minority. In fact, six months before the article appeared, General Casey had briefed the President that "Anbarites are tired of violence," and a wedge existed between the Sunni resistance groups and al-Qaida in Iraq.[21] We had been working assiduously over 2006 to expand and exploit those differences. By late summer, the efforts were beginning to bear fruit.

Since 2003, I had encouraged our military and the CPA to form alliances with local tribal leaders, particularly as part of an outreach effort to Sunnis.[22] Abizaid was an early and consistent advocate of approaching the Sunnis with financial and other assistance. And as early as 2005, Sunni tribal sheikhs in parts of Iraq formed alliances with our military to take on the jihadists, most of them non-Iraqis, who had established roots in some Sunni cities and neighborhoods. In post-Saddam Iraq, many Sunnis had until that point pursued a strategy of allying with foreign jihadists to kill Shia, create maximum disorder, and hope to ultimately drive out the impatient Americans. The theory was that the Sunnis would inherit the chaos and restore themselves to power.

But Iraq's Sunnis were contemplating a major change in their strategy just as our military commanders were pursuing new tactics. In late 2005, our commanders had brought to bear new counterinsurgency tactics and forged alliances with Sunni tribal leaders in the western cities of Tal Afar and Qaim.[23] Enterprising colonels such as H. R. McMaster and Sean MacFarland were forging new operational techniques and tactics and applying the art of counterinsurgency.[24] U.S. troops were clearing neighborhoods infiltrated with insurgents and al-Qaida. They held the ground until Iraqi security forces were sufficiently capable of maintaining security. The yields were impressive in a part of Iraq that many had written off to the enemy.

Though the terrorists often invoked the lessons of Vietnam and Lebanon, they did not heed all of them. Unlike other successful insurgency movements, al-Qaida in Iraq and its many affiliated organizations did not offer the Iraqis the promise of a better life. Instead, they offered the Iraqi people brutality and terror. Their approach was to bully and intimidate the local people into submission. Al-Qaida's vision was a kind of nihilism cloaked in the trappings of a twisted version of their religion.

The local population had an opportunity to see the kind of a future that al-Qaida would offer them and the rest of Iraq. Iraq's Sunnis recognized the need to break with the Islamist insurgency and to seek the protection U.S. forces could provide from their violence-obsessed former allies in al-Qaida and from the retribution of Iraq's Shia. The barbaric behavior of al-Qaida and its affiliated organizations had frayed their relations with Sunni tribes. Al-Qaida members were skilled in the arts of intimidation: They would "marry"—an al-Qaida euphemism for sexual assault—local women, push tribes off their land, and seize profitable activities traditionally under tribal purview. Rather than integrating with the Sunni tribes, al-Qaida sought to colonize Iraq's western provinces and turn them into the "Islamic State of Iraq." Raising revenues through smuggling and extortion, al-Qaida achieved tribal acquiescence by kidnapping, torturing, and murdering the tribal leaders and their families who stood in their way.

So in August 2006, even as some in the media were mistakenly proclaiming Anbar "lost" to the enemy, our military was actively negotiating with tribal sheikhs for them to turn against al-Qaida and join the side of the Iraqi government and our forces. In Anbar's capital of Ramadi, Army officers were establishing small outposts in the heart of enemy territory, enduring fierce enemy fire in the process. They pressed ahead on reconstruction projects and began crafting deals with the local sheikhs. If the sheikhs encouraged tribal members to join the police, Army commanders agreed to let them protect their own localities. Police recruits tripled in both June and in July. In August alone, there were close to one thousand new recruits.[25]

Part of the reason Sunni sheikhs were willing to change sides was their growing understanding that our forces would stay in Iraq only as long as necessary. In September 2006, a fledgling movement among Iraqi tribal sheikhs around Ramadi was starting to take shape, which became known as "the Awakening."[26] By October 2006, we were briefing the President on the Anbar tribal leaders leading the resistance.[27] And by the end of 2006, this alliance, also called "the Sons of Iraq," was one hundred thousand strong. The Sons of Iraq took the lead in reclaiming Anbar province for the Iraqi people and in driving al-Qaida out.

Unquestionably, the rise of this movement was an essential factor in the later turnaround in Iraq. But there was still another significant change afoot.

As calls for a fundamental reassessment of the Iraq strategy grew louder, former vice chief of the Army, retired General Jack Keane, came to visit me on the afternoon of Tuesday, September 19, 2006. He got right to the point. Violence in Iraq was spiraling upward. The American people were fed up and ready to get out. He did not think Generals Abizaid and Casey were sufficiently aware of the gravity of the situation and how perilously close the nation was to withdrawing its support.

Though I didn't share with Keane our internal deliberations or my discussions with the President, his thoughts largely dovetailed with mine. What we were doing in Iraq was not working well enough or fast enough. This also was not the first time I had heard the suggestion that Abizaid and Casey should come home. General Pace and I already had been giving thought to their replacements. Casey had originally gone to Iraq on a twelve-month tour, and he had agreed to stay for two six-month extensions. Abizaid had already come to me and told me he believed we needed, as he put it, "fresh eyes" on the situation. As early as June 2006, Pace and I had begun discussing with the President potential candidates for both positions.*

No one on the National Security Council or Joint Chiefs of Staff had recommended to me that either Abizaid or Casey should be removed. Nor were there even suggestions from anyone on the NSC that they were doing a poor job. To the contrary, by autumn 2006, the President was making a strong pitch to keep Abizaid working for him and had offered Abizaid a post in the White House to oversee the war on terror after he left CENTCOM. Bush also was considering Abizaid for director of national intelligence. As the wheels were in motion to replace Abizaid and Casey, perhaps by assigning them to new duties, Pace, Vice Chairman Ed Giambastiani, Deputy Secretary Gordon England, and I had narrowed the short list of replacements for Casey to Lieutenant Generals David Petraeus, Stan McChrystal, Pete Chiarelli, and Martin Dempsey. For CENTCOM commander, we were considering McChrystal, Chiarelli, and Dempsey.

In one Friday morning meeting on October 20, with Pace and Eric Edelman, the undersecretary of defense for policy, and Abizaid and Casey reporting via secure video teleconference, there were signs that there was little new thinking about our course of action. With an NSC meeting at the White House scheduled for the following morning, I wanted us prepared to answer the President's likely questions. He had been growing impatient. Again I raised the possibility of deploying more troops into Iraq. I asked Abizaid and Casey if that could help stem the violence.

"If we put another division into Baghdad it could actually be more damaging," Casey responded. By Casey's logic, someone could reasonably ask if we needed to reduce our forces. That didn't seem like the right course of action,

*Some analysts and pundits cited Lincoln's decision to remove General McClellan as a template for President Bush. The analogy was flawed. Lincoln had given orders to McClellan that McClellan refused to obey. He was insubordinate to the commander in chief. That was certainly not the case in Iraq. Abizaid and Casey were not defying President Bush. They were carrying out a policy that the President, General Pace, the Joint Chiefs of Staff, and I had supported. The generals offered us their best advice and the President and I took it.

so I asked, "General, if that's true, would pulling one division out of Baghdad be helpful?"[28]

He responded that he believed that with some fifteen thousand U.S. troops in Baghdad we had the right number. Two months earlier, we had sent more than five thousand additional U.S. troops and more than six thousand Iraqi troops into the capital as part of Operation Together Forward II to curb the violence across the city. The operation had yielded few visible dividends. Frustration with the lack of progress was growing within the Pentagon and the administration. With the declining public confidence in the war, the Commander in Chief was readying a different plan—one that would involve a new strategy with new generals and a new secretary of defense.

CHAPTER 49

Farewells

Personnel changes occur in every presidential administration. Some are by mutual consent, some are not. By the fall of 2006, only two of George W. Bush's original cabinet members remained: Secretary of Labor Elaine Chao and me. I had tried to resign twice in the wake of the abuse at Abu Ghraib, but President Bush had opposed my leaving. At his insistence that I stay in 2004, I had acquiesced, but in the months that followed, I became increasingly convinced that I should have left.

The start of the President's second term in 2005 was a natural transition point, a time for new beginnings and an opportunity to take a fresh look at his national security policies. But President Bush may have felt uncomfortable changing both his secretary of defense and his secretary of state in a time of war. I too felt obligated to remain if the President wanted me to do so. I thought it would be almost unpatriotic to resign from the Department when we had so many troops engaged abroad and over the President's request that I stay. I knew our troops couldn't walk away from their jobs. I felt reluctant to walk away from mine.

In the spring of 2006 another flap erupted when a small group of retired generals called for me to step down. A few of the most vocal seemed to align themselves with the Democrats, speaking out against the invasion and appearing before what was billed as a Senate "oversight hearing"—in actuality, a partisan forum set up on Capitol Hill by some Senate Democrats and opponents of the President.[1] At least two called for the election of Democrats in the November general election.[2]

The most curious aspect of the retired generals' grievances was that I didn't listen to the advice of the military.[3] I met with military leaders constantly and routinely deferred to those on the battlefield for making decisions on everything from troop levels to how to pursue insurgents. There were many times when the decisions on the ground didn't seem right—such as the first battle of Fallujah—but I took pains to try not to micromanage with the proverbial five-thousand-mile screwdriver. I encouraged generals to form their own relationships with the President. The senior military had been given ample opportunity to express their views to the President, even if those views might have differed from mine. Indeed, I thought that a more accurate criticism would have been that I too often deferred to the views, opinions, and decisions of the generals who were in charge.

I took heart that those I worked closely with were supportive. General Myers, who had retired as chairman of the Joint Chiefs of Staff, came to my defense, as did Generals Mike DeLong, Tommy Franks, and others.[4] Still, the idea of retired generals publicly calling for the removal of a sitting secretary of defense was troubling. With notable exceptions, most military officers avoided becoming politicized after leaving active duty. I knew President Bush would not favor a precedent whereby a handful of disgruntled retired officers could determine who the elected President of the United States had as secretary of defense. Indeed, President Bush proclaimed himself "the decider" on the subject and announced I would stay on.[5]

By the summer of 2006, with declining public support for the Iraq war and for the administration, I had made up my mind that I definitely would not remain if the Democrats took control of either house of the Congress in the November elections as they seemed likely to do. Even if Republicans held the House and Senate, I was giving serious thought to leaving so that President Bush could have new leadership at the Department. If the Democrats took power in the legislative branch, the President knew as well as I did that it would not be productive to have a secretary of defense constantly being summoned by members of Congress for hearings designed to promote partisan politics in the run-up to the 2008 presidential election. By then, many Democrats were campaigning against the Iraq war and would press to cut its funding. They would use their positions on congressional committees to relitigate old questions such as prewar intelligence on Iraq for their political advantage. Some were even considering impeachment hearings against President Bush.[6] All of this meant there would have to be changes in personnel and strategy if the country was to avoid the ugly ending in Iraq that new congressional majorities would be counseling.

In early October 2006, Vice President Cheney mused after a meeting in the Oval Office, "The good news is that there are only 794 days left until the end of the term."

"Dick, there are 794 days left for you," I said. "Not for me."[7]

President Bush then said something that confused the tea-leaf readers, not to mention Joyce and me. Asked on November 1 if he still had confidence in me as secretary of defense, and if he wanted me to stay on, the President announced that he wanted me to stay in his administration "until the end."[8] This ran against everything I had discussed with Joyce and suggested to Cheney, who I assumed might have passed on my less than subtle comments that I was likely to leave if the Democrats were victorious on Election Day.

In the days before the November election, it looked as though Republicans would lose the House. Americans had soured on congressional Republican scandals and profligate spending. Republicans would be lucky if they held the Senate.

Joyce and I were having dinner with some friends one evening shortly before the election when I received a phone call from the Vice President. "Don," Cheney said matter-of-factly, "the President has decided to make a change. He wants to see you Tuesday." He did not elaborate on the President's decision.

"Fair enough," I said to Cheney. "I'll prepare a letter of resignation. It makes sense."

"We're going to lose the House of Representatives, and the next two years are going to be rough," Cheney said.

"I agree. It's not helpful for the military if I stay. Fresh eyes are a good thing," I responded.[9]

Thirty-one years earlier, Dick Cheney had been the one who called me to urge that I accept President Gerald Ford's request to become secretary of defense. In August 1976, he had called me on behalf of President Ford to let me know I would not be Ford's vice presidential nominee. And in December 2000, Cheney called me in Taos to say President-elect Bush wanted me to become his defense secretary. Now Dick was on the phone one more time, confirming what Joyce and I had already concluded. Two and a half years earlier I had given President Bush a signed note saying he had my resignation whenever it might be helpful to him. That time now had come.

Several days later, as millions of Americans went to the polls on November 7, I sat in the Oval Office alone with the President. Bush was visibly uncomfortable. I tried to make the situation easier for him.

"Mr. President," I said, "I've prepared this letter for you."

I handed him a single sheet of paper. "With my resignation as Secretary of Defense comes my deep appreciation to you for providing me this unexpected opportunity to serve," the letter began. "I leave with great respect for you and for the leadership you have provided during a most challenging time for our country. . . . It has been the highest honor of my long life to have been able to serve our country at such a critical time in our history and to have had the privilege of working so closely with the truly amazing young men and women in uniform. . . . It is time to conclude my service."[10]

As he took the letter from me, Bush's first thoughts were personal. "Is Joyce all right?" he asked.

"She's fine. And she's ready," I said. "She even typed the letter for me."

I could see that the President was still concerned. I said, "Look, Joyce and I are tracking with you on this."

"This is hard for me," Bush said, shaking his head slowly. "You are a pro. You're a hell of a lot better than others in this town."

We talked briefly about my successor, Robert Gates. During the 1991 Gulf War, Gates had been deputy national security adviser under Brent Scowcroft. He later became CIA director. Gates had been a member of the Iraq Study Group, led by former Congressman Lee Hamilton and Jim Baker, which had counseled a withdrawal in light of their conclusion that "stability in Iraq remains elusive and the situation is deteriorating."[11] The President expressed confidence that despite those recommendations, Gates would hang tough on Iraq.[12]

Bush did not appear to be considering a wholesale change in strategy. In fact, he discussed his efforts to bring General Abizaid to Washington to help coordinate the war effort from the White House. I told the President that my impression from Abizaid was that as a professional soldier he felt he would be uncomfortable with a position in the White House. With General Casey slated to leave his post in Iraq, the President was planning to nominate Casey to be chief of staff of the Army. He asked for my opinion on who might replace Abizaid and Casey. I again mentioned David Petraeus.[13]

After twenty minutes, we stood up and shook hands.

As the election returns came in later that evening, it became clear that November 7 would not be good for Republicans. Democrats won a sizable victory in the House and defeated incumbent Republicans in the United States Senate, putting Democrats in control of both houses. Representative Nancy Pelosi, a liberal representative from San Francisco, would become the first female Speaker of the House.

With the midterm elections over, attention soon turned to the 2008 presidential election. Senators planning to seek the presidency, such as Hillary Clinton and Joe Biden, would use their new majority to hammer away at the administration and try to burnish their liberal credentials for the Democratic primary voters. John McCain, in turn, was going to serve as ranking member of the Armed Services Committee. Without mentioning the President by name, he had been opportunistically undermining the administration's policies in his quest for the Republican nomination for the presidency. It seemed to be his way of separating himself from President Bush and burnishing his image as a maverick without directly taking him on.

The day after the election, I stood with the President and Bob Gates in the Oval Office for the announcement of my resignation and Gates' nomination. I wished my successor well. I couldn't resist quoting Winston Churchill to the effect, "I have benefitted greatly from criticism and at no time have I suffered from a lack thereof."[14] I thanked the President for giving me the opportunity to serve and for the privilege of working so closely with the men and women in uniform.

There were many who sent well wishes over the next few days. Russia's defense minister, Sergei Ivanov, telephoned. Referring to his wife, he joked, "Irina said this morning, 'Don is a free man. I envy Joyce.'"[15] Henry Kissinger called me at home. He was disappointed by my departure, saying, "The irony is you are being attacked for overruling the generals, and, the truth is, if anything you may have overruled them too little."[16] He may have been right.

I appreciated the many kind comments I received. One of the more personal came from Congressman John Dingell, that, in a way, closed a loop on my public career. The Michigan Democrat was one of the first people I met when I had been elected to the U.S. House of Representatives back in 1962. We had played paddleball together in the House gymnasium and had been friends since, now more than forty years. "I look forward to shaking your hand and recalling the old days," he said fondly.[17] It was a nice memory for me of how the Congress had once been.*

I promptly shifted from leading the Department of Defense to simply presiding over it, while Gates prepared for his confirmation hearings. I would be available if a crisis occurred, but I decided to remove myself from policy making to the extent possible so that the new secretary would have all of his options open when he arrived.

On a bright Friday in December, with the sun pouring onto the Pentagon's parade field and with the President and Vice President of the United States and the Chairman of the Joint Chiefs beside me, I attended my second and, as I mused at the time, my last farewell ceremony as secretary of defense. My departure was not what Joyce and I had envisioned. I had planned on a smaller Department-only event. Then word came from the White House that the President and Vice President would be attending and speaking. I was pleased our three grown children had come in for the day to be there alongside Joyce and me. My family had been through it all with me and I had relied heavily on their unfailing support. Despite the ups and downs of public life, they never wavered.

Cheney spoke at the ceremony, not only as the current vice president and a former secretary of defense, but also as a friend.[19] Our time together in public service had started more than thirty-five years earlier and was now at an end. As I listened to his thoughtful words, I wished for a moment that more people could know Dick as Joyce and I did. There are facets of his personality that the public rarely, if ever, had a chance to see. Many years ago, our family took a trip with the Cheneys. One evening after a long day, one of the Cheney girls fell asleep in the living room and Dick gently lifted his child to carry her to bed. It was not an unusual gesture for a father, but it struck me then that his tenderness contrasted sharply with what most people, even his admirers, saw of Cheney. Few know the dedicated husband and father—not to mention friend—behind the calm and professional public servant.

President Bush introduced me and offered generous remarks. "There has been more profound change at the Department of Defense over the past six years than at any time since the Department's creation in the late 1940s."[20]

* Another loop was closed the day after my resignation, when I traveled to Manhattan, Kansas, to deliver the Landon Lecture at Kansas State University. Joyce and I were met by retired General and Kansas native Dick Myers and his wife, Mary Jo. Joyce and I felt good to be back in the Midwest and out of Washington, D.C.—we were at peace and knew the events of the past few days were for the best. Myers made some moving and gracious remarks about our service together. He recalled I used to joke that I spent more time with him than with Joyce.[18]

Working to reorient a department of three million people had been grueling but invigorating work. I knew I would miss it. And I knew I would miss working alongside a commander in chief who not only had strong convictions but also the courage to stand by them under withering criticism.

When it was my time to speak, I looked out on the sea of faces. It was a considerably larger crowd than I had expected—so many friends and colleagues in the Department with whom I'd worked so closely over so many years confronting such dangerous and difficult times for our country. It was an emotional moment. Those gathered there meant a great deal to me.

I wanted my remarks to be about the future, not the past.[21] I wanted to speak to the men and women in the Department of Defense who would continue the long, hard slog against a twisted and deadly ideology. I returned to a theme that had stuck with me throughout my public career—during the days of Vietnam when I served in Congress, during the Cold War when I had served as ambassador to NATO and then as secretary of defense, during the time of the Lebanon crisis as Middle East envoy, and throughout the terror and challenges of 9/11 and wars in Afghanistan and Iraq: Weakness is provocative. I knew America must not lose the will and the heart to persevere in long and difficult struggles. I knew that a loss of will was the only way America could lose any struggle.

"Today, it should be clear that not only is weakness provocative," I cautioned, recalling what I had said to then President-elect Bush in 2000, "but the perception of weakness on our part can be provocative as well."

I noted, "A conclusion by our enemies that the United States lacks the will or the resolve to carry out missions that demand sacrifice and demand patience is every bit as dangerous as an imbalance of conventional military power."[22]

I told those gathered that the most inspiring moments of my tenure were my meetings with the troops, all volunteers. I had met tens of thousands of dedicated soldiers, sailors, airmen, and Marines deployed in the defense of our country, many of whom had enlisted after 9/11 just as my father had done after Pearl Harbor. Whenever Joyce and I met with wounded troops at Walter Reed Medical Center, Bethesda Naval Hospital, and in the field hospitals in Afghanistan and Iraq, I knew they had reason for regret, bitterness, or sadness. Instead, what I found time and again was that they were strong, upbeat and wanted to get well so they could return to their units. We remembered those who had fallen as well as those who survived their time on the battlefield but saw their lives changed forever. And I remembered my times with their families who I knew sacrificed as well. It was the highest honor of my life to have served with and known them.

CHAPTER 50

After Tides and Hurricanes

"Never, never, never believe any war will be smooth and easy, or that anyone who embarks on the strange voyage can measure the tides and hurricanes he will encounter."

—*Winston Churchill,* My Early Life: A Roving Commission

On December 30, 2006, fifteen days after I left the Department of Defense, the Iraqi government executed Saddam Hussein. As he approached the noose, the former strongman struggled for a moment with his guards before regaining his composure. He had kept the salt-and-pepper beard he had favored since his capture, but his hair was again jet black, as I remembered it from our meeting in 1983. The country he had ruled had once been one of the most advanced and hopeful Arab nations in the Middle East, even a potential American ally. As Saddam met the judgment of his people for crimes against humanity, I could not help but reflect on the tragic waste he had made of his country during his long years in power. After the thick rope was placed around his neck, the vanquished dictator said only a few words. The small door below his feet snapped open.

The execution was greeted by dancing in the streets and guns fired into the air in most of Iraq. Along with euphoria and celebration, there was relief.

Saddam had lingered in a cell far longer than suited many Iraqis. Some feared American forces might have been keeping Saddam alive as a bargaining chip with the Sunni insurgents, or that he might even be released if major groups agreed to lay down their arms. Many had bitter memories of an earlier Bush administration that had encouraged Iraqis to rise up against the Baathist regime in 1991 but then stood by as Saddam regained his power and massacred those who rose up. Now the man who had dominated and darkened their lives for decades, whose portrait had been in schools and restaurants, on television screens and buildings, was truly, finally gone. Though not all of Iraq's demons were exorcised, Saddam's death offered his oppressed people a psychological release that is impossible for outsiders to fully gauge.

The U.S. military involvement in Iraq has come at a high price. Combat took the lives of thousands of American servicemen and -women and left many more wounded. The U.S. Treasury spent hundreds of billions of dollars. The prolonged war also poisoned our politics at home. Political campaigns used the war as a bludgeon against President Bush, his administration, and his party.

Since Saddam Hussein's statue was brought down in Firdos Square in March 2003, the United States' goals—replacing Saddam's government with one that did not attack its neighbors, or develop WMDs, and was respectful of the country's diverse ethnic and religious minorities—had migrated into a more ambitious effort. Bush administration officials increasingly spoke about the imperative of creating a democracy, particularly after it was discovered that Saddam Hussein didn't have the ready stockpiles of WMD our intelligence community believed we would uncover. This shift in emphasis suggested that Iraq's intentions and capability for building WMD had somehow not been threatening. Many Americans and others around the world accordingly came to believe that the war had been unnecessary.

The Bush administration should have pointed out that, while Saddam Hussein did not have WMD stockpiles, he did in fact maintain dual-use facilities that could produce chemical and biological weapons. Given Saddam's record of using chemical weapons against his own people, those facilities were effectively as dangerous as stockpiles. The Duelfer Report, the product of the Iraq Survey Group that examined Saddam's WMD programs after the war, carefully documents the scope of his ambitions. Saddam wanted to "[preserve] the capability to reconstitute his weapons of mass destruction (WMD) when sanctions were lifted."[1] He remained intent on reconstituting his WMD programs and kept many of them "on the shelf," which would allow him to begin producing biological and chemical weapons within several weeks' time.[2] Instead of pointing out these facts, the White House decided not to dispute the matter to avoid "relitigating" the past and changed the subject to democracy promotion. Some assumed that the justification for the war and the need to remove Saddam were self-evident. "[O]ne of the biggest mistakes of the Bush years," senior Bush adviser Karl Rove later acknowledged, was not "engaging" with administration critics, which "let more of the public come to believe dangerous falsehoods about the war: that Bush lied, that Saddam Hussein never had and never wanted WMD, that we claimed Iraq had been behind 9/11."[3] The damage from this error in judgment was substantial. It allowed critics to whitewash Saddam's record and political opponents to build a deceitful narrative about the rationale for going to war.

In the weeks leading up to Saddam's death in December 2006, Democrats who had gained control of Congress were poised to finally succeed in their efforts to cut off war funding, which would bring U.S. involvement in Iraq to a forced end. President Bush knew that if they prevailed, it would ensure the defeat of the U.S.-led coalition and victory for the jihadists, insurgents, and other enemies of a potentially peaceful and responsible Iraq. He believed that the outcome would be not only a military calamity, but would also force the United States to endure the humiliation of a precipitous withdrawal while plunging Iraq into a further humanitarian disaster.

Bush realized that a political strategy with the new Congress was now as important as a military strategy. The President was frustrated that progress was too slow, but he believed that with some additional time and patience, the situation could improve. His challenge was to convince the opposition party, led by incoming House Speaker Nancy Pelosi and Senate Majority Leader Harry Reid, that the administration had developed a promising new approach and deserved additional time. The President undoubtedly hoped that the sweeping personnel changes underway—new commanders at CENTCOM and in Iraq and a new secretary of defense—offered a concrete demonstration to the public that the commander in chief was pursuing a different course. Accordingly, President Bush took one of the boldest political and strategic maneuvers in recent American history: the 2007 surge.

Talk of executing a surge of additional U.S. troops began in November 2006 with a White House review of Iraq strategy led by J. D. Crouch and Bill Luti, both of whom had come to the NSC from the Defense Department. At the same time, officials in the Pentagon were undertaking our own review. Assistant Defense Secretary Peter Rodman and I sought to develop a DoD position that recognized the approach we had taken over the last year was not working "well enough or fast enough."[4] Though I had largely removed myself from policy making after the announcement of my resignation, I continued to oversee this review in the hope that the administration's new course would have the support of the country's top military officials.

We drew up a working paper in early December summarizing the options that the Pentagon's civilian and military leaders were considering. "[F]ailure in Iraq will place the American people in even greater danger," my cover memo for the paper began.[5] We suggested further accelerating the buildup of the Iraqi Security Forces and renewed efforts at befriending the Sunnis, now that the Awakening movement in Anbar province was blossoming.[6] We also suggested new efforts to curb Iran's hostile involvement, particularly its training of sectarian Shia militia death squads and its clandestine attacks on U.S. troops.

The Defense Department's summary paper was developed from a memo I had written the previous month to provide Bush with some "illustrative new courses of action." One proposed course was to "[i]ncrease Brigade Combat Teams and U.S. forces in Iraq substantially."[7] Since a surge of military forces still lacked support among military leaders, that suggestion was placed in my memo "below the line"—in other words, as a less favored option.[8]

Generals Abizaid and Casey were still uneasy with the idea of deploying more troops without a clear and agreed military mission for them. The Joint Chiefs also had questions about surging more troops into Iraq without a parallel surge by the State Department and other civilian agencies. Army Chief of Staff Pete Schoomaker and Marine Corps Commandant Michael Hagee were concerned about the toll more combat tours would take on their ground forces. Surging more U.S. troops would mean that some units' tours would need to be extended to fifteen months—a step that could not be taken lightly. The senior military leadership had the proper concern that military power alone could not solve Iraq's problems. I agreed with them that any surge of U.S. forces would have to be accompanied by more effective diplomatic and economic surges from other departments and agencies, and, of critical importance, by considerably greater political progress by Iraq's elected leaders.

The President understood his surge proposal already ran against the conventional wisdom of the foreign policy establishment, his State Department, and congressional Democrats as well as some Republicans in Congress. Without support from senior military leaders, it would be fatally wounded before it was ever proposed.[9]

Gradually, opinions were changing at the Pentagon. Pace had assembled a council of colonels to conduct a military review for the Joint Chiefs. The colonels, many of whom had spent more than one deployment in Iraq, were open to the idea of sending several additional brigades if they had a clear mission. Pace and I worked to allay any concerns Casey, Abizaid, and the Joint Chiefs might have. For instance, to address the Army's and Marine Corps' concerns about stress on their forces from continued deployments, the President endorsed an increase in the size of both services.

The skepticism of senior military leaders, however, was mild in comparison with the opposition within the State Department. Rice argued that surging more U.S. troops would further antagonize American allies and erode domestic political support. State Department officials recommended reducing U.S. troop levels and redeploying what forces were left on the ground into large bases away from the fighting.[10]

On December 13, 2006, President Bush came to the Pentagon for a meeting on Iraq. Present were the incoming secretary of defense, Bob Gates, and the senior military and civilian Defense Department leadership. The President urged everyone at the table to propose anything that could "show noticeable change in the situation in Baghdad."[11]

"What I want to hear from you," Bush said firmly, "is how we're going to win, not how we're going to leave."[12]

The President knew that if he were to avoid a congressionally mandated defeat in Iraq, he needed a political and military game changer that would give the progress underway a chance to develop fully. Though I was a latecomer in supporting the surge, by the time I left the Pentagon I felt that there were solid arguments for its two main military features: a somewhat heavier U.S. footprint and a new operational approach that centered on securing the population.

The new commander in Iraq, General David Petraeus, had distilled the lessons of counterinsurgency warfare after a year of research at Fort Leavenworth, where he had been assigned after his second tour in Iraq. He believed it was time to emphasize protecting the population now that the Sunni tribal leaders had decided to break with al-Qaida and needed the U.S. military to shield them from the jihadists' retribution. In 2005 and 2006, local commanders had tried some of the classic counterinsurgency techniques, such as living in small outposts and cordoning off neighborhoods with cement barriers to protect the population, but not in Baghdad, where violence was escalating. Petraeus proposed to take back the capital city from al-Qaida, radical Shia militias, and death squads by securing the local population block by block.

To ensure that these gains would last, Petraeus requested and received an additional twenty thousand troops that began deploying in January 2007. More troops, however, were not the sole reason for the success of the surge. In 2005 we had twice increased U.S. troops by twenty thousand. Yet the 2005 surges did not lead to the impressive progress that was achieved in 2007. The 2007 surge coincided with seismic shifts in the Iraqi political landscape. The Sunni Awakening, which had begun in the late summer of 2006 in Anbar province, was by then a full-fledged antiterrorist movement.

Sunni Iraqis were reclaiming their towns from al-Qaida one by one. Sunni leaders in Anbar, like Sheikh Abdul Sattar al-Rishawi, were willing to risk violent death—al-Qaida murdered Rishawi in 2007—to finally disavow the extremists that had taken sanctuary in their towns and villages. Muqtada al-Sadr declared a cease-fire against the coalition and the government, effectively ending a latent Shia rebellion. An elected government, seated in mid-2006, had finally formed, and its leaders were gaining enough confidence to take on the extremists, even within their own religious sect. Shia leaders like Nouri al-Maliki were prepared to win back Basra by defeating Iran-funded Shia militias. Perhaps most important, the surge also coincided with the time when the Iraqi security forces had finally reached a critical mass in number and capability. By December 2006, some 320,000 Iraqis had been trained, equipped, and deployed, producing the forces needed to help hold difficult neighborhoods; they joined in patrols with the surge troops, putting an Iraqi face on the new strategy.

The surge recognized these major political and military changes in the environment and adopted a new approach to take advantage of them. But ultimately, the true genius of the surge was the political effect it had in the United States, where the conflict's true center of gravity had migrated. The surge began first and foremost with a major shift in the administration's political strategy at home, by tempering the defeatist mood on Capitol Hill.* Petraeus' embedding of U.S. forces with Iraqi troops in violent neighborhoods also gave Iraqis a renewed confidence that the United States stood with them. It improved intelligence collection, with more tips and cooperation coming from Iraqi citizens. As more neighborhoods became calm, citizens started moving back, reopening their businesses, and once again taking their

* It is worth noting, however, that before the surge's success was known, Senate Majority Leader Harry Reid declared it a failure, and noted, "[T]his war is lost." Senator Barack Obama also expressed concern that the surge would not succeed.[13]

children to neighborhood parks. The terror that had aided the insurgents' cause began to subside.

While Petraeus brought a new operational approach to Iraq, ultimately he continued the existing strategy: building up Iraqi capabilities while containing the violent threats to the new political order so Iraqis would soon be able to take charge of their own problems. This was the same sensible and modest strategy we had set out before the war. It was the same strategy that—though altered with the establishment of a longer-term Coalition Provisional Authority—we reaffirmed in our October 2003 strategic review, when I intervened to bring an early end to the CPA. It is the strategy that President Barack Obama continued to pursue in the first years of his presidency.

As I had repeatedly argued in the Defense Department and in interagency meetings, success should not be defined as our solving all of Iraq's problems. Our strategy was not to create (for the first time in its history) a noncorrupt, prosperous democracy, with all the protections afforded by due process. Such goals were desirable, but not within the limits of American capabilities or patience. Because Iraq would be plagued for years by some level of violence, ethnic tensions, and a poor economic infrastructure, I thought our strategy should be to try to contain those problems and build up the abilities of Iraqis to deal with them so that they could manage their own affairs and not be a security problem for the region, the United States, or our allies.

I have been asked on occasion if I believed the war was worth the costs, particularly since WMD stockpiles were not found. It is a fair question. Any calculation of the costs and benefits of the Iraq war has to take into account what Iraq and the world might look like if Saddam and his sons were still in power. While the road not traveled always looks smoother, the cold reality of a Hussein regime in Baghdad most likely would mean a Middle East far more perilous than it is today: Iran and Iraq locked in a struggle to field nuclear weapons, which could give rise to a regional arms race among Egypt, Libya, Saudi Arabia, and Syria; continued support for terrorists from an Iraqi regime enriched by rising oil prices; wars of aggression launched against neighboring countries in the Gulf; the torture and death of thousands more Iraqis suspected of opposing the regime; and a United Nations even more discredited than it is today, as its sanctions crumbled. Our failure to confront Iraq would have sent a message to other nations that neither America nor any other nation was willing to stand in the way of their support for terrorism and pursuit of weapons of mass destruction.

President Bush made the decision to invade Iraq and topple Saddam

Hussein knowing there would be consequences that neither he nor anyone else could foresee. We had discussed many of the potential risks, but there are no methodologies or formulas that can substitute for judgment and intuition in dealing with the challenges of statecraft. There are always factors that turn out to be important, but were unanticipated. I have no doubt that given the facts that were available to President Bush in 2003, I would have made the same decision. Further, knowing what we later learned and recognizing the costs, there is not a persuasive argument to be made that the United States would be in a stronger strategic position or that Iraq and the Middle East would be better off if Saddam were still in power. In short, ridding the region of Saddam's brutal regime has created a more stable and secure world.

In 2010, Iraq had the twelfth fastest growing economy in the world.[14] Though al-Qaida still has the ability to pull off spectacular attacks, it no longer finds sanctuary in any corner of that country. Over the coming years, with a moderate, representative government, Iraq has the potential to become a positive influence in the Middle East, a region that is sorely in need of good influences. It could become a valued long-term partner of the United States and a bulwark against Iran, a role that will prove critical if Tehran continues on its belligerent path toward a nuclear arsenal.

Any optimistic prognosis for Iraq is quite a change from how things looked in 2006. But making policy and formulating strategy are not exact sciences in which outcomes are certain and measurable. Though it makes officials in both the executive and legislative branches of government uncomfortable, strategic thinking requires acknowledgment of the inevitability of considerable uncertainty.

Postulating a world in which Saddam Hussein remained in power is of course a theoretical exercise. It involves numerous known unknowns and undoubtedly some unknown unknowns. The only known certainty is that those who made the decisions with imperfect knowledge will be judged in hindsight by those with considerably more information at their disposal and time for reflection. Indeed, my own analysis—and criticisms—in this book benefit from both.

It is of note that during Bob McNamara's confirmation hearing to become secretary of defense in 1961, not a single U.S. senator asked him a question about Vietnam. In Dick Cheney's confirmation hearing in 1989, not a single U.S. senator asked him about Iraq. In my confirmation hearing in 2001, not a single U.S. senator asked me about Afghanistan. Yet in each case, the questions not asked dominated our tenures. The lesson is that we should learn to expect to be surprised. The limits of intelligence—of both human intellect and the products of our government's intelligence agencies—are a reality that should make us all humble. We need to be confident but also intellectually flexible to alter course as required. Being prepared for the unknown and agile enough to respond to the unforeseen is the essence of strategy.

Over my years in both the public and private sectors, I have come to see strategy and decision making as a four-step process that requires periodic recalibration and adjustment. At its most fundamental level, grand strategy is setting large, longer-term goals that are realistic and can be balanced with the means available to achieve them. It requires continual review of the goals in light of the means and of new circumstances as they come to light.

The first step of strategy is precisely defining one's goals. "If you get the objectives right," George Marshall is widely reported to have said, "a lieutenant can write the strategy." Setting clear goals may sound obvious, but it is remarkable how rarely governments—or other organizations, for that matter—take the time and care to start a policy-making process by formulating strategic goals precisely and in writing. Failure to do so can doom an enterprise before it begins. There is a tendency to deal with challenging situations by plunging into discussions of options or courses of action. That approach takes for granted that the goals are self-evident and shared by everyone involved, and that the options to be considered are appropriate to the goals. When officials fail to define their objectives with care, it's difficult for the entire government to make and execute decisions that advance them. Without a well-understood strategy, decisions can be random and even counterproductive. Setting priorities and defining limits can help to avoid what the military calls "mission creep"—the tendency to gradually increase a commitment without fully understanding the consequences and costs of doing so.

The number of goals has to be limited. Listing more than four or five means they are probably not at the strategic level. In early 2005, for example, I suggested to President Bush the three major goals in the struggle against Islamist terrorists: defending the homeland; disrupting terrorist networks abroad; and countering ideological support for terrorism.[15] We had to make some hard choices about what to leave off that list—things that would have been desirable but that I ultimately concluded were not essential and could have become distracting, such as eradicating terrorist funding through the narcotics trade or promoting democracy. Without identifying which goals are the most important, one ends up with little more than a wish list that will not provide critical strategic direction. Strategy begins by planting a clear, recognizable flag in the distance that others can see and work toward.

The second step of strategy is identifying the major assumptions associated with the challenge at hand, always recognizing that they are based on imperfect information that can change or even turn out to have been incorrect. For an entrepreneur, a major assumption might be that a company's newly developed product will receive patent protection from competition for a period of time. A major assumption in planning military action might be that a foreign country will cooperate by granting basing or overflight rights to an air force. These assumptions can turn out to be wrong. In war, for example, a common mistake is creating a picture of the battlefield based on a static picture of the enemy that fails to recognize that the enemy has a brain and will react and change his strategy, which in turn will require changing assumptions and plans.

The third step is evaluating the possible courses of action in light of the assumptions. At the upper levels of policy making almost all possible courses of action entail negative consequences that need to be weighed. This is particularly so when it comes to ones that must be made by a president. By the time he engages on an issue, most if not all of the good options often have been attempted by others at lower levels. In July 2001, for example, when I wrote the other members of the NSC suggesting various courses of action we should consider with respect to Iraq, none were ideal.[16] Ending the UN-imposed no-fly zones could embolden Saddam. Terminating the UN sanctions could give him the space to rebuild his WMD programs. Engaging with him could legitimize and prolong his regime. Pushing for regime change could alienate some of our traditional allies.

The fourth and final stage in formulating strategy is executing the chosen course of action. And this too can change based on circumstances. For example, we had to make multiple adjustments to our assumptions about the formation, development, focus, and deployment of Iraqi security forces as the situation changed over time, but we remained consistent in our emphasis on helping them develop their own capabilities. No matter how careful the preparation, fortune plays a role in all plans and necessitates the recalibration or abandonment of key assumptions, and therefore major changes in the plan. Oversight of these constant adjustments requires careful balance to avoid the extremes of disengagement and micromanagement. Kissinger once described Anwar Sadat, one of the most impressive men I have ever met, as "free of the obsession with detail by which mediocre leaders think they are mastering events, only to be engulfed by them."[17]

Strategy is not linear. It is never completed until the challenge at hand has been resolved. The means must be continually reviewed to see whether they still serve the goals, and if the goals are sensible and realistic in light of one's means and unfolding events. There is a danger that policies and courses of action can acquire a momentum of their own. Continuing them without adjustment or reconsideration is often easier than developing new ones. Inertia can be an obstacle to formulating and maintaining sound strategy.

In wartime, strategy and statesmanship require a clear-eyed understanding of the enemy and its ideology and a clear articulation of both by the nation's leaders. After 9/11, though, our government never came to such an understanding. With the benefit of nearly a decade of hindsight, we ought to have more precisely labeled our enemies as violent Islamists. President Bush and others were properly careful not to foster or be seen as fostering the idea that Islam—a faith observed by more than one billion people across the world—was our enemy. To succeed we would require the assistance of millions of Muslims—the only ones who could forcefully reject, marginalize, and ultimately defeat the extremist elements within their faith who are our enemies. We did not want to unintentionally antagonize the overwhelming majority who shared our views. But we were wrong not to forcefully communicate that we are fighting an extremist ideology rooted in Islam.

Islamists who preach and lay the foundations for jihadist violence pose a serious challenge to liberal democracy. Paradoxically, America's finest traits—our respect for religion and individual liberty—make our country particularly vulnerable to an enemy whose ideology is based in religion. But reluctance to face up to Islamism, to confront it directly and work actively to counter it, has been and remains even at this writing a serious and costly hesitation in our body politic since 9/11.

According to their own utterances, writings, and propaganda, Islamists seek to reestablish the caliphate, an empire that stretched from Spain to India in the tenth century, and expand it around the globe. The network of our terrorist enemies comprises a diverse group of people, but what links them are totalitarian, expansionist, and revolutionary distortions of Islam. Some Islamist ideals are represented by Shia ayatollahs in Iran; others by Bin Laden and Sunni al-Qaida terrorists in Pakistan. All Islamists, however, promote replacement of the world's international system of nation-states with a single theocratic empire that imposes and enforces sharia (Muslim holy law). Islamist ideology rejects democracy, civil liberties, and laws made by men. Those of us who embrace such practices are despised and detested as an insult to Allah. Though his statement was mocked and ridiculed by some, President Bush was correct—profoundly so—when he said that the terrorists who struck on 9/11 "hate our freedoms—our freedom of religion, our freedom of speech, our freedom to vote and assemble and disagree with each other."[18]

Still, we never successfully translated that basic vision into a message that explained to Americans and the world who we were fighting and why they had attacked us. In fact, we often seemed to do the opposite, out of fear of being labeled anti-Muslim—a pattern that the Obama administration has taken to a dangerous extreme in initially denying the ideological links among the terrorist plots in Times Square, Fort Hood, and Detroit.

While those of us in the Bush administration did not engage in the debate needed to identify the enemy's ideology, we did at least recognize that the challenge we faced was fundamentally ideological. "The important point is that what we face is an ideologically-based challenge," I wrote in 2004, when we were engaged in both Iraq and Afghanistan. "Radical Islamists may be centered in the Middle East, but their reach is worldwide and their goals are global." My memo continued:

> If it is an ideological challenge, our task is not simply to defend, but to preempt, to go on the offensive, and to keep the radicals off balance. We learned this lesson in the Soviet Union cold war case. For one thing, we will need to show the moderates in the religion that they have support. . . . [T]hey must take up the battle and defend their religion against those who would hijack it. . . . [I]deologies can be defeated. The Soviet collapse teaches us this. If Islamism's goal is the fantasy of a new "Caliphate," we can deflate it by, over time, demonstrating its certain futility. Simply by not giving in to terrorist blackmail—by not being driven out of the Middle East—we will demonstrate over time that the extremists' ideology cannot deliver.[19]

One of the three components of the strategy we developed in the months after 9/11 addressed how to counter the enemy's ideology. We knew that wars in Afghanistan and Iraq would not end Islamist terrorism and, in fact, in the short term could give the enemy opportunities to attract more recruits and cite the inevitable casualties as proof that the United States was warring against Islam. As long as madrassas and mosques from Jakarta to Hamburg preached Islamism and justified terrorism in its service, military action could make only limited headway. After circulating our 2005 national defense strategy, the State Department objected to the inclusion of "countering ideological support" as a goal.[20] While some in the administration recognized the problem, there was never any resolution and as a result we are not able to fashion and execute a plan to confront it effectively.

I favored a major effort to win over those Muslims who were sitting on the fence—those not supporting al-Qaida but who were not actively opposing the extremists either. Our extremist enemies did not terrorize only Westerners, but their fellow Muslims. I thought we needed a campaign to win over friends and allies in the Muslim world and "mobilize moderate Muslims," as I argued in July 2005.[21] We needed to tell the truth about the Islamist extremists—about their brutality, injustice, and totalitarian political ambitions. The best way to communicate that message was not for American political leaders to do it, but to find ways to get more Muslims around the world publicly speaking out against them. But the United States and other Western countries have been notably unsuccessful in encouraging Muslim political, religious, and educational leaders to take a stand against Islamism and the preaching of violence and terror.

This failure has been a serious deficiency in the West's struggle against the extremists. Our inability to compete in the battle of ideas and to counter our enemies' ideology has invited them to focus on communicating through the media, where they have enjoyed consistent and sustained success. This is the essence of asymmetric warfare. Instead of engaging our military forces, they engage us where we and all democracies are most vulnerable: our public will and staying power. They seek to demoralize free people and cause their nations to withdraw from the world into isolationism.

Our enemies know that a single attack cannot break our will. They also know that a single attack, skillfully handled, with accompanying grisly pictures and video, can affect public opinion dramatically and quickly. In Iraq and Afghanistan our enemies' goal was to sour U.S. public opinion on the wars and cause members of Congress to do what the enemy fighters could not do: force the U.S. military to stop fighting. They worked to inflict at least a few casualties on us every day, providing more negative images and headlines for the next news cycle. They hope to achieve what they have sought since they successfully defeated the Soviet empire in Afghanistan: the humiliation of another superpower. They almost achieved exactly that in 2007, when Speaker Pelosi and Majority Leader Reid pushed to cut funding for the Iraq war. Their efforts, if successful, would have led to precisely the kind of rout the enemy hoped for—the kind I remembered all too well from the difficult days in the spring of 1975 at the end of the Vietnam War.

Though I disagreed with those who argued to end our efforts in Iraq abruptly, I continue to believe that military missions undertaken by the United States need to be realistic in intent and limited in scope. Strategy and statesmanship require recognizing and understanding that our nation's capabilities are finite. Further, the American public is not tolerant of the long-term involvement of U.S. forces in combat. Wars threaten to change free societies, which is why it is difficult for democracies to wage prolonged bloody conflicts. This laudable aversion to war makes it all the more challenging when U.S. military efforts are required and must be sustained.

For a time, a popular maxim about Iraq was "If you break it, you own it." But to be clear, the United States did not "break" Iraq. It was broken by a dictator who over twenty-five years ran his country into the ground. Nor did the United States break Afghanistan, a land that had been broken, at least by Western standards, for centuries. We can encourage, assist, and advise, but we should not take on the responsibility as the prime actor. Local Afghans and Iraqis know far better than we do how to form and at what pace to evolve their societies. Solving corruption in Afghanistan or building a secular democracy in the Middle East are not America's problems to tackle. They are not our broken societies to fix.

The futures of Afghanistan and Iraq have yet to be decided, and circumstances could still deteriorate. Afghans, Iraqis, and their elected leaders may make wrong choices in the years ahead and lose some of the hard-won gains of the U.S. military. Nonetheless, it must be said that America has given them a chance at success. Because of American sacrifice, they have been given the opportunity to build better, more secure, more prosperous, and freer societies than they ever knew under the Taliban or Saddam Hussein. They are now challenged with the responsibilities of sustaining their free societies, just as Americans are responsible for sustaining ours.

In the late 1970s, after two decades in government and my early years in business, Joyce and I had saved enough to purchase a small place in El Prado, New Mexico, just north of Taos, then a sleepy town of a few thousand people—a haven for artists, skiers, self-described free spirits, and graying hippies. For decades it had been a crossroads of Hispanic, Indian, and Western cultures, combining the millennia-old traditions of the original inhabitants of the continent with the pioneering spirit of the settlers who first headed West.

Next to our farm is the Taos Pueblo, thought to be the oldest, continuously inhabited community in North America. The Native American tribe that founded it has made the area its home for more than a thousand years, centuries before the first Europeans set sail for the New World and well before a Declaration of Independence pitted thirteen colonies against an empire. Few other places in America serve as a more vivid reminder of how young our nation is, which for me only makes even more miraculous what has been achieved in its short existence. When I am in New Mexico and see the majestic landscape and endless blue skies, I sense what this great land of ours represents: promise, possibility, and renewal.

A few years after New Mexico became part of U.S. territory, the American Civil War began. During that conflict, deep divisions between those loyal to the North and South led to skirmishes in the area, including efforts by Confederate sympathizers to take down the American flag flying over the Taos Plaza. Eventually, a group of men, including the legendary frontiersman Kit Carson, resolved to nail the Union flag to a tall wooden pole, where it was kept under twenty-four-hour watch. Though federal regulations prevented municipalities from flying the Stars and Stripes after sundown, Congress passed a special law authorizing Taos to be the first city in the nation allowed to fly the flag day and night. And there the flag has flown ever since, through times of war, economic despair, disease, and disaster—in the cruelest of times as well as the best of times.

Our still-young country has withstood tragedies and trauma of unimagined scope. And yet it has continued to thrive, thanks to proud and resilient citizens and leaders from both political parties who have done their best to guide the nation. "If those young Americans who have the advantage of education, perspective, and self-discipline do not participate to the fullest extent of their ability," Adlai Stevenson once said, "America will stumble, and if America stumbles the world falls." He warned, "For the power, for good or evil, of this American political organization is virtually beyond measurement. The decisions which it makes, the uses to which it devotes its immense resources, the leadership which it provides on moral as well as material questions, all appear likely to determine the fate of the modern world."[22] Those words remain as true and profound today as when I first heard them at my senior class banquet at Princeton University in 1954.

Those who have been privileged to serve our country have been the guardians of one of the greatest achievements of mankind. Our United States of America, at once imperfect and extraordinary, has offered more opportunity and improved more lives, both at home and throughout the world, than any other nation in history. In writing this book I have looked back over a life enriched beyond measure by those opportunities. I hope readers will come away with a conviction that service to America is an obligation to be fulfilled, as well as an honor to be embraced.

Acknowledgments

This book has been four years in the making. To help organize its writing, as well as to put order into my voluminous documentary record and establish the supporting website, I have relied on an extraordinary team of individuals. The core group was headed by Keith Urbahn, my chief of staff and a Navy reserve intelligence officer, who has taken on historical, creative, and managerial responsibilities well beyond his years. Victoria Coates brought an academic perspective and a relentless insistence on documentation and precision—invaluable assistance from an art historian, of all things. Matt Latimer, an attorney and former Pentagon and White House speechwriter, contributed not only his considerable knowledge and talent but also his boundless interest in Richard M. Nixon.

This group was ably supported by our outstanding staff led by our office manager, Linda Figura. Aliza Kwiatek was an intrepid and meticulous fact checker. Will Cappelletti, Pratik Chougule, and Brice Long spent many long hours researching subjects related to this book; Sarah Conant, Steve Duggan, Elizabeth Goss, Lisa Ricks, and Kailey Walczak did yeoman's duty transcribing the seemingly endless streams of dictation and interviews and fielding requests for illustrations and documents. Nancy Pardo, my longtime and valued assistant in Chicago, has undertaken hundreds of hours of dictation transcription and been an all-around personal oracle. The publisher at Sentinel, Adrian Zackheim and his associates, provided experienced advice, as did Patti Pirooz and John McElroy in my reading of the audio version. Bob Barnett's unique perspective on the entire process has proved invaluable.

I have benefited from a group of stalwart if painfully honest readers, including Pete Biester, Steve Cambone, Torie Clarke, Larry Di Rita, Doug Feith, Anne Gardner, Admiral Ed Giambastiani, and Jean Edward Smith.

I also consulted directly with associates who participated in many of the events I describe, so that I could take into account their distinct perspectives as well. They include some of the most honorable and patriotic men I've had the privilege of serving alongside—men who dedicated their careers to serving our nation in the uniform of the U.S. military:

Lt. Gen. David Barno
Lt. Gen. Steven Blum
Lt. Gen. Jerry Boykin
Col. Steven Bucci
Adm. Vern Clark
Gen. Bantz Craddock
Lt. Gen. Michael DeLong
Gen. Tommy Franks
Gen. John Handy
Vice Adm. Staser Holcomb
Gen. Jack Keane
Adm. Timothy Keating
Lt. Gen. Michael Maples
Gen. Richard Myers
Gen. Peter Pace
Lt. Gen. Gus Pagonis
Gen. Gene Renuart
Gen. Peter Schoomaker
Adm. James Stavridis
Capt. Troy Stoner
Vice Adm. Stan Szemborski

They also include other colleagues, patriots, and friends who have served their country in many ways:

Karen Ballard
Brad Berkson
Marshall Billingslea
Frank Carlucci
Lee Casey
Lynne Cheney
David Chu
J. D. Crouch
James Denny
François DeRose
Anthony Dolan
Raymond DuBois
Jaymie Durnan
Eric Edelman
Robert Ellsworth
Bob Gardner
Peter Geren
Jack Goldsmith
Alan Greenspan
Richard Haver
Jim Haynes
Ryan Henry
Charles Hill
Andy Hoehn
Marty Hoffmann
Ron James
Ned Jannotta
Reuben Jeffery
Jerry Jones
Zalmay Khalilzad
Henry Kissinger
Ken Krieg

Bruce Ladd
Art Laffer
Richard Lawless
Lewis Libby
William Luti
James MacDougall
Paul McHale
Thomas Miller
Newt Minow
Jeb Nadaner
John Negroponte
Luke Nichter
Roger Pardo-Maurer
Michael Pillsbury
Robert Rangel
Paul Rester
David Rivkin
Eric Ruff
Benjamin Runkle
Suzanne Schaffrath
William J. Schneider
Abram Shulsky
George Shultz
Laurence Silberman
Daniel Stanley
S. Frederick Starr
Dick Stevens
Cully Stimson
Christopher Straub
Marin Strmecki
Marc Thiessen
Ted Vogt
James Wade
Bill Walker
Joe Wassel
Ruth Wedgewood
Robert Wilkie
Brenda Williams
Christopher Williams
Paul Wolfowitz
Frank Zarb

One drawback to living so long is that there are friends and colleagues who are no longer with us. I first considered writing a book in the 1990s in consultation with John Robson, a friend of more than fifty years. While John died before this iteration of the project was launched, his guidance and recommendations have stayed with me—particularly his knack for getting me to look at issues from different viewpoints and his admonition to keep living life to the fullest regardless of age or infirmity. Three other friends stand out who were with us at the outset of this project but were not able to see the final product: Peter Rodman, who encouraged me to make full use of my archival material; Bill Safire, who shared his friendship and superb writing expertise; and Bob Goldwin, who was the same intellectual sounding board he had been during the Nixon and Ford administrations.

Thanks are also due to Margaret McAleer, John Haynes, and the staff of the Library of Congress, where the bulk of my papers are on deposit. Bob Storer of the Defense Department's Washington Headquarters Services has been an invaluable help with my DoD records. I also appreciate the contributions of David Horrocks and Bill McNitt and the staff at the Gerald R. Ford Library as well as assistance from the Lyndon Baines Johnson Library, the Richard M. Nixon Library, the Ronald Reagan Library, and the George W. Bush Presidential Center. Pulitzer Prize–winning photographer David Hume Kennerly contributed not only the front and back jackets of this book, but also unpublished photographs for the illustration sections.

Finally, I want to acknowledge my great fortune in having a family that has been a source of encouragement and inspiration: my two loving parents, George and Jeannette Rumsfeld, and my sister, Joan Ramsay. I am most of all indebted to the person to whom this memoir is dedicated. As well as her love, Joyce has brought insight, grace, and her trademark joy to my life for our now more than fifty-six years together. She and our three children, Valerie, Marcy, and Nick, have been with me every step of the way with their support and always with good-humored perspective. This memoir is, after all, their story as well as mine.

Even given the hundreds of hours of consultation, research, and review as well as the extensive documentation employed, I recognize it is inevitable that some errors have crept into a book of this scale. As regrettable as it is to accept this human reality, the responsibility for them is mine.

My proceeds from the project will go to the programs my foundation supports for the men and women in uniform, including the wounded and their families. If this book does nothing else but reflect my respect and appreciation for them, that will be enough.

List of Acronyms

ABM: Anti-Ballistic Missile
AID: Agency for International Development
ANA: Afghan National Army
AOR: area of responsibility
BRAC: base realignment and closure
CBW: chemical or biological weapon
CENTCOM: U.S. Central Command
CERP: Commander's Emergency Response Program
CJCS: Chairman of the Joint Chiefs of Staff
CLC: Cost of Living Council
COIN: counterinsurgency
CPA: Coalition Provisional Authority in Iraq
Defcon: Defense condition
DHS: Department of Homeland Security
DNI: director of national intelligence
DoD: Department of Defense
EFP: explosively formed penetrator
EPA: Environmental Protection Agency
FAA: Federal Aviation Administration
FARC: Revolutionary Armed Forces of Colombia
FCC: Federal Communications Commission
FEMA: Federal Emergency Management Agency
FOIA: Freedom of Information Act
GI: General Instrument Corporation
HEW: Department of Health, Education, and Welfare
ICC: International Criminal Court
IED: improvised explosive device
IGC: Iraqi Governing Council
IIA: Iraqi Interim Authority
INL: Bureau of International Narcotics and Law Enforcement Affairs, U.S. Department of State
ISAF: International Security Assistance Force—Afghanistan
ISF: Iraqi Security Forces
ISG: Iraq Survey Group
JCS: Joint Chiefs of Staff
JSOC: Joint Special Operations Command
JSTARS: Joint Surveillance and Target Attack Radar System
LAF: Lebanese armed forces

MARSOC: Marine Corps Special Operations Command
MCA: Military Commission Act of 2006
MEF: Marine Expeditionary Force
MNF: multinational force
MRAP: mine resistant ambush protected vehicle
NATO: North Atlantic Treaty Organization
NGO: nongovernmental organization
NIC: National Intelligence Council
NIE: national intelligence estimate
NMCC: National Military Command Center
NORAD: North American Aerospace Defense Command
NORTHCOM: U.S. Northern Command
NSA: National Security Agency
NSC: National Security Council
NSPD: national security policy directive
ODA: Operational Detachment Alpha
OEO: Office of Economic Opportunity
OLC: Office of Legal Counsel, U.S. Department of Justice
OMB: Office of Management and Budget
OPLAN: operation plan
ORHA: Office of Reconstruction and Humanitarian Assistance—Iraq
OSD: Office of the Secretary of Defense
PA&E: program analysis and evaluation
PKK: Kurdistan Workers' Party
POW: prisoner of war
PRC: People's Republic of China
PRT: provincial reconstruction team
ROTC: Reserve Officers' Training Corps
RPG: rocket-propelled grenade
SAS: British Special Air Service
SALT: Strategic Arms Limitation Treaty
SLRG: Senior Level Review Group, U.S. Department of Defense
SOCOM: U.S. Special Operations Command
SOF: U.S. Special Operations Forces
SOUTHCOM: U.S. Southern Command
SVTC: secure video teleconference
TPFDD: time-phased force and deployment data
UAV: unmanned aerial vehicle
WMD: weapons of mass destruction

List of Illustrations

First Insert

1. Donald and Joan Rumsfeld, c. 1938. (Rumsfeld Collection)
2. Lt. George Rumsfeld and Jeannette Rumsfeld, Coronado, California, c. 1944. (Rumsfeld Collection)
3. The Philmont Scout Ranch guides, Cimarron, New Mexico, 1949. (Rumsfeld Collection)
4. The Princeton University Varsity wrestling team, Princeton, New Jersey, 1953. (Bric-A-Brac [1954], Princeton University Archives.)
5. Donald Rumsfeld and Joyce Pierson, Princeton, New Jersey, June 15, 1954. (Rumsfeld Collection)
6. The crew of a Navy S2F, Naval Air Station Glenview, Glenview, Illinois, c. 1961. (Rumsfeld Collection)
7. Marcy, Joyce, Valerie, and Donald Rumsfeld, Glenview, Illinois, 1962. (Rumsfeld Collection)
8. Donald Rumsfeld, Ned Jannotta, et al., Rumsfeld for Congress headquarters, Winnetka, Illinois, April 10, 1962. (Courtesy of Chicago History Museum, ICHi-62635, Photographer: *Chicago Daily News*)
9. Dwight D. Eisenhower and Donald Rumsfeld, 1962. (Rumsfeld Collection)
10. Donald Rumsfeld and Gerald Ford, U.S. Capitol Building, 1964. (Norman Matheny, 1964, *The Christian Science Monitor,* www.CSMonitor.com)
11. Donald and Marcy Rumsfeld, Vice President Hubert Humphrey, and Virgil Grissom, U.S. Capitol Building, c. 1965. (U.S. Government)
12. Donald Rumsfeld, President Lyndon Baines Johnson, et al., East Room of the White House, April 11, 1968. (Lyndon Baines Johnson Library, Photograph by Yoichi Okamoto)
13. President Richard Nixon, Donald Rumsfeld, Joyce Rumsfeld, Nick Rumsfeld, et al., Rose Garden, the White House, May 26, 1969. (Bettmann Collection, Corbis Images)
14. Donald Rumsfeld, Office of Economic Opportunity office, Washington, D.C., c. 1969. (Office of Economic Opportunity, U.S. Government)

Second Insert

Third Insert

Notes

A large selection of the documents referenced in this book are available at **www.rumsfeld.com.** Readers can both browse the endnotes by chapter and search a broader archive of related personal papers by keyword and subject.

Unless otherwise noted, primary documents are housed in Donald Rumsfeld's personal collection, at the National Archives and Records Administration, at the U.S. Department of Defense, at the U.S. Department of State, or on deposit at the Library of Congress.

AUTHOR'S NOTE

1. Thomas Schelling, foreword, in Roberta Wohlstetter, *Pearl Harbor: Warning and Decision* (Stanford, CA: Stanford University Press, 1962), p. viii.
2. Carl von Clausewitz, *On War,* edited and translated by Michael Howard and Peter Paret (Princeton, NJ: Princeton University Press, 1984).
3. Plato, *The Apology, Phaedo and Crito of Plato,* translated by Benjamin Jowett (New York: P. F. Collier & Son, 1909), pp. 7–8.

PART ONE Lessons in Terror

1. Neil King Jr., "Rumsfeld Handshake Proves Popular," *Wall Street Journal,* September 8, 2006.
2. Rumsfeld to Shultz, State Department cable, "Rumsfeld One-on-One Meeting with Iraqi Deputy Prime Minister and Foreign Minister Tariq Aziz," December 21, 1983.
3. Rumsfeld to Shultz, State Department cable, "Rumsfeld Mission: December 20 Meeting with Iraqi President Saddam Hussein," December 21, 1983.
4. George P. Shultz, *Turmoil and Triumph: My Years as Secretary of State* (New York: Charles Scribner's Sons, 1993), p. 238.
5. Rumsfeld to Shultz, State Department cable, "Rumsfeld Mission: December 20 Meeting with Iraqi President Saddam Hussein," December 21, 1983.
6. Rumsfeld to Shultz, State Department cable, "Rumsfeld Mission: December 20 Meeting with Iraqi President Saddam Hussein," December 21, 1983.

CHAPTER 1 Smiling Death

1. Nicholas Blanford, "The Lasting Impact of 1983 Beirut Attack," *Christian Science Monitor,* October 23, 2008.
2. John Roberts, "Marine Barracks Bombing," *CNN Presents,* CNN, August 13, 2006.
3. Ronald Reagan, *An American Life: The Autobiography* (New York: Simon & Schuster, 1990), p. 437.
4. John Roberts, "Marine Barracks Bombing," *CNN Presents,* CNN, August 13, 2006.
5. Tom Clancy with General Carl Stiner (Ret.) and Tony Koltz, *Shadow Warriors: Inside the Special Forces* (New York: Berkley Publishing Group, 2002), pp. 254–55.
6. Ronald Reagan, remarks, "The Appointment of Donald Rumsfeld as Middle East Envoy," November 3, 1983.
7. Rumsfeld to Shultz, "The Swamp," November 23, 1983.
8. Ronald Reagan, remarks, "The Appointment of Donald Rumsfeld as Middle East Envoy," November 3, 1983.
9. Ronald Reagan, radio address, "The Situation in Lebanon," December 10, 1983.
10. Caspar Weinberger, *Fighting for Peace: Seven Critical Years in the Pentagon* (New York: Warner Books, Inc., 1991), pp. 167–68.
11. George H. W. Bush, *All the Best, George Bush: My Life in Letters and Other Writings* (New York: Scribner, 1999), pp. 330–31.
12. Rumsfeld to Shultz, State Department cable, "Rumsfeld Mission: December 20 Meeting with Iraqi President Saddam Hussein," December 21, 1983.

CHAPTER 2 Into the Swamp

1. Rumsfeld to Shultz, "The Swamp," November 23, 1983.
2. Rumsfeld to Shultz, "The Swamp," November 23, 1983.
3. Rumsfeld to Shultz, "The Swamp," November 23, 1983.
4. Rumsfeld to Shultz, "The Swamp," November 23, 1983.
5. Tom Clancy with General Carl Stiner (Ret.) and Tony Koltz, *Shadow Warriors: Inside the Special Forces* (New York: Berkley Publishing Group, 2002), pp. 235–36.
6. U.S. Department of Defense, *Report of the DoD Commission on Beirut International Airport Terrorist Act, October 23, 1983* (Long Commission Report), December 20, 1983.
7. Ronald Reagan, remarks and question-and-answer session with reporters, "On the Pentagon Report on the Security of United States Marines in Lebanon," December 27, 1983.
8. Ronald Reagan, remarks and question-and-answer session with reporters, "On the Pentagon Report on the Security of United States Marines in Lebanon," December 27, 1983.
9. John Roberts, "Marine Barracks Bombing," *CNN Presents,* CNN, August 13, 2006.
10. Saul Friedman, "Reagan Pressured," Knight-Ridder News Service, January 4, 1984.
11. Rumsfeld to Shultz, "The Swamp," November 23, 1983.
12. Margaret Thatcher, *The Downing Street Years* (New York: HarperCollins, 1993), p. 327.
13. State Department cable, "Middle East Mission Meeting with Mrs. Thatcher, January 20, 1984," January 21, 1984.
14. Rumsfeld, "Lebanese Strategy," undated.

15. Ronald Reagan, radio address, "On the Budget Deficit, Central America, and Lebanon," February 4, 1984.
16. Rumsfeld to Shultz, State Department cable, "Next Steps in Lebanon," January 31, 1984.
17. Lou Cannon, *President Reagan: The Role of a Lifetime* (New York: PublicAffairs, 2000), pp. 399–400.
18. McFarlane to Rumsfeld, cable, "Implementation of NSDD-123," February 4, 1984.
19. Shultz to American Embassy Beirut, State Department cable, "Rumsfeld Report, 2/8/84," February 10, 1984.
20. Ronald Reagan, "Statement on the Situation in Lebanon," February 7, 1984.
21. George P. Shultz, *Turmoil and Triumph: My Years as Secretary of State* (New York: Charles Scribner's Sons, 1993), p. 231.
22. Rick Hampson, "25 Years Later, Bombing in Beirut Still Resonates," *USA Today*, October 15, 2008.
23. Osama bin Laden, transcript of Al Jazeera tape, Reuters, October 29, 2004; Mohamad Bazzi, "'A Thousand New bin Ladens,'" *Newsday*, July 31, 2006.
24. Rumsfeld, remarks, "On the Awarding of the George Catlett Marshall Medal," October 17, 1984.
25. George Shultz, address, "Terrorism and the Modern World," New York, Park Avenue Synagogue, October 25, 1984.

PART TWO An American, Chicago Born

1. Saul Bellow, *The Adventures of Augie March* (New York: Knopf, 1995), p. 5.
2. KTU radio broadcast, Honolulu, Hawaii, NBC Radio Blue Network (Washington, D.C.: Library of Congress, December 7, 1941), disc 21920, cut A2.
3. Louis M. Lyons, "Kennedy Says Democracy All Done in Britain, Maybe Here; Pinch Coming in Loss of Trade," *Boston Sunday Globe*, November 10, 1940.
4. NBC radio broadcast (Washington, D.C.: Library of Congress, December 7, 1941), box C48-E41-85, disc 21918B, cut A1; Newsflashes with Baukhage (Washington, D.C.: Library of Congress, December 7, 1941), box E41, disc 21930, cut A3.
5. Franklin Delano Roosevelt, "Address to Congress Requesting a Declaration of War," December 8, 1941.

CHAPTER 3 The Last of Spring

1. William Manchester, *The Glory and the Dream: A Narrative History of America, 1932–1972* (New York: Bantam Books, 1975), p. 32.
2. Adam Cohen and Elizabeth Taylor, *American Pharaoh: Mayor Richard J. Daley—His Battle for Chicago and the Nation* (Boston: Little, Brown, 2000), p. 55.
3. Rumsfeld, "My Autobiography," January 11, 1946.
4. Adam Cohen and Elizabeth Taylor, *American Pharaoh: Mayor Richard J. Daley—His Battle for Chicago and the Nation* (Boston: Little, Brown, 2000), p. 14.
5. Lincoln Steffens, *The Autobiography of Lincoln Steffens* (Berkeley: Heyday Books, 2005), p. 428.
6. Jeannette Rumsfeld, letter to George Rumsfeld, November 14, 1944.
7. George Rumsfeld, letter to Jeannette Rumsfeld, August 11, 1944.
8. Jeannette Rumsfeld, letter to George Rumsfeld, October 17, 1944.

9. Jeannette Rumsfeld, letter to George Rumsfeld, March 10, 1945.
10. Donald Rumsfeld, letter to George Rumsfeld, March 11, 1945.
11. George Rumsfeld, letter to Jeannette Rumsfeld, August 10, 1945.
12. Secretary of the Navy James Forrestal, letter to George Rumsfeld, October 31, 1945.
13. Rumsfeld, senior thesis, "The Steel Seizure Case of 1952 and Its Effects on Presidential Powers," Princeton University, April 26, 1954.
14. Adlai E. Stevenson, address at the Senior Class Banquet, Princeton Class of 1954, March 22, 1954.

CHAPTER 4 The Longest of Long Shots

1. Donald Rumsfeld, letter to Jeannette Rumsfeld, March 16, 1962.
2. Editorial, "Rumsfeld for Congress," *Chicago Sun-Times,* January 27, 1962.
3. Campaign advertisement, "Marion E. Burks for Congress," *Evanston Review,* April 5, 1962.
4. Richard T. Stout, "GOP's New Star—Donald Rumsfeld: Recent Political Unknown in Sweeping Win Over Burks," *Chicago Daily News,* April 11, 1962.
5. Robert L. Peabody, *The Ford-Halleck Minority Leadership Contest, 1965* (New York: McGraw-Hill, 1966), pp. 3–4.

PART THREE The U.S. Congress: From Camelot to Quagmire

1. Rumsfeld, "Draft of Comments on the Briefing at The White House on Friday, February 25, 1966," February 25, 1966.
2. Congressman John Anderson, "Impressions of Briefing held at The White House on February 25, 1966," March 10, 1966.
3. Rumsfeld, "Draft of Comments on the Briefing at The White House on Friday, February 25, 1966," February 25, 1966.
4. Rumsfeld, "Draft of Comments on the Briefing at The White House on Friday, February 25, 1966," February 25, 1966.
5. Rumsfeld, "Draft of Comments on the Briefing at The White House on Friday, February 25, 1966," February 25, 1966.
6. Rumsfeld, "Draft of Comments on the Briefing at The White House on Friday, February 25, 1966," February 25, 1966.
7. Rumsfeld voting record, "Southeast Asia—H. J. Res. 1145," 88th Cong., 2d sess., August 7, 1964.
8. Rumsfeld, "Draft of Comments on the Briefing at The White House on Friday, February 25, 1966," February 25, 1966.

CHAPTER 5 "Here, Sir, the People Govern"

1. John F. Kennedy, "Special Message to the Congress on Urgent National Needs," May 25, 1961.
2. Rumsfeld, "Space and the Cold War," *Washington Report*, American Security Council, November 18, 1963.
3. "Wernher von Braun: Rocket Man for War and Peace, Part 1," *In Focus*, DW-TV Europa, October 4, 2007.
4. "Wernher von Braun: Rocket Man for War and Peace, Part 1," *In Focus*, DW-TV Europa, October 4, 2007.

5. Rumsfeld, letter to Lowenstein, December 20, 1965.
6. Lowenstein, letter to Rumsfeld, March 10, 1962.
7. "Top Nixon Aide Voices 'Respect' for Lowenstein," *Long Island Press,* October 14, 1970.
8. "Key Nixon Adviser Defends Lowenstein," *Long Island Press,* October 14, 1970.
9. Lady Bird Johnson, *A White House Diary* (New York: Holt, Rinehart and Winston, 1970), p. 734.
10. "Consent by Injunction," *Chicago Tribune,* February 20, 1964; "Lopsided Law," *Chicago Tribune,* February 27, 1964.
11. "Lopsided Law," *Chicago Tribune,* February 27, 1964.
12. "Civil Rights," *Congressman Donald Rumsfeld Reports,* vol. 1, no. 4, November 22, 1963.
13. Rumsfeld voting record, "Civil Rights—HR 7152," 88th Cong., 2d sess., February 10, 1964.
14. Rowland Evans and Robert Novak, "James Farmer's GOP Candidacy Born at Kenyon College Conference," *Washington Post,* July 22, 1968.
15. William McGaffin, "How Rumsfeld Aided Candidate," *Chicago Daily News,* May 23, 1968; "Farmer Tells Why GOP Endorsed Him," *New York Post,* May 20, 1968.
16. "Caucuses Begin Today for Hill Leadership," *Washington Post,* January 2, 1969.
17. Richard Nixon, *RN: The Memoirs of Richard Nixon* (New York: Grosset & Dunlap, 1978), p. 245.
18. Nixon, letter to Rumsfeld, November 16, 1962.
19. Robert F. Kennedy, Jr., afterword, in Barry M. Goldwater, *The Conscience of a Conservative* (Princeton, NJ: Princeton University Press, 2007), p. 123.
20. "Running Mate," *Time,* July 24, 1964.
21. John Chamberlain, "A Vote for Goldwater," *Washington Post,* October 30, 1964.
22. Barry M. Goldwater, speech, acceptance of Republican presidential nomination, twenty-eighth Republican National Convention, July 16, 1964.
23. Barry M. Goldwater, speech, acceptance of Republican presidential nomination, twenty-eighth Republican National Convention, July 16, 1964.
24. "The Record Rep. Rumsfeld Made for You," Committee to Elect Lynn A. Williams to the U.S. Congress, undated.

CHAPTER 6 Young Turks

1. Rumsfeld, "The Ford-Halleck Race 1964-1965," June 7, 2000.
2. Rowland Evans and Robert Novak, "House GOP to Hold Non-Halleck Caucus," *Chicago Sun-Times,* December 1, 1964.
3. William McGaffin, "House GOP 'Young Turks' Study Gains," *Chicago Daily News,* December 17, 1964.
4. Rowland Evans and Robert Novak, "House GOP to Hold Non-Halleck Caucus," *Chicago Sun-Times,* December 1, 1964.
5. "Challenge to Charlie," *Time,* December 25, 1964.
6. "These Are My Guys," *Time,* November 17, 1975.
7. Rumsfeld, "Republican Congressmen—1965—89th Congress," tally sheet for Ford-Halleck Race, January 1965.
8. Rumsfeld, "The Ford-Halleck Race 1964–1965," June 7, 2000.
9. Yanek Mieczkowski, *Gerald Ford and the Challenges of the 1970s* (Lexington, KY: The University Press of Kentucky, 2005), pp. 10–11; Gerald R. Ford, *A Time to Heal: The Autobiography of Gerald R. Ford* (New York: Harper & Row, 1979), p. 77.

10. Michael Beschloss, ed., *Reaching for Glory: Lyndon Johnson's Secret White House Tapes, 1964–1965* (New York: Simon & Schuster, 2001), p. 164.
11. Michael Beschloss, ed., *Reaching for Glory: Lyndon Johnson's Secret White House Tapes, 1964–1965* (New York: Simon & Schuster, 2001), p.164.
12. Rumsfeld voting record, "Vietnam Appropriation—H. J. Res 447," 89th Cong., 1st sess., May 5, 1965.
13. "The Second Session of the 89th Congress Is Well Underway," *Congressman Donald Rumsfeld Reports*, vol. 2, no. 5, March 1966.
14. "Undercurrent of Doubt in Tonkin Gulf Affair," Republican National Committee Radio News, June 12, 1966.
15. Rumsfeld, draft, "Remarks on the U.S. Problem in South Viet Nam," April 11, 1966.
16. Rumsfeld and Callaway, interviewed by Lisagor and Nicodemus, May 31, 1966, rough transcript.
17. "The Situation in South Vietnam," *Congressman Donald Rumsfeld Reports*, vol. 3, no. 5, May 1968.
18. "The Situation in South Vietnam," *Congressman Donald Rumsfeld Reports*, vol. 3, no. 5, May 1968.
19. Rumsfeld voting record, "Defense Authorization, FY 1966 — HR 12889," 89th Cong., 2d sess., March 1, 1966.
20. Roy P. Basler, ed., *The Collected Works of Abraham Lincoln*, vol. 3 (New Brunswick, NJ: Rutgers University Press, 1953), p. 16.
21. House Concurrent Resolution 508, 90th Cong., 1st sess., September 25, 1967.
22. Rumsfeld, "Statement Before the Joint Committee on the Organization of the Congress," June 2, 1965.
23. "U.S. Conduct of War Ripped by Rumsfeld," *Chicago Tribune*, April 13, 1966.
24. "U.S. Conduct of War Ripped by Rumsfeld," *Chicago Tribune*, April 13, 1966.
25. "Selective Service," *Congressman Donald Rumsfeld Reports*, vol. 3, no. 1, April 10, 1967.
26. "Selective Service," *Congressman Donald Rumsfeld Reports*, vol. 3, no. 1, April 10, 1967.
27. Rumsfeld, statement prepared for presentation to the House Committee on Armed Services, quoting Harold Wool, Director of the Office of Procurement Policy and General Research (Manpower), May 2, 1967.
28. "Selective Service Act," *Congressman Donald Rumsfeld Reports*, vol. 3, no. 2, September 1967.
29. Lyndon B. Johnson, "Address to the Nation Announcing Steps to Limit the War in Vietnam and Reporting His Decision Not to Seek Reelection," March 31, 1968.

PART FOUR In Nixon's Arena

1. Rumsfeld, "Memorandum—Rumsfeld Personal File," August 1974.

CHAPTER 7 1968: Year of Turmoil

1. Rumsfeld, "Confidential Memo—1968 Nixon Meeting to Discuss Vice Presidential Nomination," August 8, 1968.
2. Rumsfeld, "Confidential Memo—1968 Nixon Meeting to Discuss Vice Presidential Nomination," August 8, 1968.
3. Rumsfeld, "Confidential Memo—1968 Nixon Meeting to Discuss Vice Presidential Nomination," August 8, 1968; Rumsfeld, interviewed by Deborah Hart Strober and Gerald Strober, February 18, 1994, transcript.

4. Rumsfeld, "Confidential Memo—1968 Nixon Meeting to Discuss Vice Presidential Nomination," August 8, 1968.
5. Rumsfeld, "Confidential Memo—1968 Nixon Meeting to Discuss Vice Presidential Nomination," August 8, 1968.
6. Rumsfeld, "Confidential Memo—1968 Nixon Meeting to Discuss Vice Presidential Nomination," August 8, 1968.
7. "Now the Republic," *Time,* August 16, 1968.
8. "Nixon Picks Agnew as Running Mate," *Chicago Tribune,* August 9, 1968.
9. Rumsfeld, statement, "Concerning Activity in the City of Chicago, Illinois, During the Democratic National Convention," October 1, 1968.
10. Jeffrey Kimball, *Nixon's Vietnam War* (Lawrence, KS: University Press of Kansas, 1998), p. 32.
11. Rumsfeld, [No Subject], October 15, 1968.
12. Rumsfeld, [No Subject], October 15, 1968.

CHAPTER 8 The Job That Couldn't Be Done

1. Richard Nixon, speech, acceptance of Republican presidential nomination, twenty-ninth Republican National Convention, August 8, 1968.
2. Rumsfeld voting record, "Anti-Poverty—Economic Opportunity Act—HR 11377," 88th Cong., 2d sess., August 8, 1964.
3. Rumsfeld, [No Subject], April 4, 1969.
4. William H. Rehnquist, "Re: Appointment of Congressman to the Office of Director of the Office of Economic Opportunity," April 14, 1969.
5. Jack Anderson, "Anti-Poverty Czar Embellishes Office," *Washington Post,* September 22, 1969.
6. Jack Anderson, "Anti-Poverty Czar Embellishes Office," *Washington Post,* September 22, 1969.
7. Rumsfeld, "The Washington Merry-Go-Round Column by Jack Anderson titled: 'Anti-Poverty Czar Embellishes Office' (The Washington Post—Monday, September 22, 1969)," undated.
8. "Scoops On Target and Off," *Time,* April 3, 1972; "The Case of the O.E.O. Office," *New York Times,* August 13, 1972.
9. Milton and Rose D. Friedman, *Two Lucky People: Memoirs* (Chicago, IL: University of Chicago Press, 1998), pp. 344–45.
10. Eric Wentworth, "OEO Plans Test of Education Vouchers," *Washington Post,* December 26, 1970.
11. Terry Lenzner, as quoted in Rowan Scarborough, *Rumsfeld's War: The Untold Story of America's Anti-Terrorist Commander* (Washington, D.C.: Regnery Publishing, 2004), p. 73.
12. Rumsfeld, letter to Hoover, November 11, 1969.

CHAPTER 9 Counsellor

1. Rebecca Roberts, "Kent State Shooting Divided Campus and Country," *Talk of the Nation,* WKSU/National Public Radio, Kent, OH: May 3, 2010.
2. Donald Murdoch to Rumsfeld, "Jackson Visit," May 18, 1970.
3. Charles W. Colson, *Born Again* (Peabody, MA: Hendrickson Publishers, 1995), p. 77.

4. H. R. Haldeman to Bob Ehrlichman, Bob Finch, Bryce Harlow, Donald Rumsfeld, and George Shultz, [No Subject], June 15, 1970.
5. Stephen E. Ambrose, "Comparing and Contrasting Ike and Dick," in *Richard M. Nixon: Politician, President, Administrator,* edited by Leon Friedman and William F. Levantrosser (Westport, CT: Greenwood Press, 1991), p. 15.
6. Rumsfeld to Nixon, "The Administration and Minorities," March 18, 1971.
7. Rumsfeld, "Cabinet Meeting, Friday, July 10, 1970," July 10, 1970; Kissinger, handwritten note, July 10, 1970.
8. Rumsfeld, [No Subject], January 15, 1971.
9. Nixon and Rumsfeld, taped conversation, July 22, 1971.
10. Rumsfeld, "Key Biscayne Meeting," November 7, 1970.
11. Rumsfeld voting record, "Dept. of Housing & Urban Development, Establish—HR 6927," 89th Cong., 1st sess., June 16, 1965.
12. James Reston, Jr., *The Lone Star: The Life of John Connally* (New York: Harper & Row, Publishers, 1989), pp. 396–97.
13. Richard Nixon, Executive Order 11615: "Providing for Stabilization of Prices, Rents, Wages, and Salaries," August 15, 1971.
14. Rumsfeld, interviewed by Deborah Hart Strober and Gerald Strober, February 18, 1994, transcript.
15. John Cassidy, "The Hayek Century," *Hoover Digest,* no. 3, 2000.
16. Rumsfeld, interviewed by Deborah Hart Strober and Gerald Strober, February 18, 1994, transcript.
17. Rumsfeld, interviewed by Deborah Hart Strober and Gerald Strober, February 18, 1994, transcript.
18. Rumsfeld, interviewed by Deborah Hart Strober and Gerald Strober, February 18, 1994, transcript.
19. Rumsfeld to Haldeman, "Response to your Memo of June 12th on the President and the Campaign," June 16, 1972 (Richard Nixon Presidential Library and Museum).
20. Bob Woodward and Carl Bernstein, "GOP Security Aide Among Five Arrested in Bugging Affair," *Washington Post,* June 19, 1972.
21. Bob Woodward and Carl Bernstein, "GOP Security Aide Among Five Arrested in Bugging Affair," *Washington Post,* June 19, 1972.
22. Jonathan Aitken, *Charles W. Colson: A Life Redeemed* (New York: Doubleday, 2005), p. 167.
23. Rumsfeld, "Watergate," August 9, 1973.
24. Rumsfeld, "Cabinet Meeting," November 8, 1972.
25. Rumsfeld, "Cabinet Meeting," November 8, 1972.
26. Rumsfeld, "Cabinet Meeting," November 8, 1972.
27. Charles W. Colson, *Born Again* (Peabody, MA: Hendrickson Publishers, 1995), p. 8.
28. White House memo, "Post-Election Activities," November 8, 1972.
29. Richard Reeves, *President Nixon: Alone in the White House* (New York: Simon & Schuster, 2001), p. 550.
30. Rumsfeld, "At Camp David," November 20, 1972.
31. Nixon and Rumsfeld, taped conversation, July 22, 1971.
32. David S. Broder, "Rumsfeld Says New Job Rounds Out Education," *Washington Post,* December 5, 1972.

CHAPTER 10 NATO and Nixon's Fall

1. Rumsfeld, draft, "Talking Points on Use of Government Vehicles," undated.

2. Laurence Stern and Haynes Johnson, "3 Top Nixon Aides, Kleindienst Out," *Washington Post,* June 1, 1973.
3. Hearing of the House Committee on Foreign Affairs and Subcommittee on Europe, "Proposals to Reduce American Troop Level in Europe," statement of Donald Rumsfeld, Washington, D.C., July 12, 1973.
4. Rumsfeld, "Notes for Rumsfeld File," October 1973.
5. Rumsfeld, interviewed by Deborah Hart Strober and Gerald Strober, February 18, 1994, transcript.
6. Charles W. Colson, *Born Again* (Peabody, MA: Hendrickson Publishers, 1995), p. 77.
7. Rumsfeld, "Memorandum of Telephone Conversation from Gen. Al Haig," July 22, 1974.
8. Rumsfeld, "Memorandum of Telephone Conversation from Gen. Al Haig," July 22, 1974.
9. Rumsfeld, "Meeting with SYG Luns," July 16, 1974.
10. Richard Nixon, *RN: The Memoirs of Richard Nixon* (New York: Grosset & Dunlap, 1978), p. 1042.
11. Rumsfeld, "Phone Conversation with President Richard Nixon on 8/12/83," August 12, 1983.
12. Martin Weil and Eleanor Randolph, "Richard M. Nixon, 37th President, Dies," *Washington Post,* April 23, 1994.
13. Martin Weil and Eleanor Randolph, "Richard M. Nixon, 37th President, Dies," *Washington Post,* April 23, 1994.
14. Rumsfeld, [No Subject], May 13, 1994.

PART FIVE Javelin Catcher: Inside the Ford White House

1. Gerald R. Ford, *A Time to Heal: The Autobiography of Gerald R. Ford* (New York: Harper & Row, 1979), pp. 59–60.
2. Gerald R. Ford, *A Time to Heal: The Autobiography of Gerald R. Ford* (New York: Harper & Row, 1979), p. 60.

CHAPTER 11 Restoring Trust

1. Scranton and Whitehead, letter to Rumsfeld, August 9, 1974; Rumsfeld, "Memorandum—Rumsfeld Personal File," August 1974; Jerry terHorst, news conference at the White House, August 10, 1974 (Press Briefing, 8/10/74, Box 1, Ron Nessen Files, Gerald R. Ford Library).
2. Gerald R. Ford, *A Time to Heal: The Autobiography of Gerald R. Ford* (New York: Harper & Row, 1979), p. 126.
3. Rumsfeld, "Meeting in the Cabinet Room," August 9, 1974.
4. Marjorie Hunter, "Kissinger Will Remain Secretary of State; Ford Likely to Keep Other Aides Also," *New York Times,* August 9, 1974.
5. Rumsfeld, "Meeting in the Cabinet Room," August 9, 1974.
6. Rumsfeld, [No Subject], October 2, 1974.
7. Philip Shabecoff, "Ford Bids Cabinet and Agency Heads Remain in Posts," *New York Times,* August 11, 1974; Rumsfeld to Ford, "A Vice President," August 13, 1974.
8. "The Veepstakes," *Newsweek,* August 26, 1974.
9. John Herbers, "Optimism Voiced," *New York Times,* August 21, 1974.
10. "The Veepstakes," *Newsweek,* August 26, 1974.

11. Rumsfeld, "Memorandum of Meeting with the President, Oval Office," August 15, 1974.
12. Rumsfeld, "Meeting with the President," August 20, 1974, 10:00 a.m.
13. John Herbers, "Optimism Voiced," *New York Times*, August 21, 1974.
14. Rumsfeld, "Meeting with the President," August 20, 1974, [time unknown].
15. John Herbers, "Optimism Voiced," *New York Times*, August 21, 1974.
16. Christopher Lydon, "G.O.P. Still Faces the Realities of Decay and Minority Status," *New York Times*, September 1, 1974.
17. John Herbers, "Optimism Voiced," *New York Times*, August 21, 1974.
18. Rumsfeld, "Cabinet Meeting: Ford Administration," August 10, 1974.
19. Transition Team memo, "Personnel," hand-delivered by Rumsfeld to Ford on August 20, 1974; Lady Bird Johnson, *A White House Diary* (New York: Holt, Rinehart and Winston, 1970), pp. 733–34.
20. "'The Sun Is Shining Again,'" *Newsweek*, August 26, 1974.
21. Rumsfeld, "Cabinet Meeting: Ford Administration," August 10, 1974.
22. Gerald R. Ford, "Remarks on Signing a Proclamation Granting Pardon to Richard Nixon," September 8, 1974.
23. Gerald R. Ford, *A Time to Heal: The Autobiography of Gerald R. Ford* (New York: Harper & Row, 1979), pp. 196–99.
24. Adam Clymer, "Ford Wins Kennedy Award for 'Courage' of Nixon Pardon," *New York Times*, May 22, 2001; Bill Boyarsky, "Kennedy Says He Doubts Public Will Stand for Pardon," *Los Angeles Times*, September 14, 1974.
25. Donald Rumsfeld, letter to George Rumsfeld, October 15, 1954.
26. Rumsfeld, "Memorandum of Telephone Conversation from the President," September 19, 1974.
27. Gerald R. Ford, *A Time to Heal: The Autobiography of Gerald R. Ford* (New York: Harper & Row, 1979), p. 186.
28. Rumsfeld, "Memorandum of Conversation with President," September 22, 1974.

CHAPTER 12 A Rocky Start

1. Rumsfeld to Buchen, [No Subject], September 29, 1974.
2. Rumsfeld, "Safe in Haig's Office," September 29, 1974; Cheney, "Safe with Attached Receipt," September 29, 1974.
3. Gannon, letter to Rumsfeld, October 31, 1974.
4. Rumsfeld, "Memorandum for the File," October 5, 1974.
5. Rumsfeld, "Meeting with the President," October 3, 1974.
6. Rumsfeld, "Memorandum for the File," October 5, 1974; Rumsfeld, "Phone call from Ron Ziegler, 8:20 AM (5:20 AM in California)," October 5, 1974.
7. Rumsfeld to Cheney, [No Subject], filed October 13, 1974.
8. Rumsfeld, "Memo: Meeting with the President," October 11, 1974 .
9. Rumsfeld, "Meeting with the President," October 17, 1974.
10. Gerald R. Ford, *A Time to Heal: The Autobiography of Gerald R. Ford* (New York: Harper & Row, 1979), p. 187.
11. Gerald R. Ford, *A Time to Heal: The Autobiography of Gerald R. Ford* (New York: Harper & Row, 1979), p. 187.
12. Rumsfeld, "Meeting with the President," November 13, 1974.
13. Rumsfeld, "Meeting with the President (10/18/74) from 1:10 to 1:14," October 18, 1974; Rumsfeld, "Meeting with the President," October 23, 1974.
14. Jesse Helms and Strom Thurmond, letter to Ford, June 23, 1975.

15. Rowland Evans and Robert Novak, "Solzhenitsyn, Kissinger and Détente," *Washington Post,* July 20, 1975.
16. Rumsfeld, "Meeting with the President," July 9, 1975, 11:32; Rumsfeld, "Meeting with the President," July 9, 1975, 17:28; Cheney to Rumsfeld, "Solzhenitsyn," July 8, 1975.
17. Rowland Evans and Robert Novak, "Snubbing Solzhenitsyn," *Washington Post,* July 17, 1975.
18. Rumsfeld, "Memorandum of Telephone Conversation from the President," September 19, 1974.
19. Rumsfeld, "Meeting with the President: Oval Office," October 8, 1974.
20. Rumsfeld, "Meeting with the President: Oval Office," October 8, 1974; Rumsfeld, "Meeting with the President," December 2, 1974.
21. Rumsfeld, "Meeting with the President: Oval Office," October 8, 1974.
22. Rumsfeld, handwritten note, September 16, 1975; Jude Wanniski, "Taxes, Revenues, and the 'Laffer Curve,'" *Public Interest* (Winter 1978).
23. Rumsfeld, "Meeting with the President: Pearl Harbor Day," December 7, 1974.
24. Rumsfeld, "Meeting with the President," December 19, 1974.
25. Rumsfeld, "Meeting with the President," October 1, 1974.
26. Rumsfeld, "Meeting with the President," December 21, 1974.
27. Rumsfeld, "Meeting with the President," December 21, 1974.
28. Rumsfeld, "Meeting with the President," January 3, 1975.
29. Joseph E. Persico, *The Imperial Rockefeller: A Biography of Nelson A. Rockefeller* (New York: Simon & Schuster, 1982), p. 261.
30. Sam Roberts, "Serving as Ford's No. 2, Rockefeller Never Took His Eye Off Top Job," *New York Times,* December 31, 2006.
31. David Burnham, "Rockefeller Plan Splits Ford Aides," *New York Times,* September 5, 1975; Rumsfeld, "Continuation: Meeting with the President," August 27, 1975.
32. Rumsfeld, interviewed by Cary Reich, November 5, 1991, transcript.
33. David Burnham, "Greenspan Asserts Energy Loan Plan Could Have Potential for Corruption," *New York Times,* September 6, 1975.
34. Gerald R. Ford, *A Time to Heal: The Autobiography of Gerald R. Ford* (New York: Harper & Row, 1979), p. 327.
35. William Brink, "Ford to City: Drop Dead," *Daily News,* October 30, 1975.
36. Rumsfeld, "Meeting with the President," October 24, 1975.
37. Hobart Rowen, "Energy Plan is Victory for Rockefeller," *Washington Post,* September 24, 1975; Joseph Lelyveld, "Rockefeller Making an Impact on Policy," *New York Times,* September 27, 1975.
38. "Thinking Big," *Wall Street Journal,* September 25, 1975; Nicholas von Hoffman, "Ford Puts Strain on Marketplace," *Chicago Tribune,* September 27, 1975.
39. Mary Russell, "House Rejects Fuel Plan," *Washington Post,* December 12, 1975.
40. Sidney Blumenthal, "The Imperial Vice Presidency," *Salon.com,* June 28, 2007.
41. Don Oberdorfer, "He Wants to Be Speaker of the House," *New York Times,* April 30, 1967.
42. White House memorandum, "Meetings at Camp David," December 4, 1974.
43. Reuters, "Chevy Chase recalls Ford as 'a terrific guy,'" MSNBC, December 27, 2006.
44. Betty Ford, "Remarks to the American Cancer Society," New York City, November 7, 1975; Betty Ford with Chris Chase, *Betty: A Glad Awakening* (New York: Doubleday, 1987).
45. "Vice President Ford: 'Why I Will Not Run in '76,'" *U.S. News & World Report,* December 17, 1973.

46. Gerald R. Ford, "Recollections of President Gerald R. Ford," September 5, 1975, transcribed by Leona M. Goodell.
47. Special Agent Larry M. Buendorf, United States Secret Service, statement, Senator Hotel, Sacramento, California, September 5, 1975; Tom Matthews, Thomas M. DeFrank, Gerald C. Lubenow, William J. Cook, and Hal Bruno, "Ford's Brush with Death," *Newsweek*, September 15, 1975.
48. Rumsfeld, interviewed by Don Fulsom, Air Force One, September 22, 1975, transcript.
49. David M. Alpen with Peter S. Greenberg, Thomas DeFrank, and Tom Joyce, "Can the Risk Be Cut," *Newsweek*, October 6, 1975; Philip Shabecoff, *New York Times*, September 23, 1975.
50. Gerald R. Ford, *A Time to Heal: The Autobiography of Gerald R. Ford* (New York: Harper & Row, 1979), p. 312.
51. Eileen Keerdoja, "Squeaky and Sara Jane," *Newsweek*, November 8, 1976.
52. Gerald R. Ford, *A Time to Heal: The Autobiography of Gerald R. Ford* (New York: Harper & Row, 1979), p. 312.
53. Gerald R. Ford, "Remarks of the President Upon His Arrival at the White House," September 22, 1975.
54. Rumsfeld, "Meeting with the President," September 24, 1975.
55. Tom Mathews, Thomas M. DeFrank, John J. Lindsay, and Tony Fuller, "How Sick Is the GOP?" *Newsweek*, August 23, 1976.

CHAPTER 13 An Agonizing Reappraisal

1. Rumsfeld, "Meeting with the President," October 22, 1975.
2. Rumsfeld, "Meeting with the President," October 22, 1975.
3. Rumsfeld, "Meeting with the President," October 23, 1975.
4. Rumsfeld, "Meeting with the President," October 23, 1975.
5. Rumsfeld, "Meeting with the President," October 24, 1975, 16:20.
6. Rumsfeld, "Meeting with the President," October 24, 1975, 21:32.
7. Rumsfeld and Cheney to Ford, [No Subject], October 24, 1975.
8. Rumsfeld, "Meeting with the President," October 25, 1975.
9. Gerald R. Ford, *A Time to Heal: The Autobiography of Gerald R. Ford* (New York: Harper & Row, 1979), p. 326; Henry Kissinger, *Years of Renewal* (New York: Simon & Schuster, 1999), pp. 836–37.
10. Gerald R. Ford, *A Time to Heal: The Autobiography of Gerald R. Ford* (New York: Harper & Row, 1979), pp. 326–27.
11. Rumsfeld, "Meeting with the President," October 27, 1975.
12. Rumsfeld, "Continuation of Meeting with the President," October 28, 1975.
13. Congressional Record, vol. 109, pt. 15, October 21, 1963, pp. 19971–19974.
14. Rumsfeld, "Meeting with the President," November 1, 1975.
15. George H. W. Bush with Victor Gold, *Looking Forward: An Autobiography* (New York: Doubleday, 1987), p. 158; Herbert S. Parmet, *George Bush: The Life of a Lone Star Yankee* (Brunswick, NJ: Transaction Publishers, 2001), p. 188.
16. Rumsfeld to Ford, "CIA Director," undated.
17. Howard J. Osborn to Executive Secretary, CIA Management Committee, "Family Jewels," May 16, 1973 (Central Intelligence Agency).
18. Gerald R. Ford, *A Time to Heal: The Autobiography of Gerald R. Ford* (New York: Harper & Row, 1979), p. 325.
19. Barbara Bush, *Barbara Bush: A Memoir* (New York: Scribner, 1994), p. 134.

20. Herbert S. Parmet, *George Bush: The Life of a Lone Star Yankee* (Brunswick, NJ: Transaction Publishers, 2001), p. 189.
21. Gerald R. Ford, *A Time to Heal: The Autobiography of Gerald R. Ford* (New York: Harper & Row, 1979), pp. 337–38.
22. "Rumsfeld for Defense," *Wall Street Journal,* March 10, 1989.
23. Rumsfeld, letter to Ford with attachments, March 28, 1989.
24. Ford, letter to Rumsfeld, April 3, 1989.
25. Lou Cannon, "Rumsfeld: Silent Architect, Chief of Staff Seen as Force Behind Shake-Up," *Washington Post,* November 4, 1975.
26. Nelson A. Rockefeller, interviewed by Hugh Morrow, November 22, 1977, transcript, p. 27 (Rockefeller Archive Center).
27. Gerald R. Ford, *A Time to Heal: The Autobiography of Gerald R. Ford* (New York: Harper & Row, 1979), p. 327.
28. Gerald R. Ford, *A Time to Heal: The Autobiography of Gerald R. Ford* (New York: Harper & Row, 1979), p. 345.

PART SIX Fighting the Cold War

1. Rumsfeld, "Eulogy for President Ford," Grand Rapids, Michigan, January 3, 2007.

CHAPTER 14 Unfinished Business

1. Douglas Brinkley, "Of Ladders and Letters," *Time,* April 24, 2000.
2. Rumsfeld, "Memorandum: Meeting with the President," April 29, 1975, 15:42.
3. Ron Nessen, *It Sure Looks Different from the Inside* (Chicago, IL: Playboy Press, 1978), p. 110.
4. Rumsfeld, "Meeting with the President," April 29, 1975, 17:10.
5. Kissinger, news conference, April 29, 1975 (*The Department of State Bulletin,* vol. LXXII, no. 1873, May 19, 1975).
6. Rumsfeld, "Meeting with the President," April 30, 1975, 8:31 a.m.
7. Ron Nessen, *It Sure Looks Different from the Inside* (Chicago, IL: Playboy Press, 1978), p. 113.
8. Rumsfeld, "Meeting with the President," April 30, 1975, 10:00 a.m.
9. General Fred C. Weyand, "Report to the President of the United States on the Situation in South Vietnam," and cover memo, April 4, 1975 (Gerald R. Ford Library, National Security Adviser, Presidential Country Files for East Asia and the Pacific, Box 19, Folder: "Vietnam [13]").
10. Rumsfeld, "Meeting with the President: National Security Council Meeting in the Cabinet Room," May 12, 1975.
11. Comptroller General of the United States, "The Seizure of the Mayaguez—A Case Study of Crisis Management" (Washington, D.C.: U.S. Government Printing Office, 1976), p. 63.
12. Rumsfeld to Ford, "Cambodia," May 14, 1975.
13. Rumsfeld, "Meeting with the President," May 14, 1975; Rumsfeld to Ford, "Cambodia," May 14, 1975.
14. Rumsfeld, "Meeting with the President: National Security Council Meeting on Cambodia," May 14, 1975.
15. Richard J. Levine, "Success of *Mayaguez* Recovery Bolsters Ford's Political Stock, Military Morale," *Wall Street Journal,* May 16, 1975.

CHAPTER 15 Turning On the Lights

1. Rowan Scarborough, *Rumsfeld's War: The Untold Story of America's Anti-Terrorist Commander* (Washington, D.C.: Regnery Publishing, 2004), p. 81.
2. David Binder, "Senate Votes to Cut Off Covert Aid for Angolans; Ford Predicts a 'Tragedy,'" *New York Times,* December 20, 1975.
3. Rumsfeld, "Meeting with the President," February 27, 1976.
4. Leonid Brezhnev, excerpted in "The 25th Party Congress," *Survival,* vol. 18, no. 3 (May/June 1976), pp. 123–26.
5. Arnaud De Borchgrave, "'Sleepers' in NATO," *Newsweek,* March 8, 1976.
6. Arnaud De Borchgrave, "'Sleepers' in NATO," *Newsweek,* March 8, 1976.
7. "Excerpts from Brezhnev's Appeal for World Red Meeting," *New York Times,* November 7, 1964.
8. Pulitzer Prize Board, "Statement on Walter Duranty's 1932 Prize," November 21, 2003; Arnold Beichman, "Pulitzer-Winning Lies," *Weekly Standard,* June 12, 2003.
9. Hearing of the Senate Armed Services Committee, "Nomination of Donald Rumsfeld to be Secretary of Defense," Washington, D.C., November 12–13, 1975.
10. Daniel Lewis, "Philip Berrigan, Former Priest and Peace Advocate in the Vietnam War Era, Dies at 79," *New York Times,* December 8, 2002.
11. "6 Jailed for Demonstration Against Nuclear Weapons," *New York Times,* January 8, 1977.
12. "Three Arrested for Digging Up Rumsfeld Lawn," *Washington Post,* August 29, 1976.
13. Rumsfeld, "Memo," November 29, 1995.
14. John W. Finney, "Rumsfeld Fights Lynn on Arms Budget Cuts," *New York Times,* December 6, 1975.
15. Rumsfeld to Secretaries of the Military Departments et al., "NATO Weapon Systems Standardization," January 28, 1976.
16. Rowland Evans and Robert Novak, "Tank Trouble," *Washington Post,* August 6, 1976.
17. Rumsfeld, "Statement by Secretary of Defense Donald Rumsfeld," September 21, 1976.
18. Melvin Price, letter to Rumsfeld, July 30, 1976; Melvin Price, letter to Rumsfeld, August 5, 1976; Rumsfeld, letter to Melvin Price, August 6, 1976.

CHAPTER 16 Hold the SALT: Tension over Détente

1. "Ford's Costly Purge," *Time,* November 17, 1975.
2. Kissinger and James (Scotty) Reston, phone conversation, November 3, 1975, transcript.
3. Kissinger and Secretary William Simon, phone conversation, November 3, 1975, transcript.
4. Kissinger and Secretary William Simon, phone conversation, November 3, 1975, transcript.
5. "Total NODIS Cables Processed by the Cable Branch," December 1976.
6. John W. Finney, "Rumsfeld Fights Lynn on Arms Budget Cuts," *New York Times,* December 6, 1975.
7. John W. Finney, "Rumsfeld Calls for More Funds, Citing Increasing Soviet Power," *New York Times,* January 28, 1976.
8. Marshall to Rumsfeld, "Key Military Balances," December 6, 1975.
9. Rumsfeld, *U.S. Defense Perspectives: Fiscal Year 1977,* July 1976.

10. Rumsfeld, *U.S. Defense Perspectives: Fiscal Year 1978*, January 1977; Rumsfeld, interviewed by Dr. Alfred Goldberg and Dr. Roger Trask, OSD Historical Office, August 2, 1994, transcript, pp. 3–5.
11. Rumsfeld, interviewed by Dr. Alfred Goldberg and Dr. Roger Trask, OSD Historical Office, July 12, 1994, transcript, pp. 20–21.
12. Rumsfeld, interviewed by Dr. Alfred Goldberg and Dr. Roger Trask, OSD Historical Office, August 2, 1994, transcript, pp. 3–4; "Hughes/Currie Briefing Attendance Summary (Presentations to Members of the 94th Congress)," undated.
13. Defense Department cable, "Soviets Attack Sec Def Rumsfeld and Growing US Defense Budget," September 22, 1976.
14. Linwood B. Carter and Thomas Coipuram Jr., "Defense Authorization and Appropriations Bills: A Chronology, FY1970–FY2006," CRS Report for Congress, 98-756C, updated May 23, 2005.
15. Lou Cannon, *Governor Reagan: His Rise to Power* (New York: Public Affairs, 2003), pp. 416–17.
16. Gerald R. Ford, "Remarks and a Question-and-Answer Session," Everett McKinley Dirksen Forum, Peoria, Illinois, March 5, 1976.
17. Jon Nordheimer, "Reagan Sharpens His Criticism of Ford, Citing Canal Talks and Two in Cabinet," *New York Times*, February 29, 1976.
18. Ronald Reagan, TV address to the nation, "To Restore America," March 31, 1976; Jon Nordheimer, "Reagan Appeals for Wide Support," *New York Times*, April 1, 1976.
19. Memorandum of conversation, Ford, Kissinger, Rumsfeld, and Scowcroft, Oval Office, March 29, 1976 (Gerald R. Ford Library).
20. Memorandum of conversation, Ford, Kissinger, Rumsfeld, and Scowcroft, Oval Office, March 29, 1976 (Gerald R. Ford Library).
21. Rumsfeld, interviewed by Dr. Alfred Goldberg and Dr. Roger Trask, OSD Historical Office, July 12, 1994, transcript, pp. 33–34.
22. Henry Kissinger, *Years of Renewal* (New York: Simon & Schuster, 1999), p. 176.
23. Rumsfeld to Ford, "'Cruise Missile' Definition," August 2, 1976.
24. Rumsfeld, "Continuation: Meeting with the President," February 15, 1976.
25. Brezhnev, letter to Ford, March 17, 1976.

CHAPTER 17 The 1976 Defeat

1. Rumsfeld, handwritten note, August 7, 1976.
2. Christopher Lydon, "G.O.P. Still Faces the Realities of Decay and Minority Status," *New York Times*, September 1, 1974.
3. Gerald R. Ford and Jimmy Carter, first presidential debate, moderated by Edwin Newman, Walnut Street Theatre, Philadelphia, Pennsylvania, September 23, 1976, transcript; "What the Voters Say," *Newsweek*, October 4, 1976.
4. Gerald R. Ford and Jimmy Carter, second presidential debate, moderated by Pauline Frederick, Palace of Fine Arts Theatre, San Francisco, California, October 6, 1976, transcript.
5. George S. Brown, interviewed by Ranan Lurie, April 12, 1976, transcript.
6. Lee Lescaze, "Gen. Brown Is in Hot Water Again," *Washington Post*, October 19, 1976.
7. Lee Lescaze, "Gen. Brown Is in Hot Water Again," *Washington Post*, October 19, 1976.
8. Rumsfeld and Brown, news conference, Pentagon, October 18, 1976, transcript.
9. "Together in Defeat," *Chicago Sun-Times*, November 4, 1976.
10. Rumsfeld, "Meeting with the President," November 5, 1976.

11. Memorandum of conversation, Carter, Mondale, Rumsfeld et al., Blair House, November 22, 1976.
12. Memorandum of conversation, Carter, Mondale, Rumsfeld et al., Blair House, November 22, 1976.
13. Rumsfeld, "President-elect's Visit, 10 December 1976," December 10, 1976.
14. Rumsfeld to Ford, "Review of Alternatives to the B-1 Bomber," October 23, 1976; Edward E. David, Jr., Michael M. May, and Paul H. Nitze, letter to Thomas C. Reed, Secretary of the Air Force, October 8, 1976.
15. Rumsfeld, "Meeting with the President," November 22, 1976.

PART SEVEN Back to Reality

CHAPTER 18 Searle's Sweet Success

1. Joann S. Lublin, "Searle Confirms Rumsfeld Will Become President, Chief Executive Officer June 1," *Wall Street Journal,* April 18, 1977.
2. Jim Denny, "G. D. Searle & Co.: A Brief History as Recalled by Jim Denny," June 17, 2010.
3. OECD Health Data 2010, Organization for Economic Cooperation and Development, June 2010.
4. Hugh D. Menzies, "The Ten Toughest Bosses," *Fortune,* April 21, 1980.
5. Robert H. Mazur, "Discovery of Aspartame," in *Aspartame: Physiology and Biochemistry,* eds. Lewis D. Stegink and Lloyd J. Filer, Jr. (New York: Marcel Dekker, Inc., 1984), pp. 3–4; John E. Robson, "Aspartame Chronology," July 30, 1986.
6. "Study of G. D. Searle Shows 'Sloppy' Tests of Drugs, FDA Says," *Wall Street Journal,* January 21, 1976; "FDA Calls for Grand Jury Investigation of G. D. Searle's Drug-Testing Practices," *Wall Street Journal,* April 9, 1976.
7. Donald R. Murdoch, letter to Dan Rather, July 17, 1984.
8. Rumsfeld, [No Subject], July 12, 1984.
9. Rumsfeld, "NutraSweet," October 22, 1990.
10. "Searle: Rallying a Drug Company with an Injection of New Vitality," *BusinessWeek,* February 8, 1982.
11. Patricia Szymczak, "Monsanto, Searle Make Sweet Deal," *St. Louis Globe-Democrat,* July 19, 1985.
12. "Searle 1888–1985," shareholder report, January 31, 1986.

CHAPTER 19 From Malaise to Morning in America

1. Carter, letter to Rumsfeld, October 24, 1978; Carter, letter to Rumsfeld, November 15, 1978; Rumsfeld-Searle, letter to Carter, December 6, 1978; Rumsfeld, letter to Carter, December 6, 1978.
2. "My Opinion of the Russians Has Changed Most Drastically . . ." *Time,* January 14, 1980.
3. "My Opinion of the Russians Has Changed Most Drastically . . ." *Time,* January 14, 1980.
4. Hearing of the Senate Armed Services Committee, statement of Donald Rumsfeld, October 11, 1979.
5. Rumsfeld, "Meeting at the White House," January 9, 1980.

6. Zbigniew Brzezinski, *Power and Principle: Memoirs of the National Security Adviser, 1977–1981* (New York: Farrar, Straus and Giroux, 1983), p. 433.
7. "My Opinion of the Russians Has Changed Most Drastically . . ." *Time,* January 14, 1980.
8. Jimmy Carter, address on Afghanistan, January 4, 1980, transcript.
9. Rumsfeld, "Soviet Invasion of Afghanistan," January 9, 1980.
10. Reagan for President News, July 1, 1980.
11. Rumsfeld, remarks at the Republican National Convention, Detroit, Michigan, July 14, 1980, transcript.
12. Hedrick Smith, "Running-Mate List Trimmed by Reagan," *New York Times,* July 1, 1980.
13. Robert A. Goldwin, "John Locke and the Law of the Sea," *Commentary* (June 1981).
14. Rumsfeld, "Meeting with President Reagan on October 13, [1982]," January 24, 1983.
15. Rumsfeld to Reagan, "Law of the Sea," December 11, 1982.
16. Rumsfeld to Reagan, "Law of the Sea," December 11, 1982.
17. Rumsfeld, [No Subject], December 10, 1986.
18. Rumsfeld, "Meeting with Fahrenkopf and Bill Greener, III," November 10, 1986.
19. Rumsfeld to Bernie Windon and Linda Schaefer, "Thoughts on the Iowa Trip," October 15, 1986.
20. Ann Reilly Dowd, "Who's Ahead in the '88 Money Race," *Fortune,* vol. 115, no. 12, June 8, 1987.
21. Richard L. Berke, "Campaign Loans Often Risky," *New York Times,* June 16, 1987.
22. Glenn, letter to Rumsfeld, April 27, 1987; Rumsfeld, letter to Glenn, May 21, 1987.

CHAPTER 20 Our Rural Period, Interrupted

1. William Safire, "Spectrum Squatters," *New York Times,* October 9, 2000.
2. Rumsfeld, "1996 GOP Convention," August 28, 1996.
3. Rumsfeld, handwritten note, October 31, 1996.
4. Roger Longman, "Gilead's Metamorphoses," *In Vivo: The Business and Medicine Report* (March 1996), pp. 35–45.
5. Rumsfeld to Shultz, "Gilead Board," November 9, 1998.
6. Rumsfeld, letter to Rice, March 29, 1999.
7. Rumsfeld, [No Subject], February 1, 1999.
8. Rumsfeld, [No Subject], February 1, 1999.
9. Rumsfeld, letter to Bolten, cc: Rice, April 28, 1999.
10. Alison Mitchell, "Bush Says U.S. Should Reduce Nuclear Arms," *New York Times,* May 24, 2000.
11. Rumsfeld, "Bush Administration," December 28, 2000.
12. Rumsfeld, [No Subject], December 28, 2000.

PART EIGHT Leaning Forward

1. Rumsfeld, handwritten note from meeting with George W. Bush, December 22, 2000.
2. John H. Cushman, "Gay Rights; Top Military Officers Object to Lifting Homosexual Ban," *New York Times,* November 14, 1992.
3. Richard L. Berke, "Timing Awry, Clinton Trips into a Brawl," *New York Times,* January 28, 1993.

4. Rumsfeld to Secretaries of the Military Departments et al., "The Title 'Commander in Chief,'" October 24, 2002.
5. Rumsfeld, handwritten note from meeting with George W. Bush, December 22, 2000.
6. Rumsfeld, "Weakening of Deterrent," December 10, 2001.

CHAPTER 21 Here We Go Again

1. Rumsfeld, [No Subject], December 28, 2000.
2. Rumsfeld, [No Subject], December 28, 2000.
3. Rumsfeld, "Meeting with Secretary Bill Cohen and Don Rumsfeld," May 21, 2001.
4. Francis Fukuyama, *The End of History and the Last Man* (New York: Free Press, 2006).
5. Dean Rusk, speech, American Bar Association, Atlanta, Georgia, October 22, 1964, as reported in the *Atlanta Constitution*, October 23, 1964.
6. Rumsfeld, "Memorandum," May 31, 2001.
7. Editorial, "Invitation to an Arms Race," *New York Times*, June 20, 2001.
8. Hearing of the Senate Armed Services Committee, "Nomination of Donald Rumsfeld to Be Secretary of Defense," Washington, D.C., January 11, 2001.
9. Hearing of the Senate Armed Services Committee, "Nomination of Donald Rumsfeld to Be Secretary of Defense," Washington, D.C., January 11, 2001.
10. Hearing of the Senate Armed Services Committee, "Nomination of Donald Rumsfeld to Be Secretary of Defense," Washington, D.C., January 11, 2001.
11. Dick Cheney, remarks, "Swearing-in of the Secretary of Defense," Oval Office, the White House, Washington, D.C., January 26, 2001.

CHAPTER 22 Dogs Don't Bark at Parked Cars

1. Rumsfeld, "Cost-Cutting," July 11, 2001.
2. Rumsfeld, "Meeting with the Chiefs 1/23/01, my 2nd day," May 21, 2001.
3. Rumsfeld to Pete Aldridge et al., "Joint Chiefs," November 12, 2001.
4. Rumsfeld, "Some Thoughts on the Senior Level Review Group (SLRG) and the Strategic Planning Council (SPC)," November 18, 2005.
5. Rumsfeld, "Meeting with the Chiefs 1/23/01, my 2nd day," May 21, 2001.
6. Rumsfeld to Andy Card, "Presidential Appointment Process," December 1, 2005; "Summary of Time Lapse Data in the Senate Confirmation Process for PAS Appointees Since the Beginning of the Administration," February 18, 2004.
7. Rumsfeld, "Meeting with the Chiefs 1/23/01, my 2nd day," May 21, 2001.
8. Rumsfeld, handwritten note, February 6, 2001.
9. George W. Bush, remarks, "A Period of Consequences," The Citadel, South Carolina, September 23, 1999.
10. Rumsfeld, "Memorandum," May 31, 2001.
11. Department of Defense, preface, *Quadrennial Defense Review Report,* February 6, 2006.
12. Rumsfeld, "The DoD Challenge," June 25, 2001.
13. Steve/John Young to Chairman Ted Stevens, "FY 77 vs. FY 01 Authorization and Appropriation Bills," February 8, 2001.
14. Rumsfeld, "Memorandum," May 31, 2001.
15. Christopher Duffy, *Frederick the Great: A Military Life* (New York: Routledge, 1988), p. 301.

16. Rumsfeld, "Characteristics for the Next Chairman, Joint Chiefs of Staff (CJCS)," April 27, 2001.
17. Rumsfeld to Wolfowitz, "Deployments and Mil-to-Mil," April 16, 2001; Rumsfeld, "Deployments and Military-to-Military Activities," April 3, 2001.
18. Rumsfeld to Nixon, "Okinawa," November 3, 1969.
19. Al-Qaida, fatwa, February 23, 1998.
20. Leigh Sales and Reuters, "Bush Announces Troop Realignment," Australian Broadcasting Corporation, August 17, 2004; John F. Kerry, "Remarks to the Veterans of Foreign Wars 105th Annual Convention," Cincinnati, Ohio, August 18, 2004.
21. Rumsfeld, "Continuing U.S. Government Efforts," September 7, 2004.
22. Jane Perlez, "Rumsfeld Seeks to Withdraw American Troops from Sinai," *New York Times,* April 19, 2001.
23. Rumsfeld to Powell, "Iceland," July 11, 2001; Rumsfeld to Powell and Rice, "Cost of Iceland," May 29, 2003.
24. Powell, letter to Rumsfeld, July 12, 2001; Principals Committee, notes from meeting on Iraq, February 6, 2003.

CHAPTER 23 Bears in the Woods

1. Rumsfeld, "Rough Notes on SecDef's remarks to MoD Ivanov on June 8, 2001," June 20, 2001.
2. Rumsfeld, "Discussions with Russia," July 12, 2001.
3. Rumsfeld, "Meeting with President Nixon—1/20/94," February 3, 1994.
4. Rumsfeld, "Meeting with President Nixon—1/20/94," February 3, 1994.
5. Rumsfeld, "Discussions with Russia," July 12, 2001.
6. Rumsfeld, "Rough Notes on SecDef's remarks to MoD Ivanov on June 8, 2001," June 20, 2001.
7. Committee of One Million Against the Admission of Communist China to the United Nations, press release, "Dem and GOP Congressmen Call on Rusk to Issue Strong Statement Against Admission of Red China to UN," October 15, 1965.
8. Memorandum of Conversation, Beijing, November 28, 1974 (U.S. Department of State, Office of the Historian, *Foreign Relations of the United States, 1969–1976,* vol. XVIII, China, 1973–1976, Document 98).
9. Rumsfeld, "Kissinger's Thoughts on PRC and Russia," June 20, 2005.
10. Sun Tzu, *The Art of War,* translated by Thomas F. Cleary (Boston: Shambhala, 2005), p. 82; Sun Tzu, *The Art of War,* translated by Samuel B. Griffith (London: Oxford University Press, 1963), p. 83.
11. Rumsfeld, "Some Additional Thoughts on Asia," February 11, 1998.
12. Rumsfeld, "China and Asia," February 25, 2001.
13. Rumsfeld, "Meeting with Andy Marshall," April 17, 2000.
14. Rumsfeld, "China and Asia," February 25, 2001.
15. Dan Dell'Orto to Rumsfeld and Wolfowitz, "EP-3 Incident—Guidance on Legal Issues," April 6, 2001.
16. Peter Felstead, "'Inside' account further exonerates EP-3 pilot," *janes.com,* May 18, 2001.
17. Department of Defense news transcript, "Secretary Rumsfeld Briefs on EP-3 Collision," April 13, 2001.
18. Peter Felstead, "'Inside' account further exonerates EP-3 pilot," *janes.com,* May 18, 2001.

19. Jennifer H. Svan, "EP-3E crewmembers hold vivid memories of ordeal in China," *Star and Stripes*, May 30, 2001.
20. "Chinese FM Spokesman Gives Full Account of Air Collision," Xinhua News Agency, April 4, 2001.
21. Ambassador Joseph W. Prueher, letter to Chinese Minister of Foreign Affairs Tang Jiaxuan, April 11, 2001.

CHAPTER 24 The National Security Council

1. National Security Act of 1947, Title I, Section 101, July 26, 1947.
2. Rumsfeld, [No Subject], February 8, 2001.
3. Jane Perlez, "A Dual Path in Diplomacy," *New York Times*, December 18, 2000.
4. Dana Milbank and Mike Allen, "Powell Is Named Secretary of State; Nominee 1st African American Tapped for Post," *Washington Post*, December 17, 2000.
5. Thomas L. Friedman, "The Powell Perplex," *New York Times*, December 19, 2000.
6. Laurence Silberman, "Toward Presidential Control of the State Department," *Foreign Affairs*, vol. 57, no. 4 (Spring, 1979).
7. Colin Powell, remarks, "Secretary Powell Greets State Department Employees," Washington, D.C., January 22, 2001.
8. Peter Rodman, *Presidential Command: Power, Leadership, and the Making of Foreign Policy from Richard Nixon to George W. Bush* (New York: Alfred A. Knopf, 2009), p. 239.
9. Jane Perlez, "Washington Memo; Divergent Voices Heard in Bush Foreign Policy," *New York Times*, March 12, 2001.
10. Greg Pierce, "Biden vs. Rumsfeld," *Washington Times*, June 22, 2001.
11. Rumsfeld, "Washington Times Article," June 23, 2001; Greg Pierce, "Biden vs. Rumsfeld," *Washington Times*, June 22, 2001.
12. Dana Milbank and Thomas E. Ricks, "Powell and Joint Chiefs Nudged Bush Toward U.N.," *Washington Post*, September 4, 2003; Sarah Baxter, "Powell Tried to Talk Bush Out of War," *Sunday Times*, July 8, 2007; Suzanne Goldenberg and Richard Norton-Taylor, "Powell's Doubts Over CIA Intelligence on Iraq Prompted Him to Set Up Secret Review," *The Guardian*, June 2, 2003.
13. "Falling on His Sword," *Washington Post Magazine*, October 1, 2006.
14. Rumsfeld to Rice, "Chain of Command," December 2, 2002.
15. Rumsfeld to Rice, "Interagency Process," August 20, 2002, and attachment to Rice, "Thoughts on the Interagency Process," August 20, 2002.
16. Rumsfeld to Rice, "Approval for Memos," December 27, 2001.
17. Rumsfeld to Rice, "NSC Meetings," October 10, 2001; Rumsfeld to Rice, cc: Powell, "Schedule," October 26, 2001; Rumsfeld to Rice, "PC Meeting," December 13, 2001; Rumsfeld to Rice, "Approval for Memos," December 27, 2001; Rumsfeld to Rice, "Approving NSC Documents," December 31, 2001; Rumsfeld to Rice, "NSC Meeting October 9—Middle East," October 16, 2002; Rumsfeld to Rice, "Chain of Command," December 2, 2002; Rumsfeld to Rice, "Briefing," January 6, 2003; Rumsfeld to Rice, "NSC Meetings," October 30, 2003; Rumsfeld to Rice, "Agendas and Schedules for PC and NSC Meetings," November 5, 2003; Rumsfeld to Rice, "Contacting Combatant Commanders," November 11, 2003; Rumsfeld to Rice, "PC Meetings," December 17, 2003.
18. Rumsfeld to Rice, "Interagency Process," August 20, 2002.
19. Lieutenant General Bantz Craddock to Rumsfeld, "PC & NSC Meetings: Are we improving?" May 29, 2004.

20. Peter Rodman, *Presidential Command: Power, Leadership, and the Making of Foreign Policy from Richard Nixon to George W. Bush* (New York: Alfred A. Knopf, 2009), p. 249.

CHAPTER 25 The Agony of Surprise

1. Rumsfeld, "Memorandum," May 31, 2001.
2. Rumsfeld, "Force Reductions," January 11, 2002.
3. Rumsfeld, handwritten note, May 31, 2001.
4. Robert Kagan, "Indefensible Defense Budget," *Washington Post,* July 20, 2001.
5. Al Kamen, "Donny, We Hardly Knew Ye," *Washington Post,* September 7, 2001.
6. Rumsfeld, speech, "DOD Acquisition and Logistics Excellence Week Kickoff—Bureaucracy to Battlefield," September 10, 2001.
7. "Rumsfeld Declares War on Bureaucracy," Voice of America, September 10, 2001.
8. Rumsfeld, speech, "DOD Acquisition and Logistics Excellence Week Kickoff—Bureaucracy to Battlefield," September 10, 2001.
9. Rumsfeld, "Pearl Harbor Post-Mortem," July 23, 2001.
10. Thomas Schelling, foreword, in Roberta Wohlstetter, *Pearl Harbor: Warning and Decision* (Stanford, CA: Stanford University Press, 1962).
11. Steve Vogel, *The Pentagon: A History* (New York: Random House, 2007), p. 450.
12. Steve Vogel, *The Pentagon: A History* (New York: Random House, 2007), pp. 417–18.
13. Stephen A. Cambone, handwritten notes, September 11, 2001.
14. Victoria Clarke, handwritten notes, September 11, 2001.
15. Stephen A. Cambone, handwritten notes, September 11, 2001.
16. Stephen A. Cambone, handwritten notes, September 11, 2001.
17. Lawrence Di Rita, handwritten notes, September 11, 2001.
18. *The 9/11 Commission Report: Final Report of the National Commission on Terrorist Attacks Upon the United States* (New York: W. W. Norton, 2004), p. 43.
19. Victoria Clarke, handwritten notes, September 11, 2001.
20. Victoria Clarke, handwritten notes, September 11, 2001.
21. General Richard B. Myers, USAF (Ret.), with Malcolm McConnell, *Eyes on the Horizon: Serving on the Front Lines of National Security* (New York: Threshold Editions, 2009), pp. 157–58.
22. *The 9/11 Commission Report: Final Report of the National Commission on Terrorist Attacks Upon the United States* (New York: W. W. Norton, 2004), p. 208.
23. Victoria Clarke, handwritten notes, September 11, 2001.
24. Stephen A. Cambone, handwritten notes, September 11, 2001.
25. Stephen A. Cambone, handwritten notes, September 11, 2001.
26. Stephen A. Cambone, handwritten notes, September 11, 2001.
27. Steve Vogel, *The Pentagon: A History* (New York: Random House, 2007), p. 431.
28. Rumsfeld, remarks, "On the Awarding of the George Catlett Marshall Medal," October 17, 1984.
29. Rumsfeld, "Weakening of Deterrent," December 10, 2001.
30. Victoria Clarke, handwritten notes, September 11, 2001.
31. Victoria Clarke, handwritten notes, September 11, 2001.
32. Stephen A. Cambone, handwritten notes, September 11, 2001.
33. *The 9/11 Commission Report: Final Report of the National Commission on Terrorist Attacks Upon the United States* (New York: W. W. Norton, 2004), pp. 266–72.
34. Victoria Clarke, handwritten notes, September 11, 2001.
35. Department of Defense news transcript, "DoD News Briefing on Pentagon Attack," September 11, 2001.

36. Department of Defense news transcript, "DoD News Briefing on Pentagon Attack," September 11, 2001.
37. Department of Defense news transcript, "DoD News Briefing on Pentagon Attack," September 11, 2001.
38. Steven Erlanger, "European Nations Stand with U.S., Ready to Respond," *New York Times,* September 12, 2001; Michael White and Patrick Wintour, "Blair Calls for World Fight Against Terror," *The Guardian,* September 12, 2001; Jean-Marie Colombani, "Nous sommes tous Américains," *Le Monde,* September 13, 2001.
39. Howard Schneider and Lee Hockstader, "As Mideast Officials Offer Condolences, Some Arabs Rejoice," *Washington Post,* September 12, 2001; Neil MacFarquhar, "Condemnations from Arab Governments, but Widely Different Attitudes on the Street," *New York Times,* September 12, 2001; Saudi Embassy, "Kingdom Condemns Attacks on United States," Press Release, September 11, 2001.
40. Department of Defense, "Saddam Hussein: In His Own Words—Quotes from Saddam and Iraq's Regime-Controlled Media," October 22, 2002; Borzou Daragahi and David Lamb, "Violence Marked His Rise, Rule and Fall," *Los Angeles Times,* December 30, 2006; Cameron S. Brown, "The Shot Seen Around the World: The Middle East Reacts to September 11th," *Middle East Review of International Affairs,* vol. 5, no. 4, December 2001.
41. Department of Defense, "Saddam Hussein: In His Own Words—Quotes from Saddam and Iraq's Regime-Controlled Media," October 22, 2002.
42. Rumsfeld to Feith, "Mubarak," September 13, 2001.
43. Rumsfeld to Feith, "Foreign Reaction to Events September 11, 2001," September 14, 2001.

CHAPTER 26 War President

1. Frank J. Murray, "Infamy; Hijacked Planes Destroy World Trade Center, Ram Pentagon," *Washington Times,* September 12, 2001.
2. The North Atlantic Treaty, Article 5, Washington, D.C., April 4, 1949.
3. Editorial, "The National Defense," *New York Times,* September 12, 2001.
4. Authorization for Use of Military Force (Public Law 107-40), 107th Cong., 1st sess., September 18, 2001, sec. 2(a).
5. Rumsfeld, speech, "Cabinet Meeting Prayer on the National Day of Prayer and Remembrance," September 14, 2001.
6. Rumsfeld, "Vocabulary," September 23, 2001.
7. Rumsfeld to Bush, "Global War on Terror," June 18, 2004; Abizaid to Rumsfeld and Myers, "Response to 18 June Paper," July 16, 2004; Rumsfeld to Steve Hadley, cc: Eric Edelman, "Nature of the Long Struggle," August 4, 2006.
8. Tom Regan, "The 'Rebranding' of the War on Terror," *Christian Science Monitor,* July 28, 2005; Eric Schmitt and Thom Shanker, "U.S. Officials Retool Slogan for Terror War," *New York Times,* July 26, 2005; Matthew Davis, "New Name for 'War on Terror,'" BBC News, July 27, 2005.
9. Rumsfeld to Bush, "Coalitions," September 22, 2001.
10. Rumsfeld to Bush et al., [No Subject], September 19, 2001.
11. Department of State, Proliferation Security Initiative, launched May 31, 2003.
12. Department of Defense, *Campaign Against Terrorism: Strategic Guidance for the US Department of Defense,* October 2, 2001.
13. "Dark Winter—Bioterrorism Exercise," developed and produced by Johns Hopkins Center for Civilian Biodefense, Center for Strategic and International Studies,

ANSER Institute for Homeland Security, and Memorial Institute for the Prevention of Terrorism, conducted June 22–23, 2001, Andrews Air Force Base; Sheryl Gay Stolberg, "Some Experts Say U.S. Is Vulnerable to a Germ Attack," *New York Times*, September 30, 2001.

14. Rumsfeld to Bush et al., [No Subject], September 19, 2001.
15. Rumsfeld to Bush et al., [No Subject], September 19, 2001.
16. American Consulate (Peshawar) to Warren Christopher, State Department cable, "Afghanistan: Taliban Agree to Visits of Militant Training Camps, Admit bin Laden Is Their Guest," January 9, 1997.
17. Barry Bearak, "Condemning Attacks, Taliban Says bin Laden Not Involved," *New York Times*, September 12, 2001.
18. Wolfowitz to Rumsfeld, "Using Special Forces on 'Our Side' of the Line," September 23, 2001.
19. George W. Bush, remarks to airline employees, Chicago, Illinois, September 27, 2001.
20. Rumsfeld to Cheney et al., "Saudi Arabia," December 6, 2001.
21. Rumsfeld to Feith, "Saudi Arabia", December 3, 2001.
22. Barry Bearak, "Condemning Attacks, Taliban Says bin Laden Not Involved," *New York Times*, September 12, 2001.
23. Rumsfeld to Rice and Powell, "Khobar Towers and USS Cole," February 5, 2001.

PART NINE Into the Graveyard of Empires

1. Jill Smolowe, Paul Hofheinz, and Cristina Lamb, "Afghanistan Without a Look Back," *Time*, February 20, 1989.
2. Bill Keller, "Last Soviet Soldiers Leave Afghanistan," *New York Times*, February 16, 1989.
3. Bill Keller, "Last Soviet Soldiers Leave Afghanistan," *New York Times*, February 16, 1989.
4. Jill Smolowe, Paul Hofheinz, and Cristina Lamb, "Afghanistan Without a Look Back," *Time*, February 20, 1989.
5. Jill Smolowe, Paul Hofheinz, and Cristina Lamb, "Afghanistan Without a Look Back," *Time*, February 20, 1989.
6. Pepe Escobar, "Backstage at the Theater of 'Terror,'" *Asia Times Online*, February 27, 2009.
7. David Johnston, "Wilson the Warrior," *New York Times*, May 25, 2003.
8. David Johnston, "Wilson the Warrior," *New York Times*, May 25, 2003; Steve Coll, *Ghost Wars: The Secret History of the CIA, Afghanistan, and bin Laden, From the Soviet Invasion to September 10, 2001* (New York: Penguin Books, 2004), p. 185.

CHAPTER 27 Special Operations

1. Stephen Tanner, *Afghanistan: A Military History from Alexander the Great to the War Against the Taliban* (New York: Da Capo Press, 2002), pp. 176–87.
2. Milton Bearden, "Afghanistan, Graveyard of Empires," *Foreign Affairs*, vol. 80, no. 6 (November/December 2001).
3. Rumsfeld, "The President," December 5, 2001.
4. Wolfowitz to Rumsfeld, "Using Special Forces on 'Our Side' of the Line," September 23, 2001.

5. General Tommy Franks with Malcolm McConnell, *American Soldier* (New York: Regan Books, 2004), p. 281.
6. *The 9/11 Commission Report: Final Report of the National Commission on Terrorist Attacks Upon the United States* (New York: W. W. Norton, 2004), p. 139.
7. Rumsfeld to Bush et al., "Strategic Thoughts," September 30, 2001.
8. Rumsfeld to Bush et al., "Strategic Thoughts," September 30, 2001.
9. Rumsfeld to Bush et al., "Strategic Thoughts," September 30, 2001.
10. Department of Defense Office of Public Affairs, "Fact Sheet: International Contributions to the War Against Terrorism," June 7, 2002 (revised June 14, 2002).
11. Bob Woodward, *Bush at War* (New York: Simon & Schuster, 2002).
12. Milton Bearden, "Afghanistan, Graveyard of Empires," *Foreign Affairs*, vol. 80, no. 6 (November/December 2001).
13. Rohrabacher, letter to Rumsfeld, September 26, 2001.

CHAPTER 28 Little Birds in a Nest

1. William Luti, Jim MacDougall, Mira Ricardel, Marc Thiessen, and John Craddock to Rumsfeld, [No Subject], undated.
2. Rumsfeld to Bush et al., "My Visits to Saudi Arabia, Oman, Egypt, Uzbekistan and Turkey," October 6, 2001.
3. Rumsfeld to Bush et al., "My Visits to Saudi Arabia, Oman, Egypt, Uzbekistan and Turkey," October 6, 2001.
4. Rumsfeld to Bush et al., "My Visits to Saudi Arabia, Oman, Egypt, Uzbekistan and Turkey," October 6, 2001.
5. U.S. Defense Attaché Office Tashkent to Rumsfeld, Department of Defense cable, "Draft Report of DefSec Meeting with President Karimov," October 5, 2001.
6. Rumsfeld to Bush et al., "My Visits to Saudi Arabia, Oman, Egypt, Uzbekistan and Turkey," October 6, 2001.
7. Rumsfeld to Powell and Rice, "Uzbekistan," October 7, 2001.
8. Department of Defense news transcript, "Secretary Rumsfeld Press Conference with President of Uzbekistan," October 5, 2001.
9. Department of Defense news transcript, "Secretary Rumsfeld En Route to Saudi Arabia," October 2, 2001.
10. Rumsfeld, "Turkey," December 28, 2001.
11. General Tommy Franks with Malcolm McConnell, *American Soldier* (New York: Regan Books, 2004), p. 285.
12. Rumsfeld to Feith, "Strategy," October 30, 2001.
13. Department of Defense news transcript, "Rumsfeld and Myers Briefing on Enduring Freedom," October 7, 2001.
14. Lieutenant General Michael DeLong, USMC (Ret.), with Noah Lukeman, *Inside CentCom: The Unvarnished Truth About the Wars in Afghanistan and Iraq* (Washington, D.C.: Regnery Publishing, 2004), p. 39.
15. Vice Admiral Giambastiani and Larry Di Rita, "Memorandum of 21 October Secure Conference Call with CinCent," October 24, 2001.
16. Rumsfeld, "Taliban and the NGOs," October 31, 2001.
17. Department of Defense news transcript, "Secretary Rumsfeld Remarks at Stakeout Outside ABC TV," October 28, 2001; Department of Defense news transcript, "DoD News Briefing—Secretary Rumsfeld and Gen. Myers," October 29, 2001.
18. Rumsfeld to Myers et al., "What Will Be the Military Role in the War on Terrorism," October 10, 2001.

19. Kathy Gannon, "Afghanistan's Terrain a Challenge," Associated Press, September 18, 2001.
20. Editorial, "The Quagmire Issue; U.S. Should Prepare for a Long Struggle," *Dallas Morning News,* October 26, 2001.
21. Maureen Dowd, "Liberties; Can Bush Bushkazi?," *New York Times,* October 28, 2001.
22. R. W. Apple, Jr., "A Military Quagmire Remembered: Afghanistan as Vietnam," *New York Times,* October 31, 2001.
23. Rumsfeld to Larry Di Rita, "War on Terrorism," September 23, 2001.

CHAPTER 29 Kabul Falls, Karzai Rises

1. Robin Moore, *The Hunt for bin Laden: Task Force Dagger* (New York: Random House, 2003), p. 28.
2. General Tommy Franks with Malcolm McConnell, *American Soldier* (New York: Regan Books, 2004), p. 303.
3. Lieutenant General Michael DeLong, USMC (Ret.), with Noah Lukeman, *Inside CentCom: The Unvarnished Truth About the Wars in Afghanistan and Iraq* (Washington, D.C.: Regnery Publishing, 2004), p. 40.
4. Vernon Loeb and Susan B. Glasser, "Tajikistan Allows U.S. to Assess 3 Air Bases," *Washington Post,* November 4, 2001.
5. Michael Wines, "Rumsfeld Visits Russia and Central Asia to Bolster Coalition," *New York Times,* November 4, 2001.
6. Celia W. Dugger, "U.S. and India Map Path to Military Cooperation; More Arms Sales Are Seen," *New York Times,* November 6, 2001.
7. Steven Lee Myers, "Clinton to Impose Penalties on India Over Atomic Tests," *New York Times,* May 13, 1998.
8. Rumsfeld, handwritten note, "Phone Call from an Aircraft w/POTUS," November 6, 2001.
9. Peter Rodman to Rumsfeld, "Why Time Is of the Essence in the Afghan Campaign," October 12, 2001.
10. Michael R. Gordon, "Key Players Confer at U.N. on a Post-Taliban Regime," *New York Times,* November 12, 2001.
11. Rumsfeld to Bush et al., "Kabul," November 13, 2001.
12. Lieutenant General Michael DeLong, USMC (Ret.), with Noah Lukeman, *Inside CentCom: The Unvarnished Truth About the Wars in Afghanistan and Iraq* (Washington, D.C.: Regnery Publishing, 2004), p. 53.
13. Thom Shanker, "Rumsfeld Pays Call on Troops and Afghans," *New York Times,* December 17, 2001.
14. Department of Defense speech transcript, "Address to the Men and Women of Fort Bragg/Pope AFB," November 21, 2001.
15. Rumsfeld to Tenet, "Ali," December 20, 2001.
16. Rumsfeld, "Discuss w/Franks," January 4, 2002.
17. Evan Thomas, "Into Thin Air," *Newsweek,* September 3, 2007; Peter Bergen, "The Battle for Tora Bora," *The New Republic,* December 22, 2009.
18. Gary Berntsen and Ralph Pezzullo, *Jawbreaker: The Attack on Bin Laden and Al-Qaeda: A Personal Account by the CIA's Key Field Commander* (New York: Crown, 2005).
19. Peter Rodman to Rumsfeld, "Further Report on Afghan Talks in Bonn," November 27, 2001.

20. Thom Shanker, "Rumsfeld Pays Call on Troops and Afghans," *New York Times,* December 17, 2001.
21. Department of Defense news transcript, "Secretary Rumsfeld Media Availability en route to Brussels," December 17, 2001.
22. Vernon Loeb, "Rumsfeld: Mission Far From Over; Defense Secretary Meets Officials, U.S. Troops in Afghanistan," *Washington Post,* December 17, 2001.
23. Vernon Loeb, "Rumsfeld: Mission Far From Over; Defense Secretary Meets Officials, U.S. Troops in Afghanistan," *Washington Post,* December 17, 2001.
24. Dwight Jon Zimmerman and John D. Gresham, *Beyond Hell and Back: How America's Special Operations Forces Became the World's Greatest Fighting Unit* (New York: St. Martin's Press, 2007), p. 215.
25. Michael Ignatieff, "Nation-Building Lite," *New York Times Magazine,* July 28, 2002; Simon Robinson, "Karzai's Kabul: Fit for a King?," *Time,* April 18, 2002.
26. Rumsfeld to Bush et al., "US Role in Gardez Situation—or, more broadly, whether or not the US should intervene in Afghan vs. Afghan conflicts," May 10, 2002.
27. Rumsfeld to Bush et al., "US Role in Gardez Situation—or, more broadly, whether or not the US should intervene in Afghan vs. Afghan conflicts," May 10, 2002.
28. Douglas J. Feith, *War and Decision: Inside the Pentagon at the Dawn of the War on Terrorism* (New York: HarperCollins, 2008), pp. 145–46.
29. Vernon Loeb, "Rumsfeld: Mission Far From Over; Defense Secretary Meets Officials, U.S. Troops in Afghanistan," *Washington Post,* December 17, 2001.

PART TEN Saddam's Miscalculation

1. George H. W. Bush, "Address to the Nation on the Invasion of Iraq," January 16, 1991; Directorate of Intelligence, Central Intelligence Agency, *Prewar Status of Iraq's Weapons of Mass Destruction,* March 1991.
2. George H. W. Bush, "Address to the Nation on the Invasion of Iraq," January 16, 1991.
3. Robert Gates, "The Gulf War: Oral History," *Frontline,* PBS, posted January 9, 1996.
4. James Baker, "The Gulf War: Oral History," *Frontline,* PBS, posted January 9, 1996.
5. Colin Powell, "The Gulf War: Oral History," *Frontline,* PBS, posted January 9, 1996.
6. Elaine Sciolino, "Gore Says Bush's Efforts to Befriend Iraqi Leader Led to Gulf War," *New York Times,* September 30, 1992.
7. Margaret Thatcher, "The Gulf War: Oral History," *Frontline,* PBS, posted January 9, 1996.
8. Colin Powell, "The Gulf War: Part B," *Frontline,* PBS, broadcast January 10, 1996.

CHAPTER 30 Out of the Box

1. Sarah Graham-Brown, "No-Fly Zones: Rhetoric and Real Intentions," *Middle East Report Online,* February 20, 2001.
2. Charles Duelfer, "Comprehensive Report of the Special Advisor to the DCI on Iraq's WMD" (Duelfer Report), vol. III, September 30, 2004, pp. 2, 13, 38 (Biological section), pp. 90–91 (Chemical section).
3. United Nations Security Council, Resolution 1194 (S/RES/1194), 3924th Meeting, September 9, 1998.
4. Rumsfeld et al., letter to Clinton, January 26, 1998.
5. Rumsfeld et al., letter to Clinton, January 26, 1998.

6. Madeleine K. Albright, press remarks following meeting with European Union, New York City, September 14, 2000.
7. Hearing of the Senate Armed Services Committee, testimony of Charles Duelfer, Special Adviser to the Director of Central Intelligence for Iraqi Weapons of Mass Destruction, October 6, 2004; Charles Duelfer, "Comprehensive Report of the Special Advisor to the DCI on Iraq's WMD" (Duelfer Report), vol. I, September 30, 2004, p. 1 (Regime Strategic Intent section).
8. Independent Inquiry Committee into the United Nations Oil-For-Food Programme, *Manipulation of the Oil-For-Food Programme by the Iraqi Regime,* October 27, 2005.
9. Doug Wead, "Bush Completes Father's Unfinished Business," *USA Today,* June 15, 2003; "Is Bush Continuing His Dad's Iraq Policy?" ABC News, February 16, 2001.
10. Hearing of the House Armed Services Committee, "United States Policy Toward Iraq," testimony of General Richard Myers, September 18, 2002.
11. Jones to Hugh Shelton, "U.S. Military Responses in Iraq," August 31, 2001; Rumsfeld to Jones, "Iraq," September 10, 2001.
12. Rumsfeld to Rice et al., "Iraq," July 27, 2001.
13. Saddam Hussein, conversation with SSA George L. Piro, Baghdad Operations Center, June 11, 2004 (Federal Bureau of Investigation).
14. George W. Bush, State of the Union Address, January 29, 2002.
15. Tenet, letter to Senator Bob Graham, October 7, 2002; Department of Defense news transcript, "DoD News Briefing—Secretary Rumsfeld and Gen. Pace," September 26, 2002.
16. James Woolsey, interviewed by Peter Jennings, "America Under Attack," ABC News Special Report, September 11, 2001.
17. Senate Select Committee on Intelligence, *Report on the U.S. Intelligence Community's Prewar Intelligence Assessments on Iraq* (S. Rep. 108-301), 108th Cong., 2d sess., July 9, 2004, pp. 318–21; Department of State, Office of the Coordinator for Counterterrorism, "Chapter 6: Terrorist Organizations," *Country Reports on Terrorism 2008,* April 30, 2009.
18. Department of State, *Patterns of Global Terrorism 2003,* April 2004, p. 114.
19. Kevin M. Woods with James Lacey, *Iraqi Perspectives Project: Saddam and Terrorism: Emerging Insights from Captured Iraqi Documents,* vol. I (redacted), Institute for Defense Analyses, November 2007, p. 18.
20. Kevin M. Woods with James Lacey, *Iraqi Perspectives Project: Saddam and Terrorism: Emerging Insights from Captured Iraqi Documents,* vol. I (redacted), Institute for Defense Analyses, November 2007, p. 18; Kevin M. Woods with Michael R. Pease, Mark E. Stout, Williamson Murray, and James G. Lacey, *Iraqi Perspectives Project: A View of Operation Iraqi Freedom from Saddam's Senior Leadership* (Joint Center for Operational Analysis, U.S. Joint Forces Command, March 2006), p. 54.
21. OSD Policy, "Sovereignty and Anticipatory Self-Defense," August 24, 2002.
22. OSD Policy, "Sovereignty and Anticipatory Self-Defense," August 24, 2002.
23. Rumsfeld, "Saddam Hussein," September 21, 2001.

CHAPTER 31 The Case for Regime Change

1. General Richard B. Myers, USAF (Ret.), with Malcolm McConnell, *Eyes on the Horizon: Serving on the Front Lines of National Security* (New York: Threshold Editions, 2009), p. 215.
2. Lieutenant General William G. Pagonis with Jeffrey L. Cruikshank, *Moving Mountains: Lessons in Leadership and Logistics from the Gulf War* (Boston: Harvard

Business School Press, 1992), pp. 157–58; George C. Wilson, "The Logistics Behind a War on Iraq," *National Journal*, vol. 34, issue 47/48, November 23, 2002.

3. Rumsfeld, "Assumptions," October 18, 2002.
4. "Iraq Tested Missile to Carry A-Bomb, a U.N. Report Says," *New York Times*, October 5, 1991.
5. Commission to Assess the Ballistic Missile Threat to the United States, Intelligence Side Letter to Tenet, March 18, 1999.
6. Rumsfeld, handwritten note, August 28, 2002.
7. Rumsfeld, handwritten note, August 28, 2002.
8. Central Intelligence Agency, "Key Judgments," *National Intelligence Estimate: Iraq's Continuing Programs for Weapons of Mass Destruction*, October 2002.
9. James Graff and Bruce Crumley, "France Is Not a Pacifist Country," *Time*, February 16, 2003.
10. Jeffrey Goldberg, "The Great Terror," *The New Yorker*, March 25, 2002.
11. Rumsfeld, "WMD," March 15, 2004.
12. Department of Defense news transcript, "Secretary Rumsfeld Remarks on ABC 'This Week with George Stephanopoulos,'" March 30, 2003.
13. Rumsfeld to Clarke, "Arguments," February 18, 2003.
14. Authorization for Use of Military Force Against Iraq Resolution of 2002 (Public Law 107–243), October 16, 2002.
15. Joseph Biden, interviewed by Tim Russert, *Meet the Press*, NBC News, August 4, 2002.
16. Hillary Rodham Clinton, statement, "Authorization of the Use of United States Armed Forces Against Iraq," 107th Cong., 2d sess., Congressional Record, vol. 148, no. 133, October 10, 2002, p. S10288.
17. John Kerry, statement, "Authorization of the Use of United States Armed Forces Against Iraq—Continued," 107th Cong., 2d sess., Congressional Record, vol. 148, no. 132, October 9, 2002, p. S10174.
18. Al Gore, "Iraq and the War on Terrorism," The Commonwealth Club, San Francisco, California, September 23, 2002.
19. General Tommy Franks with Malcolm McConnell, *American Soldier* (New York: Regan Books, 2004), p. 394.
20. "Powell Says He Made Prewar Push for More Troops," *New York Times*, April 30, 2006.
21. Rumsfeld, "Conversation with the President and Condi," May 15, 2006.
22. "Offers of support for Phase I-III (48 countries)," May 13, 2003.
23. Lindsey Graham, interviewed by Bob Schieffer, *Face the Nation*, CBS News, August 9, 2009; David Brooks, "Making the Surge Work," *New York Times*, January 7, 2007.
24. Eliot A. Cohen, *Supreme Command: Soldiers, Statesmen, and Leadership in Wartime* (New York: Free Press, 2002), pp. 185–88.
25. Rumsfeld, "Illustrative List of Recent Examples of French Opposition to the United States," October 23, 2002.
26. Rumsfeld to Shultz, State Department cable, "Rumsfeld Mission: December 20 Meeting with Iraqi President Saddam Hussein," December 21, 1983.
27. John Keegan, *The Iraq War* (New York: Vintage, 2005), p. 108.
28. Independent Inquiry Committee into the United Nations Oil-For-Food Programme, *The Management of the United Nations Oil-for-Food Programme*, vol. 1, September 7, 2005, p. 2.
29. United Nations Security Council, Resolution 1441 (S/Res/1441), 4644th Meeting, November 8, 2002.

30. Barbara Slavin and Bill Nichols, "U.S. Says Omissions Put Iraq in 'Material Breach,'" *USA Today,* December 20, 2002.
31. Hans Blix, statement to the United Nations Security Council, January 27, 2003.

CHAPTER 32 A Failure of Diplomacy

1. Department of Defense news transcript, "Secretary Rumsfeld Briefs at the Foreign Press Center," January 22, 2003.
2. "'Old Europe' Hits Back at Rumsfeld," CNN, January 24, 2003.
3. Rumsfeld, "Europe," February 18, 2003.
4. Statement of the Vilnius Group Countries, February 5, 2003.
5. John Kerry, speech, The Commonwealth Club, San Francisco, California, March 13, 2003; Dan Balz, "Kerry Assails Bush Over States' Plight," *Washington Post,* March 14, 2003.
6. Steven R. Weisman with Julia Preston, "Powell Will Press U.S. Case in Security Council Next Week," *New York Times,* January 29, 2003.
7. Michiko Kakutani, "Under a Microscope, Bush and His Presidency," *New York Times,* December 7, 2007; Bruce B. Auster, Mark Mazzetti, and Edward T. Pound, "Truth and Consequences: New Questions About U.S. Intelligence Regarding Iraq's Weapons of Mass Terror," *U.S. News & World Report,* June 1, 2003; Suzanne Goldenberg and Richard Norton-Taylor, "Powell's Doubts Over CIA Intelligence on Iraq Prompted Him to Set Up Secret Review," *The Guardian,* June 2, 2003; Karen DeYoung, *Soldier: The Life of Colin Powell* (New York: Knopf, 2006).
8. Micah Zenko, "Foregoing Limited Force: The George W. Bush Administration's Decision Not to Attack Ansar al-Islam," *Journal of Strategic Studies,* vol. 32, no. 4, August 2009, p. 640.
9. Senate Select Committee on Intelligence, *Report on the U.S. Intelligence Community's Prewar Intelligence Assessments on Iraq* (S. Rep. 108-301), 108th Cong., 2d sess., July 9, 2004, p. 336; Micah Zenko, "Foregoing Limited Force: The George W. Bush Administration's Decision Not to Attack Ansar al-Islam," *Journal of Strategic Studies,* vol. 32, no. 4, August 2009, p. 632.
10. Senate Select Committee on Intelligence, *Report on the U.S. Intelligence Community's Prewar Intelligence Assessments on Iraq* (S. Rep. 108–301), 108th Cong., 2d sess., July 9, 2004, p. 337.
11. Micah Zenko, "Foregoing Limited Force: The George W. Bush Administration's Decision Not to Attack Ansar al-Islam," *Journal of Strategic Studies,* vol. 32, no. 4, August 2009, p. 629.
12. Department of Defense notes of NSC meeting, February 3, 2003.
13. Colin Powell, remarks, United Nations Security Council, New York City, February 5, 2003.
14. Colin Powell, remarks, United Nations Security Council, New York City, February 5, 2003.
15. Colin Powell, remarks, United Nations Security Council, New York City, February 5, 2003.
16. Gregory Fontenot, E. J. Degen, and David Tohn, *On Point: The United States Army in Operation Iraqi Freedom* (Annapolis, MD: Naval Institute Press, 2005), p. 250.
17. Micah Zenko, "Foregoing Limited Force: The George W. Bush Administration's Decision Not to Attack Ansar al-Islam," *Journal of Strategic Studies,* vol. 32, no. 4, August 2009, p. 640; Linda Robinson, *Masters of Chaos: The Secret History of the Special Forces* (New York: Public Affairs, 2004), pp. 320–21; Senate Select Committee

on Intelligence, *Report on Postwar Findings About Iraq's WMD Programs and Links to Terrorism and How They Compare with Prewar Assessments,* 109th Cong., 2d sess., September 8, 2006, pp. 93–94.

18. Steven R. Weisman, "Powell Calls His U.N. Speech a Lasting Blot on His Record," *New York Times,* September 9, 2005.
19. Colin Powell, interviewed by Tim Russert, *Meet the Press,* MSNBC, June 10, 2007.
20. Rumsfeld, handwritten note, January 11, 2003.
21. Rumsfeld, "Turkey," December 28, 2001.
22. Eric Schmitt, "U.S. Plan for Iraq Is Said to Include Attack on 3 Sides," *New York Times,* July 5, 2002.
23. Rumsfeld, "Leaks," August 5, 2002.
24. Thomas E. Ricks, *The Gamble: General David Petraeus and the American Military Adventure in Iraq, 2006–2008* (New York: The Penguin Press, 2009), p. 103; Barbara Slavin and Dave Moniz, "War in Iraq's Aftermath Hits Troops Hard," *USA Today,* July 21, 2003.
25. Thomas E. Ricks, "Projection on Fall of Hussein Disputed; Ground Forces Chiefs, Pentagon at Odds," *Washington Post,* December 18, 2002.
26. Myers to Rumsfeld, "Joint Chiefs of Staff Opportunities to Express Military Advice," undated.
27. Rumsfeld, "Military Advice to POTUS," September 29, 2004.
28. Rumsfeld, handwritten note, December 18, 2002.
29. Rumsfeld, handwritten note, December 18, 2002.
30. Thom Shanker, "New Strategy Vindicates Ex-Army Chief Shinseki," *New York Times,* January 12, 2007.
31. Jamie McIntyre, "Myth of Shinseki Lingers," CNN, December 8, 2008.
32. Hearing of the Senate Armed Services Committee, "The Fiscal Year 2004 Defense Budget," testimony of Eric Shinseki, February 25, 2003.
33. Jamie McIntyre, "Myth of Shinseki Lingers," CNN, December 8, 2008; Ann Scott Tyson, "Shinseki Says He Would Modernize VA," *Washington Post,* January 15, 2009; Georgie Anne Geyer, "Straight-Talking Jones Has Kept His Integrity Intact," Universal Press Syndicate, December 4, 2008; Philip Rucker, "Obama Picks Shinseki to Lead Veterans Affairs," *Washington Post,* December 7, 2008; Paul D. Eaton, "A Top-Down Review for the Pentagon," *New York Times,* March 19, 2006; Maureen Dowd, "Alan (Not Atlas) Shrugged," *New York Times,* September 19, 2007; Thom Shanker, "New Strategy Vindicates Ex-Army Chief Shinseki," *New York Times,* January 12, 2007; Andrew Cockburn, "No, He Wasn't a Good Manager," *Washington Post,* February 25, 2007; Richard Cohen, "Vietnam's Forgotten Lessons," *Washington Post,* April 11, 2006.
34. Shinseki to Rumsfeld, "End of Tour Memorandum," June 10, 2003.
35. Rumsfeld to Hank Crumpton, "Speaking Up," May 3, 2002.
36. Rumsfeld, "Talk to VP," September 30, 2002.
37. George W. Bush, address to the nation, March 17, 2003.
38. "Bush Offers Ultimatum to Saddam in Address to Nation," Fox News, March 18, 2003.

CHAPTER 33 Exit the Butcher of Baghdad

1. "Iraq War Begins," PBS *NewsHour,* March 20, 2003.
2. "U.S. Launches Cruise Missiles at Saddam," CNN, March 20, 2003.
3. Captured document dated March 11, 2003, "Military Command Memos Concerned with the Arabian Volunteers to the Iraqi Special Forces," cited in Kevin M.

Woods with Michael R. Pease, Mark E. Stout, Williamson Murray, and James G. Lacey, *Iraqi Perspectives Project: A View of Operation Iraqi Freedom from Saddam's Senior Leadership* (Joint Center for Operational Analysis, U.S. Joint Forces Command, March 2006), p. 156.

4. Captured document dated March 11, 2003, "Military Command Memos Concerned with the Arabian Volunteers to the Iraqi Special Forces," cited in Kevin M. Woods with Michael R. Pease, Mark E. Stout, Williamson Murray, and James G. Lacey, *Iraqi Perspectives Project: A View of Operation Iraqi Freedom from Saddam's Senior Leadership* (Joint Center for Operational Analysis, U.S. Joint Forces Command, March 2006), p. 156.
5. Captured document dated March 27, 2003, "Memorandum to Director of the IIS, Subject: Hamas," cited in Kevin M. Woods with Michael R. Pease, Mark E. Stout, Williamson Murray, and James G. Lacey, *Iraqi Perspectives Project: A View of Operation Iraqi Freedom from Saddam's Senior Leadership* (Joint Center for Operational Analysis, U.S. Joint Forces Command, March 2006), pp. 132, 153.
6. Captured document dated April 2, 2003, "Written Summaries for the 37th Division 20 March–2 April 2003," cited in Kevin M. Woods with Michael R. Pease, Mark E. Stout, Williamson Murray, and James G. Lacey, *Iraqi Perspectives Project: A View of Operation Iraqi Freedom from Saddam's Senior Leadership* (Joint Center for Operational Analysis, U.S. Joint Forces Command, March 2006), pp. 131–32, 153.
7. Captured document dated April 4, 2003, "General Military Intelligence Directorate to the 8th Adjutant Confirming Saddam Hussein's Order to Treat the Arab Fedayeen Volunteers the Same Way as Special Forces Troops in Terms of Their Salaries and Supplies," cited in Kevin M. Woods with Michael R. Pease, Mark E. Stout, Williamson Murray, and James G. Lacey, *Iraqi Perspectives Project: A View of Operation Iraqi Freedom from Saddam's Senior Leadership* (Joint Center for Operational Analysis, U.S. Joint Forces Command, March 2006), pp. 150, 156.
8. Ryan Chilcote, "Sandstorm Paralyzes U.S. Copters," CNN, March 26, 2003.
9. Editorial, "Diminished Expectations in Iraq," *New York Times*, March 25, 2003; Rick Atkinson and Thomas E. Ricks, "War's Military, Political Goals Begin to Diverge," *Washington Post*, March 30, 2003; Monica Davey, "For Some Uncertain About War, Anxiety Builds in First Week," *New York Times*, March 27, 2003.
10. Department of Defense news transcript, "Deputy Assistant Secretary Whitman Interview with Egyptian TV," April 14, 2003.
11. "Iraq: Journalists in Danger," Committee to Protect Journalists, updates concluded in October 2009.
12. Eason Jordan, "The News We Kept to Ourselves," *New York Times*, April 11, 2003.
13. Dave Moniz, John Diamond, and David J. Lynch, "A Virtual Certainty: Baghdad Falls. What's Uncertain: Cost of Battle," *USA Today*, April 3, 2003.
14. Kevin M. Woods with Michael R. Pease, Mark E. Stout, Williamson Murray, and James G. Lacey, *Iraqi Perspectives Project: A View of Operation Iraqi Freedom from Saddam's Senior Leadership* (Joint Center for Operational Analysis, U.S. Joint Forces Command, March 2006), pp. 29–30.
15. "The Collected Quotations of 'Baghdad Bob,' Muhammed Saeed al-Sahaf: The Iraqi Minister of DisInformation," posted by the Center for Individual Freedom, April 10, 2003.
16. Gayle MacDonald, "Take My Country…Please! His Barefaced Lies and Poker-Faced Bravado Have Made Comical Ali a Pop-Culture Hit," *The Globe and Mail*, May 6, 2003.

PART ELEVEN The Occupation of Iraq

1. John F. Burns, "Pillagers Strip Iraqi Museum of Its Treasure," *New York Times,* April 13, 2003.
2. John F. Burns, "Pillagers Strip Iraqi Museum of Its Treasure," *New York Times,* April 13, 2003.
3. Michele Norris, Robert Siegel, Anne Garrels, and Dr. Dorry George, *All Things Considered,* NPR, April 14, 2003.
4. Ann Talbot, "US Government Implicated in Planned Theft of Iraqi Artistic Treasures," *World Socialist,* April 19, 2003; Heather Cottin, "Looting of Iraqi Museum Was Long Planned," *Workers World,* May 1, 2003.
5. Frank Rich, "And Now: 'Operation Iraqi Looting,'" *New York Times,* April 27, 2003.
6. "Secretary-General's Statement on Safeguarding Iraqi Cultural Heritage," Secretary General Office of the Spokesperson, United Nations, New York, April 15, 2003.
7. Jacques Chirac, press conference at the ceremony of the signature of the Treaty of Accession of the new member states to the EU, Athens, Greece, April 16, 2003.
8. Leon Harris, "Secretary of State, Kuwaiti Foreign Minister Address Reporters," *CNN Live Event/Special,* CNN, April 14, 2003.
9. Matthew Bogdanos with William Patrick, *Thieves of Baghdad* (New York: Bloomsbury, 2005), pp. 210–11.
10. Rumsfeld to Abizaid et al., "Looting," July 9, 2003.
11. Special Inspector General for Iraq Reconstruction interview with Lieutenant General David McKiernan, December 5, 2006, as cited in Special Inspector General for Iraq Reconstruction, *Hard Lessons: The Iraq Reconstruction Experience* (Washington, D.C.: U.S. Government Printing Office, 2009), p. 57.
12. Department of Defense notes of principals meeting, February 26, 2003; "Summary of Public Order Plan: Phase One," March 2003.
13. Department of Defense news transcript, "DoD News Briefing—Secretary Rumsfeld and Gen. Myers," April 11, 2003.
14. David Stafford, "Iraq Is a Mess. But Germany Was, Too," *Washington Post,* April 6, 2008.
15. Guy Gugliotta, "Iraq Museum Is Slowly Recovering Artifacts," *Washington Post,* September 15, 2003.
16. Melik Kaylan, "So Much for the 'Looted Sites,'" *Wall Street Journal,* July 15, 2008.
17. Melik Kaylan, "So Much for the 'Looted Sites,'" *Wall Street Journal,* July 15, 2008.
18. Matthew Bogdanos with William Patrick, *Thieves of Baghdad* (New York: Bloomsbury, 2005), p. 155.
19. Robert D. Kaplan, *Warrior Politics: Why Leadership Demands a Pagan Ethos* (New York: Random House, 2002), p. 129.
20. Alex Spillius, "Media Blamed for Exaggerating Loss of Antiquities," *London Telegraph,* May 22, 2003.
21. William Booth and Guy Gugliotta, "All Along, Most Iraqi Relics Were 'Safe and Sound,'" *Washington Post,* June 9, 2003.

CHAPTER 34 Catastrophic Success

1. Ken Adelman, "Cakewalk in Iraq," *Washington Post,* February 13, 2002.
2. Rumsfeld, "Iraq: An Illustrative List of Potential Problems to Be Considered and Addressed," October 15, 2002.
3. Rumsfeld, "Iraq: An Illustrative List of Potential Problems to Be Considered and Addressed," October 15, 2002.

4. Rumsfeld, "Iraq: An Illustrative List of Potential Problems to Be Considered and Addressed," October 15, 2002.
5. Rumsfeld, "Iraq: An Illustrative List of Potential Problems to Be Considered and Addressed," October 15, 2002.
6. Rumsfeld, "Guidelines When Considering Committing U.S. Forces," March 2001.
7. Judy Dempsey, "NATO Committed to Presence in Bosnia," *Financial Times,* May 19, 2001.
8. "The Second Gore-Bush Presidential Debate," Commission on Presidential Debates, debate transcript, October 11, 2000.
9. Rumsfeld, "Guidelines When Considering Committing U.S. Forces," March 2001.
10. Zakheim to Rumsfeld, "Report on Contributions to Afghanistan Reconstruction, Global War on Terrorism (GWOT), and Iraq," April 3, 2003.
11. Rodman to Rumsfeld, "Who Will Govern Iraq?" August 15, 2002.
12. Rodman to Rumsfeld, "Who Will Govern Iraq?" August 15, 2002.
13. Rumsfeld to Cheney et al., "Supporting the Iraqi Opposition," July 1, 2002.
14. General Richard B. Myers, USAF (Ret.), with Malcolm McConnell, *Eyes on the Horizon: Serving on the Front Lines of National Security* (New York: Threshold Editions, 2009), p. 225.
15. General Tommy Franks with Malcolm McConnell, *American Soldier* (New York: Regan Books, 2004), p. 531.
16. Department of State, "Future of Iraq Project," May 12, 2003.
17. "The Lost Year in Iraq: Planning For a Postwar Iraq," *Frontline,* PBS, posted October 17, 2006.
18. Bradley Graham, "Prewar Memo Warned of Gaps in Iraq Plans," *Washington Post,* August 18, 2005.
19. John Ware, "Blair Was Warned of Looming Disaster in Iraq," *The Telegraph,* October 28, 2007.
20. Feith to Rumsfeld, "Establishing the DoD Postwar Planning Office," January 9, 2003.
21. Mark Fineman, Robin Wright, and Doyle McManus, "Preparing for War, Stumbling to Peace," *Los Angeles Times,* July 18, 2003.
22. Rumsfeld to Secretaries of the Military Departments et al., "Support for the Office of Reconstruction and Humanitarian Assistance," April 2, 2003.
23. Paul Vallely, "Jay Garner: The US General Waiting to Replace Saddam," *The Independent,* April 5, 2003.
24. Jane Perlez, "U.S. Overseer Set to Remake Iraq," *New York Times,* April 15, 2003.
25. George Tenet with Bill Harlow, *At the Center of the Storm: My Years at the CIA* (New York: HarperCollins, 2007), p. 419.
26. George Tenet with Bill Harlow, *At the Center of the Storm: My Years at the CIA* (New York: HarperCollins, 2007), p. 398.
27. Rumsfeld to Myers, "Planning Guidance for Iraqi Opposition Training," August 12, 2002.
28. Rumsfeld to Rice, "Military Assistance Under the Iraq Liberation Act (ILA)," August 12, 2002.
29. Rodman to Rumsfeld, "Who Will Govern Iraq?" August 15, 2002.
30. Powell to Rumsfeld et al., [No Subject], March 1, 2003; Marc J. Susser to Powell, "Occupation and Postwar Government: Precedents and Options," February 28, 2003.
31. OSD Policy, "Iraqi Interim Authority Implementation Concept—Summary," March 30, 2003; OSD Policy, "Iraqi Interim Authority Action Plan," March 30, 2003.
32. Rumsfeld, handwritten note, March 11, 2003.

CHAPTER 35 Mission Accomplished?

1. Rumsfeld to Bush, "Iraqi Interim Authority," April 1, 2003.
2. Rumsfeld to Bush, "Iraqi Interim Authority," April 1, 2003.
3. Rumsfeld to Bush et al., "Visit to the Persian Gulf, Iraq, Afghanistan & United Kingdom," May 5, 2003.
4. Rumsfeld to Bush et al., "Visit to the Persian Gulf, Iraq, Afghanistan & United Kingdom," May 5, 2003.
5. Rumsfeld to Bush et al., "Visit to the Persian Gulf, Iraq, Afghanistan & United Kingdom," May 5, 2003.
6. Rumsfeld to Bush et al., "Visit to the Persian Gulf, Iraq, Afghanistan & United Kingdom," May 5, 2003.
7. Department of Defense news transcript, "Secretary Rumsfeld Town Hall Meeting in Baghdad," April 30, 2003.
8. General Tommy Franks with Malcolm McConnell, *American Soldier* (New York: Regan Books, 2004), p. 523.
9. Franks to Rumsfeld, Department of Defense cable, "Operation Iraqi Freedom," April 16, 2003.
10. George W. Bush, speech aboard the USS *Abraham Lincoln,* May 1, 2003.
11. Rumsfeld, "DoD Edits of POTUS Speeches," December 3, 2003.
12. Department of Defense news transcript, "Secretary Rumsfeld Joint Media Availability with British Secretary of State for Defence," May 2, 2003.
13. William Safire, *Safire's Political Dictionary* (New York: Oxford University Press, 2008), p. 389.
14. Rumsfeld to Feith, "Oil and Democracy," May 21, 2003.
15. Rumsfeld, "Talk to POTUS About Democracy," April 19, 2006.
16. Charles Duelfer, "Comprehensive Report of the Special Advisor to the DCI on Iraq's WMD" (Duelfer Report), September 30, 2004.
17. Rumsfeld to Myers, "Manning Requests," November 1, 2004.
18. Rumsfeld to Bush, "Jay Garner," May 9, 2003.
19. Steven R. Weisman, "U.S. Set to Name Civilian to Oversee Iraq," *New York Times,* May 2, 2003.
20. Steven R. Weisman, "U.S. Set to Name Civilian to Oversee Iraq," *New York Times,* May 2, 2003.
21. Rumsfeld, handwritten note, March 31, 2003.
22. Rumsfeld to Card, cc: Cheney, "Press Reports," April 7, 2003.
23. Rumsfeld, handwritten note, March 31, 2003.
24. Rumsfeld, "Memorandum," September 6, 2001.
25. Rumsfeld, handwritten note, October 1, 2003.
26. Rumsfeld, handwritten note, October 2, 2003.
27. Rumsfeld to Card, "Ambassador Paul Bremer," April 24, 2003.
28. Rumsfeld, "Principles for Iraq—Policy Guidelines," May 13, 2003.
29. Rumsfeld, handwritten note, May 6, 2003.
30. Ambassador L. Paul Bremer III with Malcolm McConnell, *My Year in Iraq: The Struggle to Build a Future of Hope* (New York: Simon & Schuster, 2005), p. 12.

CHAPTER 36 Too Many Hands on the Steering Wheel

1. Ambassador L. Paul Bremer III with Malcolm McConnell, *My Year in Iraq: The Struggle to Build a Future of Hope* (New York: Simon & Schuster, 2005), pp. 36–37.

2. Rory Stewart, *The Prince of the Marshes: And Other Occupational Hazards of a Year in Iraq* (Orlando, FL: Harcourt, 2006), p. 109.
3. James Dobbins, Seth G. Jones, Benjamin Runkle, and Siddharth Mohandas, *Occupying Iraq: A History of the Coalition Provisional Authority* (Santa Monica, CA: RAND, 2009), p. 248.
4. James Dobbins, Seth G. Jones, Benjamin Runkle, and Siddharth Mohandas, *Occupying Iraq: A History of the Coalition Provisional Authority* (Santa Monica, CA: RAND, 2009), p. 249.
5. George Packer, *The Assassins' Gate: America in Iraq* (New York: Farrar, Straus and Giroux, 2005), p. 396.
6. Rumsfeld to Powell et al., "Iraq Personnel," September 16, 2003.
7. Commander, U.S. Joint Forces Command, "Joint Lessons Learned: Operational Insights," August 8, 2003; Commander, U.S. Joint Forces Command, "Joint Lessons Learned: Stability, Transition and Reconstruction Operations—Operational Insights," May 25, 2004.
8. Ambassador L. Paul Bremer III with Malcolm McConnell, *My Year in Iraq: The Struggle to Build a Future of Hope* (New York: Simon & Schuster, 2005), p. 12.
9. Douglas Jehl and Jane Perlez, "Pentagon Sending a Team of Exiles to Help Run Iraq," *New York Times,* April 26, 2003.
10. Special Inspector General for Iraq Reconstruction interview with Ambassador L. Paul Bremer III, March 18, 2008, as cited in Special Inspector General for Iraq Reconstruction, *Hard Lessons: The Iraq Reconstruction Experience* (Washington, D.C.: U.S. Government Printing Office, 2009), p. 69.
11. Bremer to Rumsfeld, "Meeting with Iraqi Political Leaders," June 2, 2003.
12. Rumsfeld to Bremer, "Why We Need an IA Sooner Rather Than Later," June 9, 2003; Rumsfeld to Bremer, "Forming the Interim Administration," June 21, 2003.
13. Douglas J. Feith, *War and Decision: Inside the Pentagon at the Dawn of the War on Terrorism* (New York: HarperCollins, 2008), p. 439.
14. Patrick E. Tyler, "Overseer Adjusts Strategy as Turmoil Grows in Iraq," *New York Times,* July 13, 2003.
15. Ambassador L. Paul Bremer III with Malcolm McConnell, *My Year in Iraq: The Struggle to Build a Future of Hope* (New York: Simon & Schuster, 2005), p. 171.
16. Rumsfeld to Bremer et al., "Recognition of Governing Council," September 11, 2003.
17. David Rohde, "Iraqis Were Set to Vote, but U.S. Wielded a Veto," *New York Times,* June 19, 2003.
18. Wolfowitz to Rumsfeld, "CERP Funds," November 28, 2003.
19. Coalition Provisional Authority, "Achieving the Vision to Restore Full Sovereignty to the Iraqi People (Strategic Plan)," working document as of October 1, 2003 (Baghdad, Iraq).
20. Coalition Provisional Authority, "Achieving the Vision to Restore Full Sovereignty to the Iraqi People (Strategic Plan)," working document as of October 1, 2003 (Baghdad, Iraq).
21. Douglas J. Feith, *War and Decision: Inside the Pentagon at the Dawn of the War on Terrorism* (New York: HarperCollins, 2008), pp. 497–98.
22. Coalition Provisional Authority, "Implementation of De-Ba'athification Order No. 1," May 16, 2003.
23. Rumsfeld to Bush et al., "Visit to the Persian Gulf, Iraq, Afghanistan & United Kingdom," May 5, 2003.
24. James Dobbins, Seth G. Jones, Benjamin Runkle, and Siddharth Mohandas, *Occupying*

Iraq: A History of the Coalition Provisional Authority (Santa Monica, CA: RAND, 2009), pp. xxvi–xxvii.

25. Ali A. Allawi, *The Occupation of Iraq: Winning the War, Losing the Peace* (New Haven: Yale University Press, 2007), p. 150.
26. Department of Defense notes of NSC meeting, March 26, 2003.
27. Department of Defense, "Rebuilding the Iraqi Military," January 21, 2003.
28. Department of Defense notes of principals meeting, February 26, 2003.
29. Rodman to Rumsfeld, "Disbanding the Iraqi Army," May 24, 2006.
30. James Dobbins, Seth G. Jones, Benjamin Runkle, and Siddharth Mohandas, *Occupying Iraq: A History of the Coalition Provisional Authority* (Santa Monica, CA: RAND, 2009), p. 55.
31. Michael R. Gordon, "Fateful Choice on Iraq Army Bypassed Debate," *New York Times,* March 17, 2008.
32. Ambassador L. Paul Bremer III with Malcolm McConnell, *My Year in Iraq: The Struggle to Build a Future of Hope* (New York: Simon & Schuster, 2005), p. 224.
33. Bremer to Rumsfeld et al., "Dissolution of the Ministry of Defense and Related Entities," May 19, 2003.
34. James Dobbins, Seth G. Jones, Benjamin Runkle, and Siddharth Mohandas, *Occupying Iraq: A History of the Coalition Provisional Authority* (Santa Monica, CA: RAND, 2009), p. 57.
35. Rumsfeld to Bremer, "Response to your 'should we pay the ex-military' proposal," June 19, 2003.
36. Douglas J. Feith, *War and Decision: Inside the Pentagon at the Dawn of the War on Terrorism* (New York: HarperCollins, 2008), pp. 433–34; James Dobbins, Seth G. Jones, Benjamin Runkle, and Siddharth Mohandas, *Occupying Iraq: A History of the Coalition Provisional Authority* (Santa Monica, CA: RAND, 2009), p. 60.
37. Rumsfeld to Bremer et al., "Iraqi Army," October 15, 2003.
38. Rumsfeld to Abizaid et al., "Iraqi Security Elements," November 10, 2003; Rumsfeld, letter to Carl Levin et al., December 29, 2003.
39. Ambassador L. Paul Bremer III with Malcolm McConnell, *My Year in Iraq: The Struggle to Build a Future of Hope* (New York: Simon & Schuster, 2005), p. 236.
40. Hannah Hickey, "Bremer Defends Disbanding Iraqi Army as the 'Most Important Decision I Made,'" *Stanford Report,* April 27, 2005.
41. L. Paul Bremer III, "How I Didn't Dismantle Iraq's Army," *New York Times,* September 6, 2007.
42. Bremer to Rumsfeld et al., "Dissolution of the Ministry of Defense and Related Entities," May 19, 2003.
43. James Dobbins, Seth G. Jones, Benjamin Runkle, and Siddharth Mohandas, *Occupying Iraq: A History of the Coalition Provisional Authority* (Santa Monica, CA: RAND, 2009), p. 57.
44. Christopher Hitchens, "It Was Right to Dissolve the Iraqi Army," *Slate,* September 17, 2007.
45. Myers to Rumsfeld, "Police," July 22, 2003.
46. Rumsfeld to Bremer et al., "Training Iraqi Police," September 29, 2003.
47. Bremer to Rumsfeld, "Security Assessment," February 3, 2004.
48. Associated Press, "Saddam's Amnesty Blamed for Iraq's Crime," *New York Times,* May 16, 2003.
49. George Tenet with Bill Harlow, *At the Center of the Storm: My Years at the CIA* (New York: HarperCollins, 2007), p. 318.
50. Gary Anderson, "Saddam's Greater Game," *Washington Post,* April 2, 2003.

51. Rumsfeld to Abizaid et al., "Post-Saddam," May 22, 2003.
52. Department of Defense news transcript, "DoD News Briefing—Mr. Di Rita and Gen. Abizaid," July 16, 2003.
53. Rumsfeld to Steven Bucci, "DoD Dictionary," July 23, 2003; Rumsfeld to Abizaid, cc: Myers, "Definitions," July 23, 2003.
54. Rumsfeld to Wolfowitz et al., "Terminology," January 7, 2004.
55. Rumsfeld to Di Rita, "History of Insurgency," November 12, 2003.
56. L. Paul Bremer III, "Iraq's Path to Sovereignty," *Washington Post,* September 8, 2003.
57. Douglas J. Feith, *War and Decision: Inside the Pentagon at the Dawn of the War on Terrorism* (New York: HarperCollins, 2008), p. 459.
58. Ambassador L. Paul Bremer III with Malcolm McConnell, *My Year in Iraq: The Struggle to Build a Future of Hope* (New York: Simon & Schuster, 2005), p. 164.
59. Ambassador L. Paul Bremer III with Malcolm McConnell, *My Year in Iraq: The Struggle to Build a Future of Hope* (New York: Simon & Schuster, 2005), p. 208.
60. Rumsfeld to Bremer, "Memos on Iraq," July 8, 2003; Rumsfeld to Bremer, [No Subject], June 1, 2004.

CHAPTER 37 Liberation from the Occupation

1. Douglas J. Feith and Lieutenant General Walter L. Sharp (principal drafters), "Strategic Review: Stay the Course—Faster," October 28, 2003, as cited in Douglas J. Feith, *War and Decision: Inside the Pentagon at the Dawn of the War on Terrorism* (New York: HarperCollins, 2008), pp. 460, 644.
2. Rumsfeld, "Plan for Iraq," October 14, 2003.
3. Rumsfeld, "Risk in the Way Ahead in Iraq," October 28, 2003.
4. Ambassador L. Paul Bremer III with Malcolm McConnell, *My Year in Iraq: The Struggle to Build a Future of Hope* (New York: Simon & Schuster, 2005), p. 227.
5. Judy Keen,"Rice Will Manage Iraq's 'New Phase,'" *USA Today,* October 6, 2003.
6. David E. Sanger, "White House to Overhaul Iraq and Afghan Missions," *New York Times,* October 6, 2003.
7. "Rumsfeld Avoids Questions on Iraq Role," CNN, October 9, 2003.
8. Rumsfeld to Rice, "Cartoon," October 15, 2003.
9. David E. Sanger, "White House to Overhaul Iraq and Afghan Missions," *New York Times,* October 6, 2003.
10. Rumsfeld to Powell, "Afghanistan—Embassy Kabul Staffing," March 26, 2004.
11. Rumsfeld to Bush et al., "Iraq Reporting Relationships," October 6, 2003.
12. Rumsfeld to Bush et al., "Iraq Reporting Relationships," October 6, 2003.
13. Rumsfeld to Bush et al., "Iraq Reporting Relationships," October 6, 2003.
14. Rumsfeld, handwritten note, October 14, 2003.
15. Rumsfeld, "Alternative Approaches to Operate the NSC—Consensus v. Options for POTUS," April 1, 2004; Rumsfeld to Rice, "Interagency Process," August 20, 2002.
16. Rumsfeld, "Conversation with Jerry Bremer," December 10, 2003.
17. Rumsfeld, "Fight to the Death," July 24, 2003.
18. Alexandar Vasovic, "Saddam: 'I'm Willing to Negotiate,' Raising Hopes Insurgency Might Weaken," Associated Press, December 15, 2003.
19. Department of Defense notes of NSC meeting, April 9, 2003.
20. Department of Defense notes of NSC meeting, April 9, 2003; Ambassador L. Paul Bremer III with Malcolm McConnell, *My Year in Iraq: The Struggle to Build a Future of Hope* (New York: Simon & Schuster, 2005), p. 334.
21. Department of Defense notes of NSC meeting, April 10, 2003.

22. International Monetary Fund, "Iraq: Third and Fourth Reviews Under the Stand-By Arrangement, Financing Assurances Review, and Requests for Extension of the Arrangement and for Waiver of Nonobservance of a Performance Criterion," IMF Country Report No. 07/115, March 2007, p. 13.
23. Coalition Provisional Authority, "Law of Administration for the State of Iraq for the Transitional Period," adopted March 8, 2004.
24. Department of Defense news transcript, "Defense Department Operational Update Briefing," April 20, 2004.
25. Rumsfeld to Abizaid et al., "Sunni Engagement," December 19, 2003.
26. Rumsfeld to Bremer, "Sunni Outreach," April 12, 2004.
27. Glen D. Shaffer, Director for Intelligence (J-2) to Myers et al., "The Importance of the Tribes in Post-Saddam Iraq," April 8, 2003.
28. Bing West, *No True Glory: A Frontline Account of the Battle for Fallujah* (New York: Bantam Books, 2005), p. 61.
29. Stephan Faris, "Islamic Justice: The Religious Militia Muscles In," *Time,* March 1, 2004.
30. Rumsfeld to Abizaid et al., "SADR," August 30, 2003.
31. Rumsfeld to Abizaid et al., "SADR," August 30, 2003.
32. OSD Policy, "Apprehension of Moqtada al Sadr," January 7, 2004.
33. Edward Wong, "Truce Extended in Falluja Siege, and Talks Go On," *New York Times,* April 26, 2004.
34. Edward Wong, "Truce Extended in Falluja Siege, and Talks Go On," *New York Times,* April 26, 2004.
35. Ambassador L. Paul Bremer III with Malcolm McConnell, *My Year in Iraq: The Struggle to Build a Future of Hope* (New York: Simon & Schuster, 2005), pp. 135–36.
36. Rodman to Rumsfeld, "Decision Not to Go After Sadr," December 6, 2005.
37. Paul Bremer, statement to the Iraqi people, March 3, 2004; Paul Bremer, statement on UN Envoy Lakhdar Brahimi's announcement regarding Iraq's political transition, April 14, 2004.
38. Dexter Filkins, "U.S. Transfers Power to Iraq 2 Days Early," *New York Times,* June 29, 2004.

PART TWELVE Wartime Detention

1. Department of Defense, "DoD Chains of Command until 19 Nov 03 (Abu Ghraib abuses: Sep–Dec 03)," undated.
2. Associated Press, "Vatican Calls Prison Abuse a Bigger Blow to U.S. than Sept. 11," *USA Today,* May 12, 2004.
3. Tom Curry, "Will Rumsfeld Survive Abuse Scandal?" MSNBC, May 6, 2004.
4. Edward Kennedy, statement, "The Prisoner Abuse Resolution," 108th Cong., 2d sess., Congressional Record, vol. 150, no. 64 , May 10, 2004, p. S5058.
5. Colin Powell, interviewed by Larry King, *Larry King Live,* CNN, May 4, 2004.
6. Seymour M. Hersh, "Torture at Abu Ghraib," *The New Yorker,* May 10, 2004.
7. Al Gore, remarks, New York University, New York, May 26, 2004.
8. Rumsfeld, handwritten letter to Bush, May 5, 2004.
9. Hearings of the Senate and House Armed Services Committees, "Testimony of Secretary of Defense Donald H. Rumsfeld," May 7, 2004.
10. Hearings of the Senate and House Armed Services Committees, "Testimony of Secretary of Defense Donald H. Rumsfeld," May 7, 2004.

11. Hearings of the Senate and House Armed Services Committees, "Testimony of Secretary of Defense Donald H. Rumsfeld," May 7, 2004.
12. "Death in the Night," *Time,* May 5, 1952.
13. Rumsfeld, handwritten letter to Bush, May 9, 2004.
14. Kate Zernike, "Cited as Symbol of Abu Ghraib, Man Admits He Is Not in Photo," *New York Times,* March 18, 2006.
15. "Review of Department of Defense Detention Operations and Detainee Interrogation Techniques" (Church Report), March 7, 2005.
16. "Final Report of the Independent Panel to Review DoD Detention Operations" (Schlesinger Panel), August 24, 2004.
17. "Report on Detention and Corrections Operations in Iraq" (MG Ryder Report), November 5, 2003; "Assessment of DoD Counterterrorism Interrogation and Detention Operations in Iraq" (MG Miller Report), September 9, 2003; "Article 15-6 Investigation of the 800th Military Police Brigade" (Taguba Report), March 12, 2004; "Review of Department of Defense Detention Operations and Detainee Interrogation Techniques" (Church Report), March 7, 2005; "CFC-A AO Detainee Operations: Report of Inspection" (Jacoby Report), June 26, 2004; "Detainee Operations Inspection" (Mikolashek Report), July 21, 2004; "Final Report of the Independent Panel to Review DoD Detention Operations" (Schlesinger Panel), August 24, 2004; "Investigation of Intelligence Activities at Abu Ghraib" (Fay/Jones Report), August 23, 2004; "Article 15-6 Investigation of CJSOTF-AP and 5th SF Group Detention Operations" (Formica Report), November 8, 2004; "Final Report: Assessment of Detainee Medical Operations for OEF, Gitmo, and OIF" (LTG Kiley Medical Review), April 13, 2005; "Army Regulation 15-6: Final Report—Investigation into FBI Allegations of Detainee Abuse at Guantánamo Bay, Cuba Detention Facility" (Schmidt-Furlow Report), amended June 9, 2005; "Review of DoD-Directed Investigations of Detainee Abuse," August 25, 2006.
18. Rumsfeld, "Memorandum," June 1, 2004.

CHAPTER 38 The Least Worst Place

1. Rick Atkinson, *The Day of Battle: The War in Sicily and Italy, 1943–1944* (New York: Holt, 2008), pp. 118–19; Thomas Farragher, "Vengeance at Dachau," *Boston Globe,* July 2, 2001.
2. Associated Press, "60,000 Inmates Sexually Abused Every Year," CBS News, June 23, 2009; editorial, "Sexual Abuse Behind Bars," *Washington Post,* September 15, 2009.
3. Rumsfeld to Hadley et al., "Transferring Responsibilities to Afghanistan and Iraq," February 3, 2005.
4. Haynes to Rumsfeld, "President's Military Order on Detention, Treatment, and Trial of Certain Non-Citizens in the War Against Terrorism," November 14, 2001.
5. Haynes to Rumsfeld, "President's Military Order on Detention, Treatment, and Trial of Certain Non-Citizens in the War Against Terrorism," November 14, 2001.
6. *Ex parte Quirin,* 317 U.S. 1 (1942).
7. Haynes to Rumsfeld, "President's Military Order on Detention, Treatment, and Trial of Certain Non-Citizens in the War Against Terrorism," November 14, 2001.
8. Rumsfeld to Myers, "Status of Taliban and Al Qaida," January 19, 2002.
9. David Hackett Fischer, *Washington's Crossing* (New York: Oxford University Press, 2004), p. 379.

10. Alex Perry, "Inside the Battle at Qala-I-Jangi," *Time,* December 1, 2001.
11. Alex Perry, "Inside the Battle at Qala-I-Jangi," *Time,* December 1, 2001.
12. Alex Perry, "Inside the Battle at Qala-I-Jangi," *Time,* December 1, 2001.
13. Carlotta Gall, "In Tunnels Full of Bodies, One of Them Kept Firing," *New York Times,* November 30, 2001.
14. Alex Perry, "Inside the Battle at Qala-I-Jangi," *Time,* December 1, 2001.
15. Ronald Reagan, "Message to the Senate Transmitting a Protocol to the 1949 Geneva Conventions," January 29, 1987.
16. Ronald Reagan, "Message to the Senate Transmitting a Protocol to the 1949 Geneva Conventions," January 29, 1987.
17. Editorial, "Hijacking the Geneva Conventions," *Washington Post,* February 18, 1987.
18. Editorial, "Denied: A Shield for Terrorists," *New York Times,* February 17, 1987.
19. Editorial, "The Guantánamo Story," *Washington Post,* January 25, 2002; editorial, "Justice at Guantánamo," *New York Times,* January 29, 2002.
20. Eric Holder, interviewed by Paula Zahn, *American Morning with Paula Zahn,* CNN, January 28, 2002.
21. International Committee of the Red Cross (ICRC), "Convention (III) Relative to the Treatment of Prisoners of War," Article 17, Geneva, August 12, 1949.
22. International Committee of the Red Cross (ICRC), "Convention (III) Relative to the Treatment of Prisoners of War," Article 25, Geneva, August 12, 1949.
23. Richard A. Clarke, "Blinded by Hindsight," *New York Times,* October 1, 2006; Warren Richey, "Sorting Out Guantánamo Detainees," *Christian Science Monitor,* January 22, 2009; Charlie Savage and Scott Shane, "Terror-War Fallout Lingers Over Bush Lawyers," *New York Times,* March 9, 2009.
24. Taft to Gonzales, "Comments on Your Paper on the Geneva Convention," February 2, 2002, as quoted in Jack Goldsmith, *The Terror Presidency: Law and Judgment Inside the Bush Administration* (New York: W. W. Norton, 2007), p. 113.
25. Powell to Gonzales and Rice, "Draft Decision Memorandum for the President on the Applicability of the Geneva Convention to the Conflict in Afghanistan," January 26, 2002.
26. Douglas J. Feith, *War and Decision: Inside the Pentagon at the Dawn of the War on Terrorism* (New York: HarperCollins, 2008), p. 164; Jay S. Bybee to Gonzales and Haynes, "Re: Application of Treaties and Laws to al Qaeda and Taliban Detainees," January 22, 2002.
27. Katharine Q. Seelye and David E. Sanger, "Bush Reconsiders Stand on Treating Captives of War," *New York Times,* January 29, 2002.
28. Rumsfeld to Powell and Rice, "Geneva Convention," February 4, 2002.
29. Department of Defense, "Points for 2/4/02 NSC Meeting on Geneva Convention," February 3, 2002.
30. Department of Defense, "Points for 2/4/02 NSC Meeting on Geneva Convention," February 3, 2002.
31. Department of Defense, "Points for 2/4/02 NSC Meeting on Geneva Convention," February 3, 2002.
32. Powell to Gonzales and Rice, "Draft Decision Memorandum for the President on the Applicability of the Geneva Convention to the Conflict in Afghanistan," January 25, 2002.
33. Bush to Cheney et al., "Humane Treatment of al Qaeda and Taliban Detainees," February 7, 2002.

34. Rumsfeld to Hadley et al., "Transferring Responsibilities to Afghanistan and Iraq," February 3, 2005.
35. Haynes to Rumsfeld, "Detention Facilities in the Continental United States," December 27, 2001.
36. Department of Defense news transcript, "DoD News Briefing—Secretary Rumsfeld and Gen. Myers," December 27, 2001.
37. Rumsfeld to Myers and Franks, "Low-Level Enemy Combatants," April 21, 2003.
38. Rumsfeld to Powell et al., "Making Afghans Responsible for Holding 'Low-Level' Enemy Combatants in the Afghan System," April 21, 2003.
39. Rumsfeld to Feith, "Detainees," January 3, 2003.
40. Rumsfeld to Feith, "Detainees," January 8, 2003.
41. Rumsfeld to Haynes and Feith, "Detainees," April 11, 2003.
42. Rumsfeld to Powell et al., "Negotiating Transfer Agreements With Foreign Nations," April 21, 2003.
43. "Lesson Eighteen: Prisons and Detention Centers," Manchester Document, al-Qaida Training Manual.
44. "Lesson Eighteen: Prisons and Detention Centers," Manchester Document, al-Qaida Training Manual.
45. Michael Isikoff and John Barry, "Gitmo: SouthCom Showdown," *Newsweek,* May 9, 2005.
46. Mark Whitaker, "The Editor's Desk," *Newsweek,* May 23, 2005.
47. Reuters, "Guantánamo Better Than Belgian Prisons: OSCE Expert," Australian Broadcasting Corporation, March 7, 2006.
48. Department of Defense Office of Public Affairs, "Ten Facts about Guantánamo," September 14, 2006; Spc. Shanita Simmons, USA, "Detainee Literacy Rates Improve Through Education Programs," American Forces Press Service; Jane Sutton, "Guantánamo Convict Eligible for 'Movie Night,'" Reuters, August 8, 2008.
49. Chris Hedges, "Ex-Judge vs. the Government's Law-Free Zone," *New York Times,* February 6, 2004; Johan Steyn, "Guantánamo Bay: The Legal Black Hole," Twenty-Seventh FA Mann Lecture, British Institute of International and Comparative Law and Herbert Smith, Lincoln's Inn Old Hall, November 25, 2003.
50. Alan Cowell, "U.S. 'Thumbs Its Nose' at Rights, Amnesty Says," *New York Times,* May 26, 2005.
51. Dan Balz, "Durbin Defends Guantánamo Comments," *Washington Post,* June 17, 2005.
52. Helene Cooper and William Glaberson, "At White House, Renewed Debate on Guantánamo," *New York Times,* June 23, 2007; Walter Pincus, "Powell Calls for Closure of Military Prison at Guantánamo," *Washington Post,* June 11, 2007.
53. Helene Cooper and William Glaberson, "At White House, Renewed Debate on Guantánamo," *New York Times,* June 23, 2007.
54. Rumsfeld to Powell et al., "Guantánamo Detainees," December 19, 2003.
55. Rumsfeld to Powell et al., "Guantánamo Detainees," December 19, 2003.
56. Mark H. Buzby, "Guantánamo Is a Model Prison (Really)," *Wall Street Journal,* June 4, 2008.
57. Department of Defense news transcript, "Secretary Rumsfeld Remarks to Greater Miami Chamber of Commerce," February 13, 2004.
58. Scott Higham and Peter Finn, "At Least $500 Million Has Been Spent Since 9/11 on Renovating Guantánamo Bay," *Washington Post,* June 7, 2010.
59. Barack Obama, Executive Order 13492, "Review and Disposition of Individuals Detained at the Guantánamo Bay Naval Base and Closure of Detention Facilities," January 22, 2009.

CHAPTER 39 The Twentieth Hijacker

1. "Statement of Jose E. Melendez-Perez to the National Commission on Terrorist Attacks Upon the United States," seventh public hearing of the National Commission on Terrorist Attacks Upon the United States, January 26, 2004.
2. "Statement of Jose E. Melendez-Perez to the National Commission on Terrorist Attacks Upon the United States," seventh public hearing of the National Commission on Terrorist Attacks Upon the United States, January 26, 2004.
3. Press briefing by White House Counsel Judge Alberto Gonzales, DoD General Counsel William Haynes, DoD Deputy General Counsel Daniel Dell'Orto, and Army Deputy Chief of Staff for Intelligence General Keith Alexander, June 22, 2004.
4. Department of Defense, Office for the Administrative Review of the Detention of Enemy Combatants at U.S. Naval Base Guantánamo Bay, Cuba, "Unclassified Summary of Evidence for Administrative Review Board in the Case of Al Qahtani, Maad," January 17, 2008.
5. *The 9/11 Commission Report: Final Report of the National Commission on Terrorist Attacks Upon the United States* (New York: W. W. Norton, 2004), p. 248.
6. Department of Defense MC Form 458 (January 2007) for Khalid Sheikh Muhammed, Walid Muhammed Salih Mubarak Bin 'Attash, Ramzi Binalshibh, Ali Abdul Aziz Ali, Mustafa Ahmed Adam al Hawsawi, and Mohamed Al Kahtani.
7. "Substitution for the Testimony of Mohammad Manea Ahmad Al-Qahtani," *United States v. Moussaoui* (Cr. No. 01-455-A).
8. *The 9/11 Commission Report: Final Report of the National Commission on Terrorist Attacks Upon the United States* (New York: W. W. Norton, 2004), pp. 11, 235.
9. Department of Defense news release, "Guantánamo Provides Valuable Intelligence Information," June 12, 2005.
10. Chris Mackey and Greg Miller, *The Interrogators: Task Force 500 and America's Secret War Against al Qaeda* (New York: Back Bay Books, 2005), p. 472.
11. Department of Justice, Office of the Inspector General, "A Review of the FBI's Involvement in and Observations of Detainee Interrogations in Guantánamo Bay, Afghanistan, and Iraq," revised October 2009.
12. Hill to Myers, "Counter-Resistance Techniques," October 25, 2002.
13. Lieutenant Colonel Jerald Phifer to Major General Michael B. Dunlavey, "Request for Approval of Counter-Resistance Strategies," October 11, 2002.
14. Lieutenant Colonel Jerald Phifer to Major General Michael B. Dunlavey, "Request for Approval of Counter-Resistance Strategies," October 11, 2002.
15. Lieutenant Colonel Jerald Phifer to Major General Michael B. Dunlavey, "Request for Approval of Counter-Resistance Strategies," October 11, 2002.
16. Haynes to Rumsfeld, "Counter-Resistance Techniques," November 27, 2002.
17. Haynes to Rumsfeld, "Counter-Resistance Techniques," November 27, 2002.
18. Haynes to Rumsfeld, "Counter-Resistance Techniques," November 27, 2002.
19. Philippe Sands, *Torture Team: Rumsfeld's Memo and the Betrayal of American Values* (New York: Palgrave Macmillan, 2008).
20. Press briefing by White House Counsel Judge Alberto Gonzales, DoD General Counsel William Haynes, DoD Deputy General Counsel Daniel Dell'Orto, and Army Deputy Chief of Staff for Intelligence General Keith Alexander, June 22, 2004.
21. Press briefing by White House Counsel Judge Alberto Gonzales, DoD General Counsel William Haynes, DoD Deputy General Counsel Daniel Dell'Orto,

and Army Deputy Chief of Staff for Intelligence General Keith Alexander, June 22, 2004.

22. "Final Report of the Independent Panel to Review DoD Detention Operations" (Schlesinger Panel), August 24, 2004, p. 8.
23. "Army Regulation 15-6: Final Report, Investigation into FBI Allegations of Detainee Abuse at Guantánamo Bay, Cuba Detention Facility" (Schmidt-Furlow Report), amended June 9, 2005, p. 20.
24. Marc A. Thiessen, *Courting Disaster: How the CIA Kept America Safe and How Barack Obama Is Inviting the Next Attack* (Washington, D.C.: Regnery, 2010), pp. 284–85; "Review of Department of Defense Detention Operations and Detainee Interrogation Techniques" (Church Report), March 7, 2005.
25. "Review of Department of Defense Detention Operations and Detainee Interrogation Techniques" (Church Report), March 7, 2005.
26. "Review of Department of Defense Detention Operations and Detainee Interrogation Techniques" (Church Report), March 7, 2005.
27. Geren to Rumsfeld, "Allegations in Admiral Church Hearing—SNOWFLAKE," April 20, 2005.
28. "Working Group Report on Detainee Interrogations in the Global War on Terrorism: Assessment of Legal, Historical, Policy, and Operational Considerations," April 4, 2003.
29. "Inside the Interrogation of Detainee 063," *Time,* June 12, 2005.
30. Rumsfeld to Myers, "Status of Taliban and Al Qaida," January 19, 2002.
31. Marc A. Thiessen, *Courting Disaster: How the CIA Kept America Safe and How Barack Obama Is Inviting the Next Attack* (Washington, D.C.: Regnery, 2010), p. 23.
32. Senate Select Committee on Intelligence, "OLC Opinions on the CIA Detention and Interrogation Program," April 22, 2009; Joby Warrick and Dan Eggen, "Hill Briefed on Waterboarding in 2002," *Washington Post,* December 9, 2007.
33. Hearing of the Senate Select Committee on Intelligence, "Current and Projected National Security Threats," testimony of Michael Hayden, February 5, 2008.
34. Dana Priest, "CIA Holds Terror Suspects in Secret Prisons," *Washington Post,* November 2, 2005.
35. Michael Hayden and Michael B. Mukasey, "The President Ties His Own Hands on Terror," *Wall Street Journal,* April 17, 2009; Central Intelligence Agency Inspector General, "Counterterrorism Detention and Interrogation Activities, September 2001–October 2008," May 7, 2004, pp. 85, 88; Central Intelligence Agency, "Detainee Reporting Pivotal for the War Against Al-Qa'ida," June 3, 2005, appendix; Peter Finn, Joby Warrick, and Julie Tate, "How a Detainee Became an Asset," *Washington Post,* August 29, 2009; Central Intelligence Agency, "Khalid Shaykh Muhammed: Preeminent Source on Al-Qa'ida," July 13, 2004, p. 1.

CHAPTER 40 Law in a Time of War

1. Andrew C. McCarthy, *Willful Blindness: A Memoir of the Jihad* (New York: Encounter Books, 2008), pp. 304–5; Andrew C. McCarthy, "The Intelligence Mess: How It Happened, What to Do About It," *Commentary,* April 2004, p. 16; Ronald Kessler, *The CIA at War: Inside the Secret Campaign Against Terror* (New York: St. Martin's Press, 2003), pp. 226–27.
2. "Military Order of November 13, 2001—Detention, Treatment, and Trial of Certain Non-Citizens in the War Against Terrorism," Federal Register, vol. 66, no. 222, November 16, 2001.

3. "Military Commissions," *Time,* May 18, 2009; William Winthrop, *Military Law and Precedents,* 2nd edition (Boston: Little, Brown, 1896), vol. II, pp. 1297–1298.
4. Francis Biddle, *In Brief Authority* (Garden City, NY: Doubleday, 1962), p. 330.
5. Editorial, "A Travesty of Justice," *New York Times,* November 16, 2001; Hearing of the Senate Judiciary Committee, "DOJ Oversight: Preserving Our Freedoms While Defending Against Terrorism," opening statement of Senator Patrick Leahy, November 28, 2001.
6. William Safire, "Kangaroo Courts," *New York Times,* November 26, 2001.
7. Department of Defense Military Commission Order No. 1, March 21, 2002.
8. Editorial, "Refining Military Tribunals," *New York Times,* March 22, 2002.
9. William Safire, "Military Tribunals Modified," *New York Times,* March 21, 2002.
10. *Hamdan v. Rumsfeld,* 548 U.S. 557 (2006).
11. *Ex parte Quirin,* 317 U.S. 1 (1942).
12. *Ex parte Quirin,* 317 U.S. 1, 35 (1942).
13. *Johnson v. Eisentrager,* 339 U.S. 763 (1950).
14. *Hamdan v. Rumsfeld,* 548 U.S. 557 (2006).
15. International Committee of the Red Cross (ICRC), "Convention (III) Relative to the Treatment of Prisoners of War," Article 3, Geneva, August 12, 1949.
16. Department of Defense Directive 2310.01E, "The Department of Defense Detainee Program," September 5, 2006.
17. Rumsfeld to Cambone, "Finalization of New Army Field Manual," December 19, 2005.
18. *Boumediene v. Bush,* 553 U.S. 723, 811 (2008) (Roberts, C. J., dissenting).
19. *Johnson v. Eisentrager,* 339 U.S., 763, 779 (1950).
20. David Rivkin and Lee Casey, "Lawfare," *Wall Street Journal,* February 23, 2007; Charles J. Dunlap, Jr., "Lawfare: A Decisive Element of 21st-Century Conflicts?" *Joint Forces Quarterly,* issue 54, 3rd quarter, 2009.
21. James Ridgeway with Ariston-Lizabeth Anderson and Sandra Bisin, "Manhattan's Milosevic: How You Can Do What the Government Won't: Arrest Henry Kissinger," *Village Voice,* August 15, 2001.
22. "US Warned on Deadly Drone Attacks," BBC News, October 28, 2009.
23. Ian Black and Ewen MacAskill, "US Threatens Nato Boycott Over Belgian War Crimes Law," *The Guardian,* June 13, 2003.
24. Rumsfeld to Cheney et al., "Judicialization of International Politics," April 9, 2003.

CHAPTER 41 The Road Not Traveled

1. Rumsfeld to Hadley, "Deputies' Committee Meeting," January 6, 2005.
2. Jack Goldsmith, *The Terror Presidency: Law and Judgment Inside the Bush Administration* (New York: W. W. Norton, 2007), pp. 206–10.
3. Alexander Hamilton, "The Federalist No. 70: The Executive Department Further Considered," *Independent Journal,* March 15, 1788.
4. William J. Haynes II, "Lewis F. Powell Lecture," American College of Trial Lawyers, Tucson, Arizona, March 8, 2008.
5. Rumsfeld to Bush et al., [No Subject], September 19, 2001.
6. Rumsfeld to Haynes, cc: England, "Idea for Congressional Involvement," March 30, 2005.
7. Andrew C. McCarthy, "A Quick Way Forward After Boumediene," *National Review Online,* June 16, 2008.

PART THIRTEEN Pulling On Our Boots: Challenges and Controversies Beyond the War Zones

1. Elizabeth Becker, "Congress Passes Antimissile Defense Policy," *New York Times*, May 21, 1999.
2. Department of Defense news release, "Missile Intercept Test Successful," October 14, 2002.

CHAPTER 42 Katrina and the Challenge of New Institutions

1. Office of Assistant Secretary of Defense for Homeland Defense, "Hurricane Katrina Interim Timeline (August-September 2005)," October 17, 2005.
2. Rumsfeld to Myers, "USG's Ability to Deal with Catastrophic Events—Natural or Terrorist," September 20, 2005.
3. OSD Policy, "Gaps and Seams in Protecting the US Homeland," August 11, 2005.
4. Rumsfeld, "Homeland Defense," May 25, 2004.
5. Active-Duty Unit Timeline, September 3, 2005.
6. Joint Hearing of the House Subcommittee on Emergency Preparedness, Science, and Technology of the Committee on Homeland Security and the Subcommittee on Terrorism, Unconventional Threats, and Capabilities of the Armed Services Committee, "Military and National Guard Roles in Disaster Response," statement of Paul McHale, Assistant Secretary of Defense for Homeland Defense, 109th Cong., 1st sess., November 9, 2005.
7. Rumsfeld to Bush et al., "Daily Update on Department of Defense KATRINA Activity," September 9, 2005.
8. Rumsfeld to Myers, "USG's Ability to Deal with Catastrophic Events—Natural or Terrorist," September 20, 2005.
9. Joint Hearing of the House Subcommittee on Emergency Preparedness, Science, and Technology of the Committee on Homeland Security and the Subcommittee on Terrorism, Unconventional Threats, and Capabilities of the Armed Services Committee, "Military and National Guard Roles in Disaster Response," statement of Paul McHale, Assistant Secretary of Defense for Homeland Defense, 109th Cong., 1st sess., November 9, 2005.
10. Maureen Dowd, "United States of Shame," *New York Times*, September 3, 2005; Howard Dean, interviewed by Wolf Blitzer, *The Situation Room*, CNN, September 9, 2005.
11. Rumsfeld to Bush et al., "Some Illustrative New Approaches and Initiatives to Meet the 21st Century Challenges," April 21, 2006.
12. Rumsfeld, "Intel Issue," September 8, 2004; Rumsfeld to Bush, "Intelligence 'Reform,'" September 11, 2004; Rumsfeld to Card et al., "Possible Talking Points," October 22, 2004; Philip Shenon, "Joint Chiefs Chairman Urges Curbs on New Intelligence Post," *New York Times*, October 23, 2004.
13. Rumsfeld, "Goldwater-Nichols for the USG," February 8, 2004.
14. Rumsfeld to Card et al., "Transforming the USG," August 25, 2004.
15. Department of Defense news transcript, "Secretary Rumsfeld Remarks at the Truman Library, Independence, Mo.," March 2, 2006.
16. Rumsfeld to Bush et al., "Some Illustrative New Approaches and Initiatives to Meet the 21st Century Challenges," April 21, 2006.
17. Rumsfeld, "Role of US Military," March 26, 2004.

18. "A Major Change of Public Opinion In the Muslim World: Results from a New Poll of Indonesians," Terror Free Tomorrow: The Center for Public Opinion, poll conducted February 1-6, 2005.
19. "US Senate Passes Resolution Based on Terror Free Tomorrow's Findings," Terror Free Tomorrow: The Center for Public Opinion, 2006; S. Res. 356, 109th Cong., 2d sess., January 27, 2006.
20. Rumsfeld, "A Nation and the Civilized World at War in the 21st Century," January 18, 2005.

CHAPTER 43 Gardening

1. George P. Shultz, *Turmoil and Triumph: My Years as Secretary of State* (New York: Charles Scribner's Sons, 1993), p. 128.
2. "Popularity of Colombia's Uribe Soars After Rescue," Reuters, July 6, 2008.
3. Robert G. Joseph, *Countering WMD: The Libyan Experience* (Fairfax, VA: National Institute Press, 2009).
4. Rumsfeld, "Pressure on Terrorists," January 17, 2006; Rumsfeld to Pace, "Thoughts on Being in Place for Any Possible Future AQ Movements," January 12, 2006.
5. Condoleezza Rice, interviewed by George Stephanopoulos, *This Week*, ABC, November 11, 2007.
6. Shirin Akiner, "Violence in Andijan, 13 May 2005: An Independent Assessment," Silk Road Paper, July 2005.
7. L. E. Jacoby to Rumsfeld, "Uzbekistan: Review of Information on Unrest in Andijon, 12–13 May 2005," July 30, 2005.
8. L. E. Jacoby to Rumsfeld, "Uzbekistan: Review of Information on Unrest in Andijon, 12–13 May 2005," July 30, 2005.
9. L. E. Jacoby to Rumsfeld, "Uzbekistan: Review of Information on Unrest in Andijon, 12–13 May 2005," July 30, 2005.
10. "'Bullets Were Falling Like Rain': The Andijan Massacre, May 13, 2005," Human Rights Watch, vol. 17, no. 5(D), June 2005; "Uzbekistan: Lifting the Siege on the Truth About Andizhan," Amnesty International, September 19, 2005; "The Andijan Massacre: One Year Later, Still No Justice," Human Rights Watch, May 11, 2006; "Uzbekistan: Andijan Crisis Aftermath," Human Rights Watch, background document, 2005.
11. "Punishment Please," *The Economist*, August 27, 2005.
12. Press conference of Senators John McCain, John Sununu, and Lindsey Graham, Tashkent, Uzbekistan, May 29, 2005.
13. McCain et al., letter to Rumsfeld, September 19, 2005.
14. Rumsfeld, letter to McCain, undated.
15. Rumsfeld to Feith et al., "Uzbekistan," July 24, 2005.
16. Rumsfeld to Jim MacDougall et al., "Congressional Amendment on Uzbekistan," October 18, 2005.
17. Rumsfeld to Cambone, "Uzbekistan," July 27, 2005.
18. R. Nicholas Burns, interviewed by Pahlavon Turghunov, BBC Uzbek Service, August 2, 2005.
19. Vladimir Socor, "The Unfolding of the U.S.-Uzbekistan Crisis," published as part of *Anatomy of a Crisis: U.S.-Uzbekistan Relations, 2001–2005*, edited by S. Frederick Starr (Central Asia-Caucasus Institute and Silk Road Studies Program, 2006), p. 50.
20. Vladimir Socor, "The Unfolding of the U.S.-Uzbekistan Crisis," published as part of *Anatomy of a Crisis: U.S.-Uzbekistan Relations, 2001–2005*, edited by S. Frederick Starr (Central Asia–Caucasus Institute and Silk Road Studies Program, 2006), p. 61.

21. Vladimir Socor, "The Unfolding of the U.S.-Uzbekistan Crisis," published as part of *Anatomy of a Crisis: U.S.-Uzbekistan Relations, 2001–2005,* edited by S. Frederick Starr (Central Asia–Caucasus Institute and Silk Road Studies Program, 2006), p. 62.
22. Rumsfeld to Hadley et al., "Central Asia," July 13, 2006.
23. Rumsfeld to Hadley et al., "Central Asia," July 13, 2006.
24. Rumsfeld to Pace, "Acting on Intelligence," November 7, 2006.
25. Rumsfeld, "Talk to Hadley about U.S.-Iran Talks," April 3, 2006.
26. Rumsfeld to Bush, cc: Hadley, "Thoughts on Syria," July 31, 2006.
27. "Hezbollah Denies Link to Hariri Murder," CNN, May 24, 2009; Ayaz Nanji, "Bush Says Syria Is 'Out of Step,'" CBS News, February 17, 2005.
28. Rumsfeld to Cheney et al., "Remaining Firm on North Korea," December 26, 2002.
29. Rumsfeld to Cheney et al., "Approaching China with a Political Solution on North Korea," March 14, 2003.
30. Max Hastings, *The Korean War* (New York: Simon & Schuster, 1987), p. 324.

CHAPTER 44 The Army We Had

1. Department of Defense news transcript, "Secretary Rumsfeld Town Hall Meeting in Kuwait," December 8, 2004.
2. Department of Defense news transcript, "Secretary Rumsfeld Town Hall Meeting in Kuwait," December 8, 2004.
3. Department of Defense news transcript, "Secretary Rumsfeld Town Hall Meeting in Kuwait," December 8, 2004.
4. Thomas E. Ricks, "Rumsfeld Gets Earful From Troops," *Washington Post,* December 9, 2004.
5. Rick Atkinson, "'The IED Problem Is Getting Out of Control. We've Got to Stop the Bleeding,'" *Washington Post,* September 30, 2007.
6. Rick Atkinson, "'There Was a Two-Year Learning Curve . . . and a Lot of People Died in Those Two Years,'" *Washington Post,* October 1, 2007.
7. Rick Atkinson, "'The IED Problem Is Getting Out of Control. We've Got to Stop the Bleeding,'" *Washington Post,* September 30, 2007.
8. Rick Atkinson, "'The IED Problem Is Getting Out of Control. We've Got to Stop the Bleeding,'" *Washington Post,* September 30, 2007.
9. Rick Atkinson, "'You Can't Armor Your Way Out of This Problem,'" *Washington Post,* October 2, 2007.
10. Rick Atkinson, "'There Was a Two-Year Learning Curve . . . and a Lot of People Died in Those Two Years,'" *Washington Post,* October 1, 2007.
11. Rumsfeld to Myers et al., "Armored Vehicles," December 21, 2004.
12. Rumsfeld to Myers et al., "Meeting AOR Needs," December 14, 2004.
13. Rumsfeld to Di Rita, "Armored Vehicle Issue," December 20, 2004.
14. Department of Defense, "Defense Transformation Update," August 2006.
15. "USAF Faces Further Push to Boost UAVs in Afghanistan, Iraq," *janes.com,* April 24, 2008.
16. Caspar W. Weinberger, speech, "The Uses of Military Power," National Press Club, Washington, D.C., November 28, 1984; Colin L. Powell, "U.S. Forces: Challenges Ahead," *Foreign Affairs,* vol. 71, no. 5 (Winter 1992), pp. 32-45.
17. Department of Defense news transcript, "DoD News Briefing—Secretary Rumsfeld," May 8, 2002.
18. *Armed Forces Journal,* cover page, June 2002.
19. "Crusader Talking Points," May 1, 2002.

20. "Crusader Talking Points," May 1, 2002.
21. "DoD—Highlights of Accomplishments: The First Five Years," March 20, 2006; General Wayne Downing to Rumsfeld and Pace, "Special Operations Forces Assessment," November 9, 2005.
22. Rumsfeld to Di Rita, "Briefing on SOF," December 10, 2004; Rumsfeld to General Doug Brown et al., "Marines Special Operations Command," February 5, 2005.
23. Francis J. Harvey to Rumsfeld, "Snowflake Response: Army Modularity—Open Issues," February 2, 2005.
24. Robert D. Kaplan, "What Rumsfeld Got Right," *The Atlantic*, July/August 2008.

PART FOURTEEN The Long, Hard Slog

1. Department of Defense news transcript, "DoD News Briefing with Secretary Rumsfeld and Gen. Pace," March 7, 2006.
2. Rumsfeld to Edelman, cc: Pace, "U.S. Response to Mosque Attack," February 22, 2006.

CHAPTER 45 Hands Off the Bicycle Seat

1. Ambassador L. Paul Bremer III with Malcolm McConnell, *My Year in Iraq: The Struggle to Build a Future of Hope* (New York: Simon & Schuster, 2005), p. 357.
2. Department of Defense news transcript, "Ambassador Bremer Conference Call with Editorial Writers," July 24, 2003.
3. Department of Defense news transcript, "Ambassador Paul Bremer Interview on *Meet the Press,*" July 20, 2003.
4. Bremer to Rumsfeld et al., "Nation-Building: Lessons Learned," May 4, 2003; L. Paul Bremer, interviewed by Tim Russert, *Meet the Press,* NBC News, January 15, 2006.
5. Ambassador L. Paul Bremer III with Malcolm McConnell, *My Year in Iraq: The Struggle to Build a Future of Hope* (New York: Simon & Schuster, 2005), p. 357; Rumsfeld to Bremer, "Force Estimate," May 24, 2004.
6. Rumsfeld to Myers, cc: Wolfowitz, "Force Estimate for Iraq," May 21, 2004.
7. Myers to Rumsfeld, "Iraqi Force Estimate," July 13, 2004.
8. Myers to Rumsfeld, "Iraqi Force Estimate," July 13, 2004.
9. Myers to Rumsfeld, "Iraqi Force Estimate," July 13, 2004.
10. Rumsfeld, "Military Advice," April 26, 2004; Rumsfeld, "Giving Good Military Advice," April 26, 2004.
11. Rumsfeld to Pace, cc: Myers, "Views from Generals," January 3, 2005.
12. Rumsfeld to Pace, cc: Myers, "Views from Generals," January 4, 2005.
13. Rumsfeld to Pace, cc: Myers, "Views from Generals," January 4, 2005.
14. Dave Moniz and Tom Squitieri, "Defense Memo: A Grim Outlook," *USA Today,* October 22, 2003.
15. Rumsfeld to Myers et al., "Global War on Terrorism," October 16, 2003.
16. Chairman of the Joint Chiefs of Staff, *National Military Strategic Plan for the War on Terrorism* (Washington, D.C.: Department of Defense, 2006); President of the United States, *The National Security Strategy of the United States of America* (Washington, D.C.: The White House, 2006).
17. William Safire, "Slog," *New York Times,* November 9, 2003.

CHAPTER 46 The Dead Enders

1. Eric Schmitt, "A Low-Key Commander With 4 Stars to Tame the Iraqi Furies," *New York Times,* July 5, 2004.
2. Rumsfeld to Feith et al., "Foreign Troops," February 20, 2004.
3. Rumsfeld to Bush et al.,"Muslim Force for Iraq," January 3, 2005.
4. Ambassador L. Paul Bremer III with Malcolm McConnell, *My Year in Iraq: The Struggle to Build a Future of Hope* (New York: Simon & Schuster, 2005), p. 162.
5. Jonas to Rumsfeld and Wolfowitz, "Cost for a Soldier," February 15, 2005.
6. Rumsfeld to Matt Latimer, "Statement on Iraq," October 21, 2004.
7. Rumsfeld to Franks, cc: Myers, "Codel Restrictions," May 20, 2003.
8. OSD Policy, "Security Update: Update on Training the ISF," April 21, 2005.
9. Department of Defense news transcript, "Defense Department Operational Update Briefing," April 20, 2004.
10. Ann Scott Tyson, "Insurgents in Iraq Show Signs of Acting as a Network," *Christian Science Monitor,* April 28, 2004.
11. Department of Defense news transcript, "Secretary Rumsfeld Interview with CNN Live Today," March 8, 2002.
12. Ambassador L. Paul Bremer III with Malcolm McConnell, *My Year in Iraq: The Struggle to Build a Future of Hope* (New York: Simon & Schuster, 2005), p. 127.
13. Malcolm W. Nance, *The Terrorists of Iraq: Inside the Strategy and Tactics of the Iraq Insurgency* (Charleston, SC: BookSurge Publishing, 2007), p. 21.
14. Edward T. Pound, "Seeds of Chaos," *U.S. News & World Report,* December 12, 2004.
15. Department of Defense news transcript, "Secretary Rumsfeld Remarks at Greater Dallas Chamber of Commerce," August 2, 2005.
16. "Fact Sheet: Defining Victory in Fallujah," November 12, 2004.
17. Associated Press, "Purported Al-Zarqawi Tape Declares War on Democracy," Fox News, January 23, 2005.
18. "Iraq's Lost Election," *The Nation,* January 20, 2005; Rory McCarthy, "Violence Will Not Stop Poll, Says UN Official," *The Guardian,* January 21, 2005; Associated Press, "Bush Confident About Iraq Elections Despite Violence," *USA Today*, January 7, 2005.
19. Anas Shallal, "Postpone Iraq's Elections," *Foreign Policy in Focus,* January 13, 2005.
20. Anas Shallal, "Postpone Iraq's Elections," *Foreign Policy in Focus,* January 13, 2005.
21. Anthony Shadid, "Iraqis Defy Threats as Millions Vote," *Washington Post,* January 31, 2005.
22. Anthony Shadid, "Iraqis Defy Threats as Millions Vote," *Washington Post,* January 31, 2005.
23. Joseph R. Biden, Jr., and Leslie H. Gelb, "Unity Through Autonomy in Iraq," *New York Times,* May 1, 2006.
24. Department of Defense notes of NSC meeting, November 2, 2005.
25. Rumsfeld to Bush et al., "Progress in Iraq," November 29, 2005.
26. Ellen Knickmeyer and K.I. Ibrahim, "Bombing Shatters Mosque in Iraq," *Washington Post,* February 23, 2006.

CHAPTER 47 Eyes on Afghanistan

1. Joint Chiefs of Staff, "Forces in Afghanistan September 2001–May 2007 (Boots on the Ground)," undated.
2. Rumsfeld to Abizaid et al., "Karzai's Strategy on Warlordism," September 15, 2003.

3. Rumsfeld to Franks et al., "Afghan National Army," January 28, 2002; Rumsfeld to Feith et al., "Afghanistan," May 2, 2003.
4. OSD Policy, "Principles for Afghanistan—Policy Guidelines," July 7, 2003.
5. David Rohde and David E. Sanger, "How a 'Good War' in Afghanistan Went Bad," *New York Times,* August 12, 2007; "Will Afghanistan Be Obama's Iraq?" *The Week,* December 8, 2008; Don Gonyea, "Is Obama in an 'Afghan Box'?" NPR, September 29, 2009.
6. Jason H. Campbell and Jeremy Shapiro, "Afghanistan Index: Tracking Variables of Reconstruction & Security in Post-9/11 Afghanistan," Brookings Institution, October 28, 2008.
7. Rumsfeld to Bush et al., "Afghanistan," August 20, 2002.
8. Rice to Cheney et al., "'Accelerating Success in Afghanistan' in 2004: An Assessment," January 18, 2005.
9. Powell, letter to Rumsfeld, April 16, 2002; Rumsfeld to Wolfowitz et al., "Afghanistan Funding," September 15, 2004; Rumsfeld to Feith, cc: Wolfowitz, "Afghan Army," October 22, 2003; Rumsfeld to Abizaid et al., "Afghan Security Forces," December 19, 2003.
10. Rumsfeld to Rice, "Afghan National Police," February 23, 2005.
11. David Rohde, "Overhaul of Afghan Police Is New Priority," *New York Times,* October 18, 2007.
12. Rumsfeld to Rice, "Afghan National Police," February 23, 2005.
13. Rumsfeld to Myers et al., "Afghan Security Responsibility," April 7, 2004; Rumsfeld to Powell, "Afghanistan Briefing Papers," September 21, 2004.
14. Rep. Robert Andrews and Rep. Mark Kirk, cochairs, *Integrating 21st Century Development and Security Assistance: Final Report of the Task Force on Nontraditional Security Assistance,* Center for Strategic & International Studies, January 2008, p. 7.
15. Rumsfeld to Abizaid et al., "Training and Equipping of Police in Afghanistan and Iraq," August 2, 2006.
16. Rumsfeld to Hadley, "Afghan National Police," March 4, 2005.
17. David Rohde, "Overhaul of Afghan Police Is New Priority," *New York Times,* October 18, 2007.
18. "Foreign Assistance Reform," draft working paper, May 19, 2005.
19. National Defense Authorization Act for Fiscal Year 2006 (Public Law 109-163), January 6, 2006.
20. Combined Forces Command—Afghanistan, "What Has Changed?" December 6, 2004.
21. Rumsfeld to Hadley, cc: Edelman, "Staffing PRTs in Afghanistan," August 18, 2006, with attachment, "Staffing of PRTs in Afghanistan as of August 1, 2006"; "Status of Civilianizing PRTs in Afghanistan," April 19, 2005.
22. Rumsfeld to Bush et al., "Decision on Ambassador to Afghanistan," January 21, 2005.
23. Rumsfeld to Hadley, "Ambassador to Iraq," March 6, 2006.
24. Rumsfeld to Edelman, "Strmecki," May 18, 2006; Rumsfeld to Cheney et al., "Marin Strmecki and Afghanistan Briefing," August 25, 2006.
25. Marin Strmecki, "Afghanistan at a Crossroads: Challenges, Opportunities, and a Way Ahead," August 17, 2006.
26. Rumsfeld to Cheney et al., "Marin Strmecki and Afghanistan Briefing," August 25, 2006; Rumsfeld to Cheney et al., "Briefing by Marin Strmecki on Afghanistan," September 22, 2006; Rumsfeld to Hadley, cc: Edelman, "Strmecki Brief," October 17, 2006.

27. Marin Strmecki, "Afghanistan at a Crossroads: Challenges, Opportunities, and a Way Ahead," August 17, 2006.
28. Marin Strmecki, "Afghanistan at a Crossroads: Challenges, Opportunities, and a Way Ahead," August 17, 2006.
29. Marin Strmecki, "Afghanistan at a Crossroads: Challenges, Opportunities, and a Way Ahead," August 17, 2006.
30. Mira R. Ricardel to Rumsfeld, "Concept Paper on Merging ISAF and OEF into a Single Command," October 12, 2004.
31. Rumsfeld to Powell, "Afghanistan—Embassy Kabul Staffing," March 26, 2004.
32. Luti to Rumsfeld, "Embassy Kabul Staffing," January 26, 2004.
33. Rumsfeld to Hadley, "PRT Memos," January 26, 2006.
34. Rumsfeld, handwritten note, May 26, 2006.
35. Rumsfeld to Bush et al., "What to Do When 'Succeeding' Requires More Than Military Power Alone," October 10, 2006.
36. Rumsfeld to Cheney et al., "Marin Strmecki and Afghanistan Briefing," August 25, 2006; Rumsfeld to Cheney et al., "Briefing by Marin Strmecki on Afghanistan," September 22, 2006; Rumsfeld to Hadley, cc: Edelman, "Strmecki Brief," October 17, 2006.

CHAPTER 48 Iraq's Summer of Violence

1. Michael E. O'Hanlon and Jason H. Campbell, "Iraq Index: Tracking Variables of Reconstruction & Security in Post-Saddam Iraq," Brookings Institution, October 1, 2007, p. 30.
2. Jim Clancy and Pam Benson, "Al-Zarqawi Claims Responsibility for Wave of Attacks," CNN, April 6, 2004.
3. Associated Press-Ipsos poll, conducted by Ipsos Public Affairs, January 8–10, 2007; CBS News Poll, December 8–10, 2006.
4. Jason Burke and Rory Carroll, "Poor Bedouin Who Became a Butcher," *The Guardian,* June 9, 2006.
5. "Defiant al-Zarqawi Shows Face on Video," CNN, April 25, 2006.
6. Rumsfeld to Casey et al., "Zarqawi," June 8, 2006.
7. Rumsfeld to Myers and Cambone, "Meeting with POTUS," May 19, 2005.
8. Rumsfeld to McChrystal et al., "Congratulations," June 8, 2006.
9. Vickers to Bush, "Transitioning to an Indirect Approach in Iraq," June 12, 2006.
10. Rumsfeld to Abizaid et al., "Presence in Cities and Training Officers," November 15, 2005.
11. Abizaid to Rumsfeld, "Paper by Michael Vickers," June 21, 2006.
12. Rumsfeld to Bush et al., "Abizaid's Comments on the Paper by Mike Vickers," June 22, 2006.
13. Rumsfeld to Hadley et al., "Update on Security in Baghdad," July 14, 2006.
14. Department of Defense notes of NSC meeting, July 19, 2006.
15. Rumsfeld to Casey et al., "Integration and Militia," May 12, 2006.
16. Department of Defense notes of NSC meeting, July 22, 2006.
17. Rumsfeld, "Measures of Success in Iraq," September 18, 2006.
18. Rumsfeld to Casey et al., "Decision on Stryker Brigade," August 2, 2006; Casey to Rumsfeld et al., "snowflake response," August 11, 2006.
19. Eric Lidji, "Final Strykers Return Home," *Stryker Brigade News,* December 19, 2006.
20. Thomas E. Ricks, "Situation Called Dire in West Iraq," *Washington Post,* September 11,

2006; Jim Miklaszewski, "Iraq's Anbar Province a Lost Cause?" MSNBC, September 12, 2006.

21. National Security Council, "Al Anbar Update," March 22, 2006.
22. Rumsfeld to Bremer, "Sunni Outreach," April 12, 2004.
23. Rumsfeld to Abizaid et al., "Counterinsurgency," January 2, 2004.
24. Major Niel Smith, U.S. Army, and Colonel Sean MacFarland, U.S. Army, "Anbar Awakens: The Tipping Point," *Military Review*, March–April 2008, p. 41.
25. Multi-National Corps—Iraq, Public Affairs Office, "Most Successful Iraqi Police Recruiting Drive," Release No. 20060818-01, August 18, 2006.
26. Major Niel Smith, U.S. Army, and Colonel Sean MacFarland, U.S. Army, "Anbar Awakens: The Tipping Point," *Military Review*, March–April 2008, pp. 41-52.
27. OSD Policy, "Security Update: Situation in al-Anbar," October 26, 2006.
28. Rumsfeld, handwritten note, October 20, 2006.

CHAPTER 49 Farewells

1. William Branigin, "Three Retired Officers Demand Rumsfeld's Resignation," *Washington Post*, September 25, 2006.
2. Mark Benjamin, "U.S. Generals Call for Democratic Takeover," *Salon.com*, October 25, 2006.
3. David S. Cloud and Eric Schmitt, "More Retired Generals Call for Rumsfeld's Resignation," *New York Times*, April 14, 2006.
4. Rowan Scarborough, "Generals Defend Rumsfeld," *Washington Times*, April 15, 2006.
5. "Bush: 'I'm the Decider' on Rumsfeld," CNN, April 18, 2006.
6. Associated Press, "Rep. Cynthia McKinney Introduces Bush Impeachment Bill," Fox News, December 8, 2006.
7. Rumsfeld, handwritten note, October 11, 2006.
8. Associated Press, "Bush: Rumsfeld and Cheney Should Stay," MSNBC, November 1, 2006.
9. Rumsfeld, handwritten note, November 5, 2006.
10. Rumsfeld, letter of resignation, November 6, 2006.
11. James A. Baker III and Lee H. Hamilton, cochairs, *The Iraq Study Group Report* (New York: Vintage Books, 2006), p. 32.
12. Rumsfeld, handwritten note, November 7, 2006.
13. Rumsfeld, handwritten note, November 7, 2006.
14. Rumsfeld, "Secretary Rumsfeld's Remarks at the White House," November 8, 2006.
15. Rumsfeld, "Phone Conversation with Sergey Ivanov on November 11, 2006," November 14, 2006.
16. Rumsfeld, "November 11 Phone call with Henry Kissinger," November 14, 2006.
17. Rumsfeld, "November 10 Phone Call from John Dingell," November 13, 2006.
18. General Richard B. Myers, remarks at the Landon Lecture of Public Affairs, Kansas State University, November 9, 2006; Department of Defense news transcript, "Remarks by Secretary Rumsfeld at the Landon Lecture at Kansas State University, Manhattan, Kan.," November 9, 2006.
19. Dick Cheney, "Vice President's Remarks at the Armed Forces Full Honor Review in Honor of Secretary of Defense Donald Rumsfeld," Office of the Vice President, December 15, 2006.
20. George W. Bush, "President Attends Armed Forces Full Honor Review for Secretary Rumsfeld," Office of the Press Secretary, December 15, 2006.

21. Rumsfeld, "Farewell Remarks—The Pentagon," December 15, 2006.
22. Rumsfeld, "Farewell Remarks—The Pentagon," December 15, 2006; Jim Rutenberg, "In Farewell, Rumsfeld Warns Weakness Is 'Provocative,'" *New York Times,* December 16, 2006.

CHAPTER 50 After Tides and Hurricanes

1. Charles Duelfer, "Comprehensive Report of the Special Advisor to the DCI on Iraq's WMD" (Duelfer Report), vol. I, September 30, 2004, p. 1 (Regime Strategic Intent section).
2. Charles Duelfer, "Comprehensive Report of the Special Advisor to the DCI on Iraq's WMD" (Duelfer Report), vol. I, September 30, 2004, p. 51 (Regime Strategic Intent section).
3. Karl Rove, *Courage and Consequence: My Life as a Conservative in the Fight* (New York: Threshold Editions, 2010), p. 342.
4. Rumsfeld to Bush et al., "Alternative Approaches to Iraq," November 6, 2006.
5. Rumsfeld to Bush et al., "Iraq Policy: Proposal for the New Phase," December 8, 2006.
6. OSD Policy, "Security Update: Situation in al-Anbar," October 26, 2006.
7. Rumsfeld, "Iraq—Illustrative New Courses of Action," November 6, 2006.
8. Rumsfeld, "Iraq—Illustrative New Courses of Action," November 6, 2006.
9. Peter W. Rodman, *Presidential Command: Power, Leadership, and the Making of Foreign Policy from Richard Nixon to George W. Bush* (New York: Alfred A. Knopf, 2009), p. 266.
10. Peter Rodman, *Presidential Command: Power, Leadership, and the Making of Foreign Policy from Richard Nixon to George W. Bush* (New York: Alfred A. Knopf, 2009), p. 267.
11. Department of Defense notes of NSC meeting, December 13, 2006.
12. Peter Rodman, *Presidential Command: Power, Leadership, and the Making of Foreign Policy from Richard Nixon to George W. Bush* (New York: Alfred A. Knopf, 2009), p. 268.
13. Joel Roberts, "Senator Reid on Iraq: 'This War Is Lost,'" CBS News, April 20, 2007; Barack Obama, interviewed by Tim Russert, *Meet the Press,* NBC News, October 22, 2006.
14. Juan Abdel Nasser, "The 12 Fastest Growing Economies in 2010," EconomyWatch.com, October 13, 2009.
15. Department of Defense, *The National Defense Strategy of the United States of America,* March 2005.
16. Rumsfeld to Rice et al., "Iraq," July 27, 2001.
17. Henry Kissinger, *Years of Upheaval* (Boston: Little, Brown, 1982), p. 638.
18. George W. Bush, address, Joint Session of Congress, Washington, D.C., September 20, 2001.
19. Rumsfeld, "What Are We Fighting? Is It a Global War on Terror?" June 18, 2004.
20. Wolfowitz to Rumsfeld, "National Defense Strategy," February 7, 2005.
21. Rumsfeld to Card et al., "Mobilizing Moderate Muslims," July 19, 2005.
22. Adlai E. Stevenson, address at the Senior Class Banquet, Princeton Class of 1954, March 22, 1954.

Index

Page numbers in *italics* refer to illustrations.